STUDIES IN THE BUDDHISTIC CULTURE OF INDIA

Studies in the Buddhistic Culture of India

(*During the 7th and 8th centuries* A.D.)

LAL MANI JOSHI M.A., Ph.D.
Professor of Religious Studies,
Punjabi University, Patiala

MOTILAL BANARSIDASS
Delhi :: Varanasi :: Patna

Indological Publishers & Booksellers
Head Office : BUNGALOW ROAD, JAWAHAR NAGAR, DELHI-7
Branches : 1. CHOWK, VARANASI-1 (U.P.)
2. ASHOK-RAJPATH, PATNA-4 (BIHAR)

First Edition : *Delhi*, 1967
Second Revised Edition : *Delhi*, 1977
Price : Rs. 100.00
$28.00

Printed in India
BY SHANTILAL JAIN, AT SHRI JAINENDRA PRESS, A-45, PHASE-I, INDUSTRIAL AREA, NARAINA, NEW DELHI-28 AND PUBLISHED BY SUNDARLAL JAIN, FOR MOTILAL BANARSIDASS, BUNGALOW ROAD, JAWAHAR NAGAR, DELHI-7

CONTENTS

V. *Ethical and Spiritual Culture*

VI. *Buddhist Education and its Centres* 121

FOREWORD

WHILE IN one sense Buddhistic culture is part of the wider stream of Indian Civilization, in another sense, it transcends the quality of any purely nationalistic culture. That is because of its particular but genuine spiritualism. Like man, culture has a double origin, natural and spiritual. In fact, man's cultural life arises from his spiritual aspirations working from within the limited but modifiable circuits of his natural or instinctive life. Just as a *nyagrodha* has roots above and below, so culture is conditioned by material, social and historical circumstances and yet aspires after an eternal and universal ideal. The quest for security, for example, produces diverse historically circumscribed systems of economic, social and political institutions, all of them really seeking to express and spell out in a realm of contingent multiplicity different aspects of man's vision of the protecting Deity whether as symbolized by the bounteous goddess holding the cornucopia or as the Heavenly Father (*pitāmaha*) or as the Lord wielding the sceptre of authority. Whether man's protecting deity be real or imaginary, it cannot be gainsaid that man tends to evolve the consciousness of an ideal of security, of a universal order where each individual would receive the care a child would from a bounteous, loving and just father. Whether such an order is in some sense eternal or a future possibility, personal or impersonal, is less significant than the fact that it is not yet a perfected actuality on the historical plane and that its notion imparts a universal direction and intelligibility to man's history as governed by the quest for security. The other quests of man, for knowledge, for love and for freedom, operate similarly in history. Thus it is that culture appears as an evolving complex with a historical matrix and a transcendent ideal.

Compared to other forms of culture, spiritual culture is more universal and more self-conscious of its universality. Buddhism is in a way the most universal of all the historical forms of spirituality. It had no hesitation in adopting the linguistic and material modes of culture prevalent in the societies where it happened to spread. Thus Buddhist literature was readily created in Tibetan, Mongolian and Chinese and was held fully authoritative. The Buddha himself discredited the notion of any originally authentic language or of an absolutely sacrosanct canon. He asked his followers to accept his words only after due testing and critical examination. Buddhist monks and teachers spread this catholic and rational message wherever they could. Even Buddhist mysticism depends on the scientific analysis of psychic and parapsychic phenomena and a system of moral and mental training depending on this analysis and testable by personal experience. Perception and inference alone are accepted as the valid means of knowledge and there is no scope for blind faith, obscurantism or transcendent, metaphysical entities. Relying on experience and reason and rejecting the compulsive authority of any definitive but archaic scriptures that could not be questioned, Buddhism became a dynamic and expansive world-religion. As such, while Indian by birth, Buddhism became universal by choice.

The fact, however, is that the essence of Indian culture is not nationalistic but universal. We should not identify the core elements of Indian culture with particular obsolescent institutions like caste or detailed Dharmaśāstra regulations or specific temple rituals. It is the absract notions of *dharma* and *mokṣa*, *karman*, *jñāna*, *yoga* and *bhakti* and the tradition of genuine spiritual experience out of which these concepts were articulated that constitute the heart of Indian culture. Buddhism impersonalised the notions of *dharma* and *mokṣa*, sought to rid the salvation-seeker of soteriological egoism, emphasized moral rather than ritual *karman*, emancipated *jñāna* from *śabda*, provided *yoga* with a purely psychological foundation and made an ideal man the proper object of *bhakti*. Buddhism thus provided an ideal version of Indian culture for those who should have a tough mind, intellectual, self-reliant, public-spirited and altruistic. Unfortunately, the lure of an easy religion of mechanical worship, attractive symbols and the possibility of gaining all without losing any, overcome the Indian psyche gradually from the seventh century A.D.

It is not that Tantra and Haṭhayoga, which are as much Buddhistic in this period as non-Buddhistic, should be regarded as delusive. The fact is that in point of psycho-spiritua linsight and acumen Tantra and Haṭhayoga represent a new climax in Indian culture. They represent the one and only genuine parapsychology so far known and sought to be utilized in a spiritual and religious context. Unfortunately, they are also capable of being put to trivial personal and material uses. As such, they only recoil on the person and soon become quite delusive. If wrongly motived, even ordinary prayer and worship become a danger to mental health. If the highly potent techniques of Tantra and Yoga are used, the danger becomes all the greater. On the national plane the misunderstanding and misapplication of Tantra spelled disaster. The worshippers of *śakti* were quickly run over by Turkish hordes. In a recent novel Sri Hazari Prasad Dwivedi who has studied Siddha literature so well, sketches the tragic delusions of such worshippers in a revealing manner.

My old and beloved pupil L.M. Joshi devotes his present work to the analysis of Buddhistic culture in India in the seventh and eighth centuries A.D. With painstaking scholarship and a learned vision he has sought to make the subject alive and luminous. The work is indeed excellently done and opens the way to a more philosophical and intellectual study of the whole period of early middle ages where only dynasties and temples and material culture have so far attracted genuine scholarly attention. The work is remarkably comprehensive and presents a cultural epoch in its impressive and varied *zusammenhang*. Reading it is like entering a Gothic cathedral, spacious and high, lit in a sober light from multicoloured windows.

March, 1967 G.C. PANDE
Rajasthan University, Jaipur

EXCERPTS FROM PREFACE TO FIRST EDITION

CULTURE is generally regarded as a tradition or pattern of life and thought in a community. While it manifests itself historically in education and learning, art and literature, philosophy and religious movements, its inner being is constituted by a configuration of values. Values have a diverse character—instrumental and final, central and peripheral—and are conceived under many particular upādhis; nevertheless it cannot be gainsaid that they aspire after universality.

From this point of view, one should be able to speak of one concrete entity, the culture of all mankind. Actually, however, the vision of a universal human culture, which would be concrete in the Hegelian sense, belongs largely to the future. Human history appears as a long and painful travail toward the realization of such a vision ever moving cyclically from narrower to larger units and conceptions. One cannot, of course, speak of any strict law or predictability in history, and the historian as distinguished from the philosopher has to content himself with recording the past vicissitudes of actual cultural movements, in the course of which larger conceptions have often emerged from narrower beginnings.

The task of the historical researcher is often further constricted by the inevitable discipline imposed by the requirements of detail and rigour which tend to exclude a great deal of plausible, but in the last analysis only hypothetical, interpretation. The historical researcher can only hope to furnish some significant material to the general historian for his larger construction and interpretation, so that the work of general historian may at last aspire to stimulate the philosopher in his vision of the destiny of mankind. On the other hand, the light of philosophy also, without any dogmatic pre-conceptions, of course, must to some extent guide the historical worker.

The purpose of the following pages is to present authentic materials for the historical reconstruction and critical appreciation of some aspects of Buddhistic culture in India during the seventh and eighth centuries A.D. Although the changes in

Indian Buddhism and its achievements during this period are full of varied interests and intricate problems, and although many scholars have commented on several of its aspects in different contexts, no systematic and integral study of the subject has so far been made. The older works of Kern, Keith and Thomas or the latest of Professors Lamotte, Conze and Pande, on the history of Buddhism in India, hardly deal with this period or do so very sparingly. The poor picture of Buddhist history, philosophy and culture presented in a Government of India publication, the 2500 *Years of Buddhism* (New Delhi, 1956) indicates rather the unfortunate fact that in no other country of the world today Buddhist studies receive so negligible and scant a treatment as in the homeland of Buddhism. Below is an humble attempt, perhaps incomplete in some respects, to study in some detail, faithfully but critically, the Indian literary and archaeological sources, bearing only on two centuries of Buddhist history and culture in India. The attempt is throughout historical and critical and the approach integral; elements of Buddhist culture have been analyzed and studied within the framework of India's cultural history as a whole.

The significance of the subject and the period selected here can hardly be exaggerated. It was the age when Buddhist logic and dialectics were perfected by Dharmakīrti and Śāntarakṣita; when Buddhist moral and spiritual fervour received supreme expression at the hands of Śāntideva and Kamalaśīla; when some of the masterminds of ancient India, including Śāntideva, Candrakīrti, Dharmakīrti, Śāntarakṣita, Uddyotakara, Kumārila and Śaṃkara, were busy in a life and death struggle for the defence of their own doctrines; when Buddhist logicians like Śaṃkarānanda and Brahmanical teachers like Gauḍapāda were trying to harmonize the tenets of Buddhist and Brahmanical philosophies; when Tāntrika adepts like Sarahapāda, Nāgārjuna II, and others began to broadcast that Esoteric Gospel which soon transformed Śākyamuni's Gospel, dominated the whole medieval period of Indian culture, and which, through Gorakhanātha, Kabīradāsa, Nānaka and others, was transmitted down to Rāmakrishṇa, Ramaṇa Maharṣi and Sri Aurobindo of our own days; it was during this most critical and decisive period in the history of Indian Buddhism, in fact, of Indian culture as a whole, that while a host of Buddhist Doctors of Indian Buddhist Universities were engaged in their scientific and cultural missions in distant parts of Asia, their Brahmanical counter-parts at home were actively engaged in organizing a country-wide intellectual and cultural crusade against Buddhist ideals and practices; when Brahmanism, re-armed with Buddhist arsenal, sacked its rival creditor; when Tāntrikism washed off distinctive traits of Buddhism and swept all religious sects of the country in one massive stream of devotional mysticism; when Buddhism began to recede into the background and Brahmanism reshaped itself into 'Hinduism'; considerably refined and enriched by constant contacts with Buddhist ideals and practices, and re-modelled according to the new circum-stances brought about by the growth and popularity of Śramaṇic idealogies for centuries, Brahmanism now emerged, under its Purāṇic garb as the undisputed national 'Hindu' culture. In the twofold process of assimilation and condemnation of Buddhism, the Brahmanical priests sacrificed at the altar of mythical Viṣṇu even the most historical and overwhelmingly non-Brahmanical personality of Buddha and mystified the historical existence of Buddhism as a delusive trick of a Purāṇic God. "This well-conceived and bold stroke of policy", remarks R.C. Majumdar, "cut the ground from under the feet of Buddhism which was already steadily losing ground and the ultimate result was the complete effacement of Buddhism from India as a separate sect." (*The Cultural Heritage of India*, 2nd edn., vol. IV, p. 48). The transformation of Brahmanism or the birth of Hinduism, we may add, had been the eclipse of Buddhism in its homeland—one of the major tragedies in the annals of Indian culture—a fact frequently overlooked or confused by most of our historians.

But a volume primarily devoted to a study of some aspects of Buddhist life and thought cannot be expected to do full justice to all these outstanding events and changes of far-reaching consequences that characterized this period. A comprehensive study of inter-relations between Brahmanism and Buddhism is in itself the task of a life-time; a discussion of the polemics of near contemporary Naiyāyika and Vaiyākaraṇa thinkers against

Buddhist thought would have required two more chapters in an already bulky volume. I would have liked to include a survey of Buddhism in contemporary Nepal, Tibet, Burma and Ceylon, a more detailed treatment of Buddhist art and iconography of the period, a fuller evaluation of the thought of Dharmakīrti, and a comparative study of Brahmanical and Buddhist Tantras. But all this would have needed twice as much labour and leisure as have gone into the production of these pages.

The changes which came over Buddhism during this period were the clear manifestations of tendencies which had been at work long ago. The first chapter of this work, therefore, seeks to trace the earlier background with a view to restating the origins of the new phase of Buddhism and its connection with the past tradition.

The next chapter describes the general state of Buddhism in the seventh and eighth centuries in different regions of India.

The third chapter deals with the achievements of Buddhist art as it developed especially within the monasteries. Here the connection between Tāntrika Buddhism and plastic art has also been sought to be briefly analysed.

In the fourth chapter, a detailed picture of life and discipline in the monasteries is sought to be depicted. Historical examples of Buddhist piety and endowments and maintenance of monasteries have been gleaned from contemporary inscriptions and supplemented by Chinese accounts of India and Indian literary documents.

The fifth chapter seeks to elucidate the moral ideas and religious practices inculcated by both forms of Buddhism, Hīnayāna and Mahāyāna, the former represented chiefly by I-tsing, the latter by Śāntideva. It is sought to be emphasized that despite predominance of Mahāyāna and the emergence of Vajrayāna, old ascetic Buddhism was still very much alive in some parts of the country.

The sixth and the seventh chapters attempt to weave together a picture of Buddhist education, learning and literature. It would be seen that Buddhist Universities for the first time in India's history provided her with the best and greatest centres of higher learning, and being international in character, rose above sectarian horizon to impart training in sacred as well as secular branches of learning. To be alive is to produce, and there can be no doubt that while Buddhist educational system had justly elicited universal admiration, its fruits have been no less impressive.

The eighth chapter attempts a systematic, though necessarily concise, delineation and review of the numerous doctrinal controversies and divisions with which the Buddhist thought of this period bristled. In this connection an attempt has also been made to relate the leading tendencies in thought to their sources in spiritual experience, historical tradition or rational dialectic. It has been kept in mind that while Buddhism remains mystical at heart, it develops the arsenal of logic to defend its basic mystical position.

The ninth chapter looks at Buddhist thought from the window provided by the polemics of Kumārila and Śaṃkara. On the whole the representation of the *pūrvapakṣa* in these authors has an extraordinary fidelity and penetration. Their criticism, of course, reflects not so much the weakness or inconsistencies of Buddhist reasoning as the differences in the basic point of view and presuppositions of these eminent Brahmanical critics and opponents of Buddhistic systems. Of the two, Kumārila definitely proved his subtler logical acumen and superior grasp of Buddhist principles than Śaṃkara, whose unjustified fame as the foremost Brahmanical philosopher has kept many modern scholars ignorant of Kumārila's profounder contribution to Brahmanical logic, epistemology and dialectics.

The tenth and the eleventh chapters seek to explain the development and principal contents of Tāntrika Buddhism. The subject is full of difficulties of diverse kinds, not the least of which is the fact that the Tantras are written in a language and employ terms which can become fully intelligible only to those who have actaally trodden the esoteric path. In connection with the language of modern science it has been emphasized by some thinkers that only an operational definition is possible for the terms which it uses. If the claim of the Tantra to be a practical way to the Highest be valid, it is obvious that its terms and concepts could be understood only in a similar operational manner.

The attempt to express profound metapsychological verities in terms of common experience must necessarily lead to a kind of allegorical or code-language. The interpretation of Tāntrika principles, therefore, can only be done in the light of such explanations as the Tāntrikas, past and present, have offered.

The twelfth chapter seeks to assess the beginnings of the decline of Buddhism in India. Various views, largely hypothetical, expressed on the subject, are examined here in the light of all the available evidence. Internal and external factors in the process of decline of Buddhism have been analyzed and documented.

Chinese records and Tibetan annals have been freely utilized in modern translations. New evidence has been brought to the notice of scholars from old publications and some older views have been either strengthened or weakened by evidence from recent publications. For example, the suggestions that Bhāvaviveka was a contemporary of Dharmapāla, the teacher of Śīlabhadra, and hence flourished in the last half of the sixth and the first quarter of the seventh century and not in c.500 A.D. as is generally supposed; that the institution of married monks was prevalent in Sindha in the first half of the seventh century A.D., that a king Vikramāditya of Śrāvastī, identifiable with Skandagupta, was instrumental in causing Manoratha, the Sarvāstivāda teacher, to commit suicide; and that a Sātavāhana prince, identifiable with Gautamīputra Śātakarṇi, was responsible for the murder of the Mādhyamika philosopher Nāgārjuna, have been made in these pages and are based chiefly on the authority of old publications.

A new identification of the famous Tāntrika *pīṭha* called Pūrṇāgiri with modern Pūrṇāgiri, a famous Śākta *tīrtha* overlooking Nepal in Nainital District of U.P. has been proposed. Potalaka Parvata has been suggested as a third possible early seat of the origin of Vajrayāna in the far south apart from Dhānyakaṭaka and Śrīparvata; this suggestion is based on the authority of Hsüan-tsang, the *Sādhanamālā* and the Gilgit text of the *Sarvatathāgatādhiṣṭhāna-sattvāvalokana-Buddhakṣetra-sandarśanavyūha*. South Indian origin of Tāntrika Buddhism, already suggested many years ago by the late Pt. Rāhula Sāṃkṛtyāyana, has been further strengthened by fresh evidence extracted from the *Sekoddeśāṭīkā*, the *Blue Annals*, the *Biography of Dharmasvāmin* and the above mentioned Gilgit text. These authorities finally overthrow the generally accepted theory of Bengali origin of Tāntrika Buddhism. It would not be too much to say that a historical, critical and systematic study into the origin and early evolution of Tāntrika tendencies in Buddhism has been attempted for the first time in this work. Possibility of the existence of a few seeds of Tāntrikism in the protohistoric civilization of western India and Pakistan, chiefly represented by Harappa and Mohenjodaro, suggested for the first time by the present author, may take the rudimentary beginnings of esoterism back to the third millennium B.C. The views that, constant Brahmanical hostility towards Buddhism both in letter and spirit seems to have been the foremost factor in loosening its hold on Indian classes and masses, and that the anti-Buddhist propaganda in Brahmanical literature was not a mere "war of the pen" but was periodically accompanied with its social counterpart, such as a social boycott and royal edicts against those who violated the "divinely ordained" scheme of *cāturvarṇya*, and forceful confiscation of landed property of Buddhist establishments by Brahmanical kings, etc. have been put forward for the reconsideration of our historians who account for the decay of Buddhism by exaggerating the effects of Turkish conquest of India.

A new English translation of the memorial verses of the *Śikṣāsamuccaya* has been incorporated in this work. That the compound *mahāsukha* occurs already in the *Nairātmya-paripṛcchāsūtra* in the same sense in which it is expressed by the Siddhas; that there is epigraphic evidence for the existence of some Buddhist monk-artists in the University of Nālandā; that Siddha Nāgārjuna may have been the author of the *Guhya-samāja-tantra*, that the goddess Ekajaṭā, or Vajraikajaṭā, whose worship he is reported to have 'rescued' from Tibet, is mentioned in this text also; that I-tsing already refers to the abuses of esoteric mysticism; that Bhāvaviveka belonged to that critical school of Buddhist philosophy which was started by Kumāra-labdha and which grew with Vasubandhu and Diṅnāga and drawing materials from Sautrāntika, Vijñānavāda and Mādh-yamika systems, was perfected by Sāntarakṣita, and that Gauḍapāda's synthetic attempts were quite in keeping with the time's general policy of *rapprochement* between Brahmanism and Buddhism, and numerous other minor observations and suggestions have been made in the following pages.

It has not been possible for the author to accept the generally held and widely published theory of the genesis of Buddhism and its relation to Brahmanism. He has briefly criticized the view which traces the origin of Buddhism to Vedic religion and has distinguished between Brahmanism and Hinduism on the one hand, and between Buddhism or Śramanism and Brahmanism or Vedicism on the other. The author agrees with Prof. G. C. Pande (*Studies in the Origins of Buddhism*, p. 317) that Ascetic Culture or Śramanic thought of India is of non-Vedic and pre-Āryan origin but differs from him with respect to the mutual relationship and relative chronology of the teachings of Śākyamuni and those of the oldest Upaniṣads. In the author's view no Upaniṣad text can be proved to be pre-Buddhist in date, and the partial agreement between Buddha's teachings and those of the early Upaniṣads is due to the fact that these Vedic texts were composed between the age of Buddha and that of Aśoka, and their thought was deeply influenced by the non-Vedic doctrines of early Yoga, the early Sāṃkhya, early Buddhism and early Jainism.

It is for the Buddhist scholars and historians of ancient Indian thought and culture to judge the merits and demerits of this work.

It is impossible to mention the names of all the scholars whose publications have been utilised here. There are over twentyfive hundred notes and references in this book and acknowledgment due to modern scholars has been made at proper places. I am especially thankful and express my tribute of respect to Padmavibhūṣaṇa Mahāmahopādhyāya Dr. Gopinatha Kaviraja, Professor of Tantra-Śāstra, Vārāṇaseya Saṃskrita Viśvavidyālaya, Varanasi, Rev. Lama Anagārika Govinda, Ācārya, Ārya Maitreya Maṇḍala and a distinguished authority on Buddhism, Rev. Professor Jagdish Kashyap, Director, Nava Nālandā Mahāvihāra, Nalanda, and Professor Ksetresachandra Chaṭṭopādhyāya, Ex-Director, Research Institute, Vārāṇaseya Saṃskrita Viśvavidyālaya, Varanasi, for their valuable criticism and warm appreciation of this work even before its publication.

It is with pleasure that I express my sense of gratitude to Professor A.C. Chatterji, D.Sc., Ex-Vice-Chancellor, University of Gorakhpur, for providing me with facilities for research and study-tours; to the authorities of the University Grants Commission, Government of India, for awarding me a post-graduate Research Fellowship in Humanities; and to Professor Madan Mohan, Vice-Chancellor, University of Gorakhphur, for his keen interest in the progress of my academic endeavours and for kindly sanctioning a substantial amount of money to partly finance the publication of this Doctoral Dissertation out of the U. G. C. Research Publication Fund at the disposal of the University of Gorakhpur.

The task involved in writing this book was accomplished largely in the libraries of various Universities, Institutions, and Museums of Northern India. I thank the authorities and the staff of all those educational centres which provided me with library facilities during my study tours in 1960-1963. My thanks are due also to Rev. M. Sangharatana, Nayaka Thera, Secretary, Maha Bodhi Society of India, Sarnath, for giving me permission to reproduce here my English Translation of the *Śikṣāsamuccaya-kārikās*, published by him in 1965.

My deepest debt of gratitude goes to Prof. Govind Chandra Pande, M. A., D. Phil., formerly Professor and Head of the Department of Ancient History, Archaeology and Culture, and Dean, Faculty of Arts, University of Gorakhpur, now Tagore Professor of Indian Culture and Head of the History and Indian Culture Department, University of Rajasthan, Jaipur. At my request he kindly agreed to open a special paper on the 'History and Philosophy of Buddhism' in M.A. courses of study in the Ancient History Department of Gorakhpur in 1959, and I had the good fortune of studying Buddhism under him for about four years in that University. He suggested the scheme of the present research work and supervised its progress. He has further honoured me by writing a *Foreword* to this book which embodies his profound scholarship and depth of vision.

Buddha Jayanti, 1967,
University of Gorakhpur. L. M. Joshi

PREFACE TO SECOND EDITION

THE FIRST edition of *Studies in the Buddhistic Culture of India* (during the seventh and eighth centuries A.D.) was published in 1967. In spite of editorial defects and numerous printing errors, the first edition of the book went out of print within five years of its publication. During the last five years the demand for the book has been increasing and the publishers have been pressing for a second revised edition of it.

The original plan of the book has been retained in the present edition. Important changes have been made in the arrangement of the material. Of the five appendixes published in the first edition, three have been omitted and two have been incorporated in other chapters. An entirely new chapter, the thirteenth, dealing with the 'Buddhist Contribution to Indian Culture' has been added to the present edition. Notes and references have been edited and revised wherever necessary and placed at the end of the text. The bibliography also has been revised and made uptodate. This edition is thus a completely revised and partly rewritten version of the book.

I am thankful to Dr A.N. Sinha for his paintstaking help in the preparation of the press copy and in the task of proof reading. My thanks are due also to my wife for her manifold assistance in my life and academic endeavours.

Buddha Jayanti, 1977
PUNJABI UNIVERSITY,
PATIALA.

L. M. JOSHI

CHAPTER I

BACKGROUND OF EARLIER DEVELOPMENT

From Buddha to Nāgārjuna

THE NEW CURRENT which the Buddha started within Indian culture has ultimately come to be an essential part of world culture as a whole. The basic moral and spiritual ideas which the Buddha preached carried forward a certain ancient religious and cultural tradition and became in turn the source of a manifold development which expressed itself not only by setting up a high and refined moral ideal promoting charitable activities among the laity, and ascetic renunciation and mystical contemplation especially among the monks and nuns, but also by the creation of truly remarkable educational, literary, artistic and intellectual activities.

This rich stream of cultural life inspired by the Buddha progressed during the centuries following his *parinirvāṇa*, gradually acquiring a varied and individual aspect but ever remaining a tributary of that larger stream of Indian Culture. Buddha's teachings differed according to the intellectual level of his hearers, and the Pāli Canon contains seeds of many later developments.

After the death of the Buddha there arose great controversies among his followers with regard to the interpretation of the utterances of the Teacher and also about the rules of discipline. The germs of these controversies are discernible in the most ancient canon. To settle these disputes great Councils (*saṃgītis*) were held from time to time. There were men like Purāṇa who held it better to abide by what they had heard from the Teacher's mouth rather than to accept the conclusions arrived at in the First Council. With the gradual spread of Buddhism in Northern India, geographical and local influences also seem to have contributed towards the growth of controversies in things doctrinal and disciplinary.

In the Second Council held at Vaiśālī about a century after Buddha's *parinirvāṇa*, the controversy is known to have resulted in a schism within the *saṃgha*. The dissenters convoked another great assembly (*mahāsaṃgha*) and worked out a separate doctrinal section with its 'unorthodox' canon. This new or rather 'democratic' party of the monastics came to be known as the Mahāsāṃghika, the upholders of orthodox views were known as the Theravādins. Not long afterwards, these two sections of the Buddhist *saṃgha* gave rise to further sub-sects.[1] Simhalese histories affirm that Aśoka convened the Third Council at Pāṭaliputra in order to reorganize the *saṃgha* and put an end to heretical growth.[2] The *Kathāvatthu*, a canonical treatise supposed to have been compiled during this time by Tissa, discusses and criticises the tenets of these various sects. Buddhism seems to have undergone significant changes during the reign of Aśoka. It emerged as a distinct religion with great potentialities for growth and expansion; while the imperial patronage had a permanent influence on the *saṃgha*, the latter began to grow as an institution of faith and culture. The laity also came to play an important part in the life of the doctrine and its development.

The *Mahāvastu*, a canonical text of the Lokottaravādins of Madhyadeśa, displays a particular and significant phase of transformation of Buddhism. It reflects the nucleus of Mahāyānism. Daring docetic speculations concerning Buddha were effected by the Mahāsāṃghikas and their offshoots.[3]

The Kuṣāna monarch, Kaniṣka I, is said to have convened the Fourth Council in about the second half of the first century A.D. The accounts of Kaniṣka's Council exhibit not only the prominence of the Theravāda, Sarvāstivāda and the Buddha-*bhakti*, but also allude to the appearance of the Mahāyāna as contrasted with the Hīnayāna.[4]

The catholic inspiration of Buddha's teachings led in course of time to two distinct lines of thought and practice. The two well known historical divisions into which Buddhism developed are the Hīnayāna (Little Vehicle) and the Mahāyāna (Great Vehicle).

The term 'Hīnayāna' is usually employed for ancient Buddhism, while the term 'Mahāyāna' for developed Buddhism. In older days the two vehicles (*yānas*)[5] were co-extensive and did not appear so mutually opposed or hostile to each other as might seem to a casual observer of Buddhist practices in modern times.[6] Although the terms Hīnayāna and Mahāyāna bear a sense of 'inferiority' and 'superiority' respectively, yet of their mutual relationship, historical as well as doctrinal, there can be no doubt. A seventh century Buddhist authority found that both the vehicles were in accordance with the sayings of the Buddha, and both led to Nirvāṇa.[7] The Mahāyāna grows out of the Original Buddhism, and it traces its final authority to Buddha himself.[8] It accepts the *vinaya* of the Hīnayānists,[9] and the seeds of the Mahāyāna are discernible in the Pāli Tipiṭaka.[10] According to Nāgārjuna, Hīnayāna represents the 'manifest' (*vyakta*) teaching while the Mahāyāna represents the 'esoteric' (*guhya*) teaching of the Buddha.[11] Maitreyanātha and Asaṅga too believed both the vehicles to be contemporaneous.[12]

Emergence of Mahāyāna

Much has been written on the origins of Mahāyāna Buddhism[13] and its literature. The rise of Mahāyānism was a historical necessity in the evolution of Indian Buddhism. It was the Mahāyāna that became the main spirit and source of cultural activity of the Buddhists of India during the 7th and the 8th centuries A.D. The beginnings of this significant movement may be traced to the Mahāsāṃghikas. The Buddhological speculations of the Lokottaravādins of Madhyadeśa are preserved in the *Mahāvastu*.[14] The fundamental doctrinal ideas of Mahāyāna are expounded in the Prajñāpāramitā group of literature. The earliest work of this class of Mahāyāna literature, viz. the *Aṣṭasāhasrikā-prajñā-pāramitā*, has been placed in the first century B.C.[15] According to this text the Prajñāpāramitā doctrines (i.e., the Mahāyāna) appeared in the south, spread to the east and flourished in the northern region.[16] This statement seems to be historically correct and is supported by other sources as well. The Tibetan tradition[17] avers that the Śaila Schools were the subsects of the Mahāsāṃghikas who, according to Hsüan-tsang had an independent collection called *Dhāraṇī-piṭaka*.[18] The appearance of the Mahāyāna is associated with the name of the celebrated Buddhist philosopher and dialectician Nāgārjuna. He was a South Indian, probably a *brāhmaṇa* of Āndhradeśa, and flourished in the period cir. 80 B.C.-120 A.D.[19] All authorities agree that Śrīparvata and Dhānyakaṭaka were the centres of Nāgārjuna's religious activities. Literary traditions also indicate that the origin of Mahāyāna should be considered to have taken place in the south.[20] A number of Mahāyāna Sūtras, like the *Aṣṭasāhasrikā*, the *Sukhāvatīvyūha* and the *Saddharmapuṇḍarīka sūtra*, which contain the basic ideas of Mahāyānism, seem to have been produced early in the first century B.C. The Mahāyāna Buddhism was systematised by Nāgārjuna and his successors.

The rise of Mahāyāna in about the first century B.C. effected a significant revolution in Buddhism, both in thought and in practice. It was indeed 'Great' (*mahā*) for various reasons; for its universal sympathy, it invited all to aspire for the highest goal of Buddhahood; its outlook was broad and its aim was infinitely great like the infinite sky; its all embracing doctrine of universal emptiness and also of universal compassion; its capacity to accommodate various shades of religious beliefs and popular practices; and its uncompromising intellectualism, and so on. All these factors contributed towards its growth and popularity.

Mahāyāna and its Cultural Inspiration

Mahāyāna is also called Bodhisattvayāna,[21] the vehicle of the future Buddhas. The ideal of a Bodhisattva is the hall-mark of Mahāyāna.[22] The Mahāyānists claim superiority over their Hīnayānist counterparts. One text[23] declares that without embarking on the Great Vehicle, the ocean of misery cannot be crossed; another text[24] of the Mahāyānists states that the Śrāvakas and the Pratyeka-Buddhas[25] (i.e. the Hīnayānists) are of lesser intelligence than the Bodhisattvas. The Buddha taught Hīnayāna as an expedient means (*upāya-kauśalya*). His real intention was Mahāyāna. The Buddha does not lead through Hīnayāna. In fact, there is only one vehicle which is the Great Vehicle.[26] According to Maitreyanātha and Asaṅga, Hīnayāna is a narrow doctrine, narrow in its aim and narrow in its methods and equipment.[27] Vasubandhu regarded Hīnayāna as milk and Mahāyāna as the cream of milk.[28] Śāntideva held that Hīnayāna belongs to the realm of relative truth, and its followers are on a path that has no issue.[29] Kamalaśīla also holds that the Śrāvakayāna cannot lead to the proper elimination of the two-fold obstructions (of *kleśa* and *jñeya*)'.[30]

The Mahāyāna is characterised by the following features: the doctrine of universal emptiness as a new ontological theory;[31] the doctrine of the plurality of Buddhas and of their divinity; the ideal of Bodhisattva and of Perfect Virtues (*pāramitās*); the worship of Buddhas, Bodhisattvas and other gods and goddesses; a special doctrine of salvation by faith; use of spells (*dhāraṇīs*) and *mantras* for attaining emancipation; and adoption of Sanskrit and Buddhist Sanskrit, for literary purposes. Systematic defence of Buddhist tenets by means of a critique of the non-Buddhist, specially the Brāhmanical systems of thought, is also a notable feature of the Mahāyāna treatises. As Mahāyāna made little difference between a layman (*upāsaka*) and a monk (*bhikṣu*), for both could develop *bodhicitta* and aspire for the highest goal by practising the perfections, laity came to play an important part in the growth of the Buddhistic culture. On the other hand, the ideal of a *paiṇḍapātika* or of a *rukkhamūlika* began to disappear.[32] Instead, the growth of magnificent *saṃghārāmas* and *vihāras*, with vast population of monks and nuns and laymen and laywomen, as servants to serve the monastics and take care of their establishments, seems to have coincided with the growth of Mahāyāna.

Mahāyānism became an infinite source of literary and scholastic activities among the Buddhists. The earliest literature of Mahāyāna is known as the Mahāyāna Sūtras; a *sūtra* (Tibetan 'mDo') is traditionally regarded as proclaimed by the Buddha; it begins with the remark—*evaṃ mayā śrutaṃ*, 'Thus have I heard.' The Buddhist Dictionary *Mahāvyutpatti*[33] mentions one hundred and five Mahāyāna texts, while the *Śikṣāsamuccaya* quotes excerpts from about one hundred and ten Mahāyāna Sūtras. A large number of Mahāyāna texts are still preserved in Nepal,[34] Tibet,[35] and China.[36]

The most famous and the most representative and at the same time the most ancient literature of Mahāyāna is the Prajñāpāramitā literature.[37] *Prajñāpāramitā* means both the 'perfection of wisdom' and a treatise treating of it. The biggest text of this class is said to be in one lakh *ślokas*, while the smallest is of one *śloka* only. There are numerous Prajñā texts, but the contents of all of them could be summed up in one word, to wit, *śūnyatā*.[38]

Equally important are the Navadharmas[39] or nine sacred texts famous in Nepal. They are *Lalita-vistara*, *Samādhirāja-sūtra*, *Laṅkāvatāra*, *Aṣṭasāhasrikā-Prajñāpāramitā*, *Gaṇḍavyūha*, *Saddharma-puṇḍarīka*, *Daśabhūmika*, *Suvarṇaprabhāsa*, and *Tathāgataguhyaka*. Hardly less famous are the *Sukhāvatīvyūhas*, the *Amitāyus sūtra*, the *Kāraṇḍa-vyūha* and the *Mañjuśrīmūla-*

kalpa. An important place in early Mahāyāna literature is occupied by the Avadānas and the works of Aśvaghoṣa and Mātṛceta.

Mahāyānism and Hinduism

The growth of Mahāyāna seems to have resulted in a visible approach to Hinduism. Image-worship and *bhakti* became common features of Mahāyānism and Hinduism. While the Brāhmanical Purāṇas and Dharmaśāstras started a process of modifying and transforming old Brāhmanical doctrines and practices with a view to countering the power and popularity of Buddhism, the Mahāyāna Sūtras also popularized devotional and liturgical texts and rituals. The popularity of *stotras*, *dhāraṇīs* and *mantras* among the Buddhists is attested by early Mahāyāna Sūtras.

The Bodhisattvas, such as Mañjuśrī and Avalokiteśvara and goddesses, like Tārā and Hārīti appeared for all practical purposes like Viṣṇu, Śiva, Lakṣmī and Pārvatī, etc. From the stand-point of the common people there were no important differences between Buddhism of the Mahāyāna Sūtras and Hinduism of the Purāṇas. There are remarkable parallels between the *Bhagavadgītā* and the *Saddharmapuṇḍarīka-sūtra*; the absolutistic and idealistic ideas of Mahāyāna philosophers were soon echoed in the writings of Advaita philosophers belonging to the Vedic tradition. The Buddha was accepted as the ninth *avatāra* of God and basic Buddhist moral ideals and ideas came to be assimilated by the Brāhmanical Hindus. A large number of Jātaka stories illustrative of high altruistic ideals of the Bodhisattva found their way into the didactic poetry of the *Mahābhārata* and the Purāṇas. Several rulers of Indian states who flourished during the first half of the first millennium of Christian era took pride in following Buddhism and at the same time patronizing either Vaiṣṇavism or Śaivism. Already Aśoka had introduced and zealously practised the policy of religious tolerance and inter-religious understanding. The king who came after Aśoka tried to imitate him. Thus the Kuṣāṇas, the Vākāṭakas, the Guptas, the Vardhanas, the Kārakoṭas and the Pālas, all helped in harmonizing Buddhism and Brāhmanism. Some aspects of the historical interaction between Buddhism and Hinduism have been discussed in the concluding chapter of this book.

Development of Buddhism under the Guptas

The prosperous rule of the Guptas has been regarded as the golden age of Indian civilization; this period saw an all round progress of Indian culture including Buddhism. Although most of the Gupta kings were Vaiṣṇavas by faith, they were tolerant and benevolent towards other faiths and patronised the learned and the men of letters.

Buddhist thought grew during this period both in Hīnayāna and Mahāyāna quarters. Sarvāstivāda[40] philosophy was perfected by Vasubandhu, author of the *Abhidharmakośa*. Tradition has it that he was patronised by a King Vikramāditya.[41] Contemporary with this Vasubandhu were Manoratha, his teacher, and Saṃghabhadra, his opponent; the last named scholar wrote the *Nyāyānusāra-śāstra.*[42] Harivarman, author of the *Satyasiddhi-śāstra* and the founder of the Satyasiddhi school, flourished in the 3rd century A.D.[43]

The Madhyamaka school[44] founded by Nāgārjuna was further developed by his pupil Āryadeva.[45] Towards the middle of the 6th century A.D. the school was split into Svātantrika and Prāsaṅgika sections, the former was headed by Bhāvaviveka and the latter by Buddhapālita.[46] Of Buddhapālita we know almost nothing except that he wrote a commentary on the *Madhyamaka-śāstra,* and considered the essence of the Madhyamaka system to consist in *prasaṅga-vākya,* i.e. *reductio ad absurdum* method.

Bhāvaviveka founded the Svātantrika branch of the Madhyamaka school. Externally he appeared in the Sāṃkhya garb, but internally he was deeply versed in Nāgārjuna's thought.[47] Besides a commentary called *Prajñāpradīpa*,[48] on the *Madhyamakaśāstra,* he wrote *Madhyamakahṛdayakārikā* with auto-commentary called *Tarkajvālā*,[49] *Mahāyāna-Karatalaratna*,[50] and the *Madhyamakārtha-saṃgraha.*[51]

It was the Yogācāra (Vijñānavāda) school of Mahāyāna philosophy that reached its climax during the Gupta age. The school had been founded by Maitreyanātha[52] probably in the 3rd century A.D. The classical phase in the history of the school was the age of Asaṅga and his brother Vasubandhu. Asaṅga[53] was the pupil of Maitreyanātha and wrote commentaries on the works of his master. Among his works are *Mahāyāna-Saṃparigraha,* *Prakaraṇa-Āryavācā,* *Mahāyāna-Abhidharma-Saṃ-*

gīti-Śāstra and a commentary on the *Vajracchedikā*. In Tibetan and Chinese traditions, works written by Maitreyanātha (mystified as celestial Maitreya) are attributed to Asaṅga.[54]

Vasubandhu[55] is famed in legend as 'the Master of a thousand manuals.' Besides the commentaries on Mahāyāna-sūtras, Vasubandhu wrote *Viṃśatikā* and *Triṃśikā*—two classical works on *vijñaptimātratā*—the theory that Consciousness alone is real. Besides being a great Buddhist Idealist,[56] Vasubandhu was a logician also, and wrote three logical works; *Vādavidhi*, *Vādavidhāna* and *Vādahṛdaya*. His last work is said to be a devotional one, the *Aparimitāyus-Sūtropadeśa*.

Towards the end of the fifth and beginning of the sixth century A.D., lived and worked Diṅnāga, 'the father of Indian logic.' He inaugurated a new school of 'critical philosophy', and Buddhist doctrines were reoriented after him. The *Pramāṇa-samuccaya*, *Ālaṃbanaparīkṣā*, *Trikālaparīkṣā* and *Nyāyamukha* are his chief works. The tradition of Diṅnāga was continued by Śaṃkarasvāmī and Īśvarasena; Śaṃkarasvāmī wrote the *Nyāyapraveśa*.[57]

The Gupta rulers patronised Brāhmanism and showed a marked tolerance towards Buddhism. This fact of common patronage of two faiths naturally brought Buddhism nearer to Hinduism. About the middle of the 6th century A.D. Buddha seems to have been accepted as an *avatāra* of Viṣṇu in the Purāṇas.[58] However, the Buddhists of the fourth century A.D. seem to have developed a theory of the Ādibuddha.[59] Among the Mahāyānists, Mañjuśrī, Avalokiteśvara and the goddess Prajñāpāramitā had assumed paramount position.[60] The cult of Amitābha Buddha and of his Sukhāvatī seems to have attracted even such eminent philosophers as Vasubandhu. Among the Hīnayānists, Abhidharma and Vinaya books were revered just as the Prajñā texts were revered by the Mahāyānists, and Ānanda had assumed a sacred position among the Buddhist nuns.[61] Worship of images of Buddha and Bodhisattvas with elaborate ceremonial ritualism had become a universal practice. Likewise, the practice of reciting *dhāraṇīs* for sacred as well as secular purposes, was perhaps one of the most notable features of Buddhism during this period.[62] The popularity of the doctrine of *karma* and of the cult of *pāramitās* is evidenced by the prevalence of Jātaka tales and art illustrations of the period.

Buddhist literature, both in Pāli and Sanskrit was further enriched by the Buddhist monks of the Gupta age. The most famous Pāli scholar and commentator of Pāli scriptures, Buddhaghoṣa flourished during this time.[63] Āryaśūra, the author of the *Jātakamālā*, "the forerunner of the poets of classical, chaste and ornate Sanskrit,"[64] lived in the Gupta age. It was during the fourth, fifth and the sixth centuries that Asaṅga, Vasubandhu, Diṅnāga and Bhāvaviveka enriched the Buddhist philosophical literature in Sanskrit. A large number of texts, Sūtras, Śāstras, Dhāraṇīs and commentaries were translated into Chinese during the Gupta period. The missionary and literary activities of Fa-hsien, Buddhabhadra, Dharmakṣema, Kumārajīva and Paramārtha, greatly contributed towards the growth and diffusion of Buddhist literature.[65] A number of works which display the growth of magical practices, popularity of folk beliefs and development of the germs of Tāntrika religion, were probably composed during this age. Of special interest are the *Mahāmāyūrī*, the *Rāṣṭrapālasūtra*, the *Mañjuśrīmūlakalpa* and the *Suvarṇaprabhāsasūtra*, works which indicate the beginnings of the decline of Buddhism and the rise of Mantrayāna, and which are ascribable to this period.[66]

Buddhist art reached its classic perfection during the Gupta age. The best examples of Buddhist painting belong to this period; Buddhist rock-cut sanctuaries and *saṃghārāmas*, and the plastic deities that the Buddhist artists of the Gupta period worked out, are according to experts among the best specimens of the world art.

Except for the short lived destructive persecution by the Hūṇas,[67] Buddhism in both Hīnayāna and Mahāyāna forms continued to flourish during the rule of the Gupta kings. *Stūpas*, *caityas* and *vihāras* continued to be built and maintained except at old sites, like Kapilavastu, Śrāvasti and Gayā, which to Fa-hsien appeared in desolate and ruinous state. The monasteries at Mathurā and Pāṭaliputra were active centres of monastics; the great monastery of Nālandā, which in course of time became the greatest centre of Buddhist learning in Asia, was founded by Kumāragupta Mahendrāditya.[68] The wonderful rock-cut *caitya*-halls with their remarkable sculpture and frescoes at Ajaṇṭā are largely the creation of the Gupta period. Art centres of the period like Sāranātha, Mathurā and Nālandā have yielded a large number of images of Buddhas, Bodhisattvas and other Buddhist divinities.

Two Tendencies in the Sixth Century A.D.

The foregoing sketch of the background of earlier development reveals that in about the sixth century A.D. Buddhism in India was marked by two principal tendencies. These were (a) the emergence of the Buddhist version of the science of logic and beginning of intense controversy between the Buddhist and the Brāhmanical schools, and (b) the definite emergence of Esoteric Buddhism or Vajrayāna.

Although the works of Nāgārjuna, Maitreyanātha, Asaṅga and Vasubandhu had furnished considerable background for the development of logic in Buddhist quarters,[69] it was Diṅnāga who put it on firm foundations and started a scientific study of *pramāṇas* or 'means of proof'. He is therefore truly regarded as 'the Father of Indian Logic', more correctly of Buddhist Logic.[70] Diṅnāga may be considered also as the founder of a 'critical school of philosophy' in Buddhism[71] and one who inaugurated an age of philosophical controversies and intellectual tournaments. His system shows an admixture of Sautrāntika and Vijñānavāda tenets, and he is known to have criticised Naiyāyika logical theories.[72] With him, therefore, begins a new epoch in the history of Buddhist thought and in that of Indian philosophy also. Thenceforward, the Buddhist thinkers began to take an active part in philosophical debates and a keen interest in logical theories.[73] The system of Diṅnāga had one more important result, namely, the doctrinal controversies among the Buddhistic schools. It was in about the same time that the Madhyamaka school was divided into two factions, one headed by Bhāvaviveka which emphasised logical reasoning and independent arguments; the other headed by Buddhapālita, which was purely dialectical and applied the method of *reductio ad absurdum*. Moreover, Diṅnāga himself is said to have criticised Vasubandhu's views, and Diṅnāga's pupil Īśvarasena is criticised by Dharmakīrti.[74] Nor were the followers of Vijñānavāda, who came after Vasubandhu and lived before Hsüan-tsang's visit to India, in agreement among themselves[75]. Far more important was the controversy with the Brāhmanical thinkers. Uddyotakara is said to have composed his monumental polemical treatise, the *Nyāyavārttika*, in defence of Vātsyāyana and against the theories of Diṅnāga.[76] This controversy became more vigorous and intense during the centuries that followed.

The second important tendency, equally manifest but of far reaching consequences for it completely transformed Buddhism into a new faith, was the emergence of Tāntrika Buddhism. In the growth of *dhāraṇīs* and *mantras*, the popularity of spells and charms, the cult of Avalokita and Tārā, the worship of many male and female divinities with Ādibuddha at the head of the pantheon, and the Buddhist approaches to popular aspects of Hinduism, one can see the gradual but continuous development of the Vajrayāna, which during the next two centuries became the dominant form of Buddhism in India.

The earliest Tāntrika Buddhist literature would seem to have been a part of the Mahāyāna Sūtras. The *Saddharma-puṇḍarīka* has a whole chapter on the *dhāraṇīs*.[77] The popularity of magical charms in the fifth and sixth centuries A.D. is borne out by the *Mahāmāyūri* and the *Si-yu-ki* of Hsüan-tsang. The *Kāraṇḍavyūha* expounds the deified cult of Avalokita, and Maheśvara and Umā are among his devotees.[78] This appears very like the Śaiva cult. The *Suvarṇaprabhāsasūtra*, "for a great part, already bears the stamp of a Tantra."[79] The *Mañjuśrīmūla-kalpa*, while claiming to be a Mahāyāna-vaipulya-sūtra, contains clear elements of Vajrayāna.[80]

Chapter II

BUDDHISM DURING THE 7TH AND 8TH CENTURIES

Buddhism in Uttarāpatha

Hsüan-tsang begins his description of India with Lan-po or Lampa. According to the *Life*, all countries to the north of it are called 'frontier lands' or '*mleccha* lands.'[1] The territory has been identified by Cunnigham with Lamghan or Lughman in the Kabul Valley.[2] There were here above ten monasteries with some Mahāyāna monks. The non-Buddhists were numerous who commanded over a score of Deva-temples.[3]

Nagarahāra (Na-ka lo-ho) probably corresponded to the Jalālābād district. It is not unlikely that Nagarahāra may have been identical with the old republic of Nyas referred to by Arrian.[4] The people of Nagarahāra respected Buddhism; there were several Buddhist establishments with few monks. In this kingdom in the city called Hi-lo (Hidda) there were Buddha's relics enshrined in a two-storeyed building.[5] It is noteworthy that near the 'Shadow Cave' near Nagar there was a great monastery with 700 monks in the fifth century A.D., a fact noted by Fa-hsien,[6] of which Hsüan-tsang speaks nothing. This may point to the decline of this community and its monastery.

In old days Gāndhāra (Kan-to-lo) had produced many Śāstra-Doctors and was a famous centre of the Buddhists. But in the seventh century over a thousand monasteries were in ruinous state and most of the *stūpas* had decayed.[7] The people of Gāndhāra were fond of practical arts and were mostly non-Buddhists. There were some followers of Buddhism. Around Puṣkalāvati (Peshawar) there were about 100 Deva-temples with votaries of various non-Buddhist sects; many of them were Śaiva-Pāśupatas. However, in an old monastery built by Kaniṣka, there were still "a few Brethren all Hīnayānists". This, as Thomas Watters pointed out, may have been apparently the 'Kaṇika-Caitya' mentioned by Alberuni. A few Hīnayāna monks were also in existence at the time of Hsüan-tsang in an old monastery where the master Dharmatrāta had once lived. The Pilgrim also met with some Mahāyāna monks near the city of Peshawar who were living in an old monastery.[8]

This country, according to Hsüan-tsang, commences North India. Wu-chang-na or Udyāna (Uḍḍiyāna in Swat valley), according to Cunningham, comprised the modern districts of Pangkora, Bijawar, Swat and Bunir.[9] There were in older days 1,400 monasteries on both the sides of the river Swat; they had been tenanted by as many as 18,000 Brethren. But in the 7th century A.D. there lived only a few Brethren who followed Mahāyāna Buddhism. They practised silent meditation, recited the texts with ease but without understanding their deep meaning. "They lived strictly according to their rules and were especially expert in magical exorcisms." Though the Buddhists of Udyāna were Mahāyānists yet Hsüan-tsang found that they followed the *vinaya* of the Dharmagupta, Mahīśāsaka, Kāśyapīya, Sarvāstivādin and the Mahāsāṃghika sects—all belonging to the so called Hīnayāna. Besides, there were various other sectarians and above ten Deva-temples. In the vicinity of the city called Meng-kie (ka) li or "Muṅgali" (Beal) or 'Mangkil' (Watters) which was the principal royal seat of Udyāna, there was a Buddhist temple in which was an image of Avalokiteśvara. People offered regular worship to this image and the site was a place of Buddhist pilgrimage.[10] In Ta-li-lo (Darel) the old capital of Udyāna, the pilgrim reports that he saw a "wooden image" of Bodhisattva Maitreya, "100 feet high", a work of Arhat Madhyāntika.[11] The latter may be the same person who is mentioned in the Ceylonese Chronicles as an apostle of Buddhism in N.W. Himālayan region.[12] This image is referred to by Fa-hsien also who gives its height as 80 feet.[13] It is strange that a wooden image could have survived from the time of Aśoka when Madhyāntika lived, till the 7th century A.D. when Hsüan-tsang did homage to it.

In Po-lu-lo or Bolor of later times, modern Little Tibet, Hsüan-tsang found some hundreds of monasteries and some thousands of monks, who, however, were, without definite learning. Their observances of the rules of the *saṃgha* were also defective; they had been careless in moral conduct.[14]

The plucky people of Takṣaśilā, Ta-cha-shi-lo, were followers of Buddhism. There were many Buddhist monasteries, several of them being desolate; the monks, few in number, were Mahāyānists. In the neighbourhood of Takṣaśilā there was an old monastery where once Kumāralabdha had lived, and which was occupied by a few Brethren.[15]

The territory called Seng-ha-pu-lo or Siṃhapura lay to the south-east of Takṣaśilā. Cunningham identified its capital with modern Ketas situated on the north side of the Salt Range. Siṃhapura, a province of the Kingdom of Kashmir, had many old vestiges of Buddhist establishments; Hsüan-tsang found here in flourishing state the followers of 'the white-clothes sect', i.e. the Śvetāṃbara Jainas. They had many characteristics of the Buddhists, such as the gradation of monks into *bhikṣu* and *śrāmanera* and the observances of rituals.

Near the Manikyala stone *stūpa*, an imposing Buddhist structure in this country, there lived a small community of Mahāyāna monks, about one hundred in number. Hsüan-tsang also found some Mahāyāna monks living in the monasteries of Uraśa or Urakṣa (Wu-la-cha) located in Dhantawar near Muzfarbad. In the fifth century A.D. a Chinese pilgrim monk, Fa-sheng by name, had seen here a large Buddhist establishment frequented by about 5,000 monks. In the seventh century A.D. the conditions of Buddhism seem to have declined.[16]

The territory of Ka-sse-mi-lo or Ko-shih-mi Kashmir has been regarded as the cradle of Sanskrit Buddhism.[17] This ancient land had produced a number of famous Buddhist commentators, poets and philosophers in the first millennium of Christian era.

In the first-half of the seventh century A.D., however, the conditions of Buddhism in Kashmir were not very well. At one place Hsüan-tsang says that the "good looking but deceitful people" of Kashmir embraced both Buddhism and other faiths; the strength of the *bhikṣus* was above 5,000 who lived in above 100 monasteries. It is not specified as to what system of Buddhism these monks belonged, but from other sources we learn that both Hīnayāna and Mahāyāna monks were living together in Kashmir. The country was also rich in old establishments containing sacred relics.[18]

Hsüan-tsang observes[19] that owing to the predominance of the 'Kritiya' race which hated the Buddhists, the country in his time, had no faith in Buddhism and was devoted to other sects.

The King, whose name is not given, was favourable to Buddhism, he received Hsüan-tsang in a *dharmaśālā* along with the members of the royal household and showed a marked respect for the distinguished pilgrim. There were a number of Buddhist establishments, noted scholars and sanctuaries, and Hsüan-tsang spent two years in study and learning in Kashmir. He stayed in the Jayendra-vihāra, where he was assisted by some Kashmirian monks in the task of religious offerings and doctrinal discussions. There was an old eminent monk of 70 years who was the chief Sthavira of Jayendra-vihāra. Under him the pilgrim studied various Śāstras and Sūtras.[20] Jayendra-vihāra seems to have been a thriving centre of Buddhist scholars. Kalhaṇa also mentions this *vihāra*; it was built by Jayendra, the maternal uncle of King Pravarasena of Kashmir, who also installed an image of Buddha.[21] There was also a temple (probably a *caitya*-cum-*vihāra*) which was built by Huṣkara where the pilgrim spent one night.[22] Kalhaṇa refers to Huṣka (Huviṣka) along with Kaniṣka and Juṣka (?) who built *vihāras* and founded cities in Kashmir.[23]

There was yet another monastery here wherein lay the celebrated Tooth-relic, in length about an inch and a half, of yellowish-white colour. This Tooth-relic was taken away by Śīlāditya (Harṣa) from the king of Kashmir; the monastery had about three hundred monks at this time.[24] Near the monastery of Tooth-relic there was an old large monastic establishment. In the seventh century A.D. only a double-storeyed building in a corner of it was inhabited by about thirty Mahāyāna monks. Besides, Kashmir had also a monastery not far from the capital, wherein lived 100 monks of the Mahāsāṃghika school.[25] The *Life* mentions in Kashmir among the most famous Buddhist Doctors the following : Viśuddhasiṃha and Jinabandhu who were Mahāyānists; Sugatamitra and Vasumitra of the Sarvāstivāda school; Sūryadeva and Jinatrāta of the Mahāsāṃghika school. At the capital city the foremost sage was Ch'eng or Yaśa.[26]

Kalhaṇa has recorded the patronage of Buddhism by some rulers whose dates are not quite certain. Among the kings who ruled in Kashmir after Mihirakula and Toramāṇa (early 6th century A.D.) and who might be placed in the seventh century A.D. is King Meghavāhana. He was brought from Gāndhāra and placed on the throne by the people; most probably he was a Buddhist and propagated the cult of *ahiṃsā* and erected a *maṭha* (convent).

His queen Amṛtaprabhā built Amṛtabhavana for the use of Buddhist monks and erected a high *vihāra* also. Her teacher was Stonpa who was probably a Tibetan and a native of Ladakh and lived in Kashmir. Yūkadevī, another queen of Meghavāhana, also constructed a large monastery in Nadavana. In this monastery one half was occupied by monks of good conduct, and the other half by those 'monks' who had wives, children and the cattle. Indradevī, a third queen of this king, is said to have built a four-storeyed monastery and a *stūpa*. His other queens, Khādanā, Sammā etc. are also reported to have constructed many monasteries and *stūpas* for the Buddhists.[27] One of these is located at Khādanīya near Varāhmūla on the Vitastā river.[28] Kalhaṇa seems to suggest that Meghavāhana was a pious king who may be said to have atoned for the sins committed by his forefathers like Mihirakula.[29]

Buddhism and Kashmir Śaivism : It is remarkable that in Kashmir, Buddhism and Śaivism, despite their apparent differences, remained very close to each other. Already in the time of Kuṣāṇas, Buddha and Śiva were worshipped by the members of the same family. In the *Kāraṇḍavyūhasūtra*, Maheśvara (Śiva) is included among the devotees of Avalokiteśvara, and he himself is addressed as 'Maheśvara'. In the *Saddharmapuṇḍarīkasūtra* also it is stated that in order to convert and preach the people, Avalokiteśvara assumes the form of Maheśvara. We learn from Bāṇa Bhaṭṭa and Hsüan-tsang that in Emperor Harṣa's family Buddha was worshipped along with Śiva and Sūrya. Kalhaṇa informs us that a number of kings of Kashmir patronised both Śaivism and Buddhism. Hsüan-tsang notes that in Potalaka mountain in the far south, Avalokiteśvara used to give vision to his devotees in the guise of Pāśupata-Tīrthika or Śiva. Hūṇas, however, are known to have patronised Śaivism to the exclusion and persecution of Buddhism.

What is interesting and striking in this context is the fact that a noted Buddhist logician is seen writing authoritatively not only on Buddhism but also on Kashmir Śaivism. This scholar was Śaṃkarānanda (also called Ānanda and Śaṃkaranandana). He was a pupil of Dharmottara and wrote several works on Buddhist logic and may have lived towards the end of 8th and and beginning of 9th century A.D. He also wrote a work called *Prajñālaṅkāra*, which is not included in the list of his works translated into Tibetan, and seems to have been lost. But this work is quoted by Abhinavagupta who notes that Śaṃkarānanda controverted Dharmottara. Doctrinally there is a great similarity between the Mahāyāna tenet of Wisdom or Consciousness and the Gnosticism of Kashmir Śivaites. It seems that Kashmir Śaivism owes much to Mahāyāna idealism and gnosticism, and the *Prajñālaṅkāra* of Śaṃkarānanda is a bridge between Buddhist idealism and Śivaite idealism of Kashmir, just as the *Māṇḍūkyakārikās* of Gauḍapāda had been a bridge between the Madhyamaka absolutism and Vedāntika non-dualism. Recently, Prof. Raniero Gnoli has thrown some desired light on the philosophical position of Śaṃkarānanda and his influence on Kashmir Śaivism. He places Śaṃkarānanda in the 9th or 10th century A.D. His brief discussion has eminently proved that the *Prajñālaṅkāra* was "held in high esteem by Abhinavagupta, who constantly gives Śaṃkarānanda the title of *bhaṭṭa* and once even of *guru*, and recognises in him a true precursor of the doctrine of knowledge adopted by his school." He rightly holds, following the indications given by Abhinavagupta and Tārānātha, that Śaṃkarānanda may have left Buddhism and espoused Śaivism, and hence his "double attitude" towards thought. I think that the hybrid name (Śaṃkara+Ānanda) Śaṃkarānanda is in keeping with his hybrid thought. According to Prof. Gnoli Abhinavagupta has quoted several passages from the *Prajñālaṅkāra* of Śaṃkarānanda in the *Īśvarapratyabhijñāvivṛtivimarśini*, in the *Tantrāloka* and in the *Mālinīvijayavārttikaṃ* where he is called *guru*. The Buddhist logical text of Śaṃkarānanda, the *Apohasiddhi*, is also quoted in the first work of Abhinavagupta mentioned above. Besides, Jayaratha, in his commentary on the *Tantrāloka* has also quoted the *Prajñālaṅkāra*.[30]

In the 7th century A.D. three scholars from Kashmir, viz. Buddhapāla, Ratnacintā, and Arjuna, proceeded to China and translated a number of Buddhist books into Chinese.[31]

Although the kings of Kashmir who ruled after Meghavāhana were Śivaites, yet they seem to have been tolerant towards Buddhism. During the reign of Yudhiṣṭhira II, son and successor of Pravarasena, his ministers were Buddhists who constructed *vihāras* and *caityas*. One of these is Skandabhavana-vihāra, built by the minister named Skandagupta.[32] In the reign of King

Raṇāditya, one of his queens named Amṛtaprabhā, installed a beautiful statue of Buddha in the *vihāra* built by the queen of Meghavāhana. Galuṇa, a minister under King Vikramāditya, son and successor of Raṇāditya, had caused a *vihāra* to be constructed in the name of his wife Ratnāvali. The last king of this line was Bālāditya.

Bālāditya was succeeded by his son-in-law, Durlabhavardhana, whose queen set up the Anaṅgabhavana-vihāra.[33] This monument was seen by the Chinese monk-pilgrim, Ou K'ong, who refers to it as Ānanda-or Anaṅga-vihāra.[34]

The most famous ruler of this line was the great Lalitāditya-Muktāpīḍa, a contemporary and conqueror of Yaśovarman of Kanauj. He was a Vaiṣṇava but extended his benefactions to other faiths and built temples of Viṣṇu, Śiva and also Buddhist *stūpas* and *vihāras*. King Lalitāditya flourished most probably in the early part of the 8th century A.D., when Vākpati, Bhavabhūti and Yaśovarman had already become famous.[35]

Lalitāditya built a large *vihāra* and a *stūpa*[36] in Huṣkapura (identified with Ushkur inside the Bārāmūla pass). The king spent, reports Kalhaṇa, 84 thousand *tolās* of gold in the construction of a Rāja-vihāra decorated with large Buddha images, grand *caityas* and four-storeyed palaces.[37] Not only this, Lalitāditya, as if to rival Aśoka, caused to be prepared 84 thousand high Buddha-images which seemed to reach the sky. They were made of bronze alloy. He got these images installed in 84 thousand beautiful *caityas* specially made for thepurpose.[38]

His vassal, King Kayya of Lāṭa, built a *vihāra* in which Bhikṣu Sarvajñamitra, 'a Second Buddha', the author of the *Sragdharāstotra*, used to live. This latter was a nephew of king of Kashmir. But the most zealous Buddhist in the court of Lalitāditya was Caṅkuṇa. Caṅkuṇa was a native of Tukhāra country and was the Prime Minister of Lalitāditya. He set up two *vihāras*, one of which was very lofty and contained golden images of Buddha. His son-in-law Īśānacandra, who was a physician in the royal palace, constructed a large and fine *vihāra*. Caṅkuṇa was probably expert in Tāntrika practices and magical arts by means of which he charmed the Emperor. At the latter's request, he imparted the charms to him and received in return the great image of Buddha which had been brought by Lalitāditya from Magadha. Its existence is borne out not only by Kalhaṇa but also by the 8th century Chinese pilgrim, Ou K'ong.

One of the notable kings of the family of Lalitāditya was Jayāpīḍa, who may have ruled in the later half of the 8th century A.D. He founded a large *vihāra* and set up three images of Buddha in Jayapura, a city which he had established in Kashmir. He also adopted a special name, Vinayāditya, 'the sun of discipline.' King Jayāpīḍa also patronised a 'Dravidian Sorcerer' who performed miracles, and the famous logician Dharmottara.[39]

In the second half of the 8th century, a Chinese pilgrim came to Kashmir via Kipin, Kabul valley and Gāndhāra, and lived there for four years in the Moung-ti or Mundi-vihāra. He found more than 300 monasteries in the kingdom and a large number of *stūpas* and images. Besides the Moung-ti-vihāra, he mentions the following seven Buddhist establishments in Kashmir : (1) Amitabhavana; (2) Anaṅga or Ānandabhavana; (3) Ki-tche; (4) Nao-ye-le; (5) Je-je; (6) Yi-li-t' e-le; and (7) K'o-toen.[40]

The first Buddhist establishment seems to be identical with the Amṛtabhavana built by the queen Amṛtaprabhā noted above. The second one is evidently the *vihāra* of the same name built by the queen of Durlabhavardhana as reported by Kalhaṇa. According to Sten Konow the ruins of a *stūpa* in the village of Uskur (Huṣkapura) are the remains of Moung-ti-vihāra referred to by Ou K' ong. He also noticed the ruins of the monastery built by queen Khādanā in the village of Khādanīyar.[41] One would be tempted to suggest that the Moung-ti-vihāra referred to by Ou-K' ong may be identical with the Rāja-vihāra built by Lalitāditya-Muktāpīḍa.

The people of Pan-nu-tso (Punach or Punats to south-west of Kashmir's capital) were in the time of Hsüan-tsang, sincere believers in Buddhism. The State was subject to Kashmir and most of Buddhist establishments here were in ruins, there were only a few monks living in a *vihāra* near the capital city. To the south-east of Punats lay the territory called Rājapura (modern Rājauri). There were ten monasteries here and a few Buddhist monks.[42]

In the kingdom of Cheh-ka or Ṭakka[43] which lay between the Beas and the Indus rivers, few people believed in Buddhism. Most of the population was devoted to Devas which means that they were Śivaite. Accordingly there were only ten monasteries but hundreds of Deva-temples. One marked feature of this country, which seems to have been an example of Buddhistic and Aśokan piety, was the existence of numerous *puṇyaśālās* where free rest-houses for the relief of the needy and the distressed, medicine and food for the sick and the hungry, were supplied.[44] From the *Life* we learn that Hsüan-tsang spent a night at Jayapura (Jammu) in a non-Buddhist temple. From this he went to Śākala (Sialkot) where Mihirakula had wrought devastations in earlier days. In the 7th century there were one hundred Hīnayāna monks in a *saṃghārāma* of Sialkot.[45]

In the eastern part of the Cheh-ka country, the pilgrim found a large city in an Āmra-grove (mango-garden) wherein lived "a Brahmin 700 years old, looking like a man of 30 years and having all his mental and bodily powers." He had been a disciple of Nāgārjuna and was well acquainted with the sacred lore of Brāhmanism and Buddhism. He had thoroughly studied the following two texts, *Prāṇyamūla* and *Śataśāstra*; he had two pupils each of whom was a centenarian. Hsüan-tsang lived with him for about a month and studied some Sūtras as also the *Śataśāstra* and *Śataśāstra-vaipulya*. However, only a few people in this city were Buddhist.[46]

The capital city of Cīnabhukti has been equated to the present Patli, an old town 10 miles to the west of the river Beas. The people of this province were both Buddhist and non-Buddhist. There were ten monasteries of the Buddhist monks. One of these is called in the *Life* Tosa-sana (T'u-she-sa-na, 'Pleasure-giving') where Hsüan-tsang resided for 14 months. In this monastery lived a great Buddhist sage, by name Vinītaprabha, a master of the Tripiṭaka and Doctor of Śāstras, who taught the Chinese pilgrim.[47]

Near the capital of Cīnabhukti, there was a splendid and spacious monastery known as Tamasavana-vihāra. The original of Tamasavana (dark-forest) may have been probably Tapovana. The place is mentioned in the *Divyāvadāna* and must have been a flourishing centre of Buddhistic culture in older days. Hsüan-tsang found here thousands of relic-*stūpas* all round the monastery, ruins of numerous monasteries, caves and images including an Aśokan *stūpa*, 200 feet in height. In the Tamasavana Monastery there were at this time 300 learned monks of the Sarvāstivāda school. They lived a pure and strict life and were well versed in Hīnayāna.[48]

Comparatively speaking, Buddhism was in a more flourishing condition in Jālandhara than in other parts of the Punjab. There were 50 monasteries here and more than 2,000 monks who made special studies of Hīnayāna or Mahāyāna as they liked. The city had more than 500 professed non-Buddhists, the Pāśupatas. According to *Life* of Hsüan-tsang, he visited Jālandhara for a second time and then a king of Northern India who had his capital here, honoured him. This king's name was Wu-ti-to or Udita. He had previously honoured another Chinese monk Hsüan chao who had lived here for four years in the thirties of the 7th century.[49] In Jālandhara, on entering the country, Hsüan-tsang lived in the Nagardhana-vihāra where there was Candravarman, a master of Tripiṭaka.[50]

In the district of Kullu, in the upper valley of the Beas, the pilgrim noticed twenty monasteries in which more than one thousand Brethren lived. They were for the most part followers of Mahāyāna, a few being Hīnayānists.[51]

In the district of Śatadru on the Sutlej river, there were many desolate monasteries and a small number of the monks. The inhabitants lived a moral life, were devoted to Buddhism but observed social distinctions.[52] This shows that even the Buddhist laity was not free from Brahmanical rules of caste.

The province of Pāryātra has been identified with Bairat, the site from where a copy of Aśoka's Minor Rock Edict has been recovered. It was ruled over by a Vaiśya king, the people were not Buddhists, but Brahmanical Deva-worshippers. There were eight Buddhist monasteries in bad state of ruin. The monks who were very few in number, were Hīnayānists.[53]

Thāneśvara or Sthāṇvīśvara[54] in Ambala district of Punjab, had only three Buddhist monasteries wherein lived above 700 Hīnayāna monks. Votaries of Hinduistic sects were more numerous who had more than one hundred Deva-temples.[55]

Buddhism in Madhyadesa

In Mathurā, the famous city on the Yamunā, the Chinese pilgrim found people of good manners, who believed in the Law of karma and respected moral and intellectual eminence.[56] There were in the Mathurā district more than twenty monasteries and over two thousand Buddhist monastics, who zealously followed both Hīnayāna and Mahāyāna. This seems to indicate that some were zealous Hīnayānists, the others zealous Mahāyānists.

Mathurā had many Buddhist relics of the past. There were *stūpas* containing the sacred relics of Tathāgata, Śāriputra, Mudgalaputra (Maudgalyāyana), Pūrṇamaitrāyanīputra, Upāli, Ānanda and Rāhula, as also the *stūpas* built for some Bodhisattvas like Mañjuśrī. Every year, on religious festival days, the *bhikṣus* and the *upāsakas*, both male and female, used to gather here, and vied with each other in offering worship to their respective idols. The followers of Mahāyāna worshipped the Bodhisattvas.[57] Hsüan-tsang also mentions a cave where Upagupta had lived.[58]

The district of Srughna (Lu-le-na, or Su-lu-ki-na) may be identical with modern 'village of Sugh surrounded on three sides by the old bed of Jumna',[59] but its true location is still awaiting. The people of Srughna were not Buddhists but they were honest and esteemed religious wisdom. There were five Buddhist monasteries and more than 1,000 Buddhist monks, most of whom were Hīnayānists, a few adhering to 'other schools.' The phrase 'other schools' may be an allusion to Sautrāntikas. But the phrase is rather puzzling, it cannot refer to the sects of Hīnayāna as the majority of the monks are clearly said to be Hīnayānists and all the 18 sects were of the Hīnayāna; nor can it refer to the Mahāyānists, for it is characteristic of Hsüan-tsang to mention the Mahāyānists prominently.

The *bhikṣus* of Srughna were specialists and lucid exponents of the subtle and deep principles. Celebrated Buddhist scholars from other places used to come to them to get their doubts cleared.[60] From the *Life* we learn that Hsüan-tsang enjoyed the company of a learned Doctor of Sautrāntika thought, Jayagupta by name, who dwelt in this district. Hsüan-tsang spent one winter and half the spring season in order to study Sautrāntika tenets under him.[61]

The territory of Mo-ti-pu-lo (Matipura) has been identified by Cunningham with Mandawar near Bijnor. The people were practical minded and 'well versed in magical arts', and were equally divided between Buddhism and non-Buddhist religious sects. The king, a *śūdra* by caste, was not a

Buddhist but a Deva-worshipper, and there were more than fifty Deva-temples.

The numerical strength of the Buddhist monks was more than 800 who lived in more than ten monasteries. They were Sarvāstivādins. Close to the capital was a small monastery in which Guṇaprabha had composed 100 treatises including *Tattvanirdeśa-Śāstra*. This Guṇaprabha, a native of Kashmir, has been a student of Saṃghabhadra whose monastery was also still extant in the seventh century. Both Guṇaprabha and Saṃghabhadra belonged to the late 5th and early 6th century A.D. There were about fifty monks, followers of Guṇaprabha who lived in the monastery of that Doctor; in the *saṃghārāma* of Saṃghabhadra which lay close to the former, lived about 200 Hīnayāna (that is to say Vaibhāṣika) monks. Close to the monastery of Saṃghabhadra there was a *stūpa* containing the relics of Vimalamitra, a native of Kashmir, a Sarvāstivādin Hīnayānist by faith, and a successor and supporter of Saṃghabhadra. He flourished probably in the sixth century A.D.[62] There also lived in Matipura, Mitrasena, an eminent Buddhist sage, a Doctor of Śāstras, a pupil of Guṇaprabha, who, at the age of 90 years, taught Hsüan-tsang for half the spring and the summer following. The texts studied by the pilgrim under him included among others, the *Tattvanirdeśa-Śāstra* of Guṇaprabha and the *Jñānaprasthānaśāstra* of Kātyāyanīputra.[63] From this one may conclude that Mitrasena was a Sarvāstivādin probably of the Vaibhāṣika designation.

Hsüan-tsang refers to Haridwar and its religious activities, but does not allude to the existence of Buddhists in that city.

In Brahmapura country, 'in the districts of Gaṛhwal and Kumaon', the population pursued gain, there were five Buddhist monasteries but the monks were very few. In the country called Suvarṇa-gotra which lay north of Brahmapura and touched Tibet (T'u-fan) on the east and Khotan on the north, which was ruled over by women, there was probably no Buddhism in Hsüan-tsang's days.[64]

The old country of Ku-pi-sang-na of Chinese records, restored as Goviṣāṇa, corresponds to modern districts of Kashipur, Rampur and Pilibhit.[65] Most of the people of this kingdom were non-Buddhists, but they were fond of learning and religious merit. There were about 100 Buddhist monks belonging to

Hīnayāna, they lived in two monasteries. The country had some Buddha relics in old *stūpas* of the time of Aśoka.[66]

Hsüan-tsang found in Ahicchatra (in Eastern Rohilkhand) people of academic temperament and honest ways. There were more than a thousand monks of the Sammitīya school[67] of Hīnayāna. They occupied above ten *vihāras*. The number of Deva-temples was nine and the Pāśupata-Śaivas were also more than three hundred in number.[68]

This territory, tentatively restored as 'Virasana', 'Vilasana' or 'Bhilasana' by Julien, Beal and Watters, is difficult to identify. Its capital is equated with the mound of Atranjikherā on the river Kālī, to the north of Etah on the Grand Trunk Road, by Cunningham.[69] Its people were mostly non-Buddhist but a few were faithful. There were two Buddhist monasteries which accommodated 300 Mahāyāna monks. The capital city had some old monuments of Buddhistic cult.[70]

According to Chinese sources the old name of Kapitha (Kah-pi-t'a) was Sankāśya or Sheng-ka-she. It is the sacred spot where according to Buddhist tradition Lord Buddha descended from the Trayastriṃśa Heaven.[71] The modern village of Sankisā lies on the meeting grounds of Farrukhabad, Etah and Mainpuri districts of U.P. In Hsüan-tsang's time there were four Buddhist monasteries and 1,000 monks of the Sammitīya sect in the capital of Sankāśya.[72]

The original name of Kanauj was Kanyā-kubja (nowadays also called Kānyakubja), 'city of the humped backed women'.[73] The historic city on the west bank of the Gaṅgā, was the capital of the Buddhist Emperor Harṣavardhana and, then of Yaśovarman in the 7th and 8th centuries A.D. It was one of the principal centres of Indian culture and also a hot bed of political conflicts and conspiracies during our period.[74] Its people were cultured and refined, devoted to arts, learning and debates. Both Buddhism and Hinduism had their 'equal' votaries here. In Buddhism, both the systems, the Hīnayāna and the Mahāyāna, were thriving together. The Chinese Master of the Doctrine estimated the numerical strength of the monasteries as above 100 and of the monks over 10,000.[75]

Emperor Harṣa of the *vaiśya* caste, was a liberal patron of philosophers, poets, sages and of the faiths, Hinduistic as well as Buddhistic. He practised some of the Aśokan ideals of piety and shared the military vigour and skill of Samudragupta. He was the contemporary of such noted Buddhist monarchs as Aṃśurvarman of Nepal and Sroṅ-btsan-gampo of Tibet, and was the greatest friend and the most enthusiastic patron of Hsüan-tsang, 'the Mahāyānadeva' as the latter was styled by the graduates of Nālandā, and who presided over that great philosophical conference convoked by Harṣa in his royal city which was attended not only by thousands of Buddhists, Jaina and Brahmanical theologians and debators, but also by a host of kings and chieftains.[76] Harṣa honoured not only Buddha and Avalokiteśvara, but also Śiva and Sūrya, his family gods. His brother, Rājyavardhana, was "a devout Buddhist" (*parama saugata sugata 'iva*),[77] his sister Rājyaśrī was an intelligent, accomplished lady, actively interested in Buddhism[78] and well versed in Sammitīya school. The Emperor did personal homage to such eminent Buddhist savants and sages as Śīlabhadra, Divākaramitra, Jayasena, Hsüan-tsang, and others. "His qualifications", says Hwui-li, "moved heaven and men."[79] "He forgot sleep and food in his devotion to good works", says Hsüan-tsang.[80] His virtues and powers exceeded, writes Bāṇa Bhaṭṭa, those of Viṣṇu, Paśupati, Yama, Varuṇa, Kubera and other deities; his sacrifices, his wisdom, poetic faculty and gusto were incomparable.[81]

Harṣa erected thousands of *stūpas* on the banks of the Gaṅgā, built monasteries on the sacred places of the Buddhists; he bore the expenses of the upkeep of the Nālandā Mahāvihāra, raised a brass monastery there, and enclosed the entire Buddhist establishment with a high wall. He brought the monks together, punished the sinners and rewarded the meritorious. He fed every day in his royal lodge 1,000 Buddhists and 500 *brāhmaṇās*.[82] He was perhaps the greatest *upāsaka* in the 7th century. In the vicinity of Kanauj, close to the Gaṅgā, were three monasteries enclosed by a common wall but each having its own gate. The inhabitant monks were dignified and reserved, and they had thousands of lay Buddhists to serve them.

Not very far from Kanauj was another city called Navadevakula. To the east of this city were three Buddhist monasteries enclosed within one wall but with separate gates; above 500 Sarvāstivādin monks lived in these monasteries.[83]

It is thus clear that Harṣa extended his patronage to all schools of Buddhism. His approaching to Bodhisattava Avalokiteśvara[84] shows that he was attached to Mahāyāna. This is also the conclusion to be drawn from his special respect for Hsüan-tsang who was a zealous Yogācārin. Emperor's sister Rājyaśrī seems to have been attached to the Sammitīya school.[85] The system or plan of three monasteries being enclosed within one wall providing each with an independent gate, which the Sarvāstivādins of Navadevakula had been occupying, also seems to have been a royal plan. In the *Life*, however, Harṣa is represented as showing his disapproval of Hīnayāna doctrines.[86]

In Ayodhyā in modern Faizabad district on the bank of the Sarayū river (Hsüan-tsang says on the south of the Gaṅgā, but apparently by mistake), there were more than one hundred Buddhist monastic establishments with more than 3,000 monks belonging to both Hīnayāna and Mahāyāna. The city was rich with a number of old Buddhist *stūpas* and monasteries now in ruins.[87]

Like the people of Ayodhyā, those of Ayamukha (supposed to be modern Daṇḍikherā on the northern bank of the Gaṅgā) were also good, devoted to learning and pious activities. Ayamukha was a centre of the Sammitīya monks, Hsüan-tsang found here five monasteries in which more than 100 *bhikṣus* of the Sammitīya school resided. Not very far from the capital was the old monastery of Buddhadāsa, a Sarvāstivādin Doctor; in the seventh centuty A.D. about 200 monks were living in this beautiful monastery.[88] According to the *Life* while Hsüan-tsang was going to Ayamukha with about 84 fellow-passengers on board, his boat was captured by the pirates who were worshippers of Durgā (i.e. the Śāktas). They wanted to kill the Chinese Master as a sacrifice to the Goddess, but he was saved by supernatural intervention of Bodhisattva Maitreya.[89]

At Prayāga Hsüan-tsang found the dominance of the Brahmanical culture; there were hundreds of Deva-temples and most of the people were followers of non-Buddhist faiths. One peculiar feature, current at this time at the confluence of the Gaṅgā and the Yamunā, the pilgrim reports, was the custom of religious suicide.[90] Professor K. Chattopadhyaya has thrown some welcome light on this practice of the Hindus.[91] I-tsing also testifies to the prevalence of religious suicide in Buddha-Gayā and on the Gaṅgā.[92]

There were only two Buddhist monasteries at Prayāga in the time of Hsüan-tsang, the number of monks was small, they were Hīnayānists. A notable custom at Prayāga followed by kings and liberal minded wealthy nobles since ancient times, was to hold sessions of charity or the assembly of *mokṣa.* There was a sacred spot on the holy *saṃgama* which was actually named the 'Field of Great Beneficence'. During Hsüan-tsang's sojourn here, Emperor Harṣavardhana performed this great *dāna-yajña* for about 75 days, in course of which this 'Sun of Morality' (Śīlāditya) gave away in charity everything he had, and exhausted the Imperial Treasury. Everyone, from the sacred Buddha, Dharma and Saṃgha, down to the poorest orphan, was benefited by this gift.[93]

The ancient city of Kosambī, celebrated equally in Buddhist and Brahmanical literature of ancient times,[94] has been identified with modern village of Kosām in Allahabad district. About ten monasteries were in ruinous state when Hsüan-tsang visited the site. Early in the 5th century A.D. Fa-hsien testifies to the existence of one 'Shrine' built by Ghochiravana where there still lived some Hīnayāna monks.[95] This 'Ghochira' is most plausibly the same as 'Goṣira' of Hwui-li and 'Ghoṣila' of Hsüan-tsang's *Si-yu-ki.*[96] In the seventh century it was in ruins. G. R. Sharma has thoroughly excavated the site of Kauśāmbī and has laid bare the beautiful Ghoṣitārāma monastery complex.[97] An inscription found at the site also refers to this *vihāra*, while a seal of Toramāṇa, the Hūṇa chief, found here seems to allude to the destruction of the establishment by his outlandish army. Nevertheless, about 300 monks of the Hīnayāna still lived at Kauśāmbī in the first half of the seventh century A.D. The pilgrim also refers to a large Buddhist temple and the images of Buddha of the time of Kauśāmbī's king Udayana, the Vatsarāja. He also records the tradition that the Doctrine of Buddha would cease to exist at Kauśāmbī.[98]

In 'Pi-sho-ka' (Viśoka) which is sometimes identified with Sāket near Ayodhyā, the people were religious and studious. There were more than twenty Buddhist monasteries occupied by 3,000 monks of the Sammitīya school. Near the capital was a large monastery where two *arhats*, Devaśarman, the author of *Abhidharma-Vijñānakāyapāda-Śāstra* and Gopa, the author of a

'Śāstra on the essential realities of Buddhism', had advanced mutually conflicting arguments. The former denied the existence of 'Ego and non-Ego', while the latter affirmed the existence of both. They seem to have belonged to the first century A.D. At this large monastery also, Dharmapāla (Hu-fa) had debated and defeated the Hīnayāna doctors. The pilgrim also observed in this monastery "a marvellous tree, six or seven feet high, developed from a tooth-stick which the Buddha after using it had cast down."[99]

In the city of Śrāvasti[100] (Hsüan-tsang wrongly calls the 'Śrāvasti country', the name of the country or kingdom was Kośala, Śrāvasti being its capital), hundreds of Buddhist monasteries were in ruins. There were few monks, the votaries of the Sammitīya sect. The people who were devoted to good ways and fond of learning, were mostly non-Buddhist. Hsüan-tsang estimated the number of Deva-temples as one hundred. The great Jetavana-vihāra now lay in ruins.[101]

The well celebrated holy city of Kapilavastu was in utter ruins; "the district had been left desolate for a very long time" says Hsüan-tsang. It was a pitiable sight to see the ruins of more than 1,000 Buddhist monasteries here. There was still one monastery existing with 30 monks of the Sammitīya school. The Deva-worshippers, however, had two temples to their credit. This country in the Nepalese Tarai, seems to have had a system of the city states as Hsüan-tsang found "each city having its own chief."[102]

The account of Kapilavastu as given by Fa-hsien and Hsüan-tsang is in sharp contrast with the one preserved in the *Shui-ching-chu* by a 6th century A.D. Chinese official, Li Tao-Yuan by name. This authority supplies following new information concerning Kapilavastu. He says the kingdom of Kapila had no king then; the city was deserted and dirty. But there were some *upāsakas* (lay-devotees) about 20 Śākya families, descended from Śuddhodana. They still maintained their old spirit of religious energy. They repaired the old dilapidated *stūpas*. The king of Siṃhala sent gifts as an aid to finish this task of preserving the old *stūpas*. At that time there were only 12 monks in the city.[103] At Lumminī (Lumbinī, Rummindei) which lay at a distance of 50 li eastward from Kapilavastu (both sites are in Basti district of U.P. bordering on Nepal),[104]

Hsüan-tsang refers to old relics, Aśoka's stone pillar and *stūpas*, but no mention is made of the monks living here. It means that there were none in his time,[105] and the birth place of Buddha was without Buddhists. The neighbouring district of Rāmagrāma was likewise devoid of Buddhist population: it had a 'Śrāmanera monastery.' There were few Buddhist monks who were very hospitable to Hsüan-tsang. Kuśīnagara (Kasiā in Deoriā district of U.P.) was also in ruins, 'the interior of the city being a wild waste.' Hwui-li records : "There is a great *vihāra* here, built of bricks, within which is a figure of the Nirvāṇa of Tathāgata; his head is towards the north, and his appearance is as if he were asleep. By the side of *vihāra* is a *stūpa* about 200 feet high, constructed by Aśoka rāja." Modern archaeological excavations have shown the truth of this account. No mention is made of the monks who do not seem to have been in existence at Kuśīnagara in the 7th century A.D.[106]

The capital of Kāśī country, now the 'sacred city of the Hindus' since long, was the most sacred place of the Buddhists in ancient times, and seems to have remained so till the Gupta rule. It was in the vicinity of Vārāṇasī that the Blessed One set in motion the Wheel of the Doctrine. The people of Vārāṇasī[107] believed in other systems, only a few of them were Buddhist by faith. But all of them were courteous and esteemed learning; they were very wealthy. There were more than thirty Buddhist monasteries with more than 3,000 monks who adhered to the Sammitīya school of Hīnayāna. This report of Hsüan-tsang's *Si-yu-ki* is at variance with the one recorded in his *Life*. According to the *Life* the number of the Brethren in Vārāṇasī was 2,000 and they were Sarvāstivādins.[108]

But there were more than 100 Deva temples and more than 10,000 'professed adherents of other sects', i.e. *yogins* or ascetics, Śaiva-Pāśupatas and others who practised austerities. The object of worship in these Deva-temples was the *liṅgaṃ*, and in one of them, the *liṅgaṃ* was 100 feet high.[109]

In contrast to the 'sacred city of the Hindus' or rather of the Śivaite Hindus, Sāranātha or 'Deer Park' was, still in the 7th century A.D., an exclusively Buddhistic and a flourishing centre of the faith. It was a large living monastic establishment. The sacred spot of Dharma-cakra-pravartana was marked by an Aśokan *stūpa* and a pillar of polished stone, of greenish colour lustrous as a mirror. The monastic establishment here had eight divisions, all enclosed within one wall. Over one thousand and five hundred *bhikṣus* of the Sammitīya school were living here; the handsome *vihāra* had a number of beautiful buildings including one life-size statue of the Lord in *dharmacakra-pravartana-mudrā*. In and around the 'Deer Park' there were a number of sacred structures, mostly *stūpas*, one of them being 300 feet in height.[110]

Cunningham had identified Chan-chu with Gazipur District of U.P. This identification has been generally accepted. In the time of Hsüan-tsang's visit there were above ten Buddhist *vihāras* here and nearly one thousand monks of Hīnayāna. In and around the capital city, there were some old Buddhist monuments. In this district there was the Aviddhakarṇa-Saṃghārāma, i.e., "the monastery of the *bhikṣus* with unpierced ears," built for the monks of the Tukhāra country by the king of Gazipur territory. It is said that two monks from Tukhāra land whose ears were not pierced (*aviddha-karṇa*) had come to India to visit the sacred sites. But their Indian Brethren did not give them shelter and treated them with disdain owing to their being strange and foreigners. They were, however, patronised by the king of Chan-Chu who constructed a monastery exclusively for them. Near this monastery there were many other monasteries in bad conditions wherein few Mahāyāna *bhikṣus* were seen by the Chinese pilgrim.[111]

Buddhism in Magadha and the East

Magadha[112] had been the cradle of Buddhism and in this territory the religion continued to flourish till the last when it was wiped away by the arms of Islam.[113] Some of the most famous centres of Buddhism lay in ancient Magadha or modern Bihar, viz. Buddha-Gayā,[114] Rājagṛha,[115] Nālandā,[116] Vaiśālī[117] and Pāṭaliputra.[118]

The picture of Buddhism in the province of Magadha during the seventh and the eighth centuries A.D. was as follows. Buddhist establishments in the city of Vaiśālī were mostly dilapidated; a small number of monks lived in 3 or 4 of them that were intact. Digaṃbara Jainas and other sectarians had gained popularity in this city. In a monastery near the old royal house lived some monks of the Sammitīya school; it was believed that Buddha had delivered the *Vimalakīrtinirdeśa-sūtra*[119] at this monastery. The house of Vimalakīrti was also in ruins, so was the famous garden of Āmrapāli. A little south of Vaiśālī lay the monastery of Śvetapura in which some Mahāyānist monks lived a strict moral life.[120]

In Vṛji country Hsüan-tsang found few Buddhists. There were ten monasteries in which less than one thousand monk students and adherents of both the Great and Little Vehicle were living together. The non-Buddhists were numerous. It seems that the Vajjian monks were divided into both Hīnayāna and Mahāyāna systems. The pilgrim reports such 'mixed' faithful people in other parts of the country also as will be seen hereafter.

In Magadha proper, Buddhism seems to have enjoyed perhaps the best position in this period. Hsüan-tsang reports the existence of more than fifty Buddhist monasteries and more than 10,000 Buddhist monks, most of whom were Mahāyānists.[121] I-tsing who came to Magadha about forty years after Hsüan-tsang's visit, says that in Magadha although the doctrines of the 'four Nikāyas', to wit, the Mahāsāṃghika, the Sthavira, the Mūlasarvāstivāda and the Sammitīya, were generally in practice, yet the Sarvāstivāda Nikāya flourished the most.[122] The far famed Kusumapura (Pāṭaliputra) had long been a wilderness. There were mere ruins of the old *stūpas*, temples and monasteries all around the city. Among the more notable vestiges were the Kukkuṭārāma monastery built by Aśoka, Buddha's foot-prints on stone, and the 'Gong-Call-Tope'. The sacred stone had recently been thrown away by Śaśāṅka but it had been replaced.[123] At a small distance from the Kukkuṭārāma lay the Tilaḍaka monastery in which one thousand Mahāyāna Buddhist monks were living. They were all masters of the Tripiṭaka and greeted Hsüan-tsang cordially. On his way back to China, the pilgrim re-visited Nālandā and learned that close to Nālandā was a learned Doctor Prajñābhadra by name, who lived in Tilaḍaka monastery. I-tsing also mentions the Tilaḍha monastery near Nālandā and in his time the most famous teacher there was Jñānacandra.[124] These references show that in the later half of the 7th century A.D. Tilaḍaka was a flourishing centre of Buddhism.[125]

Next, there was yet another monastery on the slope of the hills, the high chambers of which had been hewn out of the rock; this rock-cut *vihāra* had been built in honour of Guṇamati the famous Doctor who had defeated the heretics here. In the seventh century A.D. there were 50 Mahāyāna monks in this monastery.[126]

Quite close to the Guṇamati monastery was a monastery built by Śīlabhadra, the famous teacher of Hsüan-tsang and the Head of the Nālandā University. The inmates of Śīlabhadra's monastery were maintained by the revenue of the city which had been bestowed on this Doctor for his victory in a doctrinal discussion with a *brāhmaṇa*.[127] The event took place probably early in the seventh century A.D. when Dharmapāla was alive.

Crossing the Nairañjanā, Hsüan-tsang found that the city of Gayā had very few inhabitants; there were only above 1000 *brāhmaṇa* families who were respected by all and enjoyed the freedom from royal control. The Bodhi Tree was protected by a strong wall from all sides; although, in "recent times Śaśāṅka, the enemy and oppressor of Buddhism, cut down the Bodhi Tree, destroyed its roots down to the water, and burned what remained. A few months afterwards Pūrṇavarman, by pious efforts brought the tree back to life and in one night it became ten feet high. This king then built round it a stone wall 24 feet high." In the centre of the Bodhi-Tree-Inclosure lay the Vajrāsana or Bodhi-Maṇḍala, 'the centre of the Universe'. Around this were the sitting images of Bodhisattva Avalokiteśvara one of which was sinking down showing thereby the decay of the Doctrine. The princes and the laymen as also the monks were as a rule in the habit of coming to the Tree to bathe it, worship it and to make offerings here.

Then there was the Mahābodhi Temple, 160 feet high, a large, fine and rich sanctuary, decorated with gold images. On the left and the right of the Shrine were the figures in silver of Avalokita and Maitreya. There was a beautiful image of Buddha in this temple showing him under the Bodhi Tree in *bhūsparśamudrā*. The abortive attempts of Śaśāṅka to destroy the image in order to replace one of Śiva, had not been proved successful.[128] Outside of the north-gate of the Bodhi-Tree-Inclosure was the Mahābodhi *saṃghārāma* built by a former king of Ceylon.[129] It was a superb architectural piece decorated with perfect sculpture and enriched by Buddha images of gold and silver. It contained several *stūpas* wherein were enshrined the sacred relics of Buddha. There were in this monastery nearly 1,000 monks, "all Mahāyānists of the Sthavira school, and all perfect in *vinaya* observances."[130] The Mahābodhi Monastery is also mentioned several times by I-tsing, but the details are to be found only in Hsüan-tsang.

The ruins of the ancient Buddhist establishment at Nālandā, the greatest and the most flourishing centre of Buddhism during this period, have been laid bare by the spade of the archaeologists near the village of Baḍagāon, 7 miles north of Rājagṛha, 55 miles south-east of Patna, in Bihar. It was a large monastic centre, splendidly built and well-maintained by many generations of kings.

Hsüan-tsang and I-tsing have left graphic descritpions of Buddhist activities in Nālandā in the seventh century A.D. In the first half of the 8th century A.D. we find valuable information from an Inscription of Mālāda, a minister of king Yaśovarman, probably of Kanauj. According to Hwui-li, about 10,000 monks lived at Nālandā Mahāvihāra. But from Hsüan-tsang and I-tsing the strength seems to have been between three thousand and four thousand.[131] In the neighbourhood of Nālandā there was a monastery on the Indra-śaila-guhā, in which some Hīnayāna monks were living. Hsüan-tsang narrates an incident by means of which he indicates their appreciation of the Mahāyāna ways of life. At some distance from this Indra-cave-mountain was another monastic abode called the Kapotaka Monastery in which Hsüan-tsang found over 200 Sarvāstivādin monks. Not far from this monastery was an Aśokan *stūpa*, and a temple with an image of Avalokita P'usa, erected by a king of Ceylon. In its vicinity was a monastery on a hill top in which about 50 Hīnayāna monks were living. To the north-east of this monastery, on the Gaṅgā was a thickly populated town, in which there were many well adorned Deva-temples.[132]

A large monastic establishment was flourishing in a monastery on the Hiraṇya-Parvata, identified with modern Monghyr. There were more than ten monasteries and over 4,000 Hīnayāna monks. According to the *Life* most of them were Sarvāstivādins, in the *Record* they are said to have been of the Sammitīya school. In early days of the seventh century a king of the eastern frontier had bestowed the capital city upon the monks and had built two large monasteries each of which accommodated about 1,000 monks of the Sarvāstivāda school. No other definite source has been known about the identity of this king.[133]

In Campā identified with modern Bhagalpur district, Hsüan-tsang found in ruinous condition several tens of monasteries. Yet there were over 200 Hīnayāna monks in Campā. In his biography, however, the monasteries are reported to be ten and without any reference to their ruinous state; moreover, the number of monks is given as 300.[134]

In Ka-chu-wen-ki-lo ('Khajughire' or 'Kankjol' or 'Kajangala' in modern Rājamahal), the people were honest and esteemed learning. Recently king Śīlāditya Harṣa had built a royal subheadquarters here. There were about 6 or 7 monasteries of the Buddhists in which nearly 300 monks were living in the middle of the 7th century A.D.[135]

The Gunaighar[136] record of the reign of Vainyagupta, belonging to the first decade of the 6th century A.D. records the grants of land for the Buddhists of the Avaivarttika-saṃgha, of Mahāyāna. This *saṃgha* was said to have been founded by one Śāntideva and was residing in a monastery called Āśrama-vihāra. The inscription also refers to two other *vihāras* in this locality of south eastern Bengal.[137] In Puṇḍravardhana there were 20 monasteries and more than three thousand monks belonging to both Hīnayāna and the Mahāyāna in the middle of the 7th century A.D.[138] Besides, there were 100 Deva-temples and the Digaṃbara Jainas were also numerous. Not far from the capital of Puṇḍra-vardhana towards west was a magnificent *saṃghārāma* called 'Po-shih-po' or 'Po-chisha' (Vasibhasaṃghārāma.) It had spacious halls and tall storied chambers occupied by more than 700 monks of Mahāyāna Buddhism. Close to this establishment was a temple with an image of Avalokiteśvara. In this monastery many distinguished Buddhist monk scholars from eastern India had also been living when Hsüan-tsang visited it.[139]

In Bengal, Buddhism received royal patronage under the Pāla kings, and it was generally speaking in flourishing state throughout the province. The first Pāla ruler, Gopāla is reported to have been a devoted benefactor of the faith. He erected several *vihāras* in his territory and maintained them from the royal sources.[140] His contemporary king in the west was Vibharatta, king of Kaccha who had Buddhistic leanings. In his kingdom, a Tāntrika teacher, Virūpa the younger, had consecrated the Amṛtakuṃbha temple.[141] As for the form of Buddhism in Bengal, I-tsing reports that all the 'four Nikāyas' were popular side by side.[142] In Samataṭa Hsüan-tsang observed thirty monasteries with more than 2,000 monks, "all adherents of the Sthavira school."[143] I-tsing, however, reports that in the last quarter of the 7th century A.D. when another Chinese pilgrim Sheng-chi was in India, the latter found king Rājabhaṭṭa ruling over Samataṭa. This king, supposed to have belonged to the Khaḍga dynasty which ruled over Southern and Eastern Bengal in the second half of the 7th century A.D., was, according to this pilgrim, a fervent devotee of Buddhist faith. During his reign there were 4,000 monks and nuns in Samataṭa.[144] It would appear that the number of monastics had doubled owing apparently to the patronage of Rājabhaṭṭa. Moreover, the form of Buddhism now seems to have been rather Mahāyānistic since the king worshipped the images of Buddha, revered Avalokiteśvara and recited the *Mahāprajñāpāramitā-sūtra.*[145]

In Karṇasuvarṇa, Hsüan-tsang noticed more than 2,000 monks of the Sammitīya school living in ten monasteries. He also found here three monasteries in which the resident monks were the followers of the teachings of Devadatta, the disreputed cousin of the Buddha, who made the first schism. Near the capital was a magnificent monastery famous for being the resort of illustrious monks.

A very flourishing centre of Buddhism in the second half of the seventh century A.D. in Bengal was Tāmralipti on the sea coast (modern Tamluk). There were more than ten Buddhist monastic establishments here with above 1,000 monks in the days of Hsüan-tsang. The population of Tāmralipti was divided into both Buddhist and non-Buddhist faiths.[146] Hsüan-tsang does not specify the particular school to which the Buddhist monks of Tāmralipti were attached. But it seems that they were Sarvāstivādins and this was a seat of Sarvāstivādin lore. We find not only I-tsing who was a Sarvāstivādin, living in this city for sometime,[147] but also Tao-lin staying for 3 years, and Ch'eng-teng staying in Tāmralipti for a period of 12 years. Tao-lin was initiated to the Sarvāstivāda school in this monastery.[148]

Before the establishment of the Pāla dynasty by Gopāla in the later half of the 8th century A.D., a number of petty local dynasts seem to have held sway over various parts of Bengal. Śīlabhadra, the Head of Nālandā Vihāra, came from a royal family of Samataṭa. The Nidhanapur copper plate of Bhāskaravarman mentions Jyeṣṭhabhadra as a vassal chief. He may have been connected with Śīlabhadra although there is no clear positive evidence.[149] It seems that besides the Pālas, the Bhadras and the Khaḍgas were also patrons and followers of the Doctrine.[150]

The Kailan inscription of Śrīdharana Rāta, placed on palaeographic grounds in the middle of the seventh century A.D., also points to the popularity of Buddhism in Samataṭa. This king is said to have made land grants to a Buddhist monastery for the provision of food and clothing of monks. This pious act he did at the request of his minister Jayanātha.[151]

Tārānātha in his celebrated *Chos hbyuṅ*[152] gives a detailed account of some Candra kings, who ruled in Bengal just before the Pālas. Many of these Candras were Buddhists. Several coins, inscriptions and Burmese chronicles also corroborate the rule of these kings whose names ended in Candra. In an inscription known as the Rāmapāla copper plate, Suvarṇacandra, the second king in the genealogical list, appears to be a follower of Buddha. His descendants were staunch Buddhists. This is proved by the facts that they invoked Buddha at the opening of their copper plate grants, adopted the epithet *paramasaugata* and employed the Wheel of the Law on their seals. R. C. Majumdar suggests that these Candra kings ruled in East Bengal from about the 6th to 8th century A.D.[153]

That the Khaḍga kings of Bengal were Buddhists like the Pālas, has already been pointed out. King Rājabhaṭa was a devout Buddhist, a follower of Mahāyāna faith.[154]

Gopāla's patronage of Buddhism is referred to in the *Mañjuśrīmūlakalpa*.[155] He is said to have built a monastery at Nālandā.[156] It was in his reign, the tradition goes, that a lay follower of Buddhism constructed the lofty monastery of Odantapura.[157] Dharmapāla (*cir.* 770-810 A.D.), a *paramasaugata*, was the founder of the famous Vikramaśilā-Mahāvihāra. He patronised the Prajñāpāramitā study and Haribhadra lived in his time in Traikuṭaka-vihāra. He also founded the well-known Somapurī monastery. Tārānātha makes him the founder of fifty religious institutions. Archaeological finds have borne out, to a great extent, the truth of these statements of the Tibetans. The successors of Dharmapāla were also patrons of Buddhist faith.[158]

Buddhism seems to have been introduced into the country

of Assam[159] late in the 6th or the 7th century A.D. Hsüan-tsang found only faint traces of Buddhism in the kingdom of Kāmarūpa. The Assamese of Kāmarūpa "worshipped the *devas* and did not believe in Buddhism. So there had never been a Buddhist monastery in the land, and whatever Buddhists there were in it performed their acts of devotion secretly". The king, Bhāskaravarman alias Kumāra, a *brāhmaṇa* by caste, "was not a Buddhist" but he respected accomplished *śramaṇas* such as Hsüan-tsang himself.[160]

Buddhism was quite in flourishing condition in Orissa during our period. The Śailodbhava kings who ruled in this province in the sixth and seventh centuries A.D. were pro-Brahmanic and Tārānātha leaves the impression that in their time the Buddhist monks in Orissa declined in number. But with the advent of the Bhaumakāra house in Orissa, Buddhism again received royal patronage. Under this danasty which continued to rule up to the 10th century A.D. Orissa was the abode of many Buddhist scholars.[161]

In the middle of the 7th century A.D. there were 100 Buddhist monasteries and a myriad monks all Mahāyānists. From the *Life* we get the information that the monks of Orissa were all Hīnayānists who often criticised the Mahāyāna doctrines taught in Nālandā Mahāvihāra.[162]

Some Bhaumakāra rulers had apparently Buddhistic epithets e.g., *paramopāsaka*, *paramatathāgata*, and Śubhākaradeva (A.D. 790) had the epithet *paramasaugata*.[163] The Dhenkānāl inscription of Tribhuvana Mahādevī, queen of King Śivakara III (A.D. 884) records the Buddhist patronage of her predecessors and forefathers in eulogistic terms. They had "exhausted treasures of their vast empire on religious works in order to enlighten their country and others who decorated the earth by constructing in unbroken continuity various *maṭhas*, monasteries and sanctuaries."[164] A number of archaeological finds in Orissa including the ruins of monasteries, *stūpas* and images of Buddha, Bodhisattvas, Tārā, also testify to the flourishing conditions of Mahāyāna Buddhism in early medieval Orissa.[165]

The neighbouring tract, around the Chilka Lake, supposed to be the modern representative of Konyodha, now the district of Ganjam, was entirely populated by the Deva-worshippers, and there were ten thousand non-Buddhist sectarians.

In Kaliṅga country, there were about ten Buddhist monasteries occupied by 500 monks who followed "the Mahāyānist Sthavira System." The number of Deva-worshippers and Nirgranthas was also very large.[166]

Buddhism in Dakṣiṇāpatha

The country of Dakṣiṇa Kośala corresponded to Rāipur-Bilaspur-Sambalpur region of Madhya Pradesh and Orissa. Hsüan-tsang found a *kṣatriya* king ruling here; this king was a Buddhist by faith and was noted for his benevolence. Who this king was, cannot be said definitely. The Pāṇḍuvaṃśis[167] had been ruling in southern Kośala in the 6th and the 7th centuries A.D. Dakṣiṇa Kośala had been marked by the fame of Nāgārjuna, the Mādhyamika philosopher. But the monastery in which he had lived was now desolate. Yet there were over 10,000 monks of the Mahāyāna living in over 100 monasteries.[168]

In the early centuries of Christian era Āndhra was one of the most flourishing centres of Buddhism.[169] There were more than twenty monasteries and above 3,000 monks in Āndhra in the middle of the seventh century A.D. The monastery of Acara and the *stūpa* of Diṅnāga were now old and without any monks.[170]

Although Buddhism in South India during the 7th and the 8th centuries had ceased to receive royal patronage, since the Pallavas and their rival dynasties were followers of Brahmanical religion, yet it continued to face the rising opposition from Jainism and Śaivism.[171]

In Dhānyakaṭaka or Dharaṇikoṭa on the Kṛṣṇā, many Buddhist monasteries were now in ruins when Hsüan-tsang visited the province. Still about 20 of them were occupied by about 1,000 Mahāsāṃghika monks. The famous Pūrvaśaila and Avaraśaila monasteries near the capital city (modern Bezwaḍa) as also Amarāvatī, were still extant, but without any monks. In the time of Hsüan-tsang only "the local deities guarded the monasteries."[172]

In 'Chu-li-yo' (Cola) country most of the Buddhist monasteries were in ruins, and only a few were still occupied by some monks. The Tīrthikas and the Digambaras were flourishing and were most numerous.[173]

The province of Draviḍa proper, was, however, still an important centre of Buddhism.[174] Its capital, Kāñcīpura (modern

Conjeevaram), had been associated with Diṅnāga (*cir.* 470-550 A.D.), Bodhidharma (*cir.* 600 A.D.) and Dharmapāla (*cir.* 550-610 A.D.), and in the time of Narasiṃhavarman I, the Pallava king of Kāñcī in about the year A.D. 640, when Hsüan-tsang visited Draviḍa land, there were more than ten thousand Sthaviravādin monks living in more than one hundred monasteries. The number of Digambaras seems to have exceeded that of the Deva-wroshippers or the Śivaite Hindus. Quite recently this capital city (Kāñcī) had produced an eminent scholar Dharmapāla who was the son of a city official. Near the capital was another large monastery which was a rendezvous for the most eminent men of the land.[175]

In the far south, Malakūṭa (Travancore-Cochin) had few Buddhist monasteries in the state of preservation; there were remains of old *saṃghārāmas*; the Brethren were few in number. On the contrary, Deva-worshippers and Digambaras were very numerous. The Potalaka mountain in this country was the favourite resort of Avalokiteśvara who still appeared before his devotees in the guise of 'Pāśupata Tīrthika or as Maheśvara.'[176] This last passage seems to indicate that Avalokita who had many attributes of Śiva,[177] was now in the process of being converted into Hindu god Śiva.

The Pallava king Narasiṃhavarman II is said to have built in 720 A.D. a Buddhist shrine in Nāgapaṭṭinam. I-tsing also refers to this place as a centre of Buddhism where Wu-hing lived for 30 days.[178] Both Hīnayāna and Mahāyāna monks were living together in the monasteries of Koṅkaṇ (northern Mysore). In this province Hsüan-tsang found more than one hundred Buddhist monasteries with about ten thousand monks belonging to both the Vehicles. Near the capital city (probably Banavāsī) was a large Buddhist monastery in which over 300 monks, all distinguished for their learning, were living. The monastery was decorated with Buddha images. In the vicinity there were other monasteries, one of them noted for the image of Maitreya, and a *stūpa* containing the relics of Arhat Śrotaviṃśakoṭi.[179]

The Hiregutti (North Kanara District) record assigned to the 6th century A.D. discloses the gift of a village named Sundarika for the benefit of a Buddhist *vihāra* in Dīpaka Viṣaya.

The record opens with an invocation to Buddha, the gift was made by Asaṃkita, a king of Bhoja family.[180]

In Mahārāṣṭra during the reign of king Pulakeśin II Caulukya, Hsüan-tsang found over 5,000 Buddhist monks occupying about 100 monasteries and belonging to both Hīnayāna and Mahāyāna. These monasteries were rich with *stūpas* and images. More notable among these was a monastery on the hill top built by Acara, an Arhat of West India. Its shrine was 100 ft. high, within was an image in stone of Buddha 70 ft. high. Walls of the temple were decorated with the scenes of Buddha's life.[181] This report seems to refer to an Ajaṇṭā rock-cut *vihāra.*

Buddhism in Western India

In certain localities of western India Buddhism seems to have been in fairly flourishing condition during the seventh and the eighth centuries A.D. In Bharukaccha (Broach) people were following both Hinduism and Buddhism. There were more than ten Buddhist monasteries with 300 monks "all students of the Mahāyānist Sthavira school."[182]

Likewise the population of Malwa seems to have been divided into "miscellaneous belief in orthodoxy and heterodoxy". The Deva-temples and Śaiva-Pāśupatas were very numerous. Yet the Buddhists of the Sammitīya school held their banner aloft. Hsüan-tsang reports that they had several hundreds of monasteries in Malwa and their number exceeded 20,000. There is no reason to doubt this report though the number of monks seems to be sufficiently high. A number of kings of Western India, who ruled in the 6th, 7th and the 8th centuries A.D. in Malwa region, are known from inscriptions to have patronised Buddhist establishments. Hsüan-tsang himself records of one Śīlāditya who ruled about 60 years before his visit, that this king was a devout Buddhist and had built a magnificent Buddhist temple with beautiful images of 7 Buddhas.[183]

The pilgrim further tells us that this king Śīlāditya was in the habit of arranging annually a Religious Assembly in which were invited monks and sages from all quarters and the king presented them the robes and other valuables. In this kingdom was a small town called Brāhmaṇapura, so called because a proud *brāhmaṇa* who had been defeated in debate by *bhikṣu*

Bodhiruci 'a consummate logician and well versed in the non-Buddhist *Śāstras*', went down alive into a pit in this city.[184]

This whole description, historically speaking, does not seem to be far removed in time from our period. A number of kings of Kathiawar peninsula, belonging to Kaṭachuri and Maitraka dynasties that ruled here from 6th to the 8th centuries, bore the epithet 'Śīlāditya' or 'Sun of Morality'[185] and had a soft corner for Buddhism.

It seems that 'Śīlāditya' of the above narrative is perhaps identifiable with Śīlāditya I Dharmāditya, a Maitraka king of Valabhī, known from inscriptions. His dates range between A.D. 606-612. The Buddhist Doctor, Bodhiruci flourished in the sixth century A.D. and translated *Daśabhūmikāsūtra* in Chinese.[186] The religious activities of Śīlāditya I fit in well with his another epithet Dharmāditya, 'the Sun of Righteousness'. One of his inscriptions records a grant to the Buddhist monastery of Vaṃsakaṭa.[187] In K'i-t'a ('Kheda', 'Kaira', modern Kaccha) the Chinese pilgrim found more than ten monasteries where above one thousand monks belonging to both Hīnayāna and Mahāyāna lived.

One of the most famous centres of Buddhism in the 7th and the 8th centuries was Valabhī; this is testified to by Hsüan-tsang, I-tsing and by the epigraphic records of the period. The district around Fa-la-pi maintained in the time of Hsüan-tsang, over 100 Buddhist monastic establishments with about 6,000 monks of Hīnayāna belonging to the Sammitīya sect. The ruling king Tu-lo-p'o-po-t'a (Dhruvabhaṭa, probably identical with Dhruvasena II, Bālāditya of Valabhi one of whose known dates is A.D. 639, (Gupta Era 320)[188] was, a *kṣatriya* by birth, nephew of the former king Śīlāditya of Malwa, and the son-in-law of Emperor Harṣavardhana, the Śīlāditya of Kanauj. Dhruvasena II was a sincere believer in Buddhism. Near the capital city was a large monastery in which famous Buddhist Doctors like Guṇamati and Sthiramati had lived and wrote treatises.[189] I-tsing includes these two Buddhist teachers among the celebrities of 'recent age' (*cir.* 500-670 A.D.). He also describes Valabhī as a centre of Buddhist learning like Nālandā.[190] A copper plate grant dated A.D. 580 from Valabhī also refers to Sthiramati.[191] In the district of Ānandapura (in Ahmedabad District) which was a dependency of Malwa, there were nearly

1,000 Hīnayāna monks of the Sammitīya sect living in about more than ten monasteries. In Surat the Chinese pilgrim found about 3,000 monks, most of whom belonged to the Mahāyānist Sthavira System. There were more than 50 Buddhist monasteries in Surat. Near the capital was a rock-cut *vihāra* which was well maintained and frequented by sages and scholars. In Ku-che-lo (Gurjara) few people believed in Buddhism. Hsüan-tsang found here only one Buddhist monastery in which about 100 monks of Sarvāstivāda were living. The ruler of this province was a patron of the learned and "a profound believer in Buddhism."[192]

Above picture of Buddhism in Gujarat-Kathiawar and Malwa regions as presented by the Chinese pilgrims may be taken in the light of the royal patronage of several kings of this region, all of whom were not Buddhists yet endowed the Buddhist monasteries with material goods.

Mahārāja Guhāsena of Valabhī (one of whose known dates is 567 A.D.) records in his copper plate that he arranged water facilities for the Śākya *bhikṣus* belonging to 18 sects. This gift was attached to the Mahāvihāra built by Duddā. This Duddā was the daughter of Dhruvasena I's sister. In another inscription the same king is seen recording a grant to the foreign monks belonging to 18 schools and living in Abhyantarika-vihāra built by the venerable Miṃma.[193]

An inscription of Maitraka king Śīlāditya III, dated (G.E. 343) 663 A.D. from Wālā (Kathiawar) records a grant to the Buddhist monastery of Vimalagupta.[194] Another inscription of this ruler also records a grant to the Buddhist monastery built by Duddā near Valabhi.[195]

An inscription of Dhruvasena III (Maitraka ruler), one of whose known dates is (G.E. 334) A.D. 653, records a grant to the monastery of Duddā near Valabhi.[196] The Duddā-vihāra was a famous centre of Buddhist monks in the seventh century A.D. The kings of this dynasty continued, as late as the time of Śīlāditya VII of Valabhi (one of whose dates is G.E. 447, A.D. 766), to contribute to the gifts for the Buddhist monks. These gifts included grants for the monks and the students, foundation of a library, and the ceremonies of Buddha worship.[197]

A Buddhist inscription of Devadatta dated (Vikrama Era 847 = A.D. 789) found in Shergaṛh (Koṭā State) proves that

Buddhism was not extinct in this part of Rajasthan in the 8th century A.D.[198]

Inscriptions from Berar (Vidarbha) region also point to the existence of Buddhist laity in the seventh and the eighth centuries in Western part of the Central Provinces.

The Gandheśvara temple compound has yielded a large Buddha image in which the Buddhist credo '*ye dhammā hetuppabhavā*' is inscribed in the letters of 8th or 9th century A.D. The inscription is known as Sirpur Buddha image inscription. A Bhāṇḍaka Buddhist inscription from Chāndā District which extols king Sūryaghoṣa (?), opens with 4 verses glorifying the Buddha under the name of Jina and Tāyī.[199]

In Ujayana or Ujjain Hsüan-tsang found a *brāhmaṇa* ruler, learned in heterodox lore, but a non-Buddhist.[200] Buddhist monasteries were mostly in ruins. Only three or four of them were in good condition and they were occupied by about 300 monks belonging to both Hīnayāna and Mahāyāna.[201] An interesting side light is thrown on the state of Buddhist monks of Ujjainī in about our period in the celebrated *Mṛcchakaṭikaṃ*, attributed to Śūdraka by some, and to Daṇḍin by others.[202] Buddhism does not seem to have been a dominant religion in Ujjainī. Thus Hsüan-tsang's report seems to be corroborated by the play *Mṛcchakaṭikam*. On the contrary, the site of a Buddhist monk was considered to be inauspicious and was to be avoided. Buddhist monks led a strict life; their career was supposed to be very austere. There were some Buddhist establishments and monks and nuns as would appear from the fact that a shampooer-monk is shown leading Vasantasenā to a Buddhist nun in a *vihāra* near the royal garden. A Saṃvāhaka-bhikṣu is represented as the Head of the Buddhist monasteries of the country and the king himself seems to have been the supreme controller of all the religious endowments in the State.[203]

According to both Hsüan-tsang and I-tsing, Buddhist monks of the Sammitīya school were most numerous in Sindh in their times. The people of Sindh were thorough believers in Buddhism but their learning was superficial. The king who was a *śūdra* by caste, was an honest man and a devout Buddhist by faith.

There were, according to Hsüan-tsang, many hundred Buddhist monasteries and more than ten thousand monks of the Sammitīya school of Hīnayāna. "Most of these were indolent worthless persons, of the superior Brethren who, leading lives of lonely seclusion, never relaxed in perseverance, many attained arhatship."

Along the Indus river bank in the low marshes there were several hundreds of Buddhist families. They reared cattle, killed animals; they were without government and observed no social distinctions. "They shaved their hair and wore the *bhikṣu* garb, looking like *bhikṣus* yet living in the world; they were bigotted in their narrow views and reviled the Great Vehicle."[204] This perhaps refers to the institution of married monks.

The above account of the monks of Sindh shows that the rules of monastic celebacy had been greatly relaxed. This feature of Saindhava *bhikṣus* seems to be corroborated by the *Chācha-nāmā*. It is reported that the king of Sindh, in the time of invasion of Brāhmaṇābād by Chācha, was under the influence of a "samanī' (*śramaṇa*) named Buddha-Raku (Buddha-rakṣita); the latter was an expert in magic and had family. Reference is also made to a Nau-vihāra at Sawandisi and to an old damaged Buddhist temple.[205]

In Mūlasthānapura (modern Multan) on the eastern side of the river Sindhu, there were few who believed in Buddhism; Buddhist monasteries were mostly in ruins and there were only very few monks. To further north east of Multan lay the kingdom of Parvata. Both these territories were dependencies of the kingdom of Ṭakka. In Parvata there were some *stūpas*, more than ten Buddhist monasteries and about 1,000 monks belonging to both Hīnayāna and Mahāyāna. Near the capital city was a large monastery exclusively Mahāyānist wherein lived more than 100 monks in the time of Hsüan-tsang. From his biography we learn that Hsüan-tsang stayed in the monasteries of Parvata for two years in order to study under a few learned monks who dwelt in this country. The monastery in which Śāstra-Masters, Bhadraruci and Guṇaprabha, had been converted and, where Śāstra-Master Jinaputra (*cir.* sixth century A.D.) had composed a *ṭīkā* called *Yogācāra-bhūmi-śāstra-vyākhyā*, was now in ruins.

In the small kingdom called A-tien-po-chih-lo (?) which was a province of Sindh bordering on the Arabian Sea, Hsüan-tsang noticed more than 80 Buddhist monasteries with over 5,000 monks of the Sammitīya sect. The most imposing religious object in the capital city was, however, 'a large handsomely ornamented Maheśvara temple.' In the westernmost part of India, beyond the Indus there was the province of Lang-ka-lo, subject to Persia, in this region there were more than 6,000 monks, belonging to both Hīnayāna and Mahāyāna, living in over 100 Buddhist monasteries.[206]

Chapter III

BUDDHIST ART IN THE MONASTERIES

The following pages, dealing with the Buddhist art of the period, based on information supplied by Hsüan-tsang and corroborated by corresponding references to extant archaeological remains and other sources referable to this period, are intended to supplement the general picture of Buddhism sketched above.

While speaking of the cities, houses and buildings of India in general, Hsüan-tsang observes that "the Buddhist monasteries are of the most remarkable architecture. They have a tower at each of the four corners of the quadrangle and three high halls in a tier. The rafters and roof beams are carved with strange figures, and the doors, windows, and walls are painted in various colours." Continuing his remarkable description the pilgrim tells us of the design of the houses of the Buddhist house-holders. He says that "the houses of the laity are sumptuous inside and economical outside. The inner rooms and the central hall vary in their dimensions, and there is no rule for form or construction for the tiers of the terraces or the rows of high rooms. Their doors open to the east, and the throne faces east."[1] The 'throne' probably refers to the *siṃhāsana* ('lion seat') wherein the image of Buddha was enshrined in the houses of the laity. Near the capital of Na-kie-lo-ho there stood many old Buddhist sacred buildings mostly in ruinous condition. But a large *stūpa* made of stone, said to have been built by Aśoka, was still in tact; it contained marvellous sculptures and was more than 300 feet in height. At some distance from this city, was "a stone monastery with lofty halls and tiers of chambers all silent and un-occupied." In this establishment there was, moreover, an Aśokan *stūpa*, 200 feet high.[2]

In the entire record of Hsüan-tsang, nothing strikes us more than the dimensions of a *stūpa* built by Kaniṣka in Gāndhāra. It was one and a half li in circuit at the base; the plinth was 150 feet high in five stages; the *stūpa* itself was 400 feet in height. It was thus an extraordinary architectural piece. The tiers of the *stūpa* were decorated with gilt copper disks. Around the Great Tope were several smaller buildings. Two images of Buddha, one four and the other six feet high, representing him in cross-legged seated posture under the Bodhi-Tree, seem to have flanked the main entrance of the monument. On the southern face of the ascent to the *stūpa* was a peculiar painting which appears to have been unparalleled. It was a painting of Buddha, "16 feet high with two heads from one body." Close to the south-east of the Great Tope was another Buddha image in white stone, 18 feet in height. Not far from this *stūpa* was a monastery built by Kaniṣka, which had many storeys and terraces and was an example of "rare art."[3]

Near the Mahāvana monastery in Uḍḍiyāna the pilgrim found a hundred feet high *stūpa* by the side of which was a large square stone bearing Buddha's foot-prints. In this same territory was a *stūpa*, 80 feet high, situated near the Sarpauṣadhī monastery.[4] Near the city of Mongkil, the capital of Uḍḍiyāna, was an *adbhuta-stūpa*, above 40 feet high, built of stone. Not far from it lay an image of Bodhisattva Avalokiteśvara in a Buddhist temple. In the valley of the river Darel was a great *vihāra* which contained a carved wooden image of Bodhisattva Maitreya, 100 feet in height of brilliant golden hue.[5] A number of *stūpas* built by Aśoka were still in existence in Takṣaśilā in the middle of the 7th century A.D. A 200 feet high stone *stūpa* built by Aśoka is reported by the pilgrim in Siṃhapura,[6] and yet another Asokan *stūpa* of stone and of similar height was found by him in the vicinity of Takṣaśilā. This *stūpa* has been identified with the Manikyāla *stūpa*, about 34 miles south-east from Shāhdherī. Another 200 feet high Aśokan *stūpa* stood near the capital of Urasha.[7]

Four Aśokan *stūpas* and several magnificent monasteries were seen by Hsüan-tsang; Ou-K'ong noticed as many as seven edifices. Notable among them were the Huṣkara-vihāra, the Jayendra-vihāra, the Ānanda-bhavana, the Muṇḍi-vihāra, and a large number of *stūpas* and images of Buddha. Kalhaṇa records the construction of a number of artistic and magnificent *vihāras*, *caityas*, and the erection of lofty Buddha images by the kings, queens and ministers of Kashmir in the seventh and eighth centuries. The testimony of Hsüan-tsang is corroborated by Kalhaṇa and confirmed by archaeological exploration. Mention may be made of a Buddha image which Lalitāditya brought from Magadha, probably from Nālandā.[8]

An Aśokan *stūpa* built of bright orange bricks stood near the capital of Thāneśvara; there was here a beautiful monastery which "had high chambers in close succession and detached terraces."[9] In Mathurā, Hsüan-tsang observed three *stūpas* built by Aśoka, besides a multitude of other *stūpas* containing relics of Buddha's disciples.

Attractive architectural and sculptural pieces existed at Saṅkisā (Dist. Farrukhabad, U.P.).[10] It is the traditional spot where Buddha is supposed to have descended from the Trayastriṃśa Heaven. According to the *Shui-Ching-Chu*, Aśoka had built on this spot a *stūpa* and a stone pillar surmounted by the image of a lion.[11] Hsüan-tsang found at this place (Saṅkisā or Kapitha) that three precious stairs built of gold, crystal and silver by Indra, had now disappeared, and in their place there existed stairs of bricks and stones built by previous kings. "The present stairs were about 70 feet high" with a Buddhist temple on the top in which was a stone image of Buddha, and images of Brahmā and Indra were at the top of the right and left stairs respectively.

By the side of these edifices were an "Aśoka-pillar of lustrous violet colour and very hard with a croaching lion on the top facing the stairs; quaintly carved figures were on each side of the pillar." Besides, there were other *stūpas*, a shrine, a large stone platform 50 paces long and seven feet high where the Buddha used to take exercise. This platform was enclosed by a wall.[12]

The monasteries (*saṃghārāma, vihāra*) in ancient India were usually planned as a square block formed by four rows of monastic rooms along the four sides of an inner courtyard. They were raised on a platform of brick or stone. The building materials in earlier periods were usually wood and bricks, but during our period bricks and stones of diverse colour and variety seem to have been in universal use. It was a regular feature to enclose a monastic establishment within a boundary wall with one main gate. Instances of several monasteries being enclosed within one wall are also known.

Thus in Kānyakubja (Kanauj) there were, close to the Gaṅgā, "three monasteries enclosed by a common wall but each having its own gate." These *vihāras* were adorned with beautiful images.

In a monastery in Hayamukha (supposed to be Dauṇḍiākherā, on the northern bank of the Gaṅgā) Hsüan-tsang observed an Aśokan *stūpa*, another 'a dark-blue-stone tope with the Buddha-relics', and 'a beautiful life-like image of the Buddha'. The halls and chambers of this monastery were lofty and were of exquisite workmanship.[13]

In Kauśāmbi,[14] the pilgrim found several ruined edifices, including the house of Ghoṣita, a Buddhist temple, a hair-and-nail-relic *stūpa*, and the ruins of Buddha's bath-room. Not far from the city was the Ghoṣitārāma—the monastery built by Ghoṣita—with a *stūpa*, about 200 feet high, built by Aśoka. To the south-east of the Ghoṣitārāma was 'a two-storeyed building with an old brick upper-chamber' wherein the great Vasubandhu had lodged for some time.[15]

In Kāsapura, north of the Gaṅgā, there were ruins of a monastery with an Aśokan *stūpa*, of which 200 feet still remained above ground.

In Śrāvastī, most of the Buddhist edifices were in ruinous state. At the east gate of Jetavana-vihāra, two stone pillars, one on each side of the gate, eighty feet high, built by Aśoka, were still standing.

The pillar on the left side was surmounted by a sculptured wheel and that on the right side by an ox or bull.[16] These are the well known Aśokan styles of the 'Bull Capital' and the 'Dharma-Cakra Capital'. It was quite in the fitness of things that the great Buddhist Emperor raised here a pillar with the sacred Dharmacakra at the top, because the Jetavana monastery was hallowed by Buddha's numerous discourses. The excellent example of this type is the so-called 'Lion Capital' from Sāranātha, now the exalted emblem of the Indian Union. It is in fact the 'Dharma-Cakra-Capital' and not the 'Lion Capital'. Originally, the pillar of Sāranātha was crowned by a wheel placed in a deep socket between the heads of the lions. Not only the seven fragments of the wheel extant in the Sāranātha piece but also the above words of Hsüan-tsang prove that this was a Dharma-Cakra-Capital and not a Lion-Capital, though the latter name has attained wide renown. Its right designation should be Dharma-Cakra-Capital. V. S. Agrawala observes: "There is nothing in the range of Buddhist art so meaningful in its symbolism and at the same time so powerful and beautiful in execution as the Aśokan pillar. The long tapering column with its bright polish is a charming conception and an appropriate support for so worthy a monument as the intended capital."[17] In the lonely brick shrine at the site of the Jetavana monastery the pilgrim found an old and beautiful image of Buddha, five feet high, said to have been made in the time of King Prasenajit of Kośala; close by this monastery was a temple, more than sixty feet high, which contained a sitting image of Buddha with his face towards the east.[18]

In the vicinity of Kapilavastu, on the Indo-Nepal border in U.P., Hsüan-tsang observed a *stūpa* and a stone pillar, above 30 feet high, with a carved lion on the top, erected by Aśoka to commemorate the spot connected with Krakucchanda, a previous Buddha. The pillar had an inscription recording the decease of this Past Buddha. Not very far from this place was another *stūpa*, marking the birth place of another Past Buddha, Kanakamuni; yet another *stūpa* marking the spot of his attaining Bodhi, and a stone pillar, more than 20 feet high, with a lion on the top, and an epigraph recording the death of Kanakamuni, all set up by Aśoka.[19] This last monument with the inscription has come down to our age, and once more testifies to the authenticity of our pilgrim's descriptions. At Lumminī, Hsüan-tsang already found the Aśokan pillar with a 'Horse-Capital' broken in the middle, that is, half of it, probably by a thunderbolt. The pilgrim does not refer to the inscription on it, which, however, still exists and is the best readable and clear Brāhmī inscription.[20]

These archaeological monuments dating from the third century B.C. suggest that the ancient Buddhists believed in the historical existence of Buddhas, like Krakucchanda, Kanakamuni or Koṇāgamana and Kāśyapa who flourished before Śākyamuni Buddha. This is an important, though late, tradition corroborating the theory of the existence of *munis* and *śramaṇas* in pre-Buddhistic times.

In the capital city of Rāmagrāma, about 40 miles east of Lumminī, was a *stūpa* 100 feet high, built of bricks by the rulers of that country, i.e., the Mallas, who received a portion of the relics of Buddha.[21] The great *stūpa* at Kuśīnagara, the scene of Buddha's Mahāparinirvāṇa, which was built by Aśoka, was still 200 feet high; in front of it stood a stone pillar with an inscription describing the Great Decease. In the great temple or *caitya*, built of bricks, was a large image of Buddha, lying down with his head towards the north.[22]

The pilgrim found some of the best specimens of Buddhist art at Sāranātha.[23] First of all, there was an Aśokan *stūpa* above 100 feet high; in front of it was "a stone pillar, of polished green stone, clear and lustrous as a mirror." The Deer Park Monastery nearby was a magnificent architectural whole. It was in 8 divisions, i.e., 8 groups of *vihāras*, all enclosed within one wall, "the tiers of balconies and the rows of halls were extremely artistic". Inside the boundary wall was a temple or *caitya*, more than 200 feet high, crowned by an embossed gilt *āmra*-fruit (*āmalaka*); the plinth and the steps were of stone; but the upper portion was built of bricks; in the brick portion were more than 100 rows of niches, each containing a gilt image of Buddha; inside the temple was a metal image of Buddha, life-size, representing him in the *dharmacakra-pravartana-mudrā*.[24]

This 200 feet high temple noticed by Hsūan-tsang has been identified with the Mulagandha-kuṭī-vihāra, dating from the Gupta period.[25]

The most imposing Buddhist structure at Sāranātha is the Dhamekha-stūpa, 'a solid cylindrical tower, 93 feet in diameter at base and 143 feet in height including its foundations.'[26] It is supposed to date from the sixth century A.D.

The seated Buddha in preaching posture from Sāranātha has been assigned to the Gupta period, and is one of the best and most well known plastic Buddhas all the world over.[27]

At the sacred spot where Buddha preached his religion for the first time were ruins of a *stūpa* of which 100 feet still remained above ground. In front of this was 'a stone pillar, above 70 feet high, which had the softness of jade and was of dazzling brightness'. Both these monuments dated from the time of Aśoka.

A standing image of Buddha, "grand and majestic, with long hair from the top of head (from the *uṣṇīṣa*) of noted and conspicuous miraculous powers", existed on an artificial platform, more than 50 paces long and seven feet high, in the Sāranātha complex.

About two or three li to the south-west of the great Buddhist establishment of Mṛgadāva, was a unique *stūpa*. It was more than 300 feet in height with a broad high base which was ornamented with precious substances; the *stūpa* had no storeys of niches for images, but was covered by a dome, and it had a spire but without circular bells.

In Vaiśālī, among the living edifices were a *stūpa* and a stone pillar, about 50 feet high, with a lion capital.[28]

Interesting reference to the House of Vimalakīrti, the famous building near Vaiśālī where the Sūtra called the *Vimala-kīrti-nirdeśa* was collected, are given in the *Shui-Ching-Chu* and in Hsüan-tsang. The Chinese ambassador, Wang-Hsüan-tse, is said to have measured its dimensions.[29] The Śvetapura monastery in the country of Vaiśālī, wherefrom Hsüan-tsang obtained a copy of the *Bodhisattva-piṭaka*,[30] had "sunny terraces and bright coloured halls of two storeys."[31]

One of the 84,000 *stūpas*, the construction of which is ascribed to Aśoka, was at Pāṭaliputra, the dome of which was ornamented with precious substances and stone balustrade. In the Temple of Relics at this ancient metropolis, was the sacred stone bearing the foot-prints of Buddha which were still visible.

The foot-prints were "18 inches long by 6 inches wide; on the right and left sides were wheels or discs; each of the ten toes had artistic venation; the lamination was distinct, and at times shed a bright light." There was also a stone pillar 30 feet high, with an inscription recording Aśoka's benefactions and strong faith in Buddhism.[32]

The monastery at Tilaḍha near Nālandā was a beautiful specimen of monastic architecture and sculpture of the period. The establishment had four courts with three storeyed halls, lofty terraces and a succession of open passages. It was the rendezvous of eminent scholars. At the head of the road, through the middle gate, were three temples with discs on the roofs and hung with small bells. Their bases were surrounded by balustrades, doors, windows, beams, walls, and stairs were ornamented with gilt-work in relief. The middle temple had a stone image of Buddha thirty feet high; the left side temple had an image of goddess Tārā (Tārā Bodhisattva); and the right hand side temple had an image of Bodhisattva Avalokiteśvara. These images were all of bronze.[33]

On a nearby hill was the Guṇamati-vihāra, a rock-cut monastery, 'the high bases of which were backed by the ridge, the high chambers being hewn out of the cliff'. In this locality in another hill was a monastery built by Śīlabhadra.

In the Gayā Mountain (Gayāśīrṣa) there was a stone *stūpa*, 100 feet high, built by Aśoka at the spot where the *Ratnamegha-sūtra* was revealed. The sacred Bodhi-Tree was enclosed by a brick wall, high and strong; this enclosure was long from east to west, and narrow from north to south, and was about 500 paces in circuit. The main gate opened to the east towards the Nairañjanā river; it had three other gates towards west, south and north which last opened towards the walls of a large monastery. Around the Tree were numerous sacred structures of old.[34]

Within the Bo-Tree inclosure, was the 'Adamant Seat' or 'Diamond-Throne', which originated with the origin of the world. "It is the very central point of the Universe, and goes down to the Golden Wheel, from whence it rises upwards to the earth's surface. It is perfected of diamond, and is about 100 paces round. In using the word diamond we mean that it is firm and indestructible, and able to resist all things." There were images of Avalokiteśvara all round this seat. King Pūrṇavarman of Magadha had recently raised a stone wall, 24 feet high, around the Bo-Tree.[35]

One of the most remarkable examples of Buddhist sacred architecture of the period was the Mahābodhi Temple near Bodhi-Tree.[36] "To the east of the Bodhi Tree was a temple above 160 feet high, and with a front breadth at the base of above twenty paces. This temple was made of bricks and coated with lime; it had tiers of niches with gold images; its four walls were adorned with exquisite carvings of pearl-strings and genii; on the roof was a gilt copper *āmalaka*. Connected with the east side of the temple were three lofty halls one behind the other; the wood work of these halls was adorned with gold and silver carvings and studded with precious stones of various colours; and an open passage through them communicated with the inner chamber." Such was the architectural outline of this great temple as it existed in *cir*. 637 A.D.

On the left and right hand sides of the outer door of these halls were images of Avalokiteśvara and Maitreya respectively, each made of silver and over 10 feet in height. Within the temple was an image of Buddha in *bhū-sparśa-mudrā* sitting under the Bodhi-Tree.[37]

The Mahābodhi Temple, as it now stands, appears as a building with straight sides forming 'a square truncated pyramid', '48 feet at its base and between 160 and 170 feet in height'. 'It is built of bluish bricks, with a coating of plaster'. "There can be no reasonable doubt that it is, in spite of all its repairs and alterations, the same building which was described by the Chinese pilgrim."[38]

There were other smaller temples and Buddha images within this monastic establishment; an image of Buddha gazing with uplifted eyes (on the Bo-Tree under which he obtained Bodhi); another standing image of Buddha made of bronze and decorated with precious stones, and placed in a nearby temple; a *stūpa* 100 feet high built by Aśoka and other artistic objects. Summarising his account of Gayā, Hsüan-tsang says that within this inclosure the sacred memorials were crowded together; and 'it would be impossible to enumerate them.'[39]

Outside the North gate of the Bodhi-Tree was 'the Mahābodhi-saṃghārāma built by a former King of Ceylon.' Its building formed six courts, with terraces and halls of three storeys, enclosed by walls between 30 and 40 feet high; "the sculpture and painting were perfect."

The image of Buddha was made of gold and silver, and ornamented by precious stones of various colours. There were, in this monastery, several elegant *stūpas*, lofty and spacious, containing the relics of Buddha.[40]

This *saṃghārāma* seems to have been constructed in the 4th century A.D. by the Ceylonese King Śrī Meghavarṇa, a contemporary of the Gupta sovereign Samudragupta. In the middle of the seventh century A.D., the Chinese envoy Wang Hsüan-tse incidentally refers to the despatch of two Buddhist monks, Mahānāma and Upa (-sena) with valuable presents by King Meghavarṇa of Ceylon to King Samudragupta of India for the latter's permission to build the monastery at Bodh-Gayā for the use of the monks from Siṃhala.[41]

The Vajrāsana-mahābodhi-monastery is mentioned again in about A.D. 670 by the pilgrim Hwi-Lun, as the same as the one built by a King of Ceylon, in which priests of that country formerly dwelt.

The Mahābodhi-saṃghārāma,[42] built by the Ceylonese King, was a separate establishment, complete in itself. Its remains have been identified. The mound is from 1,500 to 2,000 feet in length from west to east, and nearly 1,000 feet in breadth from north to south. The outer wall was nine feet thick with massive round towers at the four corners.[43] A seventh century inscription on the coping of the old stone-railing refers to the fact that the great temple was adorned with a new coating of plaster and paint at the cost of 250 *dīnārs*. B. M. Barua identified the donor of this adornment with a Buddhist *śramaṇa* of Ceylon, Prakhyātakīrti by name, who came on pilgrimage to Bodh-Gayā in the 7th or 6th century A.D., a fact recorded in another inscription on the same stone-railing.[44]

In Gṛdhrakūṭa hill near Rājagṛha, the pilgrim found 'a magnificent brick-hall (*ching-she*, temple), opening to the east'; within this hall was "a life-size image of the Buddha in the attitude of preaching."[45] Archaeological excavations at the site of Rājagṛha have brought to light antiquities dating from the days of Bimbisāra and Ajātaśatru onwards to 10th century A.D.[46]

The Nālandā Saṃghārāma was "the most remarkable for grandeur and height.[47] The original monastery built by King Śakrāditya (probably Kumāragupta I, A.D. 415-455) became the centre of monasteries that were added to it by kings of succeeding generations. This monastic complex may be indicated through a plan as follows :—

1. *saṃghārāma* built by Kumāragupta I, on 'a lucky spot' in Nālandā;
2. to the south of this, *saṃghārāma* built by Skandagupta;
3. to the east of this, *saṃghārāma* built by Purugupta;
4. on the north-east side, *saṃghārāma* built by Narasiṃhagupta ('College of Bālāditya-Raja');
5. on the west side (*Life*, p. 111, 'to the north') probably of the first *saṃghārāma*, was the *saṃghārāma* built by Kumāragupta II;
6. to the north of this, a great *saṃghārāma* built by Harṣa;
7. on the western side of the *saṃghārāma*, at no great distance, a *vihāra*;
8. to the south, 100 paces or so, a small *stūpa*;
9. on this southern side, a standing figure of Avalokiteśvara;
10. to the south of this figure a *stūpa* with Buddha's relics;

11. to the east of this, outside the wall and by the side of a tank, a *stūpa*; beside this tank was a tree with a two-fold trunk;
12. next to the last, was a great *vihāra*, about 200 feet high;
13. to the north of this, another *vihāra* with a statue of Avalokiteśvara;
14. to the north of this, another great *vihāra*, about 300 feet high, built by Bālāditya;
15. to the north-east of this, a *stūpa*;
16. to the south, was a *vihāra* built by Śīlāditya (Harṣa);
17. next to the east, outside the wall, a giant statue of Buddha, standing upright and made of copper. Its height was about 80 feet; a pavilion of 6 stages was required to install it, this pavilion was built by Pūrṇavarman;
18. to the north of this gigantic statue, at a small distance, was a *vihāra* built of bricks which contained a figure of Tārā Bodhisattva;
19. within the southern gate of the wall was a large well;
20. a high wall built round these edifices, made of bricks by Harṣa;
21. the only gate to enter the premises of the Mahāvihāra; this gate was southern.[48]

Archaeological excavations at Nālandā have unearthed, more than 11 large monastery sites and several temple sites,[49] besides numerous Buddhist and Brahmanical antiquities belonging to the Gupta and post-Gupta periods upto 11th century A.D.[50]

In the great monastic establishment of Nālandā, "the work of a succession of sovereigns," says Hsüan-tsang, "the sculpture was perfect and really beautiful." It seems that the best artistic skill of the golden age of the Guptas and the best intellectual and religious spirit of the best days of Mahāyānism had been employed in perfecting this wonderful Buddhist centre of art, literature, philosophy and learning. A graphic and enthusiastic picture of the architecture, sculpture and the general physical beauty of the Nālandā establishment is recorded in the biography of Hsüan-tsang, which deserves citation *in extenso*.

"The whole establishment is surrounded by a brick wall, which encloses the entire convent from without. One gate opens into the Great College, from which are separated eight other halls, standing in the middle (of the *saṃghārāma*). The richly adorned towers, and the fairy like turrets, like pointed hill-tops, are congregated together. The observatories seem to be lost in the vapour (of the morning), and the upper rooms tower above the clouds.

"From the windows one may see how the winds and the clouds (produce new forms), and above the soaring eaves the conjunctions of the sun and moon (may be observed).

"And then we may add how the deep, translucent ponds, bear on their surface the blue lotus, intermingled with the *kie-ni* (*kanaka,* Butea Frondosa) flower, of deep red colour, and at intervals the *āmra* groves spread, over all, their shade.

"All the outside courts, in which are the priest's chambers, are of four stages. The stages have dragon projections and coloured eaves, the pearl-red pillars, carved and ornamented, the richly adorned balustrades, and roofs covered with tiles that reflect the light in a thousand shades, these things add to the beauty of the scene."[51]

This contemporary piece of rare observation reveals the existence of many sotreyed buildings and large academic halls of the monastics. The pointed roofs of these structures were very high as to reach the sky, so to say. Besides, there were astronomical observatories, lofty and strong, through the windows of which the sun eclipse and the moon eclipse were observed and studied.

The Great Vihāra maintained gardens of mango trees and flowers, and fairly good ponds with lotus flowers of different kinds.

Not only the collegiate buildings, but also the residential buildings of the Buddhist sages, scholars and students of Nālandā, were four storeyed. Their style of construction, their exterior projections being dragon-like with lower edges of roofs coloured, sculptured pillars and beautified and exhuberant rows of balusters and parapets with covered copings, it was a city complete in itself and may have attracted even princes to come to its precincts. There is no reason to doubt the trustworthiness of the above description of a seventh century observer. It is corroborated by an epigraph dating from the middle of the 8th century A.D. and found from the site itself.

We read in the inscription of Mālāda that Balāditya had erected a Buddhist temple at Nālandā, "as if with a view to see Kailāśa mountain surpassed." Nālandā which had scholars reputed for their knowledge of the scriptures and the arts (*āgama-kalā-vikhyāta-vidvajjanāḥ*) was full of "the beams of the rays of the *caityas* shining and bright like white clouds." "She was mocking, as it were, at all the cities of the kings who had acquired wealth by tearing asunder the temples in hostile lands.

"Nālandā had a row of *vihāras*, the line of whose tops touched the clouds. That (row of *vihāras*) was, so to say, the beautiful festoon of the earth, made by the creator, which looked resplendent in going upwards.

"Its temples were made brilliant on account of the net work of the rays of the various jewels set in them and was the pleasant abode of the learned and the virtuous *saṃgha* and resembled Sumeru, the charming residence of the noble *vidyādharas*."[52]

It has been noted above that this inscription of Mālāda belongs to the time of Yaśovarman of Kanauj, and that Mālāda was one of the benefactors of Nālandā. In the Kapotaka-vihāra in Magadha, there were many "buildings with miraculous powers and executed with consummate art." In the main temple was a small image of Kuan-tzu-tsai P'usa (i.e., Bodhisattva Avalokiteśvara), "majestic and grave, holding a lotus in one hand, and having an image of Buddha above his forehead." This temple, the pilgrim further records, was erected by a king of Ceylon. The *Life* adds that the marvellous image of Kuan-tzu-tsai P'usa was made of sandal-wood, and was enclosed by railings.[53]

The Po-kih-po monastery in Puṇḍravardhana, "which had spacious halls and tall storeyed chambers" and which could make room for seven hundred monks, as reported by Hsüan-tsang,[54] has been identified with the ruins of Bhasuā-vihāra near Mahāsthāna, where a great mound, approximately 800 feet × 750 feet × 40 feet still exists.[55]

The Buddhist artistic remains in Assam probably date from the 9th and 10th centuries onward.[56] Hsüan-tsang found no Buddhist edifices in Kāmarūpa. In Samataṭa he found in a monastery "a dark blue jade image of the Buddha, eight feet high, showing all the distinctive characteristics."[57]

The ruins of Dharmapāla's Somapura-vihāra (modern Ompur

in Bengal) have been recognised through archaeological exploration. In a number of sealings from 8th century A.D. onwards, reference is made to this monastery of a community of monks built by Dharmapāla (*śrī-somapura-śrī dharmapāla-deva-mahā-vihāriy-ārya-bhikṣu-saṃghasya*).[58] The great monastery finds mention in inscriptions from Gayā[59] and Nālandā.[60] The entire establishment occupied a quadrangle measuring more than 900 feet externally on each side, had high enclosure walls lined on the inside with nearly 177 cells, excluding the cells of the central block in each section.[61] K. N. Diksit observes that "no single monastery of such dimensions has come to light in India."[62]

Bengal has yielded a large number of images of Buddhist deities—mostly Tāntrika Buddhist gods and goddesses—belonging to the period from the 7th and 8th centuries onwards. These include Vajrasattva, Jaṃbhala, Avalokiteśvara, Mañjuśrī, Tārā, Prajñāpāramitā, and some forms of fierce goddesses. Most of them are products of the Pāla and Sena periods.[63]

The Pāla rulers were professed Buddhists but Brahmanism also flourished vigorously during their rule. They developed a luxurious and pompous taste, their aesthetic sense seems to have appreciated "over-sensitiveness of form and gestures, a sensuous worldliness and meticulous details of ornamentation."

The sculptures of the Pāla period are generally carved out of black-stone (*kaṣṭi-pāthara*), either fine or coarse-grained. Images in metal, cast in brass or in octo-alloy (*aṣṭa-dhātu*) and wood carvings are also known. The stone and metal images are generally carved in relief, though some statues are modelled in the round.

The central point of the Pāla sculptures is the human figure which combines in itself both spiritual and physical symbolism. In the Tāntrika literature, e.g. in the *sādhanamālā*, we see that religious suggestiveness and realistic vision go together; spiritual gusto and sensuous beauty go hand in hand. Likewise the images of Buddhist deities, e.g. those in *yab-yuṃ* posture, give a picture of full fleshy and graceful vigorous male and female divinities. The erotic symbolism of the Tāntrika texts finds in these images a genuine plastic expression.[64] One noteworthy feature of the iconography of this period is the tendency to represent Bodhisattvas and other divinities with many heads and arms.

"The eleven-headed Avalokiteśvara, which has become so popular in Tibet, originated in India. It is found in one of the caves of Kānheri."[65] To this archaeological evidence, may be added the literary evidence of the *Ekādaśamukhaṃ* a *dhāraṇī* of Avalokita discovered in Gilgit,[66] which mentions this form of Avalokiteśvara.

Some writers seem to think that the classical Buddhist art traditions declined with the decay of the Gupta rule. This is not true. "During the two hundred years which immediately followed the Gupta period, i.e. A.D. 600-800, Buddhist art had an aftermath in which the great traditions continued to be an inspiration."[67]

It is true that the art centres became confined to the places of pilgrimage, such as Sāranātha, Gayā, Nālandā, and other places in Magadha. The religious enthusiasm of the pious *upāsakas* and the devotional offerings of the devout laity kept the artistic creation alive. Buddha images were still numerous, even after the Tāntrikism had become supreme, but the mass production and careless execution seem to have robbed them of the spiritual calm which characterised early Buddhist images. Exceptions, however, were not unknown. The Buddha image from Kurkīhār, for instance, belonging to 9th century A.D., now preserved in Lucknow Museum, which was a gift from one Vinītabuddhi of Benaras, "is a work of great merit", and is "marked by simplicity and severity of line, the background, on the contrary, displays a profusion of decorative detail."[68]

Orissa has yielded a large number of images of Mahāyāna and Tāntrika Buddhist deities. The Buddhist remains of Sālīhuṇḍaṃ and Śaṅkaraṃ have been dated to the 6th century onwards.[69] The Tāntrika temples of Tārā at Bankad and of Baud, are regarded to be the 'gems of art' in Orissa.[70]

A colossal image of two armed Avalokita, now broken into two pieces, flanked on the right and left by the images of four armed Bhṛkuṭī and Hayagrīva, respectively, and bearing on its forehead an effigy of Amitābha, found in Udayagiri, is assigned to 8th century A.D. on palaeographical grounds.[71]

Images of Prajñāpāramitā, of Buddha in *bhūmi-sparśa-mudrā*, of Dhyānī-Buddha Amitābha and several varieties of the form of Avalokiteśvara, especially, Khaṣarpaṇa-Lokeśvara and Jaṭāmukuṭa-Lokeśvara, which are assignable to the 8th and 9th centuries, have also been discovered in Orissa.[72]

Two of the active centres of Mahāyānism and Tāntrika Buddhism, namely, Śrīparvata and Dhānyakaṭaka were in the South. They were art centres also. The bronze Buddhas from Amarāvatī dating from the 6th century. A.D. may be said to continue the earlier tradition. A bronze Buddha from Amarāvatī of about 6th century. A.D., a granite standing Buddha from Amarāvatī of about 6th century. A.D., a granite standing Buddha from Kāñcīpura, belonging to the 7th century A.D., a figure of Siṃhanāda (granite) from Amarāvatī, belonging to 8th century A.D., a figure of Mañjughoṣa (granite) from Amarāvatī of cir. 8th-9th century A.D., and the beautiful standing image of Maitreya (bronze-gilt) found in Tanjore District assigned to the 8th century A.D., are specially noteworthy.[73]

The history of Buddhist art at Ajaṇṭā covers more than seven hundred years, from the first century B.C. to the 7th century A.D. The following pieces of architecture, sculpture and painting at Ajaṇṭā are assignable to the seventh century A.D. The wall painting in cave I depicting the attack of Māra on Buddha; Māra's attack and temptation in cave XXVI; the Mahāpariniravāṇa scene on stone in the same cave; the facade of the Caitya Hall in cave XIX; and the Caitya Hall in cave XXVI.[74]

The rock-cut Buddhist cave III of Aurangabad, showing a group of men and women worshipping, has been placed in the 7th century. A.D.[75] The worshippers, men and women, kneel into two groups carved almost in the round against the right and left walls of the cave temple, and face towards the image of Buddha which is enthroned in the middle, against the back wall. Stella Kramrisch observes that "the varied coiffures and ornaments of these figures belong to one and the same type of form as the differentiated countenances with their diversified expressions of expectant prayer and devotional surrender."[76]

Among other stray pieces of noteworthy art of the period mention may be made of the Sirpur Buddha image with a halo upon which is engraved the famous *gāthā* '*ye dharmā....*' in the letters of the 8th century A.D.[77] The Viśvakarmā cave of Ellora is also probably a product of the 7th century A.D.[78] A beautiful image of goddess Tārā with attendant deities (bronze) from Madhyapradesh is said to belong to the 8th-9th century A.D.[79]

The varied and diverse pantheon of Mahāyāna Buddhism

was, in fact, the creation of esoteric Buddhism. The esoteric Buddhist pantheon revolves round the conception of the holy pentad—the five Dhyāni-Buddhas—these are celestial Buddhas who are the heads of five families of divinities of Tāntrika Buddhism.

Certain Vajrayāna texts seem to refute the generally current view that Mahāyāna worship was a gross idolatory. B. Bhattacharya also points out that the Buddhist worship was not a mere idolatory.[80] In the *Sādhanamālā* and the *Advayavajrasaṃgraha*, the manifestation of deities is described and it is pointed out that they are merely ideal; the icons symbolise *śūnyatā* and *niḥsvabhāvatā*.

The abode of the gods is said to be the *akaniṣṭha* heaven, which is the uppermost of the *Rūpa* heavens.[81] Śāntarakṣita says at one place that "In the excellent *akaniṣṭha* heaven, which is beyond the *śuddhāvāsa* heaven, the Bodhisattva attains omniscience, and (under his influence) a Buddha is born in this world.'[82] This points to a profound philosophy behind the Buddhist patheon.

The ascetic produces mentally, so to say, in meditation through a subtle psychic process, the deity of his choice out of a seed syllable (*bīja-mantra*) appropriately assigned to that deity. In his meditation and vision he perceives certain form and attributes which are then represented in icon for purposes of worship.[83]

In the *Advayavajrasaṃgraha* it is said that "the form of the deity is an explosion of *śūnya.* It is by nature non-existent. Whenever there is an explosion it must be *śūnya* in essence."[84] Elsewhere in the same work we find the process of evolution of the deity described in the following manner. "From the right perception of *śūnyatā* proceeds the germ-syllable, from the germ-syllable proceeds the conception of an icon, and from the icon its external representations. The whole process therefore is one of dependent origination."[85]

In the *Guhyasamāja-tantra* evolution of the five Buddhas of Meditation is described. Here it is shown that these gods originate out of Sarvatathāgatasvāmin, who is also known as Vajrasattva from other sources. The Lord sat in different *samādhis*, recited different *mantras* whence-from originated these Buddhas, their female partners, and the guardians of the four quarters. The five Buddhas thus manifested were Akṣobhya (the Unshakable), Vairocana (the Brilliant One), Ratnaketu or Ratnasaṃbhava (the Matrix of the Jewel or The Jewel Born), Amitābha (the Infinite Light), and Amoghavajra or Amoghasiddhi (the Infallible Success).[86] As G. Tucci points out, according to Vajrayāna, the original consciousness symbolised by Vajrasattva or Akṣobhya, is radiated into these five Buddhas.[87] They are therefore not different from the original Essence represented by Vajrasattva. As Advayavajra says, Vajrasattva is the unity of *śūnyatā* and *jñānamātratā*.

In a passage of the *Sādhanamālā* these Buddhas are described thus : the Jinas are Variocana of white colour, exhibiting *bodhyaṅgī-mudrā*; Ratnasaṃbhava of yellow colour, exhibiting *varada-mudrā*; Amitābha of red colour, showing *dhyāna-mudrā*; Amoghasiddhi of green colour, showing *abhaya-mudrā*, and Akśobhya of blue colour, exhibiting the *bhū-sparśa-mudrā*.[88] When represented in painting or plastic forms, each Dhyānī-Buddha bears on his forehead a miniature figure of Vajrasattva. From these Dhyāni-Buddhas emanate numerous gods and goddesses that fill the esoteric pantheon.

We owe to Tāntrika Buddhism a large number of imges and paintings of Dhyānī-Buddhas and of other divinities associated with their *kulas* or 'families'. Often Puranic deities such as Gaṇeśa, Sarasvatī, Mahākāla, etc. were incorporated into Tāntrika Buddhist pantheon.[89] It may be mentioned that except for some exceptional examples, few and far between, the figures of Buddha, the historic Śākyamuni, became rare during this period. He being relegated to the position of Mānuṣī-Buddhas, the Dhyānī-Buddhas became famous and popular. True it is that the images of Avalokiteśvara, Mañjuśri and Maitreya, the most famous Bodhisattvas of Mahāyāna, still continued to be popular as is evidenced by their numerous images still extant and dating from the seventh and eighth centuries.[90]

The Buddha image of stone belonging to 8th century A.D. found from Amarāvatī,[91] shows clear deviations from the classical style. The much mutilated figure of standing Buddha with scenes of Mahāparinirvāṇa, though of considerable interest, does not reflect the spiritual dignity characteristic of ancient plastic Buddhas. Here and there we find examples depicting the episodes in the life of Buddha. But these classical episodes, e.g. the Nālagiri-taming, are treated conventionally.

The influence of Tāntrika Buddhism on Buddhist art is evidenced by other features also. Thus we find prominent place occupied by female divinities, like Prajñāpāramitā, Tārās of various colours and forms, Parṇaśavarī, Mārīci, Nairātmā, Hārīti, Bhṛkuṭi, Ekajaṭā, Vajravarāhī, etc.[92] In early Mahāyāna female Bodhisattvas were extremely rare; Tārā as a goddess is not known even to the *Kāraṇḍavyūha* which treats of the cult of Avalokita, whose consort Tārā becomes a very popular deity during our period. Even Śāntideva testifies to this view when he prays, 'may all the women become men so that they may espouse the career of a Bodhisattva'.

But in Tāntrika Buddhist literature, not only the Buddhas but also the Bodhisattvas are associated with *śaktis* or female coefficients. We find Vajrasattva often represented in *yab-yum* posture, in tight embrace with his *yoginī*, touching all the vital points of contact.[93] So is the case with Heruka and Nairātmā.[94] The images of these goddesses are fleshy, youthful and sensuous.

On the other hand, a large majority of images represents fierce and angry-looking deities who occupy such an important place in Tāntrika texts, especialy in the *sādhanas*. Thus a unique image of Buddha-kapāla is preserved in the Baroda Museum. It is a terrific posture, "with three blood-shot eyes rolling in anger, distorted face, canine teeth, ornaments made of bones, a garland of severed heads, and an attitude of menacing dance."[95] In the *Sādhanamālā* he is described in an embrace with his śakti (*prajñālingitaṃ*).[96] It may be noted that Sarahapāda, the first Siddha, wrote a Tantra called the *Buddha-kapāla-tantra*. The art illustrations of the god Mahākāla, whose popularity is testified by I-tsing, and whose worship is described in the *Sādhanamālā*, are equally fearful.

Yet another distinguishing feature of the Buddhist art of the period is the tendency to represent gods and goddesses with many faces and arms. This tendency too, is attributable to Tāntrika influence. It may be noted, however, that a Mahāyānasūtra already describes Avalokiteśvara not only with the atributes of Brahmanical gods like Śiva and Brahmā, but also as having 11 heads, a hundred thousand arms and incalculable eyes.[97] Goddesses like Tārā, Mārīci, Parṇaśavarī, etc. are shown with many arms.[98]

CHAPTER IV

MONASTIC LIFE AND DISCIPLINE

IT GOES without saying that the corner-stone of Buddhist movement consisted of *bhikṣus* or monks. In the time of the Buddha many ascetic mendicants lived a peripatetic life, they were called *paribbājakas* or 'wanderers'. A *bhikṣu* is by definition a sharer, living on alms, having no permanent abode. The *bhikṣu-saṃgha* was an 'Order of the Homeless Ones'; it had been, from the very start, an essential member of the Buddhist Trinity, called the *tri-ratna*. Quite early in the history of Buddhism, *vihāras* or monasteries came to be established and the *saṃgha* began to have a permanent residence. Though the ideals of *piṇḍa pātika* were never completely abandoned, yet the Buddhist monks now on began to live a settled life in the monastic abodes. Life in these monasteries was regulated by a code of moral conduct, a body of the rules of ethical training and monastic organization, known as the Vinaya(*vi-nayati*—'to lead to discipline').

It has been observed that "The greatest genius of the Buddha lay in the organization of the ascetic order and the creation of a code of rules and regulations for the conduct of monastic life."[1] The present chapter is intended to give a picture of this life during our period.

Endowment and Maintenance of Monasteries

Buddhist monasteries came into existence as a result of the donations made by the kings, officials of the State and merchant-princes. Their maintenance also was due to the charitable endowments and periodical contributions made by royal and rich persons of the society for the upkeep of their inmates.

Right from the days of the Buddha, "the kings, elders, and the gentry of the countries round about, built shrines for making offerings to the priests, and gave them land, houses, gardens, with men and bullocks for cultivation. Binding title-deeds were written out, and subsequent kings have handed these down one to another without daring to disregard them, in unbroken succession to this day. Rooms with beds and mattresses, food and clothes, are provided for resident and travelling priests, without fail, and this is the same in all places."[2]

This account, given by Fa-hsien in the early years of the fifth century A.D., applies almost *in toto* to the seventh and eighth centuries A.D.

The example of the development of the Nālandā-Mahāvihāra would illustrate the position clearly. According to Hsüan-tsang, the ground of the monastic establishment was originally a Mango-garden belonging to a *śreṣṭhin* or merchant-prince whose name was probably Amara.[3] It was purchased for ten lacs (or *koṭis*)[4] of gold pieces by a group of 500 merchants who gifted it to the Buddhist *saṃgha*. Laterly king Śakrāditya (identified with Mahendrāditya Kumāragupta I, *cir.* A.D. 415-455) built a monastery here. His son and successor, king Buddhagupta built another monastery to the south of this; king Tathāgatagupta built a third one to the east; king Bālāditya built a fourth one to the north-east. The son and successor of Bālāditya was king Vajra who constructed another monastery to the west; and to the north of this a king of Mid-India (identified by Father Heras with Emperor Harṣa) erected a large monastery. Then a lofty enclosing wall was built round the whole establishment with one main gate, probably by the same king of Mid-India.

The bounty of king Śakrāditya was still being enjoyed by monks, and about 40 Buddhist monks took their daily meals in that monastery.[5] The Nālandā monastery had a farm-house where Hsüan-tsang was given a refreshment before entering the Mahāvihāra.[6]

In Nālandā he first lodged in the monastery built by Bālāditya where he was entertained by Buddhabhadra for seven days. Subsequently he lived in the abode of Dharmapāla. Here he was regularly served with rice, fruits, oil, camphor and butter; besides, he was provided with two menial servants and a riding elephant. The Head of the Nālandā-mahāvihāra used to entertain in this fashion a myriad monkṣ.[7]

Among the royal patrons of Nālandā-mahāvihāra[8] during our period mention may be made of Emperor Harṣavardhana, king Pūraṇavarman of Magadha, Kumāra Bhāskaravarman of Kāmarūpa, and perhaps king Aṃśuvarman of Nepal in the seventh century A.D. Among the royal patrons belonging to the eighth century A.D., Gopāla and Dharmapāla, the first two kings of the Pāla dynasty, seem to occupy the first place. Most likely the Tibetan king Khri-sroṅ-lde-btsan (*cir.* A.D. 755-797) was also a patron of this monastery. Among the lay-followers the most noted patron of Nālandā seems to have been Mālāda, son of Tegina, a minister of king Yaśovarman of Kanauj. Besides, a number of seals of Maukharīs, of the kings of Prāgjyotiṣapura and of other non-official personages have been unearthed at Nālandā.

Hwui-li records that the king of the country (probably the country of Magadha wherein lay the Mahāvihāra) had remitted the revenues of one hundred villages for the upkeep of the Monastery at Nālandā. Two hundred householders of these villages, day by day, contributed several hundred piculs (1 picul=133$\frac{1}{3}$ lb.) of rice, several hundred catties (1 catty= 160 lb.) of butter and milk. In this way the clothes, food, beds and the medicines were supplied to the inmates.[9]

In the time of I-tsing, the endowments bestowed on Nālandā had doubled. There were now more than 200 villages in its possession. They had been bestowed by kings of many generations.[10]

The kings who made endowments and land grants for the convents of Buddhist monks also took care to upkeep them. The clepsydrae, which were regularly used in the Indian monasteries, during this period, were also supplied by the kings of many generations, together with some boy-servants to watch and announce the hours.[11] I-tsing found it a universal custom in India that gifts of images, garments, incense, utensils and eatables and articles of daily use were received from the householders—the lay Buddhists, and were distributed among the monks. Apart from the gifts, the monasteries seem to have earned some income from their corn-fields and fruit-gardens. The monasteries usually received one-sixth of the produce of the land belonging to them and cultivated by hired labour. When any resident monk died his belongings became the property of the *saṃgha*. The monasteries had a common fund out of which the inmates were supplied clothing. This fund was pooled not only by gifts but also by the produce of the farms and gardens. Sometimes, the endowments and provisions exceeded the needs of the monasteries so that they could have "great wealth, granaries full of rotten corn, many servants, male and female, money and treasures hoarded in the treasury."[12]

I-tsing lends us a glimpse of the material possessions of some Buddhist monks who were distinguished and received special favours. Thus among articles in possesion of such a Buddhist monk, we find the following : lands, houses, shops, bedgear, wooden-seats, and iron or copper implements, which were not distributable and became the *saṃgha* property. But small iron or copper bowls, door-keys, needles, razors, knives, axes, chisels, earthen pots, water-basins, etc. were distributable among the monks.

Animals, including elephants, horses, mules, horses for riding were to be offered to the Royal House; bulls and sheep were to be made *saṃgha* property. Paints of good quality were sent to the temple for colouring images and decorating the sanctuary. Wine was either to be buried or to be thrown away. All medical substances were to be kept in the monastic hospital for the use of sick persons. Valuables, precious stones, gems and the like were to be divided into two portions. One portion was to be used in sacred affairs such as in building or maintaining the Lion Seat or copying of the scriptures; this portion was called *dhammika*. The other portion, called *saṃghika*, was to be divided among those who were present there. The chairs inlaid with jewels or gold and silver were to be offered to the residents, if not sufficient for all, only the elders took them. But scriptural texts and commentaries were to be deposited in the library of the *saṃgha* to be read by members. If deeds and contracts were due, they were to be kept in the Treasury of the Order. Gold, silver, raw or worked, shells (*cowrie*) and coins were divided equally into three parts each went to each member of the Holy Trinity.[13]

Among the important examples of endowments and munificence of the time of Hsüan-tsang's itinerary, mention may be made of Pūrṇavarman of Magadha probably a Maukharī ruler. He patronised the learned and the virtuous men and assigned the revenue of twenty large towns to support a savant Jayasena by name.[14] It was he who revived the Bodhi-Tree, which had been destroyed by Śaśāṅka; he also erected a protective wall round the Sacred Tree, made of stone, rising 24 feet in height.[15] Two Maukharī seals have been found in the monasteries excavated at Nālandā which also point to their association with the endowments.[16]

The most lavish religious endowments were made by Śrī Harṣa Sīlādityarāja, the subduer of Five Indias. He had constructed one of the largest monasteries at Nālandā, and built the boundary wall around the whole establishment.[17] The construction of a large brass monastery, financed by him was still going on in Nālandā when Hsüan-tsang visited it.[18] He had offered the revenue of 80 large towns in Orissa for the comfort and support of Jayasena.[19] He offered to Hsüan-tsang 10,000 pieces of gold, 30,000 pieces of silver (pieces probably refer to gold and silver coinage of the king) and 100 garments of superior cotton. Besides, the kings and chieftains of 19 states—including perhaps Kumāra of Kāmarūpa, Pūraṇavarman of Magadha, Dhruvabhaṭa of Valabhī and others whose names are not recorded—presented him with rare jewels. Harṣa's piety and charity can hardly be recorded adequately. His charities at the Allahabad Arena of Charity continued for several months, which exhausted the imperial resources of the empire accumulated during a period of five years. It seems that in this great *dāna-yajña*, Harṣa was probably supported by his allies, particularly Bhāskaravarman, Dhruvabhaṭa and Pūrṇavarman and other vassals. But this Assembly of Mokṣa was held every five years and its duration was seventyfive days; its beneficiaries included the *brāhmaṇas* and *śramaṇas* of all the Five Indias besides lay-men, the poor, destitute and the orphans.[20] In the session witnessed by Hsüan-tsang at Prayāga, Harṣa had invited 10,000 Buddhist monks, each of whom received 100 gold pieces, one pearl, one cotton garment and sumptuous drinks and meats, flowers and perfumes.[21]

On the advice of Bodhisattva Avalokiteśvara, Harṣa assumed the sovereignty and endeavoured to "raise Buddhism from the ruin into which it had been brought by the king of Karṇasuvarṇa". Besides this, Harṣa erected thousands of *stūpas* on the banks of the Gaṅgā, built Buddhist monasteries and public rest-houses; "he furnished the chapels and liberally adorned the common halls of the monasteries. Owing to his influence, the neighbouring princes and the statesmen also became zealous in good works. At his royal lodge everyday meals were supplied to 1,000 Buddhist monks and 500 Brahmins."[22]

Reference may be made to the endowments made by the Pāla kings of Bengal. According to Tārānātha in the time of Gopāla, an *upāsaka* founded the Odantapurī or Uddaṇḍapura Monastery near Nālandā, now identified with Bihar shariff in Patna district. This king revived the monastery of Nālandā and built several monasteries in his kingdom.[23] A Vāgīśvarī image inscription found at Nālandā refers to king Gopāla, evidently of the Pāla lineage and probably Gopāla I, who flourished in the later half of the 8th century A.D.[24] The *Mañjuśrīmūlakalpa* describes in detail the religious endowments made by Gopāla. He is represented as making *vihāras*, *caityas*, gardens, reservoirs, free inns and caves.[25] The Vāgīśvarī image may have been one of his gifts.

Gopāla's successor Dharmapāla was also a great patron and builder of Buddhist establishments. He founded the Vikramaśīlā Monastery (identified with Pātharaghāṭa in Bhāgalpur District). It had 108 rooms, 54 rooms for the general use of monks and 54 for esoteric practices; in the centre was the great hall. These were surrounded by a wall with 6 gates. The king maintained 108 eminent Buddhist scholars to carry on the religious and educational activity of this institution. Besides the students other residents were also maintained by the State. Dharmapāla also patronised the Nālandā-vihāra.[26]

Reference has already been made to the Buddhist leanings of the Khaḍga kings of Samataṭa in Bengal. One of these kings, Rājabhaṭa by name, was according to Sheng-chi, a great *upāsaka*. He used to prepare everyday hundred thousand icons of Buddha with earth, and recited hundred thousand verses of the *Mahāprajñāpāramitā-sūtra*. It was a custom with him to take out processions in honour of Buddha, with an image of Bodhisattva Avalokiteśvara at the front, and make pious gifts. In his royal city, there were 4,000 monks and nuns.[27]

The Bhauma-kāra kings of Orissa are known to have made large religious endowments in favour of Buddhists along with the Brahmanical followers. Their capital city, Virajā (modern Jājapura) has yielded many Buddhist images and monuments.

The Dhenkānāl plate of Tribhuvana Mahādevi, queen of Śivakara III (884 A.D.) a devout Buddhist, records the munificence of her predecessors who had decorated the earth with many monasteries and sanctuaries that were like staircases to ascend to the city of Purandara.[28] The site of Solanapura north of Jājapura, had yielded many Tāntrika Buddhist images belonging to the 8th and 9th centuries A.D.[29] An inscribed image of Avalokiteśvara found at Khaḍīpadā was installed by a Tāntrika Buddhist called Parama-guru Rāhularuci, in the reign of Śubhakaradeva (790 A.D.).[30]

Ratnagiri in Orissa, which had yielded many pieces of Buddhist art, was also a famous centre of the Buddhistic culture during this period. A Buddhist monk named Prajñā, a native of Kapiśā, is known from Chinese sources to have lived and studied at the monastery of Ratnagiri. The king of Wu-ch'a (Uḍra, Orissa) named Su-ba-ka-ra-sim-ha, who patronised this institution, is said to have sent a section of the *Avataṃsaka* to the Chinese emperor Te-tsong through Prajñā. This Orissan king is identified with Śubhakara I (A.D. 790).[31]

A copper plate grant of 9th century A.D. informs us of the fact that in Jayāśrama-vihāra, in Northern Tosala, king Śivakaradeva III donated the revenue of a village called Kallam for the god Buddhabhaṭṭāraka. The temple of Buddhabhaṭṭāraka, enshrining an image of Buddha, was built by Amubhaṭṭāraka in the precincts of the Jayāśrama-vihāra. In this *vihāra* both monks and nuns were living together, and there were ten servants to look after the comforts of the nuns.[22]

An inscription incised on one of the caves at Dhaulī hill reveals the existence of a Buddhist monastery called Arghyakā Varāṭikā. The inscription belongs to early 9th century A.D. The monastery was built in A.D. 829 by Bhīmaṭa and Loyamaka during the reign of king Śāntikaradeva.[33]

The *Rājataraṅgiṇī* records in its third and fourth books, the lavish endowments made by the kings of Kashmir upon the Buddhist monks during the two centuries of our period. King Meghavāhana was a pious person and well understood the sanctity of life; Kalhaṇa compares him with Buddha and Bodhisattvas. He stopped killing of animals in his realm and compelled his neighbouring princes to follow the ideal of non-violence.

His queen Amṛtaprabhā constructed a large and lofty monastery for foreign monks; in this monastery lived a Tibetan Buddhist monk Ston-pa by name. The king's maternal uncle built the Jayendra-vihāra and placed therein a colossal statue of Buddha (*bṛhadbuddha*).[34]

Religious endowments continued to be made during the reigns of Yuddhiṣṭhira, Raṇāditya, and Vikramāditya, specially by the queens and the ministers of the state. During the reign of Lalitāditya Muktāpīḍa, we find the golden days of the Kashmirian Buddhists. The endowments of the king, of his queens and ministers have been already referred to. The most famous Buddhist *upāsaka* in Kashmir in the 8th century A.D. was Caṅkuṇa, the Chief Minister of Lalitāditya. The testimony of Kalhaṇa is corroborated partly by Hsüan-tsang and Ou K'ong and partly by archaeological remains.[35]

Reference has been made above to the patronage of Buddhism under king Śīlāditya of Malava, who seems to have vied with Aśoka in his religieux. Śīlāditya of Malava of Hsüan-tsang's records is most likely identical with Śīlāditya I who also bore the epithet Dharmāditya and one of whose known dates is A.D. 606. This may be taken to correspond, more or less, with Hsüan-tsang's statement that the king flourished about 60 years before his visit.

Śīlāditya I Dharmāditya of Malava is known from some records which also support the account of Hsüan-tsang. He founded several monasteries and granted endowments for many Buddhist establishments. The following description of his piety justifies his assumption of the title of Dharmāditya. He built a large temple and installed in it seven images of Buddha; he convoked a quinquennial charitable session regularly and lavished precious and rare articles, garments and gold pieces on the Brethren. His mission of piety was continued by his successors. He was so careful an observer of the doctrine of *ahiṃsā* as to supply strained water to his elephants and horses, and himself never killed even an ant. He constructed temporary residences on the largest and the grandest scale and made pious gifts. Other endowments of the Maitraka kings of Valabhī have been discussed above.[36]

Another example of a rare benevolent king is to be found in the person of Dhruvabhaṭa of Valabhī, son-in-law of Emperor Harṣa. He was a typical personality, hasty and impulsive by nature, heavy and dull in manners, but he respected virtue and promoted learning. Although he was 'an Eternal Warrior' (Dhruvabhaṭa), yet he was a devout Buddhist; deeply given to the *tri-ratna*; he convoked a great assembly annually and, for seven days entertained monks from all over the country and "bestowed on them food of the best description, choice jewels, bedding and clothes, with varieties of medicaments and other things of different kinds."[37]

A very comprehensive and interesting record relating to the benefactions of a rich lay-man at Nālandā, is a stone inscription found at Nālandā[38] belonging to the reign of king Yaśovarmadeva, indentified with Emperor Yaśovarman of Kanauj (died *cir.* A.D. 740). This lay-devotee is Mālāda, son of Tegina, a minister of Yaśovarman. The record opens with a grand eulogy of and reverent salutations to Buddha. A detailed description of the great Buddhist temple built by king Bālāditya at Nālandā is given and the Mahāvihāra with its noble inmates is also eulogised. But the purpose and the burden of the epigraph is to record Mālāda's charity. The epigraph supplies the following important notice with regard to the endowments and provisions for the maintenance of Nālandā Mahāvihāra made by *upāsaka* Mālāda in the middle of 8th century.

He brought, in person, with profound devotion to Buddha, the pious permanent grant, pure and cool water mixed with fragrant powder, a bright lamp and offerings of clarified butter and curd. Under the orders of the community of Brethren, he distributed daily, in a befitting manner, various preparations of rice, curds and copious *ghee* to the monks of the four quarters. He also distributed among them pure and scented water (perfumed with *tvak*, *elā*, *patraka* and *nāga-kesara*) daily at the session (*sattra*). Not satisfied with this charity, Mālāda purchased everything here at Nālandā from the revered *saṃgha* and then gave it back to the *bhikṣus*, according to rites, barring the monk's robe. Mālāda also 'gave away to the Buddhist monks a common dwelling place, wherein to spend time happily, upto and beyond Narddarikā, excepting a place for himself'. Commenting on this last sentence, Hirānanda Śāstrī wrote that "It means that Mālāda became a Buddhist monk for some time and after that again became a *gṛhastha*."[39]

A Shāhpur stone image inscription of 66th year (Harṣa Era=A.D. 672-673) belonging to the reign of Ādityasena, the later Gupta king, records a pious gift by Śālapakṣa (the Balādhikṛta of Ādityasena) for the Nālandā-Mahā-(-gra-) vihāra.[40]

Monastic Organization and Administration

Buddhist monasteries seem to have been organized and administered according to the traditional laws of the *saṃgha.*[41] In their internal management they enjoyed more or less complete autonomy from any external secular authority. But the kings and the royal patrons seem to have exercised some power over the institutions they maintained or that were in their dominion. The ideal of universal brotherhood, equality of opportunity and respect for virtue and learning were observed without any consideration of nationality, caste or age. Thus in the 9th century, a Buddhist monk-scholar of Jalālābād, who was on a pilgrimage to the sites in Bihar, was elected to be the Chief of a College.[42] Hsüan-tsang, though a foreigner monk-scholar, received the highest honours and the best comforts in Indian monasteries wherever he went.

In a few cases, instances of royal control on the monasteries are known to us. King Kumāra of Kāmarūpa is seen threatening through a messenger to Śīlabhadra, that he would demolish the Nālandā Mahāvihāra in case his request for despatching Hsüan-tsang immediately to his court was not complied with.[43] This shows that the Kāmarūpa king could exert his influence on that monastic institution.

Likewise, Emperor Harṣa is said to have "brought the Brethren together for examination and discussion, giving rewards and punishments according to merit and demerit. Those Brethren who kept the rules of their Order strictly and were thoroughly sound in theory and practice he advanced to the Lion's Throne (that is promoted to the highest place) and from these he received religious instruction; those who, though perfect in the observance of the ceremonial code were not learned in the past, he merely honoured with formal reverence; those who neglected the ceremonial observances of the Order, and whose immoral conduct was notorious, were banished from his presence and from the country."[44]

In the *Mṛcchakaṭika* we find *bhikṣu* Saṃvāhaka being appointed Head of all the Buddhist monasteries (*kulapati*) at the recommendation of Cārudatta, by the king who seems to have had the ultimate supreme authority on all religious endowments in the kingdom.[45]

From Tārānātha we learn that Head of the Vikramaśilā Monastery, built by Dharmapāla, had control over Nālandā Monastery also.[46] This points to the royal control which the Pāla kings exercised over the monasteries within their state.

In Kashmir the king is seen appointing some score of monks headed by *bhadanta* Yaśa from among the monks, to help Hsüan-tsang when the latter stayed there.[47]

As already observed, in their internal management the monasteries enjoyed full freedom. A regulated papal hierarchy seems to have been evolved by the monastics. At the head of the Monastery was a Chief Priest or Head Abbot (*sthavira, kulapati*).

Character, learning, seniority and general ability were the qualifications of a monk who could rise up to this distinction. In Kashmir, *bhadanta* Yaśa was the *sthavira* of the monastery;[48] in Tāmralipti Monastery, Rāhulamitra was the *sthavira*, and all monasteries of Bengal were under his supervision.[49] In the Tilaḍha Monastery near Nālandā, Jñānacandra was the *sthavira*;[50] a Jñānacandra is mentioned by Hsüan-tsang in Nālandā as a man of exceptional virtue and learning; the same scholar seems to have become the Head of Tilaḍha-vihāra in the time of I-tsing. In the forty's of the 7th century A.D., Śīlbhadra alias Treasure of the Good Law, "whose perfect excellence was buried in obscurity", was the *kulapati* of Nālandā.[51] In the time of I-tsing this exalted position seems to have been occupied by Ratnasiṃha who is mentioned as the most distinguished teacher at Nālandā.[52] Divākaramitra was the Head of the Forest Monastery in eastern Vindhya Hills, and under him lived ascetics of various faiths and philosophies.[53]

The *sthavira* or *kulapati* may be described as Director of the convent; every one respected him and obeyed his orders, all important activities were preceded by his deliberation; he enjoyed the best possible facilities available in the monastery. On religious functions he presided over the gathering; he would salute the image and make offerings first, all others will follow him. When king Kumāra of Kāmarūpa wanted to invite Hsüan-tsang he sought the sanction of Śīlabhadra; when Emperor Harṣa wished to hold philosophical debates he sought the views of Śīlabhadra.[54]

Next to *kulapati*, in position and authority, was a monk called *karmadāna* or *vihārasvāmi* or *vihāra-pāla*. He was in fact the Deputy Director of Monastery, and conducted the whole affairs thereof. He regulated the time-table, the hours of the meal and other daily programmes; in the time of Hsüan-tsang, the Deputy Director of Nālandā was probably Buddhabhadra, of 70 years' age, who lived in a four-storeyed building in the College built by Bālādityarāja. When Hsüan-tsang entered Nālandā-vihāra, the *karmadāna* was directed by the *kulapati* to sound the gong and proclaim the arrival of the distinguished guest and to arrange the requirements of the latter.[55]

By far the supreme executive body of the monastics living in a monastery or a group of monasteries, was the *pariṣad* or Assembly. All powers concerning sacred and secular affairs of the monastic establishment were vested in this Assembly of monks, which symbolised the entire Brotherhood or *saṃgha*. As an eternal member of the Holy Trinity, its dignity and authority were paramount.

No one was admitted to the Order or ordained as a *bhikṣu* or *bhikṣuṇī* without the sanction of the Assembly; admission to the Order, gradation of the members of the Order, arrangement of the *uposatha* ceremony, proper recitation and observation of the *prātimokṣa* rules, arrangement of the affairs of the dead monks and the disposal of the latter's belongings and the management of economic life, such as clothing, meals, articles of worship, construction, cultivation and preservation of monastic fields and gardens etc. were the principal functions of the Assembly.[56]

Nālandā stone inscription of Mālāda refers to the authority and management of the Order of monks. He could make endowments and charities with the permission of the Order. As many as 775 specimens of monastic seals have been recovered at the sites of the convents of Nālandā complex; they bear the inscription: *śrī-Nālandā-mahāvihāra-āryabhikṣu-saṃghasya*. These seals point to the administration of the *saṃgha*.[57]

The monasteries also maintained some inferior staff and servants. These were probably of two types: *māṇavas* and *brahmacārins*. In the three monasteries in Kanauj presumably built by king Harṣa, there were thousands of lay Buddhists to serve them.[58] At Nālandā Hsüan-tsang was given two personal servants to wait on him. On one occasion, he had sent "an attendant" to tear out a heretical document pasted on the wall of the

Monastery. On being asked as to his identity, the attendant replied : "I am the servant of Mahāyānadeva."[59] Monastic servants are referred to in Chinese records as 'pure men' and *upāsakas*. I-tsing gives more information about their work. The 'pure man' takes the chair and utensils when a monk proceeds to receive a guest; he takes out the remnant of the meals eaten by "priests who order their servants to carry it to the monastery."[60] These servants were also employed to cultivate the gardens, they also beat the time-drum (such watch-keepers were usually bestowed by the kings), but servants were not entitled to sound the gong (*ghaṇṭā*) announcing the hour of a religious service, which was announced by the Deputy Director (*karmadāna*).[61] But all other "unimportant affairs were done by the servants (pure men) and porters."[62]

Life and Discipline in the Monasteries

Resident monks in the monasteries were divided into classes or grades; the criteria being the monastic seniority, learning or knowledge and spiritual excellence. There were, according to I-tsing,[63] three classes of monks who could not be led in one and the same way; they were the superiors, the mediocres, and the inferiors. "The four refuges,[64] the four (proper) actions,[65] and the thirteen *dhutāṅgas*[66] were ordained for men of superior faculties. The possession of rooms, the acceptance of gifts and the thirteen necessaries[67] were allowed both to the mediocre and the inferior classes of monks.

But this three-fold classification, based upon the degree of asceticism practised by each class, seems to have been rather theoretical. The actual grounds, on which the gradation of monks seems to have been based during this period, were mainly three : monastic seniority, knowledge of Tripiṭaka and high moral character. Those possessing these merits appear to have enjoyed certain privileges and formed a distinct and upper class among the monks and nuns. The following extracts, gleaned from I-tsing's *Record*, will give an idea of the gradation of monks.

(1) With regard to the allotment of rooms in the monastery, we find that the respectable and learned monks, as also those versed in the Piṭakas, were allotted some of the best rooms and servants. Not only "venerable priests, if very learned", but also "to the elders (*sthaviras*), better rooms were given and

thus gradually to the lowest." Thus three categories were distinguished in the matter of distribution of cells.[68]

(2) The senior monks and the venerable priests used small chairs to sit on at a dinner, while for the junior members of the Order, blocks of wood were used instead.[69]

(3) If such men delivered daily lectures or sermons, they were freed from the normal duties imposed upon the monks; while going out, they could ride on sedan-chairs, though not on horses.[70]

(4) With respect to the distribution of articles, valuables or other commodities, if they were not sufficient for all the monks of the monastery, only the elders took them.[71]

(5) Seniority was counted from the date and actual, precise time of the ordination (*upasaṃpadā*); those who had spent ten rain-retreats, were designated *sthaviras*, 'of settled position', ordinary monks were called *śrāmaṇeras*. A *sthavira* could live by himself, "without living under a teacher's care", while a *śrāmaṇera* had to live at least five summers, under the tutelage of some elder.[72]

(6) In ceremonial meets of the monastery, the monks took their seats according to their respective ranks.[73]

(7) Those who were worthy of receiving salutation, did not salute to their juniors or inferiors.[74]

(8) In observing the *uposatha* and the *pravāraṇā* ceremonies also, the monks and the nuns preceded or followed each other according to their rank, 'first *bhikṣus*, next *bhikṣuṇīs*, then the lower classes of the members."[75]

Rules and regulations concerning the admission of persons to the *saṃgha* and ordination of the monks, were similar to those of ancient times and corresponded with those laid down in the *Vinaya-piṭaka*. I-tsing's account of the entire procedure of ordination is as follows.

Any one wishing to embrace the monkhood had to approach a teacher of his own choice and request him to be initiated; there was no caste barrier; a minor, a matricide, a patricide, and a eunuch and the like were disqualified for admission to the Order of monks. The selected teacher had to get the permission of the *saṃgha* and after this he imparted the Five Precepts to the candidate. Only a *sthavira* could act as an *upādhyāya*, and no one could attain the position of a *sthavira* without spending ten rain-retreats (*varṣāvāsa*).

The ordination (*upasampadā*) ceremony was conducted by a priest called *karmācārya*; only an elder of pure character and well up in the *Vinaya-piṭaka* could officiate as a *karmācārya*.

The *upāsaka* shaved off his head and beard, received an under-garment (*nivāsana*), a cloak (*saṃghāṭi*), a side-covering cloth (*saṅkaṣikā*), a bowl (*pātra*), and a water-filter (*pariśrāvana*).

While imparting the Ten Precepts (*sikṣāpadas*) to the *pravrajita* and during his full ordination (*upasampadā*), perfect dignity, sobriety, and pure attitude of mind were maintained. The early morning hours were preferred for the ceremony of ordination.[76] I-tsing testifies to the fact that the Indian Buddhist monasteries maintained a register in which stranger monks visiting the monastery were noted, and another register wherein the name, etc. of a newly ordained monk were registered.

Study of the *Prātimokṣa* and the *Vinaya-piṭaka* under the *upādhyāya* went on for a long time; having mastered the *Vinaya-piṭaka*, the novice proceeded to learn other *śāstras*. In the path of progress towards higher religious life, certain distinct stages are note-worthy.[77] The first stage was that of an *upāsaka*, a faithful believer in the *tri-ratna*, who observed the *pañca-sīla* (five moral precepts); the next stage was that of a *pravrajita*, an ordained monk, 'homeless one'; in the third stage when he had received ten (moral) lessons (*śikṣāpadas*), he was called a *śrāmaṇera*. Then, after receiving the full *upasampadā* and having mastered the *Prātimokṣa* and the *Vinaya-piṭaka*, he was called *dahara* or a 'minor teacher'. In the fifth stage, when he had completed ten years in monastic life, he became a *sthavira*, of 'settled position' and he could then live by himself, without living under a teacher's care.[78] It is needless to mention that, throughout India, Buddhist monks shaved their heads and faces and wore *kāṣāya* garments.[79]

Pilgrimage to the holy Buddhist places sanctified by Lord Buddha's association seems to have been much in vogue during this period. It is well known that the Lord himself had advised the followers to visit four places, viz., Lumbinī, Buddha Gayā, Sāranātha and Kuśīnagara, sacred spots connected with Birth, Enlightenment, Dharma-cakra-pravartana and Mahāparinirvāṇa.[80] *Caityas* of Rajagṛha, Bodhi-tree (Buddha Gayā) Gṛdhrakūṭa-hill, Deer-Park and the holy place of the sāla trees

(Kuśīnagara), are especially mentioned by I-tsing as the places of Buddhist pilgrimage.[81]

A Buddhist monk took with him, while travelling, a jar, a bowl, necessary clothes, hanging them from over his shoulders, and an umbrella in his hand. "This is the manner of the Buddhist priest in travelling." Besides these, he took a separate jar for unclean water and leather shoes in a bag, at the same time holding a metal-staff and going about at ease. In this way the monks used to "assemble by thousands in every one of the above places day after day from every quarter." Revered and erudite monks of Śrī Nālandā Vihāra used to ride in sedan-chairs; the monks of the Mahārāja monastery did the same. In this case, necessary luggage was carried by other persons or taken by boys.

All the Five Assemblies (*pariṣads*)[82] of the homeless ones had to observe the rain-retreat (*varṣāvāsa*). The Brethren in India entered on Retreat on the first day of the month of Śrāvaṇa and went out of Retreat on the last day of the month of Āśvin, that is, from July-August to September-October. It was customary to assign rooms to every member before the commencement of the season; better rooms were given to the elders and thus gradually to the lowest. A member of the lower rank could absent himself in case of necessity by requesting another member to apply for permission on his behalf. If there be a sick person or an emergent affair to be attended to, a member could go off; when anyone wanted to absent oneself from the rain-retreat one had to obtain the permission of the Assembly; the maximum time allowed for stay-out was forty nights. The summer or rain Retreat lasted for three months. According to both Hsüan-tsang and I-tsing, two periods of Retreat were observed by the professed Buddhists of India. At the end of the Retreat, monks and the lay-followers performed a great ceremony of offerings.[83]

At the close of the Retreat, the community observed *sui-i* (lit. according to one's wish) that is, *pravāraṇā* : "pointing out the fault of others, as one likes, according to the three points (i.e. what one has seen, what one has heard, and what one has suspected). Then followed confession and atoning for faults."[84]

For the offences against the *vinaya*, the Order had a gradation of penalties; for a light offence a reprimand was ordered; for an offence next above this gravity, cessation of oral intercourse with the Brethren was to be added. When the offence was serious, the offender was expelled and excommunicated. Expelled from a community, the monk became a miserable vagrant and often returned to the homelife of previous state.[85] Therefore, the *karmadāna's* duty of superintending the monastic life and discipline was a very strict custom.[86]

The *uposatha* (*poṣadha*[87]) day is the fast-day; it is the day of religious observance, feasting and celebration for the lay-men, and the monks. It is a weekly festival when the lay-follower goes to see the monk and takes upon himself the *uposatha* vows viz. to observe the eight *śīlas* during the day.

The host first went to the monks, saluted them and invited them for the festival. Utter cleanliness of utensils, chairs and the dining hall, pure and filtered water, worship of and offerings to the images of sages and *caityas* preceded the distribution of food at the right time, when the sun was nearly at the zenith. At the end of the row of monks, an offering of food was made to the mother Hārīti. Besides Hārīti, there was another deity, Mahākāla, whose image was to be found invariably in all Indian monasteries, near the kitchen or at the porch. An abundant offering of food was regularly made to this god who 'loved' the *triratna* and 'protected' the Five Assemblies.

Articles of food included various preparations of rice, ghee, butter, milk, sugar, fruits, soup and bread. After the meal, the host offered gifts of various kinds to the priestly guests; the poor made such gifts as he could afford; a handful of food was also offered to the dead and other spirits; when the meals were over, the *dānapati* offered tooth-woods to the guests. The guests then thanked the host and read some *gāthās* from the *sūtras* and gave blessings for the good of the lay-devotee. Before the monks withdrew to their monasteries, they were offered sugar-water and betel-nuts (*śarbat and supārī*) as the finishing items.[88] Not only the chewing of *pāna* (betel-leaf) but also the taking of *cāya* (tea)[89] or 'hot-drink' was current among the laity and monks of the time. Throughout India, says I-tsing, monks as well as the lay-men did not take onions and flesh, in exceptional cases, however, these could be used.[90]

I-tsing was profoundly impressed by the purity and cleanliness maintained by the Indian monks, with regard to body, clothes, utensils, water, sleeping and dining rooms. The Indians were "proud of their own purity and excellence"; they did not eat their daily food without having first washed; before meals they washed their hands and feet; after meals they cleaned their tongue and teeth with a tooth-wood,[91] and hands with a powder made for the purpose. The ground of the house and the kitchen was strewn with cow-dung, and seats were arranged at intervals of one cubit so that persons sitting on them did not touch one another. "The peculiar distinction between purity and impurity" was a marked characteristic of the Indian monks, who did not take impure food.

Every monk kept two jugs, one of pottery or porcelain used for keeping drinking water, and another of iron or copper, employed for storing water for cleansing purposes. As a rule, water was always filtered before use; it was the duty of the chief priest of the monastery to see every morning the water of near-by well and arrange its filteration.

The dress of the Buddhist monks of India was usually of orange colour (*kāṣāya*); silken and woollen cloth was used in preparing the monk's robes. Usually, a monk possessed three garments (*cīvara*); the patches were sewn close. I-tsing does not seem to have appreciated the style of Indian garments. "The ecclesiastic garments used in the five parts of India are stitched and sewn at random, with no regard to the threads of cloth being length way or cross way." Fine silk was commonly used for monkish robes.

There were minor points of difference in the dresses of different sectarians; thus for example, among the Mūlasar-vāstivādins, the skirt of the lower garments was cut straight, while among the Sammitīyas, the Sthaviravādins and the Mahā-sāṃghikas, it was cut of irregular shape. The manner of wearing the undergarment (*nivāsana*) among the Mūlasarvāstivadins differed from the manner of those of other two Nikāyas. The mode of wearing the *nivāsana* among the Mahāsāṃghikas, says I-tsing, resembled that of an Indian woman.

The nun's mode of putting on the *nivāsana* was identical with that of a monk of her respective school. The Indians of upper classes wore only a pair of white soft clothes, the poor and lower classes had only one piece of linen. It was only the monks who 'possessed the three garments and six requisites'.[92]

As already noted, rooms in the monasteries were allotted according to the rank of the monks; when a strange monk arrived at a monastery, he was welcomed with due hospitality and supplied with food and bed-gear as suited to his rank. When the monks lodged together, the question arose whether they should be in separate rooms or to be separated by partitions made by ropes, though both methods were lawful. The Mūlasarvāsativādin community ordained separate rooms in lodgings, while the Sammitīya sect allowed separate beds in an enclosure made by ropes.[93]

All monasteries in India observed a regulated time-table; two types of time-keepers (watches) were known and maintained: sun-dial and water-clock. The sun-clock based on the measure of time with the help of the shadow of a stick, was universally used; it was known as the 'time-wheel' (*velācakra*). When the shadow of the stick was shortest, the hour was supposed to be mid-day (noon).

Besides, clepsydrae were much used in great monasteries in India. The clepsydrae of Nālandā were noted for their efficiency. These, together with some boys who watched them, were gifts made by kings. Water is filled in a copper vessel, in which a copper bowl floats. This latter had a pin-hole in its bottom through which water sprung up. At each immersion of the bowl a stroke of the drum was announced.[94]

"Though the Great Teacher has entered Nirvāṇa, yet his image exists, and we should worship it with zeal as though in his very presence. Those who constantly offer incense and flowers to it are enabled to purify their thoughts, and also those who perpetually bathe his image are enabled to overcome their sins that involve them in darkness."[95] These words of I-tsing, a seventh century Saravāstivādin teacher, are quite at one, not only with the standpoint of Hsüan-tsang and Śāntideva who were devout Mahāyānists of the same century, but also with an ancient saying contained in the *Suttanipāta:* "By faith you shall be free and go beyond the realm of death."[96]

The monasteries were decorated with the holy images of Buddha, Bodhisattvas, *caityas* containing the relics of saints, and the images of other deities such as Tārā, Hārīti and Mahākāla;[97] a portion of food was regularly offered to the two last named deities. The monks bathed and wiped the images of Buddha every morning and offered incense and flowers and lighted lamps in adoration. The case containing the sacred scriptures was placed on one side of the image; at sleeping hour the image was removed into a different room.

Besides the Buddha, Maitreya, Mañjuśrī and Avalokiteśvara, were the most popular deities worshipped by the Buddhists.[98] Among the sacred texts popularly studied, the most notable were the *dhāraṇīs*, the *Ratnakūṭasūtra*, the *Buddha-carita* and other hymns by Aśvaghoṣa, the hymns by Mātṛceta, the *Jātakamālā*, selected parts of the Tripiṭaka and the Mahāyāna Sūtras.[99]

In the forenoon, when the monks were to bathe and worship the Buddha image, the *karmadāna* of the monastery announced the time by striking a gong or by beating a drum. After streching a jewelled canopy over the court of the monastery and arranging perfumed water jars in rows at the side of the temple, an image of Buddha, either of gold, silver, copper or stone, was put into a basin of the same material, while a band of girls played music there. The image was duly anointed with multiple scents and bathed in perfumed water; having wiped it with a clean white cloth, it was set up in the shrine, amidst all sorts of beautiful flowers. The entire ceremony was performed by the resident monks under the supervision of the *karmadāna*.

In individual rooms also of a monastery, monks "bathed an image every day so carefully that no ceremony was omitted."

Besides, the monks and the *upāsakas* made *caityas* and images with earth, or impressed Buddha's figure on silk or paper, and worshipped with offerings wherever they went.[100]

In the *caityas* two kinds of sacred contents were enclosed: (i) relics of Buddha or of saints, and (ii) the famous *gāthā*, through which once Aśvajit summarised Buddha's teaching. The *gāthā* was: "All things are born of causes; the Tathāgata has explained these causes; he has also explained how to transcend them; thus the Great Sage has declared." A very large number of clay-seals, votive monuments, tablets, images and other antiquities have been found in India in modern times which bear this *gāthā*, and support I-tsing's testimony.

It was in the afternoon or at the evening twilight that the monks performed worship of the *caitya*. Bāṇa Bhaṭṭa gives a picture of the *bhikṣus* performing *caitya-vandanā* at evening twilight.[101]

Worship of Buddha by repeating his name, offering prayers to him, and singing his praise, was popular both in India and China. In the evening, all the resident monks came out of their rooms and walked three times round a *stūpa*, offering incense and flowers. The respectable and convenient manner of performing *pradakṣiṇā* was, as this compound word implied, 'walking round towards the right."[102]

All the assembled monks while taking a round of the *stūpa* or *caitya*, chanted hymns describing the virtues of Buddha; they sang "with a melodious, pure and sonorous voice, and continued to sing ten or twenty *slokas*."

In big monasteries, such as at Nālandā, where there were 300 apartments and 8 halls and the number of inmates was more than three thousand, worship took place separately.

After the *pradakṣiṇā*, the *bhikṣus* returned to the common hall of the convent; all of them being seated, one *sūtra*-reciter mounted the 'lion-seat' (*siṃhāsana*) near the seat of the *kulapati*, and read out a short text. The 'service in three parts', a collection by Aśvaghoṣa, was a favourite text for the occasion. Its first part in 10 verses consisted of Buddha's praise; second part contained some Buddha-*vacana* and the third part comprised the prayers expressing the wish to bring one's good merit to maturity. After the recitation the Chief Abbot rose to salute the Lion Seat, the seats of other saints and then the Deputy Abbot followed the same ceremony and then others. This was the usual manner of chanting ceremony observed in eastern Āryadeśa.

In Nālandā monastery, owing to the largeness of the establishment and vast number of monastics, the chanting ceremony was observed in the following way. Everyday, a precentor was sent to go round from one apartment to another, chanting hymns, being preceded by lay-servants ('pure-men') and children carrying with them incense, lamps and flowers. At every hall he chanted the service, every time three or five *ślokas* in a loud tone, so that the sound was heard all around. At twilight he finished his duty; this precentor-monk received some gifts for his special services. In the night, the monastics read such works as Nāgārajuna's *Suhṛllekha*, Candra's *Sudāna*, Aśvaghoṣa's *Buddhacarita-kāvya*, Mātṛceta's 'Hymns on Buddha' and Āryaśūra's *Jātakamālā*.[102]

Monastic Etiquette

Great was the respect the Buddhist sages received in certain sections of Indian society. The monarchs of Kashmir and Kapiśā are known to have travelled for several days to welcome and escort the Chinese Master of the Law;[104] kings of the Madhya-deśa, along with their families and officials, are seen taking their royal crowns and official caps off, in the presence of the monks, and waiting personally at the table of the latter.[105] The foremost Emperor of the time did not hestitate to describe His Majesty as the servant of the Sages of Nālandā.[106]

Hsüan-tsang enumerates nine degrees in the etiquette of showing respect. These were : (1) greeting with a kind enquiry; (2) reverentially bowing the head; (3) raising the hands to the head with an inclination of the body; (4) bowing with the hands folded on the breast; (5) bending a knee; (6) kneeling with both knees; (7) going down on the ground on hands and knees; (8) bowing down with knees, elbows, and forehead to the ground; (9) prostrating oneself to the earth. The performance of all these nine acts from the lowest to the highest is only one act of reverence.

The Buddhist monks receiving the courtesies of respect only bestowed good wish.[107] One whose date and time of ordination was earlier could claim a salute from the juniors. When a junior *bhikṣu* saw his senior, he quietly showed respect and saluted with the word *vande* (salutation), and the senior acknowledged the salutation with the word *ārogya* holding his hands right in front; this word implied one's praying that there may be no disease. "If they do not say these words, both parties are faulty......Those who are worthy of receiving salutation need not salute others who are inferior to themselves. Such is the rule among the priests of the five parts of India."[108]

Since the rooms in the monasteries of India were not spacious, and the residents were numerous, the beds were removed after the occupants had risen; they were put in a corner of the room or removed outside the doors. The floor of the room was then cleaned and strewn with cow-dung, then the small chairs and blocks of wood and mats were properly arranged, and the monks took their seats according to their rank.[109]

Everyone who fell sick had his food cut off for seven days; during this interval the patient often recovered, but if he could not regain his health, he would take medicine. Various kinds of medicines and various types of skilled medical doctors were known and available.[110]

The Buddhist monks were forbidden to wail aloud over a

departed one; on the death of a parent they read a service of gratitude.

It was a general rule among the monastics that whenever anyone perceived a person coming to the monastery, "whether he be a stranger or a friend, a disciple or pupil, or an acquaintance, he instantly proceeded to receive him, and pronounced *svāgata* (welcome). But if he found the visitor to be a 'stranger' he proceeded to pronounce another *susvāgata* ('most welcome')".[111] This was done invariably without questioning whether the new-comer was a superior or inferior to the host. Negligence of these rites was regarded contrary to the *vinaya.*

Whenever a person arrived at the monastery, the host took off the visitor's water-jug and bowl, and hung them up on pegs on the wall, and bade the new-comer rest; then having enquired about his health, offered him either tea ('hot-water') or some other drink such as one made of sugar-cane.[112]

The Chief Priest or *kulapati* of the monastery was, as a rule, "a man of high moral character. He observed with the greatest strictness the religious rules and ordinances. He was possessed of the highest intelligence, and acquainted with all the points of a true discipline. His talents were eminent, his spiritual powers exalted, and his disposition affectionate."[113]

Rāhulamitra, for instance, who was the most eminent sage in the Tāmralipti Monastery in I-tsing's time, and was honoured as the head of the Buddhist monks of Eastern Āryadeśa, was a person of exceptional moral culture. A monk, thirty years old, of excellent conduct and profound scholarship, he never had spoken, since his ordination, with women face to face, except when his mother or sister came, whom he met outside his room. On being questioned by I-tsing, he replied like a true Buddhist; "I am naturally full of worldly attachment, and without doing thus, I cannot stop its source."[114]

Śīlabhadra, the *kulapati* of the Mahāvihāra at Nālandā was possessed of unfathomable virtue and piety; he commanded so great respect among the Buddhists that they did not dare to address him except as *ching-fa-tsong*, "Treasure of the True Doctrine."[115]

Not only the Chief Priest, but all the monks of Nālandā were "spontaneously dignified and grave, so that during 700 years since the foundation of the establishment, there had been no single case of guilty rebellion against the rules."[116] I-tsing also praises the strict rules of the Nālandā Mahāvihāra, and Mālāda in his Nālandā stone epigraph, repeatedly refers to the pious and virtuous conduct of its Brethren.[117] 'On account of the priests's mutual confession, their faults were prevented before their growth."[118]

Glimpses of Buddhist Asceticism

Early Buddhism was characterised by a marked ascetic tendency; poverty, continence, homelessness, solitude, and inoffensiveness were the fundamental elements of its monastic life and discipline. Gradually, however, with the passage of time, when the faith became, widely diffused, new ideals developed and unforeseen circumstances cropped up; Mahāyānism considerably transformed the earlier ideology and the ascetic tendency got a set back. It would appear from the foregoing discussion that a large number of monasteries were fairly rich in material possessions, and monks owned considerable valuable property.

But side by side with this happy intellectually busy life in comfortable *vihāras* we find good many examples of solitary forest life and ascetic practices occasionally amounting to suicide.

There were, in this period, in India some monks who practised some of the *dhutāṅgas* or *dhūtaguṇas*; they lived in the forests, wore only three garments and ate what they received as alms. They despised the violent and cumbersome task of farming and cultivating fields and gardens in the monasteries, and thus avoiding the destruction of living beings, lived a pure and blameless life far from the madding crowd of acquisitive and greedy persons.

"Such a *bhikṣu* would not accept any invitation, and does not care for the gifts of any precious things such as gold, any more than for mucus or saliva, but lives retired in a lonely forest."[119]

Nothing is so terrible as solitude, yet nothing is so important as solitude for a person seeking inner peace and sublime joys. He speaks with Śāntideva: "The worldly man is no one's friend: for his love is never bereft of selfishness. The trees are better, they do not get angry nor demand praise; their company is joyful. When would I be their companion ? When shall I dwell away from this puzzling world without looking back on it staying in the caves under the trees near the solitary shrines ? When shall I enjoy that free environment, free movement, fearless with half covered body, wearing garments unworthy even of thieves, and with an earthen bowl as my property ?"[120]

The livelihood earned through farming by hired labour was not a 'right livelihood'; therefore, those careful in moral precepts, did not accept food given by such persons. "Because in urging on hired servants by force, one is apt to become passionate, the seeds may be broken, and insects be much injured while the soil is tilled. One's daily food does not exceed one *shang*, and who can endure hundreds of sins incurred while striving to get even that ?" Better to wander with a begging bowl.[121]

Such an ascetic "sits still in a place in a quiet forest and takes pleasure in company with birds and deer : being free from the noisy pursuit of fame and profit he practises with a view to the perfect quietude of *nirvāṇa*."[122]

Such was Rāhulamitra, the head of the priests of Eastern Āryadeśa;[123] such was Jayasena, the great relinquisher, who dwelt in the Yaṣṭivana near Nālandā; he showed a remarkable detachment to the worldly honour and wealth when he declined to accept the highest honour and vast wealth bestowed on him by king Pūrṇavarman of Magadha and Emperor Harṣa.[124] Such was Sarvajñamitra in Kashmir whose high moral excellence and self-denial made him comparable to the Buddha,[125] such was again, the sage Divākaramitra, the head of a forest-abode in the Vindhya hills, who dwelt among the trees, birds and the beasts along with a host of pupils. So great was his piety, morality and spiritual integrity that his contemporaries regarded him as "more honourable than the Buddha and more worthy of worship than Dharma."[126]

There was also a *mahāsattva* named Candra or Candradāsa, "being like a Bodhisattva endowed with great talent", who when asked : Which is the more injurious, temptation or poison ? answered : "Poison is injurious only when it is swallowed, while the other destroys (burns) one's intellect when only contemplated."[127]

A side-light is thrown on the ascetic aspects of a Buddhist monk's life during this period by Śūdraka. "They had to subdue all their senses, shave their heads, wear ochre-coloured scanty clothes, repeat prayers and dwell on the inconstancy of worldly things."[128] The life of a Buddhist monk was one of austerity.

"In the river Ganges many men drown themselves everyday.

On the hill of Buddha-Gayā too there are not infrequently cases of suicide. Some starve themselves and eat nothing. Others climb up trees and throw themselves down. Some intentionally destroy their manhood and become eunuchs. These actions are entirely out of harmony with the Vinaya Canon."[129]

Evidently, here is a reference to religious suicide prevalent among the Buddhist monks during the seventh century A.D. Hsüan-tsang notes in his general description of India that when some people became too old or suffered from some incurable disease, they were given a farewell entertainment with music, after that they drowned themselves into the Ganges.[130] But this "contemptuous" practice, performed with the hope of reaching heaven, was not shared by all. He does not specially say that the Buddhists resorted to this mode of release.

In his account of Prayāga, Hsüan-tsang gives more details of religious suicide, which are corroborated by indigenous literature.[131] It seems that not only the Brahmanical followers but also the Buddhists, presumably Hīnayānists, also believed in the efficacy of religious suicide in obtaining release. Not only human beings but also the monkeys and other wild creatures took bath in the Gaṅgā and fasted until they died.[132]

Besides religious suicide, I-tsing alludes to the prevalence of other mortifying practices such as burning the body and cutting one's flesh. In his opinion, extreme sacrifices were meant either for the laymen or for the Bodhisattvas who sacrifice themselves for the good of others without receiving the *vinaya* rules at all.

Some young monks seem to have considered the burning of the body a means of attaining Buddhahood. I-tsing disapproves this practice and elucidates his view by quoting the Buddha-*vacana*. "The *mahāsattva* offered his own eyes and body, but a *bhikṣu* need not do so. Hsien Yu (Ṛṣi-Nandita) surrendered his life, but this is not a precedent to be followed by a Vinaya student. King Maitrībala[133] sacrificed himself, but the mendicant ought not to follow his example." It appears that some Mahāyānists were inspired by the ideals of the Bodhisattvas and imitated the incidents narrated in the Jātaka stories. But I-tsing is critical of them and remarks : "It is but vain to give up our insignificant body after having studied but a few *ślokas* of the Sūtra."[134]

CHAPTER V

ETHICAL AND SPIRITUAL CULTURE

Practical Buddhism and its Sources

BUDDHIST moral and spiritual tradition derives its inspiration from the Buddha, the saviour of beings. His love of solitude and silence was matched only by his universal compassion towards the suffering creatures. Hīnayāna seems to have laid emphasis on the former, while Mahāyāna on the latter aspect of the Buddha's personality and ideal.

Accordingly, we find in developed Buddhism, a two-fold ideal and course of action. Hīnayāna grew a narrower ideal and made a narrower effort towards ethical and spiritual progress.[1] Hsüan-tsang[2] as well as I-tsing[3] testify to the practice of asceticism, specially the *dhutāṅgas*. But such ascetic practices were not unknown to the ancient Buddhists.[4] Their ancient texts do reveal that in certain monastic quarters the *dhutāṅgas*[5] were practised and ascetic ideal extolled.[6] The goal of striving was to attain the state of an *arhat*.[7] From early scriptures it appears that deliverance from *saṃsāra* was attainable through a three-pronged training : morality (*śīla*), contemplation (*samādhi*) and wisdom (*prajñā*).[8] This is indeed the basic path of progress in all Buddhism. *Śīla* is essentially moderation in conduct and purifies *karma*.[9] *Śīla* includes the entire moral code prescribed for the followers of the Buddha. This code is three-fold : bodily, vocal and mental.[10] I-tsing reports[11] that the prohibitions of the five *skandhas* (groups of offences) were commonly observed by the Mahāyānists and the Hīnayānists of the 7th century.

Samādhi and *dhyāna*[12] occupy very important place in Buddhist spiritual discipline. To attain *samādhi* is the object of the Buddhists and *dhyāna* is the most important means leading to this end. Various degrees of *dhyāna* and kinds of *samādhi* are well known to the ancient scriptures.[13] *Dhyāna* helps the control of the mind and destruction of desire, and consolidates the knowledge of four noble truths.

The third member in the triple path is *prajñā*, wisdom or gnosis. *Prajñā* is insight, the faculty of wisdom: it includes the right views and the real knowledge of things. The importance of *prajñā* in ancient Buddhism is well known and it has remained paramount throughout the history of Buddhism.[14]

The striving for *nirvāṇa* needs a good deal of constant spiritual exercises. There are four such exercises, called *brahma-vihāras*,[15] living in the spiritual realm by cherishing and practising the four *bhāvanās* or sentiments, viz. *maitrī* (benevolence), *karuṇā* (compassion), *muditā* (cheerfulness) and *upekṣā* (equanimity). Of these, compassion has been the most important and vital element in practical Buddhism throughout its history. It was out of compassion that the Buddha proceeded to disseminate his spiritual truths.[16] It is out of *mahākāruṇya* that Avalokita refuses to enter *nirvāṇa* till all beings are liberated.[17] It was out of compassion for a woman that Jyotirmāṇavaka broke his vow of continence after having practised it for 84,000 years.[18]

Mention may be made of the four 'elements of friendly treatment' or 'things to be possessed' (*saṃgrahavastūni*).[19] They are charity, affable speech, righteousness and cooperation,[20] and are recommended to both laity and the monks.

The fundamentals of the Buddhistic way and the essential elements of the Buddhist moral and spiritual culture, are the thirty seven *dharmas*, favourable to *bodhi* or Enlightenment.[21] As if to give a summary of his teachings, the Buddha is said to have discussed these principles to a body of monks before entering into *mahāparinirvāṇa*. These thirty seven *dharmas* are grouped into seven categories in the following manner: four kinds of Thoughtfulness;[22] four kinds of Right Efforts;[23] four Stages of Psychic Power;[24] five Faculties;[25] five Powers;[26] seven Constituents of Illumination;[27] and eight Limbs of the Noble Path.[28]

There is a 'Buddhism of Faith' in which *śraddhā* and *bhakti* play the prominent part. The most famous Buddhist sage of the seventh century A.D., Śāntideva, was above all a faithful devotee. Great Buddhists like Vasubandhu, Bhāvaviveka, Śāntideva, Hsüan-tsang, Harṣa and Sarvajñamitra, are seen displaying their earnest faith in and devotion to their favourite Buddhist deities. Śāntideva even believed that "faith was the supreme vehicle."[29] The sources of this devotional fervour can be traced to some early scriptures. The *Suttanipāta*[30] declares: "By faith you shall be free and go beyond the realm of death"; again "faith is the best treasure of man—by faith the flood is crossed."[31] The ancient hymnology, the *Dhammapada*,[32] clearly mentions worship of Buddha and of his noble pupils. The cult of the relic-worship is one of the oldest traits of the Doctrine.[33] In the *Saddharmapuṇḍarīka-sūtra*[34] can be seen the development of Mahāyānic worship and devotion. The *Sukhāvatīsūtras* give an obvious picture of the devotional cult of Amitābha. Likewise the cult of the coming Buddha Maitreya, mentioned at least once in the ancient canon,[35] became popular in our age. Worship of Buddhas, Bodhisattvas and female deities was a universal trait of Buddhist culture during the period.

Mahāyāna derives its inspiration from the compassionate personality of the Buddha. Its aim is higher, its outlook broader, and its aspiration more sublime than that of Hīnayāna. The fundamental principle of Mahāyāna morality is expressed in the first verse of the *Śikṣāsamuccaya*: "When to myself as to my fellow-beings, fear and pain are hateful, what justification is there that I protect my ownself and not others ?"[36] Mahāyāna is thus literally a Great Vehicle, in the true sense a doctrine for the gain of the many, for the good and bliss of all.[37] The ethical and spiritual superstructure of Mahāyāna is founded on the doctrine and ideal of the Bodhisattva, the embodiment of compassion. Here one is confronted with a new moral dimension and a clearer spiritual horizon. A Bodhisattva is called a *mahāsattva* because he leads a great multitude of beings to the highest end.[38] The Mahāyāna is so called because in it there is room for immeasurable beings and it is spacious like the space.[39] The loud declaration of Mahāyāna is that beings are potential Buddhas.[40] All can and must aspire for the highest goal of Buddhahood. The aspiration of Mahāyāna is universal because it aims at universal liberation. But since all beings cannot of themselves penetrate into the great errors, they need the help of enlightened beings, the Bodhisttvas or the *mahāsattvas*. Men espouse the career of Bodhisattva not to liberate themselves, but to work for the liberation of all the other sentient beings.[41] This career consists of great moral and spiritual deeds. The essence of the ethical and spiritual culture of Mahāyāna relates to this career of the Bodhisattva. He is the perfect man, the ideal man of

Mahāyāna. He is called Bodhisattva because "his intention or wish is fixed on Illumination."[42] He is the hope and refuge of the suffering multitude of beings. "The essential nature of all Bodhisattvas is a great loving heart (*mahākaruṇācitta*), and all sentient beings constitute the object of his love."[43]

A Bodhisattva masters certain virtues, possesses certain moral qualities and exercises spiritual powers; these are called the *pāramitās*—the transcendental perfections, the roads to freedom. The career of a Bodhisattva consists of these *pāramitās* whence the Mahāyāna is called *pāramitānaya.*[44]

Emancipation is impossible of attainment without practising the *pāramitās* or perfect virtues. The six *pāramitās* are : *dāna, śīla, kṣānti, vīrya, dhyāna and prajñā.* These *pāramitās* include all aspects of Buddhistic culture, moral, mental and spiritual. It is the *pāramitās* which establish the superiority of a Boddhisattva over an Arhat or a Pratyeka-Buddha. The ethical and spiritual superstructure of Mahāyāna Buddhism is founded on its daring metaphysics.

Bondage, in the Buddhist doctrine, is the result of ignorance (*avidyā*). Awakening or Freedom can be obtained by destroying this ignorance. From *avidyā* springs the whole lot of *saṃskāras,* and the consequent flood of misery; with the destruction of *avidyā* all its products and consequences also disappear.[46] In Mahāyāna the only way to Freedom (*nirvāṇa*) is the perception of Truth—the realization of *śūnyatā*, the destroyer of woe.[47] This means the understanding that not only the self is non-substantial (*pudgalanairātmya*), but also that the 'things' are non-substantial (*dharmanairātmya*). This great Truth is variously called '*śūnyatā, tathatā, bhūtakoṭi, dharmadhātu*' etc.[48]

Śāntarakṣita says that ignorance and passions that cover reality, entirely disappear as soon as the truth of non-egoity (*nairātmya*) is realised, just as darkness disappears in the presence of a strong light.[49] There are two kinds of veils or positive hindrances to moral and spiritual perfection, viz. the veil of ignorance and passions (*kleśāvaraṇa*), and the veil covering the ontological or cognizable reality (*jñeyāvaraṇa*).[50] Kamalaśīla establishes that the first kind of veil (i.e. of passions, etc.) can be demolished by a direct perception of the illusory character of the ego-principle (*nairātmya-darśana*), while the second kind of veil (i.e. of cognizables) is removed by a faithful, intense and prolonged meditation on non-egoity.[51]

The doctrine of non-egoity (*nairātmya*) is the central plank of Buddhist philosophy and culture. There is a constant antagonism between the self and the not-self, between egoism and altruism; or in other words, between the lower self and the higher self; the latter cannot be affirmed without denying the former.[52] Morality and spirituality cannot be practised unless one abandons the perverted belief in one's ego. This fact has been lucidly established by Kamalaśīla in the following manner.

All *kleśas* (afflictions, passions)—love, hatred and the like, are rooted in a wrong notion of the soul. They do not proceed from external things; their source is the perverted idea of a personal permanent soul which, however, is entirely false and baseless. It is a matter of logical deduction that, in the absence of ego-principle, self-love cannot develop, and attachment to external things also cannot arise if they were not affiliated with the self as conducive to self-interest and self-gratification.

In a like manner, hatred also will loose its *raison d'etre,* for a man begets hatred towards the things or persons only when they are detrimental to his self-interest. But when a person has no ground to be attached to anything, obstruction has no sense. The same applies to other passions and evils, for directly or indirectly they are founded on self-love. It is thus that a catalogue of ills and passions comes into existence because of ego-consciousness and belief in the ego principle.

These evils and passions are, however, not innate to living beings; they are exotic growths, born of egoity, and are liable to disappear with the disappearance of the idea of egoity. Whatsoever is a rising thing, that is a ceasing thing. Now, this concept of egoity is an unfounded illusion; this has been taught in the scriptures and demonstrated in the Sūtras and the Śāstras repeatedly.[53] The conception of non-egoity is pure and bereft of egoism. When this state of purity is attained through *nairātmya-darśana,* there opens a vast and free field for virtuous and righteous actions. In this way the doctrine of non-egoity is the foundation of moral and spiritual culture.[54]

This non-egoity is the same as 'vacuity' also called the 'immaculate wisdom' (*prajñāpāramitā*). The great being, who has thrown away the vulgar illusion of the ego, trains himself thus: "My own self I will place in Suchness, and so that the world might be helped, I will place all beings into Suchness, and I will lead to Nirvāṇa the whole immeasurable world of beings."[55] This Suchness is the same as the Emptiness or Absence of Ego;[56] the same is meant by the phrase Climax of Wisdom. This Climax of Wisdom consists in self-effacement, or in the extinction of the distinction between subject and object; between 'myself' and 'my neighbour'. "The Tathāgata is free from all such thought-constructions and discriminations."[57] The doctrine of Prajñā-pāramitā thus leads to the ultimate 'unity of all life', which is so essential for a righteous life and without which friendship (*maitrī*) and peace become impossible. This monistic or non-dual knowledge, that is called Prajñāpāramitā, is identical with Buddha or Tathāgata.[58] Since all beings possess the seed of Buddhahood, all beings are potential Tathāgatas. One who has realised the Climax of Wisdom equates onself with all the beings; when Buddha is in every being, His worship means the worship of every being; to love Buddha means to love our fellow-beings. Thus the logic of the doctrine of Prajñāpāramitā indubitably, leads to universal love and sympathy. When all beings are devoid of ego, when all beings have the seed of Buddhahood, and when all beings hate pain and fear, and need perfect freedom and peace, all beings are and must constitute the object of a Bodhisattva's love.[59] There can be no moral or logical justification for an egoistical effort;[60] the ego does not exist. Moral and spiritual perfection is possible only on this profound principle of Prajñāpāramitā.[61]

Śāntideva on the Ideal of the Bodhisattva

The *Śikṣāsamuccaya* means the 'sum total of teaching', or a 'compendium of doctrine'. This teaching or doctrine is Buddhistic and chiefly Mahāyānistic. The work has three parts: (i) *kārikās* or memorial verses, 27 in number, they form the text and provide a kind of framework for the whole book, (ii) second part is a commentary on these *kārikās,* written by the author himself; (iii) the third part, the bulk of the book, consists of quotations, often very long, from various older texts. These quotations taken from over a hundred *sūtras*, are meant to illustrate the teachings and duties expounded in the *kārikās*.

The *Śikṣāsamuccaya* is thus a guide to those who aspire for a moral and spiritual life; there is little philosophy in it, although the fundamental idea of *śūnyatā* is never lost sight of. Its subject matter is ethical and spiritual; it is a religious textbook and embodies all the basic ideas of Mahāyāna Buddhism. Its value as an exposition of the ethical and Buddhological doctrines of Mahāyāna has not received sufficient attention. The following pages are intended to give a picutre of the moral principles which a great thinker of this period considered to be the essentials of what he called the *śikṣā*.

As the fundamental ideas of this great work are contained in the twenty-seven memorial verses, an English translation of these gives us in a nutshell, the essentials of the *śikṣā,* which is as follows:

(1) If fear and misery are unpleasant to me as to others, what is the special (reason) that I protect myself not others ?

(2) One who wants to put an end to one's misery and gain the goal of bliss, must firmly plant the root of one's faith and direct one's thought towards Enlightenment.

(3) The Boddhisattva's vow of restraint according to Mahāyāna is manifest; therefore, one should know its vital points in order to remain blameless.

(4) You must give freely to all beings, your person, the objects of enjoyment, and the store of your merits past, present and future. To protect them (beings) is to cultivate holiness.

(5) For the enjoyment of all living creatures one's person and all things belonging to it are given; if unpreserved, how then enjoyed ? What gift is given if unenjoyed ?

(6) Therefore, for the enjoyment of creatures, preserve your person and all its belongings; (this is to be done) by never abandoning the spiritual friend and by the study of scriptures.

(7) How to protect one's person ? By avoiding the ills. How to accomplish all that ? By avoiding the fruitless waste.

(8) (This is also) accomplished by constant mindfulness; mindfulness rises from keen devotion; and devotion rises from inner peace and right understanding.

(9) Whoever is skilled (in mind) knows (well), thus spake Buddha; the mind should not move from quiescence if outward acts are avoided.

(10) Steadfast everywhere, by loving speech gently win over worthy folk, in this way you will become acceptable to all.

(11) The worldly folk that dislikes the scion of Buddha and rejects him, like the fire covered with ash, shall go to hells and burn there.

(12) Therefore, in the *Ratnameghasūtra* Buddha has summarised the essential duty (of the Bodhisattva): 'avoid strenuously that which makes living-beings unhappy'.

(13) One should duly preserve one's person by raiment and medicine; but to indulge in enjoyments for one's own desires, leads to an evil lapse.

(14) Start noble deeds and know the measure (in all things). By this precept it is not difficult to preserve goods of enjoyment.

(15) Good results are preserved by detachment from selfish fruition; do not repent it (when resigned), nor boast of your merits.

(16) Beware of gain and honour; shun highmindedness; the Bodhisattva must be glad and eradicate doubts concerning Dharma.

(17) When his person is purified, enjoyment will become wholesome, like rice well cooked and cleansed.

(18) Just as a crop choked by weeds gets diseased and does not flourish, so the shoot of Buddhahood, covered by passions does not reach its goal.

(19) Self-purification means purging it from sins and passions, to follow strenuously in the foot-steps of Buddha, else to hell we go.

(20) Have patience, seek to hear the Word (of Buddha), and then repair to the forest abode; fix your mind on intense thought and meditate on the impurities, etc.

(21) Discern how to purify the goods of enjoyment and how to purify the right livelihood; merits are purified by actions proceeding from emptiness and compassion.

(22) Good many are the receivers from thee, little thou possess; what to avail of that ? It does not beget supreme satisfaction; therefore, increase it (as much as thou can).

(23) How to increase thy body's weal? By increasing energy and by not increasing sloth and indolence; enjoyment increases by charity based on *śūnyatā* and *karuṇā*.

(24) With endeavour, first of all, make the firm resolve; and having prized compassion, strive to increase the merit.

(25) Keep the ordinance of righteous conduct, the act of adoration etc., respectfully; practise always the faith and other virtues, and remember Buddha and friendliness.

(26) In short, good of all beings in all conditions, pure and spiritual gift, mind directed towards Enlightenment, and increase of merit—these are the most desirable (things to be done).

(27) Success lies in appropriate exertions, and also in watchfulness; and this comes from proper understanding, mindfulness, and right thought.[62]

Śāntideva's *Bodhicaryāvatāra* is perhaps the best known manual of Buddhist ethical and spiritual culture. It is in fact, an authoritative and inspiring 'Introduction to Spiritual Life' written by one of the greatest contemporary Mahāyāna sages. In its Tibetan translation this work is called *Bodhisattvacaryāvatāra,* and its contents justify such a title. Like the *Śikṣāsamuccaya,* this work also is full of ideas of Mahāyāna; but it has a long and important chapter written from the Mādhyamika standpoint. However, the *Bodhicaryāvatāra* is devoted, on the whole, to expounding the course and ideal of ethical and spiritual culture of a Mahāyāna saint. By combining the contents of *Śikṣā* and the *Bodhicaryāvatāra* one gets a comprehensive picture of Mahāyānic piety and spirituality during the seventh century A.D. This is as follows:

Human Birth: Its Uses and Ills : Human birth is precious and scarce, and must therefore be devoted to sublime things.[63] Human body is essenceless; it is impure, a useless bundle of bones and flesh. It is like a temporary slave; one must not spend too much on it.[64] Its only use is that it is a means to perform meritorious acts. Human body is nothing more than a boat needed to cross the river; it has to be preserved only to be utilised in holy deeds, otherwise it is fit for the food of jackals and wolves, and death will finally throw it before them.[65]

Bodhicitta: The Lord has said that the 'will to enlightenment', the 'thought directed to illumination' is the supreme. It is the seed of all merits and virutes and a remedy for all ills.[66] It is two-fold, inasmuch as it consists of two moments : (i) the determination to attain Enlightenment (for the good of all beings), and (ii) the actual march towards Enlightenment.[67] *Bodhicitta* is precious in itself apart from the *bodhicaryā*. The two moments are comparable to two persons : one intending to go, the other actually going. The latter is superior.[68] One should never abandon the *bodhicitta*; to do so is to incur the gravest sin.[69] The *bodhicitta* is developed through the following four ways : (i) instruction by Buddha or his disciple; (ii) by hearing the praise of *bodhi* or *bodhicitta*; (iii) by developing mercy for the suffering beings; and (iv) by realising all-round perfection of the personality of Tathāgata.[70] *Bodhicitta,* when combined with joyfulness, begets great merits.[71] A person possessed of the *bodhicitta* is the supreme saint, supreme friend and most meritorious.[72]

Faith, Devotion and Worship: Faith is the supreme vehicle; the wise are full of faith and act accordingly. The Good Doctrine does not flourish among the faithless, just as burnt seeds do not germinate.[73] Faith combined with the will to *bodhi* begets all the more mertis.[74] To hate the scion of Buddha is to invite the tortures of the hellish fire.[75] The faithful offer salutations to Buddhas, Bodhisattvas and all beings.[76] The Bodhisattva, a follower of the great vehicle speaks thus : Salutations to the Three Jewels, i.e. Buddha, Dharma and Saṃgha; I offer unto the scions of Buddha all that is offerable; I offer my body and wish to be their devoted slave.[77] I bathe the icons of the Buddhas and of their scions with perfumed water in accompaniment of songs and instrumental music. I offer unto their images good coloured clothes, yellow robes; I adore them with divine, sweet, smooth and beautiful clothes and ornaments. I decorate and adore Samantabhadra, Ajita, Mañjughoṣa, Lokeśvara, and others.[78]

I worship all the *stūpas*, *caityas* and the temples, and salute all teachers and those worthy of salutation. I take refuge in Buddha, Dharma and Bodhisattvas.[79] I salute them with folded hands, I confess all my sins before them. I pray to Ākāśagarbha, Kṣitigarbha and Vajrapāṇi.[80]

Scriptural Study: Great is the merit of hearing the Word of Buddha. Seek to hear it.[81] Hear with faith that word of Buddha by hearing which the great tortures and ills of hells are destroyed.[82] The doctrine must be heard; whatever has been spoken by Maitreya, all that has been said by the Buddha.[83] Mere *prāti-mokṣa* is not sufficient; knowledge of its vital parts is necessary. Therefore, one should study the scripture.[84] Scriptural study is necessary also because through it one knows what to do, when to do. Knowledge of actions is necessary for self-purification.[85]

Sciences to be avoided : The following should not be studied : material philosophies (*lokāyataśāstras*), polity or political economy (*daṇḍanīti*), science of debate (*vāda-vidyā*), royal-sports (*kumāra-krīḍā*), magical sciences (*jaṃbhaka-vidyā*), and similar studies.[86]

How to Grow in Holiness : The increase in holiness is furthered by these three ways : (1) concern for the weal of all beings under all conditons; (2) sincere gifts of temporal and spiritual things; and (3) the thought of Enlightenment. Perfection in ethical and spiritual life comes through (i) watchfulness, (ii) mindfulness and (iii) right understanding.[87]

Marks of the Sublime Thought of Enlightenment : A saint in whom the thought of *bodhi* has taken birth, must display the following attitude : I wish that the miserables be blessed; I affirm full faith in Buddhas and Bodhisattvas; I fully affirm the ocean of production of the thought of *bodhi* for the profit and bliss of all creatures. I beseech the omnipresent Buddhas to light the Lamp of Righteous Law so that there may be no darkness in the world; I offer all my merits for ending all the sorrows of all the creatures; let me be a medicine, a physician[88] and a nurse till all their ills are destroyed; let me become their food and drink during the famines; let me become the unending treasure of the poor men. I offer my body, my person and all its belongings for the benefit of all creatures. Nirvāṇa consists in the abandonment of egoity[89] and its concomitants; I seek such Nirvāṇa and give up my ego; I have given up my body for the use of beings, let them use it as they like. I wish Enlightenment for all whether my lovers or haters; I wish to be a lamp for those who need a lamp, a couch to those who need a couch, and a slave to all those who need a slave. In short I wish to be everything for everybody. I will learn all the sciences of a Bodhisattva and abide by all the rules of a sublime career so long as all beings are not liberated.[90]

Reception of the thought of Enlightenment: The wise, having developed the thought of Enlightenment in full faith, must think thus:

Today my birth has become successful; human life is well acquired, in the family of Buddha I am now born; now I am a scion of Buddha; hence on I have to work according to the sacred traditions of the spiritual family so as not to defile this holy clan. The jewel-like *bodhicitta* has arisen in me today: this is the chemical mixture which destroys death from the world, an eternal treasure which removes poverty from the earth; an excellent medicine to control all epidemics; it is the rest house where all the fatigued pilgirms of the world take shelter; it is the open bridge to cross the ocean of *saṃsāra*; it is the new-moon to quieten the heat of passions; it is the great sun that removes the darkness of the world; it is like the cream taken out of churning of the ocean of the True Doctrine; it is the celestial meal ready for the satisfaction of all the guests—those hungry travellers of *saṃsāra*. I invite them all, the immeasurable multitude of beings, before the Tathāgata; I welcome this *bodhicitta*. Let all the gods, demons and others welcome this.[91]

Preservation of the same: The pilgrim of the path of spirituality must thus hold fast to the thought of *bodhi*. He must strenuously act according to the Teaching (of Buddha) and must fulfil his vow without delay. He has vowed to save all beings, he must not deceive them, must never abandon the sublime thought even for a moment. The Bodhisattva is the hope and refuge of innumerable beings who are crying for peace and happiness. What will happen to those in case the thought of *bodhi* is forsaken? It will be an evil shameful day and will lead to incalculable ills. Moreover, the human birth is scarce and subject to evil states like disease, old age and death; life is momentary and deceptive. It is a healthful day, the day of the origin of the thought of Enlightenment, I must make the fullest use of it. The senses are ready to enslave me; the fierce foes like passions, are ready to throw me into doom. I must keep guard, be watchful and careful in preserving this rare and precious thought of *bodhi*. I will fight these enemies, I will not bend before them even though my intestines are rotten and my head is pulled down. I will not turn back. Having firmly resolved in this way, I have to preserve the sublime thought with utter watchfulness and perseverence.[92]

Self-Preservation and Self-Abnegation: The Bodhisattva takes the vow to attain perfect Enlightenment for the sake of all beings.[93] His perfection consists in those of others; self-preservation, therefore, is in truth, self-abnegation. Self-abnegation culminates in the perfection of charity.[94] Self-preservation is effected by two ways : (i) by never abandoning the spiritual friend, and (ii) by the study of the Sūtras.[95]

Transcendental Liberality: The Bodhisattva must be an embodiment of liberality; the virtue of giving (*dāna*) is essentially a product of compassion (*karuṇā*), Compassion is the root of Bodhisattva's life. "His enlightenment is nothing but liberality or charity."[96] He thinks thus : "My neighbour suffers his pain just as I suffer mine; why should I be anxious about myself and not about him." The perfection of charity leads to the equivalence of myself and my fellow beings. "When to me, as to others, pain and fear are unpleasant, there is no special (reason) to protect my own person and not others."[97] Compassion is the only virtue to which a saint must apply himself; all other virtues will follow up naturally.[98] Nothing is superior to charity; even the vow of chastity, it is said, was violated by a certain Bodhisattva out of compassion for a woman.[99] Liberality consists not only in giving material goods, things of enjoyment, but also in giving spiritual knowledge, imparting Buddha's teachings and offering one's merits past, present and future, for the good of all beings.[100] Production of the Thought of Enlightenment is the highest expression of charity and compassion. Only the ignorant persons do not take refuge in it.[101] Liberality, born of compassion, is the supreme means (*upāya*) of conciliating creatures (*saṃgrahavastu*) by alms giving, lovable speech, kind cooperation, and by sharing the joys and woes of beings.[102]

Transcendental Morality: The essence of morality (*śīla*) is self-preservation (*ātmabhāvarakṣā*) for the sole aim of benefiting creatures. A ghost or one condemned to rebirth in hells cannot be of service to others; it is therefore necessary to ensure good rebirths in order to undertake the career of a Bodhisattva. For this purpose morality must be observed. Without self-preservation, one cannot preserve others. This self-preservation is accomplished by the constant study of the scriptures.[103] In order to increase morality one must beware of Māra's evil deeds. Evil must be avoided, frivolity must be avoided; friendship must be cultivated with those established in the Doctrine.[104] In order to protect against evil lapses, the following must be avoided : bad friends; forgetfulness of the idea of Enlightenment; despondency, and lack of enthusiasm. Evil must be discarded by active service of man, and of the Saṃgha.[105] Confession of sins before Buddhas and Bodhisattvas also contributes to moral growth.[106] The *ādikarmika* Bodhisattva must avoid eight sins and ten great transgressions.[107] Above all, carnal passion must be controlled; duties of married life must be observed.[108] Never should one sit with a lonely woman, nor sleep nor travel with her.[110]

Need of Mindfulness: Those who wish to live up to the Teaching of the Buddha must control their mind; without mind control *śīla* cannot be observed, teaching cannot be preserved. All good things will follow up as a matter of course if only the mind be controlled. Conquest of mind means conquest of the world with all its powers and fears. The Buddha has said[110] that all fears and miseries proceed from the mind.[111] The perfection of morality is nothing but a detached mind.[112]

One cannot destroy the innumerable foes but one can do so by subduing the angry mind, just as by wearing shoes one can cover the whole earth with animal hide of which the shoes are made.[113] In a like manner, one can control all the external objects (which are uncontrollable) by controlling only one's mind. Prolonged meditation and repetition of name are useless when the mind is not reposed. You must, therefore, control your mind, protect it from going astray. Thought must be guarded under all evil conditions and disturbances. "I should not spoil my mind even though all my gains, honours, body and all good things are destroyed. I beseech with folded hands all those who aspire for perfection to protect their mind, to be vigilant and mindful."[114]

Just as a diseased person is disqualified for all actions, so a mind devoid of mindfulness is unfit for all good deeds.[115] A mind bereft of watchfulness is like a broken jug which can contain nothing owing to its leakage. Such a man's hearing of the Word (of Buddha), his thought and experiences are futile. In the absence of mindfulness, all merits are lost; those thieves, the passions, creep in and kill the spiritual life. Remember the horrors of hell in order to maintain hold on the mind. Mindfulness is maintained by an attitude of fear and regard towards the teacher, the discipline and the company of preceptors; also by remembering that Buddhas are omnipresent and omniscient.[116]

Mind-Control, the Essence of Morality: Since all actions are preceded by thought, all feelings, sensations and desires proceed from the mind,[117] it is the most urgent task to control it thoroughly. It is necessary to keep the eyes fixed, as it were, in meditation. Every action, each motion of the body and its limbs should be preceded by a careful consideration and must be checked from time to time. Care should be taken to see that the elephant-like mind always remains tied to the pole of the Doctrine. When the mind is unfree from attachment and hatred, keep quiet like a wooden piece; whenever it becomes noisy, jovial, critical, self-praising, wicked and deceptive, keep quiet like a wooden piece.[118]

"When my mind runs after gain, honour, fame, and wants family and servants, I sit idle like a wooden piece; my mind has turned away from the supreme good, has become selfish; wishes association and conversation, therefore, I am lying like a wooden piece; I do likewise when it becomes intolerant, indolent, fearful, wicked, talkative and partial." These are the ways by which a brave soul brings about the control of vain and soiled mind.[119]

Self-possessed, in the lap of Truth and free from pride, I hold the mind as a created thing; I have rendered my body completely inactive, it does not react to the objects of sense.[120]

Counsels and Precepts: Be ready to learn from all, especially from those who do good to others and preach efficiently. Be thankful for good speeches, prize the merit and enjoy the praise of others; all acts are done for the sake of satisfaction which is scarce even by wealth, therefore enjoy the virtues of others, hatred begets dissatisfaction and pain.[121]

Speak clear, steady and measured words in kind and sweet voice; look at the beings with ease and spontaneously thinking that Buddhahood is obtainable by these ways and by their service. Among the six *pāramitās* (*dāna*, *śīla*, *kṣānti*, *vīrya*, *dhyāna* and *prajñā*) the succeeding ones are of greater worth; if possible, practise them all.[122]

This body is the servant of the True Doctrine; it should not be troubled for petty things. Life should not be sacrificed when the heart is impure. Doctrine must not be imparted to the faithless, the wealthy and the proud,[123] nor to those of meagre intellect, nor even to the husbandless women. Keep equal eye on both Hīnayāna and Mahāyāna; one qualified for Mahāyāna should not be instructed in Hīnayāna. Never recommend the mere study of *sūtras* or muttering of the *mantras* to one devoid of moral conduct. Avoid the company of women.[124]

The Bodhisattva's morals are innumerable, but those that purify the heart must be observed. Nothing should be done, either based on observation or tradition, that does not contribute to the benefit of beings. Never abandon the spiritual friend nor the scriptural study. Mere study is futile, practice is essential as mere study of pathology does not cure the sick.[125]

Forbearance: Good conduct, liberality and Buddha-worship practised for centuries are destroyed by hatred. Hatred is the greatest sin; forbearance is the supreme austerity;[126] therefore, practise forgiveness and endurance.[127] Hatred destroys our peace, joy, patience and sleep; it is like a boomerang, and kills its own supporter; an angry man finds peace nowhere; he who kills anger remains happy here and hereafter.[128] Forbearance or patience is of three kinds : (i) forbearance of suffering; (ii) forbearance of insight into the Doctrine, and (iii) forbearance of injuries.[129] The first and the third types of forbearance are quite well known in religious thought, the second type is perhaps peculiar to Mahāyāna and is rather a subtle concept. Poussin says on this point : "The name of patience applied to 'insight into the Law' is justified from a double point of view : (1) resistance and resignation of mind are necessary to the acceptance of the doctrine of the non-existence of the things : those who do not 'uphold the profound teaching' (*gaṃbhīra-dharmakṣānti*) are numerous; (2) this estimate of the reality of things is an essential element of patience in the ordinary sense."[130] The *anutpattika-dharmakṣānti* is a state in the career of a Bodhisattva when he adheres patiently to the doctrine of the non-origination of *dharmas*. 'I must not disturb my joyfulness even when great calamity has befallen on me; dislike destroys all merits.'[131] Suffering is the common lot of men; it is always there, without making any effort one comes across it, therefore steady your mind. When the worshippers of Caṇḍī and other Southerners (probably Bhairavācāryas) endure so many troubles in their worship, why should I not endure suffering for the sake of liberation ? Nothing is impossible of attainment by practice; by enduring small pain, greater pain becomes endurable.[132]

Do not make yourself tender by feeling ordinary things like cold, heat, rain, air, etc.; try to overcome pain like a brave man; the wise remain glad even amidst the sorrows which readily attend the constant conflict of soul with passions. They are brave who conquer foes despite blows on their chest, the rest are killers of the killed. Indeed, pain must be welcomed as it removes our pride, generates compassion for the creatures, and fear of sin and increases devotion to Buddha.[133]

Love thy foe: Pain is disliked by all; those that are in the grip of passions and torture themselves, may torture others as well. Fire will burn wherever it be; anger rises out of this fire of passion and not out of the objects. It is a pity that I dislike pain but like the body, the house of woe.[134] It is unwise to be angry with men who injure us, for they are only acting under the influence of causes and conditions; and the foremost of these causes are our own wicked deeds of previous existence. "My enemy takes a stick to beat me, and I have assumed this body, liable to be wounded, and destined to be beaten. Far from being angry with my enemy I ought to consider him almost as beneficial as the Buddhas, for he affords me the opportunity of practising patience and forgiveness of wrongs, which blots out my sins. Am I to make this principle of salvation the cause of my condemnation ? Let us rather pity our enemies who ruin themselves by their anger, and let us think of means of saving them in spite of themselves as the Buddhas do."[135]

It is because of anger that I have suffered in hells a thousand times, but have always sought after my own good. It befits my career of patience that I should welcome such pain as would help removal of the miseries of the world. Never grudge the joy of others, rather be happy by the happiness of others.[136]

He who wants Enlightenment wants everything for every body; he who is jealous of the property of others has no thought of Enlightenment.[137] Do not be misled by praise, honour or gain, they are false and deceptive.[138] The living beings are the proper field of spiritual career even as the Buddhas; worship of beings is the worship of Buddha; friendliness towards beings in fact amounts to Buddha-worship. All beings have the seed of Buddha-qualities. Our good consists in their good for whose sake the Buddhas cut their flesh and offer their limbs and the Bodhisattvas rush into the Avīci hell. The Lord is happy at their happiness and unhappy at their unhappiness. One who serves creatures serves the Lord. I therefore devote myself wholeheartedly to the service of the world, in the worship of the Tathāgata.[139]

There is no doubt that this whole world is the field of the compassionate Buddhas; it is they who appear as beings, why then disregard these beings ? This indeed is the worship of the Tathāgata; this is the right effort for self-interest; this is the proper removal of misery from the world; therefore, let it be my vow, let this be my mission.[140]

Just as a single royal officer can subdue several persons, for he is armed with the power of the king and the state, and is not therefore alone, similarly, we must not insult any weak person for, he is also powerful by the help of the kind Buddhas and the might of the guardians of the hell who are always ready (to punish). So we should respect each being even as a servant honours his stern master. But the service of beings brings greater good than any ruler can reward for his service. Moreover, a man of patience enjoys even in this life beauty, health, joy, longevity, and prosperity just as a sovereign (king) enjoys them.[141]

The Perfection of Inner Strength : Thus having perfected the virtue of patience, the Bodhisattva must grow in the virtue of inner strength or *vīrya*. Enlightenment depends on this Energy; merit is impossible without energy, even as motion is impossible without air.[142] Energy means 'the enthusiasm for doing good' (*kuśalotsāha*). (i) Indolence (ii) attachment to the pleasures of the world, and (iii) discouragement (or self-inactivity) are its enemies.[143] In order to subdue these enemies, it is necessary to think of (i) the dangers we are vulnerable to: passions and the net of becoming or rebirths; threatened always by death and the guards of hell; 'you have boarded this boat, the human state; cross this river of misery; thou fool, this is no time to sleep; when and for what price shalt thou find this boat again ? 'Death will befall abruptly, all thine programmes will be left incomplete.' (ii) to dislike the pleasures of the world which end in suffering, and to enjoy the supreme taste of meritorious acts; and (iii) to remember what Buddha had said : 'These supreme

Buddhas, Śākyamuni, Dīpaṅkara, etc. were insects, flies and little worms; it was by exerting themselves that they obtained Enlightenment of a Buddha so difficult to obtain;' 'Since I have already obtained the human birth, the most difficult part of the career is accomplished; the life of a Bodhisattva is distressful, but the hells are much more distressful and do not lead to Wisdom'.[144]

Means of Increasing Energy : In order to do good to the beings the Bodhisattva requires much energy. To increase his energy he manoeuvres his 'armies' which are the following :

(1) Desire (*chanda*) : This is the root of all merit : What an excellent task have I undertaken in the destruction of all my vices and those of others. I have to endow myself and my fellows with infinite merits which will take infinite time. I have never enjoyed the joy of Lord's worship; I have never honoured the Doctrine; nor satisfied the needy, nor given fearlessness to victims of fear; I never made the miserable happy, I took birth only to trouble my mother. I must realise the wholesome consequences of merits and the woesome consequences of sins. Will I ever abandon this desire for Dharma (*dharma-chanda*) which the Lord has declared to be the root of righteousness.

(2) Pride (*māna*) : (a) The 'pride of work' : It is upon me that so many difficult and mean works devolve; I alone have to do them; let all beings cast on me the burden of their work.

(b) 'Pride against passions' : Shall my ambition of the (spiritual) conquest of the three worlds be turned down ? Son of the Lion of Victors, should I be a slave of passions ? I have to maintain this pride. The most humiliating and the most exacting of the passions is pride. I will take pride in subduing pride.

(c) 'Pride of power' : A Bodhisattva must be proud of his power of endurance; he is inaccessible to passions. Just as the lion is not defeated by a multitude of deer, so the Bodhisattva is not prevailed upon by a multitude of passions.[145]

(3) Joy (*rati*) : It is by virtue of joy that a Bodhisattva, after finishing one task, plunges into another, just as an elephant under the midday sun plunges into a lake. He whose happiness is in action itself, seeks action nothing but action. *Rati* is the propensity for good work.

(4) Abandonment (*mukti*): The Bodhisattva measures his powers and capabilities before starting any work; he must 'postpone' the task when his powers fail.

(5) Exclusive application (*tātparya*) : The sword that is mindfulness, must be exclusively applied to avoiding the attacks of those clever enemies, the passions. In this duel, the saint is armed with the memory of the Doctrine of Buddha. If he is wounded, he grieves and reflects—What shall I do to prevent this occurring again ?

(6) Self-mastery (*ātmavidheyatā*): Never for a moment does the Bodhisattva forget Buddha's discourse on diligence (*apramāda*). He keeps his body, speech and mind alert and organised, so that he may be ready for any work at any time. Just as a cotton plant obeys the wind, coming and going under its impulse, so in body and thought the saint directs himself according to his will. It is in this way that supernatural powers are obtained and all happiness too.

Perfect Trance: Contemplation (*dhyāna*) is indispensable to the attainment of merit and wisdom. Having increased enthusiasm and vigour,[146] the Bodhisattva must plunge into trance (*samādhi*). *Dhyāna* or *samādhi* presupposes two things : (1) abstraction or isolation of the body (*kāya-viveka*), and (2) abstraction or isolation of mind (*citta-viveka*); the former implies a life of retirement, while the latter apathy to worldly desires.[147] *Dhyāna* or contemplation recommended to Bodhisattva consists in meditating on impurity of body (*aśubhabhāvanā*) which leads to the detachment of mind which gets absorbed in ecstasy. *Dhyānapāramitā* includes (i) practice of *dhyāna* and the *samāpattis* known to old Buddhism, (ii) reflexion on the four noble verities, and study of the truths (relative and absolute), (iii) meditation on impurity in order to destroy the vice of passion, (iv) meditation on kindness (*karuṇā*) in order to destroy hatred, (v) meditation on the dependent origination in order to destroy error, (vi) meditation on the four objects of mindful-reflection (*smṛtyupasthāna*),[148] and (vii) meditation on all the doctrines of *prajñā* which relate to the true nature of things.[149]

Evils of Worldly Life : A man equipped with trance and wisdom is able to destroy passions; therefore, seek ye first the concentration of mind; this, however, cannot be obtained without disregarding the world. The worldly life is impermanent; it is vain to seek here for the lovely; moreover, attachment to the beloved covers the face of truth. One who acts like the ordinary folk (*pṛthagjana*) goes to evil condition; one who differs from the ordinary folk is not liked by them. It is hard to satisfy the worldling; now they are friendly, now they become inimical. At any rate, they cannot conduce to our spiritual progress; their company is fraught with sinful dangers. Therefore, I would live alone, happy and far from the madding crowd. I would avoid the common folk; if met with any one, I would treat him affectionately like an indifferent saint and talk always of things spiritual; I would remain like an unknown stranger.[150] The wise do not wish pleasure, for wish or desire begets fear; the saint is moved neither by praise nor by abuse, knowing that both the praised and the abused disappear. The worldlings like those that benefit them, dislike those that do not; the worldly man is no one's friend, said the Tathāgata because his friendship is founded on selfishness.[151]

Merits of Forest Life: The trees are better naturally; they do not get angry, nor require praise and worship. Their association is joyous. When would I be their companion ?[152] When would I dwell, away from this confusing world, without looking back, staying in the caves under the trees in the lonely temples ? When would I enjoy the freedom of movement, fearless, with half-covered body, wearing a garment unworthy of thieves and with an earthenpot as my property ? When would I compare this body, destined to decay, with the skeletons in the cemetery? Soon a day will come when this body will go rot and even the jackals will hate it for its obnoxious smell ? Even the bones born with the body shall become dismembered what to say of the separation from relatives ? A person is born alone, dies alone, none shares his pain; of what use then are those relations that hinder the spiritual life ? Life is like a pilgrim's sojourn; better it should repair to the forest before the weeping mortals take it to the cremation ground. Let us enjoy that solitude which quietens all disturbances, is free from ills, good and gives (spiritual) benefit; carefree, I shall plunge into absorption.[153]

Evils of Love: The greatest enemy of spiritual life which begets infinite evils, is love or lust (*kāma*). It has killed many saintly careers; it renders us pauper, brings us shame and disgrace. The pleasure derived from the embrace of a bundle of bones, flesh and blood, costs all the merits of a man and leads to disasters here and hereafter.[154]

Meditation for the sake of others: As already observed, the doctrine of non-egoity is the foundation of moral and spiritual activity in Mahāyāna. In Hīnayāna meditation on this principle of non-egoity seems to lead to perfect peace and Nirvāṇa, the sage becomes cooled and completely inactive (*sitibhūto*) by destroying the 'fetters' and removing the veil of afflictions (*kleśāvaraṇa*). But Śāntideva adopts, as pointed out by Poussin,[155] an 'original plan' and subordinates the virtue of meditation to the active virtues of charity, humility and patience. In the realization of non-egoity we find, says Śāntideva, a sufficient reason for active sympathy, and a real ground for sacrificing ourselves for our fellow beings. This practice of self-abnegation destroys attachment (*rāga*) and hatred (*dveṣa*); it purifies the mind of error (*moha*), and thus removes the veil of cognisables (*jñeyāvaraṇa*). Self-abnegation, so to say, purifies the mind by emptying it (*śūnya*) of erroneous ideas.

The aspirant for moral and spiritual perfection must, therefore, practise (a) equality of self and others (*parātmasamatā*), and (b) substitution of others for self (*parātmaparivartana*). Both the practices include a clear insight into the true nature of things.

Parātmasamatā: The essence of Bodhisattva's *saṃvara* consists in making no difference between himself and others. Just as the body is composed of different parts united together so that the hand takes care of the foot, similarly in this manifold world of living creatures, pleasure and pain are common to all. What joy means for me, it means the same for others. It is so with pain also. I ought to do for others what I do for myself. I must destroy the sorrows of others just as I destroy mine, because sorrow is sorrow whether 'mine' or 'his'. I must serve others just as I serve myself, simply because they are living beings just as I am. Should one object and say: 'my neighbour's sorrow is his sorrow, not mine'; the reply is, 'what you call your sorrow is so only by an illusion; there is no permanent ego in you, but a series of mental phenomena (which series does not exist in itself, any more than a row of ants), or an aggregate of phenomena without any individual unit. There is thus no existing being to whom we can attribute sorrow, of whom we can say 'his sorrow', or who can say 'my sorrow'.

Why then contend with suffering, when there is no sufferer ? Because, all the schools agree on this point. If it is necessary to contend with it, contend with it whatever its nature ; if it is not necessary, do not make any distinction.[156]

But why should we undertake the painful career of a Bodhisattva ? This career is not painful; even if it were, yet should the suffering of one person put an end to the suffering of several, it is a career worth undertaking. It is for this reason that the Bodhisattvas, whose spirits are fortified by the equivalence of the self and the fellow beings and for whom personal joy is the sadness when their fellow-beings are suffering, plunge into the Avīci hell to take the place of the condemned. The liberation of creatures causes the river of their thoughts to overflow into an ocean of joy. Their cup of happiness is full; Nirvāṇa, in comparison with this, is insipid. Therefore, do good to others, do not boast of it, or praise yourself, or expect a reward, for you are only doing what is quite natural.[157]

Parātmaparivartana: It is because of erroneous ideas, repeated during the course of several existences, that men attach the false notion of self to this body which is a conglomeration of heterogeneous elements. Why not treat this body as foreign to us ? The Bodhisattva regards 'others' as people regard 'themselves'; he treats his 'self' as people treat foreigners. He says: 'I shall regard myself as a stranger, and I shall find my real self first among the humblest. Then I shall practise pride for the sake of others.' Our only enemy is our selfish 'ego'. 'Renounce, O my mind, the stupid hope that I have still a special interest in you. I have given you up to others.'[158]

'If I were so foolish as not to give you to the creatures, there is no doubt that you would deliver me to the demons, the guardians of hell. How often, indeed, you have handed me over (to those wretches), and for what long tortures. I remember your enmity, and I crush you, O self, the slave of your own interests.'

The Climax of Wisdom : 'If I really love myself, I must not love myself. If I wish to preserve myself, I must not preserve myself.'[159] All these, i.e. liberality etc. are, according to Tathāgata, only a means to *prajñā*; without growing in wisdom, suffering cannot be overcome.[160] All success is preceded by 'right knowledge.'[161] This 'right knowledge' is the knowledge of the true nature of things:

it is the 'non-dual perfection of wisdom which is identical with Tathāgata.'[162]

Prajñā is the application of mind to the knowledge of truth, to the knowledge of what is. Its aim is to destroy the false views concerning the self and things; it is the awareness of the true nature of things. True nature of things is their voidness; things are void, because they are born of causes and conditions (*pratītyasamutpanna*). The perfection of wisdom consists in the realization of this emptiness (*śūnyatā*) of the self and the things. It is the destroyer of suffering (*duḥkha-śamanī*); he who wants spiritual perfection must realize this great truth of *śūnyatā* and obtain ominiscience.[163]

The Bodhisattva's Prayer: There are three ways of increasing the spiritual merit: (i) an active care for the weal of all creatures under all conditions—the salvation of the whole world must be our constant mission; (ii) an earnest liberality, giving not only material gifts but also spiritual gifts; and (iii) the thought of Enlightenment which, in fact, implies all the rest. In order to succeed in this spiritual ideal it is necessary to have (i) watchfulness, (ii) mindfulness, and (iii) insight.[164] The course and the ideal of a Bodhisattva may be summed up into two words: compassion (*karuṇā*) and wisdom (*prajñā*). The former implies a life of universal love (*maitrī*) and a zealous service of the living world, guaranteed by the phenomenal truth;[165] the latter implies a clear grasp of the unreal nature of things (*śūnyatā*) which leads to detachment from all things, self as well as not-self and attainment of the truth.

Realizing the (i) hollowness of life and of all that surrounds it,[166] and the (ii) suffering of beings, the saint makes a sincere effort in the following manner:

'Let all the creatures in all quarters, who are suffering from bodily or mental pains, enjoy the bliss of my merits. Let them have undiminishing happiness so long as they are in *saṃsāra*; may the world enjoy the bliss of Enlightenment forever, may all the beings in hells go to Sukhāvatī. Let those suffering from cold have warmth; let those suffering from heat be cooled by the waters that are the Bodhisattvas.'[167]

'May the fearful messengers of Yama, the crows and the vultures be surprised at the disappearance of darkness and the appearance of the gentle light in the world that the Bodhisattva

Vajrapāṇi showers from above. Let the creatures of the hell rejoice at the appearance of the Bodhisattva, at the rise of *bodhicitta*, at the birth of the joyous mother. Let the beings in hell welcome the chief Bodhisattva Samantabhadra who would appear free from veils, perfumed with the cool and pleasant scent of my merits. May the horrible pains of beings in hells be pacified, their fears removed; those fallen in evil conditions be freed from their evils; let there be no fear of eating each other among the beasts and birds; let the ghosts be as happy as the people of Uttara-kuru. Let the ghouls be bathed, cooled and satisfied with the streams of milk flown by Avalokita. May the blind see, the deaf hear, and all pregnant women be delivered of their offspring as comfortably as did Māyādevī.

'Let all have clothes, meals, drinks and all that they need; let the sickly be healthy, enslaved be free, weak be strong; may all love all. May all beings be equipped with faith, wisdom and compassion; let the treasure of poor become unending; may the ugly become beautiful, the females become males (so that they may undertake Bodhisattva's career). Let all creatures be pious, never without *bodhicitta*; may all beings become Bodhisattvas; may the world be spiritualized; may the word death be destroyed. May all the corners be filled with Buddhas and Bodhisattvas; may there be peace and prosperity. May the monks be wise, benevolent and lawful. May the nuns be free from passions and greed. May all worship Buddha and be blessed with Enlightenment. May the Lord's Doctrine last long'.[168]

Kamalaśīla on the Bhāvanākrama

G. Tucci has published the Sanskrit text of the first *Bhāvanākrama* with Tibetan version, notes, a summary in English, and a long Introduction dealing with the debate of bSam-yas.[169] This work of Kamalaśīla (the famous commentator of the *Tattvasaṃgraha*), is partly religious and partly philosophical, and may be classed along with the *Bodhisattvabhūmi*, *Bodhicittotpādasūtraśāstra*, and the *Bodhicaryāvatāra*, which are the Mahāyānist manuals for those who seek spiritual perfection.

Kamalaśīla was invited to bSam-yas during the reign of Tibetan King K'ri-sroṅ-lde-btsaṅ (A.D. 742-797). There he was engaged in a great controversy with the Chinese scholar Mahāyāna Hva-saṅ (or Ho-shang), a follower of the Ch'an (Skt. *dhyāna*, Jap. *zen*) School of Buddhism.[170] This historical debate gave Kamalaśīla the occasion to compose three short works called *Bhāvanākrama* in which chief points of view of his school about the meditation on the Buddhist truth and the path of spiritual perfection are expounded.

The debate of bSam-yas was an important event from the viewpoint of both history and doctrines of Mahāyāna Buddhism in the eighth century A.D. It seems that the Indian Buddhist missionary party headed by Śāntarakṣita and Padmasambhava, could not prevail in Lhasa against the followers of 'heresy', i.e. the C'han Buddhism headed Hva-saṅ. Śāntarakṣita is reported to have expressed in his will, on his death bed, that should the 'heresy' become widespread in Tibet, his pupil, Kamalaśīla was to be invited from India. "It was a clash between the Indian Buddhist party and the Chinese Buddhist party, between the followers of the Gradual Path and those of the Sudden Path."[171]

The debate took place in the bSam-yas monastery (founded in the year A.D. 775) between A.D. 792 and 794.[172] In the debate Hva-saṅ spoke first, then Kamalaśīla replied. In the end Hva-saṅ was defeated and he offered the garland of victory to Kamalaśīla. The King supported Kamalaśīla's standpoint and prohibited the diffusion of the views of Hva-saṅ. Kamalaśīla held that liberation is obtainable gradually, through the realization of both *prajñā* (gnosis) and *upāya* (means, compassion). The King requested Kamalaśīla to write down the essentials of the doctrine which, by the triple method of learning, reflexion and meditation (*t'os*, *bsam*, *sgom*, or *śrutamayī-prajñā*, *cintāmayī*°, and *bhāvanāmayī*°), explains the unreality of all notions. Doctrinally, the viewpoint of Nāgārjuna was to be followed; the view of Hva-saṅ, viz. the system of 'immediateness' or sudden realization was harmful to the practice of ten virtues. So the first *Bhāvanākrama* was written.[173]

Mahāyāna comprises three things: (i) Compassion (ii) thought of Enlightenment, and (iii) realization. (i) Compassion (*karuṇā*) is the basis of all; it is the starting point of spiritual life. The perception of the omnipresence of misery produces in us a feeling of compassion for our fellow-beings, friends and foes, as well as the desire to liberate them from it. The saint takes all beings as equal to himself (*sattvasamatā*).[174] (ii) This compassion leads us to develop *bodhicitta*, the will to reach Enlightenment for the salvation of beings. *Bodhicitta* is the germ of all virtues of a Buddha.[175] It is twofold : (a) the determination (*praṇidhi*) to become a Buddha for the good of all beings, and (b) the setting in motion of that thought of Enlightenment (*prasthāna*).[176] (iii) The third aspect of Mahāyāna is practice or realization (*pratipatti*). This consists of both the paths—and this was the main contention of Indian scholars at bSam-yas—namely, gnosis or *prajñā* and means or *upāya*. These two must be practised simultaneously; no progress is possible if only one is followed to the exclusion of the other.[177] To accept *prajñā* alone is to contradict Buddha's teaching and the holy texts; to accept *upāya* alone is dangerous. Both 'gnosis' and 'means' are necessary, because 'gnosis' helps us to avoid the extreme of affirmation (*samāropa*) and 'means' helps us to avoid the extreme of negation (*apavāda*), so that the middle path is fully realized.[178]

Prajñā is threefold, viz. (i) based on the study of scriptures and the company of the learned (*śrutamayī*); (ii) based on discursive thought (*cintāmayī*); and (iii) based on comtemplative intuition (*bhāvanāmayi*). *Śrutamayī-prajñā* helps in ascertaining the truth as revealed by the Lord and expounded in the Sūtras. The *cintāmayī* aims at penetrating and investigating the truth by means of logic (*yukti*) and sacred authority (*āgama*), and ascertains clearly both implicit meaning (*neyārtha*) and the explicit one (*nītārtha*). The *bhāvanāmayī* is the knowledge of the real nature of things (*vastusvarūpa*) arrived at by contemplation of the facts previously ascertained by logic and scriptural testimony.[179]

Those who have entered the path of spiritual progress must strive for direct experience; this is possible by frequency of contemplation. For this purpose, *śamatha* is of paramount importance; it consists in the concentration of mind which is by nature unsteady like water.[180] In order to attain the concentration of mind (*cittaikāgratā*), the aspirant must be indifferent to gains etc., must observe righteous behaviour; he should also develop the capacity to endure suffering and increase inner strength (*vīrya*). Progress in *śamatha* is furthered also by charity, morality, monastic rules, such as cleanliness, worship of Buddhas and

Bodhisattvas, confession of sins, rejoicing at the good deeds of others, and concentration on the great compassion in order to help other beings in salvation. There are several obstacles in the practice of contemplation which should be avoided. These are: sloth, confusion of the object of contemplation, idleness and frivolity, lack of effort (*anābhoga*), and striving (*bhogatā*). In order to suppress them the following correctives must be practised. These are: faith, zeal, exertion, serenity, mindfulness, awareness, investigation, and indifference.[181] The first four are the correctives of sloth. Faith is characterized by complete confidence in the virtues of *samādhi*, and therefore the saint develops a desire for it. On account of this desire he starts with energy and obtains the efficiency of body and mind. Mindfulness brings back to the fore the object of comtemplation; depression and frivolity are suppressed by awareness or watchfulness. Investigation and indifference are the correctives of effortless and disturbed tranquillity. In this way *samādhi* becomes effective, and various supernatural powers are obtained.[182]

When the mind is fixed on the object of contemplation, the saint then abandons it by means of wisdom (*prajñā*). When the saint approaches the climax of his path he realizes that *dharmas* are devoid of essence. Mahāyāna is nothing but the vision of this supreme truth; this vision of the supreme truth is non-vision which dawns on the saint when he looks upon all things with the eye of gnosis.[183]

Vajrayāna and Buddhist Ethics

In Tāntrika Buddhism, especially in the Vajrayāna, which had been making a steady headway during the seventh and the eighth centuries A.D., there takes place a fundamental change in the ethical and spiritual ideals and practices of Buddhism in India. The central philosophical idea is still the same old idealistic absolute, variously designated as *vajra, śūnya, bodhicitta, vajrasattva* and *prajñopāya*, but its nature is described as *mahāsukha* or 'Great Delight'.[184]

This goal of Mahāsukha is to be realized here and now in this very life, and this is possible by practising both wisdom (*prajñā*) and means (*upāya*); *prajñā* implies the knowledge of the void nature of the self and of things, while *upāya* is the spirit of compassion. A perfect union of these two units (*prajñopāya*) is the proper ideal.

Any action performed in accordance with *prajñā* and *upāya* is good and lawful; this is to say, it is the intention behind a deed which gives to it a moral or immoral colouring, if the intention (*abhiprāya*) is good, the action also is good. In other words, 'end justifies the means'. It is the mind which is responsible for the ethical nature of an action.[185] In Tāntrika Buddhism the ascetic is regarded as beyond good and evil; the dictum, 'everything is pure for a pure man' is often expressed; the bonds of traditional ethics do not apply to him. It is not difficult to observe in these Tāntrika Buddhist texts an utter disregard for the ancient moral code of Buddhism. A few instances will make it clear. The *Guhyasamājatantra* declares that "no one can succeed in obtaining perfection by painful and difficult rules; one can easily succeed through the staisfaction of all desires."[186] Elsewhere this text forbids the worship of Buddhist holy trinity (the Buddha, Dharma and Saṃgha). At several places it seems to advocate immoral actions including some of the most cruel and obscene.[187] The *Prajñopāya-viniścaya-siddhi* states that since all things are illusory (*māyopama*), the ascetic should not consider what is worth doing and what is not, and should resort to enjoyments as he desires; among these incest is given the first place.[188] In the *Citta-viśuddhiprakaraṇa* it is stated that "the ascetic obtains liberation by those very fierce deeds which become the cause of bondage for the ordinary beings."[189] Besides, this work gives elaborate arguments in defence of its similar attitude.[190] Likewise in the *Dohākośa* of Saraha, *mantras* and *tantras*, meditation and contemplation, are described as causes of self-deception. "One goes beyond the realm of the world by eating and drinking."[191] The *Tattvasiddhi* breathes with the same unethical spirit.[192]

It is a fact that Buddhism in India became an object of contempt and indiscriminate denunciation chiefly because of the so-called revolting side of Tāntrika practices. Although we have no evidence to prove that Buddhist Tantras became popular outside the circle of Tāntrika initiates and *siddhas*, yet it has become a fashion in these days to remember Buddhism merely as an agency which propagated the supposed 'hideous practices of Vajrayāna' in India. P. V. Kane,[193] e.g., quotes, "as a counterblast to what modern encomiasts often say about Buddhism," the following words of Swāmī Vivekānanda: "The most hideous ceremonies, the most horrible, the most obscene books that human hands ever wrote or the human brain ever conceived, the most bestial forms that ever passed under the name of religion have all been the creation of degraded Buddhism." The present author feels that such a language is neither academic nor sober, and in his opinion neither Swāmi Vivekānanda nor P. V. Kane can be considered to be authorities on Buddhist Tantra, much less on Buddhism as a whole. Attention may be drawn to a rather strongly worded remark of Benoytosh Bhattacharya,[194] who, replying to those who complain about the Tantra practices and suppose that the latter encouraged corruption and immorality in society, says that "such absurd opinions are held by none except the most ignorant of men." Moreover, the critics of Buddhist Tantras must keep in mind that the so-called "hideous practices" and "obscene books" that were associated with "degraded Buddhism" were also produced by Hinduism or Neo-Brahmanism during its best and golden days (500-1500 A.D.). The five *makāras,* the six (cruel) rites, the *strī-pūjā,* incest, necromancy and human-sacrifice, etc. are commonly found in Tāntrika texts of the Śaivas, Śāktas, Vaiṣṇavas and other Tāntrika sects of Hinduism,[195] and seem to have been more popular in Brahmanical or Hinduistic quarters than in Buddhist fold.

CHAPTER VI

BUDDHIST EDUCATION AND ITS CENTRES

General Conception of Education

EDUCATION, in common parlance, is taken to mean some kind of instruction, knowledge, training or skill in any sphere of human activity. The scope of education is coextensive with the varied interests of human life. In its wider sense education may be described as a creative process of progressive development of individual and social life. As an agency or a group of agencies of cultural advancement, it has been an essential element in human civilization all through the ages.

As an agency of progress, education may be conceived as an illumination of, or an influence on human life; it gives guidance, increases knowledge and equips us with insight. Education is thus a source of power—an invisible force—which transforms human nature so as to make him or her a perfect personality, physically, morally and mentally or intellectually.

Conceived thus, educational concept takes a philosophic turn; and, in fact, education has been called the dynamic side of philosophy, and implies rather a modification of natural growth and a purposive process of development.

With regard to the ideals of education, there has never been a perfect unanimity among educational thinkers. And this is not to be wondered at, for the educational ideals are correlative to the ideals of life, and so long there is divergence of ideals of life, so long will there be divergence of educational ideals.[1]

Ideals of Ancient Indian Education

The importance of education was duly recognized and emphasized in ancient India; though we no longer possess any ancient special treatises on education, yet we do find educational concepts and maxims, methods of training and courses of study, scattered in various Brahmanical and non-Brahamanical sacred and secular works.

Forest colleges, where specialized studies were carried on, are known to a very remote period of Indian history. The forest academy of Naimiṣāraṇya was one such centre.[2] Takṣaśilā and Kāśī are famed in literature as great ancient centres of higher education and learning.[3] The education that was imparted in ancient Indian institutes was 'an education of the kind that lifted the savage to the sage and the saint, the barbarous to the fraternal, the warring to the peace.'[4]

Since the conception of Dharma[5] was a most dominant feature of ancient Indian culture, its stamp is evident on education also. The educational ideals followed the dictums and dictates of sacred Law and Tradition, and never conflicted with the general philosophy of life[6] which was built on an awareness of the temporal nature of the phenomena that surround us on the one hand, and a postulation of a supreme spiritual goal which transcends the world of sense on the other.

Thus, education in ancient India was conceived as a process of creative self-culture, and aimed at constant growth and constant illumination of life, ultimately leading to perfect awakening, resulting in the climax of all striving.[7] The aim of education was to illumine life and to give wisdom which is the supreme eye.[8] It disciplined and subdued the human instincts and rendered the individual noble and affable.[9]

Beginnings of Buddhist Education

It is in the monkish training of newly ordained disciple that the actual beginnings of the Buddhistic type of education are to be seen. When the Buddha ordained Aññātakoṇdañña (who was thus the first Buddhist monk after Buddha) at Isipattana, he said: "Come then, Brother, well taught is the Dhamma. Live the holy life for the utter destruction of woe."[10] In this way began the Samgha, Monastic Order, starting as a union of the teacher and his pupils. Every noviciate had to pass first five years under a teacher's care; the teacher was usually a *sthavira*; the system was called *nissaya*, i.e. dependence on a preceptor.

The Buddha had laid down that every novice must be properly trained in the Vinaya (Discipline) and the Dhamma (Doctrine) and must choose an *upajjhāya* (spiritual preceptor). The relations between preceptor and pupil were like that of a father and a son, based on confidence and love.[11]

Literacy in the modern sense of the term was out of question in those days. All the teaching had to be imparted orally and retained in memory; this is inferable from the non-mention of any written document or text-book among the belongings of a monk listed in the canon. Knowledge of time-reckoning, study of the *Prātimokṣa*, the Vinaya and the Dhamma, Buddhist legends and moral fables and basic tenets, these were the subjects of study. The teaching was reinforced in occasional congregational recitations (*saṃgīti*).

Monasteries as Centres of Education

Before the Buddhist 'wanderers' settled in residential monastic establishments, the *sthavira*-teacher probably took his class informally in the open air. A pre-Gāndhāra sculpture from Mathurā shows a Buddhist master standing in teaching posture with a parasol in his left hand, addressing a group of monks sitting in three lines.[12]

Growth of Abhidharma and, at least two sections of the Sutta Piṭaka, viz. the *Niddesa* and the *Paṭisaṃbhidāmagga,* testify to an early growth of intellectual bias, scholasticism and academic temper among the monastics.

Analytic and deductive method of early Buddhist scholasticism was further carried on in the early Sanskrit literature of some Buddhist sects.[13]

With the emergence of Mahāyāna, Buddhist education, scholasticism and literary activities received a tremendous impetus. Not only the doctrinal, disciplinary and sectarian problems of academic nature, but also secular arts and studies came within the scope of education and training of Bodhisattvas. Not only the monks, but the laity also came within the educational range of Buddhist monasteries. Ornate in art, poetry and literature in general, with a manifest bias for intellectual and metaphysical progress, established in richly equipped monastic halls and with a dominant tendency to uplift the mass of lay-followers, Mahāyānism with its universal cultural mission seems to have exerted a great educational influence on society from the time of its inception. Monasteries, where the masters and poets and debators of Mahāyāna lived, became the natural centres of Buddhist education and learning.

In Hsüan-tsang's account we find that every great monastery

in India had in its past record name of some eminent Buddhist scholar and saint who wrote some notable treatise, carried on doctrinal debate and converted men to Buddhism.

It has been perhaps rightly suggested that, ancient India owed the rise of her Temple-colleges and organized public educational institutions to the influence of Buddhism.[14] Buddhist monastic Colleges were the first systematic educational institutions in ancient India, and they disseminated not only Buddhist teaching but also non-Brahmanical studies and secular branches of learning as will be seen below.

Character and Purpose of Buddhist Education

In early days, the community of monks that formed the core of Buddhist movement, was almost entirely devoted to a course of ethical excellence and intuitional gnosis leading to spiritual awakening. In a spiritual discipline directed towards a transcendental goal, which was beyond the range and reach of thought and reason, there was little place for education as commonly understood in modern times. The true character of Buddhist education, therefore, must be appreciated in the light of the way to Nirvāṇa, in which literary and intellectual skill had very little place. However, it is well to remember that the Dhamma that is described as *atakkāvacaro* is also said to be *paṇḍitavedanīyo*.[15] But the spiritual eye called *paññā* was not expected to be earned through much learning; it was the grasping of the 'right view' (*samyagdṛṣṭi*), constant mindfulness and sustained contemplation on the verities (*ariyasaccāni*) that was essential to this path (*paṭipadā*).[16] In early Buddhism virtues like *brahmacarya, bala* and *ārogya* were emphasized.[17] G. C. Pande suggests that there were apparently two kinds of *brahmacarya* known in Buddha's time, which may be called *apara-brahmacarya* and *para-brahmacarya* resembling the *aparā-vidyā* and the *parā-vidyā*. The *parivrājakas*, the Brahmanic, Buddhist and Jaina monks were concerned with *para-brahmacarya*.[18] The importance of great vows, to wit, truth, non-violence, continence, non-stealing and non-possession of property, is well known to ancient Indian mendicancy.[19] Purity in thought and conduct were the back-bones of this ascetic training.

But the theory that *duḥkha* originates in *avidyā*, that the root cause of misery is ignorance whence follows the whole lot of evils, implied, nay it is clearly declared, that freedom from misery could be obtained through the destruction of ignorance. This view thus takes a turn towards a way of knowledge (*jñāna-mārga*); in Mahāyāna Buddhism the only means of attaining Enlightenment is 'wisdom' (*prajñā*, the realization of the voidness of the self and the things).

Buddhist education had a three-fold aim : moral, intellectual and spiritual. In other words, behind the evolution of Buddhist education and learning there had been three purposive factors at work. In the first place, the monastic community had to tread along the rules and regulations laid down in the Vinaya or the Book of Discipline. This meant a rigorous ethical and moral course of training as also the general code of conduct among the monks and nuns. The relations between teacher and pupil were also governed by the Vinaya.[20] The newly ordained monks had to undergo an arduous ethical training under the supervision of some elder and able monk. Gradually, not only the monks but also the lay-followers seem to have frequented the residence of such *sthaviras* in order to receive instruction on the subjects of their choice. I-tsing clearly refers to this feature when he says that 'students' (*brahmacārin*) and 'children' (*māṇavas*) came to study under the *bhikṣus* and studied either Buddhist literature or secular sciences.[21]

The second important aim of education was to help the spiritual growth of the monk. This involved both a regulated process of contemplation (*dhyāna*), self-introspection, and mastery of mental faculties. Right understanding of and meditation on the Four Noble Truths (or, Two Truths, Absolute and Relative), mastery of the four degrees of *dhyāna*,[22] the successful practice of four virtues,[23] and the gradual rise in the ten stages[24] of a Bodhisattva's career, and such subtle and spiritual pursuits came within this category. Buddhist masters, saints and authors never lost sight of the fact that it was self-introspection, self-exertion, and intuitional approach that brought about progress and success in spiritual matters.

The third important purpose, which gave incentive to the growth of Buddhist literature, learning and scholasticism, was the need of preserving and defending the tradition (*āgama*) and doctrine (*saddharma*) among themselves and against the opponents. The custom of holding philosophical conferences and doctrinal debates among the sectarians of the same system, or among the votaries of rival philosophies and religious systems, contributed not only to the growth of critical philosophy and logic, but also resulted in transforming monasteries as active centres of education, learning and literary activity.

Education in the Monastic Universities

Types of Education :

The education imparted in the Buddhist universities of this period was neither exclusively Buddhistic nor exclusively monastic. Non-Buddhist studies and secular arts and literature seem to have received their due share in the educational curriculum ofthese universities. Broadly speaking, we may distinguish technical four types of education—(i) spiritual education, (ii) moral education, (iii) literary education, and (iv) education.

Under the first type may be placed the doctrinal teaching; instructions on Buddha's teachings, Buddhist philosophical doctrines, and the essentials of spiritual progress. Besides this theoretical aspect of spiritualism, the practical ways and means of truth-realization, such as *yogic* practices (*yoga-caryā*), mystical trances (*dhyāna* and *samādhi*), mastery over the body and the mind and the attainment of gnostic powers, and so on, must have occupied much of the time of the Buddhist masters and sages in their daily life. Scriptural study becomes an aid in spiritual education and self-cultivation as a matter of course.

Moral lessons were of primary importance. Not only the records of Hsüan-tsang and I-tsing, but also the epigraphs of the time testify to the high moral conduct and ethical excellence of Buddhist monks and scholars. Moral precepts and rules of conduct were taught through practical examples; it was in the monastic colleges that the Buddhist and non-Buddhist students learnt the rules of purity, cleanliness, proper food, etiquette of salutation, respect for all forms of life and obedience to elders and so forth. Practice of five moral precepts (*pañcaśīla*) may be taken to have been the first moral lesson taught to the students.

Literary education may have been perhaps compulsory for all resident monks of these institutions. Monastic education and general literacy had progressed considerably during this age. Reading and writing, study of the Vinaya books, specially of the *Prātimokṣa*, and general knowledge of the Tripiṭaka and Sanskrit grammar seem to have been the compulsory elements of a monk's preliminary education.

Technical education, with special reference to Buddhist art—architecture, sculpture and painting, seems to have been a part of education. An inscription of the time refers to the local artists of Nālandā. The inclusion of *śilpasthānavidyā* in the list of studies also points to this fact. An inscription found from Nālandā describes the monks of that Mahāvihāra as versed in the scriptures and arts (*āgama-kalā-vikhyāta-vidvajjanāḥ*).[25]

Courses of Study : As already noted, the Buddhist tradition of education and learning entertained a very wide range of subjects of study. Well known are the five *vidyās* : (i) *adhyātmavidyā* which must have included inner science or spiritual science, metaphysics and psychology; (ii) *hetuvidyā* or *tarkaśāstra* which included logic, epistemology and the art and rules of debate; (iii) *śabdavidyā* or *vyākaraṇa* which included the linguistic, grammatical, and literary studies of Sanskrit language; (iv) *cikitsāvidyā* or medicine and pathology; and (v) *śilpasthānavidyā* or arts and crafts.[26]

In big universities like that of Nālandā, not only the doctrines and literature of the Great Vehicle and of the Eighteen Sects (of little Vehicle), but also 'ordinary works', such as the Vedas and other books on *hetuvidyā*, *śabdavidyā*, *cikitsāvidyā*, the works on magic, the Sāṃkhya and also a large number of miscellaneous works were taught and studied.[27]

Indications are not wanting to the fact that astrology and astronomy were also taught. A Nirgrantha graduate in Nālandā is seen casting the horoscope of Hsüan-tsang[28] and the University is said to have had observatories.[29] I-tsing says that throughout the five parts of India, ordinary students and Buddhist monks had to study *śabdavidyā* or grammar and elements of language.[30] To what great extent the Buddhist scholars were well versed in grammar and intricacies of Sanskrit usages, is reflected by Kamalaśīla's *Pañjikā* on the *Tattvasaṃgraha*, wherein the erudite commentator analyzes each phrase grammatically.

Hsüan-tsang himself studied in various Buddhist colleges in course of his travels, not only all the collections of the Buddhist books but also examined and penetrated the 'sacred books of the *brāhmaṇas*', besides specializing in mysticism and Vijñānavāda.[31]

Among the favourite texts studied during this period we have reports of the Mahāyānasūtras in general; Rāhulamitra studied the *Ratnakūṭasūtra* daily; I-tsing's teacher, Hui-hsi is said to have studied the *Saddharmapuṇḍarīka* daily for more than 60 years, so that the perusal amounted to twenty thousand times.[32] King Rājabhaṭa of Samataṭa used to read hundred thousand *ślokas* of the *Mahāprajñā-pāramitāśāstra* every day.[33] Bāṇa makes a casual reference to the popularity of the *Abhidharmakośa* of Vasubandhu in the Forest Academy of Divākaramitra, where even parrots recited its *kārikās*.[34] Hwui-li records that even the spirits and demons followed its doctrines.[35]

Some monasteries were catholic enough to study the doctrine and discipline of different Buddhist sects, while others specialized in a particular class of Buddhist lore. Thus in a monastery of Uḍḍiyāna the Mahāyānists taught and studied five redactions of the Vinaya, namely those of the Dharmaguptas, Mahīśāsakas, Kāśyapīyas, Sarvāstivādins, and of the Mahāsāṃghikas.[36] The monks of a monastery in Jālandhara made special studies of Mahāyāna and Hīnayāna.[37] A monastery in Laghman is known to have produced an important work on magical invocations; the monks of Uḍḍiyāna are said to have specialized in magical exorcisms, while some monasteries specialized in Yoga texts.[38] Nālandā University seems to have made provisions for specialized studies in almost all branches of learning then known in India.[39]

Method of Teaching and Learning : A candidate after receiving the *upasampadā* ordination had to pay some 'fees' or 'gift' (*dakṣiṇā*) to his two teachers, *upādhyāya* and *karmācārya*. This gift could be 'either trifling or extravagant'.

The *upādhyāya* then delivered the elementary lessons on the precepts and the offences and gave the contents of the *Prātimokṣa*. These having been mastered, the monk then proceeded to study the larger Vinaya Piṭaka. He read it regularly day and night and was 'examined every morning.'

After having got through the study of the Vinaya Piṭaka,

the monk-scholar was asked to study the Sūtras and the Śāstras, doctrinal and philosophical treatises. These two teachers were likened to parents.[40]

A live picture of the deep and intimate relations that existed between a teacher and his pupil, is drawn by I-tsing. Early in the morning everyday a pupil went, after having cleaned his mouth, to his teacher and supplied him tooth-wood, water, washing-basin and a towel. Then he went to worship the holy image and took a round (*pradakṣiṇā*) of the temple.

Returning to his teacher, he makes a salutation, holding up his cloak, and with clasped hands, touching the ground (with his head) three times, remains kneeling on the ground. Then with folded hands and bowed head he enquires of his teacher in gentle words thus 'whether my *upādhyāya* has been well through the night, whether his body has been in perfect health, whether he is active and at ease', and so forth. The teacher answered these inquiries concerning his own health. The pupil then saluted other senior persons in the neighbouring apartments. Afterwards, he read a portion of the scripture, and reflected on what he learnt. He thus 'acquired new knowledge day by day, and searched into old subjects month after month, without losing a minute.'[41]

The following was also a method of education in which the master and the pupil lived an ideal life. The pupil went to his teacher at the first and the last watch of the night. The teacher having given a comfortable seat to the student, selected some passages from the Tripiṭaka, and gave a lesson suitable to the circumstances and left no fact or theory unexplained. The teacher inspected the disciple's moral conduct and warned him of defects and transgressions. Whenever the pupil was found guilty, the teacher made him to seek remedies and repent. The pupil rubbed or massaged the teacher's body, folded or pressed his clothes and often swept the apartment and the court-yard. It was his duty to examine whether or not the water for his teacher was free from insects, etc. Thus 'if there be anything to be done, he does all on behalf of his teacher. This is the manner in which one pays respect to one's superior.'

The teacher also, on his part, lent a ready helping hand and cherished a fatherly affection for his pupil. 'In case of a pupil's illness, his teacher himself nurses him, supplies all the medicine needed, and pays attention to him as if he were his child.'[42]

Hsüan-tsang states that the primary education in India started with a work called *Siddhaṃ* or a Primer in twelve chapters, which dealt with the alphabets and the combinations of vowels and consonants. Having mastered this course, the boy at the age of five began to learn the Five Sciences[43] enumerated above. I-tsing throws a welcome light on the contents of elementary and general education prior to specialization and higher studies in the monastic colleges of the time.

A boy started his education at the age of six years with a book called *Siddhirastu* which contained 40 letters of the alphabet and 10,000 syllables arranged in 300 couplets. This Primer was finished within 6 months. Next, the student studied the *sūtras* of Pāṇini, 'the foundation of all grammatical science'. It has 1000 *ślokas*, and boys of 8 years' age could repeat it in eight months' time. Then followed the book of *dhātu* dealing with the grammatical roots. This text was studied by boys of 10 years' age and they mastered it after a diligent study of three years. This was followed by the book on three *khilas*, dealing with the details of grammar.[44]

Monks' Secondary Education : Among the most important Buddhist texts, which a monk who had completed the study of the *Prātimokṣa*, the Vinaya Piṭaka and some Sūtras and Śāstras, had to study at a secondary stage of his education, were the following texts. Aśvaghoṣa's 'Service in three parts' was a text which all monks had to learn by heart. The first text of this class was Mātṛceṭa's famous *Sārdhaśataka-buddha-praśaṁsā-gāthā* (the 'Hymn in one hundred and fifty verses'). Mātṛceṭa's another charming composition was a Hymn consisting of 400 *ślokas*. These texts treated generally of the six perfect virtues (*pāramitās*) and expounded the excellent qualities of the Buddha, 'the World Honoured One'. These two texts were taught compulsorily. Says I-tsing, throughout India everyone who becomes a monk is taught Mātṛceṭa's two hymns as soon as he can recite the five and ten precepts. This course is adopted by both the Mahāyāna and the Hīnayāna schools.[45]

These two texts were taught compulsorily because of their following six educative values. They made known the profound virtues of the Buddha; they taught how to compose verses; they ensured purity of language; their singing expanded the chest (or lungs); by reciting them nervousness in an assembly was overcome; and lastly, by acting according to them, good health and longevity were attained. There were a number of commentaries on these hymns; and the work Jina ofand Śākya-deva which were their imitations, were also popular.

Another text popularly studied was Nāgārjuna's *Suhṛllekha* which exhorted as to the right ways and eulogised wisdom and *triratna*.[46] The *Suhṛllekha* inculcated both moral and spiritual virtues because it was advised in this letter to practise the three-fold wisdom (viz., *śrutamayī-prajñā*, *cintāmayī°* ,and *bhāvanāmayī°*), helped to understand the Noble Eightfold Path and explained the Four Truths.

Indian students learned this Epistle in verse early in the course of their education, but the most devout made it their special object of study throughout their lives, because it was a piece of standard literature.

There was another work of similar character and equally famous. It was the *Jātakamālā* (the Garland of Birth-Stories) by Āryaśūra. Its popularity during the seventh century A.D. is proved not only by the paintings of Ajaṇṭā but also by an historical episode recorded by I-tsing. King Harṣa Śīlāditya, who was exceedingly fond of literature, once commanded the poets and men of letters of his age to show their best compositions. The collection thus produced amounted to five hundred bundles, and on examination it was found that most of them were based on the *Jātakamālā*. Another work popularized by Harṣa and composed in verse by himself was the *Jīmūtavāhana*.[47] Another Buddhist work which was popularly studied in all India in accompaniment with music and dance was *Sudāna*, a poetical song concerning the *Viśvantara-jātaka*, composed by Candradāsa; one of the most famous works widely studied in India and Southeast Asia was the *Buddhacarita* of Aśvaghoṣa.[48]

Besides elementary literary and grammatical courses noted above, the students had to study such standard commentaries on the *sūtras* of Pāṇini, as the *Kāśikā-vṛtti* by Jayāditya, the *Cūrṇī* or *Mahābhāṣya* of Patañjali, the *Bhartṛhari-śāstra*, and the *Vākyapadīya*, another work of Bhartṛhari consisting of 700 *ślokas* with a commentary in 7,000 *ślokas*. This great work was a treatise on the inference, supported by the authority of the sacred teaching and on inductive arguments. Besides these, the *Pie-na* or *Beḍāvṛtti*, a joint composition by Bhartṛhari and Dharmapāla, which dealt with the secrets of heaven and earth and the philosophy of man, was also a favourite work of those who wished to be *bahuśruta* or learned. In logic, Nāgārjuna's work *Nyāyadvāra-tāraka-śāstra* was the text-book of advanced students.[49]

Standard of Scholarship : The Buddhist monks often assembled together for discussion to test intellectual ability and bring moral character into prominence, to reject the worthless, and to advance the intelligent. Those who brought forward fine points of philosophy and properly appreciated the subtle principles, and who were ornate in diction, refined in speech, and rich in higher attainments, rode richly caparisoned-elephants, preceded and followed by a host of attendants. But those defeated in debate, deficient in doctrine and poor in speech, perverted the sense while keeping the language. 'The faces of such are promptly daubed with red and white clay, their bodies are covered with dirt, and they are driven out to the wilds or thrown into the ditches.' It was not necessary for a learned and virtuous man to become a monk; he could win the highest academic honours even while being a householder, as for instance, Jayasena of Yaṣṭivana.

A monk who could orally expound one treatise whether the Abhidharma or the Sūtra or the Vinaya was exempted from serving under the prior; one who could expound two was invested with the insignia and outfit of a superior. He who expounded three treatises was given subordinate monks to assist him. A monk who was a master of four treatises had lay-servants assigned to him; he who expounded five texts rode an elephant, while a master of six treatises received besides a riding elephant, a surrounding retinue; 'where the spiritual attainments are high, the distinctions conferred are extra-ordinary.'[50] We may be sure that the academic environment must have been fairly striking, and the lures of honour, gain and eminence must have sustained the zeal of scholars for more knowledge and all that it carried.

Therefore the priests studied not only the five *vidyās,* but all the Vinaya works, and investigated the Sūtras and Śāstras as well. 'They oppose heretics as they would drive beasts in the middle of a plain, and explain away disputations as boiling water melts frost. In this manner they become famous throughout Jambūdvīpa, receive respect above gods and men, and serving under the Buddha and promoting His doctrine, they lead all the people to Nirvāṇa.'[51] There were scholars who could commit to memory several texts and several thousand *ślokas.* 'This is far from being a myth, for I (I-tsing) myself have met such men.'[52]

Important Centres of Education

It is necessary to emphasize certain general features that characterized these centres of Buddhist education. It has been repeatedly pointed out above that the Buddhist monasteries were not only the true centres of Buddhistic culture in particular, but also the nurseries and repositories of Buddhist education and learning in general. In course of centuries some of these monasteries of India grew into large educational centres and had some characteristic features which justify their being described as universities.

They had a truly universal character; they were free from religious, political or national barriers; they threw open their doors to all persons irrespective of caste, colour, creed or country. This universal and catholic spirit of Buddhist culture and its centres, earned a great international reputation for India and attracted scholars from far off countries. The same cannot be said of the Brahmanical system of education and its institutions. R. K. Mookerjee rightly observes that "the necessity of a domestic environment under the Brahmanical scheme did not thus favour the expansion of the small school under an individual teacher into a larger educational federation controlled by a collective body of teachers, as was the characteristic of the Buddhist system."[53] It is, therefore, quite proper to attribute to the influence of Buddhism the rise of organized public educational institutions in ancient India.[54]

The importance of these Buddhist universities and their singular contributions towards the growth of Indian culture—India's literatures, arts, religious faiths and institutions, philosophical systems, logical theories, and technical sciences—and its expansion beyond the frontiers of India can scarcely be overestimated. If the ancient Chinese people regarded India as 'the celestial Treasure-House'[55], and if advanced scholars and truth-seekers from Ceylon, Java, China, Korea, Tibet, Mongolia, Khotan and Nepal flocked to India to grace the halls of her universities, and if today we are able to recover our valuable Buddhist scriptures from Sinhalese, Tibetan, Chinese, Khotanese, and Mongolian languages, and if we look to-day to the Ceylonese chronicalers, Tibetan *lot-sa-bas* and Chinese annalists with an earnest hope of getting useful information concerning our past, and if the Indian historian of today can boast of his country's righteous conquest and cultural empire in bygone days, the credit goes to these Buddhist universities and their scholars.

University of Nālandā : The ruins of this ancient monastic University have been unearthed near the village of Bargaon, 55 miles south-east of Patna in Bihar State. The early history and growth of Nālandā Monastery has been discussed above. The general layout of its buildings, their architectural and sculptural features have been noted above. Only a brief outline of its educational activity needs to be discussed here.

Nālandā-mahāvihāra was both a monastery and a university; its boarding and lodging arrangements were almost modern. Large lecture-halls, hostel-rooms for students, special chambers and many-storeyed buildings for erudite and dignified professors, an efficient clipsydrae and a gong to announce the hours, a menial staff and watch-and-ward, a large fertile farm and a rich garden, a high astronomical observatory, spacious library buildings, and a high boundary wall of stone and brick around the entire establishment with the revenue of 200 villages and a host of kings, petty chiefs and moneyed officials of State to maintain its physical existence and economic prosperity—these in brief were the material equipments of this greatest Buddhist centre of culture and higher learning that ever existed in the history of Buddhism.

The University of Nālandā was a centre of higher education and advanced studies; only such students as possessed necessary qualifications were admitted to its post-graduate courses. It was the rendezvous of 'eminent and accomplished men' who assembled there 'in crowds', to spend two or three years to complete their highest education and to 'discuss possible and impossible doctrines.'[56] As such admissions were restricted and preceded by a pre-admission test of the candidates.

A monk-scholar acted as pre-admission examiner; he was called the 'gate-keeper' and preferably *dvāra-paṇḍita.* He asked some hard questions, many were unable to answer and were refused admission. Only twenty to thirty per cent of those seeking admission succeeded at the 'entrance examination'. Hsüan-tsang writes that 'those who were deeply versed in old and modern learning were admitted, only two or three out of ten succeeding.'[57]

In the last quarter of the 7th cenury A.D. I-tsing reported that there were more than three thousand resident monks in Nālandā.[58] But Hsüan-tsang did not give any precise number of its scholars. His biographer, however, records that the number of scholars at Nālandā would always reach 10,000.[59] Relying on this report of Hwui-li, R. K. Mokerjee writes that there were 1,500 teachers and 8,500 students at Nālandā.[60] But the figures given by Hwui-li can hardly be taken at their face value, he had never seen Nālandā himself and the number seems to be a round one.

The students and teachers of Nālanda lived a very academic and moral life; they were all men of great learning, ability and eminence; they strictly observed the moral precepts and the rules of their order. 'They were looked upto as models by all India; learning and discussing they found the day too short; day and night they admonished each other, juniors and seniors mutually helping to perfection. If among them were any who did not talk of the mysteries of the Tripiṭaka, such persons, being ashamed, lived aloof. Hence foreign students came to the establishment to put an end to their doubts and then became celebrated, and those who stole the name of the Nālandā Brother were all treated with respect wherever they went.'[61]

This testimony of Hsüan-tsang is corroborated by a contemporary epigraphic record from Nālandā. The Nālandā stone inscription of Mālāda refers to Nālandā-mahāvihāra as 'the pleasant abode of the learned and virtuous *saṃgha*'; its inmates were 'erudite scholars, famous for their knowledge of the sacred lore (*āgama*) and the arts (*kalā*).'[62]

From the *Life* we learn that in the Philosophical Conference, organized by Emperor Harṣa at Kanauj, one thousand eminent monk-scholars from Nālandā were present. Elsewhere, the same source tells us that there were 1000 scholars at Nālandā who could explain 20 collections of the Sūtras and Śāstras; 500 scholars who could explain 30 collections, and perhaps 10 including the Master of the Law (i.e. Hsüan-tsang) who could explain 50 collections but the Chancellor of the University, Śīlabhadra, was the person who had 'studied and understood the whole number.'[63]

Not less than one hundred chairs or pulpits were arranged every day in the University for lecture purposes. This would indicate that as many as one hundred topics were discussed every day, and the students are said to have attended to them regularly, 'without any fail, even for a minute.'[64]

The patrons and professors of the University of Nālandā realized that a monastic University without a good library was like a large granary without corn. The University, therefore, maintained a splendid and well-equipped library for the use of hundreds of teachers and thousands of students. The Tibetan sources tell us that there were three huge buildings for housing books located in an area known as the 'Treasure of Religion' (*dharma-gañja*). These three library buildings were named poetically, Ratnasāgara, Ratnodadhi and Ratnarañjaka. Of these, Ratnasāgara housed the collection of *Prajñā-pāramitā-sūtras* and the Tāntrika texts.[65]

Nālandā University Library was the only standard place where foreign scholars and translators could get authoritative texts. Hsüan-tsang had taken to China with him copies of 124 Mahāyāna texts and other works amounting to 520 fasciculi.[66] I-tsing got copies of 400 Sanskrit works at Nālandā which amounted to 500,000 verses.[67] Inscriptions refer to the Sumātran monks copying manuscripts at Nālandā.[68] It is also reported that the monks also kept their private libraries which after their death were to be deposited in the Central Library.

Nālandā University produced a large number of eminent scholars, debaters and authors who flourished during the 7th and the 8th centuries A.D. Mention may be made of Dharmapāla, Candrapāla (perhaps Candrakīrti), Dharmakīrti, Śīlabhadra, Buddhabhadra, Jayasena, Guṇamati, Sthiramati, Jñānacandra

Ratnasiṃha, Jinamitra, Prabhamitra, Sāgaramati, Siṃharaśmi, Prajñāraśmi, Candradāsa, and Śāntideva, all of whom flourished in the seventh century A.D. and are mentioned either by Hsüan-tsang or by I-tsing or by Hwui-li.

In the 8th century A.D. also, the University had many distinguished scholars as its teachers and students. Sarvajñamitra of Kashmir who studied Tantras here, Śāntarakṣita who was probably the most learned philosopher and Chancellor of Nālandā in the middle of the century, and Kamalaśīla who was the professor of Tantras here. Besides these, Dharmottara of Kashmir, Padmasaṃbhava of Uḍḍiyāna and Prajñākaramati, and Śubhākarasiṃha were also associated with the academic activity of Nālandā.[69]

University of Valabhī: According to I-tsing another Buddhist centre of higher education in India which rivalled Nālandā in fame, was in the city of Valabhī or Valabhīpura in Wālā State of Kathiawar.[70] A number of inscriptions of the Maitraka kings belonging to the 5th to the 8th centuries A.D. refer to the great educational and religious activities in their dominions. But Valabhī, their capital city, was the foremost centre.

The first building of this monastic college was raised by Princess Duddā, the daughter of the sister of Dhruvasena I. Other buildings of this monastic establishment were the Ābhyantarika-vihāra of Venerable Mimma and the Bappapāda-vihāra of Bhadanta Sthiramati. Not far from the city was another monastic college built by Arhat Acala.[71] In the seventh century, Dhruvabhaṭa, son-in-law of Emperor Harṣa, was the greatest patron of this University.

Just as Nālandā specialized in Mahāyāna studies so the University of Valabhī was the rival centre of Hīnayāna studies, for most of its scholars studied the Little Vehicle.[72] Hsüan-tsang found about a hundred monastic buildings in Valabhī, the strength of the monk-students amounted to six thousand. Names of three most important scholars who had received higher education in the University of Valabhī are known to us; they were Jayasena, a native of Saurāṣṭra, Guṇamati and Sthiramati; all these scholars subsequently lived in or around the Nālandā Mahāvihāra. Hwui-li says that the dominant system studied in Valabhī was that of the Sammitīya school of Hīnayāna.[73] From I-tsing's account we gather that Valabhī like Nālandā imparted higher education on secular subjects also. These were the two academies in India where eminent and accomplished men assembled in crowds, discussed possible and impossible doctrines, and after having been assured of the excellence of their opinions by wise men, became famous in India.

'To try the sharpness of their wit, they proceed to the King's court to lay down before it the sharp weapon of their abilities; there they present their schemes and show their political talent, seeking to be appointed in the practical government.' On being proved successful, they were advanced to high rank and could follow whatever profession they liked. Their famous names were written in white on their lofty gates.[74] This account would indicate that these two Universities turned out not only Buddhist Doctors, but also statesmen, administrators and economists who received appointments in royal courts and governments.

Epigraphical evidence proves that the Valabhī University maintained a library financed by the royal wealth and the rich contribution of the citizens.[75]

The echo of the great academic fame of Valabhī finds mention in the *Kathāsaritsāgara* of Somadeva, which shows that even the *brāhmaṇas* of Gangetic plain used to send their sons to Valabhī for higher education. It is related in this work that a *brāhmaṇa* Vasudatta by name, sent his son Viṣṇudatta, when the latter had completed sixteen years of age, to Valabhīpuraṃ for education from his home in Antarvedi (in Central Doab). It would appear that the dutiful *brāhmaṇa* considered Valabhī more suitable place of education than either Vārāṇasī or Nālandā which were nearer his home province.[76]

University of Vikramaśīlā : Among the later centres of Buddhist studies that throve after the best days of Nālandā, the most famous was the Mahāvihāra of Vikramaśīlā or Vikramapurī, founded by King Dharmpāla (*cir.* A.D. 770-810). The site of Vikramaśīlā has been identified with Sultangañja area in Bhāgalpur District of Bihar.[77] The Monastery is mentioned not only in Tibetan records but also in the late Sanskrit Buddhist texts.[78] The reference to this Vihāra as 'Śrīmad-Vikramaśīla-deva-mahāvihāra' would suggest that 'Vikramaśīla was the epithet' of the founder. According to Sumpā' mkhan po the Vikramaśīlā Monastery was situated on a hill top on the right bank of the Gaṅgā in Magadha.[79]

There were 108 temples and 6 colleges in the monastic establishment of Vikramaśīlā.[80] One hundred and eight Buddhist scholars (*paṇḍitas*) maintained by the State, looked after its educational and religious activities. Out of 108 chambers, fifty-three were meant for esoteric practices and fifty-four for general use of the monks. Although the institution was a seat specially of Tantrikism, yet other topics like grammar, philosophy, logic, etc. were also taught. Buddhajñānapāda, a disciple of Haribhadra, performed the consecration ceremony of this monastic College, and he became its first Ācārya. A large number of Tibetan scholars lived and studied in this college; besides the study of Prajñā texts and the Tantras, Vikramaśīlā University gave facilities for translation of Sanskrit Buddhist works into Tibetan.

King Dharmapāla, its temporal head, is known to have awarded the title of 'Paṇḍita' to its able scholars. He is reported to have appointed 'an Ācārya for wood-offering, an Ācārya for ordination, another for fire-offering, a superintendent of works, a guard of pigeons, and a supplier of temple servants.'[81]

Other Centres: There were a number of minor centres of Buddhist education and monastic learning in India during this period. Odantapurī or Uddaṇḍapura (located in modern Bihar-shariff) founded by Dharmapāla became a famous centre of Buddhist Tāntrika learning.[82] It was on the model of Odanpurī-vihāra that the first regular monastery was built at bsam-yas in Tibet.[83] Very little is known of the educational activities of this monastic college during our period. Jayendra-Vihāra in Kashmir was also a famous seat of Buddhist learning. About 1000 monk-scholars of this college came to greet Hsüan-tsang when the latter arrived in the capital. The King assigned 20 eminent scholars to help the Chinese scholar in his studies. The most famous saint-scholar was Yaśa, who taught Hsüan-tsang; he is said to have explained the *Abhidharmakośa*, the *Nyāyānusāra-śāstra* and the *Hetuvidyā-śāstra*. The College had some noted Buddhist scholars belonging to different schools. Viśuddhasiṃha and Jinabandhu were of Mahāyāna; Sugatamitra and Vasumitra were of Sarvāstivāda; Sūryadeva and Jinatrāta were of the Mahāsāṃghika lore. Under these savants Hsüan-tsang studied for two years.[84] In the monastery of Chi-na-po-ti lived a Tripiṭakācārya and a Śāstra Master, Vinītaprabha by name. He was the author of commentaries on the

Pañcaskandha-śāstra and *Vidyāmātrasiddhi-śāstra*, and seems to have been well-versed in Abhidharma philosophy, idealism and logic. Under him Hsüan-tsang studied for 14 months the following texts : *Abhidharmaśāstra, Abhidharma-prakaraṇa-śāsana-śāstra, Nyāya-dvāra-tāraka-śāstra* and other treatises.[85]

In the monastic college of Matipura lived a great saint and scholar, Mitrasena by name; under him studied about 200 monk-scholars. Hsüan-tsang studied with him the *Tattva-satyaśāstra*, the *Abhidharma-jñāna-prasthāna*, and other Śāstras. Though the monastic college headed by Mitrasena was chiefly a centre of Abhidharma learning, yet the mention of the people of Matipura as well-versed in magical arts indicates prominence of Tantrikism.[86] Another centre of Vaibhāṣika learning was the Bhadra-vihāra in Kanauj; its head was Vīryasena, a Doctor of the Tripiṭaka, who taught the *Varma-vibhāṣā-vyākaraṇa* of Buddhadāsa to Hsüan-tsang.[87] In the *Harṣacarita* we find that the Forest Academy in the Vindhya hills, headed by Divākaramitra, was a centre of universal learning; there lived scholars of Buddhism, Jainism, Sāṃkhya, Vaiśeṣika, Vedānta, Pāñcarātra, Purāṇic lore, and many other religious systems.[88]

Foreign Students in India

Buddhist monastic universities and colleges in India attracted a large number of foreign students and scholars who came to study here during the seventh and the eighth centuries A.D. Hsüan-tsang was the most famous of them. He spent 16 years in travels and studies in Central Asian and Indian Buddhist centres. To him we owe much of the account of Buddhist education and its centres discussed above. Hardly less famous is I-tsing, who spent 10 years in Eastern Indian monasteries, especially at Nālandā, and specialized in the Vinaya lore and the Sanskrit grammar. After him came Ou-k'ong[89] (751-790 A.D.) also known as Dharmadhātu. He travelled in Kipin, Gāndhāra and studied Sanskrit and the Vinaya in Kashmir for four years. Between Hsüan-tsang and I-tsing came more than forty monk-scholars[90] from different Asian countries and studied in Indian monastic colleges. More notable of them are the following:—

Hiuen-chiu, a Chinese monk, nick-named Prakāśamati, spent 4 years in Jālandhara in order to learn Sanskrit, 7 years in Mahābodhi and Nālandā; at Nālandā he was met by I-tsing; he died in Amarāvati. Another Chinese monk-scholar, named Taou-hi (Indian name, Śrīdeva), spent many years in Nālandā and besides studying the Sanskrit language, Mahāyāna, the Vinaya, he translated many Śāstras into Chinese.

Sse-pin, a Chinese monk who was well versed in 'the Sanskrit forms of magic incantation', studied in India along with Hiuen-chiu. A Korean monk, Āryavarman, studied in Nālandā and copied many Sūtras; Hwui-nich, also a Korean student, studied and died at Nālandā; I-tsing found his writings and Sanskrit manuscript left by him. Hiuen-tai and Hiuen-chau, both Korean monk-scholars also came to Mahābodhi Temple at Gayā. Buddhadharma, a Tokhārian by birth, 'a man of great size and strength', was studying at Nālandā when I-tsing came there. Taou-sing, a Chinese scholar studied at Nālandā for some time but spent many years in the study of the Hīnayāna Tripiṭaka in a monastery near Nālandā. Wong-po (Matisiṃha) a fellow-student of Sse-pin, having studied Sanskrit language, returned home via Nepal. Another Chinese 'Doctor of the Law', Yuan-Hwui by name, dwelt in Kashmir and took charge of the royal elephants. Lung, probably a Chinese student, took with him a copy of the *Saddharmapuṇḍarīka-sūtra* from Mid-India.

Tāmralipti seems to have been an important centre of Buddhist Sanskrit learning. Besides I-tsing, a Mahāyāna monk of China, Tang by name, spent 12 years at Tāmralipti, and perfected himself in Sanskrit. His full name was probably Ta-cheng-teng. Another Chinese priest, Tao-lin, lived here for 3 years, learnt Sanskrit and was converted to Sarvāstivāda school. At Nālandā he studied the *Kośa.*[91]

The famous Tibetan scholar and a Minister of King Sroṅ-btsan-sgam-po, whose name is spelt as Thonmi Sambhoṭa, tells us that he studied in Magadha (probably in Nālandā) under a Paṇḍita, Devavitsiṃha, and became master of both Buddhist and Brahmanical lore.[92]

CHAPTER VII

BUDDHIST LEARNING AND LITERATURE

Character of Buddhist Learning

EMPHASIS on intellectualism and metaphysical enquiry had been a dominant note of Mahāyāna Buddhism from the very beginning. With the spread of education and growth of logical reasoning, the intellectual bias and metaphysical quest received further impetus in Buddhist fold. Consequently we find intellectualism and scholasticism to be the prominent features of Buddhist learning during this period.

After Diṅnāga, the Buddhist scholars had to take a keen interest in philosophical controversies and logical development as a matter of necessity. The Buddhist authors and masters could not ignore the growing need of the art of disputation nor tolerate quietly the waves of Brahmanical attacks often bordering on sectarian animosity. It was, therefore, as a matter of historical necessity that we find the centre of interest being shifted from spiritual endeavour to intellectual endeavour; the Buddhist is now more a philosopher rather than a seer of truth;[1] his efforts became directed not so much to truth-realization as to the explanation and vindication of it. This dominant note of Buddhistic culture had the following objects in view. (i) In the domain of logic proper, the Buddhist scholars elaborated the rules of debate, and tried to distinguish with utmost precision the valid inference from the invalid inferences. (ii) Besides logic, they developed epistemology, and discussed the problems concerning the origin, nature and sources of knowledge or *pramāṇas*. (iii) Allied to these epistemological problems, was an exacting theory, namely the theory of the meaning or import of words. (iv) In the field of ontology proper, we find that the Buddhist philosophers of our period adduced elaborate arguments in defence of Buddhist doctrines based on reasoning alone. (v) On the other hand, they refuted the ontological doctrines of their opponents with the help of logical reasoning and scientific argumentation. Lastly, (vi) victory of Buddhist doctrines in public debates was desirable, because it assured the physical existence and resources of the order.

Branches of Learning

It is well to remember that one of the virtues to be perfected by a Buddhist saint, a Bodhisattva, is what is called the *upāya-kauśalya* or 'skill in means'.[2] It is his avowed mission to further the good of the beings, to endeavour for their weal and therefore to propagate the Law of the Buddha. For this missionary task, he must learn various sciences and arts. Although the ultimate truth could be affirmed best by maintaining a 'noble silence' (*ārya-tūṣṇīṃbhāva*), yet the saint has to take his stand on the relative truth (*saṃvṛti*) in order to do his sacred duty.[3]

Broadly speaking, one can divide the mass of learning current during the seventh and the eighth centuries A.D. into two groups : (i) sacred, and (ii) secular. Within the first category may be distinguished (a) the purely polemical learning which, however, involved a mastery of all the Indian philosophical systems and the latest logical theories, (b) the esoteric learning which included a knowledge of magic, mysticism, *yoga*, the technique of propitiating auspicious and inauspicious deities or demons. Besides these, exegetical learning or the intellectual capacity to explain and comment on standard treatises (*śāstras*) would also come within the sacred learning. It is needless to mention that the knowledge of the Tripiṭaka and a thorough study of the Sūtras and the Śāstras of various sects of Buddhism was the first and foremost constituent of the body of Buddhist sacred learning.

The second category of learning, the secular learning, included a study of such subjects as Sanskrit language and its grammar, knowledge of Chinese and Tibetan in order to translate the sacred texts into those languages, especially for those scholars who went to Tibet and China to propagate the Doctrine[4] and a knowledge of magic, medicine, arts and crafts. Also ability to teach polity, statesmanship, non-Buddhist studies such as the Vedas, and useful sciences such as astrology, astronomy, alchemy and ability to compose verse and good prose, especially memorial verses, came within this group of studies.

That all these branches of learning were actually prevalent

among the Buddhist men of letters has been indicated in the preceding chapter.

Types of Literatures

One of the most significant facts in the history of Indian Buddhism during our period is the decline of Pāli language and literature. It is said that even in Ceylon, the study of Pāli received a set-back during the seventh and the eighth centuries A.D. owing to the unfavourable political conditions in that island.[5] The Buddhist literature in this period flourished in several languages. At least five categories of it may be enumerated and substantiated by still extant examples of them : (i) Buddhist literature in pure Sanskrit, (ii) Buddhist literature in mixed Sanskrit or 'hybrid' Sanskrit, (iii) Buddhist literature in Apabhraṃśa, (iv) Buddhist literature in Chinese, and (v) Buddhist literature in Tibetan. The last two categories belonged to outside India.

Of the first category we have some examples. The philosophical texts, logical treatises, and ethical manuals of Mahāyāna masters and poets are in pure and standard Sanskrit, e.g. the *Tattvasaṃgraha* and its *Pañjikā*, the *Bodhicaryāvatāra* and its *Pañjikā*, the *Nyāyabindu* and its *Ṭīkā*, and the works of Candrakīrti and Bhartṛhari. To the class of mixed or hybrid Sanskrit belong most of the Mahāyānasūtras, *dhāraṇīs*, *stotras*, *māhātmyas*, *tantras* and *sādhanas*. It should be observed, however, that there is some difference between the hybrid Sanskrit of the Mahāyānasūtras, such as the Sūtras quoted in the *Śikṣāsamuccaya*, the *Gaṇḍavyūha*, the Prajñāpāramitas on the one hand, and the hybrid Sanskrit of the *sādhanas*, the *Guhyasamāja*, the *Hevajratantra* and the *Niṣpannayogāvali* on the other.

The difference consists (i) in the use of some foreign words, e.g. *chomā*, *dākinī*, *sākinī*, *hākinī- lāmo*, etc.[6] and (ii) in the description of erotic situations and pestilent doctrines which are peculiar to the Tantras.

Some features, e.g. defective construction of compounds and sentences, irregularity of the metre of verses, the use of both prose and verse, and frequent use of Prākrit words, are common to this class of literature. To the third type of Buddhist literature, i.e. the Apabhraṃśa, belong the mystic songs, *dohās* and *caryāpadas* of Buddhist Sahajiā saints and poets, most of whom flourished in the late 8th century and after. Their language is traditionally called the *sandhā-bhāṣā*.[7] This peculiar language belongs to the transitional stage forming a link between the Prakrit and the hybrid Sanskrit as well as between the old Hindi, Oriya and Bengali and their modern forms.[8]

To the fourth and the fifth types of Buddhist literature are referable those numerous works which were translated during this period into Chinese and Tibetan by Indian and foreign scholars.[9] A large number of Buddhist texts in Sanskrit, Sūtras, Śāstras, Commentaries and Tantras were rendered into Chinese by Hsüan-tsang, I-tsing, Vajrabodhi, Amoghavajra, Bodhiruci, and into Tibetan by Thonmi Saṃbhoṭa, Padmasaṃbhava, Śāntarakṣita, Kamalaśīla, and their partymen who went to Tibet in the 8th century A.D.

Buddhist Masters and Authors

Considerable progress in Buddhist thought and in its dissemination in India and abroad was made during the seventh and the eighth centuries A.D. A large number of Buddhist logicians, philosophers, poets, commentators, scholars and mystics lived and worked during these two centuries. A brief account of the life and works of some of the important personalities of this period will not only substantiate this statement but also give us an idea of the enormous amount of the varied and extensive Buddhist literature that was produced during this period.

Dharmapāla : Perhaps the most important Vijñānavāda philosopher after Vasubandhu was Hu-fa or Dharmapāla. He was born in the city of Kāñcī in a *brāhmaṇa* family as the son of a minister of the King of Draviḍa country; he conducted doctrinal discussions successfully in Uttar Pradesh near Kausāmbī and Viśākhā. He wrote an important commentary on Vasubandhu's *Vijñaptimātratāsiddhi* which was translated by Hsüan-tsang. Dharmapāla was for some time the chief Professor of Vijñānavāda philosophy in the University of Nālandā. His approximate date is A.D. 540-610. This date is suggested by the fact that he was a contemporary of Bhāvaviveka, Bhartṛhari and a teacher of Śīlabhadra.[10]

Candrakīrti : One of the most important Mādhyamika philosopher and a commentator of unequalled merit was Candrakīrti. I-tsing does not mention him; one is tempted to identify

Candrapāla,[11] mentioned in Nālandā by Hsüan-tsang, with Candrakīrti. According to Tibetan authorities, Candrakīrti was born in South in Samanta; he was a pupil of Kamalabuddhi, the latter had been a disciple of Buddhapālita and Bhāvaviveka. As Bhāvaviveka lived about the second half of the sixth century A.D. and was a contemporary of Dharmapāla, the immediate predecessor of Śīlabhadra (*cir.* 640 A.D.) at Nālandā, Candrakīrti who criticizes Bhāvaviveka may be placed between 560-620 A.D.

Candrakīrti wrote many works : the *Prasannapadā* or *Mādhyamikavṛtti*, the *Catuḥśatakavṛtti*, the *Yuktiṣaṣṭikāvṛtti*, the *Śūnyatā-saptati-vṛtti*, and an original work, the *Madhyamakāvatāra* with an auto-commentary (*bhāṣya*).[12] He is the most faithful commentator of Nāgārjuna and an erudite dialectician.

Dharmakīrti : One of the towering personalities in the history of Buddhism, whose contribution to critical philosophy has perhaps never been surpassed before or since, was Dharmakīrti. The Tibetan historians represent him as a South Indian *brāhmaṇa*, born in Tirumalai in the Kingdom of Cūḍāmaṇi (probably Coḷa country). The name of his father is given as Korunanda. Bu-ston, Tārānātha and Sumpā make him a contemporary and a rival of Kumārilabhaṭṭa; this may be true. He is said to have been a pupil of Īśvarasena and also of Dharmapāla. His immediate pupil was Devendrabuddhi. He is the author of (i) *Pramāṇavārttika*, (ii) *Pramāṇaviniścaya*, (iii) *Nyāyabindu*, (iv) *Hetubindu*, (v) *Sambandhaparīkṣā*, (vi) *Vādanyāya*, and (vii) *Santānāntarasiddhi*. Besides, he also wrote commentaries on the first chapter of the *Pramāṇavārttika* and on the *Sambandhaparīkṣā*.[13] According to Tārānātha Dharmakīrti was a pupil of Dharmapāla and a contemporary of Sroṅ-btsan-gam-po. This Tibetan King died in *cir.* 698 A.D.[14] I-tsing, writing in about 691 A.D., says that Dharmakīrti flourished in recent years.[15] In some Tibetan chronicles of Buddhism, Dharmakīrti is represented as a pupil of Īśvarasena, this latter was a direct pupil of Diṅnāga.[16] All these pieces of evidence put together would indicate that Dharmakīrti flourished in the first half of the seventh century A.D., his approximate date seems to be *cir.* A.D. 580-650. It is a moot point that Hsüan-tsang who may have come to Nālandā in 635 A.D. does not mention Dharmakīrti.

Of the seven treatises, the best and the greatest work of Dharmakīrti is the *Pramāṇavārttika*; it is not merely a commentary on Diṅnāga's *Pramāṇasamuccaya*, but is an original explanation of the elements of logic and critical philosophy. The work consists of four chapters : Inference (*svārthānumāna*), Validity of knowledge (*pramāṇasiddhi*), Perception (*pratyakṣa*), and Syllogism (*parārthānumāna*). This order of chapters is not a standard one which latter should have been as follows: validity of knowledge, perception, inference and syllogism.[17]

The *Nyāyabindu* has got three chapters dealing with perception, inference and syllogism. It is his best known short work and gives in brief the essentials of Buddhist logic. The *Pramāṇaviniścaya* is an abridgement of the *Pramāṇavārttika,* and deals with perception, inference and syllogism in three chapters respectively. The *Hetubindu* is a short classification of logical reasons. The *Sambandhaparīkṣā* is a short work which treats of the problem of relations. The *Codanāprakaraṇa* discusses the art of disputation; it is also known as *Vādanyāya.* The *Santānāntarasiddhi* treats the reality of other minds, and criticizes solipsism. In the Tibetan collection three more works are attributed to Dharmakīrti, viz. a poetical work, and commentaries on Āryaśūra's *Jātakamālā* and the *Vinayasūtra.* Non-Buddhist literary works also seem to suggest that Dharmakīrti was a poet of some merit. Philosophically, Dharmakīrti belonged to that school of critical philosophy which was founded by Diṅnāga. He represents the culmination of the Buddha's dynamic philosophy in which Buddha is conceived as an Embodiment of Right Knowledge (*pramāṇabhūta*). All subsequent creative minds of India seem to revolve round the magnificent and almost invulnerable thought-structure built by this subtle genius. According to an eminent scholar, Dharmakīrti "was never excelled by anyone in his critical reasoning, bold analysis and clear thinking."[18]

Bu-ston says that even his contemporary heretical *paṇḍitas* were convinced of the subtlety and excellence of Dharmakīrti's intellectual powers and treatises, but out of jealousy and envy they "fastened them to the tail of a dog" and let the animal run through the streets and hamlets with a view to destroying the leaves of his works.[19]

A king of Vindhya region, who was an admirer of the

philosopher is reported to have inscribed on a slab on his royal gate the following lines. "If Dharmakīrti, the sun among disputants, sets and his doctrines sleep or die, the false doctrines of the *tīrthikas* will then rise."[20] The colophon of the *Pramāṇavārttika* reads that Śrī Dharmakīrti exposed the errors of all the *tīrthikas* and was an unrivalled sage.[21]

Śāntideva : Bu-ston says that Śāntideva before becoming a *bhikṣu* at Nālandā under Jayadeva was known as Śāntivarman and was the son of king Kalyāṇavarman of Saurāṣṭra. His favourite deity was Mañjuśrī; he travelled widely in India and converted many heretics to Buddhism; he was expert in exorcism and performed many miracles in South where he spent some years in Śrīparvata.

This biographical account is corroborated by Tārānātha and Sumpā mkhan-po. They add that Śāntideva served as a minister to a king of Magadha named Pañcasiṃha. A 14th century Nepalese manuscript brought to light by H. P. Sastri gives more or less a similar biography of Śāntideva. But it adds that the name of his father was Rājā Mañjuvarmā, and his teacher was Mañjuvajra-samādhi; Śāntideva became a 'Rāut, i.e. a military officer' under the name Acalasena in Madhyadeśa.

Three of these four sources, to wit, Bu-ston, Sumpā mkhan-po and the Sanskrit biography found in Nepal, further record that Śāntideva was known as Bhū-sū-kū and he wrote the *Śikṣāsamuccaya*, the *Sūtrasamuccaya* and the *Bodhicaryāvatāra*, besides many Tāntrika works.[22]

The accounts of the life and works of Śāntideva, the Mahāyāna philosopher and poet, given above seem to be confused. There is evidence to the fact that there was a second Tāntrika Śāntideva whose name was Bhū-sū-kū or Bhūsukupā;[23] he is one of the 84 Siddhas and the author of three esoteric texts, mentioned and attributed to him in the Tenjur, viz. *Guhyasamāja-mahāyoga-tantra-bali-vidhi*, *Sahajagīti*, and *Cittacaitanya-śamanopāya*.[24]

Bu-ston, Sumpā and the fourteenth century Nepalese biographer who must have been a Tāntrika author, it seems to us, have confounded the Mahāyāna author and poet with the Tāntrika Siddha namesake.

It is important to note that Tārānātha is free from this

confusion; he does not identify Bhūsūkū with Śāntideva and regards the former as a contemporary of Dīpaṅkara Śrījñāna (*cir.* 1000 A.D.) and therefore much later than the author of the *Śikṣāsamuccaya.* It is also clear that Śāntideva's teacher was Jayadeva, while Bhūsūkū's *guru* was Mañjuvajra; Śāntideva's father was Kalyāṇavarman, king of Saurāṣṭra, while Bhūsūkū's father is named Mañjuvarman; Śantideva is said to have served as a minister of Pañcasiṃha, a king of Magadha, while Bhūsūkū became a Rāut or military officer under the name Acalasena in Madhyadeśa. H.P. Sastri believed that Śāntideva, the author of the *Śikṣāsamuccaya* was identical with Bhūsūkū or Bhūsukupāda, the author of Tantras and Dohās. He further held that Śāntideva was a Bengali. "The capital city of Śāntideva's father was probably in Bengal though in the manuscript it is destroyed". He supported this view by citing a line of a song of Bhūsukupā, '*aji bhūsuku bengāli bhayilī.*'[25] Rahula Samkrtyayana rightly observed that a person who was a Bengali by birth would never say that "today I have become a Bengali." Moreover, the word *bhayilī* is not a Bengālī word; it is a word of Bhojapurī, still used in eastern Uttar Pradesh and Bihar.[26] This leads to the conclusion that Bhūsukupāw as not a Bengālī but a Bihārī, a man of Magadha, as his biographers say.

Moreover, as is clear from the above discussion, Bhūsukupāda is a different person; he too was known previously (before becoming a Siddha) as Śāntideva; but he flourished much later, was contemporary of Śrījñāna as Tārānātha thinks, and also of King Devapāla (*cir.* 809-849) as is recorded in the *Caturaśīti-siddha-pravṛtti.*[27]

The peculiar epithet Bhū-sū-kū, was given to him, says the Tibetan Bu-ston, because he indulged in 'eating' (*bhū*), 'sleeping' (*sū*) and 'walking' (*kū*).[28]

Most likely Śāntideva flourished in the second half of the 7th century A.D. Tārānātha states that he was born in the days of Śīla,[29] son of Śrī Harṣa ; he also says that Śāntideva came after Dharmapāla, and was a pupil of Dharmapāla's successor at Nālandā, Jayadeva by name. The middle of the seventh century A.D. is thus the *terminus a quo.* The *Śikṣāsamuccaya* was translated into Tibetan by three persons : Jinamitra and Dānaśīla who were Indian, and Ye-śes-sde, a Tibetan. The last two scholars lived in the reign of King Khri-lde-sroṅ-btsan, A.D. 816-838. These dates would make *cir.* 800 A.D. as the *terminus ad quem.* Most scholars consider the middle of the seventh century A.D. as the most likely date of Śāntideva, while B. Bhattacharya says that he flourished "in a period between the departure of I-tsing from India in 695 and before Śāntarakṣita's first visit to Tibet in A.D. 743." A verse from the *Bodhicaryāvatāra* is found quoted in the *Tattvasiddhi*,[30] a Tāntrika text attributed to Śāntarakṣita. But it is neither possible nor necessary to push his date so late as the early 8th century A.D. The works of Śāntideva do not show any dominant influence of Tantra and he may have actually lived in the second half of the seventh century A.D. although I-tsing did not know of him.

Śāntideva is famed in the Tibetan tradition as the author of three works: *Śikṣāsamuccaya*, *Sūtrasamuccaya*, and *Bodhicaryāvatāra*.[31] But only two works, the *Śikṣāsamuccaya* (*ŚS*) and the *Bodhicaryāvatāra* (*BCA*) are known to us. P. L. Vaidya[32] suggests that the bulk of the *ŚS* consisting of citations from Sūtras may well represent the *Sūtrasamuccaya*. This suggestion is "indeed very tempting."[33] This point will be clear when the contents of the *ŚS* are analysed.

The *Śikṣāsamuccaya* or the 'compendium of (Mahāyāna) teaching' consists of three parts: (i) the *kārikā* portion, comprising 27 memorial verses, (ii) the commentary portion, and (iii) the illustrations consisting of quotations, often long, from various older Mahāyāna Sūtras. The Tibetans ascribe both the *kārikās* and the commentary to Śi-ba-lha (Śāntideva); the work is extant in Chinese and Tibetan translations as also in the original Sanskrit. Two editions[34] and an English translation[35] of the text have been published. The *ŚS* is divided into nineteen *paricchedas* (chapters). Its essential subject-matter is a Bodhisattva's ethical and spiritual life; the essential virtues of Mahāyāna piety, such as the six *pāramitās*, the *bodhipākṣika-dharmas*, austerity, faith and devotion, selfless service of the living beings, purity of life and living, worship of Buddha, and Bodhisattvas and the study of scriptures, the joys of renunciation and meditation and the peace and bliss born of the true knowledge (the knowledge of *śūnyatā*), etc. are discussed and illustrated.

The work reflects on the extraordinary erudition, extensive study and high bibliographical standard of Śāntideva. Winternitz says that the *ŚS* does not show any 'originality', only betrays "a loquacious learnedness which shows itself in a flood of quotations." But Śāntideva himself expresses this very modestly that, he has nothing new to say, that he wishes, without claiming any literary skill, to perfect his own mind.

About one hundred texts are quoted in the *ŚS* which means that these were existing in the author's age, but most of them are lost to us. A list of these texts is being reproduced here with a view to have a glimpse of the varied literature in Sanskrit that existed in the 7th century A.D. References to the published editions, in the case of the published texts, are given in the notes. To begin alphabetically[37] with (1) *Akṣayamatisūtra* which is quoted most frequently; (2) *Aṅgulimālikasūtra*; (3) *Acalopāsikā-vimokṣa,* probably a part of the *Gaṇḍavyūhasūtra*; (4) *Adhyāśayasañcodanasūtra* (5) *Anantamukha-nirhāradhāraṇī;* (6) *Anupūrvasamudgata-parivarta;* (7) *Aparарājāvavādakasūtra*; (8) *Avalokanasūtra* (9) *Avalokiteśvara-vimokṣa*; (10) *Ākāśagarbha-sūtra*; (11) *Āryasatyakaparivarta;* (12) *Ugradatta-paripṛcchā;* (13) *Uttara-jātaka;* (14) *Udayana-vatsarāja-paripṛcchā*; (15) *Upāyakauśalya-sūtra;* (16) *Upālipariрṛcchā;*[38] (17) *Karmāvaraṇa-viśuddhi-sūtra;* (18) *Kāmāpavādaka-sūtra;* (19) *Kṣitigarbhasūtra*; (20) *Gaganagañja-sūtra.* (21) *Gaṇḍavyūhasūtra*[39]*;* (22) *Gocara-pariśuddhi-sūtra;* (23) *Caturdharmakasūtra;* (24) *Candrapradīpa* or *Samādhirāja sūtra;*[40] (25) *Candrottarādārikāparipṛcchā;* (26) *Cundādhāraṇi;* (27) *Jñānāvatīparivarta;* (28) *Jñānavaipulya-sūtra;* (29) *Tathāgata-kośagarbhasūtra;* (30) *Tathāgataguhya-sūtra;* (31) *Tāthāgatabiṃba-parivarta;* (32) *Trisamayarāja;* (33) *Daśadharmakasūtra;* (34) *Daśabhūmikasūtra;*[41] (35) *Divyāvadāna;*[42] (36) *Dharmasaṃgītisūtra;* (37) *Nārāyaṇa-paripṛcchā;*[43] (38) *Niyatāniyatāvatāramudrā-sūtra*; (39) *Nirvāṇa-sūtra;* (40) *Piṭaka* (probably *Vidyādhara-piṭaka*)*;* (41) *Pitā-putrasamāgama;* (42) *Puṣpakūṭadhāraṇi;* (43) *Prajñāpāramitā* (also called *Bhagavatī, Mahatī, Aṣṭasāhasrikā*);[44] (44) *Pramuditā;* (45) *Pravrajyāntarāyasūtra;* (46) *Praśānta-viniścayaprātihārya-sūtra;* (47) *Prātimokṣa* (perhaps *prātimokṣa-sūtra*);[45] (48) *Bṛhatsāgaranāgarājaparipṛcchā;* (49) *Bodhisattvapiṭaka*; (50) *Bodhisattvaprātimokṣa;* (51) *Brahmaparipṛcchā;* (52) *Bhadra-kalpika-sūtra;* (53) *Bhadracaripraṇidhānarāja;*[46] (54) *Bhikṣu-*

prakīrṇaka;[47] (55) *Bhaiṣajyaguru-vaiḍūrya-prabharāja-sūtra*;[48] (56) *Mañjuśrī-buddhakṣetra-guṇavyūhālaṅkārasūtra* ; (57) *Mañjuśrīvikrīḍitasūtra*; (58) *Mahākaruṇāpuṇḍarīkasūtra*; (59) *Mahāmeghasūtra*;[49] (60) *Mārīci* (*vidyā*);(61) *Maitreyavimokṣa*; (62) *Ratnakaraṇḍakasūtra*; (63) *Ratnakūṭasūtra*;[50] (64) *Ratnarāśisūtra*;[51] (65) *Ratnacūḍasūtra*; (66) *Ratnamegha-sūtra*; (67) *Ratnolkā-dhāraṇi*; (68) *Rāṣṭrapālasūtra* or *Rāṣṭra-pālaparipṛcchā*;[52] (69) *Laṅkāvatārasūtra*;[53] (70) *Lalitavistara*;[54] (71) *Lokanāthavyākaraṇa*; (72) *Lokottaraparivarta*; (73) *Vajracchedikā*;[55] (74) *Vajradhvajasūtra*; (75) *Vinaya-viniścaya*; (76) *Vimalakīrtinirdesa*;[56] (77) *Vīradatta-paripṛcchā*; (78) *Śālistambasūtra*;[57] (79) *Śūraṅgama-sūtra*;[58] (80) *Śraddhā-balādhānāvatāramudrā-sūtra*; (81) *Śrāvakavinaya*;[59] (82) *Śrīmālāsiṃhanāda-sūtra*;[60] (83) *Satyakaparivartaḥ*; (84) *Saddhar-mapuṇḍarīkasūtra*;[61] (85) *Saddharma-smṛtyupasthānasūtra*;[62] (86) *Saptaikamaithuna-saṃyukta-sūtra*; (87) *Sarvadharmavai-pulyasaṃgraha-sūtra*; (88) *Sarvadharma-pravṛtti-nirdeśasūtra*; (89) *Sarvavajradharamantra*; (90) *Sarvāstivāda-vinaya*;[63] (91) *Saṃgīti-sūtra*; (92) *Saṃgharakṣitāvadāna*; (93) *Sāgaramati-paripṛcchā-sūtra*; (94) *Siṃhaparipṛcchā*; (95) *Suvarṇa-prabhāsottamasūtra*;[64] (96) *Śūkarikāvadāna*; and (97) *Hastikakṣyasūtra*.

Another important, original and celebrated work of Śāntideva is the *Bodhicaryāvatāra*.[65] It is in memorial *kārikās*; the work consists of ten chapters. Its subject-matter, like that of the *Śikṣāsamuccaya*, is also moral and religious; its ninth and the longest chapter, entitled Prajñāpāramitā, however, is entirely metaphysical and polemical; this chapter shows that the scholar, poet and Mahāyānist author of the *ŚS* was also a subtle diale-ctician and one of the most important Mādhyamika philoso-phers. Apart from its unique spiritual value as a manual of moral discipline and a textbook of the followers of Bodhisattva's career, the *Bodhicaryāvatāra* is one of the master-pieces of religious poetry in Sanskrit. This work has received great praise in modern times. Bu-ston says[66] that there were more than one hundred commentaries on the *Bodhicaryāvatāra*, and eight of them had already been translated into Tibetan in his time.

Prajñākaramati : The existence of a number of other Buddhist Sanskrit works, philosophical and religious, in the 7th and the 8th centuries is proved by some other works cited by Śāntideva in his *Bodhicaryāvatāra* and by Prajñākaramati in his *Pañjikā* on this work of Śāntideva. Many texts quoted in the *ŚS* are also quoted in the *BCAP*. But the following texts quoted in the *BCAP*, are not known from the *ŚS* : the *Kāśīrājapadmakāvadāna;* the *Gayāśīrṣa;*[67] the *Paramārthaśūnyatā-sūtra*; the *Bhārahārādi-sūtra;*[68] the *Bhikṣu-vinaya;* the *Mañjuśrī-vimokṣa;* the *Maitrī-bala-jātaka;*[69] the *Śatasāhasrikā* (*prajñāpāramitā*);[70] the *Śrīsaṃ-bhava-vimokṣa;* the *Satya-dvayāvatārasūtra*; and the *Sūtra-samuccaya* of Nāgārjuna.[71] Besides, Prajñākaramati in his *Bodhicaryāvatārapañjikā* quotes the following Buddhist Sūtras and Śāstras : the *Catuḥ-stava* of Nāgārjuna; *Tattva-saṃgraha* of Śāntarakṣita, *Dharmapada; Madhyamakāvatāra* of Candrakīrti; *Abhidharmakośa* of Vasubandhu; *Viṃśakārikā* (probably *Viṃśatikā* of Vasubandhu); *Madhyamakaśāstra* of Nāgārjuna; *Bhartṛhariśataka; Subhāṣitasaṃgraha; Madhyamakālaṅkāra-kārikā* (attributed to Śāntarakṣita by Khai-ḍub). The following works, viz. *Laṅkāvatārasūtra, Yuktiṣaṣṭikā* of Nāgārjuna, *Guṇaparyantastotra, Sugatakīrti-yaśastilaka, Anavatapta-hṛdāpakramaṇa, Pratītyasamutpādahṛdaya,* and *Prajñā-pāramitā-stava,*[72] quoted by Prajñākaramati, must also have been in existence in the Buddhist libraries of the times.

Śīlabhadra: The most outstanding Buddhist scholar at Nālandā University in the second quarter of the seventh century A.D. was, according to Hsüan-tsang, Śīlabhadra. So great was his piety and learning that the Buddhists called him 'Treasure of the Good Law' (Chinese, Ching-fa-tsong). Hwui-li records that Śīlabhadra had studied the entire collection of Buddhist books; this seems to be in eulogistic tone, and the teacher of Hsüan-tsang seems to have been an expert in Vijñānavāda studies. He is said to have been a prince of the *brāhmaṇa* caste of the Kingdom of Samataṭa.[73] A work called *Ārya-buddhabhūmī-vyākhyāna,* preserved in the Tibetan collection, is attributed to him.[74] From a letter of Hsüan-tsang written from China in A.D. 654 and addressed to Jñānagarbha of Nālandā, it appears that Śīlabhadra died shortly before that date.[75]

Siṃharaśmi : Siṃharaśmi is known from the biography of Hsüan-tsang; he was the professor of Mādhyamika philosophy at Nālandā University and was the author of two polemical treatises, viz. the *Śataśāstra* and the *Prāṇyamūlaśāstra.*[76]

Jayasena : Jayasena is mentioned by Hsüan-tsang as a versatile Buddhist scholar and author of the Śāstras. Unfortunately, no Śāstra of Jayasena is known to us. He is said to have been educated in the Valabhī University under Sthiramati and Bhadraruci, and in Nālandā University under Śīlabhadra. Hsüan-tsang himself studied at his hermitage in Yaṣṭivana near Nālandā for two years. The texts explained by Jayasena included the *Yoga-śāstra*, the *Hetuvidyā-śāstra*, the *Vidyāmātrasiddhiśāstra*, and others.[77]

Prajñāgupta : Prajñāgupta is reported by the biographer of Hsüan-tsang as a great scholar and Śāstra-master of the Sammitiya school. He wrote a polemical treatise in 700 *ślokas* against the principles of Vijñānavāda. The Nālandā scholars, at the request of Śrī Harṣa, had to accept the challenge and Hsüan-tsang is represented as critically studying the treatise of Prajñāgupta before proceeding to criticize the latter.[78]

Bhartṛhari : Little reliable is known about the life of Bhartṛhari. According to Merutuṅga, he was the brother of king Vikramāditya of Mālavā; another legend makes him a pupil of Gorakṣanātha.[79] Tārānātha relates that Bhartāharī or Bhartharī (probably the same as Bhartṛhari) was a king of Mālavā whose sister was married to king Govicandra of Bengal and East India. This event is placed in about the time of the death of Dharmakīrti, the logician. Incidentally, Tārānātha also says that Bhartāharī became a pupil of Jālandharīpāda.[80] It seems that Bhartṛhari of these legends and of those Śivaite traditions that are dramatized in the *Bhartṛhari-nirveda*, was a different person from the philosopher, grammarian and poet of the same name.

I-tsing places Bhartṛhari's death about forty years before the time of his composition of the Record, i.e. in about 651 A.D. According to him, Bhartṛhari was an eminent philosopher and scholar, a contemporary of Dharmapāla (*cir.* 540-610 A.D.) and a devout Buddhist by faith.[81] Most scholars place him in the first half of the 7th century A.D. chiefly on the evidence of I-tsing. Fresh evidence, however, has greatly modified the statement of I-tsing concerning the date of Bhartṛhari.

H.R. Rangaswamy Iyengar had pointed out that Bhartṛhari was a contemporary of Diṅnāga and lived in the 5th century A.D. Two *kārikās* quoted by Diṅnāga in his *Pramāṇasamuccaya* are found in the *Vākyapadīya* of Bhartṛhari.

Jinendrabuddhi, the author of the *Viśālāmalaṭīkā* (on *Pramāṇa-samuccaya*) says that Diṅnāga in those *kārikās* is referring to the view of Bhartṛhari. Secondly, Puṇyarāja, the commentator of Bhartṛhari, as well as the Jaina writer Siṃhasūrigaṇi, state that Vasurāta was the teacher of Bhartṛhari. From Paramārtha's life of Vasubandhu, we learn that a Vasurāta was one of the pupils of Vasubandhu. This revised date of Bhartṛhari should fall in the first half of the 6th century A.D. and not in the 5th century A.D. as Iyengar insists. Diṅnāga lived in 470-550 A.D. and his contemporary Bhartṛhari may have lived in about the same time. This view is accepted by Hajime Nakamura, E. Frauwallner and D.S. Ruegg.[82]

According to I-tsing Bhartṛhari was a Buddhist scholar and wrote the following works:—

(i) The *Bhartṛhari-śāstra*, in 25000 *ślokas*. It was a commentary on the *cūrṇi* of Patañjali on the *sūtras* of Pāṇini;

(ii) The Vākya-Discourse (*Vākyapadīya*)[83] in 700 *ślokas*, with an auto-commentary in 7000 *ślokas*.

(iii) The *Pei-na* (Veda? Beḍa? perhaps *Beḍā-vṛtti*).[84] It contained 3000 *ślokas*, written by Bhartṛhari; its commentary portion was wrilten by Dharmapāla which consisted of 14000 *ślokas*.

I-tsing further tells us that Bhartṛhari was a Buddhist by faith and believed deeply in the 'Three Jewels' (*tri-ratna*), and 'meditated on the two-fold nothingness' (i.e. *pudgalanairātmya* and *dharmanairātmya*); he was well versed in the 'doctrine of sole knowledge' (*vidyāmātra*) and 'skilfully discussed about the *hetu* and *udāharaṇa*.' This narrative shows that Bhartṛhari was a grammarian, a philosopher and a logician and a Buddhist by faith.[85] Perhaps this Bhartṛhari was also a great poet. But unfortunately, I-tsing does not specifically refer to Bhartṛhari's poetical works, the celebrated *Nītiśataka, Śṛṅgāraśataka* and *Vairāgyaśataka,* which are among the gems of classical Sanskrit literature, and through which Bhartṛhari has become immortal in tradition.

There is, therefore, a great controversy with respect to the identification of Bhartṛhari the poet and author of the Śatakas, with Bhartṛhari the philosopher and grammarian, the author of the *Vākyapadīya;* that Bhartṛhari the poet was a Buddhist by faith is also not undisputed.

Macdonell suggested that Bhartṛhari was a grammarian, philosopher and poet in one; 'only the literary training of India could make such a combination possible, and even there it has hardly a parallel.' He also noted that various commentators ascribe the *Bhaṭṭi-kāvya* to the poet andgr ammarian Bhartṛhari.[86]

Max Müller, L.D. Barnett and K.B. Pathak suggested that Bhartṛhari was a Buddhist and grammarian, philosopher and poet in one. K.T. Telang, and S.N. Dasgupta held that the poet Bhartṛhari was not a Buddhist and was not identical with the grammarian and philosopher referred to by I-tsing. Winternitz thinks that the poet with Śaiva-Vedāntic leanings may have finally been converted to Buddhism, while Keith imagined that Bhartṛhari may have abandoned Buddhism after investigating it and espoused Śaiva-Vedānta. It is possible that the author of the Śatakas is a Buddhist and identical with the grammarian namesake. The story told by I-tsing that Bhartṛhari became a Buddhist monk and lived in a monastery but being overpowered by desires returned to the laity and that he wavered in this way seven times between the quiet joys of the monastic life and the sensuous pleasures of the world, suits the author of the Śatakas very well. A poet who wrote 100 stanzas on passionate love also wrote two more centuries on wisdom and renunciation. These poems betray author's experience of the conflict between two master-passions—the cry of the senses and the urge of the spirit.

The Buddhist view of transitoriness is put by the poet in these sharp words. 'How can mortals find joy in life that is like the bubbles on the waves of the sea? For a moment man is a boy, for another moment a youth tortured by love; for a moment a pauper, for another moment at the apex of prosperity; then at the end of life's play with limbs tired owing to old age and with face adorned by wrinkles he retires like an actor, behind the curtain of death.'[87]

The *Śṛṅgāra-śataka* is not so much a poem on love as on the essential voidness of love: 'Death assails life, old age takes away the delight of youth, greed overwhelms contentment, and the serenity of inner joy is destroyed by the coquetries of young maidens.'[88]

Candra and Candragomin : I-tsing found in India "a great

man (*mahāsattva*) named Candra (or perhaps Candradāsa), being like a Bodhisattva, endowed with great talent. This man was still alive when I-tsing visited that country."[89] He was, moreover, a poet as well; and I-tsing attributes to him a poetical song about prince Viśvantara,[90] hitherto known as *Sudāna*. The people of India recited this song in dance.[91]

It does not appear probable that this Candra, a great man and a poet, who lived in the 7th century A.D. in Eastern India, was identical with Candragomin or Candrācārya, famous as a philosopher, grammarian and author of Stotras, known from Indian and Tibetan traditions. A Candrācārya, who wrote *Cāndravyākaraṇa,* and censured in it the *Mahābhāṣya* of Patañjali, is mentioned in Kashmir by Kalhaṇa.[92] A similar story is related by Sumpā mkhan-po.[93] The philosopher-grammarian Candrācārya finds mention in Bhartṛhari's *Vākyapadīya* also.[94] The *Vākyapadiya* refers to Candrācārya as one of those who contributed to the neglect of Patañjali's *Mahābhāṣya*. This indicates that Candragomin, who was a Buddhist scholar, cared little for the Pāninian rules. This might be the reason that his *Cāndravyākaraṇa,* at one time the most popular grammatical text in Kashmir, Nepal, Tibet and Ceylon, the Buddhist countries, entirely disappeared in India.[95]

According to Tārānātha[96] and Sumpā,[97] Candragomin came of a *kṣatriya* family of Vārendra in East India, lived for some time in Candradvīpa, encountered Candrakīrti the Mādhyamika teacher at Nālandā, and there became a pupil of Sthiramati. In the Tibetan Tenjur,[98] Candragomin is called a Dvaipa, i.e. an island dweller.

Candragomin can be safely placed in the 6th century A.D. According to B. Liebich, Altekar and others, Candragomin belonged to the period between A.D. 465-544.

He is credited with the authorship of a *Cāndravyākaraṇa* with an auto-commentary;[99] a drama called *Lokānanda* which is based on the Bodhisattva ideal;[100] a poetical and didactic work called the *Śiṣyalekha-dharma-kāvya,*[101] perhaps modelled on the lines of Nāgārjuna's *Suhṛllekha;* and *Āryatārā-antaravali-vidhi*[102] and other Tāntrika esoteric texts and Stotras in praise of Mañjuśrī and Tārā. It would appear from the above discussion that Candragomin was a versatile genius, a Buddhist controversialist, poet, devotee, grammarian, saint and a logician, for a logical work called *Nyāyasiddhyāloka*[103] is also attributed to him.

Not only Bhartṛhari, but also Candragomin, was an extraordinary product that the unique system of Buddhist learning produced.

An example of the wit and wisdom of Candradāsa the poet, is preserved not only in I-tsing's version, but also in its original in the *Subhāṣitāvalī*. On being asked, 'which is the more injurious, temptation or poison?', he at once answered: 'There is indeed a great difference between the two; poison is injurious only when it is swallowed, whilst the other destroys (burns) one's intellect when only contemplated.'[104]

Śāntarakṣita : One of the most important personalities in the history of Buddhism in India and Tibet and the greatest philosopher of the 8th century A.D. was Śāntarakṣita.

According to Sumpā[105] Śāntarakṣita was born in a royal family of Zahor during the reign of King Gopāla (*cir.* 750-770 A.D.) and died when King Dharmapāla (*cir.* 770-810 A.D.) was ruling. There is much difference of opinion among scholars with respect to the identity of Zahor. Some writers have identified Zahor with Sahor in Bengal, and Śāntarakṣita is regarded as a Bengali scholar; others suggest that Zahor or Sahor is modern Sabor in Bhāgalpur; still other scholars are inclined to locate Zahor in Punjab, modern Lahore or Mandi in North Western India.[106]

The legend concerning Padmasambhava that he was a prince of Uḍḍiyāna (Swat) and son of Indrabhūti, 'the great King of Uḍḍiyāna', and married Śāntarakṣita's sister, Princess Mandāravā, daughter of the King of Zahor, would indicate that the birth place of the philosopher lay probably in the Punjab, that is nearer to Swat.[107]

The only reliable source to determine the date of Śāntarakṣita is the Tibetan tradition which, however, is liable to different interpretations. B. Bhattacharya, relying on the information given from Tibetan sources by S.C. Das, placed Śāntarakṣita in A.D. 705-762, giving him a life-span of 57 years. Śāntarakṣita was invited to Tibet by its King Khri-sroṅ-lde-btsan who was born, according to S.C. Vidyabhusana, in A.D. 728 and died in A.D. 864; the monastery of bSam-yas or Sam-ye was built under Śāntarakṣita's supervision in A.D. 747-749. This chronological arrangement, however, does not seem to be in agreement with the latest studies in the history and chronology of Tibet which have been substantiated by epigraphic records.

According to the Tibetan sources consulted by Rahula Samkrtyayana,[108] Śāntarakṣita enjoyed a life-span of one hundred years, *cir*. 740-840 A.D. The *Blue Annals*[109] state that the great *vihāra* of bSam-yas was built from 'the hare year' (787 A.D.) till the 'sheep year' (791 A.D.). According to Bu-ston[110] the construction of the bSam-yas took 12 years, from 'the fire-hare year' (787 A.D.) to 'the earth-hare year' (799 A.D.). According to Tucci's chronology, King Khri-sroṅ-lde-btsan ruled from A.D. 742 to A.D. 792.[111] King Khri-sroṅ-lde-btsan is said to have been born in A.D. 742, and the bSam-yas convent is reported to have been built by this King at the age of 22 years; Śāntarakṣita had been invited by Khri-sroṅ-lde-btsan from Man-yul, near Nepal; the Indian philosopher taught ten precepts to the Tibetan monarch and established the first regular monastery at bSam-yas, probably in the year A.D. 775. Some four years later the *sad-mi* monks (i.e. the monks on probation) were ordained. The historic debate took place at bSam-yas between A.D. 792-794 when Kamalaśīla was present but Śāntarakṣita was no more. The latter died of the kick of a horse.[112]

Thus the second half of the 8th century A.D. seems to have been the most active period of Śāntarakṣita's life. Before proceeding to Nepal and thence to Lhasa he had been the Chancellor of the Nālandā University and the chief exponent of Buddhist thought in India.

The greatest and the most famous work of our philosopher is the *Tattvasaṃgraha,*[113] extant in Sanskrit as well as in Tibetan version. This polemical monumental work alone is sufficient to place Śāntarakṣita among the greatest thinkers of the world. Fortunately it has been published , translated and partly studied in modern times. It is in *kārikās* or memorial verses, numbering 3646. The whole work is divided into twenty-six chapters, and betrays an uncommon logical acumen, subtle grasp and a deep and vast knowledge not only of the entire Buddhist lore, but also of Vedānta, Sāṃkhya, Nyāya, Vaiśeṣika, Mīmāṃsā, Yoga, the Grammatical School of philosophy, the Materialist thought and Jainism. It is not without justification that the Tibetans praised Śāntarakṣita as a Bodhisattva, Mahā-upādhyāya, Bahuśruta, Ācārya and are one of the four suns who lighted the Lamp of True Doctrine in the Land of Snow.

Both Khai-ḍub and Tārānātha ascribe the *Madhyamakālaṅkāra-kārikās* with auto-comment to Śāntarakiṣta,[114] which is extant in Tibetan only. His other logical work is a commentary, the *Vādanyāya-vṛtti-vipañcitārtha.*[115] A Tibetan translation of Diṅnāga's *Hetucakraḍamaru* is also attributed to Śāntarakṣita.[116] Some Tāntrika texts extant in Tibetan,[117] and one text, entitled *Tattvasiddhi*,[118] extant in Sanskrit, are also attributed to one Śāntarakṣita. But whether they are from the pen of the author of the *Tattvasaṃgraha* is not beyond suspicion.

Kamalaśīla : The worthy pupil and commentator of Śāntarakṣita was Kamalaśīla. Nothing of his early life is known to us. Vidyabhusana says that he was the Professor of Tantra in the Nālandā University. He was a direct pupil and junior contemporary of Śāntarakṣita. We learn from the Tibetan sources that Bodhisattva mK'an-po-si-va-htso (Śāntarakṣita) the first Abbot of the bSam-yas, had recommended in his will on his death bed that if need be, his pupil Kamalaśīla should be invited from India. King K'ri-sroṅ-lde-btsan of Tibet (A.D. 742-797) invited Kamalaśīla to establish the Doctrine of Nāgārjuna and the standpoint of Śāntarakṣīta against the growing heresy of the followers of a Chinese Doctor of Dhyāna School, Mahāyāna Hva-san. A great council or debate was organized at bSam-yas, probably in A.D. 792 or 794. The Indian savant prevailed on the Chinese party; it was a clash between the Indian Buddhists who advocated the Gradual Path and the Chinese Buddhists who advocated the Sudden Path. But the Indian Philosopher was murdered, his kidneys were squeezed while he was lying on his bed; the murderers were, according to Bu-ston,[119] the followers of Hva-san, but according to old Tibetan chronicles, they were native heretics, the Bonpos.[120]

Kamalaśīla is the author of the *Tattvasaṃgrahapañjikā,*[121] which is a monument of his phenomenal learning, sharp wit and uncommon power of reasoning and debating. He has rendered the terse *kārikās* of the *TS* intelligible and has supplied the names of the thinkers criticized by his master. Another logical work of his is the *Nyāyabindu-pūrvapakṣa-saṃkṣepa*, extant only in Tibetan. Bu-ston attributes to Kamalaśīla a work called the

Mādhyamika-āloka and the three *Bhāvanākramas.*[122] The first *Bhāvanākrama* has been published in its original form in Roman letters along with a Tibetan translation.[123] The third of these, called *Uttara Bhāvanākrama*, also exists in Sanskrit original[124] and in Tibetan and Chinese versions.[125]

These three booklets were composed by Kamalaśīla during his stay at bSam-yas after the conclusion of the debate. They expound the way of gradual progress through meditation on truth from the standpoint of the Yogācāra-Mādhyamika. These three works deal with the threefold method of learning: (*t'os*), reflection (*bsam*), and meditation (*sgom*). Even the first text of the *Bhāvanākrama* discusses all these three aspects. The Tibetan Tenjur ascribes the following works also to the authorship of Kamalaśīla :

1. *Āryasaptaśatikā-prajñāpāramitā-ṭīkā;*
2. *Āryavajracchedikā-prajñāpāramitā-ṭīkā;*
3. *Prajñāpāramitā-hṛdayanāma-ṭīkā;*
4. *Ḍākinīvajraguhyagītināma-mahopadeśa.* He is said to have translated into Tibetan a work called *Mahāmudropadeśa-vajraguhyagīti.*

Sarvajñamitra : The Buddhist poet and monk-scholar of Kashmir named Sarvajñamitra, is known, not only from the Tibetan sources but, also from the *Rājataraṅgiṇī*, and his works extant in Sanskrit. He is the author of three short hymns in praise of Tārā. These are : the *Sragdharā-stotra*, the *Ekaviṃśati-stotra*, and the *Ārya-tārā-nāmāṣṭottara-śataka-stotra*.[126]

The *Sragdharā-stotra* is a beautiful poem.[127] *Sragdharā* is an epithet of goddess Tārā, and it is also the name of the metre in which the stotra is composed.

Tārānātha says that Bhikṣu Sarvajñamitra was a devotee of Tārā, a son-in-law of the King of Kashmir, and having given all his riches in charity, became a mendicant.[128] The *Pag-sam-Jon-zañ* states that Sarvajñamitra was a Kashmirian by birth but he was educated in Nālandā University and became the master of sciences.[129] Sarvajñamitra is famed in legends as a man of unbounded charity and virtue. The following story is told of him. On his way to the kingdom of Vajramukuṭa, Sarvajñamitra sold his person for its weight in gold which was given to a poor *brāhmaṇa* who needed it for his daughter's marriage. The buyer of the Bhikṣu was King Vajramukuṭa who wanted to kill 100 persons for a religious ritual in which he was to wash himself sitting on 100 skulls. He completed the number by purchasing Sarvajñamitra. When all the 100 persons were about to be killed, Sarvajñamitra prayed to Tārā and composed 37 stanzas in her eulogy, and all the victims were miraculously saved and taken to their homes. The King was abashed and surprised, and became a disciple of Sarvajñamitra.

This story which may not be entirely imaginary is related not only by Tārānātha, Sumpā-khan-po, but also by the commentator Jinarakṣita, a monk of the Vikramaśīla Mahāvihāra.[130]

With respect to the date of Sarvajñamitra we are more or less certain. The historian of Kashmir refers to this sage and compares him with Buddha (*jinopamaḥ*); he lived in Kashmir in the Kayya-vihāra, built by King Kayya of Lāṭa, a subordinate vassal of King Muktāpīḍa or Lalitāditya of Kashmir who ruled in the first half of the eighth century A.D. Sarvajñamitra is thus placeable in the middle of the eighth century A.D.

Vinītadeva : Among the noted scholars and commentators of the school of Dharmakīrti was Vinītadeva who probably flourished in the latter half of the eighth century A.D. According to Tārānātha,[131] he was a contemporary of King Lalitacandra, son of King Gopīcandra, and lived in the Nālandā University. Vinītadeva was the pupil of Prajñākaragupta (*cir.* 800 A.D.), the author of the *Pramāṇavārttikālaṅkāra*. Yamāri (*cir.* 800-900 A.D.) is the author of the *Pramāṇavārttikālaṅkāra-ṭīkā*, a commentary on the *Pramāṇavārttikālaṅkāra*[132] of Prajñākaragupta. This latter logician wrote an independent work also which exists in Tenjur; it is called the *Sahālambanirṇaya-siddhi*.

According to Bu-ston, Vinītadeva wrote commentaries on the 'Seven (Nyāya) Treatises'. Following works are attributed to Vinītadeva : the *Samayabhedoparacana-cakra*, which deals with the history of the eighteen sects of Early Buddhism;[133] besides this historical work, Vinītadeva wrote the *Nyāyabindu-ṭīkā*,[134] *Hetubindu-ṭīkā*, *Vādanyāya-vyākhyā*, *Saṃbandha-parīkṣā-ṭīkā*, *Ālambanaparīkṣā-ṭīkā*, and *Santānāntara-siddhi-ṭīkā*.[135] His views are criticised by Dharmottara.[136]

Among the less known Buddhist masters of the period, who wrote commentaries on the logical treatises of the school of Dharmakīrti, the following may be mentioned. The dates assigned to them are only tentative.

Devendrabuddhi : Devandrabuddhi or Devendramati (*cir.* 700 A.D.) who was asked by Dharmakīrti to write a commentary on the *Pramāṇavārttika.* But the great master was not satisfied with his pupil's performance.[137] His commentary on the *Pramāṇavārttika* exists in Tibetan collection. His pupil was Śākyamati (*cir.* 675 A.D.) who also wrote a commentary on this work which is called *Pramāṇavārttikapañjikāṭīkā.* Another scholar, who belonged to this school of commentators, was Śaṃkarānanda. According to Bu-ston,[138] he wrote commentaries on the seven treatises (i.e. seven treatises on logic by Dharmakīrti). In the *Blue Annals*[139] he appears under the name of Ānanda, and is the pupil of Dharmottara. He is the author of the following works : *Pratibandhasiddhi, Apohasiddhi; Saṃbandhaparīkṣānusāra*; and the *Pramāṇavārttikaṭīkā.* He also wrote a work called *Prajñālaṅkāra* which is quoted by the scholars of Kashmir Śaivism including Abhinavagupta and Jayaratha (see above pp. 16-17).

Mention must be made of Jinendrabuddhi or Jinendrabodhi. He wrote a "very detailed, thorough-going and clear commentary" on Diṅnāga's *Pramāṇa-samuccaya.*[140] He is also said to have written the well-known *Nyāsa* on the grammar of Pāṇini in the eighth century A.D.

Kalyāṇarakṣita: Kalyāṇarakṣita (*cir.* 800 A.D.) is known as the author of *Anyāpohasiddhi*; *Īśvarabhaṅga-kārikās*; *Sarvajñasiddhi-kārikā.*; *Śrutiparīkṣā-kārikā* and the *Bāhyārthasiddhi-kārikā.*[141] Evidently he was a great and original scholar. Another scholar of the eighth century was Ravigupta. He was born in Kashmir and had received education in Nālandā. According to Tārānātha and Sumpā, he was a great poet, dialectician and Tāntrika *paṇḍita*, and established 12 great religious institutions in his homeland and Magadha, and was a contemporary of King Bharṣa of Vārendra.[142] He is to be placed in the middle of the eighth century A.D. on the following considerations. He was the teacher of Sarvajñamitra, *cir.* middle of the eighth century A.D., and he is quoted by Jayanta Bhaṭṭa[143] (*cir.* 900 A.D.); a Ravigupta is mentioned in the inscription of Vasantasena (Gupta era, 435, corresponding to A.D. 754-755) as Sarvadaṇḍanāyaka and Mahāpratihāra.[144] Ravigupta is the author of the *Pramāṇavārttika-vṛtti*, a commentary on the 3rd chapter of the great work of Dharmakīrti, and perhaps of the *Āryā-kośa.*[145]

He wrote some Tāntrika works also.

Among the commentators of Dharmakīrti we have to mention Karṇakagomin, who is placed in the seventh century by some, and in the tenth century by others. His commentary on the first chapter with autocommentary of the *Pramāṇavārttika* has been published.[146] One of the less known commentators of Dharmakīrti, whose historical existence is vouched for by the later Buddhist and Jaina logical works, is a scholar named Śāntabhadra. He probably wrote a commentary on the *Nyāya-bindu* even before Dharmottara. He seems to have been an elder contemporary of Dharmottara and may be placed in the first quarter of the eighth century A.D. The existence of Śāntabhadra's work is attested not only by Durveka Miśra[147] but also by the *Nyāyabindu-ṭīkā-ṭippaṇa*.[148] His views are criticised by Dharmottara,[149] and Akalaṅka is also reported to have attacked his views.[150] Moreover, Durveka Miśra[151] mentions Vinītadeva and Śāntabhadra together, a fact which would suggest that the views of these two scholars were more or less identical. There is some uncertainty with respect to the date of Dharmākaradatta or Bhaṭṭa Arcaṭa. Rāhula Sāṃkṛtyāyana regards Arcaṭa as a different person (and places him in *cir.* 825 A.D.) from Dharmākaradatta (who is placed in *cir.* 700 A.D.).[152] Sukhlalji Sanghavī, however, shows that both names refer to the same person. Arcaṭa was his pre-Buddhistic name and when he became a monk, he was given the name Dharmākaradatta. His *Hetubindu-ṭīkā*-[153] has been published in the original; this text shows that its author also wrote two more works, viz. *Kṣaṇa-bhaṅgasiddhi*[154] and *Pramāṇadvitvasiddhi*.[155]

Dharmottara : The most famous and the ablest commentator of Dharmakīrti was Dharmottara. Bu-ston reports that according to some writers Dharmottara was the pupil of Vinītadeva, but "in the commentary it is said that Dharmottara was the pupil of Dharmākaradatta and Kalyāṇarakṣita."[156] The *Blue Annals* put Dharmottara in the "lineage of the Pramāṇavārttika" in between Jñānaśrīmitra and Śaṃkarānanda.[157] Jñānaśrīmitra is the teacher of Yamāri, noted above. It is curious that Tārānātha does not give Dharmottara's biography. "Although not a direct pupil of Dharmakīrti he was the sort of pupil the great master was wanting, for he not only accompanied his comments by weighty considerations of his own, but had also independent views and successful new formulations on important topics."[158]

With respect to the time and place of the logician's activity we are indebted to Kalhaṇa. The historian says that King Jayāpīḍa, one of the grand-sons of Lalitāditya, saw in a dream that a 'sun was rising in the west' and invited Dharmottara to live and teach in his court.[159] The reign of Jayāpīḍa is placed between *cir.* 770 A.D. and the closing years of the century.[160] His court was graced by other literary celebrities such as Kṣīra, Bhaṭṭa Udbhaṭa, Dāmodaragupta, and others.[161] Dharmottara can thus safely be placed in the latter half of the eighth century A.D. He did not write comments on the great work of Dharmakīrti, but has written two learned commentaries, they are the *Nyāyabindu-ṭīkā*[162] and *Pramāṇaviniścaya-ṭīkā.* He wrote the following original works: *Pramāṇa-parīkṣā* or *Laghupramāṇa-parīkṣā*),[163] *Apoha-prakaraṇa, Paraloka-siddhi,* and *Kṣaṇa-bhaṅga-siddhi.* Except the *Nyāyabindu-ṭīkā,* all the other treatises of Dharmottara are probably irrecoverably lost in Sanskrit but preserved in the Tibetan versions.

Haribhadra : According to Bu-ston, he was contemporary of King Mahīpāla.[164] King Mahīpāla I of the Pāla house is placed in the tenth century A.D. after A.D. 988.[165] This statement of Bu-ston, therefore, may not be true. Because from other sources we learn that his pupil was Buddhajñānapāda,[166] and this Buddhajñānapāda was the second spiritual teacher of Dharmapāla, and performed the consecration ceremony of the Vikramaśilā-vihāra founded by Dharmapāla (*cir.* A.D. 770-810) and became its first abbot. From the accounts of Sumpā and Tāranātha, Haribhadra appears as the first spiritual teacher of Dharmapāla.[167]

Haribhadra was a Yogācāra teacher and seems to have specialized in the Prajñāpāramitā literature. He is also known as Siṃhabhadra, and wrote commentaries on the Prajñāpāramitās. His *Abhisamayālaṅkārāloka,* is a commentary not only on the *Aṣṭasāhasrikā-prajñāpāramitā,* but also on the *Abhisamayālaṅkāra-kārikās* of Maitreyanātha, and reflects author's deep knowledge of the mysteries of the Prajñāpāramitās.[168] One unique feature of his commentary is that he utilized the *Pañcaviṃśatisāhasrikā-prajñāpāramitā* in his explanations, and in doing so, Haribhadra virtually made a recast of the *Pañcaviṃśati-sāhasrikā.*[169]

Bu-ston attributes to Haribhadra the following works:

a summary of the *Pañcaviṃśatisāhasrikā* in 8 chapters, the *Abhisamayālaṅkārāloka,* the commentary called *Sphuṭārthā*, the commentary on *Sañcaya,* called *Subodhinī,* and the *Prajñāpāramitā-bhāvanā,* etc.[170] From the *Blue Annals* we learn that the *Sphuṭārthā* was a short comment on the *Abhisamayālaṅkāra,* and the *Sañcaya* is probably the *Prajñāpāramitā-sañcaya-gathā.*[171] Haribhadra lived in the Traikuṭaka-vihāra and died in the 22nd year of Dharmapāla's reign.[172]

Early Tantrika Literature

A detailed discussion of some semi-Tāntrika and early Tāntrika texts, together with the date and contents of the *Mañjuśrīmūlakalpa,* the *Guhyasamāja,* the *Hevajratantra,* the *Jñānasiddhi,* and the *Prajñopāyaviniścaya-siddhi,* has been attempted below in the context of the development of esoteric Buddhism. The same need not be repeated here. A large number of Tāntrika Buddhist texts, Sādhanas and mystic songs, are extant in Buddhist Sanskrit, Apabhraṃśa and the Tibetan languages; their authors are mostly the Siddhas, the Tāntrika adepts and the Sahajiyā mystics.[173] The chronological succession of the eighty-four Siddhas is a matter of great confusion and controversy. It is extremely difficult, at the present state of our knowledge, to say precisely how many of these Tāntrika authors belonged to the eighth century A.D., and as such, it is equally difficult to decide the date of those works that are attributed to the so-called early Siddhas. Some Siddhas, however, seem to have flourished in the eighth century A.D. Thus Sarahapāda, Kaṃbalapāda, Indrabhūti, Nāgārjuna and Anaṅgavajra, are placeable in the eighth and early ninth century. But there were more than one Saraha, as pointed out by Cordier; likewise Tārānātha points to the existence of two or three Indrabhūtis.[174] Similarly there was an alchemist Nāgārjuna, probably different from the Siddha namesake.

To Sarahapāda are attributed as many as seven Tāntrika texts and sixteen collections of *dohās* or mystic songs.[175] Some of the works attributed to Saraha, the Ādisiddha, are : *Buddhakapāla-tantrapañjikā, Buddhakapālasādhana, Buddhakapāla-maṇḍala-vidhi, Trailokyavaśamkaralokeśvara-sādhana, Dohākośagīti, Dohākośa-nāma-caryāgīti, Dohākośopadeśagīti, Kāyakośāmṛta-vajragīti, Vākyakośa-rucirasvara-vajra-gīti, Cittako-*

śajavajragīti, Kāyavākcittamanasikāra, Dohākośamahāmudropadeśa, Dvādaśopadeśa-gāthā, Svādhiṣṭhāna-krama, Tattvopadeśa-śikharadohāgītikā, Mahāmudropadeśa-vajraguhyagīti etc.

Siddha Nāgārjuna is the author of two Sādhanas, viz., *Vajra-tārā-sādhana* and *Ekajaṭa-sādhana,* extant in Sanskrit, and collected in the *Sādhanamālā.*[176] To Nāgārjuna are attributed a large number of Tāntrika works, all extant in Tibetan. But many of them seem to be the works of the great Mādhyamika Nāgārjuna, for instance, the *Bodhicitta-vivaraṇa,*[177] the *Lokātīta-Paramārtha-Acintya-Nirupama-Stava.* This *Catuḥ-stava*[178] is usually ascribed to Nāgārjuna the Mādhyamika philosopher. The Siddha Nāgārjuna is the author of the five sections of the *Pañca-krama,*[179] its third section is attributed to Śākyamitra, said to be a contemporary of Devapāla of Bengal (*cir.* 850 A.D.). Among the works of Siddha Nāgārjuna, preserved in the Tenjur, mention may be made of the following : *Mantrālaṅkāra-sādhana, Kakṣapuṭapiṇḍīkṛtasādhana, Guhyasamājamaṇḍalavidhi, Sekacaturaprakaraṇa, Svabhāvasiddhyupadeśa, Vajrayāna-sthūlāpatti, Prajñāpāramitāhṛdayasādhana, Lokeśvarasādhana, Nīlāṃbaropasiddhi, Vajrapāṇimaṇḍalavidhi, Hayagrīvasādhana, Dharmadhātu-stotra, Kālatraya-traya-stotra, Sattvārādhana-stava, Prajñāpāramitā-stotra, Narakoddhāra-samādhibhāṣāṭikā,* etc.

King Indrabhūti of Uḍḍiyāna (Svat) who is one of the 84 Siddhas, is the author of a number of Vajrayāna works listed in the Tenjur. Some of these are *Cakrasaṃvaratantrarājasaṃvara-samuccayanāma-vṛtti, Cakrasaṃvara-stotra, Siddha-vajrayoginī-sādhana, Vajrayoginī-mantratattva-svādhiṣṭhāna-nirdeśa, Ānanda-puṣpamālā, Tattvāmṛtopadeśa, Mahāmāyā-sādhana, Sarvabuddha-yoga-nāma-tantra-pañjika, Vajrasattvopāyika, Sahajasiddhi, Mañjuśrīnāma-saṃgīti-vṛtti,*, etc. Two of of his works, the *Jñānasiddhi*[180] and the *Kurukullā-sādhana*[181] are available in Sanskrit also. To Buddhajñānapāda, a disciple of Haribhadra and first abbot of the Vikramaśilā monastery founded by Dharmapāla (*cir.* 770-810 A.D.) are attributed as many as fourteen works by Bu-ston.[182] Some of the works on the scripture of the *Guhyasamāja* by Buddhajñānapāda are the *Mukhyāgama, Samantabhadrasādhana, Ātmasādhanāvatāra, Viśva-cakra, Ratnajvālā, Mahāmūlajñāna, Gāthākośa, Mukti-tilaka-caturthāvatāra, Maṅgala-vyākhyā,* and works on magic.

In the *Blue Annals* (I, p. 367) Buddhajñānapāda is described as 'a *paṇḍita* learned in all the branches of knowledge.' Nothing certain can be said about the date of the composition of the *Caṇḍa-mahāroṣaṇa-tantra,*[183] the *Cakrasaṃbhāra-tantra,*[184] and the *Tārā-tantra.*[185] A large number of *stotras* and *dhāraṇis* seems to have been composed during this period. Emperor Harṣa composed morning prayer in praise of Buddha, called *Suprabhāta-stotra.*[186] The poet Vajradatta, a contemporary of King Devapāla, in early ninth century, composed the *Lokeśvara-śataka,* in praise of Avalokiteśvara.[187] S.C. Vidyābhūṣaṇa enumerates as many as ninety-six works on Tārā, extant in Tibetan collection, many of them may have been produced during our period.[188] The *Ekādaśamukhaṃ,* a *dhāraṇi* of Avalokita, is a work of sixth century A.D. and was rendered into Chiense by Hsüan-tsang in A.D. 656.[189] To the same period may be assigned the *Hayagrīvavidyā.*[190] The *Sarva-tathāgatādhiṣṭhāna - sattvāvalokana - buddhakṣetra - sandarśana-vyūha,* translated into Chinese by I-tsing (in A.D. 701) is also a work of the sixth century A.D.[191] A large number of Buddhist texts were translated into Tibetan and Chinese during the seventh and eighth centuries A.D. Mention has already been made of some translators and their works. Hsüan-tsang who died in 664 A.D. is reported to have translated into Chinese 74 works from among the Sanskrit books brought by him from India.[192] I-tsing who died in 713 A.D. translated 56 works, of which as many as 19 works are concerned with the Vinaya of the Sarvāstivāda.[193] In A.D. 654, Hsüan-tsang wrote to his Indian friend Jñānaprabha, the following words. "Among the Sūtras and Śāstras that I, Hsüan-tsang, had brought with me, I have already translated the *Yogācāra-bhūmi-śāstra* and other works in all 30 volumes. The *Kośa* and the *Nyāyā-nusāra-śāstra* are not yet fully translated. They will certainly be completed this year."[194] Among the Indian scholars who went to China and translated Buddhist scriptures into Chinese, we must mention Bodhiruci also called Dharmaruci (*cir.* 600-650 A.D.). During his stay for 20 years in China where he died, Bodhiruci translated 55 texts, including the Ratnakūṭa class of Sūtras.[195] An important Tāntrika text, namely the *Mahāvairocana-abhisaṃbodhi,* was brought to China by a Central Asian Buddhist monk, Śubhākarasiṃha by name, who died in 735 A.D.[196]

The most famous teachers of Tāntrika Buddhism in China were Amoghavajra and Vajrabodhi.[197] Vajrabodhi was a graduate of Nālandā University and perhaps also of the Valabhī University, and was a Tripiṭakācārya and a master of Tāntrika Buddhism. He travelled to Ceylon and went to China where he died in 732 A.D. having translated into Chinese 11 Tāntrika texts.[198]

His pupil Amoghavajra was a *brāhmaṇa* of Northern India. He began his journey in 741 A.D. and went to Ceylon via Java, from Canton in China, where he had proceeded along with his teacher, Vajrabodhi. In Ceylon he was honoured by King Śilāmegha in 742 A.D., and was taught by Ācārya Samantabhadra of Ceylon. It seems that Tāntrika Buddhism had established itself in Siṃhala before the eighth century A.D. For Samantabhadra is said to have performed the ceremony of Vajradhātu and Garbhadhātu maṇḍalas and to have taught the secrets of the five *abhiṣekas*. Amoghavajra collected more than 500 Tāntrika texts, Sūtras, Śāstras and other accessory texts. He also visited India and returned to China in A.D. 746.[199] According to one of Amoghavajra's letters, he had translated 77 works between 746 and 771 A.D. He died in 774 and the total number of works rendered into Chinese by Amoghavajra is said to be 108.[200]

The works of Thonmi Sambhoṭa, Śāntarakṣita, Kamalaśīla and his party of Indian *paṇḍitas,* have been alluded to in the preceding pages. According to Shyuki Yoshimura,[201] the catalogue of Den-dKarma, which is the oldest Tibetan catalogue, had been compiled in A.D. 824. In this catalogue 736 books are listed; 8 books were translated from the Chinese but the rest of them from Sanskrit. The catalogue includes, among other books, the three *Bhāvanākramas* of Kamalaśīla. Tucci, however, doubts the antiquity of this catalogue.[202]

Chapter VIII

BUDDHIST PHILOSOPHY AND DIALECTICS

Sects and Schools :

It seems that some of the eighteen sects of Hīnayāna had disappeared during this period. I-tsing mentions 'four principal schools of continuous tradition' in which are grouped the eighteen sects of ancient days. These four *nikāyas* were:

1. *Ārya-Mahāsāṃghika-Nikāya* : It was divided into seven sects and its Tripiṭaka consisted of three lacs of *ślokas*.

2. *Ārya-Sthavira-Nikāya* : It had three sub-divisions, and its Tripiṭaka was of the same length as that of the Mahāsāṃghika school.

3. *Ārya-Mūlasarvāstivāda-Nikāya* : It had four sub-sects and the strength of its Tripiṭaka was also three lacs of *ślokas*.

4. *Ārya-Sammitīya-Nikāya* : It had four sub-divisions and its Tripiṭaka consisted of two lacs of *ślokas*.

There were several different traditions concerning the origin and growth of these sects, but their position in the seventh century was as described above. "In accordance with several views and traditions, the Tripiṭakas of various sects differ from one another."[1]

I-tsing could not ascertain which of these four *nikāyas* should be included in Hīnayāna or in Mahāyāna. The special feature of the Mahāyānists was that they studied the Mahāyāna Sūtras and worshipped the Boddhisattvas; Hīnayānists did not do so. Mahāyāna had two (philosophical) divisions : the Mādhyamika and the Yoga (Yogācāra, Vijñānavāda). The Mādhyamikas held that "what is commonly called existence is in reality non-existence, and every object is but an empty show, like an illusion." The followers of Yogācāra affirmed that "there exist no outer things in reality, but only inward thoughts, and all things exist only in the mind." Both these systems were in accordance with the 'noble doctrine'; both lead us to Nirvāṇa; both were prosperous in India and did not differ from each other in essential points.[2]

I-tsing further reports that the Mahāyānists and the Hīnayānists had a common code of discipline (*vinaya*); the basic principles, like the four noble verities, and five groups of offences were common to both. Both the systems had for their aim the destruction of passions and the salvation of beings. This report is in substantial agreement with what Hsüan-tsang had observed some years before. Hsüan-tsang found that the Hīnayāna and the Mahāyāna monks lived in the same *vihāras* at Jālandhara, Mathurā, Ayodhyā, Vṛji country and Kanauj; similarly, there were 'Mahāyānists of the Sthavira School' at Buddha-Gayā, Kaliṅga, Bharoch and Surat.[3] The spirit of catholicity is evidenced from a few passages in the *Bodhicaryāvatāra* where the Buddhists are advised to look on Mahāyāna and Hīnayāna with equal favour.[4]

On the contrary, evidence is not wanting to the point that bitter quarrels were going on between the followers of Hīnayāna and Mahāyāna. We learn from the biography of Hsüan-tsang that a South Indian *brāhmaṇa*, an old scholar of the Hīnayāna, Prajñāgupta by name, had composed a treatise in 700 verses "against the Great Vehicle", and that Hsüan-tsang had to compose a similar polemical work in 1,600 verses in order to refute the same. The book written by Hsüan-tsang was entitled "the destruction of heresy." Thus the Sammitīya sect, to which Prajñāgupta belonged, was treated as heretical.[5]

The Hīnayāna monks of Orissa are seen ridiculing emperor Harṣa for the latter's patronage of Nālandā monastery, the chief centre of Mahāyāna. According to them the monks of Nālandā University were 'heretics', their doctrine was a system of "sky flower" which "was not delivered by Buddha." On being requested by Harṣa, the Chancellor of Nālandā sent Sāgaramati, Prajñāraśmi, Siṃharaśmi and Hsüan-tsang to refute the views of the Orissan monks.[6] Elsewhere, Harṣa[7] is seen complaining about one Devasena, 'the chief Sthavira of the priests' who, by advancing "his strange opinions, ever opposed the Great Vehicle."

Śāntideva also lends a glimpse into this old controversy between Hīnayāna and Mahāyāna.[8] Likewise, Kamalaśīla declares that the path of the *śrāvakas* cannot lead to complete destruction of passions because it does not destroy false views.[9]

Controversies within the Madhyamaka School

Although Nāgārjuna had perfected the Mādhyamika system by one stroke of his genius, the Mādhyamika dialectics remained open to difficulties.[10] Towards the middle of the sixth century A.D. this school was split into two branches: Prāsaṅgika and Svātantrika. Bhāvaviveka[11] was the founder of the Svātantrika school, while Buddhapālita[12] held the Prāsaṅgika standpoint. The controversies between these two Mādhyamika philosophers thus inaugurated a new phase in the history of the school, and they were called "the Mādhyamikas adhering to the different factions." The followers of the Prāsaṅgika branch were also known as "the Lokaprasiddhi-vargācāri Mādhyamikas."[13]

According to Bu-ston, Buddhapālita and Candrakīrti were the principal protagonists of the Prāsaṅgika branch, while Bhāvaviveka was the head of the Svātantrika branch of the Mādhyamikas. According to another Tibetan annalist, Khai ḍub, Buddhapālita explained the theory of Nāgārjuna and Āryadeva from the Prāsaṅgika standpoint: thereafter, Bhavya (Bhāvaviveka) refuted the comments made by Buddhapālita and founded the Svātantrika branch. Thereafter, Jñānagarbha wrote a Svātantrika work called *Satyadvaya-vibhaṅga* or *Mādhyamika Satya-dvaya.*[14] This Jñānagarbha seems to have been a disciple of Bhāvaviveka and a continuator of the Svātantrika tradition. But Bu-ston includes him among the "Yogācāra-Mādhyamikas." There was yet another scholar belonging to the tradition of Bhavya, he is Avalokitavrata, the author of the *Prajñāpradīpaṭīkā*, a sub-commentary on the commentary on the *Madhyamakaśāstra* by Bhavya.[15] The exact dates of Jñānagarbha and Avalokitavrata are not known.

The essential point of difference between the Prāsaṅgika and the Svātantrika branches of the Mādhyamika school seems to lie in the method of demonstration. Buddhapālita adopts the method of *reductio ad absurdum*, for him the essence of the Mādhyamika doctrine consisted in the method of relentless dialectics. This view of his was attacked by Bhāvaviveka; the latter seems to have believed in the efficacy of adducing independent arguments in logical reasoning.[16] Kajiyama points out that the problem which divided the Mādhyamikas was "whether the system of the relative knowledge can be, so far as the phenomenal world is concerned, recognized as valid or not, though it is always delusive from the absolute point of view."[17] It is known that the early Mādhyamika Doctors regarded *paramārtha* (Absolute) as entirely transcendental. It could be affirmed only by a relentless denial of the *saṃvṛti* (relative). This standpoint is upheld by the Prāsangika; Buddhapālita and Candrakīrti hold, along with Nāgārjuna and Deva that a true Mādhyamika can have no thesis of his own.[18] The view is criticised by Bhāvaviveka, who "tended to recognize the validity of relative knowledge"[19] and therefore held the Absolute to be immanent in the phenomenal. He had a realistic bias as would appear from Hsüan-tsang's remark that Bhāvaviveka externally wore the Sāṃkhya garb, though internally he was propagating the tenets of Nāgārjuna.[20] He also seems to have shared Sautrāntika psychology;[21] indeed the Tibetans describe him as a 'Mādhyamika Sautrāntika.'[22] His denial of the phenomenal things is invariably qualified by "from the standpoint of the Absolute."[23]

Stcherbatsky has very aptly described Candrakīrti as a mighty champion of the purely negative method of establishing Monism. It is perplexing that Hsüan-tsang and I-tsing do not mention this philosopher unless he is the same as Candrapāla. He seems to have flourished early in the seventh century A.D. and is the author of the *Madhyamakāvatāra* and *Prasannapadā*; this latter work is the best commentary on the *Madhyamakaśāstra* of Nāgārjuna, written fro m the Prāsaṅgika standpoint.

Candrakīrti supports Buddhapālita and criticises Bhāvaviveka. In fact, he became the chief representative of the Prāsaṅgika branch and attacked all Buddhist and non-Buddhist systems through the method of *reductio ad absurdum*. He considered Bhāvaviveka to be inconsistent although a Mādhyamika; the latter is attacked also for his desire to exhibit his skill as a logician; further, Bhāvaviveka is charged with inaccuracy in formulating the opponent's position.[24] Candrakīrti also disapproves Bhāvaviveka's view that the Śrāvakas and the Pratyekabuddhas could also obtain release without absolute realization of *śūnyatā*.[25]

He is also opposed to Bhāvaviveka's use of "from the standpoint of the Absolute" in denying the phenomenal, because the phenomenal world is self-contradictory, there is no logicality in it.[26] The Absolute (*paramārtha*) is nothing but Noble Silence, for it transcends illogicality of the phenomenal world and has no relation with the latter.[27]

One of the most important Mādhyamika thinkers who was also a religious poet of unequalled merit was Śāntideva. There is little philosophy in his *Śikṣāsamuccaya*, but the ninth chapter of his *Bodhicaryāvatāra* is a masterly piece of metaphysical literature of Mahāyāna. That Śāntideva was a Mādhyamika is clear from this chapter which expounds the doctrine of *śūnyatā* on the lines of Nāgārjuna. His commentator, Prajñākaramati also says that this chapter was written from the standpoint of the Mādhyamika. Śāntideva does not appear to deal with the comparative merits of the views of the Prāsaṅgika and the Svātantrika Mādhyamikas. But he himself seems to adopt the Prāsaṅgika standpoint. The main outline of his thought is identical with that of Nāgārjuna. The doctrine of two truths is stated at the beginning of the ninth chapter : the *paramārtha* is *tattva* which is transcendental to intellect; the *saṃvṛti* is equated to intellect.[28] He does not say anything of Bhāvaviveka's classification of *paramārtha* into *aparyāyaparamārtha* and *paryāyaparamārtha*, and of *saṃvṛti* into *tathya-saṃvṛti* and *mithyā-saṃvṛti*, nor does he refer to Candrakīrti's division of *saṃvṛti* into *lokasaṃvṛti* and *alokasaṃvṛti*.[29] But his commentator does refer to this latter division of Candrakīrti and elucidates the views of Śāntideva by quotations from the works of Nāgārjuna and Candrakīrti. Without realizing *śūnyatā* 'the destroyer of suffering', Nirvāṇa cannot be realized; but in order to gain spiritual merit a Bodhisattva has to resort to *saṃvṛti*.[30]

Mādhyamika Critique of Abhidharma

Candrakīrti and Śāntideva have directed polemics against their Hīnayāna brethren. The chief points attacked are concerning the (i) genuineness of the scripture, (ii) *dharmas* and (iii) causality. Śāntideva is preoccupied with answering to the criticisms of the Sarvāstivāda-Vaibhāṣika against the Śūnyavāda and its scriptures, while Candrakīrti devotes his energies largely to the refutation of causality and the realistic categories, the *dharmas*.

The fundamental dictum of Śūnyavāda that truth consists in the perception of the voidness (*śūnyatā*) of all *dharmas* as well as of the self is questioned by the Sarvāstivādin, and the debate follows.

Sarvāstivādin : "The perception of Truth leads to liberation, but what sense is there in perceiving voidness ?"

Śūnyavādin : "Because (i) that is the way to enlightenment, and (ii) that is laid down in the scriptures"[31] in fact, "there is no other way to Bodhi."[32]

Sarvāstivādin : "The Mahāyāna scriptures are not authentic."

Śūnyavādin : "How are your scriptures authentic ?"

Sarvāstivādin : "The authenticity of our scriptures is accepted by both the parties (by us and by you)."

Śūnyavādin : "This means that originally and prior to our acceptance, your scripture was not authentic."[33] "It, therefore, follows that you should respect the Mahāyāna scriptures just as we respect yours; our scripture is authentic for the same reasons by which yours has become authentic."[34]

Moreover, if you argue that the authenticity of the Mahāyāna scriptures is controversial, then we say that your scriptures too are not recognized by the heretics; further, there is controversy among the various sects of Buddhism itself, and each sect differs somehow from other sects.[35]

Again, the perception of the voidness of things is essential for uprooting passions; it is the essential ground upon which the tree of spiritual life stands. If it is refuted and passions remained undestroyed, Nirvāṇa will be impossible of attainment.[36] If it be admitted that the perception of (four noble truths) results in liberation, then the latter should follow immediately, which is not the case in fact. For it is known that even the Arhats who had destroyed their passions, had to reap the fruits of their deeds. It is evident from this that the view that Arhats are devoid of craving is incorrect. In other words, even Arhats are possessed of ignorance and therefore of craving. This is proved by the fact that craving rises from feeling, and Arhats do have feeling (*vedanā*). Thus when craving (*tṛṣṇā*) is not destroyed, the mind will continue to stick to some support here or there. It is therefore necessary to realize *śūnyatā*; without realising *śūnyatā*, bondage of mind continues to recur after occasional *samādhi*. Thus the scriptures of Mahāyāna (which teach *śūnyatā*) are quite authentic inasmuch as they lead to salvation by means of the perception of the voidness.[37]

If you say that only that scripture is authentic which is in the form of Sūtras, then the Mahāyāna Sūtras have all the same claim to authenticity, for they too, like your scriptures, are in the form of Sūtras. It is also possible to regard the words of the Buddha, scattered in so many scriptures, as one single aphorism. You cannot reasonably disregard the Mahāyāna texts only because they are deep and unintelligible to you.[38]

It is because of the salutary consequences of Emptiness that a Bodhisattva (taking his stand on relative truth) lives in the world for the good of beings, but is not defiled by the world. It is, therefore, unreasonable to find faults with *śūnyatā*, all those who wish to treat themselves spiritually must realize *śūnyatā*. It is the destroyer of both *kleśāvaraṇa* and *jñeyāvaraṇa* and leads to omniscience. *Śūnyatā* is the destroyer of suffering, why to dread it.[39]

Candrakīrti and Śāntideva have directed a sustained criticism against the Abhidharma categories and the law of causation.[40] It is well known that the Sarvāstivādins are realists and pluralists;[41] they believe in the existence of 75 *dharmas* (of mind and matter); three of these are regarded as 'incomposite' (*asaṃskṛta*) which are free from the laws of causation; the remaining 72 *dharmas* are 'composite' (*saṃskṛta*) and are subject to the laws of causation. These laws bear the general name of dependent origination (*pratītyasamutpāda*).[42] The realistic Buddhists further maintain that (i) no effect can ever be produced by a single cause,[43] and that (ii) the cause is different from the effect.[44] The Mādhyamikas refute these views from the Śūnyavāda standpoint and show their untenable position. Candrakīrti, apparently referring to the Abhidharma categories of *skandhas*, *dhātus* and *āyatanas*, says that 'the *yogīs* who abide in the vision of emptiness do not at all apprehend the *skandhas*, elements and sense-fields as if they were something in themselves."[45]

Buddha is reported to have stated : "Three are the phenomenalizing characteristics (*saṃskṛta lakṣaṇāni*) of all phenomena (*saṃskṛta*) : of the *saṃskṛta* there is origin (*utpāda*), cessation (*vyaya*) and change of state *sthityanyathātvaṃ*[46]. The Mādhyamikā points out that each one of these marks is not a complete definition of the 'composite'. For then we will have the difficulty of the origin of a thing that has no duration or cessation, of a thing that lasts but has no origination or decay, or of a thing which ceases to exist but was not born at all.[47] All the three characteristics cannot be applied to a thing simultaneously.[48] A thing cannot have contradictory characteristics like origination and cessation at the same time, nor successively.[49]

Moreover, the doctrine of the momentariness accepted by all the upholders of the theory of *saṃskṛta dharmas* also presents difficulties. If a thing is momentary, a point-instant, it exists for a moment only, how could it be said to originate, endure and cease ? The different moments are different, discreet entities. Under these conditions it is unintelligible to say that this originates and that endures.[50]

When the reality of 'composite (*saṃskṛta*) *dharma* is disproved and its marks (*lakṣaṇas*) also proved to be false (*mṛṣā*), the 'incomposite' (*asaṃskṛta*) too cannot be available. The realistic Buddhists have posited the existence of three *asaṃskṛta dharmas*: *ākāśa*, *pratisaṃkhyānirodha* and *apratisaṃkhyānirodha*. They are supposed to be permanent, unchanging realities beyond the realm of causes and conditions. Candrakīrti points out that *asaṃskṛta* is related to *saṃskṛta*, i.e. they are relative to each other, none without the other. When the Lord said that 'this depends on that', he meant that there is nothing in itself, everything is relative (void).[51]

A non-existent thing cannot be eternal; an eternal thing is non-existent, like a sky-flower. *Ākāśa* (space) is the absence of form; there is nothing like *ākāśa*; the same can be said of the two kinds of *nirodhas*.[52]

The realist's view that the things exist in past, present and future, and that they are causally connected, is also misleading. Āryadeva had declared that the present does not originate out of the past, Candrakīrti adds that what does not exist originally, cannot give rise to anything. In other words, the past is non-existent, the birth of the present out of the past is nonsensical.[53] The theory of the existence of future elements is unreasonable.[54] The Sarvāstivādins, Vaibhāṣikas and Sautrāntikas as also the Vijñānavādins hold the theory of *asatkāryavāda*.[55]

Śāntideva declares that nothing originates from causes nor without causes.[56] Prajñākaramati sums up the arguments. (1) The effect (*kārya*) does not originate out of itself (*svataḥ*), for before origination it does not exist; what is non-existent in itself cannot produce itself. (2) Nor does it originate from another (*parataḥ*) for if a thing could spring out from what is foreign to it, anything could come out from anything which is never the case. (3) Nor a thing could be produced by both (*dvābhyāṃ*); if it be urged that a thing originates from both, by itself and by what is other to it, then again the above two difficulties will come up.[57]

The Traikālyavādins (i.e. the Sarvāstivādins) say that "by force of causes and conditions, the elements proceed from the future to the present and from the present to the past. This change in time is called origination, duration and cessation."[58] Śāntideva points out that an element neither comes from some other place, nor it stays, nor even does it go to anywhere. As a matter of fact what these fools have taken to be real (*satyataḥ*) is no better than illusion.[59] To hold that an element comes, stays and goes, amounts to saying that it is a permanent entity. But you (Vaibhāṣika) hold that what exists (*saṃskṛta dharma*) is impermanent and not eternal. Thus there is contradiction in your theory. A thing which exists in three points of time cannot be *saṃskṛta* or impermanent.[60] Other arguments advanced are similar to those of Nāgārjuna.[61]

Mādhyamika Critique of Vijñānavāda

Metaphysical controversies between the two well-known schools of Mahāyāna philosophy formed one of the principal features of Buddhistic culture during the 7th and 8th centuries. It is the trenchant criticism of Candrakīrti and Śāntideva that brings out the difficulties of the Vijñānavāda and its differences from the Mādhyamika.

The Vijñānavādin asserts : (1) *vijñāna* (Idea or Mind) is real, not apparent; its nature is pure consciousness; it is self-luminous and self-cognisable; (2) *vijñāna* alone is real, not the object; the external world is unreal; objects of perception arise in mind which latter exists *ab aeterno*, and are mere reflected images.[62]

The Mādhyamika says that the texts[63] which teach the sole reality of mind (*citta*) were taught by Buddha only as a means to the doctrine of *śūnyatā*; they are only elementary teachings and not final truths.[64]

The Vijñānavādin controverts the middle way (*madhyamā pratipada*) taught by the Buddha, inasmuch as he accepts the existence of *vijñāna* and denies that of objects. Such a view is not in keeping with the real *madhyamā pratipada* which latter teaches the transcendence of both 'is' and 'is not'.[65]

The principal criticism centres round the doctrine of the self-cognizability (*sva-saṃvitti*) of Mind or Consciousness. "The mind is empty like illusion, how can it cognize itself at all ? Moreover, the Lord has declared that 'the mind does not perceive mind' just as a sword cannot cut itself."[66]

As has been said in the *Ratnacūḍasūtra*, even the sharpest sword cannot cut itself; the finger-tips cannot be touched by the same finger-tips; like-wise the *citta* cannot see itself."[67] Therefore, the theory that *citta* is self-conscious is not correct.

Furthermore, in the absence of objects, the *citta* cannot function;[68] if the objects are non-existent as the Yogācārins hold, what is cognized at all ?[69]

If you argue that the mind cognizes itself just as a lamp illuminates itself, then we reply that this analogy is incorrect, because the lamp is not illuminated (since the lamp is not hidden by darkness), the question of its illumination does not arise.[70]

An entity cannot be at the same time an 'action' (*krīyā*) as well as 'agent' (*kāraka*); Mind cannot be both knower and the known, because two different characteristics cannot apply to a single entity at a moment. Therefore, in truth the self-cognition of mind cannot be proved.[71]

"The lamp is luminous"—this is known through the mind (we see and know that lamp is luminous); but how do you know that "the mind is luminous ?" Whether the mind be luminous or not luminous, this thesis, in spite of your repeated assertions in the absence of any knower, is false, even as the beautiful gestures of the daughter of a barren woman.[72] If it be said that mind is bereft of self-consciousness then, memory will not be possible, the reply is : We recall the knowledge of an object when we experience it, because there is an invariable relation between the object of experience and its knowledge.[73] The idealist then advances the following argument. The fact that the perfected men (*yogins*) visualise the *vijñāna* of different times and places, leads us to conclude that *vijñāna* perceives *vijñāna*. But this reasoning too is not correct, for if by means of *siddhāñjana* one sees a treasure-trove buried in the earth, that treasure-trove cannot be regarded as the *siddhāñjana* itself. In other words, the two *vijñānas* are different and not identical, one is the 'knower' the other is the 'known'.[74] We don't deny the (phenomenal) reality of what is seen, heard or known; what we deny is the assumption of those who take phenomenality as ultimate reality, because such an assumption leads to suffering.[75]

The Vijñānavādin points out that the Mādhyamika interpretation of *śūnyatā* is an unwarranted extremism. *Śūnyatā* is not the total negation of everything, but of the duality of subject and object. According to Sthiramati,[76] *śūnyatā* is real as well as unreal (*yat śūnyaṃ sat, yena śūnyaṃ asat*). *Śūnyatā* is *dharmatā*, and this *dharmatā* is real in so far as it represents the real existence of *dharmas*. But it is also unreal, in so far as it consists in the negation of the duality of subject and object.[77] This constructed subject-object world (of duality) is unreal; but this does not make the *abhūtaparikalpa* unreal, because that is the substratum for the unreal duality of subject and object.[78]

Post-Vasubandhu Developments in Vijñānavāda

Out of Vasubandhu's school arose teachers, like Diṅnāga, Dharmapāla, Sthiramati, Śīlabhadra and Dharmakīrti, who are placed between the sixth and the seventh centuries. Of these, Dharmapāla is said to have been the most famous propagator of the Vijñānavāda tenets as expounded in Vasubandhu's *Vijñaptimātratā-siddhi*.[79] This work had been commented and annotated by as many as ten authorities, all of whom did not agree *in toto*.[80] These commentaries and counter-commentaries were melted into one, and translated into Chinese by Hsüan-tsang in A.D. 661.[81] But he seems to have followed chiefly[81] the interpretations of Dharmapāla. His report of the views of these commentators, therefore, "may not be exactly in accordance with the original authors' purports".[82] The crucial verse of Vasubandhu's *Triṃśikā*, which was the centre of controversies between the Vijñānavāda philosophers of the post-Vasubandhu period, runs thus :—

vijñānapariṇāmo'yaṃ vikalpo yadvikalpyate /
tena tannāsti (,) *tenedaṃ sarvaṃ vijñaptimātrakam* //[83]

The meaning of the *kārikā*, in simple English, is "This construct (=constructed world, the world of thought and constructs) is a transformation of *vijñāna*. Hence what is constructed has no reality. Therefore, all this is only *vijñāptimātra*".

Poussin, following the interpretation of Hsüan-tsang, translates the above verse as follows : "The development of *vijñāna* is the thought and what is thought, 'that which thinks and the thing which is thought'. Consequently, that (*tat* = *ātman* and *dharmas*) does not exist. Hence all this is *vijñapti* and nothing else." Commenting upon this verse, Poussin further observes that on Hsüan-tsang's interpretation, *pariṇāma* becomes real transformation after the manner of the Sāṃkhya *prakṛti*, and the diversified world of thought comes to be real in the same sense in which the world of *vikṛti* is real for the Sāṃkhya. On the other hand, the external object and the self become unreal construct. *Vikalpa* is the '*darśanabhāga*' and its object (*yadvikalpyate*) is the '*nimitta-bhāga*'. More clearly, *darśanabhāga* is the *grāhakacitta* and *nimittabhāga* is the *grāhya citta.*

Commenting upon the *kārikā* xvii of the *Triṃśikā*, Sthiramati says :

Yo'yaṃ vijñānapariṇāmastrividho' nantaramabhihitaḥ so'yaṃ vikalpaḥ. Adhyāropitārthākāraḥ traidhātukaścittacaitta vikalpa ucyate. Yathoktaṃ, 'abhūtaparikalpastu cittacaittastridhātukaḥ.

Tena trividhena vikalpenālayavijñāna kliṣṭamanaḥ pravṛttivijñāna svabhāvena sa saṃprayogena yadvikalpyate bhājanamātmā skandha-dhātvāyatana rūpa-śabdādikaṃ vastu tan nāstītyataḥ sa vijñānapariṇāmo vikalpa ucyate'.

According to Sthiramati the punctuation should be after '*vikalpaḥ*' in the first line of the *kārikā* and after '*nāsti*' in the second line. According to this interpretation the development of *vijñāna* is the *vikalpa* and that which is imagined by this imagination does not exist. *Vikalpa* is equal to *traidhātuka cittacaitta*, which is *adhyāropitārthākāra;* it is equal to (1) *ālayavijñāna*, (ii) *kliṣṭamanaḥ* and six *pravṛtti vijñānas*. *Loka*, *ātmā*, *skandha*, *dhātu*, and *āyatana* are the *arthākāras* (forms of things) which are superimposed (*adhyāropita*).[84]

Sthiramati believed in three aspects of *vijñāna*, viz. *vijñānasvabhāva* or *svābhāvika-bhāga* or *saṃvittibhāga*, the original and fundamental reality, and its two-fold transformation, *darśanabhāga* and *nimitta-bhāga*. Dharmapāla added a fourth one, *svasaṃvitti-saṃvittibhāga*; Nanda believed in only two and rejected *saṃvitti-bhāga*. All these scholars believed in the unreality of the superimposed world of things but accepted the reality of the constructing mind. They differed only in distinguishing the different phases of the transformation (*pariṇāma*). Takakusu observed that 'the assumption of the separate reality of the eight consciousnesses is Dharmapāla's special tenet, and nowhere else in Buddhism can it be seen not even in Hīnayāna'.[85]

From Poussin we learn that the Kouei-ki commentary on the *Viṃśatikā* states that before Asaṅga two *bhāgas* (of *vijñāna*) were recognized, viz. *darśana-bhāga* and *nimitta-bhāga*, of which *pratyakṣa* takes place. After Asaṅga, Diṅnāga distinguished three *bhāgas*, viz. *nimitta*, *darśana*, and *sva-saṃvitti-bhāga*, which are *pratyakṣa*. Dharmapāla distinguished 4 *bhāgas*, of which the last two *sva-saṃvitti* and *sva-saṃvitti-saṃvitti* are *pratyakṣa*.[86]

The testimony of this Chinese source is confirmed by the *Pramāṇa-samuccaya* of Diṅnāga, a verse from which is found quoted in the *Nyāyamañjari* of Jayanta Bhaṭṭa.[87] The verse runs thus :

yadābhāsaṃ prameyaṃ tat pramāṇaphalate puṇaḥ /
grāhakākārasaṃvittyostrayaṃ nātaḥ pṛthak kṛtam //[88]

The three aspects of *vijñāna* thus are, according to Diṅnāga, (i) object known (*prameya*), (ii) knowing mind (*pramāṇa*), and (iii) knowledge (*pramāṇa-phala*). The first is *nimitta*, the second is *darśana* and the third is *svasaṃvitti* of Sthiramati's view noted above.

Growth of Critical Philosophy

In order to appreciate (i) the critical philosophy of Dharmakīrti and to ascertain (ii) the correct philosophical standpoint of Śāntarakṣita and Kamalaśīla, it is necessary to discuss the main trends in the evolution of Buddhist thought up to the seventh century A.D.

Sautrāntika School : The origins of this school are traceable to the fourth Buddhist Council in the time of Kaniṣka in the first century A.D. According to the Chinese tradition, the first Doctor of the Sautrāntika school was Kumāralāta or Kumāralabdha. He was a contemporary of Nāgārjuna, Aśvaghoṣa and Āryadeva.[89] Tibetan tradition also makes him a Sautrāntika Ācārya.[90] His work, *Kalpanāmaṇḍitikā*,[91] bears witness to the fact that he branched off from the Sarvāstivāda, and in fact Doctors of Sarvāstivāda are praised in it.[92] P.V. Bapat points out that "the views ascribed by the *Vibhāṣa* to the Dārṣṭāntikas are those ascribed by *Abhidharmakośa* to the Sautrāntikas.[93]

According to Przyluski, Kumāralāta, the author of *Dārṣṭāntika-paṅkti* (a portion of the *Kalpanāmaṇḍitikā*) is known also as the Dārṣṭāntikācārya and Mūlācārya.[94] The possibility of the Dārṣṭāntikas being a branch of the Sautrāntikas is by no means ruled out.[95]

The views of the Sautrāntikas are referred to by Vasubandhu,[96] Bhāvaviveka,[97] Candrakīrti,[98] Śaṅkarācārya,[99] Haribhadra,[100] and Mādhvācārya.[101]

The Sautrāntikas were critical realists as distinguished from the Vaibhāṣikas who were dogmatic realists. Their basic tenets were:

(i) Mind knows itself, just as a lamp renders itself manifest.[102]

(ii) The external objects exist, their denial is without any proof. Their existence is proved by (a) inference, e.g. nourishment is inferred from a thriving look, nationality from language, emotion from its expression, etc. Their existence is further proved by (b) the fact that consciousness manifests itself in duality; if the objects were a manifestation of consciousness, then they should appear as consciousness and not as objects. To say that consciousness appears as external objects would be absurd if the latter did not exist. How can the mind appear in the form of a non-entity?[103]

(iii) Destruction has no cause; things are perishable by their nature; they are not transitory (*anitya*) but they are momentary (*kṣaṇika*); past and future do not exist.[104]

Two important points emerge out of the above views: (1) the Sautrāntikas started a 'critical realism' by declaring the incapability of sense-perception in ascertaining the external things which do exist, (2) by so doing they also assumed that the external is something-in-itself, a thing in itself.[105] The net result of these speculations was the emergence of logic. This is seen in Vasubandhu, who was a Vaibhāṣika with strong Sautrāntika leaning. He wrote three logical treatises[106] on *vāda* (disputation), and Buddhist logic is the outcome of these disputations. It was the critical outlook of the Saūtrāntikas that influenced the growth of Buddhist Idealism and led its upholders to make a compromise with critical realists.

The Sautrāntikas seem to have liked logic and metaphysics more than the scriptural authority (Sūtras).[107] The historicity of Śrīlabdha as a notable 'Sautrāntika Śāstra Master' is attested not only by Hsüan-tsang but also by Tārānātha.[108] Yaśomitra, the commentator of the *Abhidharmakośa*[109], was perhaps a Sautrāntika philosopher.

Diṅnāga : The critical school of Buddhist philosophy, which climaxed during our period in the works of Dharmakīrti and Śāntarakṣita, was really inaugurated by Diṅnāga, "the founder of Buddhist Logic, and one of the foremost figures in the history of Indian philosophy."[110] Stcherbatsky[111] recognized in him not only "a comprehensive system of critical philosophy", but also "a most excellent achievement of Indian mind." The sharpness of his insight and the soundness of his critical logic were so great that "no praise seems too high for him. Indeed he may fittingly be styled as the first and last of Indian logicians."[112]

Diṅnāga is represented as a pupil of Vasubandhu. Frauwallner, however, suggests that he may not have been a personal pupil of Vasubandhu.[113] Diṅnāga was a south Indian *brāhmaṇa* born in Kāñcī, was originally a Hīnayānist and later became a Mahāyānist and devoted to the study of the Science of Logic and propagation of the Yogācāra.[114]

Diṅnāga has been placed by modern writers in the fifth century A.D., mainly on the ground that he was a pupil of Vasubandhu[115]. It is, however, possible to place him in the first half of the sixth century A.D., inasmuch as his direct pupil Īśvarasena (*cir.* 600 A.D.) was the teacher of Dharmakīrti (*cir.* 580-650 A.D.). and inasmuch as I-tsing places Diṅnāga not in the "middle ages", when Asaṅga and Vasubandhu flourished, but in the "recent" years when flourished Dharmapāla, Dharmakīrti and others.[116]

Diṅnāga was a celebrated logician and controversialist, and his works were studied as text books on *hetuvidyā* during our period. His most famous work the *Pramāṇa-samuccaya*,[117] became the most authoritative śāstra of Buddhist dogmatics in seventh and eighth centuries A.D.[118]

According to an eminent Vijñānavāda authority of ancient times, Diṅnāga having heard the *Yogācārabhūmiśāstra*, gave up Hīnayānism and espoused the Great Vehicle with a view to propagate the 'Yoga system'.[119] This shows that Diṅnāga was a Yogācārin, a Vijñānavādin in philosophy. This is confirmed from his works, especially by the *Ālambanaparīkṣā*, which displays him as a champion of Vijñānavāda.[120] But he differed from the protagonists of Vijñānavāda, and in fact criticised Vasubandhu however politely.[121]

A tradition, recorded by a certain Tibetan annalist, includes Diṅnāga among the Ācāryas of the Abhidharma system.[122] Hsüan-tsang also indicates Diṅnāga's faith in Hīnayāna before his conversion to the Mahāyāna. Stcherbatsky points out that Diṅnāga quotes from the Abhidharma of the Sarvāstivādins in support of the formulas of the definition of two *pramāṇas*.[123] All these points of interest suggest that Diṅnāga represented a mixed school of philosophy which was drawn on Sarvāstivāda realism and Yogācāra idealism.

Diṅnāga's system may be described as a 'system of realistic logic'; compared to the naive realism of the Nyāya school,[124] the system of Diṅnāga appears as a critical and dialectical system; but when we compare it with Candrakīrti's method of *reductio ad absurdum*, bordering on skepticism, which condemned all experience as hopelessly false (*mṛṣā*), the doctrine of Diṅnāga appears realistic. His system may best be described as a system of transcendental realism or critical philosophy.

Diṅnāga reduces the means or sources of knowledge (*pramāṇas*) to two : (i) sense perception (*pratyakṣa*) and (ii) inference (*anumāna*).[125] The latter is twofold: for one's own sake *svārthānumāna*), and for the sake of others (*parārthānumāna*). Diṅnāga thus injured the Naiyāyika theory in which *śabda* (scriptural testimony) and *upamāna* (comparison) were established as separate means of knowledge. The Brahmanical philosophers from Uddyotakara onwards continually attacked Diṅnāga for the latter's doctrinal assault and logical acumen.[126]

"Sense-perception is that which being freed from pre-conception is unconnected with name, genus, etc."[127] This definition of direct knowledge (*pratyakṣa-jñāna*) shows that in Diṅnāga's opinion perceptual knowledge is pure and unqualified perception, stripped of characters. A clear distinction is made between sensation and imagination.

Diṅnāga's definition of inference (*anumāna*) as quoted by Uddyotakara and attested by Vācaspati Miśra, is as follows: "Experience of a thing as inseparably connected is the instrument of inference for a person who knows this inseparable connection."[128]

In the second chapter of the *Pramāṇasamuccaya*, Diṅnāga discusses the views of some logicians who from smoke (which is the middle term), infer fire (the major term), which is inseparably connected with it. He also refers to those, who from smoke infer the connection between fire (the major term) and the hill (the minor term).

Against the first mentioned logicians he says that it is already known that smoke is inseparably connected with fire; therefore, those who infer fire from smoke, obtain nothing new. Against the second type of logicians, he says that connection cannot be inferred: connection implies two things, whereas here only one thing (viz. the hill) is visible, the other (viz. the fire) is invisible. What then is really inferred from smoke ? The answer is: it is neither fire nor connection between fire and the hill, but it is the fiery hill that is inferred.[129]

The inference is divided into two kinds. Inference for oneself (*svārthānumāna*) is defined as the knowledge of an object obtained through a mark or sign having one of the three characters (i) effect (*kārya*) that is, the mark may be an effect of that which is inferred; (ii) identity (*svabhāva*), the mark may be in essence identical with the thing to be inferred; (iii) non-perception (*anupalabdhi*), the non-perception of a mark may be indicative of the non-existence of that which is to be inferred.

Inference for the sake of others (*parārthānumāna*) takes place, according to Diṅnāga, when a person demonstrates to others the conclusion drawn by him through an inference for oneself. Diṅnāga has been rightly credited with establishing the distinction between the actual process of reasoning for the ascertainment of truth and the reasoning for another, which latter is in the form of communication by a three-membered syllogism.

Before Diṅnāga, the following example of a familiar case was cited to help the understanding of the listener : "The hill is fiery; Because it has smoke; Like a kitchen (example)." Diṅnāga's distinction was that he converted an ordinary example into a universal proposition, a proposition expressive of the universal, invariable connection between the middle term and the major term. e.g. "The hill is fiery; Because it has smoke; All that has smoke is fiery, as a kitchen (homogeneous example)"; and "Whatever is not fiery has no smoke as a lake" (heterogeneous example).[130]

Dharmakīrti: Buddhist logic and critical philosophy made further remarkable progress at the hands of an Indian Kant, Dharmakīrti, whose life and works have been discussed above. As I-tsing remarks, Dharmakīrti made further progress in Buddhist logic after Diṅnāga and discussed the problem of the 'means of proof' in his *Pramāṇaviniścaya* while critically elaborating the doctrines of Diṅnāga in the *Pramāṇavārttika*.[131]

Dharmakīrti's exposition of Buddhist logical and epistemological theories may be summed up in the following pages.

Right knowledge is the knowledge not contradicted by experience. All successful human endeavours are preceded by right knowledge. The right knowledge is of two kinds: (i) direct (*pratyakṣa*) and (ii) indirect (*anumāna*). In others words, two are the sources of right knowledge: perception and inference. Perception (*pratyakṣa*) or perceptive knowledge is knowledge which is free from 'construction' (judgment) and 'illusion'; that is to say, direct knowledge is non-constructive and non-illusive cognition.[132]

Dharmakīrti, thus adds one more condition of right knowledge to the definition of Diṅnāga, namely the compound *abhrānta*, 'non-illusive'. Right knowledge should be not only 'stripped of characters' (*kalpanāpoḍha*) but also 'free from illusions' (*abhrānta*).

This direct knowledge is fourfold : (i) sensation (*indriyajñāna* (ii) mental sensation (*manovijñāna*) (iii) self-consciousness (*ātma-saṃvedana*) and (iv) mystic intuition of the saint (*yogijñāna*).

The usual definition of sense-perception states that it is a cognition produced by the senses or by a stimulus applied by an object on the senses.[133] But this definition was found defective; the Buddhist philosophers, perhaps knowingly, left out the condition of the contact between the object and the senses. By doing so they could include in direct knowledge such perceptions as *sva-saṃvitti* and *yogijñāna* which are not wholly sensuous.

The Buddhist view of sense-perception, is that it is a pure sensation, a sensuous sensation, the first moment of perception; its salient feature is that it is non-conceptual, non-constructive. In order to emphasize this, Dharmottara says that "perception is a source of knowledge whose function of making the object present in the ken is followed by the construction of its image."[134] Thi s single moment of pure sensation, a point-instant, the philosopher tells us, is an abso ute particular, beyond the reach of our knowledge.[135] But this is real and is proved by direct knowledge.[136]

After pure sensation, the next variety is that of mental sensation. Sensation is immediately followed by mental sensation; the former is thus the immediately preceding homogeneous cause; and the latter cooperates with the corresponding moment of the momentary object of sensation.[137]

Third variety of direct knowledge is revealed by the fact that "every consciousness and every mental phenomenon are self-conscious." Every mental state and every mind are self-conscious. We are conscious of our existence. This aspect of our knowledge is a direct knowledge; our knowledge is self-luminous like a lamp.[138]

The fourth variety of direct knowledge is the intuition of the saint which is "produced from the sub-culminational state of deep meditation on transcendental reality."[139] The *yogi-pratyakṣa* is, in fact, the vivid and immediate image or vision of truth which the *yogin* is capable of obtaining through special spiritual training and contemplation. Buddha's knowledge of Four Truths belongs to this category of direct knowledge.

The object of this type of right knowledge, i.e. direct knowledge, is *svalakṣaṇa*, the utterly unique, extreme particular.[140] This *svalakṣaṇa* is an entity in itself, an essence which is unique and uncommon, not shared by anything else.[141]

It is the distinction of this school of critical philosophy, to which Diṅnāga and Dharmakīrti belonged, that the 'unique particular' (which is different from the 'general') is a "thing-in-itself"; "it is the absolute particular, the limit of all synthetic construction"; it is a transcendental reality which cannot be realized in a definite representation (*jñānena prāpayituṃ aśakya-tvāt);* it is the absolute reality which underlies every effcient empirical reality (*dāhādy-artha-kriyā*).[142]

Here we find a doctrine of Absolute Reality as indescribable 'point-instant', the utter relativity or vacuity of the Mādhymikas. Candrakīrti, in spite of Diṅnāga, held even the 'Thing-in-itself' to be relative.[143] It is well known that for the Buddhists the only reality is the efficient-point-instant; to be real means to be efficient; to exist means to produce an effect (*artha-kriyā-kāritva);* all else is thought-construction, imagination and interpretation. Only particular is the real which is a moment, a point-instant (*kṣaṇa*).

Dharmottara says, "That which is apprehended in direct perception is unique." "This means that the unique particular is the exclusive object of sense-perception.[144] According to Dharmakīrti, "That alone (which is unique) represents ultimate reality, because the essence of reality is just efficiency."[145]

Further, real is only the particular, the unique point of efficient moment, not the constructed object. An object, which does not represent the unique point, is general (*sāmānya*); that is to say, 'different from the unique particular is the character of the universal (*sāmānya*)' which latter is the object of inference or indirect knowledge.[146]

The second type of right knowledge is the indirect knowledge, its source is inference. Inference (*anumāna*) is of two kinds : for oneself and for others. "A cognition which is produced (indirectly) through a mark that has a threefold aspect, and which refers to an object (not perceived, but) inferred—is internal inference (*svārthānumāna*)."[147]

The three aspects (*trairūpya*) of the mark (*liṅga*) are (i) its existence in the object cognized by i nference, (ii) its presence only in similar (*sapakṣa*) cases, and (iii) its absolute absence in dissimilar cases.[148]

Keith observed that here an advance is made on Diṅnāga in the process of examination of the conditions of a correct middle term.

Dharmakīrti further shows that the cases, where there is the invariable concomitance, are limited to three only. These three varieties of the three-aspected logical mark are : (i) negation (*anupalabdhi*), (ii) identity (*svabhāva*), and (iii) causation (*kārya*).[149] Knowledge derived through *svārthānumāna* is, therefore, of three main types : (i) here there is no jar because it is not perceived although the conditions of perception are fulfilled (negation); (ii) this is a tree, because it is a pine (relation of identity); and (iii) here there is fire , because there is smoke (relation of cause and effect) the cause (fire) is inferred from effect (smoke).[150]

Inference for the sake of others (*parārthānumāna*) or syllogism, consists in communicating the three aspects of the middle term, when the reason is set out in words to produce a conviction in others.[151] Dharmakīrti was a critical realist from logical standpoint; he was an idealist in philosophy; but his idealism is not identical with the dogmatic Vijñānavāda of the early Yogācāras. He was a transcendental idealist. Specially noteworthy is the omission of the theory of the 'store-house-consciousness' (*ālaya-vijñāna*). Stcherbatsky[152] observes that "the *Pramāṇavārttika* never mentions the *ālayavijñāna* doctrine and there is evidence enough to maintain that Dharmakīrti rejected it as a soul in disguise." According to a Tibetan authority, "Ārya Vimuktasena and Haribhadra and also Dharmakīrti in his 'seven treatises' hold that the theory of 'stored-consciousness' is an arrow shot into darkness." The same authority quotes a work called the "'Ornament of the Seven Treatises' by Gendunḍub, wherein it is stated that "those who maintain that in the systems of Seven Treatises the 'store-consciousness' doctrine is admitted, are blind men (living) in the darkness of their own ignorance."[153]

That Dharmakīrti believed in the doctrine of *sva-saṃvedana* or self-consciousness like the Vijñānavādins, and held the reality of external objects on logical grounds and in refined technology, is clear from the *Nyāyabindu* as well as the *Sarva-darśana-saṃgraha*. In the *Sarva-darśana-saṃgraha* of Mādhavācārya the view of Dharmakīrti is specifically quoted and he is referred to as a Yogācārin. His definition of sense-perception hints at his Sautrāntika side of logical reasoning. Perception according to Dharmakīrti, as we have seen, consists in the apprehension of an object in its own specific character; knowledge thus obtained is free from imagination and illusion.

The light of consciousness makes the dead matter shine and if one were to suppose that consciousness is hidden and veiled in itself and by itself, one cannot explain how knowledge can arise at all. Therefore, "self-subsistent cognition must be allowed, or it will follow that the whole universe is blind. It has conformably been proclaimed by Dharmakīrti, 'to one who dis-allows perception the vision of objects is not competent'."[154]

In the *Nyāyabindu*, as noted above, Dharmakīrti declares that "every consciousness and every mental phenomenon are self-conscious". In a number of verses of the *Pramāṇavārttika*, he affirms the *vijñaptimātratā* and *sva-saṃvitti*. Thus at one place he says that if thought reflects external objects then it should be held to have the form of that object. Now the thought will rest in the form, and the external object would be unnecessary; since the external object is never known by itself, but only in conjunction with thought, its separate assumption is groundless.

Elsewhere he says though there is no diversity, the intellect, owing to illusory perceptions appears to possess a duality of cognitions, of percepts and of percipient.[155]

The tenet of *sva-saṃvedana* is put forth more poignantly in the following *kārikā*:

> *dhiyā' tadrūpayā jñāne niruddhe'nubhavaḥ kutaḥ /*
> *svānca rūpam na sā vettītyutsanno'nubhavo'rthinaḥ //*[156]

"Perception of an object is impossible if perception itself is unperceived" (*apratyakṣopalaṃbhasya nārthadṛṣṭiḥ prasiddhyati*).[157]

The difference between the objects is due to *vāsanās* and not due to external objects; in other words, the (form of) thought is determined by *vāsanās*, and not by objects.

In short, the identity of percipient and percept is inferable. That which is cognized by consciousness is nothing else than that consciousness, e.g. the mind is no other than the cognition of the mind, and blue and other momentary objects are cognized by cognition. If there were a difference (between percept and percipient) the object could not be connected with cognition, there being no identity to determine the constant connection, and nothing to account for the rise of such a connection. As far as the interval between the object and consciousness is concerned this is an illusion, like the vision of two moons when there is only one. The cause of this illusion is the ideation of difference in a stream without beginning and without interruption. Therefore, it is declared that "as invariably cognized together, the blue and the cognition thereof are identical; and the difference should be accounted for by illusory cognitions as in the example of the single moon". The following verse quoted in the *Sarvadarśana-saṃgraha*:

> *sahopalaṃbhaniyamādabhedo nīlataddhiyoḥ /*
> *bhedaśca bhrānti-vijñānairdṛśyetendāvivādvaye //*[158]

seems to belong either to Diṅnāga or to Dharmakīrti. In Dharmakīrti's *Pramāṇavārttika*, the second line of this *śloka* occurs, and is put among the verses containing the same idea as has been above. It appears that Dharmakīrti has commented upon the line *'sahopalaṃbhaniyamādabhedo nīlataddhiyoḥ'* in the following two *ślokas:—(Pramāṇavārttika-bhāsyaṃ,* pp. 409-410, verses 388-389)*

> *sakṛtsaṃvedyamānasya niyamena dhiyā saha |*
> *viṣayasya tato'nyatvaṃ kenākāreṇa siddhyati ||*
> *bhedaśca bhrāntivijñānairdṛśyetendāvivādvayaṃ |*
> *saṃvitti niyamo nāsti bhinnayornīlapītayoḥ ||**

Besides these, the doctrine of the identity of the percept and the percipient is emphasized in the *Pramāṇavārttika-bhāṣyaṃ* (p. 397, verse 355: p. 416, verse 398 also).

Religion vis-a-vis Logic

It is important to note that in spite of the growth of intellectualism, scholasticism, logical subtleties, dialectics and disputations among the Buddhists of this period, and in spite of the fact that the sages and scholars of Mahāyāna were preoccupied with the task of rationally expounding and defending their doctrines in current logical technology, they remained religious men at heart. Candrakīrti, Dharmakīrti, Śāntarakṣita, Kamalaśīla and Dharmottara, the towering personalities in the galaxy of Buddhist philosophers of the age, never for a moment seem to forget the essential and fundamental position of Buddhist mysticism and transcendentalism. Even Diṅnāga, the father of Buddhist logic, and the systematiser of the critical philosophy of Buddhism, who inaugurated perhaps consciously an age of historical debates and tense doctrinal controversies in the history of Indian thought, observes that the Climax of Wisdom is Monism. In the very final Absolute subject and object coalesce. This Climax of Wisdom (*prajñāpāramitā*), this spiritual Non-Duality, says the philosopher, is identical with Absolute, the Buddha. Commenting upon this statement of Diṅnāga, Stcherbatsky rightly remarks that "philosophy here passes into religion". Towards the end of his great polemical treatise of three thousand six hundred and forty-six memorial verses, Śāntarakṣita points out that whatever Buddha wishes to know, He comes to know without fail; having secured the knowledge of all things, He becomes the Lord, and that, what is apprehended by the Mystic Consciousness is not that universal which is discussed by people as real; the Reality apprehended by the Mystic Consciousness is unutterable, and transcends thought and imagination.[159]

Even Dharmakīrti, despite his rich arsenal of logic, commits himself thus. "The essence of consciousness is undivided, subject and object is an illusive division. Their unity is Buddha's Omniscience, his Spiritual Body." We may also note that he gave prominent place to *yogijñāna* (mystic intuition) among the means of proof or sources of right knowledge. His definition of sense-perception and his view that the object of right knowledge is the unspeakable, unique particular, also point to his mystical and transcendental attitude.

Diṅnāga says that "*dharma* is not the subject of logical reasoning"; one who seeks to lead to Absolute Truth by way of logical reasoning "will be very far from the teaching of Buddha, and fail"; logic is uncertain (*anitya*), merely empirical and limited to conventional truth (*saṃvṛti*), and is of interest only to the foolish people (*bālāśraya*) and at best tiresome (*khedavāna*).

Candrakīrti, the unsurpassed dialectician, stoutly maintained that the ultimate reality can be cognized only in mystic intuition and that the Absolute is unspeakble and the saints maintain a 'noble silence' when questioned on this point.

What is the need of logic ? Diṅnāga answers that although logic cannot lead to Absolute, yet we study it in order to correct the mistakes of the realists: the realists are bunglers in logic; they have given wrong definitions, we only correct them; in logic we explain the daily experience of life scientifically, describe the sources of knowledge and their respective objects; but we do not accept their transcendentality.

It is thus clear that Buddhist logic and dialectics were the product of historical tradition and social circumstances. The Buddhist philosophers were mystics at heart. They developed logic and rational dialectic in order to defend their fundamental, transcendental and mystical position. When the validity of Saddharma was questioned, the omniscience of Buddha challenged, the philosopher-mystic could not face the circumstance by having a recourse to the scriptures which had no evidential value for the opponent; nor could he dissociate the truth from the intuitional gnostic experience within which it operates.

As a matter of historical necessity, therefore, the spiritual experience and meditational background had to be detached (for the sake of argument) and Buddhist truth had to be reduced to a series of rational propositions and logical conventions which were commonly accepted by both the parties. Hence the definition of perception as pure sensation (*kalpanāpoḍha*) and hence also its object as the unique particular (*svalakṣaṇa*). This definition of perception as pure sensation, bereft of all characters, is unlike any thing that is known as common sense perception; and the definition of its object as the unutterable Thing-in-itself is a pointer to the unspeakable state of Nirvāṇa which the *yogin*, free from fetters, self-possessed and calmed (*sītībhūto*) enjoys through *scientia intuitiva.*

Philosophical Standpoint of Śāntarakṣita and Kamalaśīla

There are indications in the *Tattvasaṃgraha* and its *Pañjikā*, that Buddhist philosophy of transcendental idealism, critical realism and universal flux, reached its acme in the hands of Śāntarakṣita and Kamalaśīla at the close of our period. There seems to be some confusion with regard to the correct standpoint of these two philosophers.

The structure of the *Tattvasaṃgraha* indicates its Mādhyamika character; the opening verses of it and the author's obeisance to the Teacher of the law of dependent origination, as also the method of *parīkṣā* of various theories and concepts adopted in this work, at once remind us of the techniques of Nāgārjuna, manifested in the *Madhyamakaśāstra* and the *Dvādaśamukhaśāstra.* The dominant note of the *TS* is refutation and the work is largely polemical.

Besides this, Śāntarakṣita is said to have written a work entitled *Mādhyamakālaṅkāra-kārikā.* This work is extant in Tibetan translation and as its name suggests, seems to be a Mādhyamika text. Bu-ston includes Śāntarakṣita and Kamalaśīla among the Yogācāra-Mādhyamikas. Gos-lo-tsaba puts Śāntarakṣita in the lineage of Nāgārjuna, Bhavya, Śrīgupta and Jñānagarbha.[160] Khai-ḍub states that Bhāvaviveka and Jñānagarbha were Sautrāntika-Mādhyamika-Svātantrīkas,[161] while Bu-ston expressly includes these two Doctors among the Yogācāra-Mādhyamikas along with Śrīgupta, Śāntarakṣita, Kamalaśīla and Haribhadra.[162] Besides, from the accounts of the debate of bSamyas (so-called 'Council of Lhasa'), in which Kamalaśīla defeated the *dhyāna* master Mahāyāna Hva-saṅ, we learn that in philosophy the doctrine of Nāgārjuna was decided to be followed and in practice the 'gradual method' of 'gnosis' and 'means',[163]

B. Bhattacharya held, on the basis of the *Tattvasiddhi*, a Vajrayāna work alleged to be from the pen of Śāntarakṣita, that Śāntarakṣita "was a Vijñānavādin, or more correctly a Vajrayānist." The manuscript of the *Tattvasiddhi* is said to lay emphasis on *vijñāna*, and a passage from the *Tattvasaṃgraha* is said to have been quoted in this manuscript text.[164] The *Tattva-saṃgraha* and its *Pañjikā* clearly support the doctrine of *sva-saṃvedana* and its self-luminous nature.[165] The author of the *Bhāvanākrama*, to wit, Kamalaśīla, sympathetically quotes the Vijñānavāda view that the universe is a mere ideation.[166] Both Śāntarakṣita and Kamalaśīla, accept at many places, the views of Diṅnāga and Dharmakīrti concerning the self-cognizing consciousness.[167]

According to Khai-ḍub, Śāntarakṣita founded a separate school, another school of the Mādhyamikas, after the split made by the controversies between Buddhapālita and Bhāva-viveka. The main tenets of this new school, which were expounded in the *Madhyamakālaṅkāra* by Śāntārakṣita, were as follows :

(1) denial of the reality of the external world;

(2) acceptance of the doctrine of introspective perception (i.e. *sva-saṃvitti*); and

(3) the view that consciousness was not an ultimate reality —"differing in this from the Yogācāra Vijñānavādins." Khai-ḍub designates this school as "that of Yogācārā-Mādhyamika-Svātantrika", perhaps appropriately enough.[168] According to this source Śāntarakṣita was neither thoroughly Śūnyavādin nor thoroughly Vijñānavadin.

The fact that Bhāvavivkea and Śāntarakṣita belonged to the same philosophical standpoint, as is affirmed not only by Bu-ston but also by Gos-lo-tsaba,[169] is important and sets one thinking. Bhāvaviveka, according to Hsüan-tsang, wore the "garb of the Sāṃkhya" though he was a follower of Nāgār-juna.[170] This points to the admission by Bhavya of some sort of realistic doctrines. Indeed, Khai-ḍub expressly says that Bhavya as well as Jñānagarbha (the author of a Svātantrika work, *Mādhyamika-satya-dvaya*) represented a system which "maintained the reality of external objects from the empirical standpoint."[171] Apart from these Chinese and Tibetan testimonies, the works of Bhāvaviveka also indicate that he recognized the science of logic and its efficacy, and admitted the empirical reality of the external objects (*tathya-saṃvṛti*).[172] Moreover, whenever he condemned and denied the existence of empirical world, he did so from the absolute standpoint. Like Diṅnāga, Bhavya was a logician, a critical realist in logic, and a transcendentalist in philosophy. We know that Candrakīrti attacked Bhavya for the latter's faith in logic, in *tathya-saṃvṛti* and in maintaining a positive thesis. We also know Candrakīrti's assault on Diṅnāga.

In short, Bhāvaviveka made the same revolution in Mādhyamika thought which Diṅnāga made in Vijñānavāda. Both these Doctors were influenced by the Sautrāntika doctrines, and perhaps we shall not be far from truth to suggest that Śāntarakṣita accepted the views of Bhāvaviveka and Diṅnāga and not of Vasubandhu and Candrakīrti. The fact that Śāntarakṣita does not expound the uncompromising tenets of Nāgārjuna nor of Vasubandhu, the author of the *Vijñaptimātratā-siddhi*, but adopts a logical and critically realistic standpoint, shows that the author of the *TS* and his faithful commentator, were attempting a synthesis of Mādhyamika, Yogācāra and Sautrāntika tenets.

Śāntarakṣita perhaps makes a clear reference to the views of Bhāvaviveka (though the name of this Doctor is not specified) when he says, "Even those who regard all things as featureless (devoid of characters), always have recourse to such qualifying terms as "truly' and the like."[173] As if to make the point clearer, Kamalaśīla adds that "In fact it must be admitted by all men that the fact that a thing is somehow existent is quite certainly recognized."[174] Moreover, a passage in the *Bhāvanākrama* of Kamalaśīla bears a striking resemblance to a passage in the *Karatalaratna* of Bhavya. The passage concerns the principle of non-duality.[175]

Śāntarakṣita, after having criticised at length the doctrines concerning God, matter, world, and soul, commits himself thus: "All this effort is made needlessly as all such doctrines are really set aside by the well established doctrine of the perpetual flux of things,"[176] So important and so fundamental is this doctrine of impermanence of things that, Kamalaśīla regards this as the climax of Buddhist philosophy, and says that without doing much labour we could have with one stroke only (*eka prahāreṇa eva*) demolished all these theories of permanent entities quite easily (*svalpa upāyena*) had we applied our great doctrine of momentariness.[177]

Doctrine of Momentariness : In accordance with their admission of a twofold source of knowledge (perceptive and inferential) the Buddhist philosophers of this school postulate a double existence—particular and general or universal. The first is cognized through sense perception, the second through understanding or reason. This existence, they further maintain, consists of momentary, discreet entities which are in a state of perpetual flux and are by nature impermanent. The idea of an all pervasive matter, eternal and durable, is a figment of imagination. All existence without exception is momentary; things are instantaneous.

Moment or *kṣaṇa* is that form of thing which ceases as soon as it originates, a thing which has this character is called 'momentary' or *kṣaṇika*. The nature of a thing is not different from the thing itself. The term *kṣaṇika* is applied by the wise to the thing that does not continue to exist after its coming into existence.[178] In other words existence is identical with moment; existence is a point-instant.

Kamalaśīla observes that what is normally regarded by the people as real (*vastu*), is proved by us (Buddhists) to be momentary. These real things, i.e. the objects of some purposeful actions, are called entities or things by the intelligent persons; they are so called because they are capable of producing some useful action. This rule is universal and there is no exception to this. We might even say that this feature (i.e. the capacity to produce a purposive action) is coterminous with existence. The real is, therefore, an efficient entity (*artha-kriyā-kārī*).[179] The essence of this reality (*pratītyasamutpāḍaḥ*), says Śāntarakṣita, is motion (*cala*). This real which is *cala* (*calabhāva-svarūpa*) is momentary (*kṣaṇika*). Causation, i.e. the interdependence of *kṣaṇas* following one another, produces the illusion of stability and uninterrupted continuity, but these moments are discreet and without any enduring substance in them.

The Buddhist is thus an advocate of the dynamic constitution of things, and he genuinely maintains that there is no existence, no reality which is static and stationary. Things are in perpetual motion, constantly originating, and constantly ceasing without any break (*nirantara*).

In this school of thought, 'existence', 'reality', 'change' 'efficiency' are synonymous, applicable to a real fact. For example, a jar (*ghaṭa*) which is produced by the labour of a potter, is describable as variable, as a product having an origin, as efficient and as existent. This truth is borne out by the following doctrinal declarations : "whatever is real is changing"; "whatsoever is produced by a conscious effort is impermanent."[180]

Non-existence does not exist; non-existence or annihilation is a mere name, nothing corresponds to it; a thing is never annihilated. The universal is not something residing in the particular; it is a mere idea, a pseudo-idea like the idea of space and time. Existence is efficiency, and efficiency is the thing itself; causality is the dependent origination of things originating; these things themselves are the causes; there is no causality besides their existence.[181]

Śāntarakṣita puts forth, as an argument in support of the doctrine of momentariness, a remarkable formula, namely, that "the momentary thing represents its own annihilation", that is, "the destruction in the form of the momentary thing appears along with the thing itself."[182] This means that every thing ceases as soon as it arises, it does not survive in the next moment; if it stayed on, it would be eternal and not *kṣaṇika*, because it would go on staying in the subsequent moments. But an eternal thing like *ākāśa*, etc. is a fiction, a flower growing in the sky.

The *ākāśa* and the like have been held to be uncreated and permanent (e.g. by the realistic Buddhists),[183] but these are really non-existent in the form of entities, because they are devoid of all potentiality. They cannot be called even momentary (as only the real is the momentary), like the son of a barren woman.

Space, Time, God and the rest which are supposed to be existent, could never have an existence if they were not momentary, permanent things cannot serve any purposive action, either successively or simultaneously, they are therefore, non-existent. If you accept the permanence of a thing, you cannot accept its fruitful activity as succession and simultaneity.[184]

Doctrine of 'Meaning' (*apoha*) : The philosophers of our school made, as noted above, a sharp differentiation between direct and indirect knowledge. This fact seems to have led to the development of a new and striking theory about the import of words. Ordinary experience admits some sort of a relation between a word and the object. The Buddhist holds that the word does not represent the actual object, it only negates what the object is not.

Our knowledge, our concepts, our language and all the namable things are dialectical. The words do not signify anything positive, or an essence or a universal; they merely denote an exclusion (*apoha*) or negation of everything else.

"Every word or every conception is correlative with its counterpart and that is the only definition that can be given. Therefore all our definitions are concealed classifications, taken from some special point of view. The thing defined is characterized negatively. What the colour 'blue' is, e.g. we cannot tell, but we may divide all colours in blue and non-blue. The definition of blue will be that it is not non-blue, and vice versa, the definition of non-blue that it is not the blue."[185] Such in short is the meaning of *apoha*.

It was Diṅnāga, who, for the first time, evaluated the doctrine of *apoha* in Buddhist thought in the fifth chapter of his *Pramāṇasamuccaya*. Dharmakīrti discussed the problem in the first chapter of the *Pramāṇavārttika*. His pupil Dharmottara wrote a special work on it, the *Apohanāma-prakaraṇa*, extant in Tibetan. Śāntarakṣita devoted one of the biggest chapters of his *Tattvasaṃgraha*, the xvith chapter, containing 345 verses, to the discussion of *śabda-artha-parīkṣā*, and Kamalaśīla added an equally voluminous comment thereto. Ratnakīrti wrote a short text, the *apoha-siddhi*[186] (in the 10th century A.D.), Vācaspati Miśra gives a fairly detailed account of the theory of 'neglected difference' (*bheda-agrāha*) held by the Idealistic Buddhist logicians *nyāya-vādino bauddhāḥ*.[187]

There are three distinguishable landmarks in the career of the Buddhist doctrine of *apoha*. (i) In the first place in Diṅnāga, *apoha* or *anyāpoha* had a purely negative meaning; *apoha* stood for pure negation; (ii) in the next phase, probably in Śāntarakṣita, *apoha* is given a new meaning, it was "supposed to stand for a positive conceptual construction, a purely subjective idea"; and (iii) in the hands of Ratnakīrti, we find that the old sense given to it by Diṅnāga is restored.[188]

In this school of critical philosophy, words and names do not represent the true nature of things. "The name can express its own meaning only by repudiating the opposite meaning.'[189] Knowledge that is derived from the words and names is in principle identical with inference. "Language is not a separate source of knowledge and names are not the adequate or direct expression of reality. Names correspond to images or concepts, they express only universals. As such they are in no way the reflex of reality, since reality consists of particulars, not of universals."[190]

Jinendrabuddhi, commenting upon the above view of Diṅnāga, says : "Therefore the meaning of a word consists in a repudiation of the discrepant meaning."[191] Or to put it otherwise : "the repudiation of the contrary is the exclusive meaning (of every word)."[192]

At the outset in the second *śloka* of the *Tattvasaṃgraha*, Śāntarakṣita says that "(the Truth) is amenable to words and cognitions only in an assumed (superimposed) form."[193] He as well as Kamalaśīla maintains that though the words are mere concepts and notions, there being no basis for them, "the only basis for them consists in the seed located in the purely subjective consciousness",[194] yet they indirectly refer to the particular real thing. This "thing" itself is a negation (*apoha*); it is a unique thing inasmuch as it is ontological (*arthātmaka*) negation.[195]

Śāntarakṣita and Kamalaśīla argue as follows :

The essence of entities is such that whatever is said to be object of a verbal expression is never really perceived, whether it be specific individuality or the like.[196] Specific individuality cannot be denoted by words, because it can have no connection with the time of convention and usage.[197] Because the thing conceived by convention is never met within actual usage, even within the specific individualities, e. g. the Himālaya which does not differ with time and place, there are atoms which differ with time and place, and are therefore changing and momentary.[198]

That the names and ideas do not represent realities is clear from the following : the idea of 'heat' which follows when we hear the word 'hot' is not so distinct as the perception of the hot thing brought about by sense-organ. It is therefore wrong to think of any connection between the particular and the word; nor does the 'thing' appear in the cognition brought about by the word, just as taste does not appear in the cognition of the colour. As regards the form of consciousness, it rests in the consciousness itself and does not follow the object, therefore the form of consciousness also cannot denote the import of words.[199] The examination of 'words' and 'names' is concluded thus: just as a man of diseased vision says to another man of diseased vision that 'there are two moons', so also is all verbal usage.[200]

Doctrine of Causation (*pratītyasamutpāda*) : Śāntarakṣita pays homage to the Buddha as "the best of expounders of the doctrine of *pratītyasamutpāda*", and Kamalaśīla says that "Of all the gems of Buddhist thought the doctrine of causation is the excellent gem."[201] The doctrine of causation as evaluated by the Buddhist philosophers of our period seems to be a direct outcome of their doctrine of universal momentariness. Causality, reality, efficiency and momentariness are interchangeable terms in this system.

The phrase *pratītyasamutpāda* means 'contingent co-production or 'combined dependent origination'. Existence means efficiency. This efficiency is nothing but the capacity to produce or cause something. This something is nothing but the point-instant, the efficient moment, caused by the preceding efficient moment. The universe is a moving show of these momentary entities that are the causes themselves. "Whatsoever exists is a cause; cause and existence are synonymous (*yā bhūtiḥ saiva kriyā*)."[202] Causation is kinetic. What exists is always acting, always moving; it is an illusion that a thing exists placidly, that it exists without acting; what does not act, does not exist; action is motion, this motion itself is causation.[203]

Replying to a criticism by Uddyotakara, Kamalaśīla remarks that "the Buddhists, who are conversant with Logic, hold that a non-cause is necessarily a non-reality."[204] The old formula of causation, to wit, '*asmin sati idaṃ bhavati*', is too well known.[205] But during our period the doctrine of causation, like other Buddhist doctrines, is stated dialectically; says Kamalaśīla, "The relation of an agent to the instrument and (to the object of his action) is not ultimately real because all real elements are momentary and cannot work at all."[206]

Dharmottara, in reply to a critic who remarks that if causation is only imagined, it cannot be real, says : "Yes, but although serial existences (i.e. objects having duration) are not realities, their members (*santāninas*), the points-instant, are the reality..."[207] "When an effect is produced, we do not really experience causation itself as a sensible fact (separately from the effect). But the existence of a real effect presupposes the existence of a real cause, therefore (indirectly) the relation of causality is also necessarily a real one," i.e. empirical causality is contingently real.[208]

The doctrine of momentariness proves that the cause is momentary and the effect is also momentary; cause had come into existence at the first moment and it does not exist at the second moment when the effect has appeared. Cause and effect cannot exist simultaneously; it is not the case that the effect comes into existence by firmly embracing its cause like the tight embracement of the lover and the beloved; the cause does not catch hold of the effect with a pincer. So the simultaneity of cause and effect is not possible.[209]

Kamalaśīla sums up the doctrine by saying that as a matter of fact, neither the cause nor the effect does any work, they are powerless and aimless or unemployed; the whole universe is entirely devoid of activity. It is only a metaphorical description or a conventional expression that we say a cause produces something. We should rather say that "the effect arises in functional dependence on such and such a thing."[210]

If it be asked, what is this 'function' or 'operation' and what is this 'dependence' (i.e. the 'need' of the effect), the answer is as follows : 'the effect appears immediately after the existence of the cause, hence this existence itself may be called the operation'; 'the dependence of the effect on the cause, or the need that an effect has of the cause, consists in the fact that the effect comes into existence immediately after the cause.' The cause is the 'thing' by itself, the bare thing, without any form or operation.[211]

Doctrine of Consciousness (*vijñāna*) : It has been noted above that this critical school of Buddhist philosophy, inaugurated by Diṅnāga, admits, with a peculiar adjustment and coordination, the doctrines of absolute monism, idealism and critical realism. The doctrine of the reality of 'self-consciousness (*sva-saṃvedana*) is fundamental to this school and Kamalaśīla supports his statements by citations from Diṅnāga and Dharmakīrti. It should be noted, however, that while Diṅnāga and Dharmakīrti who call themselves idealists, and are in fact realists in logic and idealistic monists in metaphysics and ontology, their successors, Śāntarakṣita and Kamalaśīla, while accepting the doctrine of *sva-saṃvitti*, are not thoroughgoing idealists. Though old arguments of idealism are given, Vijñānavāda of Śāntarakṣita and Kamalaśīla does not maintain that consciousness alone (*vijñaptimātratā*) is the one and only reality. This is clear from the following lines.

In the fourth verse, in the opening of the *Tattvasaṃgraha*, Śāntarakṣita describes *pratītyasamutpāda* (which, as we have seen, appertains to the inter-dependence of the entities or serial existences) as 'resembling the reflection of things' (*pratibiṃbādisannibhaṃ*). This, says Kamalaśīla, is the standpoint of the idealistic Buddhists who maintain that, the entire universe comprising the threefold phenomena, is mere ideation (*vijñāna*).[212] But he challenges the contention of the Vedantic monists who maintain the unique reality of the one immutable whole (*yathopaniṣadvādināṃ*). He says that the *vijñāna* of the Buddhist idealists is not like that.[213]

This consciousness (*vijñānaṃ*) is infinitely manifold (*anantaṃ*), changing every moment (*pratikṣaṇa-viśarāru*) and is pure and bright and manifests itself in all beings (*ojāyate sarvaprāṇabhṛtaṃ*). This *vijñāna* alone exists, the existence of objective, non-mental world, is impossible. It is impossible for two reasons (a) it involves contradiction, and (b) the comprehension of it (i.e. of objective world) is incomprehensible.[214]

The theory of the reality of the external world (*bahirartha*) is fraught with contradictions as would be clear from the following antinomy (*ekāneka-svabhāvaṃ*, i.e. *paramāṇu*, atom and *avayavin*, conglomeration of atoms).[215] The external object must be either simple or composite (i.e. it must be either in the form of an atom or, in the form of an aggregate of atoms); there is no third possibility.[216] If it is proved that it is neither one simple thing nor a composite thing, it would, as a matter of course, be proved that it is nothing, like a flower in the sky (*vyomotpalaṃ*). Indeed a sky flower is neither simple nor composite.

That the composite must consist of simple parts is proved by the following manner. Suppose these parts are taken one by one until the smallest uncompound remains, this last residue would be indivisible and unextended, like the point-instant, a momentary feeling; therefore, it would be incorporal, a mere idea.[217]

Another argument may thus be pressed against the realists. Granting that a simple unit, an atom, is surrounded by other such atoms, the question then arises whether it faces the surrounding atoms, the one in front and the one in the back, by the same face or not. If it faces them by the same face, the atoms will coalesce and there would be no composition. If it faces them by two different faces, it will have two faces and also two parts; it will be a composite thing.[218]

According to the theory (of the realists) says Śāntarakṣita, an atom must be a simple unit; but it cannot be so because the parts also are held (by them) to be atoms. The upshot is that the atom is a non-entity, like a sky lotus; it is neither one nor many.[219] The same fate awaits the composite said to be an aggregate of those misleading atoms.

Referring to the view of the Upaniṣadic Vedāntins that "there is nothing which is endowed with the character of apprehensibility, and all this is a mere modification of manifestations of consciousness", the philosopher says that "there is only a slight error in this philosophy, due only to the assertion that this consciousness is eternal (*nitya*)."[220] Kamalaśīla also affirms that "the view that consciousness is the only entity is quite reasonable", but the doctrine of an 'eternal consciousness' is not right.[221] It is, however, a fact that idea or consciousness alone exists.[222]

"Consciousness is different from all unconscious forms; the fact of its being 'not unconscious' constitutes its self-consciousness." "There can be no self-consciousness of the consciousness in the sense that it is both action and the agent. One and the same entity cannot be the cogniser, the cognised and the cognition. The only right view is that the self-consciousness of the consciousness is owing to its being of the very nature of consciousness. It is not possible to have a consciousness of an object apart from the consciousness itself."[223]

Kamalaśīla points out that "self-consciousness does not mean that it is the cogniser of itself, what is meant is that it shines, becomes manifest by itself, by its very nature, just like the light diffused in the atmosphere."[224]

We do not hold that consciousness bears the imprint of the object;[225] the subject to object relation is incomprehensible. It is indeed, a very poor hypothesis to imagine that consciousness moves towards an object external to it, catches hold of its form, and then comes back with this booty.[226]

The meaning of self-consciousness is that it does not need anything else for its being conscious. Consciousness by nature is self-conscious.[227] The consciousness rests within its ownself and does not apprehend any object at all, nor is it ever imprinted by the objective form.[228] At the end of this chapter, Śāntarakṣita observes : "The fact of the consciousness being the only entity has been clearly established by clever writers. We also have trodden the same path for the ascertainment of truth."[229] Kamalaśīla, however, expresses elsewhere[230] that "the view that consciousness only exists does not coincide with truth."

Buddha's Omniscience (*sarvajñatva*): The existence and possibility of an omniscient person is tacitly assumed in early Indian philosophical literature. The Upaniṣads repeatedly affirm that by knowing the *ātman* (*brahman*, ultimate reality) everything is known.[231] Buddha is held to be the omniscient in several places in the Tripiṭaka.[232] Āryadeva says: "he who sees one sees all; for voidness of one thing is the voidness of all things, voidness is the nature of all things."[233] Likewise the Jainas regarded Mahāvīra to be omniscient and held that he who knows one knows all and vice versa.[234] True it is that the Lokāyatas (Cārvākas) and the Pūrva-Mīmāṃsakas opposed the belief in omniscience. But until Kumārila systematically attacked and refuted the idea of a person being omniscient,[235] the doctrine did not receive a rational and logical support. Buddhist philosophers of our age especially, Dharmakīrti, Śāntarakṣita and Kamalaśīla, discuss the problem of omniscience at length and refute the arguments advanced by Kumārila. The *Tattvasaṃgraha* opens with a salutation to that "Omniscient Being, the best of world-teachers, who revealed the doctrine of *pratītyasamutpāda*."[236]

Kumārila says that neither sense-perception nor inference can prove the existence of an omniscient person; and that Buddha was an omniscient person can be negated both by perception and inference. (a) We do not perceive an omniscient person at the present moment. (b) Buddha was not an omniscient, because he was a man like ourselves.[237]

Dharmakīrti says at one place that a teacher who is the knower of Four Noble Verities, and leads the beings on the path of freedom from birth and death, should be taken as an authority (*pramāṇa*); it is immaterial whether or not he can see things at a great distance. A vulture (*gṛdhra*) cannot be a spiritual authority although it sees things from a great distance.[238]

Dharmakīrti refuses to accept the view that an Omniscient Being does not speak; *karuṇā* for the beings and knowledge of truths are essential for imparting instructions.[239]

Candrakīrti, likewise says that although the Ultimate Truth is 'Noble Quiescence', yet out of compassion the Buddha and Bodhisattvas speak and instruct.[240] Elsewhere Dharmakīrti also maintains that we can neither cognize nor express Omniscience. The Omniscient Being, like the Absolute Truth or Ultimate Reality, is unutterable.[241]

Kamalaśīla points out that an Omniscient Being is not amenable to sense-perception; the inapplicability of perception to Omniscient Being cannot annal the existence of the latter; ordinary beings have very limited powers of vision; only an Omniscient Being can perceive another omniscient person. Nor can inference prove the non-existence of an Omniscient Being, because it is held that inference always envisages affirmation.[242] You cannot perceive a being possessed of the knowledge of all things unless you also had the knowledge of all things. In fact, the *sarvajña* is by nature imperceptible and his existence cannot be denied on the ground of rules laid down to prove the existence of perceptible objects.[243]

Moreover, if you (the Mīmāṃsaka) deny the reality of the Omniscient Being merely on the ground of non-apprehension, then you might also deny the marriage of your mother and etc. (i.e. her relation with your father); if you persist in your dull-wittedness that your non-perception should set aside things, you are damned—it would be impossible to name your father.[244]

It is quite possible that the *sarvajña* being self-luminous (*ātmajyoti*) perceives Himself by Himself, so that there can be no certainty regarding the non-perception of the *sarvajña* by all men.[245]

It is wrong to say that the *sarvajña* who is said to have a direct perception of all things experiences impure and unclean things also. The Omniscient does not perceive all things through sense-organs as is the case with ordinary mortals. He perceives things through *citta* (consciousness). Moreover, the unclean taste and such other things appear themselves only through ignorance; but these are not perceived by the Wise One.[246]

The Buddha is the only Omniscient because the unique doctrine of 'no soul', that 'gate to the Highest Good' which is the only ultimate truth, was realized by the Buddha only; all other doctrines are lost in the false doctrine of soul.[247] The possession of the perfect knowledge of all things, the knowledge of the true nature of things (i.e. of their soul-lessness) is the sole characteristic of a Buddha. And it is the Buddha alone in whom this characteristic is seen, therefore He is the only Omniscient Being.[248]

Omniscience follows as soon as the hindrances of afflictions (*kleśāvaraṇa*) and the hindrances of cognisables (*jñeyāvaraṇa*) are removed, just as darkness disappears as soon as the bright lamp shines.[249]

The Buddha stands at the head of the list of all philosophers and seers, because it was He who for the first time expounded the truth of *nairātmya.* Therefore the omniscience belongs to Him and not to Vardhamāna, Kapila and others. Other teachers who have expounded false doctrines, cannot stand a comparison with the Blessed Lord, the knower of the complete truth, whose words are free from impurities like the gold tested by heating, cutting and touching.[250]

"The Omniscient Being whose existence we have established", says Śāntarakṣita, "is one who comprehends within a single cognitive moment the entire round of all that is to be known."[251]

"Whenever He wishes to know He comes to know it without fail; such is His power ; He has shaken off all evil. He knows things either simultaneously or in succession, just as He wishes, and having secured the knowledge of all things, he becomes the Lord."[252]

CHAPTER IX

KUMĀRILA AND ŚAṂKARA ON BUDDHISM

Kumārila's View of Buddhist Thought

KUMĀRILABHAṬṬA, the great Mīmāṃsā Doctor, was perhaps the foremost and the fiercest critic of Buddhist thought. He has devoted two long chapters of his great polemical work, the *Ślokavārttika*,[1] exclusively to the refutation of the two well-known systems of Mahāyāna philosophy, viz. the Vijñānavāda and the Mādhyamika. In course of his penetrating and sustained criticism, Kumārila has attacked the Buddhist view of Buddha's Omniscience, the theory of no-soul (*nairātmya*), the theory of momentariness, the doctrine of unique particular (*svalakṣaṇa*), and the theory of phenomenal reality (*samvṛti-satya*)—all this diverse and severe polemic only in defence of the eternality of *śabda* and the infallibility of Veda.

Nirālambanavāda : Kumārila starts by saying that all the paraphernalia of secular and sacred life will become useless if ideas or cognitions were devoid of objects (corresponding supports in the external world). In order to understand *dharma*, therefore, it is necessary to examine the question of the existence and non-existence of external objects by means of proofs. He devotes 200 *ślokas* to the consideration of Buddhist doctrine of Vijñānavāda or Vijñaptimātratā; the system is called by Kumārila Nirālaṃbanavāda, i.e. the theory that there is no external support (*ālaṃbana*) of ideas which are the only realities.[2]

The Buddhist holds that the idea alone (*jñānamātra*) is the real entity. All this manifestation (the external world) can be explained as the *saṃvṛti* (false reality), as such it is useless to adhere to the reality of the external world.[3]

But this theory (of two realities)[4] is quite untenable. There can be no reality in *saṃvṛti* (falsity), as such it cannot be a form of reality. If it is a reality how can it be *saṃvṛti* ? If it is *saṃvṛti* (false), how can it be real ? Reality cannot in common belong to two mutually contradictory objects, true (*satya*) and false (*saṃvṛti*); the character of the 'tree' cannot belong in common to a tree as well as to a lion. Moreover, the words '*saṃvṛti*' and '*mithyā*' are synonymous, and the assumption of *saṃvṛtisatya* is either meant to hoodwink ordinary men or with a view to removing the stain of atheism from Buddhist doctrine. Furthermore, when the external world is void (*śūnya*), how can consciousness assume it at all ? It, therefore, follows that what exists is real, and what does not exist is unreal; a thing is either absolutely real or absolutely unreal. Hence the doctrine of two truths is untenable.[5]

The Bauddhas (Vijñānavādins) further hold that the experiences of heaven, etc. are similar to the experiences of a dream.[6] It is for the refutation of this theory that we (the Mīmāṃsakas) seek to establish the reality of the external world. Nobody will practise *dharma* for the pleasures of a dream, for dream experiences come spontaneously to a man in sleep; the *paṇḍita* will rather lie down quietly, instead of performing sacrifices, etc. when desirous of obtaining the real results. It is for these reasons that the Mīmāṃsaka seeks to prove the truth of external things.[7]

The Bauddhas, both the Yogācārins and the Mādhyamikas, deny the external world. The former hold that ideas are without corresponding supports or realities in the external world, while the latter deny the reality of the ideas also. But the denial of the external world is common to both these classes of Buddhists.[8] The Mādhyamikas hold that inasmuch as the external object is unreal, no cognition based on it can be real. It is only after setting aside the reality of the object that they lay down the falsity (*saṃvṛti*) of the idea (*jñāna*).[9]

The denial of the external world is, according to the Bauddha, of two kinds. The first kind of denial is based upon the examination of the object itself which is as follows. Neither atoms nor a conglomeration of atoms are amenable to the senses as the aggregate too can have no existence apart from the atoms themselves. Nor can the embodied substance be sensed, for this has no existence apart from the constituent atoms which cannot be perceived by the senses. For these reasons it is concluded that there is no external object that can be perceived by the sense.[10]

The Buddhists have reasoned out yet another kind of denial, and this second kind of denial is in fact the root of the theory of Nirālaṃbanavāda. Here also the denial of the external world is introduced in two ways : first, through inference, and then, after an examination of the applicability of sense-perception through its inapplicability (to external objects). It is this kind of denial based upon inferential argument which is discussed here.[11] The Buddhist argues as follows.

(i) It has been declared that sense-perception (*pratyakṣa*) is only that which is produced by contact (of the senses) with the particular object; but there is no relation between the objects and the sense-organ in reality, while as for an assumed contact, this is present in a dream also. Therefore, it is impossible to differentiate between cognitions produced by such contact and not so produced.

(ii) Again it has been said that falsity is only of two kinds and not more, but here it is added that all cognition is false; why then should there be any such specification ?[12]

"Thus, the cognition of a pole is false, because it is a congition; because whatever is a cognition has always been found to be false for instance the cognitions in a dream."[13]

Kumārila employs logical as well as dialectical devices to refute the Buddhist argument. He has formulated the *pūrvapakṣa* in a manner that would suit his way of criticism. Thus while stating the Buddhist view he says that the Buddhist accepts the self-congnisability (*svāṃśagrāhya*) of cognition (*jñāna, vijñāna*) and denies the reality of the external objects of perception.[14] He repeats this view when he starts his own thesis (*siddhānta*) and says that when the self-cognisability (of cognitions) is refuted, what remains there (in the Buddhist theory) is only a pure denial of everything that is cognisable.[15]

But this denial, says Kumārila, cannot be sustained, because the object of sense-perception does have an existence in the external world, and hence if you deny this (external world) you would simply contradict your own theory of sense-perception.[16] Moreover, if you deny every conception, then your own theory, being a conception, would also be denied.[17] Moreover, the predicate and subject (the major and minor terms of your syllogism) being (according to you Buddhists) incapable of being cognized (i.e., being no real objects of comprehension), you would be open to the charge of having both the subject and the predicate, or only one of them such as has never been known. If the cognition of the subject and the predicate, as belonging to the speaker and the hearer, were without corresponding realities, then both of them would stand self-contradicted. Nor would any differentiation be possible between the subject and the predicate. For these reasons your declaration of the conclusion is not right.[18]

We do not admit of any such entity as not having a real corresponding object (*nirālambanatā nāma na kiñcid vastu gaṃyate*); therefore it is not right to raise any questions with respect to the absence or otherwise of such entities.[19] Kumārila asks : if the cognition is not a real entity, then in what way do you wish to explain it to us ? Or how do you yourself comprehend it ?[20]

If it be urged that "we assume its existence and then seek to prove it"—then (we reply) how can there be an assumption of something that does not exist ? And even if it is assumed, it comes out (by the mere fact of this assumption) to be an entity. If it be asked—"how do you (Mīmāṃsakas) apply cognisability to negation (which is a non-entity) ?" (we reply) that we hold negation to be a real entity.[21]

Whether (you have for your minor term 'cognition') as a property of the soul or independently by itself—in any case, your argument has the great defect, viz. of having the subject unknown. Nor is there any such thing as 'mere mind' (*vijñānamātra*) without objects, because such a mere mind cannot be recognized or specified.[22] Though for others (e.g. the Mīmāṃsakas) there is a specification in the shape of mere signification of a word, but such cannot be the case with you, for you do not accept any difference between the word and its signification.[23]

If you seek to prove the fact of being devoid of a substratum, as Universal, then you are open to the faults of having your predicate unrecognized, and that of the absence of an example.[24] If, however, you assert the fact of being devoid of substratum only partially, we also admit the cognition of taste to be devoid of colour, so that your argument becomes superfluous.[25] And again, if you seek to reject only such substratum as the form in which the cognition appears, then (we say that) inasmuch as you accept the cognition of the cognition itself (*svākāra*) such denial (of the form of cognition) would be a self-contradiction.[26]

If by *nirālambanatā* (*vijñaptimātratā*) you mean that consciousness has no such substratum (in the external world) as the pole and the like, then this would contradict a visible fact.[27]

For us (the Mīmāṃsakas) the reality or the unreality of a cognition is based upon the contact of the senses with the objects, and it is on the authority of this that we accept the cognized object as real or unreal.[28] For you, however, there being no sense-organs, there can be no other ground for holding the fact of the cognition having a real substratum than the cognition itself, and as such a denial thereof is unreasonable.[29]

Moreover, when you do not recognize the reality of any external object, how could you have such a minor term as 'cognition appears to be external ?'[30]

You will have to face graver difficulties if you go on asserting the non-difference between the object of cognition and the cognition itself.[31] There is no denotation without connection, and this connection is impossible without some difference between the word and its denotation. But you do not accept any difference between the word and its signification, therefore your argument becomes unintelligible and faulty.[32]

Further, it is impossible to impart any instruction with regard to *dharma* and the like, without ascertaining in its reality the difference between *dharma* and *adharma*, or between teacher and pupil. We, therefore, conclude that the difference of the idea (of *dharma* from *dharma* itself) is accepted even by your Teacher (Buddha). And in denying the difference between the percipient (cognition) and the perceptive (cognized) you contradict your own Master.[33]

The view (of you Buddhists) goes against the facts known to all persons who always recognize objects apart from their cognitions.[34]

Above all we press against you the following argument: 'cognitions have real substrata in the external world; and this notion is correct because it is a notion free from contradiction, like the notion of the falsity of dream-cognition'. Now if you urge that this notion is also false, then dream-cognition would never be false, and consequently it could not supply the instance (of falsity) in the argument you have brought against us. (Here the Buddhist is put into a fix: if he accepts the falsity of dream-cognition, he cannot say anything against the counter-argument put forward above, and he loses his ground; but if he does not accept to avoid this fix the falsity of dream-cognition, then he contradicts himself, for he has employed dream-cognition as an instance of false-cognition.)[35]

In the same way, if you were to accept the correctness of the notions of momentary character, distinctness and existence of cognitions, then your argument (i.e. the middle term) would become inconclusive or doubtful; while if you accept the falsity of such notions, you contradict your own theory. Moreover, there could be, in your theory, no such distinction as that into the 'bound' and the 'liberated', and hence you would have the absurdity of the fruitlessness of any efforts toward liberation.[36] Then, if all cognitions were false, there could be no idea of comparative reality or unreality of objects in regard to the sense organ concerned.[37]

For us (the Mīmāṃsaka) dream-cognition would certainly be falsified by the perception of a waking-cognition contradicting it, but for you what would constitute the difference (between the reality of waking cognition and that of dream-cognition, both of which are held by you to be equally false) ?[38]

We do not come across any such instance where a waking cognition as such is contradicted by another waking-cognition, while the whole world knows that the dream-cognitions are contradicted by waking-cognitions.[39]

If you urge that even waking-cognitions become invalidated by the contrary cognitions of a *yogin* (who knows all worldly things to be false), we reply that such *yogic* cognition does not belong to any person in this life, and as for those who have reached the state of a *yogin*, we do not know what happens to them.[40]

Kumārila, then, adduces some striking arguments which would appear to anticipate modern parapsychology and theories of dream-cognition. He says that the external substratum is not altogether absent. In all cases there is a real substratum, though in dreams appearing under diverse conditions of time and place. What is perceived in dream is some real external object that has been perceived previously either in this life or in some past life, or at some other time, and it is cognized in dreams either in the same context or under different circumstances.[41]

Thus the cause of misconception in the notion of the 'fire-brand-circle' is the fire-brand whirled with extreme rapidity; in that of 'imaginary cities' (*gandharvanagare*), the particular shape of the clouds; as also some pre-conceived notions, etc. in that of 'mirage', pre-conceived water, or sand heated by and reflecting the rays of the sun; the cause of the notion of 'hare's horns' would be either the horn of the other animals, or the peculiar character of the hare itself. And of the negation of the hare's horns, the cause is the baldness of its head. Of the notion of 'emptiness' in the object, the cause is the place untouched by any other object. And in the case of improbable utterances (e.g. 'hundreds of elephants on the tip of one's finger'), the cause lies in the objects themselves (as under the influence of extreme proximity of giving rise to such misconceptions).[42]

A typical example of Kumārilian dialectic and technique of disputation is observable in the following few lines.

Even such objects as are never perceived (e.g. the Sāṃkhya *prakṛti* according to Pārthasārathi Miśra) are comprehended by cognitions, and the origin of these cognitions lies in (its constituent elements) the earth, etc. It is a peculiarity of sense-perception (*pratyakṣa dharmaśca*) that it comprehends the objects existing at the present time, and also that it functions over objects in contact with the senses (such is not the case with inference).

How could an object, not existing, bring about a cognition ?—asks the opponent to which Kumārila answers as follows.

Whence do you conclude the capacity of non-existing objects to produce cognitions ? The point of debate between us is the fact of cognitions having external substrata and even if there be no proximity of the objects (with the sense-organ) how could that affect our theory ?[43]

After dilating on the inferential arguments, Kumārila proceeds to refute the Buddhist tenet of *vāsanā* (impression), basing his arguments chiefly on the Buddhist theory of momentariness (*kṣaṇabhaṅgavāda*).

It is impossible for the Buddhist to specify the impression (*vāsanā*), for he has no cause for specification. The idea (cognition) is said to exist by itself. It is without differentiation and hence it cannot be the cause of specification. Moreover, to say that the difference of *vāsanā* is due to the difference of idea is to land upon reciprocity and thus contradict the tenet that the idea by itself is of pure form.[44]

There is no evidence either for the existence of *vāsanā*, or the differentiation thereof; even granting its existence, *vāsanā* would only bring about the differentiation of the apprehender (*grāhaka*). Then by what would the differentiation of the apprehended (*grāhya*) be brought about ? Appearing as it does in consciousness (*saṃvitti*) alone, the *vāsanā* could only give rise to memory.[45]

Moreover, the Buddhist theory of momentariness goes against the theory of *vāsanā*. The ideas (*citteṣu*) being momentary, and their destruction being total, and their being no association of the impressed and the impresser (i.e. two do not appear together), there can be no *vāsanā*. The next moment (*uttara-kṣaṇa*) having not yet appeared, cannot be impressed by the foregoing moment (*pūrva-kṣaṇa*); and the following moment having been destroyed as soon as it appears, there can be no impression thereby by the foregoing; and even if the two moments appeared together, they could have no relation between them. Hence there can be no *vāsanā* or impression.

(The preceding and following moments) being momentary, they cannot operate upon one another, then how can that which is in the course of destruction be impressed by another which too is undergoing destruction ? It is only the permanent entities (i.e. those that last for some moments) that can be impressed by other entities which are also permanent.[46] For you (the Buddhists) who hold doctrine of momentariness of things, there can be no causal relation between the preceding cognition and the following cognition, the preceding cognition cannot produce an effect unless it is destroyed, nor can it do so after having been destroyed. Therefore, the assertion that there exists a causal relation between two ideas is wrong.[47]

Further, since the cognition is destroyed totally, whence can there be such similarity (*samāna dharmatā*) (as you would have us believe) ? As in the subsequent cognition there exists no such property as belonged to the preceding cognition, barring the sameness of properties, no other 'similarity' is possible (Pārthasārathi Miśra adds : if the property of the previous cognition persists in the subsequent cognition then the former cannot be said to have been destroyed totally).[48]

It is only on the destruction of the cause, and not otherwise, that the effect is held (by you) to appear. And hence the destruction of a single idea would bring about the destruction of all impressions (based thereupon). And then, the Universal Idea that had been brought about by all these impressions would all in a single moment disappear.[49] If you hold the potentiality of the idea to subsist even after its destruction, its momentary character would disappear and your theory of momentariness would stand contradicted.[50]

If you have assumed the existence of *vāsanā* (impression) as a false reality (i.e. *saṃvṛti satya*) only and not as true reality, then in that case no effect can ever be produced by such assumed false reality.[51]

Concluding his survey of and polemic against the Vijñānavāda (Nirālambanavāda), Kumārila makes the following remarkable observation. "As a matter of fact, this denial of (the reality of the external world) objects, following upon the assumption of such an 'impression-theory' which is incorrect and devoid of reason, was declared by the Buddha with the sole object of alienating the affections (of men from such worldly objects); and somehow or other, some people (the so-called followers of the Buddha) fell into a mistake (and accepted it to its utmost extent as the denial of all external substratum of cognitions)."[52]

Śūnyavāda : In the Śūnyavāda section of the *Ślokavārttika*, the Mīmāṃsā Doctor considers certain Buddhist doctrines, which he puts under '*śūnyavāda*' in two hundred and sixty-three verses; sixty-three of them are devoted to the *pūrvapakṣa* and the remaining two hundred to criticism of the same.[53]

The Buddhist, addressing the Mīmāṃsaka, says : 'You stick to sense-perception, and the contradiction thereof you urge as an objection against our argument; now just consider the following points'.

'Is it a fact that a cognition is able to function, only when such objects as the post and the like have an existence in the external world ? Or is it that the cognition rests only in itself as the object cognized, and not in any extraneous object ? If it is only the external object that is perceived by the cognition, then the objections urged by you are right enough; but if it is the cognition itself which is cognized, then each and every one of them falls to the ground.[54]

It must be admitted, the Buddhist states, that all living creatures are aware of the fact that the fact of cognizability belongs to objects, in the form of blue, yellow, long, short, etc.

And we do not perceive any difference in the form of the cognition and the cognized; nor do we have any clear idea of this or that property as belonging to this or that object. What is real must be cognisable, what is incognisable cannot be real; it must therefore be admitted that there exists something with a form, inasmuch as it possesses the character of congnisability. Now, if the investigators of this problem find that the cognition itself appears as having a shape, then the trustworthiness (of the existence of the form) would rest solely in cognition, and the postulation of an external object would be groundless.[55]

If however, the form belonged to the external object, then the latter would have to be accepted as really existing on the sole ground of its being cognized; and for the accomplishment of this (perception) we would also have to accept the existence of the cognition.[56]

Now, which (of the two alternatives) is correct ? It must be the consciousness itself which has the form (as perceived). Why ? Because we find that it is one and the same object which has the form and it is cognized as such. If what has the form were held to be some extraneous object, then its cognisability not being otherwise possible, we would have to postulate something else as the cogniser. But in doing so, we would be postulating a groundless cogniser, which would be formless and something foreign to the cognisable object. If, in order to avoid the postulation of a groundless entity, you were to attribute the character of the cogniser to the object itself, then the difference between us would be only nominal, (i.e. you would be holding the external object to be both the cogniser and the cognized, while we hold cognition itself to be both). In any case, we assert the identity of the cogniser (consciousness) and the cognized (the object); the assumption of either externality or internality is utterly groundless.[57]

In my theory, the Buddhist goes on, although the real character of consciousness is naturally pure,[58] yet in this beginningless world there is an agglomeration of diverse dispositions or impressions born of foregoing cognitions and it is owing to these that the cognition appears in various forms tinged with the *grāhyagrāhaka-bheda*, which latter however, is not something apart from the cognition; and as such, the cognition does not need any extraneous object. The reciprocal causality of the cognition and its faculty (in the form of dispositions) is not faulty, just as the reciprocal causality of the seed and the shoot or tree is not faulty. The assumption of one is certainly better than that of many, and the assumption of a diversity in the faculty (of an object) is better than that of a diversity in the objects themselves. For these reasons it is far more reasonable to postulate the form to belong to the cognition itself; cognition must be held to have the form, because being self-luminous it is accepted even by you to be the means of illuminating the external object which in itself is devoid of any luminosity. Moreover, without the comprehension of the cognition, the object cannot be comprehended, because such comprehension depends upon the cognition, like the jar under the light of a lamp.[59]

Even when the objects have appeared, the Buddhist continues, they are not cognized, either because there is no illumination (of consciousness) or because there is some impediment (to their cognition). For the cognition, however, when it has appeared, there is no impediment; it being ever luminous cannot but be cognized. You accept the appearance of the cognition even prior to the appearance of the object, and as such we would have the comprehension of the cognition (even prior to that of the object). If such comprehension were denied even in the absence of impediment, then we can as reasonably deny its comprehension at all times, even after the comprehension of the object.[60] Because what would accrue to the cognition subsequently (i.e. after the comprehension of the object) which did not originally belong to it and accompanied by which it has never been really comprehended, but only comes to be known subsequently as 'comprehended' ? The luminosity (the appearance of cognition) does not stand in need of the appearance of another cognition, for if it were so, then the comprehension of one cognition would require the appearance of another cognition, and so on *ad infinitum*, and there would be no resting ground for any cognition.[61]

We find that even in the absence of external objects, we have a reminiscence of their forms following upon mere ideas thereof. How could this memory be possible if the cognition did not always embrace the form of the objects, and even in the past the objects were not cognized only as preceded by such cognition ?

Even with respect to the cognition of the objects existing at the present time, we see the people asserting : 'this is a blue object, for with respect to it I have such a notion'.

It is, therefore, clear that the objects are cognized only after the cognitions having been cognized; nor is there any comprehension possible when the cognitions are without any definite forms. Because there is no difference between the objective form and the cognition, and because only such objects are cognized as have forms, it stands to reason that it is the cognition alone, and not any external object, that can ever be comprehended as having that form.[62]

We have already said that it is only after the cognition of the cognition itself that the external object is cognized. It is impossible for the form of the object to enter the inner cognition, and therefore, the form cannot be said to be super-imposed on the cognition.[63]

Moreover, there is no evidence that the object is endowed with (such) a form (as would enter the cognition); for this reason, we do not accept the position (held by the Sautrāntikas) that the form is reflected upon the cognition. It is only the person who has seen the surface of the water during the day as without any reflection of the moon, that seeing at night the moon in the sky, can recognize its reflection in water. But in the case of cognition, it has never before been seen without a form, nor there has been any idea (without cognition) of the external object being endowed with a form; and hence, in this case, there can be no notion of reflection.

And again, what sort of reflection could there be in the case of (incorporeal objects like) sound, colour, taste, etc. ? And how could there be any notion of the form belonging to the object, when it is distinctly comprehended as belonging to the cognition ?[64]

Being as they are, located (separately) in the external world, and inside (the man), there can be no mutual contact between the object and the cognition; and hence, no amount of stupidity could give rise to the notion of identity (of the form of the object and the cognition).[65]

Since we do not find any person who is not so deceived, the assumption of such stupidity is ruled out; even if such deception could be assumed, it would apply equally to both (cognition and object). For this reason it is improper to assert that the form is a property of the contact (between the cognition and the object); such a contact is improbable, because of the difference of their locations, and because of cognition being incorporeal and the object being corporeal.

Such contact cannot be said to consist of the coevality or contemporaneity, for that would apply to the whole universe. Nor is there any such position of the object as is face to face with the cognition. If such contact could be held to be universal, then taste would come to be perceived by the eye, which is impossible. Nor can it be said that the mere existence of the object, as an object of cognition, constitutes the said contact, because of what sort would the character of the object be prior to the comprehension of its forms ?[66]

Nor can it be proved that the diversity of cognitions or the diversity of forms is due to this (i.e. contact) which itself is formless; the form of the cognition cannot originate in the object which itself is also formless. We have already said that the cognisable does not exist apart from the form; the theory of contact, therefore, is without any foundation.[67]

Thus, by both affirmative and negative inferences we get at the fact of the form belonging to the idea. There is no proof for the existence of an external object independently of the idea, while we have the idea independently of the external object. The contact theory could be maintained only with reference to the impressions. It cannot be maintained that both the idea and the object have one and the same form, because (i) there is difference in their positions, (ii) there is no contact between them, and (iii) there is no definite notion of the two being distinct and different.[68]

Moreover, in the case of the use of such words as *nakṣatra* (neuter), *tārakā* (feminine), *tiṣya* (masculine) and *dārāḥ* (masculine plural) it is impossible for the contradictory genders, etc. to apply to one and the same thing. Similarly, with regard to a fair girl, for example, (a single object), there could not be such diverse notions of a corpse etc. In other words, (says the Buddhist) the terms '*nakṣatra*', '*tārā*', '*tiṣya*', all signify stars; now if the object star had any real existence in the external world then names of such contradictory genders could not be applied to it. In the same manner, the term '*dārā*' is always used in the masculine-plural, which could not be the case, if any such thing as woman (*dārā*) really existed in the external world. And again, in the case of a fair girl, the ascetic looks upon her as a disgusting corpse, the licentious man looks upon her as an object of pleasure, and the dog looks at her as an article of food, which diversity would not be possible if the fair girl had a real existence.[69]

Further, with regard to the same object we have the notions of its being long and short, in comparison with different objects, and with regard to the same object (e.g. one finger appears long in comparison with one, while shorter in comparison with another finger). A jar, e.g. is conceived as a jar, being earthly, being a substance, and being predicable—all these notions appear simultaneously in the observer; but this could never be the case, if there really existed any such single object as the jar. For, in one and the same object, the application of contradictory forms is not possible. As for the ideas, they are different in each case, and as such adjustable to the diversity in the force (of impressions).[70]

The object should be traced to the form that an idea takes, and never the vice versa; the form of the object depends on the idea, so that the existence of the external object is not possible. As for the idea, it could rest in itself.[71]

Having summarized the doctrines of Śūnyavāda as he viewed them, Kumārila proceeds to refute the same with his characteristic logical subtlety and polemical skill.

What has been said by the Buddhist, says he, is not true; you (Buddhists) hold the idea to be both cogniser and the cognized; but you cannot cite any instance wherein such a duplicate character belongs to a single entity.[72] Because, fire and the like, that are illuminators (of the jar and the like), cannot be said to be themselves illuminable, and they do not stand in need of any illuminator. And whenever they come to be cognized they are cognized through a sense-organ; the sense-organ is cognized by the idea. And this idea itself is cognized by another idea; but in no case can the same object be both cogniser and the cognized.[73]

Moreover at the time of cognising a cognisable form, such as the blue, we do not come across any idea which has the form of (this cognising) cognition.[74]

No pure idea would be possible if it were to be non-different from the object (which has a form); if the object cannot be comprehended, the cognising agency too cannot be comprehended because they are held to be non-different.[75]

And again as the comprehension of the cognizable object would not lead to that of the cognising idea—and as the comprehension of the cognising idea would not lead to that of the cognisable object—there would be non-comprehension of both these (because they are held to be non-different).[76]

The Buddhist asserts that since both idea and the object are identical in form, therefore when one is comprehended the other too is comprehended. But this is not true for this is proved neither by perception nor by inference. As a matter of fact it is only one form that is comprehended, and yet you (Buddhists) assume a second; why then cannot you assume a thousand such forms to be included in that single idea ?[77]

If, however, it is only conventionally that you call these entities '*jñāna*', then let that be so; the word '*jñāna*' when applied to the object would be explained as 'that which is known', and when applied to the cognition, it would be explained either as 'knowledge' or as 'that which cognises anything'. In any case, the duality of existence (in the form of cognition and the cognized) becomes established.[78]

There is no such distinct class as '*jñāna*' which embraces both (cognition and the cognized); you do not admit of any distinct class of *jñāna* apart from the individuals. Even if there were such a distinct category of '*jñāna*' different from the cognized and the cognition, then in that case, the character of '*jñāna*' could not belong to these two; thus there being a total absence of form or character of '*jñāna*' there would result an absolute negation of '*jñāna*'.[79] And as there is no other substance (than idea), even an '*apoha*' (negation) cannot be possible for you because the Buddhist Idealist does not admit of a non-Idea that could be negatived by *apoha*.[80]

Since ideas do not appear together, the two ideas cannot be causally related; they can have no such relation as 'conceived' and 'the means of conception' as has been said in the *Bhāṣya* (i.e. *Śābarabhāṣya*, vide K. Chaṭṭopādhyāya, 'References to Buddhist Philosophy in the *Vṛttikāragrantha* of '*Śābarabhāṣya*', *Jha Commemoration Volume*, pp. 115ff.); "it (idea) is momentary etc. Therefore, the object (of cognition) must be something other (than the idea itself).[81]

It is thus that there can be no causal relation between the two ideas even when they appeared simultaneously. The mere concomitance of the idea and the object cannot be called a causal relation. The wise people take into account the notion of sequence besides the notion of concomitance. On the contrary also, if sometimes the cow followed the horse, this mere sequence could not constitute the causal relation.[82]

Your example of the lamp and the light emitted by it as an example of the simultaneity of the cause and the effect, is unsound, because in this case also, there is a minute point of time (intervening between the appearance of the lamp and that of the light), though this is imperceptible, just as is the case with the piercing (with a needle) of the hundred petals of the lotus. The same criticism would apply even if you assert the simultaneity of the two parts (of cognition), i.e. the comprehender and the comprehended.[83]

What is comprehended by memory is nothing but a comprehended object, mixed with its past character. In dream-consciousness, however, it cannot be so, because the dream-consciousness is always false, as in dreams what is not present is cognized as present, but this is not so with the cognitions of a waking state.[84]

The theory that the cognition cognizes itself is not sound; while comprehending the object, the cognition does not approach itself (does not render itself comprehensible); though the idea illuminates other things, yet for its own illumination it needs something else; its illuminative character consists in cognising objects and not in cognising itself. As in the case of the eye, we see, though the eye illuminates things, yet its illuminative character is limited to specific objects, colour, form etc. An eye does not see itself, likewise the idea cannot know itself.[85]

For those who hold that cognitions have cognitions for their objects, the distinction between the 'cognition of a jar' and that of 'a cognition of this cognition' is impossible.[86]

Different persons comprehend one single thing in different forms so that it is possible for a thing to have different forms. There is no such hard and fast rule laid down by God that "one object must have one and only one form."[87] As a matter of fact, apart from the form of the object, there is no recognition of the idea. And the idea being recognisable by another's form cannot be the object of cognition, because it is like a mirage.[88]

The remarkable review and the trenchant criticism of the tenets of Buddhist systems reproduced above shows that Kumārila was well trained in the niceties of Buddhist dogmatics. Gopīnātha Kavirāja observes[89] that "Kumārila's knowledge of Buddhist philosophy was more profound and more accurate, though Śaṃkara is better known as having been more deeply influenced by Buddhism."

At one place (*śloka* 14, Nirālambanavāda, *S.V.*) Kumārila refers to the two well known schools of Mahāyāna philosophy (the Vijñānavāda and the Mādhyamika) and says that "the Yogācāras hold that the idea is devoid of the corresponding reality (in the external world), and the Mādhyamikas deny the reality of the idea also." The arrangement of two different sections entitled 'Nirālambanavāda' and 'Śūnyavāda' also shows that the Mīmāṃsā Doctor intended to deal with these two schools separately. But in spite of this pronounced scheme, we find that the great author of the *Ślokavārttika* has confused between the tenets of the two schools; throughout these two large sections, it is only the doctrines of Vijñānavāda school that attract his attention; the essential doctrine of Śūnyavāda is left untouched. On the whole, we find a very good review of the Vijñānavāda philosophy which is without a parallel in Brahmanical quarters.

Śaṃkara's View of Buddhist Thought

Śaṃkarācārya, the most famous among the Brahmanical philosophers and the supreme champion of Advaita Vedānta, who is now supposed to have lived in the last quarter of the eighth century A.D., presents us with an account of Buddhist philosophical systems. In keeping with the old and honoured tradition of Indian philosophers, he also gives in his commentary on the *Brahmasūtra*,[90] first the *pūrvapakṣa* and then a critique of the same afterwards. In discussing Śaṃkara's view and review of Buddhist doctrines his own plan has been followed below.

Buddhism, according to Śaṃkara, is a system of nihilism (*sarva-vaināśika*); but he distinguishes three principal systems of these 'thoroughgoing nihilists' : (1) the Sarvāstivāda, (2) the Vijñānavāda, and (3) the Śūnyavāda.

Sarvāstitvavāda : According to the Sarvāstitvavāda,[91] every thing, external as well as internal, is real; what is external is either matter (*bhūta*) or material (*bhautika*); and what is internal is either mind (*citta*) or mental (*caitta*). The elements (of matter) are the earth, water, etc.; the elemental are eye, colour, etc. The external world arises out of the four kinds of atoms which are either hard, fluid, hot or mobile, according as they are earth, water, fire and air, respectively.[92]

The internal world, which constitutes the personal existence of man, consists of the five groups (*skandhas*) of matter (*rūpa*), consciousness (*vijñāna*), feeling (*vedanā*), sensation. (*saṃjñā*), volitions (*saṃskāra*).[93]

With regard to this view, says Śaṃkara, we have to observe that neither the elements (or atoms) nor the aggregates (or groups) of elements called the *skandhas*, are able to achieve the two classes of groups assumed by the Buddhists. Because the elements of these groups are non-intelligent, nor can they enter into activity of their own accord for that would imply their ceaseless activity, (in consequence of which) there will be no liberation. The Buddhist admits of neither the existence of a self or a permanent intelligent being who enjoys, nor that of a Lord who governs, nor a chain of cognitions of one's 'ego' be said to be the cause (of the activity of these elements). For if the chain is different in character from the several momentary cognitions of which it is constituted, it would be tantamount to the acceptance of an eternal Self of the Vedānta. But if the chain too is momentary, it cannot bring about the motion in atoms so that the latter would not be able to form an aggregate, and in the absence of the aggregates the external and the internal worlds will be non-existent, and the mundane existence will disappear altogether.[94]

The Buddhist may argue as follows. Although there exists no Lord who rules, and no Soul who enjoys, yet the mundane existence is rendered possible by the force of causal links. This series in the causal chain comprises *avidyā*, *saṃskāra*, *vijñāna*, *nāma-rūpa*, *ṣaḍāyatana*, *sparśa*, *vedanā*, *tṛṣṇā*, *upādāna*, *bhava* and *jāti*, and the whole lot of painful things attending on mundane existence.[95] These links in the chain of causes and effects revolve ceaselessly like pots in a water-wheel, and explain the *saṃsāra*.[96]

But this argument, says Śaṃkara, cannot be accepted, because it merely accounts for the origin of several members in the series by reference to the preceding members of the same; it does not explain how the external and internal aggregates are formed. It has been pointed out above that even on Vaiśeṣika doctrine,[97] it cannot be proved as to how the atoms are combined, in spite of the fact that the doctrine admits the existence of permanent atoms and of the souls in which the unseen fruits of actions reside. It is much more impossible, on the Buddhist view, to explain the combination, when the atoms are held to be momentary and are bereft of any connection with souls and with the unseen fruit.

The series of *avidyā* and so on, being itself dependent on the assemblage of atoms and *skandhas*, cannot be the cause of the latter. If you (Buddhists) say that the series of *avidyā* and so on, as well as that of atoms and *skandhas* on which it depends, are simultaneously responsible for the continued existence of *saṃsāra*, we ask: are the successive aggregates of atoms and *skandhas* like unto each other or unlike ? In the first case (i.e. if they are like unto each other) a man, in spite of his good or bad deeds, will never be able to obtain the bodies of birds and animals or of angels and gods; in the second case (i.e. if they are unlike each other) a man may change at any time, even while living, into an elephant or a god. Moreover, in the absence of an eternal self it is inconceivable how a man can wait till the objects of enjoyment are formed for his sake, or till the time of his final liberation.[98]

There can be no causal relation between any two momentary things, because it is only after the first momentary entity has ceased to exist that the second momentary entity comes into existence. If it be said that the mere existence of the antecedent entity produces the consequent entity, then the doctrine of universal impermanence will be contradicted, because such an assumption would mean that the antecedent entity continues to exist in the subsequent entity.

Apart from this flaw, what does the Buddhist mean by the origination and destruction of things ? It may mean the nature of a thing, in that case, whether a thing is destroyed or not, it will continue to maintain its nature in spite of the theory of momentariness. If, however, origination and destruction are the initial and final stages of one and the same intermediate thing, then the thing would be existent during moments of time which would mean the abandonment of theory of momentariness. And finally, if the origination and destruction are absolutely different and distinct from the thing, just as a horse is different from buffalo, even then we reach the same conclusion—the thing will be permanent and will not be affected by origination and cessation. However, if origination and destruction were merely to imply the perception and non-perception of a thing, then these terms would refer to the percipient being and not to the thing at all. Hence the Buddhist view is untenable.[99]

The Bauddha may say that 'there may be an effect even if there is no cause'[100] but then, the basic tenet of the school that the mind and mental states arise on account of the four different causes (*pratyayas*)[101] will have to be abandoned. Moreover, anything may arise at any time, if no cause is required.[102]

These 'nihilists' (*vaināśikāḥ*), Śaṃkara goes on, imagine that all produced things, save the triad of 'space' (*ākāśa*), 'cessation through intellectual power' (*pratisaṃkhyānirodha*) and 'cessation through the absence of productive cause' (*apratisaṃkhyānirodha*), are momentary. This triad, they hold to be non-substantial, of negative character (*abhāvamātra*) and devoid of all positive traits.[103]

Now the twofold cessation (*nirodha-dvaya*) is impossible. Why? Because of the absence of interruption, both kinds of cessation must refer either to the series of momentary existences, or to the single members of this series. But neither of these alternatives is admissible; the series of things cannot be destroyed, as the members are causally related in an uninterruped manner; and it is equally impossible to maintain that any momentary existence should be annihilated by itself. A thing is known, either by perception or by inference, to exist in various states through which it passes, e.g. the clay is known as such whether it appears as a jar or the potsherds into which it is broken. It is for these reasons that the two kinds of cessations cannot be proved to be real;[104] nor can it be proved that they are devoid of positive characters and of non-definable nature. The scripture (*śruti*) declares that "space came forth from the Self."[105] This shows that space is a real entity; moreover, the existence of space can be inferred from the quality of sound. If you say that the *ākāśa* is simply uncovered space, then the existence of any flying bird in the sky would render the space covered, so that there would be no room for a second bird wishing to fly at the same time. If you reply that another bird may fly in another portion of the sky where there is an absence of covering body, then we point out that that portion of the sky is a positive entity, viz. space and not a mere non-existence of covering bodies.

Moreover, by defining the space negatively, you (Buddhists) go against Buddha's *ipse dixit*, for the Buddha (Sugata) says that "the air is founded on space."[106] How 'air' which is a positive entity could have its support in space (*ākāśa*) if the latter were a non-entity ? Further more, it is contradictory to say (as you do) that the two *nirodhas* and the (*ākāśa*) are non-entities and of negative character and also eternal (*śāśvata*) and not produced (*asaṃskṛta*). How can a thing which is negative and unreal be eternal ?[107]

The 'nihilist' philosopher holds the doctrine of universal momentariness of all things; he will have to extend this momentariness to the experiencing subject also. But this is rendered impossible by the fact of recollection or rememberance. It is not the case that one man cognizes things and another recognizes; recollection belongs to the same person who had previously made the perception. Even the '*vaināśika*' thinker will admit that the perceptions which he had yesterday, he remembers today; he knows that the perceptions he remembers today belonged to him in the past as surely as he knows that fire is hot.[108]

The Buddhists, says Śaṃkara, are *asatkāryavādins*; they deny the existence of permanent and stable causes and therefore believe that an entity arises from a non-entity. This belief is expressed in the following manner. The sprout comes forth after the seed is destroyed, curd is formed only when the milk ceases to be milk, and the clay ceases to be a mere lump of clay before we see a jar out of it. If effects did spring from changeless or permanent causes, all effects would originate from all causes at once, and no specification would be required.

To this Buddhist tenet we reply, says Śaṃkara, (entity does) not (spring) from non-entity; if non-entity were to produce entity, then there would be no meaning in assigning specific causes for specific effects, such as seed for sprout, clay for jar, or milk for curd. On the contrary, we will have to assume that the sprout originates from the hare's horn which is absurd. In no case would a non-existence possess causal efficiency, simply because like a hare's horn it is non-existence. Every effect wears a peculiar aspect of existence. The Buddhist view that nothing which does not change, can become a cause, is false.[109]

Vijñānāstitvamātra-vāda : The Vijñānavādin Buddhist thinker says that the Buddha indeed expounded the doctrine of the reality of the external world in order to cater some of his pupils who were too much attached to the world. But this was not his real view; Buddha's real doctrine was that nothing but the consciousness is real.[110]

(According to this system) all experience—the act of cognition, the object of cognition and the result of cognition (*pramāṇa-prameya-phala-vyavahāra*)—is an internal one, existing only in the mind (*buddhi*). Even if things existed in outside world, we cannot experience them unless the mind determines their form. But if the things existed in the external world, they would be either of the nature of atoms or of their aggregates. Obviously, things like pillars cannot be apprehended as atoms, because the latter are imperceptible; nor can they be apprehended as aggregates of atoms; for if these aggregates are different from atoms, they cannot be considered as composed of atoms; and if they are non-different, they will be as imperceptible as atoms. Hence there will be no cognition of pillars as pillars.

In a like manner, one can demonstrate that the external objects have neither universality (*jāti*) nor any other category.

The cognitions which are of uniform nature only in so far as they are various states of consciousness, undergo modifications according to their objects, so that the mind is presented now with the idea of a post, now with the idea of a wall, now with the idea of a jar, and so on. In other words, the forms of objects of our knowledge are determined by our ideas and not given by the reality of the external world.

Our knowledge of the objects in the form of ideas and of objects themselves being always simultaneously presented (*sahopalambhaniyama*) must in reality be one and the same. Had they been different, we might have been aware of one and not the other, which however, is not the case. When we are conscious of the idea we are conscious of the object also. Hence we maintain that the world of external things is unreal.[111]

One more reason for not believing in the reality of the external things is that our perceptions of waking life are similar to our experiences of dreams and illusions. The ideas present to our mind during a dream, a magical illusion, a mirage, and so on, appear in the twofold form of subject and object, in spite of the fact that there is no external object. Therefore, it is legitimate to hold that the experience of our waking life also may be independent of external things. Our perceptions of the objects are simply ideas.

The variety and diversity of ideas is not due to external objects, but due to the diversity of impressions (*vāsanās*) of past ideas. In this beginningless *saṃsāra* the ideas and impressions succeed each other as causes and effects, as necessarily as the seed and sprout succeed each other. The following affirmative and negative judgements also lead to the same conclusion. We both the Vedāntins as well as the Bauddhas admit that in dreams and illusions, there presents itself a variety of ideas which arise from mental impressions without any external objects. We (the Bauddhas) do not admit that any variety of ideas can arise from external objects without mental impressions. We therefore conclude that the external things do not exist.[112]

To all this, Śaṃkara makes the following reply. The non-existence of external things cannot be maintained, because our perceptions point to the existence of external things corresponding to our ideas. Nobody will pay heed to a man who, while eating and relishing his dinner, says that he is neither eating nor having any satisfaction out of it; let the Buddhist say as he likes. The truth is that consciousness itself points out to us that what we are aware of in perception is not perception itself, but the object of perception.

The Buddhist seems to accept this fact when he states that consciousness appears 'like something external'. How can there be 'something like external' when there is really nothing external? No one says : 'Viṣṇumitra appears like the son of a barren woman.'[113]

Moreover, the possibility and the impossibility of the objects of perception cannot be made dependent on our preconceived notions, but must depend on the authority of perception or some other means of proof. As a matter of fact, external things are apprehended by all instruments of knowledge; you cannot maintain their non-existence on the ground of such an idle dilemma as that about their difference or non-difference from atoms.[114]

Moreover, it is difficult to understand how can the ideas have the forms of objects; does it mean that forthwith the objects whose forms the ideas have are all reduced to these forms only? The fact is this that objects are perceived as external and as distinct from the ideas. Therefore, the invariable concomitance of the ideas and the objects should be construed as the expression of a causal connection between them and not as that of identity. That the idea and the object are different and distinct from each other can moreover be shown by reference to the difference between a substantive and the attributes belonging to it. Thus the perception of a white cow differs from the perception of a black cow, though the knowledge of a cow in general is the same; the knowledge of 'white' and the knowledge of 'black' are different from the generic knowledge of cow which remains the same; the same is the case with perception and rememberance of a jar, although the jar is the same.

If you (Buddhists) say that we are aware of the idea, you must admit that we are also aware of the external thing. To say that 'the idea is self-luminous' like a lamp is tantamount to the absurd statement that 'fire burns itself', while you deny the common and rational view that we are conscious of the existence of things by means of the ideas which are different from things. This is an extraordinary philosophical insight indeed, which makes a thing an object of its own activity.[115]

The lamp-like self-illuminating idea of the Vijñānavādin appears neither in need of any means of proof nor of any knowing being. But this is like believing that a thousand lamps burning inside an impenetrable rock manifest themselves.

The view that the self-luminous idea of the Vijñānavādin resembles the view of Vedāntin is not correct; the witnessing-self of the Vedāntin is one, eternal and self-manifesting, while the ideas of the Vijñānavādin are many and momentary and without any intelligent principle (i.e. *ātman*).[116]

The view that the ideas of waking life are similar to the ideas in a dream is not correct. The experience of a dream is cancelled by waking life, and the experience in the dream is due to memory or infatuation by sleep, while the experience in waking life is due to the apprehension of the presence of the objects.[117]

The view that the variety of ideas can be explained through the variety of mental impressions (*vāsanāvaicitrya*) and without any reference to external things is incorrect.[118]

If you maintain that the store-house consciousness (*ālaya-vijñāna*), assumed by you, may constitute the abode of mental impressions, we reject that, because that is momentary in character and impermanent, and therefore, cannot be the abode of impressions any more than the quasi-external cognitions (*pravṛtti-vijñāna*). Unless there be something which continues to exist and is connected with the past, present and future, or unless there is the absolutely eternal on-looker (i.e. Self) of all things, there will be no proper explanation of the whole of practical life which consists of memory, recollection and the various impressions.[119]

Śūnyavāda : With regard to the Śūnyavāda or the Sarva-śūnyatva-vāda, 'the doctrine that everything is void', Śaṃkara's treatment is striking. He says that this doctrine goes against all means of right knowledge, and therefore, it is unworthy of refutation (*tannirākaraṇāya nādaraḥ kriyate*). This apparent world, the existence of which is attested by all means of knowledge, cannot be denied except on the recognition of some other truth; a general principle is proved by the absence of contrary instances.[120]

The height of Śaṃkara's criticism of Buddhist thought reaches in his comment on the thirty-second *sūtra* of the second section of the second chapter of the *Brahmasūtras*. He says therein that no further consideration (for this system) is in fact required. From whatever point this Buddhist philosophy is examined, it collapses from all sides, like the walls of a well dug in sandy soil. It has, in fact, no foundation to rest upon, and hence it is unworthy of becoming a practical guide in life.

Moreover, Buddha by propounding the three mutually contradictory systems, viz. the reality of external world (*sarvāstitva*), the reality of ideas only (*vijñānamātra*), and genera nothingness (*śūnyavāda*), has made it clear that either he was a man given to making incoherent assertions, or else, that his hatred of all beings induced him to propound absurd doctrines by accepting which they would become thoroughly confused.

The essence of this *sūtra* is that the Buddha's doctrine should be entirely discarded by all those who wish to achieve their spiritual good.[121]

It is not possible here to give any exhaustive Buddhist answers to the strictures made by Śaṃkarācārya. It is not difficult to see that much of the foregoing animadversion is based on certain fundamental misunderstandings concerning Buddhist principles.

The epithet 'nihilist' (*vaināśika*) given to Buddhist philosopher by Śaṃkara is not in keeping with Buddhist's true position. Nowhere in the whole mass of Buddhist philosophical sūtras and śāstras can we cite any single instance to justify the epithet *vaināśika.* Right from the Buddha down to Śāntarakṣita, over a period of about fourteen centuries of Buddhism's active life in India, we find that the Buddhists have been giving warnings against falling into grave mistakes of believing in eternalism and nihilism; the Mādhyamikas had always championed the doctrine transcending both *est* and *non-est*, is and is-not, *asti* and *nāsti.*[122]

Śaṃkara's criticism of the Sarvāstivāda views is far from being sound. It does not seem to be true that "Śaṃkara had a firm grasp of the real significance as well as the limitations of Buddhist thought."[123] On the contrary, it is true that "Śaṃkara's knowledge of Buddhist philosophy was naturally superficial",[124] and that he misunderstood and "ignored the fundamental principles of Buddhism".[125]

Thus Śaṃkara is not right in identifying the mental (*adhyātman*) with the aggregate of the five *skandhas.* The *citta* or *vijñānaskandha,* in Sarvāstivāda, stands for one of the components of the aggregate. Similarly, Śaṃkara's view that the Buddhists deny that causes produce their effects is clearly wrong. The Buddhists do not deny the causal relation between things, they only say that there are no permanent causes; nothing, which is changeless and eternal, can produce an effect; the law of *pratītyasamutpāda* had always been the central plank of Buddhist philosophy. Therefore to say that the Buddhists deny the fact that causes produce effects is absolutely wrong.[126]

Śaṃkara is not right when he regards the trinity of *asaṃskṛta-dharmas* (to wit, *ākāśa*, *pratisaṃkhyānirodha* and *apratisaṃkhyānirodha*) as 'mere nothing' or 'non-existence' (*abhāvamātra*). The Vaibhāṣikas hold that they are uncompounded (*asaṃskṛta*) and immutable *dharmas*; they are positive entities though incapable of description in words. *Pratisaṃkhyānirodha*, like Upaniṣadic *ātman*, is the goal of spiritual efforts, though *anabhilāpya*, yet *pratyātmavedanīya*.

Śaṃkara's statement that the Buddha taught these doctrines out of hatred (*dveṣa*) for the people (*prajā*) and owing to his desire to confuse the people is a serious and baseless charges against the Blessed One, the All-compassionate (*sabba-bhūtānukaṃpī*) Buddha. Such a stricture, paralleled only in some Purāṇic passages,[127] can be understood only as a product of *odium theologicum*.

It is remarkable that Śaṃkara has not dealt with the doctrines of the Mādhyamika, and has summarily dismissed it as unworthy of refutation. It is well known that his grand-*guru*, Gauḍapāda's work the *Āgamaśāstra*, displays unmistakable influence of Mahāyāna philosophy. It is not unlikely that Śaṃkara discovered his own non-dual philosophy in the system of Nāgārjuna[128] and left it unexplained. His debt to Śūnyatā doctrine was so great that he quietly passed over it.

Chapter X

ORIGIN AND GROWTH OF ESOTERIC BUDDHISM

Esoterism or Tāntrikism

THE PHRASE 'esoteric Buddhism' seems to be an appropriate mode of expressing the significance and essential character of the contents of the Buddhistic Tantras. These texts profess to be meant for the initiates and their teaching is said to be 'esoteric' or 'secret' (*guhya*). Historically, this 'esoteric Buddhism', commonly described as "Tāntrika Buddhism', is the last phase of Buddhism in India, and its beginnings are wrapped up in obscurity.

Etymologically the term '*tantra*' seems to have been connected with the idea of weaving and its derivatives: warp, loom, thread. The grammarians derive the word from the root '*tan*', meaning 'to extend' or 'propagation'; the word is also used for a book, e.g. *Pañcatantra*, a collection of stories; Śaṃkara uses the word for a philosophical system,[1] and the *Amarakośa*[2] refers to various treatises as '*tantrāṇi*'.

In the *Kāmikāgama*, *tantra* is explained as a class of texts 'that deals with profound matters concerning *tattva* and *mantra*'.[3] In this sense a *tantra* would mean a manual giving the principles of truth and mystic sounds. In modern Sanskrit lexicons *tantra* is understood as "a class of works teaching magical and mystical formularies."[4] *Tantra* is also understood to mean a religious system or science (*śāstra*) dealing with the means (*sādhana*) of attaining success (*siddhi*) in secular or religious efforts.

In Tibetan, the term '*rgyud*' (*tantra*) stands for a *tāntrika* text, "a ritual book for coercing deities and for other magical ceremonies".[5] One of the large sections of the Kanjur which contains numerous Buddhist *tāntrika* texts is known as *rgyud*. It would seem from the above discussion that the word '*tantra*' connotes several meanings,[6] but its special technical meaning is a religious system now commonly called Tāntrikism and the scripture belonging to this system. Mahāyāna Buddhism came to be transformed, in course of time, into Tāntrika Buddhism, just as Mahāyāna Sūtras were supplanted by Buddhist Tantras.

The religion expounded in the Tantras is a peculiar mixture of mystic syllables (*mantras*),[7] magical diagrams (*yantras*), ritualistic circles (*maṇḍalas*),[8] physical gestures (*mudrās*) sex-play (*maithuna*), psycho-physical discipline (*yoga*),[9] a fearful pantheon, elaborate worship and ritualism, magical sorcery, necromancy, symbolism, astrology, alchemy, coefficiency of female element and a monistic philosophy.[10]

The affirmation of the material world, the dogma that all gods together with the supreme truth reside in the human body, the assumption of the principle of an apparent duality in an essential non-duality, the tenet of the coefficient female partner (*śaktisāhacarya*) as *sine qua non* in the process of liberation, a radical ethics that everything is pure for a pure men or *omnia sancta sanctis* and above all the concept of the *summum bonum* of life in terms of the Great Delight (*mahāsukha*) born of the union (*yab-yum*) of 'male' (*upāya*) and 'female' (*prajñā*)—would appear to be some of the fundamental postulates of Tāntrikism or Esoterism of the Buddhists and the Hindus alike.

Antiquity of Esoterism

The Tantras make no claims for historicity; instead, they claim to be revelations. All the Tantras, Buddhist as well as Brahmanical, ascribe their doctrines and practices to the highest personalities in their religious hierarchy.[11] The Tantras are regarded as scriptural authority par excellence,[12] and often classed with the Vedas.[13] The Purāṇas clearly recognize the Tantras as authorities on religious affairs.[14] In spite of all this, the developed Tāntrika religion as it was prevalent during our period and became popular in medieval times, is not a very old religious system of India, although its seeds may be traced back to the remotest period of Indian civilization.[15]

It has been held by some that Tantra was of foreign origin. H.P. Śāstrī, while maintaining that Śakti-worship is the *raison d'etre* of Tantra, held that "Tantra came from outside India. Most probably it came with the Magi priests of the Scythians". As an argument he pointed out that wonder is expressed in the *Niḥśvāsatattva-saṃhitā* at the novel mode of Tāntrika initiation.[16]

Likewise, B. Bhattacharya opined that "The introduction of

Śakti-worship in religion is so un-Indian that we are constrained to admit it as an external or foreign influence".[17]

P.C. Bagchi[18] pointed out some possible foreign elements in the Tantras; but they are quite late importations and belong to a period when Tāntrikism had become popular in India and when India's cultural contacts with northern neighbours had become well established. It is true that Tantras contain many un-Indian elements and in some Brahmanical texts[19] they are condemned, yet it is far from truth to regard the Tantra as a whole or Śakti-worship in particular, as un-Indian or of foreign origin.

According to H.P. Śāstrī, Tantra "really means the worship of Śakti or female energy."[20] Gopīnātha Kavirāja observes that "Tāntrika worship is the worship of Śakti".[21] It is becoming increasingly manifest that the cult of Śakti is related to the cult of the Mother Goddess[22] on the one hand, and to phallic worship and Śaiva cult on the other. Archaeological discoveries in the Indus delta have indicated that the seeds of Śāktism go back to the days of Harappā and Mohenjo-daro,[23] that is, about the third millennium B.C. Tāntrikism has so much in common with Śaivism and Śāktism that it might eventually be taken as the most ancient living faith in the world except for the elements incorporated in its body in the course of centuries.

The famous steatite seal from Mohenjo-daro described by John Marshall as a 'male god' and as "the prototype of historic Śiva"[24] may equally be regarded as the prototype of the Tāntrika Siddhas. There is much indirect and extremely suggestive evidence for Śakti worship in Harappan culture. The well-known bronze "dancing girl"[25] from Mohenjo-daro might be taken as the prototype of Tāntrika Yoginī. The continuity of this custom of female religious and professional dancer from the third millennium before Christ to the pre-Mauryan, Mauryan and pre-Kuṣāṇa days is attested by the gold plaque from Lauriyā-Nandangarh, supposed to represent Goddess Pṛthvī, [26] the so-called "Naṭī of Pāṭaliputra",[27] and a number of terra cotta statuettes from Mathurā.[28]

The association of sex with religion was a common feature of primitive beliefs; phallism has been a feature of popular religion since the dawn of civilization.[29] Vedic literature is said to bear traces of phallic worship.[30] Numerous antiquities found in Harappan sites by E. Mackay and John Marshall,[31] and in the neolithic sites in the Deccan by Bruce Foote,[32] also indicate the worship of *yoni* and *liṅga*. Possible traces of the cult of hierodule have been suggested by some writers even in the Vedic literature.[33]

A large number of Tāntrika elements, such as *mantras*, sacrifice, priestly sorcery and magical charms, use of wine, worship of semi-divine and demoniac beings were, perhaps, the legacy of the Vedic people.[34]

About a dozen hymns of the *Ṛgveda* are concerned with the magic; "magic is the main and essential subject matter of the *Atharvaveda*; it is a collection of metrical spells."[35]

The *Ṛgveda* frequently refers to the magicians and sorcerer (*yātudhāna*) and to the power of the spells. A person says : "may he lose his ten sons who falsely calls me sorcerer"[36]; at one place we read : "with mighty spells the fathers found the hidden light."[37] The *Ṛgveda* also knows men possessed of supernatural powers, "the gods had entered into them."[38] In Vedic literature the place for the practice of magic is usually a cemetery or the seat of flesh eating demons.[39]

The cult of female-worship remained subordinate throughout the great days of the Vedic Āryans, perhaps because of its being a cult of the pre-Āryan races and cultures. But popularity seems to have been enjoyed by what are known as Apsarases, lit. 'goers in the water', water nymphs.

The long-haired *muni*, with magic powers, is said to move on the path of Apsarases and Gandharvas;[40] the Gandharvas are lovers of the Apsarases. The fact that in a rite the priest points to the young men and maidens present when he means to indicate Gandharvas and Apsarases[41] would appear to be a pointer to the Tāntrika mode of addressing Vajradhara and Vajrī ('male' and 'female').

The Tāntrika idea of the unity of male and female and of the female aspect being inherent in the male aspect, may be compared to a passage in *Ṛgveda* where Indra appears as manifold by his *māyā*.[42] This concept is echoed in the *Śvetāśvatara Upaniṣad*,[43] and strongly reminds of the Śivaite theology. Mystic syllables or 'gibberish' like *svadhā*, *svāhā*, *vaṭ*, *phaṭ*, *vaṣaṭ*, *śrauṣaṭ*, etc. abound in the *Yajurveda*.[44] Of the puerilities of muttering *mantras* or spells and reciting hymns for controlling the forces of nature, subduing the foe and winning the love of a woman, "the Brāhmaṇas are never tired."[45]

According to some scholars the semi-religious and semi-magical practices of the Tantras seem to correspond to a phase of Vedic ritual represented by the *Sāmavidhāna Brāhmaṇa*, the *Ṣaḍviṃśa-Brāhmaṇa* and the *Atharvaveda*.[46]

In the *Taittirīya Upaniṣad*, the entire universe (macrocosm) with its elements and forces is equated to the human body (microcosm).[47] The *Bṛhadāraṇyaka Upaniṣad* compares the 'sacrificial horse', its limbs and organs with the universe, its forces and elements.[48] A similar symbolical account of the human personality is given in the *Chāndogya Upaniṣad*.[49] This text says that the vowels (*svara*, '*āli*') proceed from Indra, while the consonants (*varṇas*, *kāli*') proceed from Brahmā.[50] As pointed out by G.C. Pande, the *Śvetāśvatara* also presupposes a "Siddha-body".[51]

The *pañcavidyās* described in the Upaniṣads have manifest Tāntrika import. The *Bṛhadāraṇyaka* and the *Chāndogya* describe male as 'fire' and female also as 'fire'; the gods sacrifice vital energy in this 'female fire' (*yoṣāgni*); that is to say, male fire is sacrificed in the female fire.[52] The *Ṛgveda* also states that "the gods offered sacrifice of sacrifice",[53] and the *Bhagavadgītā* refers to those offering sacrifice of sacrifice itself.[54] In the Tantras, Vajrasattva and Vajravilāsinī make sacrifice into *vajra* and attain to *yab-yum*.

In the *Chāndogya*, Ghora-Āṅgirasa tells Kṛṣṇa Devakiputra that all actions of a man who sacrifices self into the self become spiritualized including, eating, laughing and *maithuna*.[55]

The worshipper of the *dahara-puṇḍarīka* is conceived as possessed of all the powers of attaining all objects of enjoyment.[56] The vision of the *nemi* and *cakra* revealed by a sage in the *Śvetāśvatara* is strikingly Tāntrika in character.[57]

A passage of the *Bṛhadāraṇyaka* describes the joyful condition of the union of *jivātman* with *paramātman*, and compares it with the state of a person embraced by his beloved. The passage hardly admits of translation and is in agreement with the language of the Tantras.[58]

The foregoing discussion should suffice to establish the indigenous origin and great antiquity of a large number of elements, theoretical and practical, which may have contributed to the evolution of Tāntrikism on Indian soil.[59] The question that now crops up is concerning the time and circumstances in which Tāntrikism came to be introduced into Buddhist fold. Such a question presupposes that early Buddhism was eatirely free from traces of Tāntrikism or Esoterism as it is now known from the Buddhist Tantras. But such a presupposition runs contrary to certain traditional accounts and the views of some modern scholars. Moreover, the Tantras themselves claim to have been 'proclaimed by Buddha'. To the examination of this aspect of the problem we now turn our attention.

Traditional Beginnings of Esoteric Buddhism

The Buddhist Tantras like the Mahāyāna Sūtras, claim to have been revealed by Buddha; the origin of Esoteric or Tāntrika Buddhism is therefore traced to Buddha himself. In the *Sekoddeśaṭīkā*, a comment on the Sekoddeśa section of the *Kālacakratantra*, it is stated that Mantrayāna had been first imparted by Buddha-Dīpaṅkara but it had to be adapted to our age by Buddha-Gautama or Śākyamuni. At the request of Sucandra, king of Śaṃbhala, Buddha Śākyamuni convened a council at Śrī Dhānyakaṭaka and delivered a discourse on esoteric path or Mantranaya, just as he had previously delivered a discourse on the Mahāyāna (Prajñāpāramitānaya) at Gṛdhrakūṭa.[60]

This tradition is confirmed by the Tibetan historians. According to Bu-ston Rinpoche, the Kālacakra system was preached by Buddha in the year of his Enlightenment. He rejects the view held by other Tibetan annalists, that the event took place in the 80th year, the year of Nirvāṇa of Buddha.[61] According to yet another Tibetan authority, Buddha performed the act of 'turning the wheel of the Law' three times: first in the year of Enlightenment at Ṛṣipatana (Sārnāth); second, ın the 13th year of Enlightenment at Gṛdhrakūṭa near Rājgīr where he taught the Mahāyāna; and third, in the 16th year of Enlightenment at Śrī Dhānyakaṭaka where he taught Mantrayāna.[62]

There is not even the slightest reliable ground to attach any historical importance to these legends. The tradition of a third *dharma-cakra-pravartana* like that of a second, seems to have been fabricated to give an air of authenticity to the 'Way of spells'. The references to Dhānyakaṭaka and to Śaṃbhala, an enigmatic country real or imaginary, are however, significant for the history of the origin and growth of Buddhist esoterism.

(1) There is no reliable evidence to assume that Buddha ever went to the far south at Dhānyakaṭaka, The Pali Tipiṭaka and the Ceylonese histories do not know this tradition. (2) That it is a late invention is apparent from the fact that the *Mañjuśrīmūlakalpa*, possibly the earliest Vaipulyasūtra whichc ontains many elements of the Mantrayāna, does not know this tradition, although it refers to Śrīparvata and to Śrī Dhānyakaṭaka as favourable seats for the practice of *mantra-siddhi.*[63](3) The *Guhyasamājatantra*, perhaps the earliest known Buddhist Tantra, which gives all essential elements of Tāntrikism is also silent on this point. (4) In fact, the *Guhyasamāja* contradicts the Tāntrika Buddhist tradition when it records that (i) Buddha, when he appeared as Dīpaṅkara, did not expound the *guhyasamāja* tenets and (ii) the graphic description of astonishment of the Bodhisattvas who fell into coma by hearing the radical teachings.[64]

A number of *sādhanas* and *mantras* are attributed to the authorship of Sugata. We read in the *Sādhanamālā* that the *sādhana* of Jāṅgulī was prepared by Buddha,[65] that the *sādhana* of Vajrasarasvatī was composed according to the instructions of Sugata;[66] and that the *mantra* '*om picu picu prajñāvardhani... svāhā*' was delivered by Buddha.[67] The *Tārātantra*, equally acknowledged by Brahmanical and Buddhist Tāntrikists, states that Buddha, while he was living in Mahācīna (China) initiated Vasiṣṭha in the secret doctrines of Cīnācāra.[68] According to the *Mahācaṇḍaroṣaṇa*, the great truth that "the Buddhahood abides in the female organ" was discovered by Śākyamuni who attained Buddhahood by practising Tāntrika rites.[69] The *Guhyasamāja tantra*[70] and the *Hevajratantra*[71] represent Buddha delivering secret doctrines while enjoying the blissful state with Vajrayoginī.

A balanced criticism of these Tāntrika traditions requires grea sympathy and an unbiased mind. Seldom will one come across any other instance wherein with less sympathy the founder of a spiritual discipline may appear to be systematically, and perhaps innocently, transformed by his own followers who advocated an easier path for salvation, composed new treatises to propagate their chosen practices, and attributed them to Śākyamuni, making him a Tāntrika of the first order.

According to Benoytosh Bhattacharya there is no room for

any doubt that "the *tantras* and *mantras*, *mudrās* and *dhāraṇīs*, were taught by the Buddha to the lay-brethren"[72] that "a clever organiser as the Buddha was, he did not fail to notice the importance of magical practices in his religion to make it popular from all points of view and thereby attract more adherents."[73] The learned scholar seems to have placed absolute reliance on the statements of the Tāntrika authors of the *sādhanas* noted above, which he himself places between A.D. 300 and 1200. It is evident that these *sādhanas* cannot be regarded as Buddha's creations or revelations. Nor is there any evidence beyond doubt which points to the existence of *tantras*, *maṇḍalas* and *dhāraṇīs* in the time of Buddha.[74]

Bhattacharya refers to two verses[75] in the *Tattvasaṃgraha* of Śāntarakṣita as explained by Kamalaśīla in his *Pañjīkā* thereon. Both these worthies lived in Tāntrika Age and flourished about thirteen centuries after the Buddha.

The passage in question in the *Tattvasaṃgraha* runs thus: "That is described as Dharma by all wise men, from which follows prosperity and the highest good; whosoever properly practises the rules laid down there, regarding *mantra*, *yoga*, and such things, becomes endowed even with obvious qualities such as knowledge, health, greatness, and so forth".[76] Kamalaśīla, commenting on these *ślokas*, says that the phrase 'and such things' (*mantra-yoga-ādi*) is meant to include '*mudrās* and *maṇḍalas*'.

But there is nothing specially Buddhistic about the first *śloka* (3486); it is borrowed from the *Vaiśeṣikasūtra* as a definition of Dharma;[77] it is not a Buddhistic definition. In the next *śloka* (3487) Śāntarakṣita refers to the merits accruing to the man who practises the *mantras*, *yoga*, etc. He does not say that Buddha taught *mudrās*, *mantras*, and *maṇḍalas* so that people may become happy and prosperous by practising them. The explanation of Kamalaśīla that etc. (*ādi*) is meant to include them is rather arbitrary; and he himself lived and wrote at a time when *mudrās*, *maṇḍalas* and *mantras* had become common features of religion. The testimony of Kamalaśīla, therefore, is a very slender thread which cannot be relied on. As Winternitz observed, "There is nothing in the Tripiṭaka or any early Buddhist document to prove that Gautama and his early disciples had anything to do with the *mudrā*, *maṇḍala* and *dhāraṇīs*."[78]

Buddha has been described as a rationalist of the first order;[79] the *Tattvasaṃgrahapañjikā* itself bears witness to the fact that Buddha discouraged superstition and recommended critical enquiry.[80] The *Vīmansakasutta* of the *Majjhimanikāya* shows that Buddha discouraged blind faith,[81] and the *Kesamuttisutta* of the *Aṅguttaranikāya* reveals that Buddha was not in favour of winning disciples unless they were satisfied after critically examining his teachings.[82] What Buddha emphasized to his pupils was the need of purity, fear from doing evil, sense-control and mindfulness.[83] Buddha's characteristic saying was that the disciples should seek refuge in themselves, should seek no other refuge.[84] The *Pāsarāsisutta* reveals Buddha's true attitude when it records that running after the enjoyments is an ignoble quest.[85] The *Kevaṭṭasutta* shows that Buddha disapproved of magical and superhuman feats, and regarded these as black arts like the Gāndhārī-vijjā.[86] In the *Brahmajālasutta* a long list of pseudo-sciences (*vijjās*) is given, but Buddha apparently condemns them as low arts.[87]

Historical Beginnings of Esoteric Buddhism

The beginnings of Esoteric Buddhism seem to be inseparable from the beginnings of the Mahāyāna; indeed the Tibetans never made any difference between Mahāyāna and Vajrayāna. What are known as *sūtras* (*mdo*) in Sanskrit are classed by them as *tantras* (*rgyud*).[88] They even went so far as to give Nāgārjuna a life-span of 600 years and attributed to him both the *Madhyamakaśāstra* as well as the *guhyasamāja* system.[89]

Mantras became so fundamental to Esoteric Buddhism that the latter is often called Mantrayāna (Mantranaya).[90] *Mantras* seem to have been developed from *dhāraṇīs*. These *dhāraṇīs* are often traced to the *parittās* known, for instance, to the *Āṭānāṭīyasutta* of the *Dīghanikāya*,[91] and to the *Milindapañha*.[92] But their sense in these texts is not identical with those of *mantras* as found, for example, in the *sādhanas*. The Mahāsāṃghikas are known to have compiled a *Vidyāharapiṭaka* or *Dhāraṇīpiṭaka*,[93] and citations from this text are still known to us.[94] *Dhāraṇīs* are known to the *Lalitavistara*,[95] the *Samādhirājasūtra*,[96] the *Sandhinirmocanasūtra*,[97] the *Saddharmapuṇḍarīkasūtra*,[98] and the *Laṅkāvatārasūtra* among the early Mahāyāna texts.

A number of texts discovered in Gilgit and assignable on

palaeographic grounds to the fifth and the sixth centuries A.D. contain *dhāraṇīs* and *mantras*. These texts are older than their script.[99] The *Kāraṇḍavyūha* attributes a *dhāraṇī* to Buddha.[100] The celebrated spell associated with Avalokita viz. *om maṇipadme hūṃ*, occurs in the *Divyāvadāna*,[101] which refers to many other spells. The *Mahāmāyūrīdhāraṇī* famed as a *vidyārājñī* had been translated into Chinese in the fourth century A.D.[102] The *Laṅkāvatāra* contains many magical formulae,[103] and the *Bodhisattvabhūmī* dwells at length on the meaning and mystic aspect of the syllables.[104] Bhāvaviveka is found reciting *Vajrapāṇīdhāraṇī* in order to have that god's vision.[105] In the sixth century A.D. *mantras* were written on birch-bark and used as amulets.[106] The *Mañjuśrīmūlakalpa* contains numerous *mantras* of numerous deities.[107] A large number of Mahāyāna Sūtras are little more than *dhāraṇīs*. To this class may be assigned the shorter Prajñāpāramitā sūtras.[108] Śāntideva quotes very many *dhāraṇīs* from earlier sūtras.[109]

B. Bhattacharya's attempt[110] to trace the evolution of the seed syllable (*bījamantra*) '*praṃ*' hints at a possible process of the developments of *mantras* from *dhāraṇīs*. '*Praṃ*' symbolizes Prajñāpāramitā. The *Aṣṭasāhasrikā* was a stupendous text which could not be recited by illiterate Mahāyāna laity. It was therefore reduced to *Prajñāpāramitāhṛdaya*. It may be noted that this shorter text was preserved in the Horiuzi convent of Japan since 609 A.D. and was considered as a *mantra* which alleviates pains.[111] The *Prajñāpāramitāhṛdayasūtra* was then reduced to *Prajñāpāramitā-ekākṣarī* and out of this latter was evolved the *bījamantra* '*praṃ*'. It was believed that by muttering '*praṃ*', *śūnyatā* would transform herself into Prajñāpāramitā, who is "a veritable metamorphosis of the Prajñāpāramitā literature".[112]

Besides the *mantras*, a vast and varied pantheon is another principal feature of esoteric Buddhism. A number of semi-divine, semi-human and even demoniac beings like Māra and his retinue, *yakkhas*, *gandhabbas*, *nāgas* and *devas* are known to old Buddhism. There they all appear as much inferior to Buddha and as protectors and devotees of the Dhamma save the evil Māra.[113] The early Indian Buddhist art of Sāñcī, Bharhut, Ajaṇṭā Amarāvatī, Mathurā and Gāndhāra, is full of the plastic forms of these beings.[114] Likewise tree and serpent worship was an equally old feature of popular Buddhism.[115]

The *Lalitavistara*, a text partly Sarvāstivādin and partly Mahāyānist, introduces Buddha in an assembly attended not only by *bhikṣus*, *bhikṣuṇīs*, *upāsikās*, but also by *devas*, *nāgas*, *yakṣas*, *gandharvas*, *garuḍas*. *kinnaras*, *mahoragas*, Śakra, Brahmā and the *lokapālas*.[116] Poussin did not find Padmapāṇī in the *Saddharmapuṇḍarīka*, the *Amitāyus*, the *Sukhāvatī*, or the *Kāraṇḍavyūha*. Padmapāṇi in later times was an epithet of Avalokita who is eulogized in the *Kāraṇḍavyūha* and the *Saddharmapuṇḍarīka*. But Padmapāṇi, originally probably a *yakṣa*, is represented in pre-Kusāṇa art of Mathurā.[117] When "the necessities of *bhakti* determined the appearance of all deities in visible forms" the old *yakṣa* figures became the model for cult images of Buddha, Bodhisattvas and other Brahmanical deities.[118] This fact points to great antiquity of Buddhist images.

The glorification and deification of Prajñāpāramitā, in the Prajñā texts indicates that she was revered as a powerful goddess. Besides, *Aṣṭasāhasrikā* also describes Gaṅgā goddess who passes from one Buddha-field to another Buddha-field. Prajñāpāramitā is the goddess supreme, the teacher and the mother of the Tathāgatas.[119].

The *Dharmasaṃgraha*, attributed to Nāgārjuna knows the following deities:[120] five Buddhas—Vairocana, Akṣobhya, Ratnasaṃbhava, Amitābha, and Amoghasiddhi; four goddesses Rocanī, Māmakī, Pāṇḍurā, and Tārā. The list of 18 *lokapālas*[121] includes, among others, Indra, Yama, Varuṇa, Kubera, Brahmā, Kṛṣṇa, Candra, Sūrya Pṛthvī, and Asura. The six *yoginīs* mentioned in it are: Vajravārāhī, Yāminī, Saṃcāraṇī, Saṃtrāsanī, and Caṇḍikā. The eight Bodhisattvas listed are : Maitreya, Gaganagañja, Samantabhadra, Vajrapāṇi, Mañjuśrī, Sarvanivaraṇaviṣkaṃbhī, Kṣitigarbha, and Khagarbha. Strangely enough, the most famous Bodhisattva, viz. Avalokiteśvara, with whom the list in the *Mahāvyutpatti* opens, is omitted here, unless he be Vajrapāṇi.

Amitābha or Amitāyu (Amitāyus) finds mention first in the *Sukhāvatīvyūha*. Vasubandhu is known to have been a devotee of Amitābha. The *Lalitavistara* mentions Maitreya and Dharaṇīśvara among 32,000 Bodhisattvas who listened to Buddha. Avalokita is eulogized in the *Saddharmapuṇḍarīka*, the *Dharma-*

saṃgīti,[122] and the *Sukhāvatīvyūha*. Fa-hsien testifies to the worship of Maitreya, Avalokiteśvara, Mañjuśrī, and deified Arhats. Hsüan-tsang describes images, temples and worship of Avalokita, Mañjuśrī, Maitreya, Tārā, Hārīti, Vajrapāṇī and *yakṣas*. I-tsing also testifies to the popular worship of Hārīti, Mahākāla, Maitreya, Mañjuśri, and Avalokiteśvara.

The prose version of the *Kāraṇḍavyūha* shows that Avalokita issued out of the primordial Tathāgata (Ādi-Buddha ?); in this text many attributes of Śiva are given to Avalokita. Thus he is *maheśvara* with eleven heads and hundred thousand arms.

Maitreyanātha testifies to the existence of the doctrine of Ādi-Buddha in the time of the *Mahāyānasūtrālaṅkāra*.[123] The *Suvarṇaprabhāsa* introduces not only four *dhyānī* Buddhas, to wit, Akṣobhya, Ratnaketu, Amitābha and Dundubhīśvara, but also Śrī Mahādevī, and Sarasvatī. Śāntideva testifies to the existence of deities like Ghoṣadatta (a Tathāgata), Gaganagañja, Mañjughoṣa, Avalokita, Nakṣatrarāja (a Tathāgata), Rutāvatī (a Sāgaradevī, 'inventress of music'), Siṃhavikrīḍita (a Tathāgata), Vidyutpradīpa (another Tathāgata), Indra, Amitābha, Ākāśagarbha, Anantaprabha (a Tathāgata), Akṣobhya, and demi-goddesses like Mārīci, Cundā, Ḍākinī, and a non-human deity Jaṃbhala.[124]

If coefficiency of female element is *sine qua non* in the esoteric career of an ascetic, and if Śakti-worship is the *raison d'etre* of Tāntrikism, one must point one's finger at the docetism and the erotic fancy of the Andhra-Vaitulyakas and the early texts of Mahāyāna known as Prajñāpāramitāsūtras. The esoteric career of a Bodhisattva who is supposed to embody in his being two great qualities, to wit, compassion (*karuṇā*) which includes skill in means and transcends the bonds of morality[125] and wisdom (*prajñā*) which from the standpoint of *śūnyatā* (*paramārtha*) teaches the utter substancelessness of all things material and mental, already detailed in early Mahāyāna Sūtras, leads to the same conclusion.

The *Kathāvatthu* records how the Vaitulyakas had made a provision that "on account of a particular intention, the saint could resort to sexual-intercourse."[126] Śāntideva refers to an old story of a saint who had broken his vow of continence out of *karuṇā* for a woman.[127] The declaration of the *Dharmasaṃgītisūtra* that "the Buddhas are beyond Nirvāṇa and *saṃsāra*'[128] might well have given the clue to the dogma that the Siddhas are beyond good and evil and they do not incur sin.[129] The virtue of Prajñāpāramitā having been deified is seen developing into a supreme Goddess and invoked like Buddha at the beginning of Sūtras. She becomes Bhagavatī to whom all Buddhas and Bodhisattvas owe their existence.[130] Avalokita, the supreme advocate of the doctrine of compassion (*upāya*) is seen as the husband of Prajñāpāramitā now called Tārā, the embodiment of wisdom (*prajñā*).[131] This development had taken place much before Hsüan-tsang. The description of *nairātmya* (i.e. *prajñā*, *śūnyatā*) in the *Nairātmyaparipṛcchā-sūtra* reads like the description of *prajñopāya*; in fact the compounds like '*mahāsukha*', '*bodhicitta*' and *prajñāpāramitā*' are used here as synonyms and this is called the Prajñāpāramitānaya.[132] This *mahāsukha*, according to Vajrayāna authorities, is impossible of attainment without Śakti, the embodiment of *karuṇā*.[133]

A few verses in the *Mahāyānasūtrālaṅkāra* of Maitreya-Asaṅga have been subjected to much critical explanation and controversy. Whether symbolical or actual, their essential import is erotic[134] and they are concerned with esoteric, erotic mysticism involving sexual-intercourse and psychophysical discipline which plays an important part in subsequent Buddhist esoterism.

Emergence of Esoteric Buddhism

The generally accepted opinion among modern scholars is that the Tāntrika Buddhism appeared in the seventh century A.D., and the Buddhist Tantras were published from the seventh century onwards.[135] B. Bhattacharya, G. Tucci, Gopīnātha Kavirāja and G.C. Pande seem to have been inclined to push the date of the emergence of Buddhist esoterism back to the time of Maitreya and Asaṅga. Rāhula Sāṃkṛtyāyana had also drawn attention to the great antiquity of Mantrayāna.[136] Yet the chronological problem concerning the approximate time of the emergence of Buddhist Tāntrikism does not seem to have finally settled. The following discussion is intended to correlate the available material with a view to suggesting a possible chronological outline of origin and growth of esoteric doctrines and literature in Buddhism. According to the Tibetan traditions,[137] Nāgārjuna, the great Mādhyamika dialectician and the putative father of Mahāyāna, was a great magician, (*mahāsiddha*); he acquired many *dhāraṇīs*, *prajñā* texts and *sādhanas* and propagated esoteric teachings. He was expert in medical sciences, alchemy and divination. He lived in Śrīparvata for 200 years and at other places enjoying a life of over five hundred years.

In all probability this Tibetan account of Nāgārjuna refers to another person of that name, a Tāntrika author and a Siddha, who flourished in about the eighth century A.D. This fact apart, the great philosopher and the author of the *Madhyamakaśāstra* and *Suhṛllekha*, a contemporary of Kaniṣka,[138] and a native of south, who spent many years in Śrīparvata, and was a teacher of Deva or Ārya (Kāṇa) Deva, is known to have been an expert in medicine and alchemy. The Mādhyamika philosopher's association with mystical system is suggested not only by the confused Tibetan traditions[139], but also by fairly reliable authorities like Hsüan-tsang, I-tsing, Bāṇabhaṭṭa, and the *Mañjuśrīmūlakalpa*.[140] Moreover, if pāramitānaya (the worship of Prajñāpāramitā) is in essence identical with Mantranaya (Tāntrikism), as seems not unlikely inasmuch as Prajñā of the Sūtras has become Śakti in the Tantras, Nāgārjuna's own encyclopaedic treatise, the *Mahāprajñāpāramitāśāstra*,[141] and his *Prajñāpāramitāstava* would lead to the same conclusion.

There are strong Tibetan and Chinese traditions concerning the intimate connection between Asaṅga and Maitreyanātha and of both with esoteric Buddhism. These traditions are confirmed by internal evidence of the treatises of these masters. Asaṅga is said to have been initiated into the esoteric path by his teacher Maitreyanātha. Both these worthies flourished probably in the third and the fourth centuries of Christian era.[142]

Asaṅga is famed in tradition to have received from Maitreya in Tuṣita heaven not only esoteric teaching but also a number of works. This Maitreya, supposed to be a celestial Bodhisattva by Hsüan-tsang and Tārānātha,[143] was a historical person, who wrote some standard texts on Buddhist mysticism which were commented upon by Asaṅga.[144]

The *Mahāyānasūtrālaṅkāra* which expounds the doctrine of *parāvṛtti* of *maithuna* is one such work, composed by Maitreyanātha and explained by Asaṅga. Bu-ston attributes to Maitreyanātha a work called *Mahāyānottaratantraśāstra*.[145] This text introduces the concept of *sahajakāya* or Innate Body which became the apex of Tāntrik mysticism. There is a common dictum among the late Mahāyānists and the Tāntrika Buddhists that "whatever is spoken by Maitreya, that is Buddha's word".[146] This Maitreya seems to be Bodhisattva Maitreya and new esoteric ideals were attributed to him with a view to ensuring their authenticity.

Moreover, as G.C. Pande has pointed out, in Asaṅga's *Abhidharmasamuccaya* also there is an allusion to erotic mysticism and the author uses the compound '*abhisandhiviniścaya*' which implied a double meaning, one manifest and the other intended; the latter was different from the manifest sense. This clearly seems to be the forerunner style of the Tāntrika *sandhābhāṣā*.[147]

Thus the names of Maitreyanātha and Asaṅga are closely associated with the emergence of (i) erotic mysticism. (ii) *sahajakāya* and (iii) mysterious language (*sandhābhāṣā*). Besides these important points Hsüan-tsang records that Asaṅga was an expert in (iv) "the law of entailing (or conferring on others) the power of *samādhi*" and that Asaṅga had a disciple named Buddhasiṃha, "a man whose secret conduct was unfathomable."[148] Tārānātha says that esoteric texts were secretly transmitted from the time of Asaṅga onwards.[149] B. Bhattacharya held the opinion that the *Prajñāpāramitā-sādhana*, attrtbuted in its colophon to Asaṅga, is also a work of this celebrated Yogācāra Doctor.[150] His view that Asaṅga was also the author of the *Guhyasamāja* stands on a very slender piece of suggestive evidence.[151] But even without making Asaṅga the author of this first known Vajrayāna text, Asaṅga's connection with esoteric Buddhism seems to be a well ascertained fact from the above discussed correlation of diverse pieces of evidence.

G. Tucci[152] had drawn a pointed attention to the fact that in the *Tattvasiddhiśāstra* of Harivarman[153] (*cir.* fourth century A.D.) there is a reference to a Tāntrika school called Na-ya-siu-mo (?Nayasauma, probably a Tāntrika Kāpālika sect) which believed in sixteen categories. These sixteen categories are enumerated in the *Madhyāntānugamaśāstra* of Maitreyanātha after the Māheśvara school. The list includes among other topics, medicine, *mantras*, stars, planets, gods and divine practices. Tucci concludes that this fact points, on the one hand, to the existence of some Tāntrika doctrines and practices in the time of Harivarman, and to the close relation between the Buddhists and the Śivaites (Kāpālikas) on the other.[154] It was probably the Somasiddhānta.

Winternitz[155] criticised the great antiquity claimed for the rise of Buddhist Tantrikism by Bhattacharya and Tucci. These scholars pointed to the fourth century A.D. as the probable time of the appearance of Vajrayāna. The preceding discussion of the growth of mantras, deities and the antecedents of erotic mysticism, should show that the historical beginnings of Buddhist esoterism go back at least to the first century B.C. when the Vaitulyakas flourished, Nāgārjuna lived, Prajñāpāramitā texts and a *Dhāraṇīpiṭaka* were composed, and when the Buddha image was published in plastic form.[156] Tāntrikism seems to have influenced some sections of the Buddhist order of monks some centuries before Asaṅga composed *Prajñāpāramitā-sādhana.* Goddess Prajñāpāramitā, '*sarvatathāgata mātā*', might well be considered as the true prototype of Tantrika Śakti or Prajñā. What Śakti is in Brahmanical Tantras, Prajñā is in Buddhist Tantras, and the evolution of Prajñā dates from 200 B.C., or perhaps even from an earlier period.

The *Kāraṇḍavyūhasūtra* possibly existed before the fourth century A.D. The cult of Avalokita is known to Fa-hsien, and his paintings of the fifth century A.D. are still extant in Ajaṇṭā. This text bears clear impact of Tantra and Purāṇic religion. It mentions Umā, Maheśvara, Mahākāla, and Mahāvidyā-maṇḍala; true it is, Tārā is not mentioned. But it glorifies the six-syllabled spell, '*om maṇipadme hūṃ*'; this is called the innermost core (*hṛdaya*) of Avalokita; this Maṇipadma, also called Ṣaḍakṣarī and Mahāvidyā-rājñī, is most likely a designation of female partner.[157]

The *Suvarṇaprabhāsasūtra*, first translated into Chinese in A.D. 414-433 by Dharmakṣema and in the sixth century by Paramārtha and in the seventh century by I-tsing, "for a great part already bears the stamp of a Tantra", and is "quite Tāntrika in its contents, formulae, and rites." Goddesses like Śrī Mahādevī and Sarasvatī are introduced in Buddhist pantheon.

The *Bhaiṣajyaguruvaidūryaprabharāja-sūtra* had been translated into Chinese by Śrīmitra between A.D. 317 and 322, by Dharmagupta in A.D. 615, and by Hsüan-tsang in A.D. 650. This text shows unmistakable influence of Tāntrikism. It refers to dreadful Tāntrika practices and spells, and includes *rākṣasas* among deities that were worshipped; those who eat flesh and blood, frequent cemetery and perform *sādhanas*, *ghora-vidyās*, are also described.[158]

A few more texts, the contents of which are quite Tāntrika, are also known. The *Mahāmāyūrī-vidyārājñī*, a Tāntrika *dhāraṇī* was translated into Chinese by Śrīmitra (A.D. 317-322) and by Kumārajīva (A.D 402-412).[159] The *Ekādaśamukhaṃ* which mentions so many spells of Avalokita was translated into Chinese by Yaśogupta (A.D. 557-581). The *Hayagrīva-vidyā* eulogises a horse-faced god and Avalokita.[160] This short work is a Tāntrika text of *mantra* and ritual; the horse-faced deity is associated with Avalokiteśvara; directions are given for drawing his image. It is significant that the Vajrayāna deity, Vajradhara, is mentioned here along with Hayagrīva; this latter is described in the *Sādhanamālā* as a minor god. The text is written in upright Gupta characters of about the fifth and sixth centuries.[161] To the same age and category belongs the semi-Tāntrika text called *Sarvatathāgatādhiṣṭhāna-sattvāvalokana-buddhakṣetra- sandarśana-vyūha*. This text was translated by I-tsing in A.D. 701. N. Dutt, the editor of the text, places this work in the fifth or sixth century A.D.

The text locates Buddha's residence at Potalaka, a mountain in South India referred to by Hsüan-tsang as the abode of Avalokiteśvara; a number of *dhāraṇīs* are recorded and also the rites given by Mahāyakṣiṇī Anopamā, Śaṅkhinī and Bhīmā Mahādevī.[162]

Among the characteristic texts containing exorcism, *mantras* and *dhāraṇīs*,mention may be made of *Nīlakaṇṭhadhāraṇī* discovered from Central Asia, and the *Mahāpratyaṅgirā-dhāraṇī*[163] which invokes Tārā and belongs to the sixth century A.D. The *Śikṣāsamuccaya* quotes from the *Anantamukha-nirhāra*, the *Cundā*, the *Puṣpakūṭa*, the *Mahāmegha*, the *Mārīci*, the *Ratnolkā*, the *Vidyādhara* and the *Sarvavajradhara*, all of which deal with *mantras* and *dhāraṇīs* and existed before the seventh century A.D.[164]

The *Mañjuśrīmūlakalpasūtra* is a ritual text of Mantrayāna dealing with numerous gods, goddesses, their iconography, *mudrās*, *mantras*, *maṇḍalas* and popular worship, although it styles itself a *Mahāyāna-vaipulya-sūtra*.[165] It is written in what is called '*gāthā* dialect' or 'mixed Sanskrit.' The printed text is a voluminous work and seems to be a compilation, reflecting not only the developed popular Mahāyānism, but also showing the growth of Tāntrika ritual and worship. The text glorifies Bodhisattva Mañjuśrī who is called Kumārabhūta and many Śaiva deities are associated with him. Goddess Tārā is introduced and her worship is prescribed. In the last two chapters goddess Vijayā is the chief speaker; in the ninth chapter the *mantra* of Mañjuśrī, viz. '*klhūṃ*' is described as a great king of sciences.

The *MMK* seems to belong to the class of later Mahāyāna sūtras, although the Tibetans put it under the '*rgyud*' section; but they did the same for the *Suvarṇaprabhāsa* which is a Mahāyānasūtra and one of the nine Dharmas. The *MMK* was translated into Chinese so late as the tenth century A.D. and it consisted at that time of only 28 chapters. The printed text in original Sanskrit contains 55 chapters. In the 53rd chapter, the text refers, among other things, to the defeat of Śaśāṅka by Harṣa, king Śīlāditya of Lāṭa (i.e. Śīlāditya I, Dharmāditya) and to the election of the first Pāla ruler, Gopāla. These facts show that the present text is placeable in the eighth century A.D. or even later. It was translated into Tibetan in the eleventh century A.D.

B. Bhattacharya placed the original text of the *MMK*, which had 28 chapters only in the second century A.D. The subsequent chapters he described as later additions. His main argument was that the *MMK* does not know a systematic theory of five *dhyānī* Buddhas and their *śaktis*. He says that its 27 chapters must be placed in the second century A.D. The dating is arrived at after comparing *MMK* with the *Guhyasamājatantra;* the latter states the theory of 5 *dhyānī* Buddhas and their *kulas*, it is therefore, later than *MMK*. The *Guhyasamāja* is placed by him in the third or fourth century A.D. and its authorship is attributed by him to Asaṅga.[166]

M. Winternitz criticised these views at length and said that *MMK* has not much to do with *GST;* the former is a *vaipulya-sūtra* of Mahāyāna, while the latter is a *mahāguhya-tantra-rāja*. Winternitz, Jayaswal and Dutt have suggested eighth century A.D. as the date of the composition of the final text of the *MMK*, while Przyluski places the final redaction of the *MMK* between eighth and tenth centuries A.D.[167]

It may be noted that Śāntideva does not quote the *MMK* which glorifies Mañjuśrī, a favourite god of this seventh century

Mahāyāna poet. But this cannot lead to any positive result. The *MMK* mentions in its older section[168] texts like the *Gaṇḍavyūha*, the *Suvarṇaprabhāsa* (said to have been explained by Kāśyapa Mātaṅga in China in the reign of Ming-ti, A.D. 58-75, but translated first in the fifth century A.D.), *Prajñāpāramitā*, and *Candrapradīpa-samādhi* (probably *Samādhirāja*, supposed to be a work of 100 A.D. and known to Candarakīrti and translated into Chinese first in 148 A.D.). In the xivth Chapter are mentioned texts which were translated in between 702 and 705 A.D.[169] Many Vajrayāna *mantras* like '*klhūṃ*' and '*bhrūṃ*' and '*jinajika*' '*ārolika*', '*vajradhṛka*', '*surāraka*', and '*pinādhṛka*'; Tāntrika *deva-kulas* like *tathāgatakula*, *padmakula* and *sarvavajrakula*, together with some names of *dhyānī* Buddhas like Amitābha, Ratnaketu, and *śaktis* like Māmakī, Locanā, and Bodhisattvas like Vajrapāṇi, Ratnapāṇi, Viśvapāṇi, are mentioned in the *MMK*.[170] The fact that erotic mysticism and disregard to ethical rules are still absent in the *MMK*[171] which otherwise is almost a Tantra, goes to show that it was and remained till the last a Mahāyāna sūtra, a Boddhisattvapiṭaka, but underwent considerable interpolations in the Gupta and post-Gupta periods.

The foregoing discussion should suffice to indicate the appearance of Tantras before the seventh century A.D. But Winternitz emphatically maintained that "the word '*tantra*' ought to be restricted to the texts connected with Śakti worship. Tantra texts in this sense cannot be proved to have existed before the seventh century".[172] This opinion should be modified in view of the fact that the *Mahāṃāyūrī*, already translated by Kumārajīva in between A.D. 402 and 412, probably mentions goddess Bhīmā or Bhīṣaṇā and her consort Śivabhadra. The temple of this Śakti or Bhīṣaṇā lay in the north-western region.[173] Attention may be drawn to a passage in the *Si-yu-ki* where Hsüan-tsang describes the image of Īśvara and goddess Bhīmā, that is Bhīmādevī or Durgā, spouse of Śiva-Maheśvara, in the state of Gāndhāra.[174] No one can deny that all the Tantras centre round two deities, one male the other female. The very word '*tantra*' occurs in an inscription of the fifth century A.D. The Gaṅgdhār stone inscription of Viśvavarman records the erection of "the very terrible abode of the Divine Mothers, filled full of Ḍākinīs..." and the performance of "tāntrika rites of their religion".[175] It is presumable that these Tāntrika rites may have been based on some Tāntrika treatises of the time; in fact the royal minister, Mayūrākṣa, who built this temple of Divine Mothers and Ḍākinīs, seems to show some knowledge of Śakti-ritual.[176]

There is yet another piece of epigraphic evidence bearing on Tāntrika Śakti-worship. The Bihar Stone Pillar Inscription of Skandagupta refers not only to Skanda-Kārttikeya, but also to the divine mothers' (*mātṛbhiśca*).[177] Varāhamihira in his *Bṛhat-saṃhitā* clearly mentions Śakti-worship and men versed in its sacred lore, i. e. those who were well versed in the *maṇḍala-krama* concerning the images of the divine mothers, and of gods, like Viṣṇu, Sūrya, Buddha, and Śaṃbhu. The commentator refers to such texts as the *Vātūlatantra* of the Pāśupatas and the *Pāraṃitās* of the Buddhists.[178]

Hsüan-tsang clearly refers to the Śāktas or worshippers of Durgā who sacrificed human beings to their deity. The pilgrim himself narrowly escaped his death at the hands of Durgā-worshippers somewhere between Ayodhyā and Ayamukha.[179] From the Siṃhalese *Nikāyasaṃgraha* it appears that Vajrayāna originated in the sixth century A.D. in the time of king Kumāradāsa of Siṃhala (515-524 A.D.)[180]

According to Schrader the Pāñcarātra system is practically concerned with one force, the Śakti.[181] He is of the opinion that the *Ahirbudhnyasaṃhitā* was written in Kashmir in about the fourth century A.D. This text mentions the *Sāttvata* and the *Jayākhya Saṃhitās* which must be still older. The Pāñcarātra is mentioned in the *Śāntiparvan* of the *Mahābhārata*.[182]

Bāṇabhaṭṭa mentions in his *Kādambarī*[183] certain Tāntrika rites involving human flesh and bloody-worship, prevalent among a lower class of people, the Śabaras. He also refers to a temple of Caṇḍikā, where a Draviḍian priest performed Tāntrika rites. In the *Harṣacarita*[184] we find a graphic description of the Tāntrika *sādhanas* and practices performed by a Tāntrikist Bhairavācārya by name; he seems to have been a Śivaite sorcerer and king Puṣpabhūti had great faith in him.

Vākpatirāja in his *Gauḍavaho*[185] shows that Tāntrika goddesses like Kālī, Cāmuṇḍā, and Gaurī were widely worshipped in his time. Kalhaṇa mentions a Pāśupata Siddha in Kashmir in the time of king Pravarasena, a successor of

Toramāṇa on the throne of Kashmir; he also testifies to the witch-craft (*abhicāra*), worship of Mahākāla, Durgā Vindhya-vāsinī, magical feats and alchemy of Caṅkuṇa, a minister of Lalitāditya, and the prevalence of Khārakhoda.[186] The *Devī-purāṇa* itself is said to have been composed in the seventh or the eighth century A.D.

Early Seats of Esoteric Buddhism

With respect to the place of the development of Esoteric Buddhism, there is a generally accepted opinion among many scholars that the cradle of Tāntrika Buddhism was Bengal in particular and Eastern India (specially Assam and Orissa) in general. Rāhula Sāṃkṛtyāyana, however, had opined that the cradle of Mantrayāna and Vajrayāna was the country around Śrīparvata and Dhānyakaṭaka in south India.[187]

In the Tantras, as is well known, there is a tradition about the four famous seats or *pīṭhas* where esoteric doctrine and Śakti-worship were first revealed. These *pīṭhas*, sacred for the Buddhist as well as Brahmanical Tāntrika followers, are[188] : (1) Kāmākhyā, (2) Śrīhaṭṭa, (3) Uḍḍiyāna and (4) Pūrṇāgirī. These are sometimes called Śāktapīṭhas owing to the legend associated with the corpse of Śakti (Dakṣa's daughter) the parts of which are said to have fallen in these places. The origin of the idea of these *pīṭhas* is known to the *Mahābhārata* and late Brahmanical Tantras,[189] and their mention in late Buddhist Tāntrika text shows that these *pīṭhas* are of late origin. They became the famous centres of Tāntrika culture, it is a fact, at a late date, from about the seventh century A.D. onwards. They are not mentioned in the *GST* nor in the earlier chapters of the *MMK.* Except Uḍḍiyāna, these *pīṭhas* were not the original seats of Buddhist esoterism.

The view that Mahāyāna Buddhism originated in Gāndhāra under the patronage of Kaniṣka and the influence of Indo-Greek culture, can hardly be supported by any ascertained fact. The attempt to prove that Orissa was the cradle of both Mahāyāna and Tāntrika Buddhism is far from historical truth. Nor is there any evidence to support the Bengali origin of Tāntrika Buddhism, while it is quite evident that it was in Bengal, Orissa and Assam and the sub-Himalayan regions that Tāntrikism flourished during the early medieval period of Indian history. One has to look for the earliest seats of Buddhist esoterism to two places, one in the far south and the other in extreme north-west of India. This suggestion may be substantiated by the following evidence.

(i) The *Aṣṭasāhasrikā*,[190] the oldest Prajñāpāramitā text, states that the Pāramitānaya originating in south (Dakṣiṇāpatha) will spread towards east in order to flourish in the north (Uttarāpatha). The Pāramitānaya gave birth to the Mantranaya.

(ii) The *Sekoddeśa-ṭīkā* of Nāropā[191] an authority on esoterism, records that the Mantrayāna was promulgated by the Lord in Śrī Dhānyakaṭaka.

(iii) Buddhist traditions preserved in Indian,[192] Chinese[193] and Tibetan literatures are unanimous on the fact that Nāgārjuna the "putative father" of Mahāyāna, who rescued the esoteric science and the Prajñā texts from the Nāgas, was a south Indian *brāhmaṇa*. All authorities further agree that Śrīparvata was the centre of the Sage's activities. The hill of Nāgārjunakoṇḍa might well have been named after him.

(iv) Hsüan-tsang[194] records that the Māhāsāṃghika brethren had a whole Piṭaka of spells or *dhāraṇīs* as a part of their canon. Āndhradeśa was the centre of the culture of sub-sects of this community as is proved by epigraphic evidence.[195] The Tibetans also attribute to them the earliest Prajñā text written in Prākṛt language.[196]

(v) The *Mañjuśrīmūlakalpa*, a book of Mantrayāna ritual and popular Mahāyānism, has been discovered from the Manalikkara Maṭhaṃ near Padmanābhapuraṃ in south India. This cannot be without significance concerning the origin of this text. At one place, the author refers to Vidiśā (modern Bhelsa, M.P.) as being situate between west and north (*paścimottarayormadhyaṃ*). Rāhula Sāṃkṛtyāyana rightly suggested that the author wrote this from a place in south, probably from Dhānyakaṭaka.[197]

(vi) In the *Mañjuśrīmūlakalpa* itself, Dhānyakaṭaka and Śrīparvata are mentioned as favourable places for Buddhist worship and *mantra-siddhi*.[198]

(vii) The *Gaṇḍavyūhasūtra*[199] mentions Sāradhvajavyūhacaitya in the city of Dhānyakaṭaka, where many devotees lived; Mañjuśrī himself proceeds from Śrāvastī to the south; Suddhana is advised to meet *kalyāṇamitras* living in south.

(viii) Hsüan-tsang further records that Bhāvaviveka came to

Dhānyakaṭaka where god Vajrapāṇi resided, and the Doctor recited the *Vajrapāṇidhāraṇī* for a long time in this country in order to have his wishes fulfilled and doubts removed.[200]

(ix) The *Sarvatathāgatādhiṣṭhāna-vyūha*, a semi-Tāntrika Buddhist text found in Gilgit and belonging to the 5th or the 6th century A.D., states that the Lord delivered this text at Potalaka *parvata*. This Potalaka is represented by Hsüan-tsang as the abode of Avalokita where this god frequently appeared to his devotees in the guise of Maheśvara (Pāśupata-tīrthika).[201] Tārānātha also represents Potalaka as the abode of Avalokita, and describes Śāntivarman's journey to this place and how this *upāsaka*-pilgrim invoked, for safety, Avalokita, Tārā and Ekajaṭā. He also represents Candragomin as going to Potalaka from Nālandā and invoking goddess Tārā on his way to the holy place.[202]

This Potalaka is located by Hsüan-tsang in Malakūṭa, identified by Cunningham with a tract between Madura, Tanjore and Travancore. Nandolal De suggested that Potalaka lay in Western Ghāṭs. N. Dutt suggests that modern Poṭiyam may represent Potalaka.[203] This Potalaka was near Dhānyakaṭaka and Śrīparvata which places have been identified with Amarāvatī and Nāgārjunakoṇḍa respectively.[204]

It is needless to state that Avalokita and Tārā whose one abode was this southern extremity played a great part in the evolution of Mahāyāna and Vajrayāna. We hardly know any place in Bengal, Assam or Orissa, which is represented at an early date as a centre of Mahāyāna and Māntrayāna in equally numerous and diverse, ancient and medieval sources, as is the case with Śrīparvata, Dhānyakaṭaka and Potalaka in south India.

(x) Rāhula Sāṃkṛtyāyana has pointed out that owing to its being an early centre of the Vajrayāna, Śrīparvata may have come to be known as Vajraparvata. This Vajraparvata is mentioned in the *Nikāya-saṃgraha;* in this text many Vajrayāna works are attributed to the authorship of the Buddhists belonging to the Vajraparvatavāsinikāya.[205] This Vajraparvatavāsinikāya seems to be identical with Vajrayāna.

(xi) The contemporary secular works of our period, e.g. the *Harṣacarita*,[206] the *Kādambarī*[207] and the *Mālatīmādhava*,[208] also testify to the fact that Śrīparvata was an early centre of *mantras* and *tantras*. Kalhaṇa, too records that a famous Siddha came from the famous Śrīparvata to show his marvels in Kashmir.[209]

Another original centre where from Tāntrikism spread in and outside India was Uḍḍiyāna or Udyāna, mentioned in the Tantras as one of the four *pīṭhas*.

Of the four *pīṭhas*, Kāmākhyā has been identified with Kāmarūpa, Śrihaṭṭa with Sylhet; Pūrṇāgiri is most likely identical with Pūṇyāgiri or Pūrṇāgiri of modern days, a famous holy centre of Śakti-pūjā in Nainital Distirct of U.P. Much controversy has been raised over the location of Uḍḍiyāna or Udyāna. B. Bhatttacharya following H.P. Śāstri, identified it with Orissa. Waddell, Levi, Tucci, and Bagchi[210] have convincingly shown that the Tibetan name Urgyan and the Chinese name Wutch'ang (Wu-chang-na) correspond to Uḍḍiyāna which is identical with modern Swat valley in the extreme north-west of India (now in Pakistan). One writer has recently made a renewed attempt to identify Uḍḍiyāna with Orissa which he regards as "the cradle of Tāntrika Buddhism".[211] But this is improbable; the Chinese sources refer to Orissa as Wu-T'u or Ota or Wu-cha, while the Tibetans refer to Orissa as Oḍiviśa which must be different from Urgyan or Wu-chang. Moreover, Orissa became a centre of Tāntrika Buddhism after the 7th century A.D.; even if the Uḍḍiyāna pīṭha of the Tantras is to be identified with Orissa, it must refer to a period posterior to Hsüan-tsang and the credit which is due to Uḍḍiyāna or Swat as an earlier centre and, in fact the second great and early seat of Buddhist Esoterism after Śrīparvata, remains unquestioned. The following points should show that the Swat valley was a centre of Tāntrika Buddhism long before 700 A.D.

In ancient Indian literature the extreme north-western region of the country, especially Uḍḍiyāna, Gāndhāra, Kapiśa and Tukhāra or Śvetadvīpa, find frequent mention. A Kuṣāṇa inscription mentions a monk Jīvaka Oḍiyānaka,[212] that is, Jīvaka of Oḍiyāna. This is probably the earliest epigraphic reference to Uḍḍiyāna. It is certainly not in Orissa or Oḍiviśa. The Vihāra of Huviṣka to which Jīvaka Oḍiyānaka made gift of a pillar was in the north-west. Hsüan-tsang entered India from the north-west route and his biographer clearly locates Udyāna's capital in the valley of the Darel.[213] Fa-hsien, who also came from that pass, clearly says that Udyāna lay in the north on the Swat river.[214]

It is of Udyāna or Wu-chang-na and not of Orissa or Wu-ṭa that Hsüan-tsang deplores when he says that the people of Uḍḍiyāna held in high esteem the magical arts and spells.[215]

Already in the Pāli Canon we find mention of *gāndhārīvijjā* which like the *bhūtavijjā* was an art of sorcery and exorcism.[216] The *Śāntiparvan*[217] relates the legend that Nārada received the *Pāñcarātra* (a Brāhmanical Tāntrika Śāstra) during 'five nights in Śvetadvīpa'. This Śvetadvīpa, like Tuṣaraśila of *Harṣacarita*, seems to be a name of north-western sub-Himalayan region.

Hsüan-tsang mentions the town of Mong-kie-li as the capital of Uḍḍiyāna; this place has been identified by Foucher with Mangakoṣṭha of a Nepali manuscript (8th-11th century A.D.), which illustrates among other gods, a Vajrapāṇi of Mangakoṣṭha in Uḍḍiyāna.[218] Hsüan-tsang also narrates the legends concerning 4 sacred places in Uḍḍiyāna (Wu-chang-na) where Buddha in his former existences as P'usa (Bodhisattva) had sacrificed his life and dismembered his limbs.[219] Whether here we have a Buddhist counterpart of the Brahmanical legend concerning the dismemberment of the body of Satī (Dakṣa's daughter, Śiva's wife) in four places, which is famed in Brāhmanical literature and the Tantras, one cannot say anything with any certainty.

It is in this north-western part, in Gāndhāra, that Hsüan-tsang found the temple of Bhīmā or Durgā, consort of Maheśvara, where the Tāntrika followers came for worship and got their wishes fulfilled through the miracles of the goddess.

In the petty hill state of Panjab, viz. Chamba, Vogel discovered numerous Tāntrika antiquities, some extant, most of them damaged, dating from the 7th-8th centuries A.D. In the upper Rāvī valley he found shrines of 84 Siddhas, early Tibetan inscriptions and temples of Śaktidevī and their paintings as also the *yoginī* bronzes.[220]

H. Goetz points out that the temple of Lakṣaṇādevī had been damaged by the Tibetans in the 8th century A.D. and that most of the monuments belonging to the period prior to the 7th century A.D. have disappeared owing to Tibetan and Muslim invasions.[221] In ancient days Chamba was probably a part of the Udumbara republic. These Udumbaras, the ancient people of Panjab, are known to have worshipped serpent deities (*nāgas*), demons like *rākṣasas* and *yakṣas*, and a cruel mother-goddess demanding human sacrifice.[222] All these references to the north-western parts of India in ancient times should clearly indicate that this part supplied a suitable climate for the rise of Tāntrikism. From the time of the composition of the *Dīghanikāya* and the *Mahābhārata* to the time of Hsüan-tsang and Padmasambhava, we have regular historical and traditional references to the prevalence of magical arts, exorcism, *tantra*, Devī-worship and *ḍākinīs* in Panjab, Gāndhāra and the Swat region.

It may be noted that Asaṅga who had so much to do with esoterism in Buddhism, hailed from Gāndhāra.[223] The Tibetans clearly say that Uḍḍiyāna lay in the west of India. Padmasambhava, the apostle of Buddhism of Tibet, Indrabhūti, the celebrated Tāntrika author, Lawapa, the rescuer of Yoginītantras, all are represented as coming from Uḍḍiyāna. Caṅkuṇa, the great exorcist prime minister of Lalitāditya, belonged to Tukhāra country.[224] It is therefore clearly established that the earliest seats of Tāntrika Buddhism were not in Bengal, Orissa and Assam, but in Uḍḍiyāna (Swat) and Āndhradeśa.

Early Esoteric Texts and Siddhācāryas

As the title of the work seems to suggest the *Guhyasamājatantra* must have been a work of those esoteric Buddhists who practised secret *yoga*, confidential rites and ceremonies, held secret gatherings, employed secret signs and mysterious language. As such the *GST* and similar esoteric texts were perhaps, not meant for modern critical and heretical study; they were meant for the initiates, for they are said to be not only sacred (*śuddha*) and unique (*anuttara*) but also 'the most secret of secrets' (*guhyātiguhya*).

B. Bhattacharya placed it in the 3rd or 4th century A.D. and attributed its authorship to Asaṅga, the famous brother of equally famous Vasubandhu, the Yogācāra Doctor. He gave two main reasons; a comparison of the *GST* and the *MMK* with respect to the doctrine of the holy pentad, *pañca*-Tathāgata shows according to Bhattacharya that the *MMK* does not give a systematic account of five *dhyāni* Buddhas and their *śaktis*, whereas the *GST* supplies this for the first time; therefore, the *MMK* must be earlier than the *GST*. Secondly, the five *dhyāni*

Buddhas and their respective *śaktis* are mentioned in the *Prajñā-pāramitā-sādhana* which is attributed in its colophon to Ācārya Asaṅgapāda. No other Asaṅga than the Yogācāra Doctor is known to us; Asaṅgapāda, therefore, is the most likely author of the *GST* also.[225]

These views of Bhattacharya have been questioned and criticized by M. Winternitz[226] and others. Winternitz held that the attribution of Sādhana No. 159 (*Prajñāpāramitā-sādhana*) to Asaṅga, the Yogācāra philosopher of 4th century A.D., is not beyond doubt. Nor the *GST* can on any authority or tradition worth the name be ascribed to him. Neither the *GST* nor the Sādhana No. 159 are mentioned in the list of the works attributed to Asaṅga and Maitreyanātha in Chinese and Tibetan traditions and literatures. The language as well as the teachings of the *GST* are much inferior to that of the *Sūtrālaṅkāra of* Maitreya-Asaṅga. With regard to the date of *GST*, he held that no Tantra concerned with Śakti-worship can be proved to have existed before the 7th century A.D.

N. Dutt[227] placed the *GST* and the *MMK* after the *Kāraṇḍa-vyūha* and before *Mahāpratyaṅgirā-dhāraṇī* 'about the fifth or sixth century A.D.' He is of the opinion that the Sādhana No. 159, ascribed to Ācārya Asaṅgapāda, is not a work of the founder of the Yogācāra school; the very name with '*pāda*' as suffix and preceded by the appellation '*ācārya*' indicates that he cannot be identified with Ārya Asaṅga.

G. C. Pande[228] opines that there is no definite evidence in support of Asaṅga's authorship of *GST*, but Asaṅga's relation with Tantra is evident and his dissociation from the author of the Sādhana No. 159 is groundless. The date and authorship of the *GST* are thus still in the melting pot; the following points, however, deserve a careful attention while considering the date and authorship of the *GST*. One line of approach is as follows:

(i) Some scholars[229] are of the opinion that the *Ārya-tathāgata-guhyasūtra* frequently quoted in the *ŚS* of Śāntideva is identical with the *Guhyasamāja-tantra*, also called *Tathāgataguhyaka*. But this opinion is apparently based on a confusion. It has been shown[230] that the text quoted in the *ŚS* is a Mahāyāna Sūtra, the teachings of which are quite ethical and noble and entirely different from the *Tathāgataguhyaka* which is a Vajrayāna Tantra and teaches things contrary to the Mahāyāna ethics. In brief the *ŚS* does not prove that the *GST* is older than it.

(ii) The fact that the *GST* was translated into Chinese so late as the 10th century and into Tibetan in the 11th century further prevents us from placing it at a very early date.

(iii) The fact that the contents of the *GST* are, for the most part, similar to that of the *MMK*, except for certain erotic elements and a particular grouping of the pantheon based on the holy-pentad, which are peculiar to the *GST*, would also indicate that the two texts belong to about the same period.

(iv) The view that Asaṅga, the Yogācāra philosopher of the 4th century A.D., was the author of the *GST* is not supported by any indubitable evidence. The oldest manuscript of the *Sādhanamālā* which contains Sādhana No. 159 and attributes it to Asaṅgapāda is dated A.D. 1165 (Newari Era, 285), and may not be a very old compilation. Most of the Siddhas who composed these Sādhanas are assigned, even in the chronology fixed by Bhattacharya, to the period 700-1200 A.D. The authority of the *Sādhanamālā* too, thus, cannot be of much help in determining an early date for the *GST*.

The above line of approach to *GST* problem would indicate that the work may have been composed in the seventh-eighth centuries A.D.

Tārānātha speaks of one Asaṅga who was a contemporary of Luipā, the disciple of Saraha; this Asaṅga may be associated with the Sādhana No. 159 and may be placed in the 8th century A.D. Thus while Ārya Asaṅga (400 A.D.) cannot be dissociated from Esoteric Buddhism, the possibility of a second Asaṅgapā who flourished some four centuries later and was a contemporary of Luipā is also not entirely groundless.

It is admitted by some noted critics that there may have been two, three or even four persons bearing the name Nāgārjuna. But there is a strong possibility of the historical existence and distinct identity of at least two Nāgārjunas. The first was the Mādhayamika philosopher (*cir.* 80 B.C. to 120 A.D.) who was a towering dialectician, scholar and mystic. The Tibetans have confounded this great Nāgārjuna with a Tāntrika Siddha namesake; supernatural powers and *yogic siddhis* can readily be admitted to have been possessed by the Mādhyamika philosopher. All sages, saints, and mystics are known to have possessed superhuman powers. Even fairly reliable and comparatively earlier authorities like Bāṇa, Hsüan-tsang and I-tsing, in whose time Siddha Nāgārjuna perhaps had not yet been born, associate our great Buddhist philosopher with *nāgas,* marvels, alchemy and medicine. Of his connection with the mysteries of Prajñā-pāramitā, there can be no doubt. He was, therefore, very likely to be mistaken by the credulous medieval Tibetan Buddhist as the actual author of Esoteric Buddhism and many of its treatises (Tantras). It appears to us that a Siddha Nāgārjuna, the author of the *Ekajaṭā-sādhana,* the *Vajratārā-sādhana* and other Vajrayāna works, a disciple of Saraha or Rāhulabhadra, and a historical person of about the 8th century A. D. is confounded and identified with Nāgārjuna, the author of the *Madhyamaka-śāstra* and the 'putative father' of the Mahāyāna Sūtras. The two persons were, however, quite different from each other.

It is very likely that Nāgārjuna II, the Siddha, and a Tāntrika author is the real writer of the *Guhyasamājatantra.* Whereas there is some evidence in support of this view, there is no contradictory evidence which can be brought forth against this suggestion. To be more precise, the view suggested here that Siddha Nāgārjuna of the eighth century A.D. may have been the author of the *Guhyasamājatantra* is based on the following considerations.

(i) According to Dharmasvāmin, who travelled around Magadha in the 13th century A.D., there were many Buddhists in India in his time who followed the "Guhyasamāja according to Nāgārjuna system".[231]

(ii) In the *Blue Annals* (Deb-ther Snoṅ-po) of Gos lo-tsaba gZoṅ-nu-dpal (A.D. 1392-1481) it is stated that the 'Ācārya Nāgārjuna and his disciples obtained the Yoga Tantras, including the *Guhyasamāja* and others (the Anuttarayoga Tantras were also called Mahāyoga Tantras, and preached them. They spread from the south.[232]

(iii) In the *Nikāyasaṃgraha,* a fourteenth century Sinhalese work '*Śrī Guhyasamāja* (*Samājatantra*) is attributed to the followers of the Vajraparvatavāsinikāya. As already explained, this Vajraparvata is the same as Śrīparvata and Siddha Nāgārjuna lived for a long time in this place, hence the followers of this Vajraparvatavāsinikāya seem to be identical with the followers of Vajrayāna. The *Nikāyasaṃgraha* thus corroborates the origin of *GST* in the south and its association with Nāgārjuna and his disciples who preached the *GST* from south as the *Blue Annals* state.

(iv) In the *Sādhanamālā* the cult of goddess Ekajaṭā is attributed to Nāgārjunapāda.[233] This goddess is clearly mentioned as Vajra-Ekajaṭā in the *GST*.[234]

(v) In the Tibetan *rgyud* section several works connected with the explanation of the *GST* are attributed to Nāgārjuna, viz. *Guhyasamājamaṇḍalavidhi; Guhyasamāja-tantrasyatantra - ṭīkā* and *Guhyasamāja-mahāyoga-tantrotpattikramaśādhana*.[235]

The foregoing discussion may perhaps finally settle one of the most complicated and controversial problems of the history of Buddhist Esoterism. The composition of the *GST*, thus may be placed in the eighth century A.D., and Siddha Nāgārjunapāda may well have been its author. It may be argued that the work is not ascribed to Nāgārjunapāda in the colophon. In fact the *GST* has no such colophon, and the text ends without any reference to its author; this is probably because of its utterly secret tenets, and their author may not have liked to openly associate his name with such doctrines as astonished even the Bodhisattvas who consequently fell into coma.

That the *GST* is perhaps the earliest Anuttarayoga Tantra, or at least one of the earliest esoteric texts,[236] seems to be indicated by the text itself. In the V chapter the Bodhisattvas express their great surprise and resentment at the unconventional and radical ethics taught by the Lord. In the XVII chapter it attempts to record the esoteric tradition of secret practices being taught by the Tathāgata. In the XVIII chapter the text tries to explain technical terms, symbols and esoteric practices and situations.

The text opens with a salutation to Śrī Vajrasattva; he is called the *sarva-tathāgata-kāya-vāk-citta* and is represented in an erotic embrace with Vajrayoṣit or Vajrayoginī. The Vajrayāna is defined as that which has recourse to '*moha*', '*dveṣa*', '*rāga*', '*vajra*', and '*rati*'. The text describes itself as the 'king of the treatises of the illustrious secret society'. It is not unlikely that the Mūlatantra (original Tantra) often quoted in Vajrayāna works, corresponds to the *GST*.[237]

After the time of Dharmakīrti many esoteric treatises and masters of esoteric science (Mahāvidyādharas, Mahāsiddhas) are known to have appeared. The life and works of the eighty-four perfected ones (Siddhas) are preserved in the Tibetan canon and the histories of Bu-ston, Gos lo-tsa-ba, Tārānātha and the *Pag-sam Jon-zaṅ* of Sumpā-khan-po. They are known from medieval Indian and Nepalese traditions, as also from their songs preserved in the original Apabhraṁśa. In spite of these sources, a connected and chronological account of the Siddhas and early Tāntrika authors has been a task of admitted difficulty. This problem has been treated below.

From the *Blue Annals* we learn that in the beginning a Tantra called the *Sarva-tathāgata-tattvasaṃgraha,* was obtained by Pradyotacandra of eastern India. After that Nāgārjuna and his disciples composed the *Guhyasamāja* and other Anuttarayoga Tantras in southern India. Then Kambala and others brought out the Yoginī Tantras from the country of Uḍḍiyāna in the west of India.[238]

Tārānātha informs us that Saraha and Kambala composed the *Hevajra tantra,* an Anuttarayoga Tantra.[239] This text has been published and is placed in the eighth century A.D. Tārānātha also attributes to Saraha a work called the *Buddha-kapāla-tantra.* A large number of mystic songs of Saraha have been published and studied in modern times. According to a Tibetan tradition, Saraha alias Rāhulabhadra, was a *brāhmaṇa* of Rājñī in east India and was the first of 84 Siddhas; he was a contemporary of the Pāla king Dharmapāla (A.D. 768-809). According to the *Mystic Tales,* Saraha was a native of Orissa and one of his pupils was Nāgārjuna.

The *Hevajratantra,* a joint creation of two teachers, Saraha and Kambala, is a Tantra of the class of *Guhyasamāja.* Its philosophical basis is derived from the Mādhyamika and the Yogācāra schools. The theory of 'two-in-one', the 'innate' (*sahaja*) and *bodhicitta,* and a symbolical analysis of the psycho-physical mechanism of human personality, find classic treatment from the Vajrayāna standpoint. The chief deity or Supreme Reality is termed Hevajra. The text treats at length of the *mantras,* secret signs, and painting of the images. Of special historical interest is the mention of the centres of esoteric culture. The list of places includes Jālandhara, Oḍḍiyāna, Paurṇāgiri, Kāmarūpa, Mālavā, Sindhu and Nagara (probably Nagarahāra of Chinese accounts).[240]

G. Tucci has published another work of Kambalapāda, the *Navaślokī;* this work is also extant in Chinese and Tibetan versions; its Sanskrit title being *Bhagavatīprajñāpāramitāpiṇḍ-ārtha.*[241] Tārānātha makes Kampala (Kambala, Kamalāmbara, Kamalī and Kambalapāda, a contemporary of king Gopīcandra and of Vinītadeva, and in his *Mystic Tales,* he represents Kambala as a teacher of Indrabhūti.

This Indrabhūti, a king of Uḍḍiyāna, was also one of the early Siddhas. One of his works on esoterism has been published in the original; it is called the *Jñānasiddhi.* In this text the *GST* is quoted several times. Tārānātha says, "the great king Indra-bhūti was master in Guhya-tantra". The *Blue Annals,* however, state that "Indrabhūti, the great king of Uḍḍiyāna", was the same as Kambala; the *Jñānasiddhi* of Indrabhūti and the *Guhya-siddhi* of Padmavajra are based on the *Guhyasamāja.* Āryadeva's work, the *Caryāmelayanapradīpa,* was also based on the *GST* system. Āryadeva is represented by Tārānātha as a pupil of Nāgārjuna and teacher of Rāhula. One of his works in Sanskrit, viz. *Cittaviśuddhi-prakaraṇa,* has been published. Anaṅgavajra whose esoteric treatise, the *Prajñopāya-viniścaya-siddhi,* has been published in Sanskrit, is said by Tārānātha to have been a teacher of Saraha. All these teachers of esoteric Buddhism seem to have flourished in the eighth century A.D.

Chronology of some Early Siddhas

Tārānātha says that during the time of the Pāla kings of Bengal many Siddhācāryas appeared and diffused the Tāntrika teachings after the time of Dharmakīrti. The Anuttarayoga Tantras appeared in the following order : (1) Saraha's *Buddhakapāla-tantra,* (2) Luipāda's *Yoginīsaṃcaryā,* (3) Kambala and Padma-vajra produced the *Hevajra tantra,* (4) Kṛṣṇa's *Samputa-tilaka,* (5) Lalitavajra's *Kṛṣṇa-yamāri-tantra,* (6) Gambhīravajra's *Vajrāmṛta,* (7) Kukkurī's *Mahāmāyā,* and (8) Piṭo's *Kālacakra.* This account is given by Tārānātha in his *Chos-ḥbyuṅ.* In his first work on Indian history, the *Mystic Tales,* he gives the following succession of these Siddhas.

Rāhulabhadra for the first time revealed the *Mahāmudrā.* He later on became known as Saroha or Saraha. After him came Nāgārjuna, Śavarī, Luipāda, Ḍombī, Tilly, Nāro, second Ḍombī and Kuśalībhadra.

It will be noticed that in these two lists of succession the first Siddha is Saraha alias Rāhulabhadra. Luipā figures in both the lists.

An entirely different list of succession of early Siddhas is given in the Tenjur which is given below: (1) Padmavajra, (2) Anaṅga-vajra, (3) Indrabhūti, (4) Bhagavatī Lakṣamī, (5) Līlāvajra, (6) Dārikapā, (7) Sahajayoginī Cintā and (8) Dombī Heruka. Two most important Siddhas, viz. Saraha and Nāgārjunapāda, it is to be noticed, are not mentioned in this group of early Siddhas.

Another tradition, preserved in the work of Sumpā-mkhan-po, gives the following list of early Siddhas : (1) Saraha, (2) Nāgārjuna, (3) Śabarīpā, (4) Luipā, (5) Vajraghaṇṭa, (6) Kacchapa, (7) Jālandharīpā, (8) Kṛṣṇācārya, (9) Guhya, (10) Vijayapā, (11) Tailopā, and (12) Nāropā. It will be observed that many names are common to the lists of Tārānātha and Sumpā. Secondly, in Tārānātha as well as in Sumpā, Saraha alias Rāhulabhadra is at the head of the list of these Siddhas.

In the *Blue Annals* are mentioned at several places, a large number of Siddhas. A certain king Pradyotacandra is credited to have first obtained the Yoga Tantras in the east. After him are placed Nāgārjuna and his disciples who introduced the *Guhyasamāja* and other Mahāyoga Tantras. Then comes Śrīkambala who introduced Yoginī Tantras from Uḍḍiyāna. After that the Boddhisattvas ("here Bodhisattvas mean the kings of Śambhala") introduced the Kālacakra and other Tantras from Śambhala.[242] Among these Bodhisattvas of Śambhala were king Indrabhūti, his sister Lakṣamīṅkarā, and his son Padmasambhava, as we shall see below.

The author of the *Blue Annals* feels that the Kālacakra system had appeared in the Āryadeśa earlier than is usually believed. According to him the chronological succession of the line of *ācāryas* of the Kālacakra system is as follows : (1) Vajraghaṇ-ṭapāda, (2) Kūrmapāda, (3) Vijayapāda, (4) Kṛṣṇapāda, (5) Bhadrapāda, (6) Vijayapāda, (7) Tilli-pā or Tailipā, and then (8) Nāropā. "Thus from Ghaṇṭa (pāda) till Nāropā there have been eight teachers in the line." Nāropā's son was Kāla-cakrapāda.[243]

It seems that there were several lines of teachers, or *āmnāyas*, i.e. mystic schools of the Tāntrika Buddhists. Some Siddhas belonging to a particular branch of mysticism may have been contemporary with those belonging to the other branch. This seems to be inferable from the fact that the *Blue Annals* enumerate groups of *gurus* or different *guruparamparās*. Thus as many as "54 Siddhas, males and females", appear as belonging to different branches of Tāntrika Buddhism, although they were, perhaps, contemporaries also. Members of one branch are : (1) Vāgīśvara, (2) Buddhagupta, (3) Godhārī, (4) Karmavajra, (5) Javāri, (6) Jñānapāda, (7) Nāgabodhi, (8) Ānanda, (9) Kṛṣṇapāda, (10) Vasudharma, and (11) Padmavajra. These teachers belonged to the lineage of the 'father' class of Tantras, and seem to have been all teachers of a great soul (*siddheśvara*), Dam-pa by name, a native of Be-ba-la in south India.[244]

Another line of teachers belonging to the 'mother' class of Tantras, is as follows :

(1) Anaṅgavajra, (2) Saroruha, (3) Indrabhūti, (4) Ḍombhīpā, (5) Vajraghaṇṭa, (6) Tillipā, (7) Kṛṣṇapā, (8) Līlāvajra, (9) Luyī-pā, (10) Virūpā, (11) Ānandagarbha, and (12) Kukkurīpā.[245] It is noticeable that in this last list are several persons belonging to the list given by Tārānātha and Sumpā.

G. Tucci[246] brought to light some interesting details concerning the Siddhas given in a Nepalese palm-leaf manuscript discovered by him. This biography of Siddhas is unfortunately very fragmentary and cannot be of much help in setting the complicated and confused history and chronology of the Siddhas. This Sanskrit biography of the Siddhas shows that a Nāgārjuna who was an alchemist was a contemporary of Śabara and Advayavajra (also called Dāmodara, Maitrīgupta). This work thus points to a different line of teachers which claimed Nāgārjuna as its head.

Rāhula Sāṃkṛtyāyana[247] has reconstructed the geneology and chronology of the Siddhas on the basis of the *Caturaśīti-siddha-pravṛtti*, preserved in the Tenjur, and has supplemented his account by other Tibetan sources.

The historicity of the 84 Siddhas of Tāntrika Buddhism is indicated not only by a number of Indian and Tibetan legends and traditions but also by some historical references to them. Besides the works of Tārānātha, Sumpā, the *Blue Annals*, the *Caturaśīti-siddha-pravṛtti* and the Sanskrit biography, mentioned above, many other Tibetan works written after the time of Bu-ston and before that the Sumpā-mkhan-po, also refer to their life and works. The *Śābaratantra* gives a list of 24 teachers of the Kāpālika sect, and Nāgārjuna, Mīnanātha, Gorakṣa, Carpaṭa and Jālandhara, are included in the list.[248] We know from other sources that these are included among the 84 Siddhas also. These 84 Siddhas are also well known to the literature of medieval Indian Chemistry and Alchemy.[249] The fifteenth century poet and mystic, Kabīradāsa refers to them in one of his songs.[250] Some of these are mentioned in the literature of the Nātha school.[251] A fourteenth century writer, Jyotirīśvara, also mentions them in his *Varṇaratnākara*.[252] The Siddhas are mentioned in the works of Guru Nānaka also. Carpaṭa and Lohārī are mentioned in the *Siddha-goṣṭhi*, while Gorakha is referred to in the *Japu*. A few Siddhas are mentioned in some inscriptions also.[253] A large number of them are known from their Tāntrika works, Sādhanas, Dohās, and commentaries, extant in Tibetan, Sanskrit and Apabhraṃśa.[254]

The list of 84 Siddhas, as preserved in the Tibetan sources, is as follows :—

(1) Luhī-pā, (2) Līlā-pā, (3) Virū-pā, (4) Ḍombī-pā, (5) Śabara (Śavarī-pā), (6) Saraha (Rāhulabhadra), (7) Kaṅkalipā, (8) Mīna-pā, (9) Gorakṣa-pā, (10) Cauraṅgī-pā, (11) Vīṇā-pā, (12) Śānti-pā, (13) Tanti-pā, (14) Carmāri (Camarīpā), (15) Khaḍga-pā, (16) Nāgārjuna, (17) Kāṇha-pā, (18) Karṇari-pā (Āryadeva), (19) Ṭhagana-pā. (20) Nāro-pā (Naḍapāda), (21) Śāli-pā (Śṛgāla-pāda), (22) Tilo-pā (Tailika-pāda), (23) Chatra-pā, (24) Bhadra-pā. (25) Dvikhaṇḍī-pā (Do-khaṇḍhi-pā), (26) Ajogi-pā, (27) Kāḍa-pāda (Kāla-pā), (28) Dhovī-pā, (29) Kaṅkaṇa-pā, (30) Kampala-pā (Kambala), (31) Geṅgi-pā (Teṅki-pā), (32) Chade-pā, (33) Taṇdhi-pā, (34) Kukkurī-pā, (35) Cujbi (Kusulī)-pā, (36) Dharma-pā, (37) Mahī-pā (38) Acinti-pā, (39) Bhalaha-pā, (40) Nalina-pā, (41) Bhūsūkū-pā, (42) Indrabhūti, (43) Megha-pā (Meko-pā) (44) Kuṭhāli-pā (Kuṭhāri), (45) Karmara, (46) Jālandhara-pā, (47) Rāhula-pā, (48) Garbhari-pā, (49) Dhakari-pā, (50) Medini-pā (51) Paṅkaja-pā (52) Ghaṇṭā-pā (53) Jogi-pā, (54) Celuka-pā, (55) Gundari-pā (56) Luñcaka-pā (57) Nirguṇa-pā, (58) Jayānanda, (59) Carpaṭi-pā, (60) Campaka-pā, (61) Bhīkhan-pā (62) Bhali-pā, (63) Kumāri-pā, (64) Cavarī (Javāri)-pā, (65) Maṇibhadrā (Yoginī), (66) Mekhalā-pā (Yoginī),

(67) Maṅkhalāpā (Yoginī), (68) Kalakala-pā, (69) Kanthali-pā, (70) Dhahuli-pā, (71) Udhali-pā, (72) Kapāla-pā, (73) Kīla-pā, (74) Sāgarapā (Puṣkara), (75) Sarvabhakṣa-pā, (76) Nāgabodhi-pā, (77) Dārika-pā, (78) Putuli-pā, (79) Upānaha-pā, (80) Kokila-pā, (81) Anaṅga-pā, (82) Lakṣamīṅkarā (Yoginī), (83) Samudra-pā, and (84) Vyāli-pā (Bhalipā).[255]

Most of the modern scholars agree in placing the 84 Siddhas between the eighth and the twelfth centuries A.D. The chronological discussion of all these Siddhas is, properly speaking, beyond our present scope, because most of them flourished after the eighth century A.D. But it is extremely difficult to decide how many of these 84 Buddhist sages flourished in the eighth century A.D. As a matter of fact, the whole problem of the history and chronology of 84 Siddhas is a confused and complex one. All attempts to reconstruct their systematic chronology at the present state of our knowledge and available evidence must be tentative.

Benoytosh Bhattacharya was perhaps the first to make such an attempt.[256] He placed Saraha in A.D. 633, a date which is too early, and perhaps cannot be substantiated by any undisputed evidence. There are indications that lead us to place Saraha in the later half of the eighth century A.D. Saraha or Rāhulabhadra, according to Sumpā-mkhan-po, was a *brāhmaṇa* born in the city of Rājñī in the east, and flourished in the reign of king Candanapāla of Prācya (East). K.L. Barua suggests that this Rājñī is probably Rānī in western Assam.[257] In Sāṃkṛtyāyana's list, Saraha seems to belong to Nālandā, and was a contemporary of king Dharmapāla (*cir.* 770-813 A.D.). Some writers suggest that Saraha was a contemporary of Ratnapāla, a king of the Brahmapāla dynasty of Kāmarūpa, who is placed in the tenth-eleventh century A.D.[258] According to Tārānātha, Rāhulabhadra alias Saraha was a *brāhmaṇa* of Oḍiviśa (Orissa).[259]

From the Tibetan Tenjur Saraha appears to be a contemporary of Śāntarakṣita and Kamalaśīla. Almost all the Tibetan sources agree on the point that Saraha's pupil was Nāgārjuna.[260] This Nāgārjuna, one of the Siddhas, flourished in the eighth century A.D. as discussed above. Sāṃkṛtyāyana informs us that Saraha was a pupil of Haribhadra, who was the *guru* of king Dharmapāla. An eighth century inscription, inscribed on the pedestal of an image of Avalokiteśvara, preserved in Orissa

Museum, and installed in the reign of Śubhakaradeva of Kāra dynasty (*cir.* 790 A.D.), refers to one Mahāmaṇḍalācārya Paramaguru Rāhularuci.[261] This Rāhularuci may be identical with Rāhulabhadra alias Saraha. Thus all these pieces of evidence put together seem to place Saraha in the second half of the eighth century A.D. Sāṃkṛtyāyana suggested that Saraha may have died in *cir.* 780 A.D. which date is probable enough.

When we fix the date of Saraha, we fix the date of some of the earliest Siddhas; Saraha, the first of 84 Siddhas, seems to have flourished in the middle of the eighth century A.D. One of his direct pupils, in Vajrayāna mysticism, was Nāgārjuna, whose Tāntrika works have been mentioned above. There were several persons bearing this name, and the Tibetan sources are full of confused legends concerning this name. Even the great Mādhyamika metaphysician and perhaps the earliest known master of Mahāyāna is brought into Tāntrika age and is confused with an alchemist and Tāntrika namesake.[262] In Sāṃkṛtyāyana's list, Nāgārjuna (Siddha 16) appears as a pupil of Saraha and a *brāhmaṇa* of Kāñcī in the south.[263] The *Blue Annals* attribute to Nāgārjuna the introduction of the *Guhyasamāja* in south India.[264] Tārānātha and Sumpā,[265] although both give a confused and legendary account of this person, inform us that Nāgārjuna came from Vidarbha in south, and met Saraha at Nālandā, and again went to south and spent many years in Śrīparvata.

B. Bhattacharya placed Nāgārjuna in 645 A.D.[266] But such an early date perhaps cannot be accepted inasmuch as he was a junior contemporary of Saraha who died in the last quarter of the eighth century A.D. G. Tucci's report shows that there were perhaps two Nāgārjunas even among the Siddhas. One Nāgārjuna is said, in the Sanskrit biography of the Siddhas, to have been in Karhāṭaka (probably Karṇātaka) and his pupil (incarnation) was Dāmodara also known as Maitrīpā and as Advayavajra.[267] Even in the list prepared by Sāṃkṛtyāyana we cannot say whether Siddha 16 (Nāgārjuna) is identical with or different from Siddha 76 (Nāgabodhi). Moreover, Nāgārjuna the pupil of Saraha (*cir.* 800 A.D.) cannot be the same as Nāgārjuna, the teacher of Advayavajra or Maitrīpā and the author of the *Advayavajra-saṃgraha, Madhyamaka-ṣaṭka* and other Tāntrika texts who lived in 1100 A.D.[268] We may also note, as pointed by Tucci, that the *Gorakṣasiddhānta-saṃgraha* knows not only a Nāgārjuna but also Malayārjuna and Sahasrārjuna.[269] It is not unlikely that a Siddha Nāgārjuna, a pupil of Sarahapāda, who introduced the *Guhyasamāja* and whose Sādhanas of Ekajaṭā and Vajratārā, have been published in the *Sādhanamālā*, flourished in the late eighth and early ninth century A.D. This date seems to find some support in a work of Tārānātha in which he says that Nāgārjuna fought many enemies of Mahāyāna including Śaṅkara.[270] This statement which does not seem to have received due attention of scholars would show that Nāgārjuna, the Siddha, was a contemporary of the great Śaṅkara, the chief exponent of Advaita Vedānta whose birth is placed in *cir.* 788 A.D.

According to Tārānātha two of Nāgārjuna's pupils were Āryadeva[271] (Siddha 18, Karṇaripā) and Śavarīpā.[272] The latter was also called younger Śaraha, Śavarī or Śabarapā, the fifth Siddha, was a *kṣatriya* by caste, and associted with Vikramaśilā; he was a pupil of Saraha also, and a teacher of Lui-pā. To him are ascribed 16 Tāntrika works in Tenjur and his Sādhana of Kurukullā is published in the *Sādhanamālā*. He seems to have flourished about the turning point of the eighth and the ninth centuries A.D. Bhattacharya, however, placed Śabarain 657 A.D. which is a very unlikely date. Āryadeva or Karṇaripā, the eighteenth Siddha, and the author of the *Cittaviśuddhi-prakaraṇa* seems to have belonged to the late eighth century.

Luhī (or Luī pā) who heads the list of the 84 Siddhas, was not the first Siddha, but was a pupil of Saraha, the Ādisiddha. According to Sāṃkṛtyāyana's sources, Luhī-pā was a *kāyastha* by profession, who belonged to Magadha and was a clerk in the employ of king Dharmapāla (*cir.* 770-810 A.D.) of Bengal. Tārānātha, however, clearly says that Luīpā, the pupil of younger Saraha, (i.e. Śabarapā) was "a writer of the King of Udyāna in the west named Samantaśubha."[273] N. Dutt writes Ujjayinī instead of Udyāna[274]. Whether there was any king named Samantaśubha in Ujjayinī (Mālawā) in the second half of the eighth and the first half of the ninth century A.D., may very well be doubted while there is numismatic evidence,[275] to prove the existence of a king named Sāmantadeva or Samantaśubha (Tibetan Kun-tu dge-ba)[276] in the Swat region, the Kabul valley and Afghanistan. It stands to reason to place Luīpā in the early ninth century A.D.

and to regard him as being a clerk of King Samantaśubha of Śhāhī family of the N.W. Frontier Province.

Kambala (Siddha 30) and his collaborator (in producing the *Hevajratantra*) *Padmavraja*, are also placeable in the second half of the eighth century A.D. Their works have been mentioned above.

Indrabhūti, one of the early Siddhas (no. 42), was the King of Udyāna in the N.W. of India. His son Padmasambhava, reputed as a second Buddha in Tibet, who was instrumental in formulating Lamaism, lived in the second half of the eighth and the first half of the ninth century A.D. A notable figure is Lakṣamīṅkarādevī, sister to Indrabhūti, who became a Siddha and may be placed in the ninth century A.D. There is no doubt that there were several persons who bore the name Indrabhūtis. Snellgrove says that there were three Indrabhūtis.[277] Tārānātha seems to refer at least to two Indrabhūtis—one Indrabhūti, king of Udyāna, was the teacher of Mahāpadmavajra; another Indrabhūti is called the 'junior' who was the pupil of Saroruha and Kambala.[278]

The other Siddhas seem to have belonged to the period between the ninth and the twelfth centuries A.D. Even the Siddhas who have been tentatively placed here in the eighth and the ninth centuries A.D. are placed by other scholars much later.

H.P. Śāstrī[279] held that the Tāntrika works, collected in the *Bauddha Gān O Dohā*, were the products of the tenth century A.D. The authors of these Dohās are mostly Siddhas. S.K. Chatterji[280] also placed the Buddhist Caryāpadas in the tenth century and after. P.C. Bagchi was of the opinion that Lui-pā was the same as Matsyendranātha and that most of the Siddhas lived in the eleventh century A.D.

Esoteric Buddhism : General Considerations

The Buddhist Tāntrika scholars and Tibetan historians make little or no clear-cut distinction between Mahāyāna as taught in the Mahāyāna Sūtras and Śāstras on the one hand, and the esoteric doctrines and practices expounded in the Tantras and Sādhanas, on the other.

Kamalaśīla was inclined to include *mantras*, *mudrās*, *maṇḍalas* and *yoga* in Dharma, i.e. Buddha's teachings.[281] Tārānātha maintained that there had been much study devoted to the

Kriyātantras and the Caryātantras from the time when Mahāyāna began to spread.[282] This view would seem to be supported by the tendency of a large number of Mahāyāna Sūtras, noted above, to incorporate many esoteric elements. However, sometimes the esoteric authorities seem to distinguish between esoterism and Mahāyānism. Thus a tenth century author, Siddha Nāropā[283] says that the Lord gave discourses on two occasions at two different places, first on Prajñāpāramitānaya (Mahāyāna) and then on Mantranaya (Esoteric Vehicle). Another esoteric authority, Maitrīpā or Advayavajra, belonging to the eleventh century A.D., while maintaining that the Mahāyāna is twofold, viz. Pāramitānaya and Mantranaya, states that whereas the former could be explained by the philosophical system of the Vaibhāṣikas, Sautrāntikas and Mādhyamikas, the latter is accessible only through the systems of Mādhyamikas and Yogācārins.[284] Moreover, as if to exalt the esoteric method, he says that Mantranaya is very abstruse and deep, its Śāstras transcend all other Śāstras and it is meant for men of sharpened faculties.[285]

Bu-ston, however, regards Mantranaya as an easy and shorter way of reaching the goal.[286] Some medieval Tibetan scholars talk of the Mahāyāna Tantras, called the old Tantras belonging to the Mantra school.[287] Bu-ston Rin-po-che, author of the famous *Chos-ḥbyuṅ* or 'History of Buddhism', who is credited with the first compilation of the Tibetan Kanjur and Tenjur,[288] did not include these *rnin-ma* Tantras in his catalogue, because they were not regarded as genuine Tantras.[289]

The esoteric texts represent a miscellaneous collection of material; they are not uniform in contents. Broadly speaking, the Tantras are divided into two types : Higher Tantras and Lower Tantras.[290] In a well-known scheme we find the following four classes of Tantras:

1. Kriyātantra (rites of ceremonial magic),
2. Caryātantra (rites of religious practice),
3. Yogatantra (rites of communion); and
4. Anuttarayogatantra (rites of supreme communion).

Tārānātha states that first two categories of Tantras appeared at about the same time when the Mahāyāna Sūtras appeared, but the Yoga and Anuttarayoga Tantra were transmitted esoterically from the time of Asaṅga to that of Dharmakīrti. The latter type of Tantras became popular during the rule of the

Pāla kings chiefly by the efforts of the Vajrācāryas and Siddhācāryas.[291]

It is interesting to note that a parallel division is to be found in the *Padma-tantra* (a Vaiṣṇava Tantra), viz. Jñānapāda, Yogapāda, Kriyāpāda and Caryāpāda.[292]

The *kriyā* and *caryā* Tantras were meant for the beginners, like the *Ādikrama* of the Mahāyāna. The Yoga Tantras and the Anuttarayoga Tantras were meant for advanced saints. Most of the Tantras now published belong to this higher class. The *MMK*, however, may be regarded as a Tantra for the beginners.

CHAPTER XI

DOCTRINES AND PRACTICES OF ESOTERIC BUDDHISM

The Philosophical Basis of Esoteric Buddhism

MYSTICISM often finds philosophical expression in a theory of absolute unity or monism or non-dualism. The esoteric Buddhism displays a manifest influence of the idealistic and absolutistic ideas of Mahāyāna; its doctrines and practices are based on the Mādhyamika and the Vijñānavāda thought. Indeed, according to one authority, the esoteric mysticism of the Buddhist Tantras can be understood only through the Mādhyamika and the Vijñānavāda systems.[1]

The Buddhist esoteric treatises often describe the Truth in negative terms; the terms, *śūnyatā*, *śūnya*, *vijñāna*, *citta* and the compounds *nairātmya*, *bhāvābhāva-vivarjita* and *nissvabhāva*, etc. frequently occur in connection with ceremonies and secret *yogic* practices. These texts do not seem to be concerned so much with metaphysics as with the practical implications of the philosophical ideas of Mahāyāna.

The description of *bodhicitta* given in the second chapter of the *Guhyasamājatantra* is thoroughly permeated by the ideas of the Śūnyavāda as well as of the Vijñānavāda. Thus it is "bereft of all existence, free from *skandhas*, *dhātus* and *āyatanas*, object and subject; and because of the substancelessness and sameness of *dharmas*, it is, from the beginning, unborn and devoid of existence."[2] At another place, it is said that "because the *dharmas* have no origin there is neither existence nor thinking; existence is like the existence of sky."[3]

Anaṅgavajra in his *Prajñopāya-viniścaya-siddhi* declares that all existence issues out of the absolute which is bereft of the thought-construction; the false conceptual construction is the source of all miseries.[4] The author argues that "it is better to imagine the world as real, rather than to regard everything as non-existent, because a burning lamp can be extinguished, but how can it be extinguished if it is not burning at all ?"[5] It means that our struggle for moral and spiritual perfection is necessitated by the presumption of a world of objectivity, in the absence of the latter, there will be no incentive for spiritual endeavour.

Elaborating the point, Anaṅgavajra says that so long as there is the notion of *bhava* or *saṃsāra*, there remains the possibility of *nirvāṇa*, but in the absence of the notion of *bhava*, there can be no final extinction, there is no possibility of destroying the beginningless voidness.[6] With respect to the ultimate Truth, the author says that "it cannot be defined, not even by the Jinas, because it can be known only by oneself (*pratyātma vedyarūpa-tvāt*) and not through external means."[7]

The *Hevajratantra* gives a negative description of the Reality (*tattva*). "In reality there is neither form nor seer, neither sound nor hearer; there is neither smell, nor one who smells neither taste nor taster; neither touch nor one who touches, neither thought nor thinker."[8] This passage strikes a note of similarity to the opening lines of *Madhyamaka-śāstra* of Nāgārjuna, containing the famous eightfold negation.[9] Kāṇhapā, comment-ing upon this passage, says : "Form refers to blue and all other attributes. It is all this that does not exist. Yet how does it not exist, for one certainly sees it ? It does not exist in its essential nature. An essential nature should be uncreated, transcen-dent, non-contingent, self-comprising and in this capacity it does not exist, because it arises from dependent causation."[10]

The ultimate Reality, says Indrabhūti, is "unsupported like the sky, all-pervasive and devoid of characteristics; it is the highest Reality and the unique *vajrajñāna*. It is known as Mahāmudrā, Samantabhadra, and Dharmakāya; it is the ideal to be known and knowledge itself."[11]

The Reality called gnosis (*prajñātattva*) is to be known by realizing the substancelessness of *dharmas* and by a careful discrimination of the knowledge and the object of knowledge.[12] The nature of *dharmas* is described in the *Guhyasamāja* by declaring that they belong neither to *kāmadhātu*, nor to *rūpa-dhātu* nor to *arūpadhātu*, and nor even to the four great ele-ments.[13]

The Vajrayāna sages speak of *saṃsāra* and *nirvāṇa* in the same vein in which Nāgārjuna the great had characterized them. "Between *nirvāṇa* and *saṃsāra* there is not the slightest shade of difference", because they both are neither produced nor annihilated.[14] In actual experience the nature of the world is identical with the nature of the Tathāgata; Tathāgata is devoid of any essence, so is this world.[15] Tathāgata is free from all concepts and thought-constructions.[16]

We read in the *Hevajratantra* that "such as is *nirvāṇa*, such is *saṃsāra*. There is no *nirvāṇa* other than *saṃsāra*, we say. *Saṃsāra* consists in form and sound and so on, in feeling and other constituents of personality, in the faculties of sense, in wrath, delusion and the rest. But all these elements are really *nirvāṇa*, and only from delusion (*moha*) do they appear as *saṃsāra*."[17] This means that all men are really Buddhas; yes, they are. "All beings are Buddhas, but this is obscured by accidental defilement (*āgantukamala*). When this is removed, they are Buddhas at once, of this there is no doubt."[18]

Another picture of this attitude towards *saṃsāra* and *nirvāṇa* is to be observed in the *Prajñopāya-viniścaya-siddhi* in the following words. "The Vajrayānist calls the *saṃsāra* as a condition of the mind which is enveloped with the darkness born of innumerable false ideations, is as ephemeral as the lightning in a storm, and is besmeared with the dirt of attachment, etc. not easily removable."[19] The same mind becomes excellent jewel when it is freed from these excretions. Hence the Vajrayānist further holds that "the excellent *nirvāṇa* is another condition of the mind when the latter is bright and luminous, free from conceptual excretions that envelop it; it (the mind) then becomes the foremost Reality which is neither objective nor subjective."[20] Advayavajra, a late Vajrayāna saint and scholar, says that, in Esoteric System "*śūnyatā* is described as *vajra*, because it is firm and sound, indivisible, impenetrable, cannot be burnt and cannot be destroyed."[21] The term *vajra*, thus stands here for the whole truth itself; although, more frequently as will be seen below, *vajra* symbolizes one of the two coefficients of truth.

The supreme Being (*sattva*) which is the goal and apex of esoteric culture, is often called Vajrasattva. Advayavajra observes that "by *vajra* is meant *śūnyatā* and by *sattva* is meant *jñānamātratā*. The identity of the two follows from the nature of Vajrasattva."[22] Thus this idea of Vajrasattva embodies both the *śūnyatā* and the *cittamātratā*. Some earlier authors, however, explain Vajrasattva in a slightly different manner. In the *Hevajratantra* we are told that "It is indivisible and so known as *vajra*. A Being which is unity of three, because of this device he is known as Vajrasattva."[23] The unity of the three is the unity of body, speech and mind; Tathāgata, the Supernal Being, is the unity of body,speech and mind as is clear from the *Guhyasamāja*.[24] Dharmakīrti, a 9th century Tāntrika Buddhist author and a commentator of the *Hevajratantra*, however, regards this unity as the unity of the three worlds, *kāmadhātu*, *rūpadhātu* and *arūpadhātu*, which is attained in the state of voidness (*śūnyatā*).[25] One is often tempted to understand Vajrasattva as a monotheistic God-head of the esoteric system. Indeed He is invoked as such and is described as the Lord and the saviour of the world.[26]

Āryadeva in his *Citta-viśuddhi-prakaraṇa* echoes the views of Vijñānavāda phenomenology. At one place he paraphrases the first verse of the *Dhammapada*. Mind is the real agent of all actions, it is the antecedent factor of all *dharmas*, it is the most important and the quickest, all our speech and actions follow the pleasure and displeasure of the mind.[27]

Sarahapāda observes that "the great tree of non-dual mind spreads throughout the three worlds in its vastness; it contains flowers and fruits of compassion—there is nothing beyond it."[28] Elsewhere, he says "mind is the universal seed; both *saṃsāra* and *nirvāṇa* spring forth from it; pay honour to this that like a wish-granting gem gives all desirable things. Thought bound brings bondage and thought released brings release; of that there is no doubt."[29]

Kamalāmbarapāda in his *Navaślokī* sets forth the Vijñānavāda philosophy when he says that all objects of perception arise in mind which exist *ab aeterno* and are similar to reflected images; so also consciousness which takes their form as a series of reflected images connected with one another (as perceiver and perceived).[30]

Some Aspects of Esoteric Buddhism

Śakti-sāhacarya (*female-coefficient*) : One of the most important aspects of Buddhist Tāntrika culture is its emphasis on the female counterpart. We may call it Śakti-worship or worship of female energy, or association with coefficient female partner in spiritual effort. The consensus of opinion among acknowledged scholars[31] is that Śakti-sādhana is the essence of Tantra, whether Hinduistic or Buddhistic. Some scholars[32] have, however, pointed out that the use of the term '*śakti*' in the context of Buddhist esoterism, is misleading.

According to Lāmā Anāgārika Govinda, "the concept of Śakti, of divine power, of the creative female aspect of the highest God or his emanations does not play any role in Buddhism. While in the Hindu Tantras the concept of power (*śakti*) forms the focus of interest, the central idea of Tāntrika Buddhism is *prajñā*, knowledge, wisdom. To the Buddhist Śakti is *māyā*, the very power that creates illusion, from which only *prajñā* can liberate us".[33] Elsewhere he remarks in this connection that "there is no need to resort to such superficial reasons as the necessity to comply with the grammatical gender of *prajñā* (feminine) and *upāya* (masculine)." He thus concludes that "the concept of Śakti has no place in Buddhism".[34]

Even granting that the Buddhist Tantras are written in an enigmatical or mysterious language which is to be interpreted symbolically rather than literally, it is quite clear from the esoteric texts, esoteric symbolism, esoteric art representation and the biographies of 84 Mahāsiddhas, that the concept of female element, commonly called '*śakti*' and symbolically described as '*yoginī*', '*prajñā*', '*mudrā*' and 'woman' is very vital and fundamental to esoteric Buddhism. It is the essential coefficient of *mahāsukha*, the goal of life.

The view that in the Hindu Tantras "the focus of interest" is power (*śakti*) does not seem to be well grounded. In Śaiva and Śākta Tantras, the relation of Śiva and Śakti, of the supreme God and the supreme Goddess, is one of identity. Śakti is the feminine aspect of the Absolute when conceived *sub specie temporis*, and in essence, is inseparable from the Lord. As such "the focus of interest" is not active, creative power, but the idea of unity (*advaya*), identity (*tādātmya*) and harmony (*sāmarasya*).

Śakti is worshipped not for the sake of power or creation, but for the sake of integration of 'male' and female' polarities; worship of Śakti is essential for the fusing of the 'two-in-one' (*yuganaddha*).

It is well known that those who worship the wisdom aspect (Śiva, male god) of Reality are known as the Śaivas, and those that worship the power aspect (Śakti, female element) are known as Śāktas; in other words, when Śiva is worshipped Śakti also is worshipped, and vice-versa, when Śakti is worshipped Śiva also is worshipped. The two are, in essence, identical; Śiva and Śakti, apparent male and female, are two essential aspects of Reality which is the unity of the two.

The same is true of the Buddhist Tantras. Here also the supreme truth is the unity of the 'male' and the 'female', called in Tibetan, *yab-yum*. We read in the *Hevajratantra* that "twofold is the Innate (*sahaja*), for wisdom is the woman and means is the man."[35] The only difference between Śākta and Buddhist Tantras concerning female element is that in the Buddhist Tantras and in the esoteric Buddhist art the female (*yum*) or *prajñā* (śe'rab) is represented embraced by an active male aspect or god, often Hevajra or Vajrasattva. In the Śākta Tantras the posture is reversed, Śakti is an active element and the god is passive. But this difference is superficial and makes no material difference in the essential doctrine of Tāntrika theology. *Prajñā* (wisdom) alone is not the central idea even as *upāya* (means) alone is insignificant. "The way of Bodhisattva consists in the practice of *prajñopāya;* neither *prajñā* alone, nor *upāya* alone." "Means without wisdom, and wisdom without means leads to bondage. Means in unison with wisdom and wisdom in unison with means leads to salvation."[36]

The argument that "to the Buddhist, Śakti is *māyā*, the very power that creates illusion, from which only *prajñā* can liberate us", advanced to differentiate *śakti* and *prajñā*, may be counter-balanced by drawing attention to the fact that the Buddhist does not make any distinction between *māyā* or *saṃsāra* and *prajñā* or *nirvāṇa*. If *śakti* stands for *māyā* which symbolizes *saṃsāra* and bondage, and *prajñā* stands for *śūnyatā* the realization of which results in *nirvāṇa*, we have the express declaration of the Mahāyānist and the Vajrayānist authorities that, from the view-point of actual experience, "there is not the slightest shade of difference between *saṃsāra* and *nirvāṇa*";[37] "Such as is *nirvāṇa*, such is *saṃsāra*. There is no *nirvāṇa* other than *saṃsāra*."[38] *Saṃsāra* (or Śakti), as a matter of fact, is not different from *nirvāṇa* (or Tathāgata); Prajñāpāramitā which is often called Bhagavatī, the female counterpart of Buddha, who is often called Bhagavān, is, says Diṅnāga, the same as the 'non-dual Gnosis, the Buddha."[39] Just as Śiva and Śakti are two sides of the same ultimate Truth, so are Tathāgata and Prajñā (*prajñāpāramitā jñānaṃ advayaṃ sā tathāgataḥ*).

Moreover, it is too much to brush aside the fact of the grammatical gender of *prajñā* (feminine) and *upāya* (masculine). These terms are used deliberately and stand for their respective genders. It would be impossible to deny that in Buddhist esoterism the term '*prajñā*' stands for female counterpart. The term '*śakti*' is also used in some standard esoteric texts.[40] The Buddhist Tāntrika *sādhaka* practises esoteric *yoga* with his female partner, this is the essential import of the Yoginī Tantras of Anuttarayoga Tantras. D.L. Snellgrove complaints that modern scholars refer to feminine element as the Śakti and says that "she is not Śakti (active power)."[41] It may be pointed out that the word '*śakti*' need not be interpreted too literally in the sense of 'power' alone. In the esoteric treatises this term is employed for woman, goddess, and *ḍākinī*, and symbolically it represents *prajñā* or *śūnyatā*. But the terms *yoginī; vajrī, mudrā, tārā, bhagvatī, vidyā, prajñā* or *prajñāpāramitā*, etc. which abound in these texts, clearly point to the fact that *śakti-sāhacarya* or *śakti-sādhana* is the most important aspect of this system. Gopīnātha Kavirāja points out that "Tāntrika worship is the worship of *Śakti*. From the Buddhist standpoint *prajñā* is essentially a form of *śakti*."[42]

Prajñopāya : The supreme Reality is often described as the unity of *prajñā* (wisdom) and *upāya* (means); it is the 'non-dual', 'two-in-one', the state of final realization. The conception of *prajñā* and *upāya*, both philosophically and esoterically is cardinal in esoteric Buddhism. *Prajñā* is the same as *śūnyatā* (voidness) and *upāya* is the same as *karuṇā* (compassion); these two terms are very well known to Mahāyānā Sūtras. Bodhisattva is the embodiment of both wisdom and compassion; by means of Prajñāpāramitā or transcendental Gnosis, he realizes the voidness of the phenomenal things and knows that this *saṃsāra* is ephemeral and miserable. Out of *karuṇā* or compassion for the beings he endeavours for the salvation of suffering beings. These two elements of wisdom and compassion, constitute the essence of the thought of enlightenment or *bodhicitta*. The Bodhisattva fixes his intention on obtaining *bodhi* or Enlightenment and this he does by constantly endeavouring for the liberation of all living beings.[43]

In Mahāyāna, *bodhicitta* is the mind directed towards Enlightenment, but in esoteric Buddhism the compound *bodhicitta* is of great technical significance and of complex nature. In short, it is a state of consciousness in which *prajñā* and *upāya*, female and male, wisdom and means, *yoginī* and *yogī*, have perfectly commingled. The description of *bodhicitta* as detailed in the second chapter of the *Guhyasamāja* gives a clear idea of its nature in esoteric Buddhism. It is the utterly indescribable reality, beginningless and endless, neither existent nor non-existent, and is non-substantial like the void and the space. It is eulogized as the pure *tattva,* born of non-substantiality, the heart of Tathāgata and the giver of Buddha's *bodhi*.[44] Elsewhere, this text declares that "*bodhicitta* is the unity of voidness (*śūnyatā*) and compassion (*karuṇā*)."[45] This last definition becomes stereotyped and standardized in all subsequent esoteric texts. The *Cittaviśuddhi-prakaraṇa* describes *advaya* or non-dual in the same terms in which *Guhyasamāja* describes *bodhicitta*. It is said to be beginningless, deathless, quiescent, free from the notions of 'is' and 'is not', devoid of thought-construction, supportless and immutable.[46]

Anaṅgavajra describes *bodhicitta* as non-dual supreme, diamond and enlightenment, and equates it with Śrī Vajrasattva and Sambuddha.[47] *Bodhicitta* is eternal, luminous, pure, the abode of Buddha; it is divine; it includes all the *dharmas* and is the root cause of the whole universe.[48] This supreme Reality is known by the self alone; it is eternal, called *prajñopāya;* it is omnipresent, good, quiescent, neither dual nor non-dual.[49]

The same Reality is called *prajñopāya* because of its two constituents, to wit, *prajñā* or wisdom and *kṛpā* or compassion; they are both absolute and without any support; they commingle together in *prajñopāya* so entirely and completely as one sky merges into another sky.[50] The *Jñānasiddhi* of Indrabhūti also describes *prajñopāya* as *bodhicitta* and as non-dual, eternal unity of wisdom and means.[51] The *Hevajratantra* uses the compound *bodhicitta* in the sense not only of the thought of enlightenment, but also in that of '*śukra*' (male energy), of '*maṇḍala*' and of the '*mahāsukha*.[52] It is clear that the compounds *prajñopāya*, *bodhicitta*, *vajrasattva* and *advaya* stand in Tāntrika Buddhism chiefly for the ultimate truth which is the unity of gnosis (female) and means (male).

Mantra : Another important feature of esoteric system is the significant place occupied in it by the *mantras*. The term '*mantra*' means a 'hymn' or 'prayer' sacred to a deity; it is also understood to mean a 'spell', a 'charm' or 'incantation'. The growth of *mantras* from *dhāraṇīs*, sketched above, would show that in its preliminary stage Tāntrika Buddhism was actually Mantranaya or Mantrayāna. According to one authority *mantras* are the special scriptures of the Mantrayāna school of Northern Buddhism.[53] These Mantras along with Tantras are the fruits of the Sūtras which are the seeds.[54]

H. Zimmer gives a brilliant analysis of the word '*mantra*' which is as follows: "In the word '*mantra*', he says, the root '*man*' ,"to think', is combined with the element '*tra*' which forms tool words. Thus '*mantra*' is a tool for thinking, a thing which creates a mental picture. With its sound it calls forth its content into a state of immediate reality."[55] *Mantra* thus renders thought more tractable; it is a help to meditation and *yogic* vision.[56]

Mantra is a symbol; thus *praṃ* symbolizes the Prajñāpāramitā;[57] *mantra* often symbolically represents a deity or even Reality; thus *oṃ* represents or rather denotes the Lord through its sound.[58] In the Upaniṣads[59], the famous monosyllabic *mantra*, '*oṃ*' is a means (*praṇavo dhanuḥ*) as well as the goal itself (*oṃ iti brahman*). *Mantra* is a power; its repeated uttering brings out certain extraordinary results, such as the subjugation of demons, destruction of enemies or controlling the forces of nature. By practising the secret *mantras* the Buddhist masters of esoteric vehicle acquired power of travelling in the sky or becoming invisible.[60]

"A *mantra*", says Evans-Wentz, "is a syllable or series of syllables of the same frequency as the thing or being (usually an invisible spiritual being, god or demon) to which it appertains; and an expert magician who knows the *mantra* of any deity or order of lesser beings can, by intoning it properly, invoke the deity or dominate the lesser beings."[61] The *mantras* seem to have been the backbone of Tāntrika worship. These *mantras*, as known to us from the esoteric Buddhist texts, are almost invariably unmeaning[62] compilation of words. For instance, "*oṃ hūṃ jinariti he hūṃ hūṃ phaṭ phaṭ svāhā*"; "*oṃ ṭakki hūṃ jaḥ*"; "*oṃ cchinda cchinda bhinda bhinda han han dah dah dīptavajra cakra kṣum phaṭ*."[63] The *mantra* for causing a city to tremble is "*oṃ a ka ca ṭa ta pa ya sa svāhā*"; the *mantra* for subduing is "*oṃ am svāhā*", and for bewitching is "*oṃ būṃ svāhā*."[64] The *mantra* of Yamāntaka is "*oṃ hrīḥ ṣṭrīḥ vikṛtānana hūṃ hūṃ phaṭ phaṭ svāhā*" ; of Maitreya is "*oṃ ṃai Maitreya svāhā*"; a *mantra* for obtaining wealth from Jambhala is "*oṃ aḥ jaṃ dhanaṃ me dehi hūṃ*."

The Tāntrika authors were formidable optimists; they believed in extra-ordinary and super-human powers of *mantras*, charms and spells. Says one author, "What is impossible for the *mantras* to perform, if they are applied according to rules ?"[66] Great emphasis is laid on the correct pronouncing of words. They are regarded as the desire-yielding fruits and their power and efficacy are said to be beyond dispute. The power generated by muttering a *mantra* is so tremendous as would astonish the whole world;[67] the *mantra* can confer even Buddhahood;[68] even an ass can memorize three hundred scriptures by muttering the *dhāraṇī* of Avalokiteśvara,[69] not to say of man. So innumerable are the merits that accrue to the reciter of the *mantra* of Mahākāla, that even all the Buddhas cannot count them for several days and nights.[70] By repeating the *mantra* of Lokanātha are washed away even the five gravest sins[71], and by muttering the *mantra* of Khaṣarpaṇa Buddhahood becomes easily accessible.[72]

The *Mañjuśrīmūlakalpa*, as we have seen above, is full of *mantras* and their merits. The *Guhyasamāja* devotes one whole chapter to *mantracaryā*,[73] while the *Hevajratantra* discusses various *mantras*, their efficacies and methodology in one full chapter[74] besides scattered discussions.

Guru : It is impossible to tread the path of esoteric culture without the kind offices of the *guru* or teacher. The preceptor has to be respected and obeyed as the very incarnation of truth. In Buddhism, as in other ancient Indian educational systems and spiritual disciplines, the importance of a preceptor was never lost sight of. But in esoterism which is concerned with secret, mystic and confidential doctrines and practices, a qualified teacher is indispensable. Accordingly we find the Buddhist esoteric texts eulogizing *guru* above everything else. A pupil has to be initiated by a worthy teacher who is well versed in the mysteries of the Vajrayāna.

The *guru* is reverenced even as the Lord; he is the destroyer of all coverings; he is wisdom embodied, supreme, eternal and full of bliss. The disciple accepts a life long status of a slave of his *guru,* for till he obtains *siddhi* and *mukti* there is no other shelter for him.[75] One who insults the preceptor, never succeeds in his efforts.[76]

In the *Advayasiddhi* attributed to Lakṣamīṅkarā, we are told that "in all the three worlds, movable and immovable, there is nothing superior to the teacher (*ācārya*), through whose grace the wise obtain manifold success.[77]

The fierce Mahākāla eats alive those who hate the preceptor and the *tri-ratna.*[78] The *Hevajratantra* declares that "even when he has attained to *siddhi* and is resplendent in his perfect knowledge, a disciple respectfully greets his master, if he wished to avoid the *avīci* hell."[79]

Almost every esoteric text bears witness to the importance of *guru*; the qualifications of an able teacher are often enumerated. The *Jñānasiddhi* repeatedly mentions the characteristics of the *guru*, and at one place the disciple eulogizes his preceptor in superlative terms.[80] It is laid down that the excellent truth can be obtained only through the kindness and grace of one's teacher, otherwise the fools remain deluded for a long time.[81]

Sādhana : The term '*sādhana*' means accomplishing by means of a *mantra* or charm or prayer; it means evocation, i.e. calling forth of a deity or demon, male or female, usually by means of repetitive recitation of the appropriate *mantra* of the idol, and by meditating over his or her form or symbol. A large number of such Sādhanas, composed by esoteric adepts, written in mixed Sanskrit, are known to us.[82] They contain eulogies of various gods and goddesses, their prayers, different forms, iconographic details, attributes, *mantras* and modes of worship.

An approximate *modus operandi* of an ascetic *sādhana,* according to esoteric Buddhist texts, is as follows.

On a chosen day the ascetic, after performing the regular ablutions, wearing a neat dress or new dress, goes to a solitary place, either auspicious, a wood or the bank of a river, or loathsome, a cemetery, according to the purpose. He sits there at ease in a purified spot and fulfils in order the different acts of Mahāyānic worship—offering of flowers, perfumes, either mental or real, to a host of Buddhas and Bodhisattvas, makes confession of sins, etc. He practises in the same style the virtues of joy, pity, friendship, impartiality and dwells on voidness.

Thus he is supposed to have acquired both merit (*puṇya*) and wisdom (*prajñā*) ; all this is only a preparation to the rite itself. The rite begins with the meditation on the seed (*bīja*) of the god who has been chosen for some technical purpose. If the god is Yamāntaka or Yamāri (the destroyer of Yama, the god of death), the seed syllable (*bīja-mantra*) is *hūṃ*. It is to be written on the disc which in the *maṇḍala*, symbolizes the sun. The *yogin* then causes to arise from *hūṃ* the angry Yamāntaka, hair-bristling, blue, with six faces, six arms and six feet, riding a bull, standing in the *ālīḍha* pose, wearing a garland of skulls, immensely fearful.

Having summoned the god in this way, the *yogin* then begins the second part of the rite; he fancies that he is a god; he realizes the metaphysical identity of himself and the god. As soon as the ascetic knows that he is a god, he acquires all the powers that belong to the god. Any wish he utters in the appropriate form—for his voice must be the voice of the god—will surely be accomplished.

In the *Guhyasamājatantra* we are told that the aim of *upasādhana* is to visualize the deity and this is to be practised for six months without any restriction with regard to the food and other desired objects. If within this time the ascetic does not visualize the deity, he should perform the same *sādhana* three times. And if, even then, the god does not present himself before the *sādhaka* and *bodhi* is not obtained, he should then, resort to the *haṭhayoga*.[84]

Upāya : The *Guhyasamājatantra*, in its 18th chapter, gives a brief outline of *vajrayoga*, called '*upāya*', to be adopted by an ascetic for obtaining *bodhi* or Englightenment. This *upāya* or the 'course' is fourfold : *sevā*, *upasādhana*, *sādhana* and *mahāsādhana*[85]. *Sevā* is again twofold : *sāmānyasevā* and *uttamasevā*; the former consists of four *vajra*-practices, while the latter consists of the ambrosia or nectar of knowledge. The four aspects of *vajra* are : (i) the awareness of vacuity (*śūnyatā*) ; (ii) the transformation of vacuity in the form of seed (*bīja*), (iii) the development of this seed in the form of a deity (*bimba*), and (iv) the outward representation of the deity (*nyāsa*).[86]

In *uttamasevā* is enjoined a sixfold *yoga*[87] : (i) *pratyāhāra*,[88] the process by which the sense organs are controlled; (ii) *dhyāna*, the 'conception of the five desired objects through the five *dhyānī* Buddhas'. *Dhyāna*[89] is also fivefold : *vitarka, vicāra, prīti, sukha* and *ekāgratā*. (iii) *Prāṇāyāma*[90] is the regulation of breath; breath is of the nature of five elements and five kinds of knowledge; it is regarded as a lump and is placed on the tip of the nose in the form of a jewel with five colours and is meditated upon. (iv) *Dhāraṇā*[91] is the concentration of one's chosen *mantra* in the heart, and the restraint of the senses placing them in the *prāṇabindu*. When this is achieved five kinds of signs (*nimittas*) make their appearance : first in the form of mirage, then in that of smoke, third in that of fire-flies, fourth in that of a light, and fifth in the form of a cloudless sky. (v) *Anusmṛti* is the constant remembrance of the object for which the exercise is undertaken, and by this revelation (*pratibhāsa*) takes place. (vi) Through the combination of wisdom and means all existing objects are meditated as one lump. Their meditation in the lump (*bimba*) and the sudden obtaining of transcendental knowledge is called *samādhi*.[92]

Esoteric Performance : An interesting account of esoteric ('erotic') mysticism as practised in Buddhist Tāntrika circles is given in the *Hevajratantra*, a summary of which is as follows.[93] In order to gain perfection in the cult of Hevajra, the ascetic proceeds thus : he wears a tiger-skin, bone necklace, sacred earrings, bracelets on his wrists and girdle round his waist. He associates himself with the five families of Tathāgata (*kulas*[94] of *vajra, padma, karma, tathāgata* and *ratna*), and meditates preferably at night beneath a lonely tree or in a cemetery, or in the mother's house (i.e. the dwelling of goddess), or in some unfrequented spot.

After having gained some 'heat' (*prabhāva*) from meditation he proceeds further on the path. He takes "a girl of a *vajra*-family,[95] fair-featured and large-eyed and endowed with youth and beauty" who has been consecrated or embraced by oneself, and has a compassionate heart. With her the practice should be performed. In case a girl of *vajra*-family is not available, any other woman[96] may be adopted and duly consecrated with the seed of enlightenment. Then the *yogin* along with the *yoginī* sings and dances in various postures of Hevajra.

While practising this esoteric performance, the ascetic

abandons desire and folly, fear and anger, and every sense of shame. He destroys the notion of a self and forgets sleep; he makes, so to say, an offering of his body, by dedicating it to the cause of liberating all the beings. Enjoying food and drinks as they come, without making discrimination between good and bad, eatables and non-eatables, suitables and unsuitables,[97] and honouring *guru* all the more, the *yogin* performs the practice.

"Free from learning and ceremony and any cause of shame, the *yogin* wanders, filled with great compassion in his possession of a nature that is common to all beings. He has passed beyond oblations, renunciation and austerities, and is freed from *mantra* and meditation. Released from all conventions of meditation the *yogin* performs the practice. Whatever demon should appear before him, even though it be the peer of Indra, he would have no fear for he wanders like a lion."[98]

Sandhābhāṣā : All modern scholars agree that the language of the Buddhist esoteric texts or the Tantras is a mixed variety of Sanskrit, and its import is 'special', 'cryptic' and 'esoteric'. *Sandhābhāṣā*[99] refers to a linguistic device of that circle of initiates which employs among its members some intentional symbols and signs called *chomā*.[100] It refers to "the real meaning of a text or doctrine opposed to its *prima facie* or superficial meaning."[101] The following extracts from a few esoteric texts would clearly elucidate this point.

It is well known that in some of their mystic songs the Siddhas address their female counterpart and say that marriage with her resulted in the attainment of great bliss. Thus in song number 10 Kāṇhapāda addresses a *ḍombī*, a low caste or out-caste female. The Sanskrit commentary clearly says that the word '*ḍombī*' is said in esoteric sense (*ḍombī śabdaḥ sandhyābhāṣayā kathayati*).[102]

Ḍombī in the above usage is explained as the *nairātmā* or the purified central *nāḍī*, called *avadhūtī* (*ḍombī pariśuddhāvadhūtī nairātmā boddhavyā*).[103] It is well known that according to the Mahāyāna, Nirvāṇa or Enlightenment is realized as soon as the vacuity or substancelessness (*nairātmya-darśana*) of all things and the self is grasped. The Siddhas say the same truth in their mysterious words.

We may take yet another example of *sandhā.* The compound *'vajrasattva'* literally would mean 'diamantine being', or 'a being whose essence or nature is thunder-bolt or diamond'. But the real and esoteric meaning of Vajrasattva, says Advayavajra, is this : "By *vajra* is implied *śūnyatā* and by *sattva* is meant *jñāna-mātratā*; *vajrasattva* is the utter unity of the two."[104]

By the compound *'tri-śaraṇa'*, i.e. taking refuge in the three, one is apt to understand that this threefold refuge is the refuge in Buddha, Dharma and Saṃgha. As a matter of fact, in this esoteric language, *tri-śaraṇa* refers to taking refuge in body, speech, and mind (*kāya, vāk, citta*) the unity of which is the *sahajakāya,* the Innate Body, also called the Body of Great Bliss (*mahāsukhakāya*).[105]

The *Hevajratantra,* one of the early Yoginī Tantras, explains at several places a number of cryptic words and devotes one whole chapter to the treatment of *chomā* or 'secret signs'; some fanciful or mysterious etymologies are explained. For instance, "*prajñā* is called the mother, because she gives birth to the world"; "she is called washer-woman (*rajakī*) because she tinges all beings (*rañjanāt*)". "Our speech is called uttering (*japa*) because it is the enunciation (*prajalpana*) of *āli* and *kāli*." The words '*āli*' and '*kāli*' stand respectively for vowels and consonants.[106] "A *maṇḍala* is a foot-mark, and it is called *maṇḍala* because it arises from pressure (*malanāt*)." "The bliss that is found in the father, that bliss is enjoyed of oneself, and that bliss by which occurs the slaying, such bliss is said to be *dhyāna*." The 'father' is Vajradhara, and 'slaying' of death is Release, according to the commentator.[107]

Two kinds of secret signs (*chomā*) were employed by the *yogins* "by which the right *yogin* and *yoginī* may be recognized with certainty"; these were : bodily signs, and verbal signs. Thus whoever showed one finger, implied : 'am I welcome?'; the showing of two implied 'he is welcome'.[108] In this way the *vajra-yogins* and *vajra-yoginīs* explained things conventionally by means of signs and counter-signs.

Maṇḍala: Literally the term *'maṇḍala'* is understood to mean 'round', 'circular', 'multitude', a 'province' or 'part', an 'association', a 'charmed circle' or a 'halo round a figure' such as of any god. But technically, and in esoteric Buddhism, *maṇḍala* implies one of the subtlest concepts of Indian mysticism. In this system *maṇḍala* denotes an 'idealized representation of existence', a 'mystic circle', a 'magical diagram', or a 'sphere of divinity'. In the *Guhyasamāja*, the *maṇḍala* is created by the five *dhyānī* Buddhas, their emanations, female counterparts, spiritual sons, and the guardians of the four quarters.[109] More deeply, *maṇḍala* is the means of 'integration', a symbol of unity and a pictorial representation of cosmic process and its forces. The origin of this idea of *maṇḍala* is of great antiquity and is wrapped up in obscurity.

Tucci has given an excellent interpretation of the esoteric theory and practice of the *maṇḍala* in a language intelligible to modern mind. "A *maṇḍala*", he says, "delineates a consecrated superficies and protects it from invasion by disintegrating forces symbolized in demoniacal cycles."[110]

Of course, a *maṇḍala* is not merely a consecrated area that must be kept pure for ritual, liturgical ends. "It is, above all, a map of the cosmos. It is the whole Universe in its essential plan, in its process of emanation and of reabsorption."[111] By means of the *maṇḍala* a disciple obtains to his eternal condition. *Maṇḍala* is the strong-hold, "the essence of all Buddhas". The Lord said : "the *maṇḍala* is the very essence, we say; it is *bodhicitta* and the great bliss itself."[112]

In its geometrical pattern in paintings, a *maṇḍala* is divided into five sections or parts; the central point is occupied by the central symbol or image, and at each of the four cardinal points, four other images or symbols are placed. This quinary grouping of images is significant from the doctrinal and psychological standpoints. They correspond to the five constituent elements of human personality (*pañcaskandhas*) ; they further correspond to the five members of the holy pentad (*pañca dhyānī* Buddhas) —Akṣobhya, Vairocana, Ratnasambhava, Amitābha and Amoghasiddhi—just as the macrocosm corresponds to the microcosm, so that external quinary complex corresponds to the internal, spiritual quinary principle.[113]

These five Tathāgatas are essentially associated with the five components of human personality, viz. *rūpa*, *vedanā*, *saṃjñā* *saṃskāra* and *vijñāna*. These five Buddhas are not remote gods ruling from distant heavens; they reside in human body;

the component parts of human personality are of the nature of five Buddhas who represent the entire cosmos and macrocosm.[114] The ascetic imagines, as he must, in course of *sādhana* and meditation that, he himself is in the centre of the *maṇḍala* as an embodiment of supreme divine Buddhahood or Vajrasattva. The seed syllable (*bīja*) which is placed at the centre of the disc in the *maṇḍala* is the symbol of that profound Reality which is the goal of Tāntrika *sādhana*.[115]

The Five Dhyānī Buddhas : Although the Mahāyāna Buddhists had long been worshipping Buddhas, Bodhisattvas, some demigods and a number of deified sages and *arhats*, yet the evolution of a Buddhist pantheon, properly so called, is attributable to the Tāntrika Buddhists of our period.[116] The first crystallization of a systematic pantheon in Buddhism seems to be reflected in the order of the holy pentad—the five Meditative Buddhas or Celestial Jinas. They are the spiritual sons of the Ādi-Buddha, called Vajrasattva in some texts, Heruka or Hevajra in others, and known as Svayambhū and Ādi-Buddha in Nepal and Tibet. Most scholars believe that this was a theistic or rather monotheistic development in Buddhism.[117] At one place in the *Hevajratantra*, we read that "the *saṃsāra* is Heruka's phenomenal aspect, and he is the Lord, the saviour of the world."[118]

The emanation of the five *dhyānī* Buddhas and of their families (*kulas*) from the meditations of the Supreme Lord is detailed in the first *paṭala* of the *Guhyasamājatantra* in the following manner. From the meditation, called *jñānapradīpa-vajra,* by uttering the *mantra* '*vajradhṛk*', the Lord produced *dhyānī* Buddha Akṣobhya ('unshakable'); from the meditation, called *samaya-sambhava-vajra,* by uttering the *mantra* '*tinatika*', was produced the *dhyānī* Buddha Vairocana (brilliant one); from the meditation, called *ratnasambhava-vajraśrī,* by uttering the *mantra* '*ratnadhṛk*', was produced the *dhyānī* Buddha Ratnaketu or Ratna-sambhava ('matrix of jewel'); from the meditation, called *mahārāgasambhava-vajra,* by uttering the *mantra* '*ārolika*', was produced the *dhyānī* Buddha Amitābha ('infinite light'); in the same way, from the meditation, called *amoghasamaya-sambhava-vajra,* by uttering the *mantra* '*prajñādhṛk*', came forth the *dhyānī* Buddha Amoghasiddhi ('infallible success').

These Buddhas of meditation belonged to five families, namely *dveṣa*, *moha*, *cintāmaṇi*, *vajra*, *rāga* and *samaya* respectively. Subsequently, the Supreme Lord transformed himself through a meditative process into five female counterparts, namely Dveṣarati, Moharati, Īrṣyārati, Rāgarati and Vajrarati, associated with each of the *dhyānī* Buddhas in the aforesaid order. As if to complete the *maṇḍala* of these divinities, the Lord produced through contemplation four guardians of the four quarters, namely Yamāntakṛt, Prajñāntakṛt, Padmāntakṛt and Vighnāntakṛt.[119]

In Buddhist Tāntrika literature an elaborate discussion of complex liturgy, iconography and philosophy of these Buddhas is frequently given. Each *dhyānī* Buddha is associated with one Śakti or female counterpart, with a human Buddha, a Bodhisattva, a family, a seed syllable, an element, a *skandha*, a vehicle, a particular direction and location in the human body.[120]

In the *Hevajratantra* the following arrangement of the five Buddhas and their associations is given. Akṣobhya has for the name of his family *vajra*, the *yoginī* affiliated with him is Vajrī or Ḍombī, and his family symbol is *viśvavajra*. Vairocana has Tathāgata as the name of the family, Brahmāṇī as *yoginī*, *cakra* as symbol. Amitābha's family is called *padma*, *yoginī* Nartī, symbol *padma*. Ratnasambhava's family is *ratna* family, *yoginī* Caṇḍālī, symbol *ratna*. Amoghasiddhi's family is called *karma*, *yogini* Rajakī and symbol *khaḍga*.[121] Akṣobhya's colour is black, of Vairocana white, of Amoghasiddhi dark-green, of Ratnasambhava yellow, and of Amitābha red. These are described as five families or classes. "He who practises the *yoga* of Heruka should frequent the five classes. These five classes that are associated together, he conceives as of one."[122] These five Buddhas are said to represent, among other things, five *skandhas* of our existence.[123]

Mahāsukha : The Buddhist conception of Nirvāṇa is envisaged as *mahāsukha* in this esoteric vehicle. Though a fully developed theory of Nirvāṇa as *mahāsukha*, 'intense bliss' or 'great delight' was elaborated by the Sahajayānists[124] yet the conception of *mahāsukha* as the goal of spiritual endeavour is found also in some esoteric texts belonging to our period. The compound '*mahāsukha*' does not occur in the *Guhyasamāja*, although the

Nairātmya-paripṛcchā already refers to it and equates its nature with *bodhicitta* which is said to be the quiescence of the phenomenon (*prapañca samatikrānta*).[125] Although often negatively described in the old canonical and philosophical texts, the idea of Nirvāṇa as the Supreme Bliss is well known to the oldest scriptures.[126] The famous *ipse dixit* of the Buddha: "There is, O *bhikṣus*,[127] an unborn, unoriginated, uncreated and uncompounded sphere", and the idea that Nirvāṇa is the cessation and opposite of *duḥkha*, [128] also point to a positive conception of Nirvāṇa in early texts. It is this positive conception that is emphasized in Tantras.

Mahāsukha is the essential nature of the final Truth in Vajrayāna, called Bhagavān or Vajrasattva; that is to say, the Ultimate Reality is of the nature of Great Bliss. This is the state of unity of *śūnyatā* and *karuṇā* or *prajñā* and *upāya*; *mahāsukha* is *prajñopāya*; the non-dual fusion of wisdom and means.[129] This is clear from the fact that sometimes goddess Nairātmā is represented in tight embracement with Lord Heruka, or the goddess Varāhī with Lord Mahāsaukhya.[130] This Lord Śrī-Mahāsukha is of the form of infinite bliss.[131] *Mahāsukha* is the Reality (*tattva*) which even the Jinas never discuss, because it transcends discussion.[132]

Mahāsukha is the wisdom of all the Tathāgatas, by nature self-knowable (*svasaṃvedya*) ; it is the supreme bliss among all forms of bliss.[133] *Mahāsukha* is described negatively also. Thus Saraha says that *Mahāsukha* is essencelessness (*nissvabhāva*), indescribable (*akatha*), devoid of self and not-self.[134]

The Social Role of Esoteric Masters

When we study carefully a few standard esoteric texts, or when we read the biographies of Siddhas recorded by the Tibetan chroniclers and translators, we at once realize the striking role and a strange, revolutionary and unconventional social circle of Tāntrika authors, their teachers and followers. The Tantras seem to have spread among the circles of outcastes, voluntary outcastes and carefree wanderers. The *Hevajratantra* refers to such circles of *yogīns* and *yoginīs*, their meeting places, performing esoteric practices, eating flesh of diverse kinds and drinking wine and blood. They used their 'special language' and 'secret signs', so that "the malicious outsiders and wanderers would be bewildered."[135] The followers of Hevajrayoga did not make any difference between classes; they regarded all classes as one.[136] Many of the technical terms used by them testify to their unorthodox origin.[137]

These masters of esoteric culture were by no means social reformers; but they reformed, so to say, indirectly a number of ugly features of Indian society; they did not care for social distinctions or the rules and regulations of *varṇāśrama* organization. When they declared that all men are Buddhas, they meant that all men are equal, and must have equal opportunity in religious life.

The fact that a large number of 84 Siddhas came from lower orders of society, about half of them being of the rank of *ḍomba, camāra, cāṇḍāla,* washerman, oilman, tailor, fisherman, woodcutter, cobbler, and so forth, indicates that the Tāntrika movement was accelerated chiefly by the members of the lower orders of society that had been always relegated to an inferior lower position in Brāhmanic theology and orthodox sociology. This movement succeeded in raising some of the lowliest of men to the status of 'adepts' or 'perfect ones' (Siddhas). These men reasserted their position by means of the powers with which they got credited, and it was by their success (*siddhi*) that they were vindicated.

These teachers, who wandered free from convention and social taboos, did teach through their teachings and doings that there is practically no distinction between a *brāhmaṇa* and a *ḍomba,* a king and a slave. Some of them like Saraha, who was a *brāhmaṇa* by caste, became voluntary out-caste; he married a girl of the mean class, a daughter of an arrowmaker. In his very first *dohā*, Saraha attacks his own former caste, that of the exalted *brāhmaṇa.* He could find no reason to regard a *brāhmaṇa* as the highest of men. The Brāhmanic practices of study, sacrifice, *saṃskāras* and rituals are ridiculed openly. Not only the priestly class, but also the scholars, magicians, Kāpālikas, Śaivas, and Jaina Kṣapaṇakas, are taken to task for their vain practices, high claims and religious exclusiveness. The daily life and practices of the Siddhas and their pupils seem to have helped in lessening caste-distinctions, bonds of *varṇa* in matters of marriage, food, education, and religious avocation.

Revolting Side and Abuses of Esoterism

What strikes to the casual reader of the Tantras as something puzzling and unconventional, is their so-called 'revolting' side. The description of esoteric practices and situations, *śakti-sāhacarya*, ceremony of secret initiation of young *yogin* and *yoginī*, details of diverse kinds of food and drinks including flesh and wine, etc. that find frequent mention in the pages of esoteric texts, have been subjected to rather much uncharitable criticism. According to H. Kern,[138] "tantrism is, so to say, a popularized and, at the same time, degraded form of *yoga* because the objects are commonly of a coarser character, and the practices partly more childish, partly more revolting". R. L. Mitra[139] declared that "no good purpose would be served by dwelling further on the absurd and often disgusting prescriptions of such works as the *Tathāgataguhyaka*", and Charles Eliot[140] held that "the details of Śāktism are an uprofitable study." Even discerning critics, like Winternitz and La Vallée Poussin, do not seem to have appreciated the language and style of the Tantras. The former found in them an "unsavoury mixture of mysticism, occult pseudo-science, magic and erotics" couched in "strange and often filthy language."[141] The latter frankly attributed to Tantrism "disgusting practices, both obscene and criminal.[142] B. Bhattacharya stigmatizes the Tantras as examples of "the worst immorality and sin"[143] and Tāntrikism as a "disease."[144]

Perhaps we may not be justified in such a whole-sale condemnation of Tāntrikism or Esoterism. It is true that the Vajrayāna *yogin* is said to find Nirvāṇa in the blissful embrace of a young girl;[145] it is stated that the Buddhahood resides in the female organ;[146] that lust is crushed by lust;[147] and that there can be no liberation without a female partner.[148] But the Tantras make it clear that their language is not to be interpreted literally and that the darker aspects of Tantra practices were not meant for the ordinary men. According to Giuseppe Tucci, apart from some exceptions, "the Tantras contain one of the highest expressions of Indian mysticism which may appear to us rather strange in its outward form, chiefly because we do not always understand the symbolical language in which they are written."[149] More recently, in his excellent work on the *maṇḍala*, where he compares the symbols of the Tantras with those of the Upaniṣads, Tucci shows the profound mystical and metaphysical import of Tāntrika symbolism.[150] The authoritative and interpretative studies concerning the doctrines and practices of the Tantras published by Gopīnātha Kavirāja, indicate that the real import of the Tantras is quite beyond our reach.[151] Reference may be made to the appropriate protest against the strictures on Tantras made by D. L. Snellgrove,[152] and the just and faithful appreciation of the Tāntrika mysticism by Lāmā Anāgārika Govinda.[153] All scholars seem to agree that Tāntrika mysticism became the subject or controversy in modern times owing mainly to its cryptic or esoteric language, technically known as the *sandhā-bhāṣā.* It is generally believed that the abuses of Tāntrika practices may have resulted in moral degeneration and the decline of Buddhism.[154]

Chapter XII

BEGINNINGS OF THE DECLINE OF BUDDHISM IN INDIA

Testimony of Chinese Pilgrims

The writings of the Chinese pilgrim-scholars, viz. Fa-hien, Song-yun, Hsüan-tsang and I-tsing, who visited India in the fifth, sixth and seventh centuries respectively, testify to the decadence of Buddhism in several parts of the country.

Travelling across the plains of the Gaṅgā in the first quarter of the fifth century A.D., Fa-hien found Buddhism generally in a prosperous condition in most places he visited save and except Kanauj, Kapilavastu, Rāmagrāma, Vaiśālī and Gayā. At Kanauj there were only two Hīnayāna monasteries.[1] Kapilavastu had "no king nor people" and was "like a wilderness, except for priests and some tens of families."[2] Rāmagrāma had only one monastery,[3] while at Vaiśālī he observed only the *vihāra* of the "Great Forest."[4] The city of Śrāvastī was also in ruinous state with a negligible population.[5]

A progressive decline in Buddhist population is evidenced by the records left by the successors of Fa-hien. What is more striking is that, Buddhism is seen giving way to Hinduism in its very strong-holds of earlier days. Thus in the time of Hsüan-tsang though the city of Vaiśālī had not fallen into ruins, yet the Buddhist establishments, some hundreds in number, were, with the exception of three or four, dilapidated and deserted, and the monks were very few. On the contrary, there were some tens of Deva-temples, the various sects of Hindus lived pell-mell and the Digambara Jains flourished.[6]

In Kanauj where in the first decade of the fifth century A.D. Fa-hien had seen two monasteries of Little Vehicle Song-yun and Tao-sheng (A.D. 518-521) found neither monks nor nuns, though the temples were numerous. It was perhaps the Hūṇa invasion and its destructive effects that had resulted in Buddhism's decline. But even Kanauj, the metropolis of Harṣa, the famed patron of Buddhism and Buddhist pilgrims in the first half of the seventh century A.D., is seen populated by anti-

Buddhist *brāhmaṇas* and Deva-worshippers and the number of temples exceeded that of the *vihāras*.[7]

In Udyāna (or Uḍḍiyāna in Swat), which had once boasted of its 1,400 monasteries and 18,000 monks, there were very few of them left in the 7th century A.D., and they understood the doctrine very poorly. What is more, they had now been addicted to magical exorcism.[8] Gāndhāra presented to Hsüan-tsang a miserable scene with its 1,000 monasteries in ruins, solitary to every inch, while heretics were numerous living in some hundred temples.[9]

The monasteries in the kingdoms of Takṣaśilā, Siṃhapura and Wu-la-shi (Urṣa) were likewise desolate.[10] In Kashmir also Buddhism was declining. Hsüan-tsang observes about Kashmir: "At the present time this kingdom is not much given to the Faith and the temples of the heretics are their sole thought."[11] Nonetheless, Buddhism was still flourishing in some parts of Kashmir,[12] and Hsüan-tsang thought it worth-while to study and participate in its scholastic debates. In Sindh, though there were numerous Buddhists, more than 10,000, and hundreds of monasteries, but most of them were "worthless persons", "as a rule, they were indolent and given to indulgence and debauchery".[13]

In Sthānvīśvara, the home province of the house of Harṣa, there were only three monasteries against some hundred Deva-temples.[14] In Mathurā, there were 20 monasteries, the same number as in the time of Fa-hien, but while in Fa-hien's days they were tenanted by 3,000 monks,[15] the number had come down to 2,000 in the time of Hsüan-tsang.[16] In Śrughma there were five monasteries as against 100 Deva-temples with many non-Buddhists; in Matipura there were 10 monasteries but 50 Deva-temples; in Brahmapura 5 monasteries to match against 10 Deva-temples; in Goviṣāṇa 2 monasteries against 30 Deva-temples; in Ahicchatra and Kapitha the Śaiva-Pāśupatas outnumbered the Buddhists. Ayamukha had five monasteries to match against 10 Deva-temples, while in Prayāga only 2 monasteries against 100 Deva-temples. In Kauśāmbī there were about 10 monasteries, "but all in utter ruin", while the number of Deva-temples was more than fifty; in P'i-shoka (Viśākhā) also the Buddhists and their sacred establishments were outnumbered by 'heretics' and their temples. In Śrāvastī most of the monasteries were in ruins with few followers, the unmber of the non-Buddhist votaries was far more numerous who commanded 100 Deva-temples.[17] In Vārāṇasī, there were 30 monasteries with 3,000 monks, but the number of Deva-temples was above 100, and their worshippers, more than ten thousand, mostly Śaivas.[18] Thus these statistics tend to suggest a progressive decay of Buddhism in comparison to Hinduistic sects. Everywhere the latter seem to be thriving at the cost of the former.

It is only in Magadha, especially around Nālandā, that Buddhism is seen to be a living and prominent religion, still holding its banner aloft as the great institution of self-culture and higher learning. This ancient land was populated by people who "esteemed learning and reverenced Buddhism. There were above fifty Buddhist monasteries and more than ten thousand ecclesiastics, for the most part adherents of the Mahāyāna system." It is legitimate to presume that this vigour of the Doctrine in Magadha may have been chiefly due to the influence of Nālandāmahāvihāra, which seems at this time to have been the greatest and the best equipped international centre of Buddhistic culture.[19]

Although Buddhism is supposed to have lasted longest in eastern India, upto as late as the 13th century A.D., yet contemporary records point out that the condition of Buddhism in the 7th century A.D. was hardly enviable in this part of the country.

In the province of Bengal, Tāmralipti (Tamluk) was a famous centre not only of sea-borne trade but also of Buddhism. However here also a palpable decline in Buddhist following is apparent from the fact that the number of monasteries in the time of Fa-hien was 24 but it had come down to 10 in that of Hsüan-tsang, while I-tsing mentions only one or two important convents in Tāmralipti.[20] In Puṇḍravardhana there were 100 Deva-temples against 20 convents; in Samataṭa 100 Deva-temples against 30 monasteries; in Karṇasuvarṇa likewise, there were 50 Deva-temples against 10 monasteries.[21] The people of Kāmarūpa did not believe in the Law of the Buddha; there were no Buddhist chapels nor monasteries at the time of Hsüan-tsang's visit. King Kumāra of Kāmarūpa, though a friend of the pilgrim, was not a Buddhist by faith.[22]

Orissa seems to have been a flourishing centre of Buddhism,[23] but its neighbouring tract of Konyodh (Kongodh, around the lake Cilkā), was bereft of Buddhist traces. In Kaliṅga there were some 'students of the Mahāyānist Sthavira school system, with only ten monasteries as against numerous adherents of heretical sects, with 100 Deva-temples, and Jainism was most prosperous.[24]

In the South,[25] Buddhism seems to have been losing ground before the rising movements of Śaivism and Jainism. Most of the monasteries of Dhānyakaṭaka were deserted, while the Deva-temples were more than one hundred with numerous followers. Similarly in the Cola country, 'the Buddhist monasteries were in ruins', only a few had some monks but they were out-numbered by several tens of Deva-temples, besides, the Nirgranthas were numerous. In Draviḍa land the strength of the Digambara Jainas was little less than that of the Buddhists. In Malakūṭa in the southern extremity (probably Travancore-Cochin), there were 'remains of old monasteries', the number of brethern being very little in comparison to those of the Jainas and others.[26]

The same phenomenon of decadence is manifest in Western India. In Kaccha, Surat, Ujjain and Maheśvarapura, everywhere the non-Buddhists out-numbered the Buddhists, while in Gurjara Buddhism was virtually extinct. In Cittor (Rājapūtānā) the majority people were non-Buddhists. Of the decadence of Buddhism in Sindh mention has already been made above.[27]

Not only Hsüan-tsang but I-tsing also leads us to conclude that "the teaching of the Buddha is becoming less prevalent in the world from day to day."[28] He asks people to be more alert in future, but in vain; the conditions had deteriorated in his time. He records this deterioration in a language full of sincerity and pathos : "When I compare what I have witnessed in my younger days with what I see today in my old age the state is altogether different, and we are bearing witness to this, and it is to be hoped that we shall be more attentive in future."[29]

But the history of Indian Buddhism after the 7th century A.D. reveals that the Buddhists never became 'more attentive', and the hopes of I-tsing were never fulfilled as the Doctrine of Śākyamuni went on declining until it finally disappeared from India. The altogether different state, was nothing but the decadent state of Buddhism in the seventh century A.D.

The foregoing survey should serve to illustrate the state of decline of Buddhism in India during this period.

Beginning of Decline of Buddhism

Some modern writers have traced the decline of Buddhism from the seventh century A.D. Thus P. C. Bagchi was of the opinion that the decline of Buddhism "commenced from the 7th century A.D.", and "the internal degeneration in the faith became manifest from the 7th century A.D."[30] Likewise R. C. Mitra traces the decline of Buddhism in India from the seventh century A.D., perhaps chiefly because of the evidence of the Chinese travellers.[31] It appears, however, that the decline of Buddhism in India had started at a considerably earlier date; it was in fact a long drawn process, slow but steady, the beginnings of which seem to go back by several centuries. It is, therefore, not advisable to fix any particular point of time for the beginning of decline. On the other hand, one can trace the process of decline from a much earlier period of Buddhist history. It is proposed here to indicate this earlier phase of decline and its detailed examination during our period.

In this connection it is interesting to note a striking phenomenon in Buddhistic tradition, viz. prophecies concerning the life-span of the Doctrine of Buddha. The relevance and significance of such ancient and medieval Buddhist traditions, preserved in Indian, Sinhalese, Tibetan and Chinese documents, of both Hīnayāna and Mahāyāna, can hardly be overestimated in the context of an historical study of the decadence of Buddhism. To begin with the tradition preserved in the Pāli canon itself. Buddha is said to have prophesied that the duration of the Doctrine would be shortened by five centuries as a result of the admission of women to the Saṃgha :

"If, Ānanda, women had not received permission to go out from the household life and enter the homeless state, under the doctrine and discipline proclaimed by the Tathāgata, then would the pure religion, Ānanda, have stood fast for a thousand years. But since, Ānanda, women now have received the permission, the pure religion, Ānanda, will not last so long, the Good Law would now stand fast for only five hundred years."[32] The purport of this passage is that the Saddhamma would begin to decay five hundred years after the Buddha, i.e. in about the first century A.D.

This ancient tradition finds support in Bu-ston's *Ch'os ḥbyuṅ.*

Quoting from an old text, 'the Sūtra of the Gratitude of Buddha', he says that "the prophecy therein lays down that if the Lord permits that women enter his congregation, the Highest Doctrine will cease to exist 500 years earlier (than it would otherwise)".

Bu-ston also records extracts from some other older works which tend to suggest 1,000 years life-span of the Doctrine. So it is said in the *Vinaya-kṣudraka*, the *Abhidharmasūtra*, and the *Abhidharmakośa-vyākhyā*. According to the *Bhadrakalpikasūtra*, "the real Doctrine is to exist for 500 years and the next 500 years there will be only a resemblance of it."[33]

The *Theragāthā*, an ancient collection of the songs of the Elders also refers to a prophecy concerning the decay of moral rules among the monks. In an answer to the question as to what the monks of the future will be like, Phussa says that the monks will be full of all the evil qualities, like anger, hatred, envy and obstinacy and that they will transgress the teachings of the Lord, and will live without any discipline.[34] It is difficult to say what precise period this prediction is referrable to; even if it refers to a later period, it is presumable from this and other similar passages in the canonical texts[35] that the ancient Buddhists themselves entertained a belief about the impending tragedy in their faith.

The well-known *Rāṣṭrapāla-paripṛcchā-sūtra* also records a prophecy, said to have been made by Buddha, concerning the lax morals of the monastics and decay of the religion. The work belongs to the sixth century A.D. and might well reflect the contemporary conditions.[36]

Hsüan-tsang has recorded with a feeling of despair a number of legends which were current in India in the seventh century A.D. and were greatly suggestive of the imminent catastrophe that was to befall on the Sacred Law. Two or three of them may be reproduced here without sharing the pilgrim's credulity in more or less imaginary tales. They are, as said above, not historic facts, but suggestive of the historical course of things.

Thus he narrates the story of Kaniṣka's *stūpa*, of which Buddha had predicted (so he heard from the people) that "when this Tope had been seven times burned and seven times rebuilt, his religion would come to an end." In the days of Hsüan-tsang it had been burned down four times, so that the fulfilment of the prophecy was nearing.[37]

At Buddha-Gayā the pilgrim saw the figures of Avalokiteśvara which were destined to sink down with the disappearance of Buddhism. "An image at the south corner had already disappeared upto the breast."[38] In his biography is recorded a dismal dream that Hsüan-tsang dreamt one night, while residing at Nālandā, that soon after the death of Śīlāditya Harṣavardhana the Doctrine of Buddha would be visited by a terrific calamity and the great halls of Nālandā would be deserted, its glorious chambers turned into the dwellings of the water-buffaloes and that a devastating fire would reduce to ashes all its structures and towns around it.[39] That this prophetic dream of Hsüan-tsang was in course of time fully materialized to its tragic climax is borne out, not only by the Muslim records,[40] but also by archaeological excavations at Nālandā.[41] Elsewhere in his *Si-yu-ki* the Chinese pilgrim records the tradition that the final extinction of the Law would take place in Kauśāmbī. According to the *Mahāmāyāsūtra*, the doctrine was to disappear after 1,500 years of Buddha's Nirvāṇa.[42]

The foregoing discussion would seem to indicate that Buddhism had declined to a considerable extent in several parts of the country in the seventh century A.D. It cannot be denied that in certain parts of India it was still in prosperous condition and in a healthy state when the Chinese pilgrims were touring. It is equally undeniable, however, that on the whole, in most places of India, Buddhism was losing its hold on people before the expanding and evergrowing tide of Hinduism, while in south India Jainism was gaining the upper hand. Thousands of monasteries throughout the length and breadth of India had been deserted and dilapidated before the seventh century was out. The various legends and prophecies concerning decline of Buddhism seem to suggest that the declining tendencies had been in progress from about the fifth century after Nirvāṇa.

Factors in the Decline of Buddhism

The decadent state of Buddhism discussed above was brought about by a number of factors. These factors were partly internal and partly external. To begin with the internal factors.

Moral Degeneration: Degeneration in moral and spiritual attainments of the Buddhist monks and nuns during the seventh and the eighth centuries is reflected in the accounts of the Chinese pilgrims and clearly alluded to in the contemporary Indian literature. Hsüan-tsang refers to the careless moral conduct of the Buddhist monks of Bolor or Balti and says that they were without any definite learning.[43] Of the worldly life and indisciplined ways of the Sammitīya monks of Sindha, Hsüan-tsang gives a graphic description. They were indolent, worthless persons given to debauchery. Though they wore the monastic dress yet killed animals, reared cattle and maintained wives and children. This may well be described as the institution of 'married monks' which became popular in Nepal and still exists in Tibet[44] and Japan.

The Kashmiri historian Kalhaṇa also alludes to this feature among the monks of that country. In the *vihāra* built by Yūkadevī, a queen of king Meghavāhana (*cir.* 600 A.D.), one half was allotted to regular monks of good conduct and the other half to those who had wives, sons and property and were thus blameworthy.[45]

Occasional cases of lax morals and transgression of the rules of monastic celebacy are not unknown to earlier phase of Buddhist history.[46]

It is quite likely that there may have been many other lesser monks than Bhartṛhari who wavered seven times between 'the joy of renunciation' in a forest abode on the one hand, and the 'voluptuous embrace' of a fair youthful lady on the other.[47]

In a number of literary works belonging to the seventh and the eighth centuries the Buddhist monks and nuns are represented as active participants in political, military and matrimonial affairs of the times.

In the *Mālatīmādhava* of Bhavabhūti we find that Kāmandakī, an old *bhikṣuṇī* along with her two associates, is engaged in bringing about a private union among the lovers. The intrigues and almost un-Buddhistic activities of Kāmandakī in this play are a pointer to the degenerate condition of the Buddhist church during this age.[48]

Likewise in the *Daśakumāracarita* of Daṇḍī, which 'reflects a corrupt state of society', the Buddhist nuns are the 'go-betweens' and a Buddhist woman is depicted as an expert in procuring lovers.[49] In the *Mattavilāsa-prahasana* of the Pallava king Mahendravarman I (*cir*. 600-630 A.D.), the Buddhist monks along with the Śaivas, are ridiculed for their lack of self-control and indulgence in sense-pleasures.[50]

Already in the *Mālavikāgnimitra* of Kālīdāsa[51] we find *parivrājikās* acting as a go-between for the lovers. In the one-actor plays, the Bhāṇas, the Buddhist sacred terminology is employed for sex purposes in quite vulgar and corrupt sections of society; the Buddhist monks and nuns are found engaged in making advances of love. Thus in the *Caturbhāṇī*,[52] a product probably of the seventh and the eighth centuries A.D., not only the princes, *brāhmaṇas*, poets and learned grammarians, but also the Buddhist *bhikṣus* are described as frequenting the houses of courtesans.[53] Monks and nuns are seen acting as *pīṭhamarda* and *pīṭhamardikā* respectively. The character of the Buddhist nun Saṃghadāsikā provokes reader's contempt for her. She is being consoled by a degraded monk who quotes Buddha-words. This dissolute *bhikṣu*, named Saṃghalika, is badly taken to task and ridiculed by a group of druken and love-sick persons given to debauchery. They also attack the doctrine of Buddha, the institution of monks, and the *saṃgha* which is being polluted by such impure monks. Saṃghalika is shown to be careful about the rule of taking food in time but abrogating the Five Precepts (*pañcaśikṣāpadas*).[54]

The 'Sūtra of the Face of Lotus' translated into Chinese in A.D. 584 records a prophecy in which it is said that "the *bhikṣus* shall then take pleasure in doing only evil deeds. They shall be given to theft, pillage, tending of meadows and cultivation of lands."[55]

Referring doubtless to the growth of wealth and greed among the monks, I-tsing laments that most of the monasteries in India maintained corn-fields, bulls and monastic servants; some of them were 'very avaricious' and did not divide the produce.[56] At another place in his record he observes that "it is unseemly for a monastery to have great wealth, granaries full of rotten corn, many servants, male and female, money and treasures hoarded in the treasury without using any of them."[57]

Bu-ston records from the *Candragarbha-paripṛcchāsūtra* that 1,300 years after the death of Lord (i.e. in about 800 A.D.) the monks shall covet riches and articles of enjoyments.[58]

The *Bhagavadajjukam*, a work ascribed to Bodhāyana by its

commentator and which, according to some, may be a work of Mahendravarman I, the Pallava king, shows that beggars flocked to the Buddhist *saṃgha* in order to get free food easily and other material comforts merely at the cost of shaving their heads and wearing the yellow robes.[59] On the other hand, some monasteries in the time of I-tsing were occupied by monks who appropriated everything among themselves, did not provide food for other resident monks and compelled the latter to seek their own food. These monasteries, where selfish and greedy monks must have been living, "did not admit a stranger to reside there. Thus those who come from any quarter are induced by these monasteries themselves to lead the unlawful life."[60]

The *Rāṣṭrapālaparipṛcchā-sūtra*, a work commonly placed in the 6th century A.D., depicts in the form of a prophecy, a life-like sketch and a satirical picture of the lax morals of the Buddhist monks. It says, for example : "My monks will be without shame and without virtue, haughty, puffed up and wrathful...... intoxicating themselves with alcoholic drinks. While they bear the banner of the Buddha, they will only be serving the householders." They will have cattle, slaves and will indulge in agriculture and trade; they will be devoid of moral conduct, deceitful and possessed of wives, sons and daughters. They will be indisciplined and uncontrolled in eating and sex-play; devoid of education and honour, they will live without Prātimokṣa rules, and as unrestrained as elephants without elephant-goad.[61] As Winternitz observes, this picture "must necessarily reflect actual facts" of the 6th century A.D..[62]

It is evident from these references that decadence of Buddhism in India is related, at least in some measure, to the decay of moral and spiritual discipline among the Buddhist monks and nuns. Indulgence in non-religious affairs by monks and nuns is testified to by the *Mṛcchakaṭika* and the accounts of the early Arab invasions of India also. Mention has already been made of a '*samanī*' of Sindha named Buddharakṣita who had family and was actively associated with the political and military affairs of the king.[63]

The *Mṛcchakaṭika* shows that the Buddhist monks were not held in honour in Ujjainī. A shampooer-monk is seen associated with the plot of the drama and is represented as leading Vasantasenā to a *bhikṣuṇi* in the *vihāra* in the precincts of the royal garden. Saṃvāhaka *bhikṣu*, to whom Cārudatta was grateful for saving the life of Vasantasenā, is shown as being appointed the head of monasteries in the kingdom at the recommendation of Cārudatta,[64]

Sectarian Disputes : Decay of moral discipline among the Buddhists was not the only factor which hastened Buddhism towards its decline from within, but another very harmful factor was the schism in the *saṃgha* and fierce disputes among the sectarians and scholars of Buddhism. Hsüan-tsang in his general description of India observes : "Buddhism now is pure or diluted according to the spiritual insight and mental capacity of its adherents. The tenets of the schools keep these isolated, and controversy runs high; heresies on special doctrines lead many ways to the same end. Each of the eighteen schools claims to have intellectual superiority; and the tenets (or practices) of the Great and Small Systems (lit. vehicles) differ widely......and many are the noisy discussions. Wherever there is a community of brethren it makes (its own) rules of gradation."[65]

Buddhism was no longer one system, it had become a family of several systems and schools and communities long before our period. Buddha had apprehended the danger of internal disunity, and *saṃghabheda* was condemned as one of the five deadly sins. But, in fact, the history of schism in Buddhism dates back from the time of Buddha himself.[66]

It has been noted above that the followers of Devadatta were still in existence and commanded three convents in Karṇasuvarṇa in the 7th century A.D.[67] It is in the philosophical controversies and doctrinal differences of the Buddhists that the most extreme form of this weakening phenomenon is visible. Not only the Sammitīyas of Sindha were reviling the Mahāyāna,[68] but one of the most famous teachers of Hīnayāna, Prajñāgupta by name, had composed "a treatise in 700 *ślokas* against the Great Vehicle," and Hsüan-tsang was inspired by Mahāyānists of Magadha to destroy the heresy by composing a polemical work in 1,600 *ślokas*.[69]

Even Śāntideva devotes so many verses of the *Bodhicaryāvatāra* to the refutation of Abhidharma systems and the Vijñānavāda.[70] Candrakīrti's fierce attacks on all non-Mādhyamika systems of Buddhist thought are too well known.[71] Śāntarakṣita devotes a long section of his *Tattvasaṃgraha* to demolish the tenets of the

Vātsiputriyas, and he as well as Kamalaśīla declares that the Pudgalavādins have no claims to be called the followers of the Buddha.[72] In short, the controversies among the Buddhists were as bitter as between the Buddhists and the non-Buddhists.

Mahāyānism and Tāntrikism : One writer has remarked that "it was to the corruptions of the Mahāyāna rather than of the Hīnayāna that the decay of Buddhism in India was due."[73] This unpleasant remark can hardly be regarded to be without some substance in it. The growth and popularity of Mahāyānism resulted not only in the increase of the votaries of the religion, but also in a corresponding qualitative decay. To a seventh century critic Mahāyāna Buddhists appeared as mere worshippers of Bodhisattvas and readers of Mahāyāna Sūtras.[74] The Great Vehicle laid emphasis on the image-worship, prayers and incantations, pompous ceremonies and rituals; it incorporated many folk-beliefs and made room for the emotional demands of the laity, and in doing so, the Buddhists made a near and clear approach to Hinduism; this process ultimately led to the destruction of distinction between the two faiths. The laymen and laywomen of India found no difference between the worship of Viṣṇu and Buddha, of Śiva and Avalokita, and of Tārā and Pārvatī.

Buddhism, taught and practised in the Nālandāvihāra, was a popularized form of Buddhism. Certain innovations of Mahāyāna doubtlessly made the religion of Buddha easily acceptable to races and classes of men, but these features in course of time resulted in the inner decay of the Faith. The Bodhisattvayāna, for instance, seems to have given birth to the institution of 'married monks' the reality of which is attested during our period by Hsüan-tsang, Kalhaṇa and *Chācha-nāmā*.[75] The Mahāyānists advocated the ideal of Bodhisattva; not only the monks but householders also could embrace Bodhisattvacaryā. Since Śākyamunī, in his earlier existences had been living in the world, it was therefore possible to embrace the career of a Bodhisattva even though married. Already the Vaitulyakas, the fore-runners of the Mahāyāna, had made provisions for the followers of this career that under special conditions '*methuno dhammo*' could be observed; Śāntideva records of a Bodhisattva's extreme case in which he broke his vow of continence after having kept it for many thousands of years. It is legitimate to conclude that this peculiar form of religious course was the source of the doctrine of co-efficiency or female element in the Tantra.

The first known Vajrayāna text, therefore, declared: *rāgacaryā kulaputrā yadut bodhisattvacaryā*". The Buddhist ascetic now went to his teacher along with a female partner.[76] Almost all the 84 Siddhas of Tāntrika Buddhism were either married or had espoused *yoginīs*.

The increasing Hinduistic manifestations in the plurality of divinities, worship, ritualism and litany had already considerably weakened the original impulse and pristine purity of Buddhism. With the introduction of Tāntrikism in Buddhist quarters, the process of decline seems to have been quickened. Tāntrikism further narrowed down the distinction and difference between Buddhism and Hinduism. Buddhist Tantras, in spite of their being "proclaimed by Buddha", are almost identical with the Śivaite and Śākta Tantras. A large number of gods and goddesses became common to the pantheons of Hinduism and Buddhism. The Śākta *pīṭhas* became equally important and holy places for Hindu and Buddhist Tāntrikists. The strange "mixture of mysticism, occult pseudo-science, magic and erotics", was a common feature of all Tāntrikism.

Moreover, the Vajrayāna texts reveal a radical departure from classical Buddhism in the domain of both doctrine and practice. The world of sense, which was considered as the source of evil, and the Buddhist saint's essential endeavour was directed towards the destruction of attachment to *saṃsāra*, is now taken as the true medium, a proper field for making spiritual progress. Liberation, according to Vajrayāna, is to be attainable here and now, in this life and through the *saṃsāra*. This *saṃsāra* is to be realized as Nirvāṇa.[77] The Vajrayāna dogma that "everything is pure to a pure man" and that the *yogins* are beyond good and evil, may have proved very dangerous. Some of the printed texts of the Vajrayāna clearly advocate a moral anarchy among the *yogins* and *yoginīs*. The Five Moral Precepts are no longer heard of; their place is taken by *pañcamakāras* and five sacraments; the ideal of incomprehensible Nirvāṇa gives way to that of Great Delight (*mahāsukha*), attainable not through *śīla*, *samādhi* and *prajñā*, not even by the noble Eightfold disciplinary course, but by a mystic union with the *yoginī*.[78]

The pessimistic odour of Buddha's sermons seems to have

been replaced by a hedonistic temper of the revelations of Vajra sattva. The rationalism and intuitionalism of early Buddhism disappears and a superstitious sorcery and erotic esoterism comes to the foreground. Early Buddhism condemned attachment as the fiercest fire, Vajrayāna regarded it as the supreme joy. In short, fundamental principles of Buddhist ethics, the spiritual elements conducive to Enlightenment, are entirely transformed in Vajrayāna mysticism. It seems that it is of the abuses of Vajrayāna that I-tsing speaks when he records : "Some have committed sins as numerous as the grains of sand of the Ganges, yet they say they have realized the state of Bodhi."[79] Among the internal factors in the decay of Buddhism in India, the abuses of Vajrayāna perhaps occupy the foremost place.

Brāhmanical Hostility : Among the external factors the most important was the Brāhmanical hostility towards Buddhism. The *brāhmaṇas* never fully accepted the growth of Buddhist faith, although at a later date they counted Buddha as one of the *avatāras*. This fact of Brāhmanical hostility to Buddhism has not usually been given the attention it deserves. Right from the days of Buddha the orthodox Hindus (the followers of Vedic, Brāhmaṇic and Paurāṇic religious doctrines and practices) have been showing a bitter hostility towards Buddha's teachings. This hostile attitude was vigorously sustained till Buddhism was overpowered in India and disappeared from the land of its birth.[80]

Bu-ston records the tradition that even after being fully convinced of the subtlety and correctness of the logical works of Dharmakīrti, the heretics of other schools fastened his treatises to the tail of a dog and drove the animal in order to destroy them.[81]

The *brāhmaṇas*, who had been the custodians of the religion of the classes and the masses, and whose hereditary superiority had been challenged by the Buddhist conception of a superior man, were naturally dissatisfied with the Buddhists, and looked at Buddhist monks with disdain. Yājñavalkya declares that the very sight of a Buddhist monk, even in dreams, is inauspicious and should be avoided.[82] The *Bṛhannāradīyapurāṇa* laid it down as a principal sin for a *brāhmaṇa* to enter the house of a Buddhist even in times of great perils. The drama *Mṛcchakaṭika* shows that in Ujjainī the Buddhist monks were despised and their sight was considered inauspicious and was to be avoided by non-

Buddhists as far as possible. The *Agnipurāṇa* declared that the son of Śuddhodana beguiled the *daityas* to become Buddhists.[83] The author of the *Vāyupurāṇa* records his contempt perhaps for Buddhists in the following words. "With white teeth, eyes brought under control, head shaved and red clothes, the *śūdras* will perform religious deeds."[84]

The *Viṣṇupurāṇa* regards Buddha as a great seducer. He is called Māyāmoha; who appeared in the world to delude the demons, taught the doctrines of *ahiṃsā* and Nirvāṇa and made people devoid of Vedic rites and religion. The followers of Māyāmoha were finally destroyed by the gods.[85]

Even the most noted philosophers of Brāhmanical thought seem to have been unfree from this sectarian jealousy. Uddyotakara's polemics against Buddhist thought were not only full of transparent sophistry and claptrap but also 'smacked of rankling jealousy.'[86] He wrote his great work with a view to refuting the doctrines of the Buddhist logician Diṅnāga.[87]

Far more fatal to Buddhism were the onslaughts of Kumārila, the fiercest critic of Buddhism. The *Ślokavārttika* shows that he was a hostile critic and avowed enemy of Buddhistic ideals.[88] He is reported, both in Indian and Tibetan traditions, to have organized a religious crusadeag ainst Buddhists. He is said to have instigated king Sudhanvan of Ujjainī to exterminate the Buddhists. This report has not been accepted by modern scholars as a genuine and historical fact. No other historical details of this pro-Brāhmanical king of Ujjainī are known to us.[89] Hsüan-tsang refers to a king of Ujjaina who was a *brāhmaṇa* by caste and 'well versed in heterodox lore, but not a Buddhist.[90] This king was ruling when the pilgrim visited the city of Ujjainī. From the *Mṛcchakaṭika* we learn that the king's brother-in-law in Ujjainī harassed the Buddhist monks. He beat with blows a newly turned mendicant, Saṃvāhaka by name, and treated other *bhikṣus* as 'bullocks by passing a nose-string through their nose and yoking them to the cart.[91] It may not be an impossibility that the evidence furnished by the *Śaṃkaradigvijaya*, Hsüan-tsang and the *Mṛcchakaṭika*—three independent sources—allude to some historical episodes in which the Brāhmanical followers persecuted the followers of Śākyamuni in the country around Ujjain.

There can be no doubt as to the fact that Kumārila was the strongest protagonist of Vedic ritualism, Brāhmanical theology and priestly superiority. The Tibetan historians[92] also record his wars against the Buddhists. The *Kerala-utpatti*[93] documents his extermination of the Buddhists from Kerala. The name of Kumārila is thus associated with the decline of Buddhism in diverse sources. According to Gopīnātha Kavirāja, Kumārila "was one of the most potent forces actively employed in bringing about this decline."

According to G.C. Pande, philosophical criticism of Buddhism by non-Buddhist thinkers cannot explain the decline of Buddhism.[94] It is true that Jainism survived the attacks of Brāhmanical thinkers, and that the Buddhist philosophers also strongly criticized the Brāhmanical systems. But it is evident from the evidence discussed here that Brāhmanical hostility to Buddhism was not confined to mere doctrinal attacks. The Purāṇas, the *Mṛcchakaṭika,* the *Yājñavalkya-smṛti,* the *Rājataraṅgiṇī* the works of Kumārila and Śaṃkara and the latter's biographies, the accounts of Chinese travellers and the histories of Bu-ston and Tārānātha, do seem to point to deeper hatred for Buddhism. It is not unlikely that there were some social factors also working behind "the war of pen" against the followers of Śākyamuni. Unfortunately only few examples of such actual social counterpart of theoretical wars against Buddhists are known to us, e.g. Puṣyamitra's activities, Śaśāṅka's activity, and Mihirakula's activity.

Gopīnātha Kavirāja observes : "The struggle between Buddhism and Hinduism was a war of the pen and not of the sword."[95] This considered opinion is true so far as the philosophical controversies and doctrinal debates of our period are concerned. But it would be evident that this "struggle" assumed the form of a severe bloody war against the Buddhists in the case of Kumārila, if any weight is to be attached to the tradition recorded in so many ancient and medieval Indian and Tibetan works. And the tradition is too weighty.

The mounting tide of anti-Buddhist propaganda in Brāhmanical literature seems to have reached its apex in the hands of the famous Śaṃkarācārya (*cir.* 788 A.D.). His debt to Buddhist thought has been well recognized by modern scholars, and while his works justify the epithet of 'crypto Buddhist' (*pracchanna-bauddha*), he himself, notwithstanding, describes, Buddhist systems as '*vaināśika*' or '*sarva-vaināśika*', and regards Madhyamaka philosophy as unworthy of consideration.[96] Thus far *odium theologicum*,[97] Śaṃkara's biographies tell us that the great *guru* led a religious expedition against the Bauddhas and caused their destruction from the Himālayas to the Indian ocean.[98]

Śaṃkara is known to have founded his Śṛṅgerī Maṭha on the site of a Buddhist monastery.[99] His anti-Buddhist activities may have been very terrible, and according to the Tibetan tradition, at his approach "the Buddhist monasteries began to tremble and the monks began to disperse pell-mell."[100] R.C. Mitra says that "no special animosity against the Buddhists is betrayed in the writings attributed to him."[101] Attention may be invited to a passage in the *Bhāṣya* on *Brahmasūtra* in which Śaṃkara says : "Buddha was an enemy of the people and taught contradictory and confusing things."[102] The statement is quite in keeping with the hostile attitude of Brāhmanical works like the Purāṇas. Thus Śaṃkara and Kumārila are the two most important representatives of Brāhmanical hostility towards Buddhism in India during this period.

Revival of Brāhmaṇism: Allied to the above discussed factor of Brāhmanical hostility there was a Brāhmanical renaissance. Besides preparing a hostile atmosphere in society for Buddhism, the protagonists of Vedicism and Brāhmanic philosophy, like Uddyotakara, Kumārila, Śaṃkara, Udayana and Vācaspati Miśra, also endeavoured to re-establish Brāhmanism on stronger grounds. They advanced all sorts of arguments in defence of Hinduistic theology and Paurāṇic mythology. They accepted as sacred authority the Purāṇas which ridiculed Buddhism.

The growth of Brāhmanical cults like those of the Bhāgavatas and the Śaivas and re-establishment of *varṇāśramadharma* during the Gupta and post-Gupta periods had a declining influence on Buddhism. The spread and the popularity of Buddhism, the prominence that Buddhist monks had been gaining since the days of Aśoka—a class of persons which did not believe in *varṇas*, questioned the authority of the Vedas, challenged the validity of law-givers (Smṛti-writers) and priestly authority, and opened the doors of higher and spiritual life for all able persons irrespective of their social status, colour and occupation—all this and the rest for which Buddhism stood, was perhaps never appreciated by the Brāhmanical custodians of Indian culture.

The reactions of the priestly section of Hindu society may be seen in the Purāṇas and the later Smṛtis. Owing to the progress of Buddhistic culture in India Brāhmanism seems to have suffered a distinct set-back during the centuries immediately preceding and following the Christian era.

Attempts to fortify the sanctity and the authority of the Vedas, to put the *varṇas*, *āśramas* and their respective *dharmas* on more powerful and popular foundations, to counter-balance the growth of Buddhist monasticism by exalting the life of a *gṛhastha*, to incorporate and accommodate the mixed-castes and to make Hinduism more appealing and more attractive to the common people by devising and prescribing various *vratas*, *upavāsas*, *saṃskāras* and so on, are perceivable in the literature of the Gupta and post-Gupta periods of Indian history.

That parts of the Purāṇas were compiled with this end in view is evident from the Purāṇas themselves. The *Devībhāgavata-purāṇa* says : "Women, *śūdras* and the *dvijabandhus* (ordinary twice-born) are not entitled to hear the Vedas; it is but for their good that the Purāṇas have been composed."[103] The *Bhāgavatapurāṇa* states that the *Mahābhārata* was written by the sage in order to enable the women, *śūdras* and the mean twice-born to perform good works.[104]

The *Mārkaṇḍeyapurāṇa* teaches that it is absolutely necessary for every person to lead a householder's life to be free from the debt to his *pitṛs*, before he could join the *saṃnyāsa*.[105]

These texts of neo-Brāhmanism seek to re-establish the exalted position of the *brāhmaṇa*, the authority of the Veda and the sanctity of the *varṇāśrama* organization by means of illustrative stories. Thus the *Matsyapurāṇa* eulogizes the *karmayoga* which is said to consist in performing five daily sacrifices, doing good to *brāhmaṇas*, with cows, money etc.[106] According to the *Viṣṇupurāṇa*, God cannot be satisfied except by one who is loyal to the duties required by one's own caste and stage of life. Non-Vedic works are declared to be delusive and leading to misfortune. The legend of Veṇa is cited to show that those who would neglect the *varṇāśramadharma* shall be killed like Veṇa.[107] The sons of Rājī were destroyed by Indra, because they espoused Jina Dharma and gave up Vedic Dharma.[108] In this way Vedicism was fortified to counteract the growth of Buddhist culture, and various kinds of horrible consequences were prescribed for those acting against the injunctions of the Vedas and conforming to the ways of the *śramaṇas*.

Rapprochement with Buddhism : It has been observed that "Buddhism perished in India, to be born again in a refined Brāhmanism."[109] To put the fact in a simple language, one may say that one of the potent factors in the decline of Buddhism in India was its assimilation to Hinduism. Hinduism appropriated or adopted many of the cardinal elements of Buddhism. The following features seem to have gone to weaken the distinct existence of Buddhism.

Most of the kings of ancient India showed a marked religious catholicity. The Gupta rulers, most of whom were devout Vaiṣṇavas (*parama-bhāgavatas*), are known to have patronized Buddhist scholars and monastic establishments. The Maitraka kings of Kāṭhiāwār peninsula made lavish grants to Buddhist monasteries and patronized Buddhist scholars though they were mostly Śivaites. King Kumāra of Kāmarūpa was not a Buddhist, yet he respected Buddha and the accomplished *śramaṇas.* The Bhauma-kāras of Orissa were Brāhmanical followers but they patronized Buddhist establishments. Emperor Harṣa, the famed patron of Mahāyāna, divided his loyalty into Śiva and Sūrya besides worshipping Buddha. His parents adored Śiva and the Sun while Rājyavardhana was a *parama-saugata.*

The Pāla kings of Bengal, reputed to be the devout patrons of Buddhist faith, were never entirely free from their Brāhmanical leanings. Throughout their rule the Brahmanic culture never ceased to be a living force in Bengal.[110] They built not only the *vihāras* for Tāntrika Buddhist monks and Tibetan *lotsabas* but also built Hindu temples. Tārānātha says that their chief ministers were generally *brāhmaṇas* who used to erect non-Buddhist images in Buddhist shrines.[111]

Kings of the Kārakoṭa dynasty in Kashmir were followers of Brāhmanical religion, but they, their queens and ministers continued to support Buddhism.

These historical instances of common patronage of Hinduism and Buddhism by kings and their officials may have made it possible for both the Buddhists and the Hindus to borrow heavily from each other. Hsüan-tsang found non-Buddhists of Siṃhapura copying the customs of the Buddhists; in

Gayā he saw the sacred Buddhist place completely populated by the *brāhmaṇas.* The Nepalese Buddhists believed both in 'true' (Buddhist) and 'false' (non-Buddhist) religions and the Deva-temples 'touched' the Buddhist monasteries.

In the Potalaka hill, Avalokita had started appearing as Pāśupata (Śiva); the people of Śatadru though Buddhists, were observing social distinctions. Dharamadāsa, a commentator of *Cāndravyākaraṇa* took pride in having Rudra as the titular deity and Buddha as the ornament of his family.[112] The Brāhmanical writers did not lag behind.

Buddha had penetrated the Indian mind very deeply; his images had covered thousands of pillars, walls, and gates of so many monasteries all over the country; his teachings had been popularized and broadcast through an almost inexhaustible mine of Pāli and Sanskrit literatures, many emperors and subtle thinkers had espoused the cause of his rational and humanitarian mission, and his praise had been sung by numerous Indians for centuries; he was too great to be neglected. He naturally came in as the most exalted member in the galaxy of *avatāras.* The acceptance of Buddha as an incarnation had been accomplished probably in the sixth century A.D. first in the *Matsyapurāṇa.* The *Matsyapurāṇa's* verse is found engraved on Pallava monuments of *cir.* 700 A.D. at Mahābalipuram, where the Buddha is mentioned as the 9th *avatāra* of Viṣṇu.[113] In early medieval Brāhmanical texts ten *avatāras* are often referred to. The *Matsyapurāṇa* (285. 6-7) reads thus.

matsyaḥ kūrmo varāhaśca nārasiṃho'tha vāmanaḥ |
rāmo rāmaśca kṛṣṇaśca buddhaḥ kalkī iti ca kramāt ||

Almost an identical verse occurs in the *Varāhapurāṇa* (IV.2). This verse is quoted by Aparārka in his commentary on the *Yājñavalkyasmṛti* (Ānandāśrama edn., p. 338). In the cave temples of Ellora there is one *daśāvatāra* cave. Varāhamihira mentions Buddha's attributes and prescribes iconographical details of his image (*Bṛhatsaṃhitā*, 57.4). Kṣemendra in his *Daśāvatāracarita* (I.2) includes Buddha (Sugatamuni) among the ten incarnations. Buddha *avatāra* is also known to Māgha (*Śiśupālavadha* XV. 58). The *Śāntiparvan* of the *Mahābhārata* mentions ten *avatāras* but it omits Buddha. The *Bhāgavata-*

purāṇa mentions Buddha as a deity and also as a god who deluded demons. This version is known to the *Viṣṇu-purāṇa* also (III. 17-18). The *Bhāgavatapurāṇa* (I.3.24) reads thus :—

tataḥ kalau sampravṛtte saṃmohāya suradviṣāṃ /
buddho nāmnā'janasutaḥ kīkaṭeṣu bhaviṣyati //

Buddha as a god occurs also in the *Bhāgavatpurāṇa* (X. 40.22). The ten *avatāras* including Buddha are mentioned in the *Merutantra* (ch. XXVI, on Buddha verses 1314-1328). A hymn of the 9th century saint Nammalwar also points to the popularity of Buddha *avatāra* in south India.[114] In a number of Brāhmanical Purāṇas compiled in the post-Gupta period, Buddha is mentioned as an *avatāra* of God.[115] P.V. Kane has collected a good number of references to ten *avatāras* from early medieval Brāhmanical texts.

Thus Buddha became a Hindu divinity and one of the makers of modern Hinduism.[116] Gayā is now the foremost of Hindu *tīrthas*. Śaṃkara organized the monastic institution of his followers on the model of Buddhist *saṃgha*.[117] His philosophical terminology, his concept of *māyā* and of the 'non-dual' are very much like those of the Mādhyamika, and his grand *guru's* attempt to synthesize Vedānta and Buddhism is too well known. Lastly, the Tantra practices harmonized the two systems so completely that Buddhism's independent existence might have appeared needless or even impossible.

Declining Royal Patronage : Decline in the royal patronage of Buddhism is regarded by some modern scholars as the foremost factor in the disappearance of Buddhism from the land of its birth. While it cannot be denied that Buddhism developed and became popular to a considerable extent by the munificence and sympathy of kings and the richer sections of the laity, it will be perhaps too much to regard Buddhism completely dependent on royal patronage. Its doctrines and practices were so sublime and so rationally appealing that numerous instances are known where the followers of other religious sects and philosophical schools are seen turning to Buddhism. The missionary zeal of some of the Buddhist sages and monks, who set their backs on the royal thrones and pleasures of the world and volunteered themselves to uplift the suffering mass of humanity, to lessen ignorance and the ills of the world, and suffered incalculable tortures, can hardly be regarded to have been inspired by the patronage of the royal dynasties.

It is, however, true that after Harṣavardhana no strong and whole-hearted patron of Buddhism in India is known, except some of the Pāla kings, who however, were patrons equally of the Brāhmanical religion. No king came forth to protect the Buddhists of Sindha when they were attacked by the Arabs; no Indian army came forward to protect Nālandā when it was sacked by the soldiers of Bakhtyar Khalji. Buddhist monks either fell before the swords of invaders or fled to Nepal and Tibet.[118]

Royal Persecution : One of the really potent factors contributing to the decline of Buddhism in the country was royal persecution, forceful ill treatment of the monks and damage to or destruction of their holy establishments by the kings. It is, however, a fact that royal persecution of Buddhism in India was only sporadic and occasional; it was not a regular feature.[119]

Hsüan-tsang has recorded a curious Buddhist legend concerning the harassment of a Buddhist philosopher Manoratha, a teacher of Vasubandhu, by a certain king Vikramāditya. It is said that Manoratha had once paid his barber one lac gold coins for shaving his head and face. The king was chagrined to hear of this news and felt ashamed. He resolved to bring public shame on the philosopher and organized a gathering of 100 learned heretical scholars to meet Manoratha in debate and issued a decree that if the Buddhist monks failed to prevail, 'they shall be exterminated'. Manoratha had defeated 99 of them, but when he was arguing with the 100th opponent, the king and the non-Buddhists cried out and disturbed the meeting. Manoratha thereupon, bit his tongue, and wrote to his pupil, Vasubandhu that "in the multitude of partisans there is no justice", and died. The pilgrim further adds that king "Vikramāditya lost his kingdom and was succeeded by a king who showed respect to men of eminence." Under him Vasubandhu washed the disgrace of his master by vanquishing all the heretics.[120]

This account has the appearance of a legend, but does not seem to be entirely bereft of historical truth although the episode is not corroborated by any other source. From the context it would appear that the 'Vikramāditya' of this legend may have been a Gupta king of the fifth century A.D. His successor was a patron of Vasubandhu. This would lead one to identify this 'Vikramāditya' with Skandagupta who bore this epithet and who lost his kingdom probably to the Hūṇas. Afterwards came Narasiṃhagupta Bālāditya[121] who was a patron of Buddhism and repulsed the Hūṇa inroads.

The greatest of royal persecutors of Buddhism in India was the Hūṇa tyrant Mihirakula (Mahiragula). His sacrilegious acts against Buddhism are recorded by Kalhaṇa and corroborated by Hsün-tsang and the *Mañjuśrīmūlakalpa.* The Kashmir historian compares Mihirakula with Yama, the god of death, for the former's atrocities.[122] At one place Kalhaṇa remarks : "One's tongue would become polluted if one attempted to record his cruelties and evil deeds in detail."[123] From this authority we learn that Mihirakula patronized *brāhmaṇas,* worshipped Śiva, and erected a temple of Śiva, called Mihireśvara in Śrīnagara.[124] His coins, also prove that Mihirakula was a Śaiva; they bear the legend : *Śrī Mihirakulaḥ jayatu vṛṣaḥ*'.[125] His name 'Mihira' ('Sun', cf. 'Mithra') points to his association with the sun god. The *Mañjuśrīmūlakalpa* also records the anti-Buddhist activity of a king who was marked with the appellation of a planet (Sun); he patronized the *brāhmaṇas.*[126] Thus from literary as well as archaeological sources Mihirakula seems to have been a follower of Brāhmaṇism and a fanatical Śaiva. Besides, he had one more reason to persecute the Buddhists—he had been enraged by the Buddhist monks who had sent to him a monk of low rank to teach him the doctrines of Buddhism. Thereupon, says Hsüan-tsang, the king ordered, "the utter extermination of the Buddhist Church throughout all his dominions". This royal edict was opposed by King Bālāditya of Magadha, who was "a zealous Buddhist", and the two monarchs came to war; Mihirakula was jailed but owing to the misplaced clemency of the queen mother, the captive was set free. He went to Kashmir for shelter, killed its ruler and usurped the throne of Kashmir and then renewed his unrighteous project. He "overthrew *stūpas,* destroyed the *saṃghārāmas,* altogether one thousand six hundred foundations." Besides, he "put to death nine hundred *koṭis* of lay-adherents of Buddhism." His evil career was cut short only by his sudden demise.[127]

According to the *Rājataraṅgiṇī*, Mihirakula killed 'three crores' of human beings and did not show mercy even to his own person and committed suicide by plunging into the fire.[128]

We learn on the authority of Watters that according to 'the Sūtra of Lotus-flower-face', Mihirakula was the exterminator of Buddhist Brethren in Ki-pin and broke the sacred bowl of Buddha.[129] According to the 'Fu-fa-tsang-yin-yuanching,' Mihirakula destroyed monasteries in Ki-pin, slaughtered Brethren and murdered the 23rd patriarch, by name Siṃha.[130]

Mention has already been made of another persecutor, king Sudhanvan of Ujjainī, who is said to have ordered the slaughter of the Buddhists all over the country. This may be an exaggeration, but the historical identity of this king remains still a problem.

Mention may be made of a seal of Toramāṇa, another Hūṇa king, found in the ruins of the Ghoṣitārāma monastery at Kauśāmbī.[131] This indicates that the Buddhist establishment here was perhaps destroyed by the Hūṇas.

According to Joseph Edkins, "at the beginning of the sixth century, the number of Indians in China was upwards of three thousand......They came as refugees from Brāhmanical persecution."[132] This may have been a consequence of the Hūṇa persecution; the Hūṇa kings were Śaivas and patronized *brāhmaṇas*.

Among the ancient Indian princes, the most notable example of anti-Buddhist Brāhmanical fanaticism after Puṣyamitra Śuṅga, is presented by Śaśāṅka, the king of Gauḍa. He had died only a few years before Hsüan-tsang's visit to India. Śaśāṅka was a *brāhmaṇa* by caste[133] and Śaiva by faith[134] as his coins testify to. Moreover, he had been a treacherous murderer of king Rājyavardhana of Thāneśvar who was a *parama-saugata*.[135] These facts seem to point out that Śaśāṅka's sacrilegious acts were rooted in his religious hatred for the Buddhists.[136] Hsüan-tsang records that Śaśāṅka exterminated Buddhist monks in the region around Kuśīnagara as a consequence of which "the groups of Brethren were all broken up." He threw into the Gaṅgā a sacred stone bearing the foot-prints of Buddha in Pāṭaliputra; he cut down the holy Bodhi-Tree at Gayā, down to the roots and burned what remained. And, as if to crown his misdeeds, he removed a Buddha image from a temple east of the Bodhi-Tree, and replaced it by that of Śiva.[137] A more systematic endeavour to destroy Buddhism was never made in India before. The testimony of Hsüan-tsang is supported by the coins of the persecutor, "the oppressor of Buddhism," he was a fanatic Śivaite.

The *Mañjuśrīmūlakalpa*, corroborating the evidence of Hsüan-tsang says: "Somākhya (Śaśāṅka) of wicked intellect will destroy the beautiful image of Buddha. He, of wicked intellect, enamoured of the words of the *tīrthikas*, will burn the great Bridge of Dharma as prophesied by the former Buddhas. Then, that angry and greedy evil-doer, of false notions and bad opinion, will bring down all the monasteries, gardens and *caityas*, and the rest-houses of the Nirgranthas."[138]

Even making due allowance for the Buddhistic bias of Hsüan-tsang and *Mañjuśrīmūlakalpa*, one cannot consider Śaśānka to be a small persecutor free from anti-Buddhist fanaticism. For, the tradition is echoed in late genealogies of Bengali *brāhmaṇas* also.[139]

Some Current Opinions

A number of scholars, including V.A. Smith,[140] S. Radhakrishnan,[141] B.M. Barua,[142] P.C. Bagchi,[143] R.C. Majumdar,[144] R.C. Mitra,[145] Sylvain Lévi[146] and others, have opined that the most important fact concerning the decline of Buddhism in India was a "gradual almost insensible assimilation of Buddhism to Hinduism." The Mahāyāna borrowed heavily from Hinduism, and the latter appropriated many cardinal elements of the former. This mutual rapprochement between Hinduism and Buddhism proved fatal to the latter faith. The acceptance of Buddha as an incarnation of Viṣṇu by Hinduism was a "well conceived and bold stroke of policy (which) cut the ground from under the feet of Buddhism." The disapproval of animal-sacrifice, the relaxation of caste rigidities in Brāhmanical quarters owing to Buddhistic influence and the organization of monastic community on the lines of Buddhist *saṃgha* by Śaṃkara, the standard-bearer of Hinduism, may have further helped the merger of Buddhism into Hinduism. The existence of Buddhist concepts, rites and ceremonies in modern Hinduism also indicates that gradually Buddha became "a maker of modern Hinduism."[147]

According to G.C. Pande, one of the most important factors

in the decline of Buddhism in India was "the social failure of Buddhism."[148] N. Dutt remarks that "Buddhism was never a social movement."[149] There is some truth in this view. Buddhism could not become a sufficiently secular movement; it did not try to evolve a complete society on its own lines; it did not prescribe any ceremonies for birth, marriage and death of the householder. The laity continued to practise the current practices and ceremonies, prescribed largely by the Brāhmanical clergy. This non-interfering attitude of Buddhism, though it helped the smooth spread of the religion, resulted in the long run in lessening its hold on society. Thus the precarious relation between the *saṃgha* and the *upāsaka*-world, the aloofness of the former from the latter, was a serious flaw which confined the Buddhistic culture to the monasteries. These monasteries were the strongholds and the only centres of Buddhistic culture; when they were invaded by indigenous or foreign rulers, or they lost royal or popular support, or when they became deserted and dilapidated by some other calamities, Buddhism also decayed. In such circumstances lay followers of Buddhism who were never made free from the influence of the traditional orthodox culture, returned more and more towards the latter. The seemingly everlasting strength of Brāhmanism (Hinduism) would appear to lie in the fact that its religion and society are inseparable. The fabric of Hinduism rests on the bed-rock of *varṇāśrama* organization, the classification of the members of society into four categories, and of each individual life into four stages, with an orthodox arrangement, fortified by sacred scriptural authority, of the duties and obligations of each caste and each stage. Hinduism survived even when the Muslims killed its ascetics and pulled down its temples; it survived in society. The leaders of Brāhmanism were priests who were usually householders. Such an inseparable and solid relation between Buddhism and its laity was never conceived in Buddhist circles. No effort was ever made to make the laity members of a special corporation,[150] the *saṃgha* had no authority over any member of the laity to punish him or her in case of transgressions. Specific Buddhist doctrines and practices were to be found in the monasteries only.

No wonder when Hsüan-tsang found the Buddhists observing caste distinctions in India, he is meticulous in recording the caste of Indians, especially of the Buddhist monks and its lay-adherents. Udayanācārya claimed that even the Bauddhas followed Hindu customs and rites. "There is no philosophy", says he, "which is free from the injunctions of the Veda; nor any people who do not abide by the Vedic rules in their rites from inception to cremation."[151] Thus, in spite of Buddhism and its doctrine of priestless, casteless and rational approach to the problems of life, the Indian mind could not be freed from priestly craft, casteism, superstition, and the like. The *upāsakas* who took 'refuge' in Buddha, Dharma and the Saṃgha, did not swear exclusive allegiance to the Holy Trinity they invoked. Perhaps this fact is essentially related to that of "assimilation' both as a cause and consequence of the latter.

In the opinion of one writer, "the historic significance of the rise of Buddhism must be realized in its proper context." This proper context, in his opinion is that "Buddhism never cut itself asunder from the parent stock of Brāhmanism," and that the great Buddha was "a child of that noble culture which is generically known as Brāhmanism." This writer further maintains that the monastic rules of the Buddhist *saṃgha* were modelled on those of the *saṃnyāsī* in the fourth *āśrama* of life.[152] A noted scholar of Hindu philosophy has observed at one place: "The Buddha did not feel that he was announcing a new religion. He was born, grew up, and died a Hindu. He was restating with a new emphasis the ancient ideals of the Indo-Aryan civilization."[153]

This has been the generally accepted and 'official' view about the origin of Buddhism and its relation to Brāhmanism. It is also frequently believed that Buddhism was a 'schism' and aimed at reforming the Brāhmanical religion.

Recent studies, however, have brought to light some new facts concerning the origin of Buddhism. It has been suggested that the ancient Vedic ideals differed in important respects from the ideals of the non-Vedic people. The culture of the *munis* and *śramaṇas* was different from those of the Vedic Āryans. Śākyamuni like Mahāvīra was a representative sage of this Śramaṇic tradition, and his teachings contained many elements which were foreign to Vedic or Brāhmanical culture.[154] Historically as well as doctrinally, the term 'Hindu' can hardly be applied to Buddha.

One is not justified in completely identifying Buddhist culture with Brāhmanical culture. The presumption that the institution of the fourth *āśrama* of life is pre-Buddhistic, is not borne out by evidence. One of the oldest Upaniṣads mentions only the first three *āśramas*,[155] and even this Upaniṣad cannot be definitely regarded to be older than the Buddha.[156] The Pālī Tripiṭakas do not know Upaniṣads nor do they refer to the idea of neuter *brahman*.[157] The concept of Buddhist Nirvāṇa and the doctrine of *pratītya-samutpāda* are, perhaps, quite new and independent discoveries of the Buddha. Indian monachism in its disciplined form is most likely a legacy of the Buddha. The Buddha distinguished his doctrine by disregarding the Vedas, animal-sacrifice and caste barriers. He did not belong to the culture of the Indo-Āryans.

Unlike Vedic religion, original Buddhism was an ascetic and monastic movement which could not at that time be looked upon as progressing within the Brāhmanical culture as then known. Later on, Brāhmanical religion imbibed a great deal of the ascetic tendency and thus came nearer Buddhism. There was considerable interchange of ideas and tendencies between Buddhist and Brāhmanical religions in course of time, and that explains sheer gradual but partial similarity of aspects.

Moreover, Brāhmanical religion is inseparable from the national culture of India and had thus in ancient times the aspect of a national religion. On the other hand, Buddhism is a truly universal religion which has never identified itself with any particular national culture. That is why Buddhism spread beyond the borders of India, and one can hardly say that the culture of Ceylon, Burma, Korea, Tibet and Japan is the child of Brāhmanical culture.

To say that the Mādhyamika thought is "a modification of the theory of name and form of scholastic Vedāntins"[158] is a radical historical anachronism. Nāgārjuna flourished several centuries before the 'scholastic Vedāntins' like Gauḍapāda and Śaṃkara. The basic hypothesis that Buddhism was a child of Hinduism has led some writers to still more hypothetical conclusions which are far removed from historical truth.

According to one writer,[159] "the ultimate result of the teachings of the Buddha was disappointment in society and chaos in the Order", and "both the rise and the decline of Buddhism began almost simultaneously." As far as the first statement is concerned, neither sober history nor any careful and impartial student of Indian history and culture can furnish any evidence in support of such a view, which, therefore, remains a mere view. And the view depends upon the view-point. The second statement contains at best a contradictory notion; 'rise' and 'decline' are two mutually opposed events, and can never take place simultaneously. The same writer further opines that one of the main causes of the decline of Buddhism in India was that the Buddhists hated the Sanskrit and adopted Pāli language.

Now, one may ask : how are we to account for the progress and continued existence of Jainism which also adopted Prākrit, a non-Sanskrit language in place of Sanskrit ? Furthermore, the Mauryas adopted Māgadhī or Pāli as their official language, will it not be an absurdity to attribute the decline of Maurya Empire to their adoption of non-Sanskrit language ? But it is not true to say that the Buddhists hated Sanskrit. The whole mass of Buddhist literature from about the second century B.C. onwards is written in Sanskrit. The Buddhists thought in Sanskrit, wrote in Sanskrit and taught its grammar as a compulsory subject in their universities. The total output of Buddhist Sanskrit authors does not seem to be less than those of the Brāhmanical authors. The numerous texts on Abhidharma, the Vinayas of so many Buddhist schools, the Prajñāpārmitā-sūtras, and the hundreds of Mahāyāna Sūtras are in Sanskrit; the philosophical treatises and commentaries by Kātyāyanīputra, Nāgārjuna, Kumāralabdha, Āryadeva, Maitreyanātha, Asaṅga, Harivarman, Vasubandhu, Manoratha, Saṅghabhadra, Diṅnāga. Bhavya, Buddhapālita, Īśvarasena, Candrakīrti, Dharmakīrti, Śāntideva, Śāntarakṣita, Kamalaśīla, Dharmottara, Haribhadra, and so on, are in chaste Sanskrit. The history of Buddhist literature from *cir.* 200 B.C. to *cir.* 1200 A.D. is an essential and important part of the growth of Sanskrit literature. Some of the greatest names in the history of Sanskrit literarure are those of Aśvaghoṣa, Āryaśūra, Bhartṛhari and Śāntideva, who were Buddhists by faith. We cannot conceive of such tremendous contribution to the development of Sanskrit language and literature by those who hate Sanskrit. Buddhists' love of Sanskrit and their contribution to it is too great to be discussed here.

P. V. Kane has reasserted the Brahmanical theory of the origin of Buddhism. According to him, the Buddha was a reformer of "the Hindu religion as practised in his time"; he did not renounce Hindu religion and referred to "Hindu sages" and "took over several beliefs current among the Hindus in his day".[160] As pointed out above, the use of the terms 'Hindu' and 'Hinduism' in the context of the age of Buddha is entirely wrong, both historically and doctrinally. There were neither Hindus nor Hinduism in the 7th and the 6th centuries before Christ. The orthodox religion of that age was what is called Vedic Brāhmanism. The other 'heterodox' religions of that age were the sects of Śramaṇism, such as Jainism, Buddhism, Ājīvikism, etc. The Buddha was a Śramaṇa, a Muni, a founder and follower of a non-Vedic and non-Brāhmanical system, the roots of which cannot be traced to Vedic religion. The beginnings of Śramaṇic systems go back to the pre-Vedic and pre-Āryan epoch of Indian culture. The ascetic, tradition of Harappan culture was continued by the *munis*, *yatis* and *vrātyas* of the Vedic age, and it culminated in the rise of Buddhism in the 6th century B.C.[161]

Chapter XIII

BUDDHIST CONTRIBUTION TO INDIAN CULTURE

Buddhist Culture and Indian Culture

A well-defined *weltanschauung*, originally peculiar to the Śramanic tradition, moral and ascetic ideas, religious practices and institutions, art and literature, education and learning, inspired by the teachings of Śākyamuni Buddha, constitute what has been called the Buddhistic culture.

The Buddhistic strands in Indian culture and civilization can be discerned and appreciated by those who are aware of the non-Vedic Śramanic background of the origins of Buddhism, the fundamental differences between old Brāhmanism and Buddhism, the transformation of old Brāhmanism into neo-Brāhmanism or Hinduism, and of the role of Buddhism in this transformation which transformed Buddhism also and ultimately produced a fusion of the two traditions.

Modern Indian culture of course is composite. It is neither entirely Buddhistic nor entirely Vedic or Brāhmanical. Christian, Islamic and Zoroastrian traditions came to India from without and made significant contributions to Indian culture and civilization. A large number of elements in the languages, arts, religions and social customs of India have been contributed by primitive folks of India and the Central Asian tribes of the Scythians, Kuṣāṇas, Hūṇas and the Tibetans. The dominant ideas in the formation of Indian culture, however, have been contributed mainly by two streams of thought, viz. Śramanic and Brāhmanic. The non-Indian elements that entered into the structure of Indian culture in historical times did not change or modify the basic patterns of thought and values of life that had been perfected in classical antiquity between B.C. 500 and A.D. 500.

The pre-historic Śramanic strands in our religious and philosophical heritage were developed and diffused by Jainism, Buddhism, Ājīvikism, the Sāṃkhya and the Yoga systems. The Brāhmanic ideas embodied in Vedic literary tradition succeeded in maintaining their vitality by making numerous compromises and by homologizing non-Brāhmanic, Śramanic as well as non-Āryan, ideas and institutions. Thus Vaiṣṇavism, Śaivism, Śāktism and numerous other minor cults came into existence as a consequence of Brāhmanization and homologization of the various non-Vedic elements of human faith and practice.

The later half of the period of classical antiquity, viz. the first five hundred years of the Christian era, witnessed the transformation and assimilation of Buddhism into the ever growing mosaic of Hinduism. To speak of the decline of Buddhism in India is true only in this sense of its transformation into refined Hinduism. As a result of assimilation of Buddhism the Vedic Brāhmanism reshaped itself into the Purānic Hinduism. The assimilation of Buddhism by Purānic Hinduism was so complete that, except for certain aspects of Vedic orthodoxy and mythology which persisted in the Brāhmanical sections of Indian society, Buddhism and Hinduism became indistinguishable from each other. This fusion of two traditions was the basis of many confusions and errors found in the writings of the older generation of Indologists of India and the west. For example, the assumption that Buddhism had originated as a protestant movement within the Brāhmanical fold and had finally merged into its parent religion, was founded partly on the ignorance of the ultimate origins of *śramaṇa* thought and partly on the medieval fusion of Buddhism and Brāhmanism.

In spite of this fusion of the Buddhistic and Brāhmanical thought-currents and the emergence in early medieval times of what is popularly called Hinduism, it is quite possible to study the history of the Buddhistic culture as distinct and different from the Hindu culture. This has been one of our major theses, and the preceding chapters are illustrative of this standpoint.

The Buddhist culture may be viewed as constituting the dominant strand in the fabric of the Indian culture. It is, of course, a serious error to identify the 'Indian culture' with the 'Hindu culture'; we cannot reduce the Indian culture to the Hindu culture unless we understand the word 'Hindu' in the sense of Hindustānī, Bhāratīya or Indian. The word 'Hinduism' is a misnomer; it can only mean 'Indianism'. But the Hindus, that is, the modern Indians who owe allegiance to the Vedic tradition and Brāhmanical ideas and practices, use the word Hinduism in the sense of Brāhmanism. A follower of the Vedic ideas and beliefs, even if they be based on the writings of Tulasīdāsa or of Swami Vivekānanda, likes to describe himself as a Hindu and his religion and philosophy as Hinduism. These usages in modern practice create confusion and lead to difficulties in scientific study of the history of ideas in India. The 'Hindu' culture forms an important element in Indian culture; the latter is wider in scope and much more composite in character than the former.

Although modern Hindu culture has a great many elements of the Buddhist culture, the two are not identical. The Hindus consider the Buddha as a maker of Hinduism and worship him as an *avatāra* of God; Hinduism has accepted all the great and noble elements of Buddhism. These facts do not alter the historical truth that Buddhism is different from Hinduism and Hinduism is different from Buddhism. The Hindus may worship the Buddha, because their religion is largely based on the teachings of the Buddha. The Buddhists do not worship either Viṣṇu or Śiva, nor is their religion based on the Vedas.

The Vedic or Brāhmanical strands in the Hindu culture have given it the aspect of a national culture. The Buddhist culture, on the other hand, has been throughout an international and universal culture. The Hindu culture, in spite of its modern official version presented by influential men, like Swami Vivekānanda, Mahātmā Gāndhi and Radhakrishnan, is still peculiar to India, whereas the Buddhist culture has been widely shared and cherished by a large section of humanity beyond the borders of India.

It is true that certain elements of the Brāhmanical Hinduism had travelled to some south-eastern Asian lands in early medieval centuries. But these elements could not retain their characteristic Brāhmanical form and were soon lost in the traditions of those lands. The Buddhist culture is still flourishing in all those countries of Asia where it had penetrated and where it could not be suppressed by the sword of Islam. While it will be absurd to describe the culture of Sri Lanka or of Japan as the Hindu culture, it is quite reasonable to describe the culture of these countries as the Buddhistic culture. One can even say that the Buddhistic strands of the Indian culture are found in all the Buddhistic countries.

The relationship between Brāhmanism and Buddhism and the historical interactions between these two traditions resulting in the evolution of Hinduism have been discussed in detail by the present writer elsewhere.[1] In the following pages we propose to briefly review some aspects of the influence of the Buddhist religion and thought on the Brāhmanical Hindu religions and philosophical traditions and to point out some of the important contributions of the Buddhist tradition to Indian culture. In this connection the remark of S.N. Dasgupta is well worth noticing. Referring to the Buddhist thought he says that 'it is impossible to overestimate the debt that the philosophy, culture and civilization of India owe to it in all her developments for many succeeding centuries.'[2] The subject is very wide in scope and complex in nature; a comprehensive and full-length study of this subject should be made in a separate volume. Here only a brief and general survey can be attempted.

Buddhist Contribution to Hinduism

According to the chronology accepted in these pages even the oldest of the extant Upaniṣads are not pre-Buddhist in date. These venerable texts of composite character and hybrid origin have been assigned by the present writer to the period between B.C. 600 and 200.[3] The partial similarity between some of the teachings of the Pāli Sūtras and those of the Upaniṣads seems to be due to the influence of *śramaṇa* thought in the Vedic circles. The anti-sacrificial tendency of a few Upaniṣadic passages seems to have been inspired by the Buddha's critical attitude towards Vedic *karmakāṇḍa*.

Some of the Upaniṣadic teachers agreed with the Buddha in criticizing Vedic priest-craft, sacrificial slaughter of animals and propitiation of many gods with a view to gaining material prosperity, progeny, longevity, etc. A few of the Upaniṣadic philosophers were in partial agreement with the Buddha in recognizing superiority of inner awakening over external ceremonies and textual learning and in stressing the law of *karman* or moral retribution, *dhyāna* and *yoga*.

Several modern writers have suggested that the Upaniṣadic conception of the ultimate Reality, called *brahman* and *ātman*, especially in its absolute aspect is similar to the Buddhist conception of the ultimate Truth, called *nirvāṇa* and *asaṃskṛta*. It is difficult to express a definite opinion on this point in spite of the fact that several passages in the Upaniṣads (*Kaṭha*, II.2.15; *Muṇḍaka*, II.2.10; *Śvetāśvatara*, VI. 14 etc.) remind us of the *Udāna*, VIII. 1-4. We should not forget that one of the basic

Buddhist doctrines teaches the absence of 'own-being' (*svabhāva*), of 'self-existence' (*ātmabhāvā*); this doctrine of *anātmavāda* is diametrically opposed to the Upaniṣadic *ātmavāda.* The present writer feels that the identity of 'the one and only Truth' (*ekaṃ hi saccaṃ*) taught in the Pāli Sūtras with 'the one indestructible God' (*ekākṣaraṃ brahma*) taught in some Upaniṣadic passages cannot be decided by scholars. This problem was finally solved, for Hinduism though, as we will presently see, by the *Bhagavadgītā* which coined the compound *brahma-nirvāṇa.*

Many writers have drawn attention to the great philosophical importance of 'consciousness' (*vijñāna*) in the Pāli Sūtras and the Upaniṣads. The *Bṛhadāraṇyaka Upaniṣad* speaks of the Reality (*bhūta*) as an 'infinite and limitless mass of consciousness'; this statement reminds us of the one found in the *Dīgha-nikāya* which describes consciousness as 'invisible, infinite and shining everywhere.'[4] The notion of liberated saints (*yatis*) who are freed from impurities (*kṣīṇadoṣa*) and whose passions have been spent up (*vītarāga*) found in a few Upaniṣads strongly reminds us of the Buddhist notion of *arhats* who are regularly described as freed from taints (*kṣīṇāsrava*).[5]

There seems to be no doubt that the *Bhagavadgītā* embodies a considerable body of Buddhist principles and practices. D.D. Kosambi who places this text between 150-350 A.D. remarks that the theory of perfection through a large succession of rebirths taught in this book 'is characteristically Buddhist' and that the *Bhagavadgītā*, II. 55-72, recited daily as prayers at Mahātmā Gāndhi's *āśrama*, would be 'impossible without Buddhism.'[6] In these verses the characteristics of a man of 'fixed understanding' (*sthitaprajña*) are described in detail. Any one acquainted with early Buddhism will at once find out that this is the description of a sage of 'calmed thought' (*samāhitacitta*), the wise one who has transcended pairs of opposites and dwells wholly detached from the phenomena. The chapter concludes by saying that such a sage (*muni*) attains the 'holy Nirvāṇa' (*brahma-nirvāṇa*). The phrase *brahma-nirvāṇa* occurs several times (*Bhagavadgītā*, II.72; V. 24-26), and at one place Peace and Nirvāṇa are identified with God (*Ibid.*, IV. 15, *śāntiṃ nirvāṇam*).

Thus, although the *Bhagavadgītā* does not mention the Buddha as an *avatāra* of God, its author seems to have tacitly assumed Buddha's identity with Brahman or God. See, for example, this verse:

> Thus ever disciplining himself,
> The man of discipline, with controlled mind,
> To peace that culminates in Nirvāṇa,
> And rests in Me, attains.[7]

Who is this 'man of discipline' or *yogin* who attains Peace and Nirvāṇa through meditation ? History knows only Śākyamuni as the first *yogin* who attained Nirvāṇa through *yoga*. The *Gītā* adds that this Nirvāṇa is identical with God. In addition to the well-known verses which describe the *sthitaprajña* and *brahma-nirvāṇa*, there are some striking verses which deal with 'Buddhist ideology' in what V.V. Gokhale[8] calls 'pregnant yet unmistakable phrases.' Below I quote two of these verses in Edgerton's translation:

> Of what is not, no coming to be occurs,
> No coming not to be occurs of what is :
> But the dividing-line of both is seen,
> Of these two, by those who see the truth.[9]

This seems to be a reference to the Buddha who taught the tenet of transcending the extreme views of existence (*bhāva*) and non-existence (*abhāva*). If so, 'those who see the truth' (*tattva-darśibhiḥ*) that lies beyond is (*asti*) and is not (*nāsti*) are the teachers of the doctrines of conditioned coproduction (*pratītya-samutpāda*) and the middle path which transcends the alternatives. Consider another verse:

> Transcending these three strands,
> That spring from the body, the embodied soul,
> From birth, death, old age, and sorrow
> Freed, attains deathlessness.[10]

The stress on *janma-mṛtyu-jarā-duḥkha* and the description of *vimukti* or Liberation as *amṛta* or deathlessness are characteristically Buddhist. The two other verses of the *Bhagavadgītā*, VI. 5-6, are clearly echoes of the *Dhammapada*, verses 160, 165 and 379.

According to V.V. Gokhale, "the Buddhist approach has found a deeply sympathetic response in the Rāma Epic, unique for its dignified ethical standards, rigidly maintained in defiance of a tragic, human fate, as well as in another powerful branch of the Epic tradition, built around the ascetic Śiva, who with his sombre, pristine meditations is known to be as ancient as the Himalayas."[11]

V. Fosböll and Max Müller[12] had long ago invited the attention of scholars to numerous parallels between passages belonging to the Pāli Canon and the Brāhmanical texts like the *Mahābhārata* and the *Manusmṛti*. We reproduce below some of these parallel verses :

Dhammapada : 'He who wishes to put on the yellow dress without having cleansed himself from sin, who disregards also temperance and truth, is unworthy of the yellow dress.'[13]

Mahābhārata : 'In my opinion, the yellow-coloured dress on a man who is unfree from impurity, serves only to increase cupidity; it is meant to supply the means of living to those ascetics, who carry their *dharma* like a flag.'[14]

Dhammapada : 'Death carries off a man who is gathering flowers and whose mind is distracted, as a flood carries off a sleeping village.'[15]

Mahābhārata: 'Death carries off a person who is gathering flowers and is not satisfied in his desires, as a flood carries off a sleeping tiger.'[16]

Dhammapada: 'Self is the master of self, who else would be the master ? With self well subdued, one finds a master, difficult to find.' Elevate Yourself by yourself; investigate yourself by yourself, in this way, self-protected and mindful, O monk, you will live happily .'[17]

Bhagavadgītā : 'Raise yourself by yourself; do not allow yourself to fall; for, self alone is the friend of self, self alone is the foe of self. His self alone is friend who has subdued himself by himself; to him who has not subdued himself even his own self acts like an enemy.'[18]

Such or similar parallels can be increased to many more verses. The *Mahābhārata*, as is well known, in its present form belongs to the fourth century A.D. Its older portions may be as old as the second century B.C. The ethics of the *Manusmṛti,* in spite of its author's strong Vedic bias, occasionally comes close to Buddhist ethics. Some of its verses seem to be direct imitations of the Pali *gāthās* :

Dhammapada : 'Four things will increase to him, viz. life (longevity), beauty, happiness and power, who constantly serves and reveres the elders.'[19]

Manusmṛti : 'He who constantly serves and reveres the elders (aged), to him will increase the four things, viz. life, knowledge, fame and power.'[20] Here 'beauty' is replaced by 'knowledge' and 'happiness' by 'fame'.

Dhammapada : 'He will not find happiness after death who seeking his own happiness, punishes or kills the beings who also long for happiness.'[21]

P.V. Bapat has also drawn attention to some of the verses of this text which reveal Buddhist influences. He says that 'the liberal attitude shown by the Buddhists in throwing the doors wide open to all who wished to participate in religious life seems to have found general acceptance as the *Gītā* (IX. 32, *striyo vaiśyās tathā śūdrās te api yānti parāṃ gatim*) indicates.' The *Bhagavadgītā* is a part of the *Mahābhārata* which contains several Buddhist verses. Bapat has cited one famous verse dealing with Buddhist piety. "The Buddha's policy of peace, self-sacrifice, kindness and charity", says he, "finds an echo in the following lines from the *Mahābhārata* :

akrodhena jayet krodhaṃ asādhuṃ sādhunā jayet,
jayet kadaryaṃ dānena jayet satyena cānṛtam.

(One should conquer anger by cool-headedness, evil by good, miserliness by charity and falsehood by truth, *Udyogaparva*, BORI edition, 30.58). This spirit moulded the lives of numerous saints in medieval India and the great minds of modern India, too, have been guided by the Buddha's teachings.

The influence that the life of the Master exercised on Mahātmā Gāndhi is self-evident."[22]

In order to show that the above lines are a translation into Sanskrit from the Pāli original, we quote verse 223 from the *Dhammapada* :

> *akkodhena jine kodhaṃ asādhuṃ sādhunā jine,*
> *jine kadarīyaṃ dānena saccena-alika vādinam.*

Max Müller rendered it as follows :

'Let a man overcome anger by love, let him overcome evil by good; let him overcome the greed by liberality, the liar by truth.' The reference to the fourfold food in the *Bhagavadgītā* (XV.14; *annaṃ caturvidhaṃ*) echoes the Buddhist view of fourfold food (*cattāro āhārā*). Similarly the teaching regarding moderation in food, sleep and waking (VI. 16-17) seems to presuppose the Buddhist stress on the Middle Way. The wise men who say that the sinful action must be abandoned (XVIII. 3) are the Buddhist teachers. In the *Aṅguttaranikāya* (vol. I, pp. 59-60, and vol.III, pp. 293-294) the Buddha says that he teaches inaction in the sense of abandoning the sinful action. All these facts show that the moral ideas of the *Bhagavadgītā* are derived from those of Buddhism.

The moral principle of *ahiṃsā* (non-violence), so characteristic of Jainism and Buddhism, though unknown to old Vedic texts, became an important feature of Hinduism also. The Buddhist texts had always placed *ahiṃsā* at the top of 'five precepts' *pañca śīla*); the *Anuśāsanaparva* of the Great Epic also declares *ahiṃsā* to be the 'supreme duty' (*paramo dharmaḥ*).

The worship of icons, images and symbols also seems to have been introduced by the Buddhists and the Jainas although its ultimate origin may be traced to the pre-Vedic Harappan culture. In historical times the art and ritual of image worship was popularized first by the Buddhists. It soon became an essential feature of all the sects of Purānic Brāhmanism. There is a remarkable correspondence in the inconography of Buddhist and Brāhmanical sculptures and paintings of gods and goddesses. The early medieval Hindu temple architecture shows, in certain respects, a striking similarity to Buddhist examples of brick-built *stūpas* and rock-cut sanctuaries of Western India. Buddhist conception of Māra finds its parallel in Brahmanical conception of Yama (known to the Vedic texts) and Kāma; the demigods, like Yakṣas, Gandharvas, Kinnaras and Nāgas, had always attracted the veneration of both Buddhist and Hindu folk.

In Tāntrika age, goddesses such as Tārā, Kālī, Cāmuṇḍā, Sarasvatī, Varāhī, Hārīti, and gods such as Mahākāla or Kāla, Gaṇeśa, etc. were worshipped by both Buddhists and Hindus. The old Vedic gods, Indra and Brahmā, have always been associated with Buddha as his pious devotees. Bodhisattva Avalokiteśvara is also called Maheśvara, an epithet of Śiva; Mañjuśrī is often called Kumārabhūta, and Kumāra is another name of god Kārttikeya; the idea of the unity of Prajñā and Upāya (or *śūnyatā* and *karuṇā*) finds its close parallel in Śaivism and Śāktism, in the idea of the unity of Śakti and Śiva. The notion of *yuganaddha* (two-in-one) is identical with the notion of *ardhanārīśvara*. The technology of Tāntrika Yoga is common to Tāntrika Buddhism and Tāntrika Hinduism; the eighty-four Siddhas are respected in Buddhist as well as Brāhmanical tradition. The Brāhmanical scriptures are written in Sanskrit language. The sacred writings of the Buddhists of many Abhidharmic and Mahāyānic systems are also in Sanskrit language. There are many significant parallels between the Buddhist texts which treat Buddha's life, such as the *Mahāvastu, Lalitavistara, Buddhacarita,* etc. on the one hand, and Hindu epics and Purāṇas, such as the *Rāmāyaṇa*, the *Mahābhārata, Harivaṃśa, Bhāgavata,* etc., which treat the biographies of Kṛṣṇa, Rāma and other superhuman and mythical sages, on the other.

The practice of visiting the holy places (*tīrthas*) possibly originated with the Buddhists. In the *Mahāparinibbānasutta*, visit to the spots sanctified by the Buddha is recommended. In the Vedic texts, a *tīrtha* was understood to mean a place where animal sacrifices were performed. But in the Epics and the Purāṇas, which teach the cult of *tīrthayātrā* or pilgrimage, killing of animals in sacrifice in holy places is prohibited. The eighth chapter of the *Laṅkāvatārasūtra* perhaps contains the strongest exposition of vegetarianism which became a central feature of Vaiṣṇavism in medieval India.

The four stages of *dhyāna* or meditation mentioned repeatedly in the Pali texts are referred to once in the *mokṣa-dharma* section of the *Śāntiparvan* of the Great Epic, while the four sublime states of meditation (*brahma-vihāra*) found their way into the *Yogasūtra.* It is possible that the word *bhagavat*, 'Blessed One', was first used by the Buddhists for their Teacher. Later on it was adopted by the Bhāgavatas or Vaiṣṇavas as an epithet of Viṣṇu—Kṛṣṇa.

The legends of Kapilamuni and the elements of his system, the Sāṃkhya, also form a bridge between Buddhism and Hinduism. Kapilamuni the founder of the Sāṃkhya system is revered in equal degree by the Buddhists and the Hindus.

The Yoga system of Patañjali (minus its subsequent theistic feature) is quite in keeping with Buddhism. The analytical, non-theistic, and pluralistic bias of early Sāṃkhya and Yoga is reminiscent of early Buddhist Abhidharmic thought.

During the early medieval centuries Buddhist and Brāhmanical traditions fused together so completely that Buddhism in India lost its separate identity. In the nineteenth century when the Indologists began to discover Buddhist literature and monumental antiquities, they were still under the influence of Purānic myth that Buddhism was a heretical sect of Brāhmanism which had merged into Hinduism. It is only recently that this myth has been exploded by modern researches.

Buddhism and the Vedānta

The Buddhist doctrines of non-origination (*ajātivāda*), of phenomenal world as illusion or mere appearance (*māyāvāda*), of twofold division of truth into ultimate (*paramārtha*) and temporal (*vyavahāra*), and of Reality (*tattva*) being without attributes (*nirguṇa*) and beyond fourfold description have become so completely Vedāntic that their origins have nearly been forgotten. One can multiply the list of the elements of what Toynbee calls the "diverse Buddhistic philosophies that are part of the mental apparatus of a post-Buddhistic Hinduism."[23] Not only the Buddhist holy places and shrines were occupied and transformed into Hindu *tīrthas* and *devālayas* and this occupation of non-Brāhmanical places and sanctuaries was strengthened by an invented myth or pseudo-history (*purāṇa*), but the best elements of the Buddhistic culture, including the Buddha, were appropriated and homologized in sacred books. To quote Toynbee again, "Hinduism despoiled a senile Buddhist philosophy in order to acquire for itself the weapons with which it drove its philosophical rival out of their common homeland in the Indic World?"[24] The *Ahirbudhnya-saṃhitā* (*cir.* fourth century A.D.) was one of the earliest Vaiṣṇavaite texts to identify the Buddha with Viṣṇu—Nārāyaṇa.[25]

An example of this philosophical plunder is furnished by the Advaita Vedānta as expounded by Gauḍapāda, Śaṃkara, Śrī Harṣa, and others. In order to substantiate this view we will briefly analyse the contents of the *Āgamaśāstra* or the *Māṇḍūkyakārikā*.

T.R.V. Murti's attempts to explain away the Buddhist elements in classical Vedānta and to exclude the possibility of doctrinal borrowings by the classical Vedāntists, like Gauḍapāda and Śaṃkara, are quite unconvincing. "It is our contention", Murti asserts, "that there could not be acceptance of any doctrinal content by either side from the other, as each had a totally different background of tradition and conception of reality." Realizing, however, that "there is no difference between the Absolute of Vedānta and that of the Mādhyamika or Vijñānavāda," he is constrained to admit that "there has been borrowing of technique and not of tenets."[26] This argument is not satisfactory, because it is contradicted by historical facts. For example, as late as the time of the Dharmaśāstras, we find that Brāhmanical tradition was against Śramanic way of life; *śramaṇas* were denounced as 'outcastes' and 'inauspicious' and the institution of the ordination of *bhikṣus* (*pravrajyā*) was attributed to *asuras* or demons. The oldest Upaniṣads (*Bṛ. Up.* and *Ch. Up.*) prove that the greatest Brāhmanical teachers like Yājñavalkya were married and householders. Other early Upaniṣads clearly reveal Śramanic influence. However, in Smṛtis and Purāṇas the institution of *saṃnyāsa* finds a respectable position showing thereby that the Brāhmanical authors had at last accepted elements of non-Brāhmanical origin. Then again, the followers of Buddhism and Brāhmanism had different background of tradition and concept of reality, yet we find the Brāhmanical priests, the compilers of the Purāṇas, accepting Buddha as an *avatāra* of Viṣṇu. Further, earliest Brāhmanism or Vedicism involved animal sacrifice and there is no mention of the principle of non-violence (*ahiṃsā*) in the entire Vedic literature prior to the *Chāndogya Upaniṣad*. But due to the popularity of Jainism and Buddhism which laid particular emphasis on *ahiṃsā* and *maitrī*, the Brāhmanical authors of the *Manusmṛti* (200 A.D.) and the *Mahābhārata* (200 B.C.—400 A.D.) and others also accepted the tenet of *ahiṃsā*, and thenceforth it became a cardinal principle in Brāhmanism also. It is impossible to deny that the Purānic Hinduism has borrowed the institution of *saṃnyāsa*, the tenet of *ahiṃsā* and reverence for *munis*, *yatis* and *yogins* from Śramanism or Buddhism and Jainism. In short, we cannot rule out the possibility of doctrinal borrowing by the Brāhmanical or Vedāntist thinkers from Buddhist thought.

But we are not going to argue that Gauḍapāda has borrowed Buddhist doctrines, or that he was himself a Buddhist. Our humble suggestion is that he made an attempt to harmonize Buddhist tenets with those of the Upaniṣadic or non-dualistic Vedānta; in the *Āgamaśāstra* we find an endeavour to synthesize and bring about a concord between Mahāyāna Buddhism and Advaita Vedānta. In this endeavour seem to have crept into Vedānta certain basic tenets of Mahāyāna philosophy, and the result was the non-dualistic Vedānta of Śaṃkara. It would be historically correct to say that the Śāṃkara Vedānta has been influenced by the Mādhyamika thought, and the link is preserved in the *Āgamaśāstra* of Gauḍapāda. Gopīnātha Kavirāja rightly maintains that the *Mādhyamika-kārikās* of Nāgārjuna had influenced the thought of the *Gauḍapādakārikās*.[27]

Vedānta and Buddhist Thought before Gauḍapāda

It is a fact that the *Vedāntasūtra* or *Brahmasūtra* of Bādarāyaṇa is theistic rather than monistic. It is equally universally admitted that the *Brahmasūtra* was commented upon before Gauḍapāda by avowed dualists. We don't know any Brāhmanical author or thinker who expounded monistic (*advaita*) doctrine before Gauḍapāda and Śaṃkara.[28] The scattered seeds of monism in the Upaniṣads were developed for the first time by Gauḍapāda (600 A.D.) and Śaṃkara (900 A.D.) who established the classical form of the Advaita Vedānta. In fact, Śaṃkara credits Gauḍapāda with the discovery of the Advaita doctrine which, according to him, lay deep in the Vedas.[29]

The necessity of conjectural explanations, viz. the fourth chapter of Gauḍapāda's work being from the pen of a Buddhist, unknown to history, and its being added to the first three chapters by some one who is also unknown to history, seems to have arisen out of an inclination to adhere to the myth of the originality of monistic absolutism of classical Vedānta. This myth disappears when we realize that pre-Gauḍapāda Vedānta is neither systematic nor monistic, and that Gauḍapāda flourished after all important Vijñānavāda and Mādhyamika philosophers had diffused their idealistic, monistic and absolutistic tenets. The *advaita* turn in Vedānta in and after Gauḍapāda can reasonably and satisfactorily be explained only by recognizing the debt of Gauḍapāda and Śaṃkara to the Mādhyamika and Vijñānavāda systems of thought.

It is a matter of historical truism that the doctrine of two truths (*satya-dvaya-vyavahāra* and *paramārtha*) was first expounded by Nāgārjuna, Āryadeva, Bhāvaviveka, Candrakīrti, and Śāntideva, but its seeds are perceivable in the Pāli Canon itself.[30] It is legitimate to suppose that the classical Vedāntists took this double-truth theory from the Mādhyamikas. Nāgārjuna was the father of the *kārikā* style in Sanskrit literature, and after his *Madhyamakakārikās*, many other Buddhist and Brāhmanical authors began to write philosophical texts in *kārikās* or memorial verses.

The doctrine that this phenomenal world is void of truth and its appearance is due to illusion (*moha*) born of ignorance (*avijjā, avidyā*) and perverted view (*dṛṣṭi āsrava*), is very well known to the Pāli sources and the Mahāyāna Sūtras and Śāstras.[31] In the Nikāyas the world is said to be void (*suñño loko ti vuccati*),[32] and is compared to a house set on fire;[33] the goal of Nibbāna is often understood to mean the 'extinction' of this fire born of *tṛṣṇā*. The method of affirming the transcendental truth by a system of relentless denial of the reality of phenomenal world was evolved first in Buddhist quarters by Nāgārjuna. The entities, the elements of mind and matter, are known as *dharmas* exclusively in Buddhist quarters. Nāgārjuna, the father of Indian system of dialectics, was the first thinker to give prominent place to the method of fourfold description (*catuḥ-koṭi*), though the method is already employed in the Pāli Nikāyas.[34]

The doctrine of non-dual idealist absolute was developed first by the Buddhists in the *Sandhinirmocanasūtra* and the *Laṅkāvatārasūtra*, and it received its classical form at the hands of Maitreyanātha, Asaṅga, and Vasubandhu. Diṅnāga had declared that "the climax of wisdom is the non-dual Absolute."[35]

Buddhism in the Āgamaśāstra

The age of Gauḍapāda was one of philosophical controversies and almost warlike activities of theologians espousing different sects. But as pointed out above, it was also the age when rapprochement between Brāhmanical theology and Mahāyāna Buddhology was nearly complete; an age when *parama-saugatas* worshipped Brāhmanical gods, supreme divine Bodhisattvas assumed the form of Pāśupata *tīrthika*, Brāhmanical images were being enshrined in Buddhist temples, Buddhist logicians were being quoted as authorities on Kashmir Śaivism and when historical Buddha was being sacrificed at the altar of mythical Viṣṇu by making him an *avatāra* for the Kali Age. In such an age it is neither curious nor surprising to find a synthesis of Buddhist absolute and that of the Vedānta. Gauḍapāda was true to the spirit of his age, therefore, he comments on the *Māṇḍūkya Upaniṣad* and pays devout homage to the Buddha.

Buddhist contents of the *Āgamśāstra* are already well known to scholars, some have acknowledged while others have them explained away. We shall briefly review the concordance between the *Āgamaśāstra* (abbr. *AŚ*) and Buddhist sources.

AŚ, I. 7 refers to those who view creations as being of the nature of dream and illusion (*svapnamāyāsarūpeti*). This obviously refers to the Buddhist view of the world.

See, e.g.—*māyādisvapnasadṛśam vipaśyanto vimucyate*, *Laṅkāvatārasūtra,* X. 25; cf. *Ibid.* X. 279, 291. etc. In the *Aṣṭasāhasrikā* we read the following:
māyā ca sattvāśca advayametadadvaidhikāram, iti hi svapnaśca sattvāśca advayam etadavaidhikāram sarva dharmā api devaputra māyopamāḥ svapnopamāḥ, p.20).

The Buddhist philosophical terms occur in the very first chapter, e.g. *AŚ*. 29, *upaśamaḥ śivaḥ*; 1.17 *prapañca* comparable to *MŚ*. opening lines, and *AŚ* 1.18, *vikalpa*. I think that the idea expressed in *AŚ*, I.22 reminds us of Buddha's perception of the triple world (*tridhātu=triṣu dhāmasu*), and 'Mahāmuniḥ' is meant to indicate the Great Ascetic Buddha.

In *AŚ*, II. 1, Gauḍapāda says like Vasubandhu, 'as in dream, so in waking, the objects seen are unreal'; compare *Viṃśatikā-kārikā*, verses 1-2. "The wise men (who) speak of the sameness of the dream and waking states", *AŚ*, II. 5, are probably Vijñāna-vādins. "The knowers of the mind" referred to in *AŚ*, II. 25, are evidently the Idealist Buddhists.[36] The term '*vitatha*' is found used in the *Vajracchedikā Prajñāpāramitā* in the sense of 'false' SOR, edn. XIII, pp. 35, 48).

There is a remarkable harmony between *MŚ*, opening lines and *AŚ*, II. 32.[37] The concept expressed in *AŚ*, II. 35 with emphasis on 'the quiescence of the phenomenon that is non-dual (*prapañcopaśamo'dvayaḥ*) at once recalls similar ideas expressed in the opening lines of *MŚ*, *Aṣṭasāhasrikā*, p. 177, and *Prajñā-pāramitā Piṇḍārtha* (in BST, no. 4) opening line. According to S.N. Dasgupta,[38] "the Buddhists were the first to use the words *prapañcopaśamaṃ śivam*." The thought of *AŚ*, II. 31 seems to be a mere repetition of some verse of the *Laṅkāvatārasūtra*, see, for instance, *Laṅkāvatāra*, X. 291.

The use of the word '*saṃghāta*' in *AŚ*, II. 3 and III. 10 for objective bodies is manifestly a Buddhist usage. The argument for the non-origination of things in *AŚ*, II. 20 strongly reminds us of the dialectical approach evinced in the *Madhya-makaśāstra* and the *Catuḥ-śataka* of Nāgārjuna and Āryadeva respectively.

At *AŚ*, III. 29-30 one feels that Gauḍapāda is giving a most faithful expression to Vijñānavāda philosophy as known from the *Laṅkāvatārasūtra* and the works of Vasubandhu. I am inclined to observe that at *AŚ*, III. 33 the first line is eminently Vijñānvādin, while the second line equally clearly Upaniṣadic. Here in this verse we find a perfect combination of the two thought-currents.

The epithets used in *AŚ*, III. 37 remind the reader of Nirvāṇa which is said to be *atarkāvacara* and *anabhilāpya*. The *Aṣṭasā-hasrikā* (p. 177) states '*sarvakalpa vikalpa prahīṇo hi Tathā-gataḥ*'. It is likely that the mention of *asparśayoga* at *AŚ*, III. 39, refers to the intangible cessation called *nirodha* or Nirvāṇa. The description given at *AŚ*, III. 47 fits in well with that of Buddha and Nirvāṇa as given in Buddhist texts. We have seen that the hypothesis of the *AŚ*, IV, being an independent treatise is not well grounded. The chapter is captioned *alātaśānti*, and we find that the course of thought in the *AŚ* reaches its logical conclusion in this chapter. The *Laṅkāvatārasūtra* (X.173) uses the word '*alātacakra*'. The use of the word '*dharma*, at *AŚ*, IV. 1, in the sense of an entity is "peculiarly Buddhistic". There can be no doubt that the opening verse of ch. IV adores the Fully Enlightened One (*sambuddha*), 'the best among men' (*dvipadāṃ varaṃ*). Likewise, *AŚ*, IV. 2 repeats the salutation to him who, being the benefactor of all beings (*sarvasattvasukho hitaḥ*, cp. *sabbabhūtānukampī*) taught the supreme contemplation (*asparśayoga*, probably *asamprajñāta samādhi*), and a doctrine which can neither be disputed nor contradicted.[39] Commenting on this verse Radhakrishnan says that "the *kārikā* is an attempt to combine in one whole the negative logic of the Mādhyamikas with the positive idealism of the Upaniṣads."[40] Eminent scholars including Jacobi, Poussin, V.S. Sukthankar, S.N. Dasgupta and V. Bhattacharya have already shown the Buddhist influence on the last chapter of the *Āgamaśāstra*. As I cannot improve upon their discussions, I feel no justification in reproducing what is already well acknowledged. In order to complete my survey I add the following notes : *AŚ*. IV. 4-5, 19 subscribe to the theory of non-origination of things; *AŚ*. IV 22-23, are comparable to *MŚ*, I.1,7 and XXI. 13 which deny causality. *AŚ*, IV. 33 contains the most common words of Buddhist philosophy, such as '*saṃvṛti*'and '*sarve dharmā mṛṣā*' (cp. Nāgārjuna's '*sarve dharmāḥ śūnyāḥ*' and Candrakīrti's '*anubhava eṣa mṛṣā*'. etc). *AŚ*, IV. 42 seems to speak in the vein of *Saddharmapuṇḍarīka-sūtra* and other early Mahāyāna Sūtras. *AŚ*, IV. 57 compares with *MŚ*, XXIV. 8-10. *AŚ*, IV. 58-59 recall *Catuḥśataka*, X. 14 and so many passages in the *Aṣṭasāhasrikā* and the *Vajracchedikā*. *AS*, IV. 61-62 compare well with the *Laṅkāvatārasūtra*, III. 65, 121. Phrases such as '*agrayāna*', *AŚ*, IV. 90; '*sarve dharmā anādayaḥ*', IV. 91, *ādibuddhāḥ*,' IV. 92, and '*ādiśāntā*, IV. 93, are obviously Buddhist in connotation.

Although most of the Brāhmanical thinkers have, generally speaking, misunderstood the awe-inspiring *śūnya* of the Buddhists, the conception of the Absolute (*nirguṇa brahman*) in Advaita Vedānta is similar to that of Emptiness. Gauḍapāda and Śaṃkara are the earliest and the greatest masters of Advaita Vedānta and both of them flourished many centuries after Nāgārjuna. It is generally acknowledged by distinguished scholars that Advaita Vedānta is deeply influenced by the

Mahāyāna thought. S.N. Dasgupta says, for example, that "Gauḍapāda seems to have assimilated all the Buddhistic Śūnyavāda and Vijñānavāda teachings, and thought that these held good of the ultimate truth preached by the Upaniṣads."[41] According to Stcherbatsky, "there is but little difference between Buddhism and Vedānta, a circumstance which Śaṃkara carefully conceals."[42] Many years ago, Swami Vivekananda had remarked that "the Advaita philosophy has a great many conclusions of the Buddhists", and that "the Vedānta has no quarrel with Buddhism."[43] Śaṃkara's exposition of Brahman as the one and only non-dual attributeless reality came so close to the Mādhyamika exposition of Śūnya that the medieval theologians like Vijñānabhikṣu and some Vaiṣṇavaite texts like the *Padma-purāṇa* described Advaita Vedāntins as 'crypto-Buddhists' (*prac-channa-bauddha*).[44] The impact of Mādhyamika dialectics is particularly predominant in the works of Śrī Harṣa, a twelfth century Vedāntist of Śaṃkara's school.

The *Yogarājopaniṣad*, a late medieval Upaniṣad, states that one certainly attains liberation by absorbing oneself in the Void (*śūnya*).[45] Another important Hindu (Vaiṣṇavaite) religious text of medieval age which employs the word '*śūnya*' exactly in the Buddhistic sense is the *Yogavāsiṣṭha-Rāmāyaṇa*. Its author has expounded a monistic doctrine of *brahman* on the lines of Śaṃkara and has made a synthesis of Mahāyānistic and Vedāntic thoughts. The fifth and the sixth chapters of this book are named 'Upaśama' and 'Nirvāṇa' respectively, words first used and popularized by Buddhism. The word '*upaśama*' in Buddhism means 'quiescence', a synonym of emptiness; the abolition or extinction of all views is called *prapañcopaśama*, another name for Nirvāṇa or Peace.

The *Yogavāsiṣṭha* describes *brahman* as *śūnya*, 'void' and as *vijñānamātra*, 'consciousness only.'[46] Here the word '*sūnya*' does not mean 'pure essencelessness' as Dasgupta renders it. This word stands for negation of all determinations; *brahman*, the Absolute, is called *śūnya* because it is devoid of all attributes (*nirguṇa*). The author of the *Yogavāsiṣṭha* considers *śūnya* as the ground of world-appearance (*yasmin śūnyaṃ jagat sthitaṃ*).[47]

The concept of the Great Void (*mahāśūnya*) as understood by Siddhas, like Sarahapāda, seems to have penetrated into the theology of Nāthapantha. In the *Haṭhayogapradīpikā* the ultimate Reality (*tattva*) is called 'void and not-void' (*śūnyāśūnya*), 'the innate nature' (*sahaja*), 'the immaculate' (*nirañjana*), and 'the supportless' (*nirālamba*). When the *yogin* awakens the great power (*mahāśakti, kuṇḍalinī*), his breath (*prāṇa*) becomes quiescent in the Void (*śūnya*). This quiescent state is called 'the state of the Innate' (*sahajāvasthā*) and 'the state of Emptiness' (*śūnyāvasthā*). He who attains this state is described as 'void within, void without, void like a pitcher in the sky; full within, full without, full like a pitcher in the ocean'. The great Void (*mahāśūnya*) is declared as the abode of all virtues and super-normal powers.[48]

The word '*śūnya*' (*sunn*) is used as a synonym of *sahaja* in the poetry of Kabir and the Sikh Gurus. These saints frequently refer to *sunn-samādhi*, emptiness-trance, and identify it with *sahaj-samādhi* and *sahaj-subhāi* (*sahaja-svabhāva*). Kabir refers to the union of individual soul and the supreme Lord as the meeting of the void with the Void (*sunnahi sunn miliā samadarsī*). Guru Nānak says that before the creation of the world that one (*eko soi*) was in *sunn-samādhi*.[49]

Several modern Hindu scholars have acknowledged Buddhist contributions to Hinduism.

Radhakrishnan says, "For us, in this country, the Buddha is an outstanding representative of our religious tradition. He left his footprints on the soil of India and his mark on the soul of the country with its habits and convictions. While the teaching of the Buddha assumed distinctive forms in the other countries of the world in conformity with their own tradition, here, in the home of the Buddha, it has entered into and become an integral part of our culture."[50]

N. Aiyaswami suggests that the Buddhist practice of dedicating merit to others has influenced the *Gītā's* teaching that action should be dedicated to God. He also agrees with our view that Gauḍapāda's exposition of *advaita* "was influenced considerably by Nāgārjuna's method of argument . . . The non-origination theory, as applied to the phenomenal world, was unknown in Advaitism before Gauḍapāda. Therefore there is no denying the fact that Gauḍapāda must have taken the idea from Nāgārjuna and adopted it suitably to provide the Advaita doctrine with a firm foundation." The Advaitins, following the Madhyamaka and Yogācāra schools of Buddhist thought, adhere to the doctrine of *māyā*-like nature of the world. "A great champion of the Advaita school, Śaṃkarācārya, took this weapon of the illusion theory and used it against his rival realists." In conclusion, this scholar observes that "Buddhism has left a permanent mark on the culture of India. Its influence is visible on all sides. The Hindu faith has absorbed the best of its ethics. A new respect for life, kindness to animals, a sense of responsibility and an endeavour after higher life have been brought home to the Indian mind with renewed force. Thanks to Buddhist influences, the Brāhmanical systems have shed those parts of their religion which were irreconcilable with humanity and reason."[51]

The learned editors of *The Cultural Heritage of India* have rightly observed that the Buddha's Middle Path "struck a new keynote in Indian religious life—a course midway between the rigorism of the Jains and the secularism of the sacrificial *Brāhmaṇas*." The grateful and enlightened Hindus are aware of India's debt to Buddhism; to quote their words, "it has left an indelible mark on our cultural heritage, particularly on language and literature, logic and philosophy, and on moral values."[52]

Some of the greatest modern Indians have been influenced by Buddhist teaching. The impact of Buddhist doctrines has been found in the life and works of Swami Vivekananda, Mahatma Gandhi, Rabindranath Thakur, Sri Aurobindo, Jawaharlal Nehru, Sarvepalli Radhakrishnan, Acharya Narendradeva, Mahamahopadhyaya Gopinatha Kaviraja, Acharya Vinoba Bhave, B. R. Ambedkar, and others. The national emblems of the Government of the Democratic Republic of India, such as the sacred *cakra* and the *siṃhanāda* sculpture from Sāranātha, symbolize the Buddhist ideals of universal peace and enlightenment. As V. V. Gokhale has remarked, "In the India of today, we see the spirit of ancient Buddhism, now attuned to the common way of life in the country, still harking back to its original, realistic purposes and still seeking for an awakening into a world of scientific inquiry, social equality and preservation of life on earth."[53]

From this standpoint it is not correct to say that Buddhism has declined in India. Satkari Mookerjee makes the correct observation when he says that Buddhism is alive as Hinduism.

"It lives for certain, but in a form totally assimilated to Hinduism, so that it is not easily discernible to a casual observer. . . .Buddhism may not exist in India as a separate sect; that is because it has permeated the entire religious and philosophic thought of India and percolated into the deepest recesses of the religious mentality of the present-day Hindus. The consequence is that it will not be incorrect to say that every Hindu is a Buddhist, in spite of all outward appearances to the contrary."[54]

In his speeches and writings Swami Vivekananda has often noted the diverse Buddhist influences on Hinduism. He has observed that "modern Hinduism is largely Paurāṇika, that is, post-Buddhistic in origin." He pointed out that Buddhism was mainly responsible for stopping or lessening the customs of drinking wine and killing living animals for sacrifice or for food in India. He rightly traced the origin of Hindu images and temples to Buddhist models. About the relation of Vaiṣṇavism to Buddhism, he has declared that "Buddhism and Vaiṣṇavism are not two different things. During the decline of Buddhism in India, Hinduism took from her a few cardinal tenets of conduct and made them her own, and these have now come to be known as Vaiṣṇavism."[55] It should be noted here that Vaiṣṇavism does not consist mainly of "a few cardinal tenets of conduct." The Swami is briefly referring to moral principles and practices, such as *ahiṃsā, karuṇā, maitrī*, respect for the *guru*, control of the mind and the senses or *yoga*, etc. which Buddhism transmitted to Vaiṣṇavism. The Bodhisattva ideal and the idea of Buddhā-vatāra also became integral parts of Vaiṣṇava theology.

Speaking of Buddhist ascetic ideals and institutions, Swami Vivekananda has said that the monastic vow and renunciation began to be preached all over India since the time of the Buddha, and "Hinduism has absorbed into itself this Buddhist spirit of renunciation." The ochre robe found a lasting home in Hinduism also. The Hindu teachers not only accepted the Buddhist institution of monks, they occupied the Buddhist monasteries also. "The many monasteries that you now see in India occupied by monks were once in the possession of Buddhism. The Hindus have only made them their own now by modifying them in their own fashion. Really speaking, the institution of *saṃnyāsa* originated with the Buddha." In conclusion, the Swami has stated that "Hinduism has become so great only by absorbing all the ideas of the Buddha."[56] Swami Vivekananda has been a pivotal figure in modern Hinduism and his opinions are representative of the educated Hindus.

Buddhism and the Dharma Cults

Buddhist beliefs and practices seem to have produced in the course of time some devotional and theistic systems of faith in eastern India. The existence of the cult of Dharmaṭhākura or Lord Dharma in Bengal was first pointed out by H.P. Sastri. In his epoch-making work, *The Discovery of Living Buddhism in Bengal*, published in 1897, he suggested that the worship of Dharmaṭhākura was a relic of Buddhism. He noted that the conception of Lord Dharma as Emptiness-Embodied (*śūnyamūrti*) and as Immaculate (*nirañjana*) as well as the worship of His images in the form of *caityas* were of Buddhist origin. In the Buddhist Tantras we find that the conception of Vajrasattva also called Śrīmahāsukha often borders on a theistic conception. A similar doctrine of Ādibuddha called Svayambhū is found in the *Svayambhūpurāṇa*.[57] It is quite likely that the system of Dharmaṭhākura developed as a theistic offshoot of the doctrine of Dharmakāya.

The stone images of Dharmaṭhākura are still worshipped in the temples of Dharma in some districts of West Bengal. Two short inscriptions on two pieces of tortoise shells found from Vajrayoginī village in Dacca District prove the existence of Dharmaṭhākura's worship as early as the tenth or the eleventh century A.D. One of these inscriptions invokes the blessings of the Buddha for the prosperity and salvation of the people.[58]

N.N. Vasu had strengthened the views of H.P. Sastri by publishing valuable archaeological and literary evidence bearing on the cult of Dharma in Orissa. He also pointed out the Buddhist foundations of a modern theistic sect of Mahimā-Dharma which originated in the nineteenth century in Orissa.[59] Maheshwar Neog had brought to light the prevalence of the Dharmaṭhākura cult in Assam.[60]

The literature of the Dharmaṭhākura cult is quite extensive. The *Śūnyapurāṇa* is its basic scripture.[61] It is atributed to Ramāī Paṇḍita who is regarded as the traditional founder of the faith. The *Dharmapūjāvidhāna* attributed to both Ramāī Paṇḍita and

Raghunandana, the *Śrīdharmapurāṇa* ascribed to Mayūrabhaṭṭa, the *Yātrāsiddharāyer Paddhati,* the *Śrīdharmamaṅgala* of Ghanarāma, and the *Anādimaṅgala* of Rāmadāsa are the representative theological and liturgical texts of this system. S.B. Dasgupta has given a detailed account of the history, literature and theological beliefs of the worshippers of Dharmaṭhākura in Bengal.[62]

It has been pointed out by scholars that the cult of Dharmaṭhākura had been current among the people of low-class, such as the Ḍomas, Hāḍīs, Bāgḍīs, Fishermen, Carpenters, etc. In the Brāhmanical social scheme these castes belong to the *śūdra* order. S.B. Dasgupta describes their religion as "a mixture of later Buddhistic ideas and practices with the popular Hindu beliefs and practices including a mass of the beliefs and practices of the non-Aryan aborigines." According to him, "Dharma cult owes many of its elements to that form of later Buddhism, which is known as Mantrayāna, and laterly and most commonly, as Vajrayāna."[63] He suggests some Muslim influences on the Dharmaṭhākura cult, and contrariwise, some Buddhist influences on the Muslims of Bengal.

It may be noted in passing that several scholars, including S.K. Chatterji and Sukumar Sen, have suggested non-Aryan and Austric origins of the Dharma cult. But all scholars agree that some relics of Buddhism are found in this system.[64]

Buddhist Contribution to Education and Letters

When the Buddha had founded at Vārāṇasi the ideal *saṃgha* consisting of sixty worthies (*arhats*), he commanded them in the following words : "Walk, monks, on your tour for the blessing of the many, for the happiness of the many, out of compassion for the world, for the welfare, the blessing and the happiness of *devas* and men. Monks, teach Dharma which is a blessing in the beginning, a blessing in the middle, and a blessing in the end". We quote this passage from the *Mahāvagga* to recall that Buddhism was, from the very beginning, a missionary movement founded on compassion, determined to spiritually transform the world of humanity, and to awaken it morally, intellectually and spiritually. Who can say how many millions of human beings had been awakened morally, intellectually and spiritually by the message of Buddhism in the course of its long history ? We can only imagine that an immeasurable multitude of creatures must have been awakened in India alone.

Buddhist monastic colleges and universities of ancient India threw open their doors to all those who wished to know, irrespective of caste, colour, creed or country. This universal attitude and catholic spirit of Buddhist culture and its educational centres earned a great international reputation for India and attracted students and scholars from far-off countries. The same cannot be said of the Brāhmanical system of education and its institutions. It is, therefore, quite proper to attribute to the influence of Buddhism the rise of organized public educational institutions in ancient India. The influence of Buddhist monastic and educational institutions on the growth and propagation of Indian culture can scarcely be overestimated. It was through Buddhism that Indian art, literature, thought, myths and morals were transmitted throughout the length and breadth of Asia during the first millennium of the Christian era.

In India it was after the Buddhist model of an organized institution of monks that Śaṃkara established *advaita* seats (*pīṭhas*) with an ordained and regulated community of Śaiva-Vedāntic monks. There is no evidence of Brāhmanical monasteries before the time of Śaṃkara (*cir.* 9th century A.D.). Charles Eliot is right when he observes that "the monastic institutions of India seem due to Buddhism," and that "Śaṃkara perceived the advantage of the cenobitic life for organizing religion and founded a number of *maṭhas* or colleges. Subsequent religious leaders imitated him."[65] One of the centres founded by Śaṃkara was located in Puri in Orissa. According to Swami Vivekananda, a leading modern teacher of Śaṃkara's school, "the temple of Jagannath is an old Buddhistic temple. We took this and others over and re-Hinduised them. We shall have to do many things like that yet."[66] Among other temples of the Buddhists took over by the Hindus, mention may be made of the one at Badrinath in Garhwal in which even the original Buddha image is still *in situ* and worshipped as that of Viṣṇu.

Buddhist contribution to Indian languages and literatures is matched only by the richness and variety of the Buddhist religion and philosophy. The development of Pali and its literature was wholly due to Buddhism. Of its great historical, cultural and literary value scholars are well aware. But Pali was not the only area which contributed to the flowering of the Buddhist tradition. The vast amount of Pali texts, canonical and non-canonical, is the contribution of only one major branch, doubtless one of the most ancient and orthodox branches of Buddhism. Several other schools of Buddhism cultivated varieties of Buddhist Sanskrit and varieties of Buddhist Prakrit. The Buddhist intellectuals of ancient India contributed not only to what is now called Buddhist Sanskrit and its varieties but also to what is called Pāṇinian or classical Sanskrit. Thus while we have the *Mahāvastu* and the Mahāyāna Sūtras in a Sanskrit peculiar to the Buddhist tradition, we also have such texts as the *Madhyamkaśāstra*, the *Jātakamālā*, and the *Tattvasaṃgraha*, to mention only three out of numerous texts, in classical Sanskrit. The Sanskrit of the Buddhist Tantras and Sādhanas presents us with yet another category of language. The language of the epigraphs of Aśoka is a kind of Prakrit, by no means uniform in all the major rock edicts and quite different from the language of what has been called the *Gāndhāri Dharmapada*. The Buddha's injunction to his disciples to learn the sacred word in their own languages (*sakāya-niruttiyā*) was fully carried out by the faithful Buddhists.

The Pali authors were the first to write hagiographies and traditional historical narratives. Some sections of the *Māhavagga* and the *Cullavagga* contain the earliest examples of what may be called Buddhist historical literature. But *Buddhavaṃsa* presents us with the oldest hagiographies of the Buddhist tradition. Parallel developments of legendary biographies and hagiographies of mythical heroes and sages can be seen in the *Mahābhārata* and the Jaina *Kalpasūtra*. The Jātakas and the Apadānas (Sanskrit Avadānas) remained a constant source of inspiration to future poets and religious authors who wrote in Sanskrit. Kṣemendra (10th century), for example, who was first a Śaiva and later on became a Bhāgavata, was inspired by Buddhist subjects and legends. He wrote the *Bodhisattvāvadānakalpalatā* in beautiful verse in which he collected one hundred and eight Avadānas. Whether it is in the *Vetālapañcaviṃśatikā* or in the *Daśakumāracarita* of Daṇḍin or in the *Kathāsaritsāgara* of Somadeva (11th century), the Buddhist fables and stories, in spite of changes due to transmission in different versions, retained their moral grandeur and psychological appeal, to the learned as well as the simple folk. The didactic portions of the Purāṇas and the Dharmaśāstras contain much that can ultimately be traced to Buddhist moral teachings. This is specially true of the *Mahābhārata*. The beginnings of epic poetry, particularly of dramatic poetry, can possibly be traced to Buddhist *ākhyāna* poetry. The numerous dramatic narrations in the form of dialogues in Pali verse or in verse mixed with prose present us with the earliest forms of Buddhist *ākhyānas* or so-called 'ballads'.

The contribution of Buddhism to the psychological literature of ancient India has perhaps never been equalled in the literature of Brāhmanism. The psychological advances made by the Abhidharma schools of Buddhist thought deserve detailed study in the light of contemporary psychology developed in the West. The problems of Abhidharma psychology have hardly been studied yet in relation to the psychology of Tāntrika *yoga* and the Siddha culture. A study of devotional meditation (*bhakti-yoga*) and of its techniques and terminology as revealed in the Hindi literature of medieval saint-poets is likely to throw important light on the transmission and transformation of the classical Buddhist system of *dhyāna* and related concepts.

It is well known that the first dramatist in the history of Sanskrit literature was a Buddhist poet, Aśvaghoṣa (first century A.D.). Fragments of three dramas in Sanskrit, including the fragments of the *Śāriputraprakaraṇa,* a drama by Aśvaghoṣa, have come to light from Central Asian Buddhist antiquities. Aśvaghoṣa was the forerunner of classical Sanskrit dramatists, like Bhāsa and Kālidāsa. Winternitz states that "the finished form of the epics together the perfect technique of the dramas of Aśvaghoṣa proves that they were composed only on some long-standing models. By itself it appears improbable that a thoroughly Buddhist poet should be the first to have composed in this style."[67] This statement makes a strange reading and no reason is given for assuming that it is improbable for a thoroughly Buddhist poet to be the pioneer in ornate style of *kāvya* and the perfect technique of dramaturgy. On the other hand, there are no models extant which can be said to have influenced Aśvaghoṣa in the techniques of the Sanskrit drama. At another place the same scholar is obliged to say that "Aśvaghoṣa, however, is the first

Indian poet who is actually known to us as an author of dramas."[68]

Although Vālmīki is traditionally considered the 'first poet' in Sanskrit, the extant *Rāmāyaṇa* attributed to his authorship is of composite character and of uncertain date. No such uncertainty attaches to Āryaśūra (fourth century A.D.), and his authorship of the *Jātakamālā* and other works. He has been described by P.L. Vaidya as "the forerunner of the poets of classical, chaste and ornate Sanskrit." In Śāntideva's *Bodhicaryāvatāra* we find the loftiest flights of religious poetry. Bu-ston's statement that there were "one hundred commentaries on this text, out of which only eight were translated into Tibetan," gives us an idea of the extent to which the Buddhist ideals were capable of inspiring men of letters.[69]

Buddhist poets were also pioneers in the composition of hymns of praise (*stotra, stava, stuti*) in Sanskrit. The *Prajñāpāramitā-stuti* may or may not be a work of Nāgārjuna (*cir.* first century A.D.), but he certainly composed the *Catuḥstava*. The earliest specimen of a hymn is possibly the *Buddhānusmṛti* section of the *Mahāvastu*, a canonical text of the Lokottaravāda sect of the Mahāsāṃghika school. The greatest writer of Buddhist hymns was, however, Mātṛceta (*cir.*first century A.D.). The following works, ascribed to him, are preserved in the Tibetan Tenjur : *Varṇārhavarṇastotra,* (also called *Catuḥśataka*), *Triratnamaṃgalastotra, Samyaksambuddhalakṣaṇastotra, Ekottarikastotra, Sugata-pañcatriṃśatstotra, Triratnatstotra, Śatapañcāśatkanāmastotra, Āryatārādevīstotra-sarvārthasiddhināmastotrarāja, Mātṛcetagīti* and *Āryatārāstotra*. Aśvaghoṣa, perhaps a contemporary of Mātṛceta, composed the *Gaṇḍīstotragāthā*. The *Miśrakastava* of Diṅnāga, the *Suprabhātastotra* of king Harṣa, and *Sragdharāstotra* of Sarvajñamitra, all these texts are of immense value from the standpoint of religious poetry. The *Bhaktiśataka* of Rāmacandra Bhāratī was perhaps one of the last hymns in praise of the Buddha composed in Sanskrit by an Indian Buddhist poet.

One of the latest contributions made by the Buddhists to the literature of India was in the form of *dohās* or *gītis* (songs) composed by Buddhist *siddhas* (adepts in Tāntrika culture) in Apabhraṃśa. This language became the mother of several modern Indian languages. The terms and concepts of Mahāyāna

Buddhism were transmitted by the *siddhas* through the medium of their Apabhraṃśa poems to medieval saint-poets. Unfortunately only a small portion of the *siddha* literature has survived to this day and much of it is still to be studied.

Finally mention may be made in passing of the contributions of Buddhist writers to Sanskrit grammar and lexicography. A Buddhist scholar, named Śarvavarman, wrote the *Kātantra* in which he tried to build a new system of Sanskrit grammar. He possibly lived in or about the second century A.D. In the eighth century a commentary was written on *Kātantra* by one Durgasiṃha. The Buddhist scholar Candragomin (*cir.* fifth century A.D.) wrote the *Cāndravyākaraṇa* with an autocommentary (*vṛtti*) on it. It became the standard grammatical treatise in most Buddhist countries of Asia. Bruno Liebich's researches have shown that an extensive literature developed around the *Cāndravyākaraṇa.* Another early grammarian was Indragomin possibly a Buddhist scholar, who wrote the *Aindravyākaraṇa.* The text was once famous in Buddhist Nepal, but it has not come down to us. The Buddhist logician Jinendrabodhi wrote the *Kāśikā-vivaraṇapañjikā* also known as *Nyāsa,* commentary on the *Kāśikā* of Jayāditya and Vāmana. In the eleventh century seem to have flourished not less than three Buddhist grammarians of Sanskrit. Śaraṇadeva wrote a work, called *Durghaṭa-vṛtti,* in which he simplified the difficult points in the *Aṣṭādhyāyī* of Pāṇini. It is said that the text of *Durghaṭavṛtti* was revised by his teacher Sarvarakṣita. Maitreyarakṣita wrote the *Tantrapradīpa,* a critical commentary on the *Nyāsa.* This author also wrote another grammatical work, called *Dhātupradīpa.* Fragments of a manuscript in eight leaves of a synonymical dictionary in Sanskrit were purchased by F. Weber at Leh in Ladakh. The author of this dictionary is believed to have been a Buddhist scholar and those fragments are supposed to be the oldest fragments of any dictionary in Sanskrit known so far.

Another Sanskrit dictionary which seems to have originated in Buddhist literary circles was the *Utpalini* compiled by Vyāḍi. The existence of this dictionary is known from quotations from it in some later commentaries. Vyāḍi may or may not have been a Buddhist by faith, but he seems to have drawn largely on the Buddhist literary sources. The most famous and earliest extant dictionary is the *Nāmaliṅgānuśāsana,* better known as

Amarakośa, by Amarasiṃha who possibly flourished in the sixth century A.D. He was a Buddhist, though he did not pay any special attention to Buddhist vocabulary in his dictionary. It is said that there are as many as fifty known commentaries on the *Amarakośa.*

Mention may be made in this connection of three important Buddhist Sanskrit texts which are well-known lexicographical collections of technical Buddhist terms. The first is the *Dharmasaṃgraha,* attributed to Nāgārjuna (?); it contains valuable lists of technical terms and important names collected under one hundred and forty headings. The other text is the *Arthaviniścayasūtra* which resembles the *Dharmasaṃgraha* to a great extent but contains also explanations of technical terms of Buddhist religion and philosophy. The third is the famous *Mahāvyutpatti,* a bilingual (Sanskrit-Tibetan) encyclopaedic lexicon of Buddhist proper names and technical terms. It was prepared jointly by Indian and Tibetan scholars in Tibet early in the ninth century. It may be mentioned here that there is also a commentary, called *Nibandhana* written on the *Arthaviniścayasūtra.*

The last Buddhist dictionary writer to be mentioned is Puruṣottamadeva (*cir.* 12th century). As a supplement to the *Amarakośa* he wrote the *Trikāṇḍaśeṣa.* The *Amarakośa* is divided into three parts, hence its secondary title 'Trikāṇḍī.' Puruṣottamadeva followed this arrangement in his work which contains rare names of the Buddha and many words that are peculiar to Buddhist Sanskrit.[70] Another dictionary by this author is called the *Hārāvali.* Before leaving this section we want to mention an interesting work by a great Buddhist poet and abbot of the Jagaddalavihāra (District Malda). This is an anthology of *Subhāṣitas* selected from the works of 227 authors and contains in all 1739 verses in the extant version and is called the *Subhāṣitaratnakośa.* Its author was Vidyākara who made the anthology in the eleventh century. Among other things this remarkable work proves that Dharmakīrti, the Buddhist logician, was also a great poet. The anthology reveals the existence of a large number of Buddhist poets whose works are now lost for ever.[71]

The Buddhists also composed what are called the Purāṇas. The *Svayambhū Purāṇa* was composed in about the tenth century A.D. while the famous *Śūnya Purāṇa* originated probably shortly after the twelfth century A.D. The last phase of transformed Buddhism in Bengal produced considerable religious literature in vernacular. A most important text of this class of literature is the *Dharmapūjāvidhāna* which expounds the theology and ritual of the Dharmaṭhākura cult of West Bengal. Many years ago N.N. Vasu had drawn attention to texts like the *Śūnya-saṃhitā*, *Anādi-saṃhitā, Yaśomati-mālikā*, etc. which originated as the works of 'modern Buddhism' in Orissa.

Buddhist Contribution to Art and Architecture

Even if we judge only by his posthumous effects on the civilization of India, Śākyamuni Buddha was certainly the greatest man to have been born in India.[72] Before becoming a major faith and a civilizing force in the world, Buddhism had been a mighty stream of thought and a tremendous fountain-head of human culture in its homeland. Ignorance or neglect of the available Buddhist literature is not the only shortcoming of the traditional approach. The fact that the knowledge of Indian archaeology is confined to a handful of scholars is another factor which has prevented most students from viewing Buddhist culture in its entirety. Mortimer Wheeler observes that "archaeologically at least we cannot treat Buddhism merely as a heresy against a prevailing and fundamental Brāhmanical orthodoxy."[73] For in spite of the ravages of time and destruction by Indian and foreign fanatics, Buddhism is still speaking vividly and majestically through its thousands of inscriptions, about one thousand rock-cut sanctuaries and monasteries, thousands of ruined *stūpas* and monastic establishments, and an incalculable number of icons, sculptures, paintings and emblems, that it prevailed universally among all the classes and masses of India for over fifteen centuries after the age of the Buddha, and that its ideas of compassion, peace, love, benevolence, rationalism, spiritualism and renunication had formed the core of the superstructure of ancient Indian thought and culture.

What is proved by Buddhist archaeology is affirmed by Buddhist philosophy and literature also. Not only the numerical strength and volume of Buddhist texts extant in Pali, Buddhist Sanskrit, classical Sanskrit, Prakrit and Apabhraṃśa, or preserved in South and South-east Asian, Tibetan, Chinese, Mongolian, Japanese and Central Asian languages and scripts, but also the variety, depth and subtlety of Buddhist literature and philosophy lead us to conclude that the religion and philosophy of Buddhist texts had captivated the Indic world. According to Swami Vivekananda, Buddhism had at one time "nearly swallowed up two-thirds of the population" of India. This is no exaggeration.

Buddhism in the Theravāda tradition has been a twofold movement : Buddhism of monks and nuns or ascetic Buddhism, and Buddhism of the laity or popular and social Buddhism. Along with the way to Nirvāṇa there was the way to 'good rebirth'. In the *Brahmajālasutta*, the *Pātimokkha*, and the *Visuddhimagga*, all worldly arts and crafts are described as unworthy of those who seek ultimate liberation. Prohibition of participation by monks and nuns in dances, songs, instrumental music, shows of entertainment, and use of articles of personal beautification is the burden of the seventh and the eighth *śikṣāpadas*. The case was different in popular Buddhism or *upāsaka-dharma*. The *Mahāparinibbānasutta* narrates how the nobles and the commoners, both men as well as women, of the Malla clan honoured the body of the Tathāgata by dancing and singing in accompaniment with instrumental music, with garlands and perfumes. Similar artistic activities full of ceremonial dignity and aesthetic sense are reported in the *Lalitavistara* and the *Buddhacarita* to have been performed by men and women of Kapilavastu at the birth of the Bodhisattva Siddhārtha.

The growth of Buddhist fine arts was due largely to the educational, religious, and devotional needs of the Buddhists. The supremely perfect and supernal personality of the Buddha (*sarvāṅgasundaram, sarvākāravaropeta*) was the greatest attraction for artists and poets and the supreme object of devout contemplation for monks and mystics. Hence the growth of Buddhology, Buddhist iconology, sculpture and painting. With the emergence of Mahāyāna, the Buddha image became the central plank of popular Buddhism and it was manufactured in a thousand plastic forms. Manufacturing religious icons and emblems was viewed as a pious deed. So was excavating *vihāras* in live rocks and erecting shrines and *stūpas*. The Pali Apadānas as well as the Sanskrit Avadānas eminently display the popular enthusiasm for adoration (*pūjā*) of emblems, such as the wheel, bowl, foot-print, the bodhi-tree and other items connected with the Master's earthly existence. From about the beginning of the Christian era images of the Buddha began to come into existence, and revolutionized rituals of worship not only in Buddhism but also in Brāhmanism. In place of sacrificial rituals temple rituals now became popular.

The style of the Buddhist *stūpa* seems to have inspired the style of Brāhmanical temples, especially those with a *śikhara.* It may be suggested that the early Buddhist practice of raising *stūpas* or sacred reliquary mounds perhaps reflected, *inter alia* a sense of time and historicity. The Vedic Āryans lacked this sense, and hence in Brāhmanism the tradition of building *stūpas* did not develop. The *Mahābhārata* and the Purāṇas considered the practice of venerating *stūpas* or *caityas* (called *eḍukas*) as a mark of the 'dark age' (*kaliyuga*). However, later on the practice was adopted by those sects of the Brāhmanical tradition which were most influenced by later Buddhism, viz. Śivaite Vedānta and Gorakhapantha.

Of all the joys that of Dhamma, *dhammapīti* was supreme. The Buddha had said that "the gift of Dhamma excels all other gifts." This was the teaching of Emperor Aśoka too.[74] The gift of Dharma included all that was conducive to nobler and higher life, including the knowledge of doctrines, articles of faith and devotion, scriptures, icons, symbols, and all the other means of growing in piety or expressing compassion and liberality. In this way Buddhism became the source of manifold artistic and literary activities reflecting the creative and aesthetic genius of its teachers and followers.

With the passage of time old inhibitions receded into the background; moreover, the theory of 'perfection in expedient means' (*upāyakauśalya pāramitā*) naturally required and encouraged proficiency in various arts and sciences. The Bodhisattva ideal of Mahāyāna left no difference between *bhikṣus* and *upāsakas.* The art and literature of Buddhism was produced through the donations not only of *upāsakas* and *upāsikās* but also of monks and nuns. For instance, there are 827 Brāhmī inscriptions on the monuments of Sānchī alone. Among the donors are mentioned the names of over two hundred monks and nuns; the rest are lay followers.[75] Similar is the case at a number of other centres of Buddhist art and culture. Hsüan-tsang has noted the names of a number of monks who established monasteries, built shrines and erected images. Mention may be made in this connection of Jayasena of Yaṣṭivana-vihāra, an *upāsaka* but a great teacher and author of Buddhist Śāstras.[76] The Nālandā Stone Inscription of Mālāda describes the monks of the University of Nālandā as 'reputed experts in true scriptures and the arts'.[77]

The community of monks became in the course of time a community of teachers of society and they have left a permanent influence on the country-people who esteem any tawny-clad person not only for his austere dress but also for his supposed proficiency in solving secular problems, such as knowledge of medicine. For example, King Duṭṭhagāmani of Śrī Laṅkā is reported to have said that 'the very sight of monks is auspicious and conducive to our protection'.[78] The 'sharers' of alms (*bhikṣus*), before whom kings and nobles bowed, had been the cultural leaders and religious teachers of society and a source of inspiration for the masses for several centuries before the sack of Nālandā Mahāvihāra by Bukhtyār Khilji.

The great mass of Buddhist art and literature, so rich, varied and deeply meaningful in both form and content, was inspired by the mystery and the norms of the Dharma. This Dharma itself was conceived as a blessing in the beginning, a blessing in the middle, and a blessing in the end. It is to be noted that the Buddhist seers made a distinction between the pursuit of abstract beauty which they found through the spotless spiritual eye of the Dharma, and the delights of its ephemeral beauty. All that is holy and wholesome and is conducive to the attainment of the supreme Goal, is indeed beautiful. This is the spiritual dimension of aesthetics.

We need hardly mention that the earliest and the best painting of ancient India is the Buddhist painting; the best sculpture of the golden days of ancient Indian culture is the Buddhist sculpture, and the earliest historical sculpture of India is also the Buddhist sculpture. In the field of architecture too, Buddhism was the pioneer source of inspiration. In both structural and rock-cut architecture of ancient India, Buddhist examples had provided a permanent legacy in planning, technique and style. The earliest historical buildings in brick are the ruins of Buddhist monasteries; the earliest man-made rock-cut halls are the *vihāras* of Buddhist and Ājīvika monks excavated under the orders of the Buddhist emperor. Last but not least the earliest and the best free standing monolithic pillars with beautiful capitals of animal figures were inspired by Buddhism and conceived by a Buddhist genius. All subsequent examples of *kīrtistambhas* and *dhvajastambhas* have been influenced by Aśokan *lāṭs*. Indian paleography and epigraphy owe a great deal to the original and pioneer inspiration of Buddhism and its lithic records. The earliest historical inscriptions of India are the Buddhist inscriptions. The *dhammalipi* of Aśoka became the mother of all subsequent varieties of Brāhmī and its derivative Indian and Asian scripts.

Buddhist Contribution to Political and Social Thought

Buddhism had contributed significantly to the development of the forms and institutions of civil government, including the ideals of kingship, in ancient India. Śākyamuni was a teacher also of the principles of righteous government, individual freedom, and the rule of law. The seven conditions of stability of a republican body which he suggested to the Magadhan diplomat Vassakāra are words of social wisdom still relevant to our contemporary political life.[79]

The influence of Buddhism on ancient Indian political theory and administrative organization could be understood in the light of (i) Buddhist speculations concerning the origin of state and government, (ii) the Buddhist organization of the *bhikṣu-saṃgha* and its impact on democratic states of ancient India, (iii) the influence of the Buddha's teachings on the kings, queens, their vassals and ministers, and (iv) certain concepts and institutions concerning political life which were inspired by Buddhist teaching. In the first place, the Buddhist theory of the origin of state and government as related in the *Aggaññasutta* is of democratic import. A similar version in the *Śāntiparvan* of the *Mahābhārata* seems to have been modelled after the Buddhist theory. The fact that many ancient Indian kings and authors of political thought felt that the king owed his authority to his subjects may have been suggested by the legend concerning Mahājanasammata, the first traditional king. The *Arthaśāstra* of Kauṭalya, the Junāgaṛh Rock Inscription of Rudradāman I, the *Mahābhārata*, the *Mañjuśrīmūlakalpa* and the *Rājataraṅgiṇī* suggest that the custom of the election of kings was continued till the twelfth century A.D. in some parts of India.[80] With respect to the second point it is a well-known fact that the organization and administration of the Buddhist *saṃgha* was based on democratic ideas, and that the democratic traditions of early Buddhist republics[81] were continued till as late as the time of Samudragupta (fourth century A.D.) who seems to have wiped out the republican states in his time. But the tradition survived in *paurajānapada* assemblies and also in village administration, and has come down to our era in the form of *grāma-pañcāyatas*.

With regard to the third point, namely the influence of the Buddha's teachings on ancient Indian kings, queens, and their ministers, there is a mass of evidence in the form of literary, epigraphic, and foreign records, and a modest volume could be written on this subject. It is impossible here even to mention the mere names of the kings, queens, nobles and ministers of ancient India who were Buddhists or were influenced by Buddhism. Among the kings who were Buddhist by faith we may include the following : Bimbisāra, Ajātaśatru, Puṣkarasārin (of Gāndhāra), Kālāśoka, Emperor Aśoka, Daśaratha Maurya, Bṛhadratha Maurya, Menander, the Greek king, Kaniṣka I, the Kuṣāṇa king, one of the Śātavāhanas, either Sīmuka or his son Kṛṣṇa, Buddhagupta, Tathāgatagupta, Narasiṃhagupta Bālāditya of the Gupta dynasty, Pūrṇavarman of Magadha, Rājabhaṭa of Bengal, Rājyavardhana and Harṣavardhana of Thāneśvara, Dhruvasena or Dhruvabhaṭa of Mālava, Śilāditya I, Dharmāditya of Mālava, Meghavāhana of Kashmir, Śubhakaradeva of Orissa, almost all the rulers of the Candra dynasty, Khaḍga dynasty, Bhadra dynasty, and the Bhaumakara dynasty of Bengal and Orissa, Gopāla and Dharmapāla and some other kings of the Pāla dynasty. This list is by no means exhaustive. Many of these kings have described themselves in their epigraphs as *paramopāsaka* or *paramasaugata*, i.e. 'devout Buddhists'. With the ignoble exception of about ten kings who persecuted Buddhism in their kingdoms, as a rule most of the kings of ancient India had sympathy and respect for Buddhism and patronized Buddhist monks and their establishments. The same is true of most of the queens and ministers whose patronage of Buddhism is known either through literature or through inscriptions or through foreign records.

It appears that India owes to Aśoka, *the idea of a welfare state* as well as *the idea of secular state*, secular in the sense not of a state without any religion, but in the sense that political administration of a state should be free, as far as possible, from sectarian principles and must respect the truly religious sentiments of different votaries that dwell in a particular state. Both these ideas are suggested by the inscriptions of Aśoka. Aśokan ideals of kingship were directly responsible for the growth of the idea of a welfare state free from the exclusive influence of a particular church. The idea of *dharmavijaya* or 'conquest by righteousness' practised and propagated by Aśoka was inspired by Buddhist morality. This grand concept remained an ideal for many kings who came after Aśoka. It does not seem to have been merely an imperial boast of Aśoka when he declared that he had gained a righteous victory by silencing the war-drums (*bherī-ghoṣa*), and by beating the drums, of righteousness (*dharma-ghoṣa*) throughout his empire and along its frontiers. The author of the Chinese *Hou Hanshu* has been quoted as saying that the people of India "practise the religion of the Buddha; it has become a habit with them not to kill and not to fight".[82] Along with this concept of conquest through righteousness Buddhism gave us the concept of an 'inoffensive sacrifice'[83] by kings, a *yajña* entirely free from *hiṃsā* and full of charity and kindness. This kind of sacrifice was performed by Emperor Aśoka and King Meghavāhana of Kashmir.[84] In the Nānāghāṭa Cave Inscription of Nāganikā we hear of this kind of sacrifice called *anārabhaniyo yaño*.[85]

Lastly it may be pointed out that ancient Indian political theory owed to Buddhism such institutions as that of *dharmamahāmātra*, *dharmasamāja*, *dharmadūta*, such royal epithets as *śīlāditya*, *vinayāditya*, *dharmāditya*, *paramasaugata*, *paramopāsaka*, etc. and to Buddhist social thought such historical examples as kingship of *brāhmaṇas*, *śūdras* and *vaiśyas*. In early Brāhmanical theory only a *kṣatriya* could be a ruler. In about the second century B.C. this rule was changed and it was declared that even a *brāhmaṇa* could be a ruler. This change in the duties of a *brāhmaṇa* was possibly inspired by Buddhist disregard for the scheme of *varṇa-dharma*. Puṣyamitra Śuṅga, a *brāhmaṇa* general of the last Maurya king, having murdered his sovereign, made himself king of the dacaying Maurya empire. Among the *brāhmaṇa* families which ruled over small areas in different periods of ancient Indian history, mention may be made of the Śuṅgas, Kāṇvas, Kadambas, Vākāṭakas and Śātavāhanas.

Many modern scholars have maintained that Buddhism developed as a monastic religion or as an ascetic movement, and that it was not a social movement. I have criticized this view elsewhere[86] and pointed out that monasticism or asceticism is only one aspect of Buddhist religious tradition and we should not mistake one part for the whole. The word '*saṃgha*' does not mean merely 'the order of monks'. The community of monks is only a part of the *saṃgha*, not the whole of it. *Saṃgha* has to be understood to mean the entire community of those human beings who take refuge (*śaraṇa*) in the Buddha, the Dharma and the Saṃgha. *Saṃgha* is the all-embracing universal society of humans wedded to the doctrine and method taught by the Sage of the Śākyas. This universal *saṃgha* includes men as well as women, ascetics as well as householders. In Buddhist words, *bhikṣus*, *bhikṣuṇīs*, *upāsakas* and *upāsikās*, all these four classes of Buddhists are members of the *saṃgha*. *Saṃgha* is the third member of the holy triad of the Buddhist tradition. In this spiritual sense *saṃgha* includes all kinds of enlightened beings, viz. the perfectly Awakened Ones (*samyaksambuddhas*), the individually Awakened Ones (*pratyekabuddhas*), the Worthy Ones (*arhats*), the Bodhisattvas, as well as those holy beings who are in different stages of purification (*viśuddhi*). This spiritual and ideal *saṃgha* is the true Refuge sought by the faithful disciples of the Buddha.

There is, however, no denying the fact that in practical life the Buddhists make a distinction between ascetic members and lay members of the *saṃgha*; for instance, they use the word *bhikṣu-saṃgha* in contradistinction to *upāsaka-saṃgha* and *bhikṣuṇī-saṃgha* to distinguish it from *bhikṣu-saṃgha*. In some old texts we find the *bodhisattva-gaṇa* contrasted with the *śrāvaka-saṃgha*. Likewise in the contemporary situation we refer to the *saṃghas* or communities of different places and countries, for example the *saṃgha* of Śrī Laṅkā, the *saṃgha* of Bangladesh or the Nepalese *saṃgha*, and so on. Sometimes in one and the same country are found *saṃghas* based on geographical separation, sectarian affiliation, etc. But these narrow and restricted meanings of the word *saṃgha* should not be allowed to obscure the vision of the *ārya-saṃgha*, the society of the enlightened beings, which is the ideal, nor should one lose sight of the universal society of human beings who are all united through their common dislike for suffering and common quest of happiness.

To describe Buddhism as a monkish or monastic religion is not right. Even the Theravāda tradition which has continuously promoted monasticism cannot be described as monkish. The Theravāda tradition did not envisage such an inseparable connection between the path of purity and the path of social life, as for example, was done in the Brāhmanical tradition through the scheme of *varṇāśrama-dharma*. In the Theravāda Buddhist view the joys of a homeless life of those who put on the ochre robe are declared to be superior to the joys of married and household life. It would, however, be erroneous to suppose that Buddhism neglected the social life altogether.

There are many discourses preserved in the Pali canon which contain principles and practices to be observed by those who live in society. A division of the *Majjhimanikāya* is called *Gahapativagga*. The *Maṃgalasutta*, which the Buddhists recite daily, is nothing short of a summary of sociologically oriented soteriology. A comprehensive picture of the social perspective of Theravāda Buddhism may be gleaned from the *Ambaṭṭhasutta*, the *Sigālovādasutta*, the *Kandarakasutta*, the *Aṭṭhakanāgarasutta*, *Upālisutta*, *Ghaṭikārasutta* and *Mahākammavibhhaṃgasutta*. Another authentic picture of the social ethics of early Buddhism is documented in the rock and pillar edicts of Emperor Aśoka.

It is true that the Pali texts make a clear distinction between ascetic and lay members of the *saṃgha*. This is as it should be in so far as their ends and means are concerned. Soteriological ends and means differ from social ends and means. Those who aspire for ultimate Freedom (*vimutti*) from *saṃsāra* are certainly superior to and different from those who aspire for rebirth in happy or heavenly abodes. The career of ascetics (*śramaṇas*) is therefore subtle, difficult, and extraordinary. The vast majority of lay members follow a less subtle, less difficult and ordinary way of life. But this way of life is guided by the teachings of the Buddha and of Buddhist sages. The relationship that has existed between the ascetic and social members of the *saṃgha* especially in South-east Asian lands, shows that those who interpret Theravāda Buddhism as ascetic and anti-social are mistaken.

The monks were never supposed to remain indifferent to social human beings and their sufferings; the *dharma-vinaya* was not meant only for those who had 'gone forth' from home-life. Śākyamuni was a perfectly Awakened One and therefore a World-Teacher. He was not the teacher of monks only, he was the teacher not only of all human beings, monks as well as the laity, but also of divine beings—*satthā deva manussānaṃ*. He is renowned as 'the Torch-bearer of mankind' (*ukkādhāro manussānaṃ*). He was 'born for the good and happiness of humanity' (*manussa-loke hitasukhāya jāto*). The beginnings of the Buddhist movement lay in the Buddha's keen concern for the freedom and happiness of human beings living in the whole world. There would have been no Buddhism, had he withheld his great compassion (*mahākaruṇā*) which was one of the corner-stones of the Buddhist movement. And compassion is a social emotion, a human virtue. It was to be practised in the world of living beings.

A movement which moves society is a social movement. And Buddhism definitely moved society wherever it spread in the course of its long history. For thousands of years it has moved men and women to a higher life, to noble truths and deeper principles; it has inspired races, peoples and nations to develop art and literature, morals and manners, science and philosophy, and to build patterns of civilization and forces of peace. The history of Buddhist civilization has been the result of Buddhist moral and social ideas and ideals which are not all ascetic or monastic.

Recently Melford E. Spiro has advanced the view that there are 'three systems of Theravāda Buddhism', viz. 'nibbanic Buddhism', 'kammatic Buddhism' and 'apotropaic Buddhism'. By the first system he means Buddhism of those who aspire direct to Nirvāṇa; by the second system he understands Buddhism as practised by those who aspire to favourable rebirth and happy states in heaven. The third system, according to him, is 'concerned with man's worldly welfare; the curing of illness, protection from demons, the prevention of droughts, and so on.'[87] This view is based on his study of Buddhist communities in Burma during the days of U Nu. We may observe in passing that these so called 'three systems' are three facets of one system, Theravāda Buddhism, and they are interrelated. Those who aim at Nirvāṇa do not, perhaps cannot, remain indifferent to the welfare of those who aim at a favourable rebirth. Contrariwise those who follow the so-called 'kammatic' religious life treat those who aspire to Nirvāṇa as the proper 'field of merit.' The worldly welfare of human beings cannot be divorced from transcendental concerns either of the monks or of the laity so that the tasks such as curing illness, overcoming droughts and famines etc. are common concerns of all grades of Buddhists. Even the Buddha is known to have discussed the problems of life with kings, ministers, generals, traders, craftsmen, priests, and all kinds of householders. As A.K. Warder remarks, "there is a general underlying assumption that beyond the immediate aim of individual peace of mind, or more probably in essential connection with it, lies the objective of the happiness of the whole of human society and the still higher objective of the happiness of all living beings."[88]

It may be pointed out that the lay Buddhists also contributed significantly to the growth of Buddhist ideas and practices. The rise of the powerful schools of the Mahāsāṃghikas and Sarvāstivādins resulted in important sociological and secularizing developments. These were matched in the Theravāda tradition by the popularity of the Apadānas and Jātakas which illustrate social ethics. At the same time *stūpa* architecture and related sculpture presented a fresh area of a concrete religious and social activity in which the monks as well as the laity joined. Another area of social life in which this cooperation was meaningfully employed was that of education of the monks as well as the laity. Its centres were monastic schools and colleges in which the monks were the teachers not only of religious doctrines and texts, but also of secular arts and letters.

But Buddhist community of casteless and classless monks exerted important influence on Indian society in general. The Brāhmanical leaders and authors were obliged to introduce the ascetic life as the fourth stage (*saṃnyāsa-āśrama*) in the theory of *āśramas*. The provision of *vikalpa* or option to embrace *saṃnyāsa* or monastic life even without going through all the preceding three stages was made possibly due to the popularity of *pravrajyā* or 'going forth' in Jaina and Buddhist circles of Indian society. The tenet of redeeming one's debt to one's 'fathers' (*pitṛs*) by producing sons was, however, never given up by the Brāhmanical tradition.

A fundamental tenet of Buddhist socio-moral ideology was that all beings are bound by their *karma*. It is the deeds of a person which determine his or her fortunes in this and the next life. The doctrine recognized the freedom of every person to select a way of life suitable to his or her equipment. In other words, it is one's inner worth and moral excellence, purity of life and nobility of character, control of the mind and the senses and an insight into the real nature of things, in short, progress in the triple training : *śīla, samādhi* and *prajñā*, which determine one's superiority over others. No distinction of birth or caste, colour or sex, race or status was of any value so far as one's higher or holier life and its ways and means were concerned. This was a revolutionary doctrine from the standpoint of the Brāhmanical tradition which zealously guarded the myth of the divine origin of four classes and their duties.

Buddhism made profound impact in Indian social life in several ways. Its leaders and teachers continuously criticized the theory of castes and ridiculed the false claims to superiority based on birth (*jāti*) and colour (*varṇa*). On the other hand, Buddhism opened the doors to higher religious life and the highest goal for all those who sought them, including the members of the lower strata of society. Although Buddhism was not directly concerned with the abolition of castes, it strongly opposed the caste-system and repeatedly taught the evils of casteism. Another aspect of Buddhist social contribution was towards the emancipation of women from social inhibitions. Buddhism along with Jainism but unlike Brāhmanism gave the equality of opportunity in religious culture to women. Some of the female members of the earliest ascetic order known to history were the Buddhist *therīs* or nuns whose religious poetry has come down to us in the *Therīgāthā*. The eminent position attained by a large number of women in Buddhist history, viz. Khemā, Paṭācārā. Dhammadinnā, Sujātā, Viśākhā, Sāmāvatī, Ambapāli, Uppalavaṇṇā, Subhā, Kisā, and Somā, etc., shows that Buddhism had done much for the emancipation of women in Indian society. The same is true with regard to the Buddhist contribution towards the upliftment of *śūdras*.

Another aspect of Buddhist contribution in ancient India lay in the area of social harmony and racial integration on a national scale. It was through Buddhist influence and teaching of social harmony and tolerance that foreign invaders, such as the Greeks, Śakas, Pahlavas, Kuṣāṇas and Hūṇas who came to India and settled here in the course of centuries immediately preceding and following the Christian era, were assimilated by Indian society. This was a permanent contribution to social integration and national growth, and it could not have been so easily accomplished in a strictly Brāhmanical scheme of social gradation without the wholesome effects of the Buddhist disregard for *varṇa*-organization and respect for the liberty of the individual. Had Buddhism been a living force during the medieval centuries the problem of Hindu-Muslim communal disharmony in medieval and modern India would not have taken such a strong turn as it did. Because of the revival of the traditional Brāhmanical social scheme, reinforced with fresh religious injunctions, and because of the decline of Buddhism in India after the tenth century A.D., the mass of early medieval Islamic followers in India could not be assimilated and digested by Indian society. Arnold J. Toynbee has rightly remarked that "if either Buddhism or Jainism had succeeded in captivating the Indic World, caste might have been got rid of. As it turned out, however, the role of universal church in the last chapter of the Indic decline and fall was played by Hinduism, a parvenu archaistic syncretism of things new and old; and one of the old things to which Hinduism gave a new lease of life was caste."[89]

The Buddhist message of social equality and communal harmony had left a deep impression on the mind of the Indian people which continued after the transformation of the classical Buddhist movement. A number of instances in the myths and stories of the *Mahābhārata* reveal that moral and intellectual attainments carried greater prestige than mere birth in a *brāhmaṇa* family. The *Bhagavadgītā*, while stating the theory of the divine origin of four castes (IV. 13), nevertheless teaches that the wise people are impartial towards a learned and disciplined *brāhmaṇa*, the cow, an elephant, a dog and an outcaste (V.18). The task of fighting the evils of casteism and untouchability was continued by the Buddhist *siddhas*, the adepts in Tāntrika culture, during the early medieval centuries. A large number of these *siddhas* came from lower caste families, but their greatness was assured by their success (*siddhi*) in esoteric culture (*sādhana*).

This work of social reform was afterwards resumed by the saint-poets of the *bhakti* movement throughout the middle ages. Though most of these saint-poets (*santas*) were, generally speaking, within the fold of the Brāhmanical 'Hindu' religiou stradition, yet they revolted freely against many fundamental dogmas and powerful customs of traditional Brāhmanism. Their social and moral teachings were more in keeping with Buddhism than with Brāhmanism. All of them disregarded the rules of the *varṇa-āśrama-dharma* scheme and attacked social distinctions based on birth and profession. Many of them were born in *śūdra* families. They became exalted through their pure character, sincere devotion and magnanimity. The saints of Karṇāṭaka and Mahārāshṭra, viz. Basaveśvara, Jñāneśvara, Nāmadeva, Rāmadāsa, Tukārāma, and Ekanātha, were all against casteism and ritualism. Likewise the saint-poets (*santas*) of north India, viz. Caitanya, Rāmānanda, Kabīrdāsa, Ravidāsa, Guru Nānak, Dhannā, Sena, Pīpā, Dādū, and the Muslim *sūfis*, were equally strong critics of the Brāhmanical scheme of castes and rituals. The social reforms initiated by the Buddhists and continued by medieval saint-poets were finally legalized and accomplished (at last in theory) by the government of the Republic of India in 1949.

NOTES AND REFERENCES

CHAPTER I

1. For an account of early Buddhist sects see Mahāvaṃsa, V; G. N. Roerich, Blue Annals, I, 24 f; Masuda, Origin and Doctrines of Early Buddhist Schools of Vasumitra's Treatise in Asia Major, II, pp. 1-78; Andre Bareau, Les Sectes Bouddhiques du petit Vehicule; N. Dutt, EMB, II, chs. VI-XI; G. C. Pande, Bauddha Dharma ke Vikāsa kā Itihāsa, ch. III.

2. Dīpavaṃsa, VI; Mahāvaṃsa, V; Beal, Si-yu-ki, p. 331; D. R. Bhandarkar, Aśoka, pp. 89-90.

3. N. Dutt, Aspects of Mahāyāna Buddhism, pp. 32-33; G. C. Pande, Bauddha Dharma, ch. IV; Etienne Lamotte, Histoire du Bouddhisme Indien, pp. 686f; Mahāvastu, tr. J.J. Jones; ERE, Art. on 'Mahāyāna', 'Docetism'.

4. Yuan Chwang, I, 270-278; N. Dutt, Aspects, ch. I; H. Kern, A Manua of Indian Buddhism, pp. 12 f., G. C. Pande, Bauddha Dharma, ch. VI.

5. R. Kimura, A Historical Study of the Terms Hīnayāna and Mahāyāna, etc. in the Journal of the Dept. of Letters, Calcutta University, vol. XII, 1925.

6 J. Takakusu, I-tsing, pp. 14-15.

7. Ibid, pp. 15, 51.

8. See the traditions of a second Dharmacakrapravartana at Gṛdhrakūṭa mount in Beal, Si-yu-ki, pp. 371-372; Sekoddeśaṭīkā, p. 4; Obermiller, Bu-ston, II, pp. 46-52; Saddharmapuṇḍarīka, II. 33-34.

9. I-tsing, pp. 15, 51; Yuan Chwang, II, 196, 241, 148.

10. ERE, vol. VIII, p. 33; N. Dutt, Aspects, pp. 38 f.

11. Kimura, op. cit., p. 56.

12. Mahāyānasūtrālaṅkāra, 1, 7.

13. D. T. Suzuki, Outlines of Mahayana Buddhism; B. L. Suzuki, Mahāyāna Buddhism; W. M. McGovern, An Introduction to Mahāyāna Buddhism; Har Dayal, Bodhisattva Doctrine in Buddhist Sanskrit Literature; R.L. Mitra, Sanskrit Buddhist Literature of Nepal; M. Winternitz, A History of Indian Literature, vol. II (pt. I); N. Dutt, Aspects of Mahāyāna Buddhism and its Relation to Hīnayāna; R. Kimura, A Historical Study of the Terms Hīnayāna and Mahāyāna and the Origins of Mahāyāna Buddhism; Edward Conze, The Prajñāpāramitā Literature, and the Thirty Years of Buddhist Studies; La Vallee Poussin's Art. on 'Mahāyāna' in ERE; Rāhula Sāmkṛtyāyana, 'Mahāyāna Bauddha Dharma kī Utpatti' in Purātattva-Nibandhāvalī; ch. 8; Hajime Nākamura, 'Historical studies of coming into existence of Mahāyāna Sūtras' in Bulletin of the Okurayama Oriental Research Institute; G. C. Pande, Bauddha Dharma, ch. 8; A. Hirakawa, 'The Rise of Mahāyāna Buddhism' in Memoirs of the Toyo Bunko, pp. 57-106.

14. Mahāvastu, vol. I, pp. 124-150.

15. N. Dutt, Aspects, Appendix, pp. 323f.; Edward Conze, 'The Oldest Prajñāpāramitā', The Middle Way, vol. XXXII, no. 4, 1957.

16. Aṣṭasāhasrikā Prajñāpāramitā, p. 112; E. Conze's transl., 79—ime khalu punaḥ Śāriputra ṣaṭpāramitā pratisamyuktāḥ sūtrāntāstathāgatasyātyayena, dakṣiṇāpathe pracariṣyanti, dakṣiṇāpathātpunareva vartanyāṃ pracariṣyanti, vartanyāḥ punaruttarāpathe pracariṣyanti.

17. N. Dutt, Aspects, p. 39; Poussin in ERE, vol. VIII, p. 334.

18. Yuan Chwang, II, 160; Śi-yu-ki, p. 381, This is also called Vidyādharapiṭaka which is quoted in the Śikṣāsamuccaya.

19. Si-yu-ki, pp. 415 f.; I-tsing, pp. 35, 165, Blue Annals, I, pp. 34-35.

20. Sekoddeśatīkā, pp. 3-4.
21. Aṣṭasāhasrikā, Eng. tr., pp. 182 f.; R Kimura, op. cit.
22. Har Dayal, Bodhisattva Doctrine; Bodhicaryāvatāra with Pañjikā and the Śikṣāsamucaya are the best ancient authorities on the subject.
23. Mahāyānaviṃsikā, last verse (MBT, I, p. 203).
24. Aṣṭasāhasrikā, Eng. tr., pp. 88, 108, 145.
25. G. P. Malalasekera, DPPN, vol. II, pp. 94-95, 294-295; Ria Kloppenborg, The Paccekabuddha, A Buddhist Ascetic.
26. Saddharamapuṇḍarīkasūtra, pp. 21 f.
27. Mahāyānasūtrālaṅkāra, I. 10.
28. R. Kimura, op. cit., p. 61.
29. BCA, IV. 7; IX 42, 49.
30. (First) Bhāvanākrama, MBT, II, pp. 172-173.
31. Frederick J. Streng, Emptiness, a Study in Religious Meaning.
32. I-tsing, pp. 54-56.
33. Mahāvyutpatti, 65.
34. R.L. Mitra, op. cit.
35. P. Cordier, Catalogue du Fonds Tibetain de la Bibliotheque Nationale; H. Ui, M. Suzuki, Y. Kanakura and T. Tada, A Complete Catalogue of the Tibetan Buddhist Canons.
36. B. Nanjio, A Catalogue of the Chinese Translation of the Buddhist Tripiṭaka.
37. The latest notices of the Prajñā-texts are by E. Conze, The Prajñāpāramitā Literature; see also Ryusho Hikata (ed.), Suvikrāntavikaramī Paripṛcchā Prajñāpāramitā, Introduction; some short Prajñāparamitās have been recently published in BST, no. 17.
38. M. Anesaki, 'Prajñāpāramitā' in ERE.
39. These texts have been re-edited in BST series.
40. On Sarvāstivāda, see J. Takakusu, , 'Sarvāstivāda' in ERE, vol. XI, pp. 198 f.; La Vallee Poussin, 'Sautrāntikas' in ERE, vol. XI, pp. 213 f; Stcherbatsky, Central Conception of Buddhism; Yamakami Sogen, Systems of Buddhistic Thought, ch. III; A.C. Banerjee, The Sarvāstivāda Literature. Some original sources: Abhidharmakośa with Bhāṣya; Abhidharmāmṛta of Ghoṣaka (Sanskrit restoration); Yaśomitra's Sphuṭārthā-Abhidharmakośavyākhyā; Tattva-saṃgraha, ch. XXI.
41. J. Takakusu, 'Life of Vasubandhu' in JRAS, 1905; E. Frauwallner, Date of Vasubandhu, SOR, III, 1951.
42. Yuan Chwang, I, pp. 210-212, 325-328; U. Wogihara, 'Vasubandhu' in ERE, vol. XII, p. 595.
43. Y. Sogen, Systems, ch. IV, pp. 172 f.; H. Ui, Vaiśeṣika Philosophy, pp. 43 f.
44. Fundamental sources: Madhyamakaśāstra with Prasannapadā; Catuḥśataka; Vigrahavyāvartani; Mahāyānakaratalaratnaśāstra; Dvādaśamukhaśāstra, Madhyamakārtha-saṃgraha in Dharmadūta, vol. 29, July-August, Sarnath, 1964; Madhyamakāvatāra, ch. VI, Sanskrit restoration in JOR, Madras, vols. IV-VI; BCA with Pañjikā; Tattva-saṃgraha. Among the modern works, the most important are — Stcherbatsky, the Conception of Buddhist Nirvāṇa; T.R.V. Murti, Central Philosophy of Buddhism; E. Conze, Buddhist Thought in India, ch. 2 of pt. III; Y. Sogen, Systems, ch. V; F. J. Streng, Emptiness; Richard Robinson, Early Mādhyamika in India and China.
45. L. M. Joshi, 'Life and Times of the Mādhyamika Philosopher Nāgārjuna', Maha Bodhi, vol. 73, nos. 1-2, 1965.
46. Obermiller (Bu-ston), II, p. 135 and ch. VIII below.
47. Yuan Chwang, I, 215-224.
48. Blue Annals, I. p. 341; Bu-ston, II, 135; Nanjio-Catalogue, no. 1185; ed. in BI by M. Walleser.
49. Rāhula Sāṃkṛtyāyana in JBORS, vol. XXVIII, pt.1, pp. 48f; chapters second and eight published in Indo-Iranian Journal, vol. XIV and Adyar Library Bulletin, vol. XXXIX.

50. Restored into Sanskrit by N. Aiyaswami Śāstri in Visvabharati Annals, vol. II.
51. Restored into Sanskrit by N. Aiyaswami Śāstri in JOR, vol. V; reproduced in Nāgarī script and tr. into Hindi with notes by L.M. Joshi in Dharmadūta, vol. 29, July-August, 1964.
52. Winternitz, op. cit., pp. 352 f.; G. Tucci, Doctrines of Maitreyanātha etc.
53. On Asaṅga see ERE, vol. II, pp. 62 f; EB, II, pp. 133-146.
54. Blue Annals, I, p. 233; Yuan Chwang, I, 355-357.
55. E. Frauwallner in SOR, III; U. Wogihara in ERE, vol. XII, pp. 595 f.
56. On Vijñānavāda see Vijñaptimātratāsiddhi Deux Traites de Vasubandhu, ed. par S. Levi; Vijñaptimātratāsiddhi La Siddhi de Hiuan Tsang, ed. par L. De La Vallee Poussin; Laṅkāvatārasūtra; D. T. Suzuki, Studies in the Laṅkāvatārasūtra; Y.Sogen, Systems, ch. VI; Narendradeva, Bauddha Dharma Darśana, pp. 422 f; A.K. Chatterjee, Yogācāra Idealism.
57. On the life and works of Diṅnāga see S. C. Vidyabhusana, History of Indian Logic, pp. 272 f.; Stcherbatsky, Buddhist Logic, vol. I, pp. 31-32; H. N. Randle, Fragments From Diṅnāga, pp. 2-3; M. Hattori, Diṅnāga on Perception.
58. Matsya Purāṇa, 208-67 ; R. C. Hazra, Studies in the Puranic Records on Hindu Rites and Customs, p. 41.
59. Mahāyāna-sūtrālaṅkāra, IX. 77; Poussin, 'Ādibuddha' in ERE, vol. I, pp. 93 f.; Svayambhupurāṇa.
60. H. A. Giles, The Travels of Fa-hsien, p. 23.
61. Ibid.
62. Yuan Chwang, II, 224; JUPHS, vol. XV, pt. 2, p. 26.
63. T. W. Rhys Davids, 'Buddhaghoṣa' in ERE, vol. II, pp. 885 f; B. C. Law, The Life and Works of Buddhaghoṣa.
64. Jātakamālā, Introduction, p. IX.
65. Rāhula Sāṃkṛtyāyana, Bauddha Saṃskṛti; P. K. Mukherji, Indian Literature in China and the Far East; P. C. Bagchi, India and China.
66. M. Winternitz, op. cit., pp. 375 f.; B. Bhattacharya (ed.), Guhyasamājatantra, Introduction; N. Dutt in HCI P, vol. IV, pp. 260 f.
67. Yuan Chwang, I, pp. 288 f.
68. Ibid., II, pp. 164 f.
69. G. Tucci, 'Buddhist Logic Before Diṅnāga' in JRAS, 1929; Doctrines of Maitreyanātha and Asaṅga; and Pre-Diṅnāga Buddhist Texts on Logic From Chinese Sources.
70. Stcherbatsky, Buddhist Logic, I, pp. 31 f.; H. N. Randle, op. cit.; S.C. Vidyābhūṣaṇa, op. cit.; Jwala Prasad, History of Indian Epistemology; Keith, Buddhist Philosophy.
71. Winternitz, op. cit., p. 363; Stcherbatsky, Ibid., I, pp. 11-13; S. Mookerjee, Buddhist Philosophy of Universal Flux, Introduction; Conze, Buddhist Thought in India.
72. Vide Nyāyavārttikatātparyaṭīkā, p. 2; Randle, Indian Logic in the Early Schools, p. 33; Stcherbatsky, Ibid., I, pp. 59 f.
73. E. Conze (Buddhist Thought, p. 265) says that logic was "at variance with the spirit of Buddhism", because "its methods implied a radical departure from the spirit of ahiṃsā". We however, think, as Conze himself notes, that the development of Buddhist logic was a historical necessity in the life of Indian Buddhism, and its methods were quite in keeping with the spirit of upāyakauśalya and the spirit of saṃvṛti.
74. Stcherbatsky, Ibid., I, pp. 35-35; R. Sāṃkṛtyāyana, Purātattva Nibandhāvalī, p. 178.
75. Narendradeva, op. cit., ch. XVIII, pp. 422 f.
76. Vide Nyāyavārttikatātparyaṭīkā, pp. 2-3; H. N. Randle, Indian Logic, p. 33; S. Radhakrishnan, Indian Philosophy, II, pp. 37-38. Gopīnātha Kavirāja, Gleanings From the History and Bibliography of Nyāya-Vaiśeṣika Literature.
77. Saddharmapuṇḍarīka, ch. XXI; Laṅkāvatāra, ch. IX.

78. Vide Mahāyānasūtra-saṃgraha, Sūtra no. 18.
79. Winternitz, op. cit., p. 399.
80. Mañjuśrīmūlakalpa, chs. 2, 3, 4, 9, 37, etc.

CHAPTER II

1. Life, p. 57; on the Lampakas see Mahābhārata, Droṇaparva, 121, 42-43.
2. Cunningham, AGI, p. 43.
3. Yuan Chwang, I, pp. 190-192.
4. V. A. Smith, Early History of India, p. 57; H. C. Raychaudhuri, Political History of Ancient India, p. 246.
5. Yuan Chwang, I, pp. 182 f.
6. Giles, Fa-hsien, p. 18.
7. On the Buddhist monuments of Gāndhāra, see John Marshall, (1) Taxila, 3 vols., (2) A Guide to Taxila, and (3) The Buddhist Art of Gāndhāra.
8. Yuan Chwang, I, 198, 222.
9. Cunningham, AGI, p. 81; G. Tucci, 'Preliminary Report on an Archaeological Survey in Swat', East and West, vol. IX, no. 4, 1958.
10. Yuan Chwang, I, 225-238.
11. Ibid., p. 239.
12. Mahāvaṃsa, V. 206; Madhyāntika is mentioned in a Sāñcī inscription also.
13. Giles, Fa-hsien, p. 9.
14. Yuan Chwang, I, 240.
15. Ibid., 240-245.
16. Yuan Chwang, I, 248-256.
17. N. Dutt, Gilgit Manuscriptsm, vol. I, Introduction; J.N. Ganhar and P. N. Ganhar, Buddhism in Kashmir and Ladakh.
18. Yuan Chwang, I, 261; Life, p. 68.
19. Yuan Chwang, I, 279.
20. Ibid., 259; Life, pp. 69-70.
21. Rājataraṅgiṇī, III, 356; see my article 'Buddhist Gleanings From the Rājataraṅgiṇī' in the Journal of the Oriental Institute, vol. XIV, 1964.
22. Life, p. 68.
23. Rājataraṅgiṇī, I, 170.
24. Yuan Chwang, I, 279.
25. Ibid., 282.
26. Life, p. 70.
27. Rājataraṅgiṇī, III, 2-14.
28. Rājataraṅgiṇī, Stein's tr., vol. I, Introduction, p. 74 note.
29. Rājataraṅgiṇī, III, 57.
30. See R. Gnoli (ed.), Pramāṇavārttikam of Dharmakīrti, Introduction, pp. XXIII-XXVI.
31. Jan Yuan Hua, 'Kashmir's Contribution to the Expansion of Buddhism in the Far East', IHQ, vol. XXVII, 1961, p. 98.
32. Rājataraṅgiṇī III, 380-381, see Stein, op, cit, p. 105 note.
33. Rājataraṅgiṇī, III, 464, 476, IV. 3.
34. See L'itineraire d' Ou K'ong (751-790), ed. and tr. by S. Levi, Journal Asiatique, 1895, pp. 341-384; Gilgit Manuscripts, vol. I, p. 36 f.
35. Rājataraṅgiṇī, IV, 127, 134, 144.
36. Ibid., IV, 188; Stein, op. cit., I, p. 140.
37. Rājataraṅgiṇī, IV, 200; Stein, op. cit., I, p. 142 and II, pp. 302-303.
38. Rājataraṅgiṇī, IV, 203-204; cf. the Buddhist traditions of 84000 śarīras or relics and of an equal number of stūpas built by Aśoka.
39. Rājataraṅgiṇī, IV, 210-11, 215-16, 259-63, 506-7, 517, 594-604, 498; Stein, op. cit., I, pp. 143-44.
40. See Gilgit Manuscripts, I, Introduction, p. 37.
41. Sten Konow, ASR, 1915-1916, p. 50; Gilgit Manuscripts, I, p. 38.

42. Yuan Chwang, I, 283 284.
43. Rājataraṅgiṇī, V, 150.
44. Yuan Chwang, I, 286.
45. Life, pp. 72-73.
46. Ibid., pp. 74-76; Yuan Chwang, I, 287, Beal thinks that '700 years' is a mistake for '170 years'.
47. Life, p. 76; Yuan Chwang, I, 291.
48. Ibid., p. 76; Yuan Chwang, I, 294.
49. Ibid., 296-297.
50. Life, p. 76.
51. Yuan Chwang, I, 298.
52. Ibid., 299.
53. Yuan Chwang, I, 300.
54. Harṣacarita, chapter III, describes Kanauj as a centre of men and women of all faiths and vocations.
55. Yuan Chwang, I, 314.
56. Giles, Fa-hsien, p. 20.
57. Takakusu, I-tsing's Record, p. 14.
58. Yuan Chwang, I, 301 f.
59. Cunningham, AGI, 345.
60. Yuan Chwang, I, 317-318.
61. Life, pp. 78-79.
62. Yuan Chwang, I, 322 f. Life, pp. 79-80.
63. Ibid., p. 81.
64. Yuan Chwang, I, 329-330.
65. Cunningham, AGI, 357.
66. Yuan Chwang, I, 330-331.
67. On Sammitīya system see Sammitīya-nikāya-śāstra, tr. in Visvabharati Annals, vol. V, 1953.
68. Yuan Chwang, I, 331.
69. AGI, 365.
70. Yuan Chwang I, 332.
71. W. W. Rockhill, Life of Buddha, p. 81; Giles, Fa-hsien, p. 24.
72. Yuan Chwang, I, 333-334; see Hīrānanda Śāstri, 'Excavations at Saṅkisā' in JUPHS, vol. III, 1927, pp. 99 f.
73. Giles, Fa-hsien, p. 29; Beal, Records of the Western World, p. 235.
74. See R. S. Tripathi, History of Kanauj; History and Culture of the Indian People, ed. by R. C. Majumdar and A. D. Pusalkar, vol. IV; and Yuan Chwang I, 345.
75. Ibid. 340; Life, pp. 82-83.
76. Ibid., p. 177; R. K. Mookerji, Men and Thought in Ancient India, ch. V.
77. See Bānsakhera copper plate inscription in D. B. Disalkar, Selections from Sanskrit Inscriptions, p. 35; Harṣacarita, ch. V; V.S. Agrawala, Harṣacarita ek Sāṃskṛtika Adhyayana, p. 113.
78. Harṣacarita, ch. VIII, Eng. tr. by Cowell and Thomas, p. 288; Life, p. 176.
79. Life, p. 83.
80. Yuan Chwang, I, 344.
81. Harṣacarita, ch. II; Agrawala, op. cit., p. 47.
82. Yuan Chwang, I, 343-344; Life, pp. 83, 111, 159.
83. Yuan Chwang, I, 352.
84. Ibid., 343.
85. Life, p. 176.
86. Ibid., pp. 175. f.
87. Yuan Chwang, I, 355; Life, p. 85.
88. Yuan Chwang, I, 359.
89. Life, pp. 86-90.
90. Yuan Chwang, I, 361.

91. K. Chattopādhyāya, 'Religious Suicide at Prayāg in JUPHS, vol. X, pt I, 1937, pp. 65 f.
92. I-tsing, Record, pp. 197-198.
93. Yuan Chwang, I, 361-363; Life, p. 90.
94. See N. N. Ghosh, Early History of Kauśāmbī; B. C. Law, 'Kauśāmbī in Ancient Literature' in MASI, no. 6, 1939.
95. Giles, Fa-hsien, pp. 61-62.
96. Life, p. 91; Yuan Chwang, I, 369.
97. G. R. Sharma, Excavations at Kauśāmbī; Ancient India, no. 9, 1955, pp. 145 f. plate LXIV.
98. Yuan Chwang, I, 365-372.
99. Ibid., I, 375-374; Serie Oriental Roma, no. II, p. 32.
100. See B. C. Law, 'Śrāvastī in Ancient Literature' in MASI, no. 50. 1935.
101. Yuan Chwang, I, 377-401; See ASI Reports, 1907-1908, pp 81 f.
102. Yuan Chwang, II, 2 ff.
103. Northern India According to the Shui-Chgin-Chu, tr. by L. Petech, SOR, II, 1950, pp. 32-35.
104. See W. C. Peppe and V. A. Smith in JRAS, 1898, pp. 573 f.; A. C. L. Carllayle in ASI Reports, vol. XII, p. 83 & vol. XIII, pp. I ff; P.C. Mukherji, Antiquities in the Tarai, ASI Reports, vol. XXVI, 1901.
105. Yuan Chwang, II, 14 ff.
106. Ibid., 14-45; Life, 96-97; ASI Reports, 1904-1905, p. 41; & 1911-1912, pp. 134 ff.; Ancient India, no. 9, p. 143; Bhikṣu Dharmarakṣita, Kuśīnagara kā Itihāsa.
107. See S O R, II, p. 50.
108. Life. p. 98; Yuan Chwang, II, 47.
109. Ibid., see Annual Bibliography of Indian History and Indology, III, p. XII f.
110. Yuan Chwang, II, 48-55; Life, p. 98; V. S. Agrawala, Sārnāth; B. Majumdar, A Guide to Sārnāth; Bhikṣu Dharmarakṣita, Sārnāth kā Itihāsa.
111. Yuan Chwang, II, 59-60; Cunningham, AGI, p. 438.
112. See Havaldar Tripathi, Bauddha Dharma aur Bihar.
113. See Biorgaphy of Dharmasvāmin, Eng. tr. by G. Roerich.
114. See B. M. Barua, Gayā and Buddha-Gayā, vol. I.
115. See B. C. Law, 'Rajagriha in Ancient Literature' in MASI, no. 58, 1938; M. H. Kuraishi and A. Ghosh, Rajgir,
116. See Hīrānanda Śāstri, 'Nālandā and its Epigraphic Material' in MASI, no. 66, 1942; A Ghosh, Nālandā.
117. See R. Sāṃkrtyāyana, Purātattva Nibandhāvāli, ch. III.
118. See Ancient India, no. 9, pp. 146-147; Satyaketu Vidyālaṅkāra, Pāṭaliputra kī Kathā.
119. Extant in Chinese and Tibetan versions, cf. SOR, II, p. 29; tr. into French by E. Lamotte, into Sanskrit by Bhikkhu Pāsādika, and into English by Charles Luk.
120. Yuan Chwang, II, 63-79; Life, pp. 100-101; Hwui Li says that his master obtained a copy of the Bodhisattva-Piṭaka from Śvetapura monastery.
121. Yuan Chwang, II, 81-83.
122. Ibid., II, 86.
123. I-tsing, pp. 7-8.
124. Yuan Chwang, II, 87 f.; Life, pp. 100 f.
125. Yuan Chwang, II, 105-106; Life, p. 103; I-tsing, p. 184; in the Life only 'some tens of priests' but in the Si-yu-ki the number is one thousand.
126. Yuan Chwang, II, 108.
127. Ibid., II, 109
128. Ibid., II, 110-116; Life, pp. 103-105; Shui-Ching-Chu in SOR, II, pp. 38-40.

129. This former king of Ceylon is King Kittisiri Meghavaṇṇa (362-389 A.D.), a contemporary of Samudragupta. On his history see Mahāvaṃsa, XXXVII, 93 ff.; cf. B. C. Law, 'Contemporary Indian and Ceylonese Kings' in JBBRAS, vol. 26, 1950, pp. 88 f.
130. Yuan Chwang, II, 136.
131. Life, p. 112; I-tsing, p. 154; Yuan Chwang, II, 165.
132. Ibid., II, 173; Life, p. 119.
133. Life, p. 127; Yuan Chwang, II, 178.
134. Life, p. 128; Yuan Chwang, II, 181.
135. Life, p. 131; Yuan Chwang, II, 182-182-183.
136. See IHQ, vol. VI, 1930, pp. 55f.
137. History of Bengal, I, p. 413.
138. Yuan Chwang, II 184.
139. Ibid., II, 148; Life, p. 131.
140. Mañjuśrīmūlakalpa, ed by T. Gaṇapati Śāstri, pt. III, p. 631.
141. See Pag Sam Jon Zang, p. 111.
142. I-tsing, p. 9; History of Bengal, I, pp. 413-425; HCIP, IV, pp. 266-272; Visvabharati Annals, VI, pp. 49-89.
143. Yuan Chwang, II, 187; Life, p. 132.
144. Cf. Life, Introduction, pp. XL-XLI; E. Chavannes's French tr. of I-tsing's Memoire on Religiux Eminents etc., p. 128, quoted in History of Bengal, I, pp. 87, 414.
145. History of Bengal, I, pp. 86-88; JASB, vol. X, p. 86.
146. Yuan Chwang, II, 191; Life p. 131.
147. Ibid., 133; Yuan Chwang, II, 190.
148. I-tsing, pp. 154, 211.
149. History of Bengal, I, p. 414; Life, p. XXXVIII.
150. History of Bengal, I, p. 86; Yuan Chwang, II, 109.
151. IHQ, 1947, p. 235; Visvabharati Annals, VI, p. 52.
152. Relevant portions from Schiefner's German tr. of it are translated by R. C. Majumdar in History of Bengal, I, pp. 182 f., and by N. Dutt in HCIP, IV, pp. 266 f.; see now Tārānātha's History of Buddhism, Eng. tr. by Lama Chimpa & A. Chattopadhyaya.
153. History of Bengal, I, pp. 192-195.
154. Ibid., I, pp. 86, 99.
155. Mañjuśrīmūlakalpa, p. 631.
156. Bu-ston, II, p. 156; Tārānātha (Schiefner), p. 204.
157. Ibid., p. 206; Bu-ston, II, p. 157 attributes its construction to Dharmapāla.
158. Tārānātha (Schiefner), p. 217; R. L. Mitra, Buddhist Sanskrit Literature of Nepal, p. 229; Bu-ston, II, p. 156. Prajñāpāramitās, vol. I, ed. by G. Tucci, pp. 563-564.
159. S. C. Goswami, 'Hidden Traces of Buddhism in Assam' in IHQ, vol. III, 1927.
160. Yuan Chwang, II, 186.
161. N. K. Sahu, Buddhism in Orissa, and Foreword to it by N. Dutt; cf. also Binayak Misra, Dynasties of Medieval Orissa.
162. Life, pp. 159 f.; Yuan Chwang, II, 193.
163. On the history and chronology of these Orissan kings, see B. Misra, op. cit.; HCIP, IV, pp. 62-68.
164. B. Misra, Orissa under the Bhauma Kings, p. 28; N. K. Sahu, op. cit., p. 86.
165. R. D. Banerji, History of Orissa; R.L. Mitra, Antiquities of Orissa.
166. Yuan Chwang, II, 196, 198.
167. HCIP, III, pp. 220 f.
168. Yuan Chwang, II, 220.
169. See V. R. R. Dikshitar, 'Buddhism in Āndhradeśa' in B. C. Law Volume, pt. I, pp. 346 ff.
170. Yuan Chwang, II, 209.

171. See K. A. Nīlakānta Śāstrī, 'An Episode in the History of Buddhism in South India' in B. C. Law Volume, pt. I, pp. 35 ff.
172. Yuan Chwang, II, 214.
173. Ibid., 224.
174. A. Aiyyapan and P. R. Srinivasan, Story of Buddhism with special reference to South India, pp. 54-55.
175. HCIP, III, p. 261; Yuan Chwang, II, 226.
176. See Tārānātha (Schiefner), pp. 141, 157; Yuan Chwang, II, 229.
177. See Kāraṇḍavyūha-sūtra; ERE, Art. on 'Avalokiteśvara'.
178. Story of Buddhism, p. 56; Takakusu's note in I-tsing, p. XLVI, quoting 'Religieux Eminents', p. 144.
179. Yuan Chwang , II, 237; Life, p. 146.
180. P. B. Desai, 'Buddhist Antiquities of Karnāṭaka' in Journal of Indian History, vol. XXXII, 1954, p. 87.
181. Yuan Chwang, II, 239.
182. Ibid., II, 241.
183. Ibid., 242; Life, p. 148.
184. Yuan Chwang, II, 242.
185. HCIP, III, chs. VIII, X, V.V. Mirashi, Corpus Inscriptionum Indicarum, vol.IV.
186. Takakusu, Essentials of Buddhist Philosophy, p. 114.
187. D. R. Bhandarkar, A List of the Inscriptions of Northern India in Brahmi etc., Appendix to Epigraphia Indica, vols. 19-23, pp. 3, 221; also Wālā Museum Plates, ed. by D. B. Disalkar, JBBRAS (n.s.), vol. I, pp. 33f.
188. D. R. Bhandarkar, List of the Inscriptions, p. 3; HCIP, III, p. 103.
189. Yuan Chwang, II, 245-246; I-tsing, p. 9.
190. I-tsing, pp. 177, 181.
191. Indian Antiquary, 1877, p. 91; Ibid., 1878, p. 80; A. S. Altekar, Education in Ancient India, p. 126.
192. Yuan Chwang, II,247-248.
193. Indian Antiquary, vol. IV, pp. 106, 175; Ibid., vol. V, p. 206.
194. D. R. Bhandarkar, List of the Inscriptions, p. 185.
195. Ibid., p. 222; see JBBRAS (n.s.), vol. I, pp. 40 f.
196. D. R. Bhandarkar, op. cit., p. 221.
197. Indian Antiquary, vol. III, p. 67; Visvabhārati Annals, vol. VI, p. 37.
198. Shyam Sundar Das, Prācīna Lekha-Maṇi-Mālā, p. 7.
199. Hira Lal, Descriptive List of Inscriptions in Central Provinces, pp. 13, 101-102.
200. Was he the Brāhmanical King Sudhanvan of Ujjainī associated in legends with Kumārila's wars against Buddhism ? see ch. XII, and Śaṃkara-digvijaya with Diṇḍima-ṭīkā, I. 93.
201. Yuan Chwang, II, 250.
202. A. A. Macdonell, History of Sanskrit Literature, p. 305, quoting Pischel's view; see HCIP, III, p. 315.
203. S. Mookerjee, 'Ujjainī in Mṛcchakaṭika' in B. C. Law Volume, pt. I, pp. 414-418.
204. Yuan Chwang, II, 252.
205. H. M. Eliot and John Dowson, History of India as told by its own Historians, vol. I, pp. 147 f; Visvabharati Annals, VI, pp. 30-31.
206. Yuan Chwang, II, 254-257; Life, pp. 152-153.

CHAPTER III

1. Yuan Chwang, I, 147.
2. Ibid., I, 183-84.
3. Ibid., I, 204, 208.
4. Ibid., I, 233, 235.

5. Ibid., I, 238-39.
6. Ibid., I, 250.
7. Ibid., I, 255-56; Cunningham, AGI, 121, 103.
8. Life, 68-69; Yuan Chwang, I, 261 ff.; Rājataraṅgiṇī, III, 355 & IV. 188 ff.; see my article, 'Buddhist Gleanings From the Rājataraṅgiṇī' in Journal of the Oriental Institute, vol. XIV, Dec. 1964.
9. Yuan Chwang, I, 216, 302.
10. See H. Sastri, 'Excavations at Saṅkisā' in JUPHS, III, 1927, pp. 99-118.
11. L. Petech, Northern India According to the Shui-Ching-Chu, pp. 30-31.
12. Life, 81-82; Yuan Chwang, I, 334.
13. Ibid., I, 352, 359.
14. See Ancient India, no. 9, pp. 145-46.
15. See G. R. Sharma, Excavations At Kauśāmbī; Yuan Chwang, I, 369-70.
16 Yuan Chwang, I, 383.
17. 'Buddhist Art—Its Four Bases' in ALB, XX, 1956, pp. 319.
18. Yuan Chwang, I, 384, 393.
19. Ibid, II, 5-6. On the 'Past Buddhas', see my article (in Hindi) in Dharmadūta, vol. 29, 1965.
20. Yuan Chwang, II, 14-15; D. C. Sircar, Inscriptions of Aśoka.
21. Yuan Chwang, II, 20; see Mahāparinibbānasutta, DN, vol. II; Dharmarakṣita, Kuśīnagara kā Itihāsa.
22. Yuan Chwang, II, 28; see A S I R, 1904-1905, pp. 41 f.; Ancient India, no. 9, p. 143.
23. See B. Majumdar, A. Guide to Sārnātha; V. S. Agrawala, Sārnātha; Dharmarakṣita, Sāranātha kā Itihāsa.
24. Yuan Chwang, II, 48.
25. Ancient India, no. 9, p. 143.
26. B. Majumdar, op. cit., p. 67.
27. V. S. Agrawala, op. cit., pp. 23 ff. plate VIII. A 9th century Buddha image in bhūsparśa-mudrā from Sāranātha (Ibid., plate XA) is now preserved in the National Museum, New Delhi.
28. Yuan Chwang, II, 52, 50, 55, 65.
29. Ibid., II, 66; L. Petech, op. cit., 28-30.
30. Nanjio, Catalogue, no. 23 (12) and no. 1005.
31. Yuan Chwang, II, 79.
32. Ibid., II, 91-93.
33. B. M. Barua, Gayā and Buddha-Gayā, vol. II, pp. 37 ff.
34. Yuan Chwang, II, 111-113.
35. Ibid., II, 115; Life, p. 103.
36. See Cunningham, Maha Bodhi or the Great Buddhist Temple at Bodha Gayā, pp. 18 ff.
37. Yuan Chwang, II, 116.
38. Cunnigham, op. cit., p. 18; B. M. Barua, op. cit., fig. 10.
39. Yuan Chwang, II, 121-126.
40. Ibid., II, 136.
41. Barua, op. cit., II, p. 35.
42. Cunningham, op. cit., p. 43.
43. Barua, op. cit., p. 37.
44. Ibid., pp. 56, 70-72.
45. Yuan Chwang, II, 151; see D. N. Sen, Rājgīr and Its Neighbourhood.
46. A Ghosh and M. H. Kuraishi, Rajgir, pp. 13 ff.
47. Life, p. 112.
48. Ibid., pp. 110-112; Yuan Chwang, II, pp. 166 ff.; H. Heras's article in JBORS, vol. XIV, 1928, pp. 1-28.
49. A. Ghosh and M. H. Kuraishi, op. cit., pp. 15-30.

50. H. Śāstri, Nālandā and its Epigraphic Material; H. D. Sankalia, The University of Nalanda.
51. Life, pp. 111-112.
52. MASI, no. 66, pp. 79, 'Nālandā hasatīva sarvanagarīḥ śubhrā' bhragaurasphuraccaityāṃśu prakarīstadāgamakalāvikhyātavidvajjanāḥ yasyāmbudharāvalehi śikharaśreṇīvihārā'vali mālevordhvavirājinī viracitā dhātrā, manojñā bhuvaḥ nānāratna-mayūkhajālakhacitaprāsādadevālayā sadvidyādhara saṃgha raṃya vasatir dhatte sumerośśriyam.'
53. Yuan Chwang, II, 176.
54. Ibid., 184.
55. History of Bengal, vol. I, p. 489.
56. See N. N. Law, 'Some Images and Traces of Mahāyāna Buddhism in Chittagong in IHQ VIII, pp. 332-341.
57. Yuan Chwang, II, 187.
58. ASIR, 1927-1928, p. 105.
59. Ibid., 1908-1909, p. 158.
60. Epigraphia Indica, vol. XXI, pp. 97, 101. The inscription of Vimalaśrīmitra refers to it as "a singular feast to the eyes of the world".
61. History of Bengal, I, pp. 490-491.
62. ASIR, 1927-1928, p. 106; see, however, the dimensions of the Nālandā Mahāvihāra given above.
63. N. K. Bhaṭṭasāli, Iconography of Buddhist and Brahmanical Sculptures in the Dacca Museum, pt. I; History of Bengal, vol. I, chapters on art and iconography; B. Bhattacharyya, The Indian Buddhist Iconography; Stella Kramrisch, The Pāla and Sena Sculpture.
64. History of Bengal, I, pp. 535 ff.; A. K. Gordon, Iconography of Tibetan Lamaism, pp. 12 ff.
65. J. Ph. Vogel, Buddhist Art in India, Ceylon and Java, Eng. tr. by Barnouw, p. 168.
66. See ch. X; A. K. Coomaraswamy, The Dance of Śiva, chapter on Indian Images with many arms.
67. J. Ph. Vogel, op. cit., p. 68.
68. Ibid., p. 70.
69. See IHQ, vol. IV, pp. 734.
70. JBORS, 1929, pp. 65-69
71. MASI, no. 44, p. 11.
72. N. K. Sahu, Buddhism in Orissa, ch. XI, pp. 187 ff.
73. See A. Aiyyappan and P. R. Srinivasan, The Story of Buddhism with Special Reference to South India, plates VI-X.
74. See The Way of the Buddha, pp. 291, 295, 305, 313; G. Yazdani, 'Wall Paintings of Ajanṭā' in JBORS, vol. XXVI, 1941; Stella Kramrisch. The Art of India Through the Ages, A Survey of Paintings in the Deccan.
75. Stella Kramrisch, The Art of India Througn the Ages, plates 96-97.
76. Ibid., p. 207.
77. Hira Lal, Descriptive List of Inscriptions in the Central Provinces and Berar, p. 101.
78. The Way of the Buddha, p. 313, plate 78.
79. Ibid., p. 314, plate 89.
80. B. Bhattacharyya, 'What a Deity Represents ?' in IHQ, IX, 1933; 'Buddhist Worship and Idolatry' in Buddhistic Studies, ed. by B. C. Law.
81. Sādhanamālā, I, pp. 47, 64; Sādhanamālā, II, Introduction, pp. CXXII ff.
82. Tattva-saṃgraha (GOS), p. 916; H. Zimmer, Philosophies of India, p. 558.
83. Sādhanamālā, I, p. 224; G. Tucci, Maṇḍala, pp. 33-34.
84 Advayavajra-saṃgraha, p. 50.
85. Ibid., p. 51; B. Bhattacharyya, Indian Buddhist Iconography, pp. 24-25.
86. Guhyasamāja-tantra (GOS), pp. 3-9.
87. G. Tucci, Maṇḍala, p. 50.

88. Sādhanamālā, II, pp. 568-69; A. K. Gordon, op. cit., pp 51-53.
89. B. Bhattacharyya, Buddhist Iconography, pp. 344 ff.; on the controversy of Hindu Gods vs. Buddhist Gods, see Sādhanamālā, II, Introduction, pp. CXXX ff.. and A.K. Coomaraswamy in JAOS, vol. 46, p. 287.
90. R. D. Banerji, Eastern India School of Medieval Sculpture, pp. 3f.; R. P. Chanda, Medieval Indian Sculpture in the British Museum, pp. 24 f.; Stella Kramrisch, Indian Sculpture, p. 183; H. Sāstrī in MASI, no. 66, p. 117; JUPHS, vol. I, pp. 62-75.
91. A. Aiyyapan and P. R. Srinivasan, op. cit., pp. 74-75, plate VII.
92. See N. K. Bhaṭṭasāli, op. cit., pt. I; B. Bhattacharyya, Buddhist Iconography, chs. VII, IX-X; History of Bengal, vol. I, pp. 466 f.; A. K. Gordon, op. cit., pp. 71 f.
93. History of Bengal, I, plate XI, 54; B. Bhattacharyya, op. cit., plate VII.
94. Vide Hevajra-tantra, I, plate facing p. 110; Sādhanamālā, II, pp. 468 ff.
95. Ibid., Introduction, pp, CLIX-CLX, plate VIII.
96. Ibid., pp. 501-502.
97. Kāraṇḍavyūha, pp. 262-263.
98. B. Bhattacharyya, Buddhist Iconography, figs. 175, 179, 182, 192, 226 and Appendix on 108 forms of Avalokita; N.K Sahu, op. cit., figs. 77, 79; A. K. Coomaraswamy, The Dance of Siva, ch. on Indian Images with many Arms' pp. 79, Heimo Rau, 'Multiple Arms in Indian God-Images' in ALB, vol. XXXIX, 1975, pp. 275 ff.

CHAPTER IV

1. The Cultural Heritage of India, vol.. I, p. 587; Eliot, Hinduism and Buddhism, vol. II, pp. 175, 211; ERE, Art. on 'Monasticism'.
2. Giles, Fa-hsien, pp. 21-22.
3. Yuan Chwang, II, 165, 'Mango-park'; Life, p. 110, 'the garden of the lord (shreṣṭin) Āmra (or Amara)'.
4. Yuan Chwang, loc. cit., 'ten koṭis of gold coins'; Life, loc. cit., 'ten lacs of gold pieces'.
5. Yuan Chwang, II, 164-65.
6. Life, pp. 105-6.
7. Ibid., pp. 109-10.
8. H. Heras, 'The Royal Patrons of the University of Nālandā in JBORS, XIV, 1928.
9. Life, pp. 112-13.
10. Takakusu, I-tsing, p. 65; R. K. Mookerjee, Ancient India Education, chs. XII-XV.
11. Takakusu, I-tsing, p. 144.
12. Ibid., pp. 192-94. He reports that the non-Buddhist texts belonging to a deceased monk were to be sold and the money acquired thereof was also distributed among the resident monks.
13. Ibid., ch. 36.
14. Life, pp. 153-54.
15. Yuan Chwang II, 115.
16. MASI, no. 66, pp. 26 ff.
17. Yuan Chwang, II, 164-65.
18. Life, pp. 158-59.
19. Ibid., p. 154.
20. Ibid., p. 180.
21. Ibid., pp. 184-87.
22. Yuan Chwang, I, 343-44.
23. Tārānātha (Schiefner), p. 204.
24. H. Sastri in MASI, no. 66, p. 74.
25. Ibid.; Mañjuśrīmūlakalpa (TSS), p. 631.

26. Tārānātha (Schiefner), p 207.
27. S. Beal's Summary of I-tsing's 'Memoire' in Life, pp. XL-XLI; History of Bengal, I, pp. 87, 414.
28. JBORS, pp. 419-27; B. Misra, Orissa under the Bhauma Kings, p. 28.
29. Epigraphia Indica, XV, p. 1.
30. Ibid., XXVI, pp. 147 ff.
31. S. Levi in Epigraphia Indica, XV, pp. 363-364; HCIP, IV, pp. 65, 80.
32. See Talcher plate of Śivakaradeva III in B. Misra, op. cit., pp. 40 ff.
33. Epigraphia Indica, XIX, pp. 363-64.
34. Rājataraṅgiṇī, III, verses 2, 4, 9-14, 27, 57, 380-81, 464, 476.
35. Rājataraṅgiṇī, IV, verses 3, 188, 201-203, 211, 215-216, 484, 507-508.
36. D. R. Bhandarkar's List of Northern Indian Inscriptions, pp. 182, 221; Life p. 148; Yuan Chwang, II, 242.
37. Life, pp. 145-150. It is wonderful that this glorious king does not find mention in K. M. Munshi's Glory that was Gūrjaradeśa. One recalls how the Purāṇic chroniclers ignored Emperor Aśoka.
38. Epigraphia Indica., XX, pp. 43 ff.; H. Śāstrī, 'Nālandā and Its Epigraphic material' in MASI, no. 66; on the controversy about the date of this epigraph see IHQ, vol. VII, p. 664; vol. VIII, pp. 288 ff., 615 ff.
39. MASI, no. 66, pp. 81-82.
40. Ibid., p. 83.
41. See Gokuldas De, Democracy in Early Buddhist Saṃgha.
42. Indian Antiquary, vol. XVIII, p. 307; Altekar, Education in Ancient India, p. 76.
43. Life, pp. 169-171.
44. Yuan Chwang, I, 344. Cf. Asoka's Minor Pillar Edict No. 1.
45. Mṛcchakaṭika, Act X.
46. Tārānātha (Schiefner), op. cit., p. 218.
47. Life, p. 69.
48. Ibid.
49. I-tsing, pp. 63-64.
50. Ibid., p. 184.
51. Yuan Chwang, II, 109, 165; Life, pp. 106, 158.
52. I-tsing, op. cit., p. 184.
53. Ibid.; Harṣacarita, VIII; R. N. Salatore, 'Divākaramitra, His date and Monastery' in Proceedings of Indian in History Congress, Annamalainagar, p. 60.
54. Life, pp. 160, 169-170.
55. Ibid., pp. XXXVII, 106, 109; I-tsing, pp. 62, 145, 153-154.
56. Ibid., pp. 87, 96, 190, 193.
57. MASI, no. 66, pp. 36, 87 ff.; see I-tsing, pp. 63, 148 on Assembly's functions.
58. Yuan Chwang, I, 352.
59. Life, p. 161.
60. I-tsing, pp. 36, 47
61. Ibid., pp. 61, 64.
62. Ibid., pp. 144-145.
63. I-tsing, pp. 56-57.
64. Four 'refuges' are concerning clothes, food, shelter, and medicine.
65. Four 'proper actions' are not returning slander for slander, not returning anger for anger, not meting insult with insult, not returning blow for blow.
66. Thirteen dhutāṅgas are enumerated below in chapter V; see Dharmasaṃgraha, 63, where only 12 are listed.
67. Thirteen 'necessaries' are—1. saṃghāṭi, 2. uttarāsaṅga, 3. antaravāsa, 4. nisīdana, 5. nivāsana, 6. pratinivāsana, 7. saṅkakṣikā, 8. pratisaṅkakṣikā, 9. kāyaproñchana, 10. mukhaproñchana, 11. keśapratigraha, 12. kandu-

pratichadama, and 13. bhaiṣajyapariṣkāra-cīvara. See Mahāvagga, chs. VI, VIII; I-tsing, pp. 54-57.

68. Ibid., pp. 64, 80.
69. Ibid., p. 82.
70. Ibid., pp. 30, 64.
71. Ibid., p. 191.
72. Ibid., pp. 103-104.
73. Ibid., p. 112.
74. Ibid., p. 115.
75. Ibid., p. 87.
76. Ibid., pp. 95 f.
77. Cf. the Daśabhūmikasūtra; Har Dayal, Bodhisattva Doctrine, ch. VI.
78. I-tsing, pp. 96-104.
79. Ibid., p. 185.
80. See DN, II, pp. 108-10.
81. I-tsing, pp. 29-30.
82. The five pariṣads of the 'homeless ones' are those of bhikṣus, bhikṣuṇīs, śikaṣāmāṇas, śrāmaṇeras, and śrāmanerīs.
83. I-tsing, pp. 85-86; Yuan Chwang, I, 144.
84. I-tsing, pp 86-87.
85. Yuan Chwang, I, 162-163.
86. I-tsing, p. 84.
87. See J. Przyluski, 'Uposatha, a Babylonian Element in Indian Civilization' in IHQ, vol. XII, 1936. This view lacks sound evidence.
88. I-tsing, pp. 35 f.
89. See R. K. Mookerjee, 'A Note on the History of Tea' in JUPHS, XII, 1935.
90. I-tsing, pp. 137-138.
91. Ibid., chapters V and VIII are devoted to the discussion of toothwood. Tooth-ache, says he, was a rare disease in India.
92. I-tsing, pp. 6-7, 58-67; Yuan Chwang, I, 148. Six 'requisites' of a monk are—saṃghāṭi, uttarāsaṅga, antaravāsa, pātra, nisīdana and pariśrāvaṇa; three robes are—lower one, upper one, and the cloak.
93. I-tsing, pp. 6-7.
94. Ibid., pp. 142-145.
95. Ibid., p. 147.
96. Suttanipāta, 1146.
97. See Yuan Chwang's description of Nālandā; I-tsing, pp. 37-38.
98. Fa-hsien (tr. Giles), pp. 9, 10, 23, 61, 74; Yuan Chwang, I, 238, 343; II, pp. 105, 107, 125, 175, 215, 219 etc; I-tsing, pp. 162, 136, 169, 196, 213; BCA, X.
99. I-tsing, pp. 14-15, and ch. 34.
100. I-tsing, ch. 31; Yuan Chwang, II, 115.
101. Harṣacarita, ch. II, kamaṇḍalu jala śucisaya caraṇeṣu caitya praṇati pareṣu pārāśariṣu.
102. I-tsing devotes a whole chapter (ch. 30) to discuss pradakṣiṇā.
103. I-tsing, ch. 31-32.
104. Life, pp. 191-192; MASI, no. 66, p. 82.
105. Fa-hsien, p. 20.
106. Life, p. 160.
107. Yuan Chwang, I, 173.
108. I-tsing, p. 116.
109. Ibid., pp. 111-112.
110. Yuan Chwang, I, 174.
111. Ibid., p. 175.
112. I-tsing, pp. 124-125; see also MASI, no. 66, p. 82.
113. Life, pp. 69 70.
114. I-tsing, pp. 63-64.
115. Ibid., p. 106; Yuan Chwang, II, 165.

116. Life, p. 112.
117. MASI, no 66, pp. 81, 83.
118. I-tsing, p. 65.
119. Ibid., p. 50.
120. BCA, ch. VIII, verses 24-29 (abridged).
121. I-tsing, p. 61.
122. Ibid.
123. Ibid., pp. 63-64.
124. Life, pp. 153-154.
125. Rājataraṅgiṇī, IV, 210; L. M Joshi, 'Buddhist Gleanings From the Rājataraṅgiṇī, in Journal of the Oriental Institute, vol. XIV, December, 1964.
126. Harṣacarita, ch. VIII.
127. I-tsing, p. 183.
128. S. Mookerjee, 'Ujjainī in Mṛcchakaṭika' in B. C. Law Volume, pt. I, pp. 416-4x7.
129. I-tsing, p. 198.
130. Yuan Chwang, I, 175.
131. See K. Chaṭṭopādhyāya in JUPHS, vol. X, pt. I, 1937.
132. Yuan Chwang, I, 364.
133. See Maitrībala-jātaka in Āryaśūra's Jātakamālā, pp. 43 ff.
134. I-tsing, pp. 196-197.

CHAPTER V

1. S. Radhakrishnan, Indian Philosophy, I, pp. 589-690, remarks that "the Hīnayāna ignored the groping of the spirit of man after something higher, and wronged the spiritual side of man". This observation is too far-fetched and by no means convincing. I-tsing found both Hīnayāna and Mahāyāna in perfect accord with Buddha's teaching. I-tsing's Record, p. 15.
2. Yuan Chwang, II, 191.
3. I-tsing, pp. 50, 54, 56-57, 66, 166.
4. C.A.F. Rhys Davids, 'Asceticism' in ERE, vol. II, p. 69.
5. The thirteen ascetic practices or dhūtaguṇas are (1) pāṃsukulika or having a garment made of rags, (2) traicīvarika or keeping only three robes at a time, (3) paiṇḍapātika or begging alms, (4) aikāsanika or rule of eating at one sitting, (5) sapadānacārika or begging from door to door, (6) pattapiṇḍika or rule of eating from one bowel only, (7) khalupaścād-bhaktika or not receiving food twice, (8) āraṇyaka or rule of living in the woods, (9) vṛkṣamūlika or residing at the foot of a tree, (10) abhyavakāsika or living in an unsheltered place, (11) śmāśānika or living in or near a cemetery, (12) yathāsanstarika or spreading a night-couch where one happens to be, and, (13) naiṣadyika or being in a sitting posture while sleeping. cf. Dharma-saṃgraha, 63, where only twelve are listed.
6. E.g. Cullavagga, pp. 196-197; Mahāvagga, p. 55; Suttanipāta, Uragasutta, Khaggavisāṇasutta, etc; Dhammapada, verses, 305-330, 353, 404; MN, I, pp. 38 f. II, pp. 231 f.; for modern discussions on this subject see Kern, Manual, pp. 75-76; S. Beal, Catena, pp. 256 f.; S. Hardy, Eastern Monachism, pp. 9, 73 f.; S. Dutt, Early Buddhist Monachism, pp. 92 f.; N. Dutt, EMB, I, 156-158.
7. See Dhammapada, Arahatavagga; ERE, Art. 'Arhat'.
8. DN, II, p. 95—sīlam samādhi paññā ca vimutti ca anuttrarā; on this triple path are based the Path of Freedom (Vimuttimagga) and the Path of Purity (Visuddhimagga); on its relative antiquity with respect to the eightfold path see G. C. Pande, Origins of Buddhism, ch. XIII.
9. See Suttanipāta, e.g. Dhammikasutta; Dhammapada, Brāhmaṇa-vagga; E. Conze, Buddhist Scriptures pt. II, ch. I, 'Morality'; Tachibana, The Ethics of Buddhism; N. Dutt, EMB, I, ch. VII.

10. DN, I, pp 5-10; Dharma-saṃgraha, 106.
11. I-tsing, p. 14.
12. On dhyāna and samādhi see Conze, Buddhist Meditation, Anesaki and Takakusu in ERE, vol. IV, pp. 702 f.; Visuddhimagga, ch. III and XI; Nyanaponika Thera, The Heart of Buddhist Meditation.
13. AN, I, pp. 150-151; DN, I, pp. 65-67; Ibid., III, p. 173; Dharma-saṃgraha 72 and 101; Yogasūtra of Patañjali; Samādhipāda, 17; Mahābhārata, Śāntiparvan, 195. 1.
14. DN, I, p. 73; AN, I, p. 14; KN, I, p. 218; MN, II, p. 235; Milindapañha, p. 230; Dhammasaṃgaṇī, pp. 20-21; Visuddhimagga, ch. XVII.
15. KN, I, p. 280; Dharma-saṃgraha, 16.
16. Mahāvagga, p. 23; Lalitavistara, p. 301.
17. Kāraṇḍavyūhasūtra, pp. 266 f.
18. ŚS, ed. by Bendall, p. 167; ed. by Vaidya, p. 93; Kathāvatthu, p. 535 where "methuno dhammopaṭisevitabbo" is alluded to and criticized.
19. ŚS, ed. by Vaidya, pp. 56, 148, 174.
20. Dharma-saṃgraha, 19—dāna, priyavacana, arthacaryā, and samānārthatā.
21. Ancient sources: Mahāparinibbānasutta, DN, II, p. 95; Kern, op. cit., pp. 66-67; N. Dutt, EMB, I, ch. XII; G. C. Pande, Origins of Buddhism, ch. XIII; E. J. Thomas, Life of Buddha, pp. 183ff; Brewester, Life of Gotama the Buddha, pp. 197 f.; Har Dayal, Boddhisattva Doctrine, ch. IV,
22. For satipaṭṭhānas see DN, II, p. 217; Ibid., III, p. 173; Dharma-samgraha, 44; the four 'fields' (*upasthānas*) of 'mindfulness' (*smṛti*) are—kāya, vedanā, citta and dharma; see The Way of Mindfulness.
23. For samyakprahāṇas see Dharma-saṃgraha, 45.
24. For ṛddhipādas, see Dharma-saṃgraha, 46; DN, III, p. 73.
25. For indriyas, see Dharma-saṃgraha, 47; MN, II, p. 169.
26. For balas, see Dharma-saṃgraha, 48; Lalitavistara, p. 231; Har Dayal op. cit., p. 144.
27. I-tsing, p. 196; DN, III, p. 82; AN, IV, p. 270; Dharma-saṃgraha, 49.
28. Mahāvagga, p. 13; DN, I, p. 133; Ibid., II, p. 94; MN, I, pp. 22, 65 f; AN, I, p. 201; Lalitavistara, p. 303; Dharma-saṃgraha, 50.
29. śraddhā hi paramaṃ yānaṃ, Daśadharmasūtra quoted in the ŚS, ed. by Bendall, p. 5; on faith in Early Buddhism see L. M. Joshi, "True Buddhsim" in The Maha Bodhi, vol. 74, nos. 1-2, 1966.
30. Suttanipāta, KN, I p. 440.
31. Ibid., I, p. 296—saddhīdha vittaṃ purisassa seṭṭhaṃ...saddhāya tarati ogham.
32. Dhammapada, vv. 195-196.
33. Mahāparinibbānasutta, DN, II, pp. 126-128.
34. Saddharmapuṇḍarīkasūtra, II. 94; XV. 21, etc.
35. DN, III, p. 60; F. L. Woodward, Some Sayings of the Buddha, pp. 317-318.
36. Śāntideva's ŚS-kārikās, ed. and tr. by L. M. Joshi, p. 9 —
yadā mama pareṣāṃ ca bhayaṃ duḥkham ca na priyaṃ /
tadātmanaḥ ko viśeṣo yattaṃ rakṣāmi netaraṃ //
Contrast Dhammapada, verse 166 and Manu-smṛti, VII 217.
37. Mahāvagga, p. 23; Lalitavistara, p. 301; Saddharmapuṇḍarīka, ch. I-III; Aṣṭasāhasrikā, ch. I.
38. Ibid., Eng. tr. by Conze, p. V.
39. Ibid., pp. 9-10 (slightly changed rendering).
40. Ratnagotravibhāga in Buddhist Texts Through the Ages, ed. and tr. by E. Conze and others, p. 189; cf. Kathāvatthu, p 523—sabbā disā Buddhā tiṭṭhanti ti ? Hevajra-tantra, pt. I, tr. by D. L. Snellgrove, p. 107; BCA, VI. 122.
41. See Aṣṭasāhasrikā, Eng. tr., p. 84; Saddharmapuṇḍarīka, chs. II-III.
42. BCAP, p 200—tatra bodhiḥ sattvam abhiprāyo'syeti bodhisattvaḥ.

43. D. T. Suzuki, Outlines of Mahāyāna Buddhism, p. 292; Clarence H. Hamilton, Buddhism : A Religion of Infinite Compassion.

44. ye sadā pāramitāsu caranti te pratipannā iho mahāyāne, Ratnolkādhāraṇī quoted in ŚS, ed. by Vaidya, p. 6; see Aṣṭasāhasrikā, p. 112; Sekoddeśaṭīkā, pp. 3-4; Advayavajra-saṃgraha, p. 14.

45. Dharma-saṃgraha, 17-18; on the pāramitās see Aṣṭasāhasrikā, pp. 40-41 and Āloka, p. 282; standard texts are the Daśabhūmikāsūtra; the BCA, the ŚS, and the Bodhicittotpādasūtra of Vasubandhu; a modern work on the subject is Har Dayal's Bodhisattva Doctrine, ch. V; for a historical survey of the terms 'pāramitā' and 'prajñāpāramitā' see Bhūmikā to Vajracchedikā, ed. by L. M. Joshi.

46. BCAP, p. 186—avidyā nirodhāt saṃskārā nirudhyante.

47. BCA, IX. 56—śūnyatā duḥkha śamanī tataḥ kiṃ jāyate bhayaṃ.

48. BCAP, p. 111. In critical school this becomes 'unique particular' or 'thing-in-itself' (svalakṣana).

49 TS, 3338; Eng. tr., II, p. 1474.

50. BCA, IX. 55—kleśajñeyāvṛtiḥ pratipakṣo hi śūnyatā; cf. also BCAP, p 211; TSP, II, p. 870.

51. TSP, II, p. 870

52. Dhammapada, vv, 160, 380; cf. Bhagavadgītā VI. 5.

53. MS, XVIII; Dvādaśamukhaśāstra, pp. 185 f; CŚ, X; Aṣṭasāhasrikā, Eng. tr., pp. 1-4; Nairātmyaparipṛcchāsūtra; TS, ch. VII and TSP.

54. TSP, II,pp. 870-857; Eng. tr., II. pp. 1474-1481; S. Mookerjee, Universal Flux, pp. 260-265.

55. Aṣṭasāhasrikā, Eng. tr., p. 84.

56. BCAP, p 171—sarvadharmāṇāṃ niḥsvabhāvatā, śūnyatā, tathatā, bhūtakoṭiḥ dharmadhāturityādi paryāyāḥ.

57. Aṣṭasāhasrikā, p. 179—sarvakalpavikalpaprahīṇo hi tathāgatah.

58. Prajñāpāramitā-piṇḍārtha, ed. in BST, p. 263—prajñāpāramitā jñānaṃ advayam sā tathāgataḥ; for other similar passages see Vajracchedikāprajñāpāramitā with Asaṅga's commentary called Triśatikā-kārikā-saptati, ed. and tr. into Hindi by L. M. Joshi, Bhūmikā; Conze (tr) Selected Sayings from the Perfection of Wisdom.

59. BCA, VI. 122; and BCAP, p. 113.

60. Cf. Thomas A. Kempis, The Imitation of Christ, p. 43—"whoever is moved by true and perfect love is never self-seeking, but desires only that God's glory may be served in all things."

61. See E. A. Burtt in Philosophy East and West, vol. V, 1955, p. 202; E. Conze, Buddhist Thought, p. 262.

62. Śāntideva's Śikṣāsamuccaya-kārikās, ed. and tr. into English by L. M. Joshi.

63. BCA, I. 4—kṣaṇasaṃpad iyaṃ sudurlabhā pratilabdhā puruṣārthasādhanī; ŚS, (BST) p. 6—durlabha satttva pṛthagjanakāyā; cf. Vivekacūḍāmaṇi, verse 2.

64. BCA, V. 64-68; cf. The Imitation of Christ, p. 57—"If you have ever seen any one die, remember that you, too, must travel the same road."

65. BCA, V. 66-67, 70; The Imitation of Christ, ch. on 'A Meditation on Death', pp. 56 f.; Visuddhimagga, ch. VIII, and Theragāthā, KN, II. pp. 376 f.

66. BCA, I. 5-14; ŚS (BST) pp. 6-9; Gaṇḍavyūhasūtra, p. 396—bodhicittaṃ hi kulaputra bījabhūtam sarva buddha dharmāṇāṃ; this important sentence is quoted in Bhāvanākrama, p. 192; Ālokavyākhyā p. 283; BCA, p. 11

67. BCA, 1. 15.

68. BCA, I. 16-17; see L. M. Joshi, ' A Survey of the Conception of the Bodhicitta' in Journal of Religious Studies, vol. III, 1971.

69. BCA, IV-12; ŚS. (BST), p. 41.

70. Ibid., p. 8.

71. BCA, I. 35.

72. Ibid., I. 29-30; see Gaṇḍavyūhasūtra, 54.

73. ŚS (BST), pp. 4-5; cf. Suttanipāta in KN, I, pp. 296, 440; Dhamma pada, verses 195-196; Bhagavadgītā, IV. 39; II. 66; Aṣṭasāhasrikā, Eng. tr., p. 63; ŚS -kārikā, 18.
74. ŚS (BST) p. 6.
75. ŚS-kārikā, 11.
76. BCA, I. 1 ; ŚS, ch. XVIII.
77. BCA, II. 1-10 : ŚS (BST), p. 94.
78. BCA, II. 11-19; I-tsing's Record, ch. XXXI.
79. The Mahāyāna Saṃgha consists of the Bodhisattvas.
80. Śāntideva's favourite deity is Mañjuśrī, see BCA, X. 58.
81. ŚS-kārikā, 20.
82. ŚS, ch. I; I-tsing, p. 167.
83. ŚS (BST), p. 12—yatkiñcinmaitreya subhāṣitaṃ sarvaṃ tadbuddhabhāṣitam. This seems to echo the Mahāyāna myth that Maitreya revealed the secret scriptures.
84. Ibid.; BCA, V. 105-106 recommend the study of the ŚS and other Sūtras.
85. BCAP, p. 80; ŚS-kārikā, 19.
86. ŚS (BST), p. 106.
87. ŚS, ch. XIX kārikā 27; cf. Bhāvanākrama, p. 157 where compassion, thought of Bodhi and realization are said to be the essentials of the Mahāyāna.
88. Medicine includes spells, and charms besides all the other pathological devices for treating the diseases, see specimen in ŚS (BST), pp. 140 f.
89. TS, 338 and TSP, p. 870.
90. BCA, III. 1-23; cf. the Imitation of Christ, p. 45.
91. BCA, III. 24-33; Bodhicittotpāda, ch. I-III, pp. 207-216; The Imitation of Christ, bk. IV, ch. 17, 'Eager Desire to receive Christ.'
92. BCA, IV. 1-48 (abridged).
93. See Kāraṇḍavyūha, p. 268.
94. ŚS, ch. I, kārikās 5-6.
95. Ibid., ch. II, pp. 23-27. On spiritual friend (kalyāṇamitra) see Gaṇḍavyūhasūtra, pp. 36 f.
96. BCA, V. 10; ŚS (BST), p. 22, quotation from the Ratnameghasūtra-dānaṃ hi bodhisattvasya bodhiḥ.
97. ŚS, kārikā 1; BCA, VIII. 95-96.
98. BCA, IX. 76; BCAP, p. 228, quotation from the Dharmasaṃgītisūtra.
99. So by Bodhisattva Jyotirmāṇavaka, ŚS (BST), p. 93; Kathāvatthu, XXIII. 219. 1, p. 535 alludes to those fore-runners of Mahāyānism who held : 'ekādhippāyena methuno dhammo paṭisevitabbo', and 'paradāro gantabbo'. We know that they were Vetullas or Vaipulyakas.
100. ŚS, kārikā 4; BCA, V. 70, 84-85; VI. 120; see I-tsing, p. 118, where he expresses his disapproval of extreme forms of liberality.
101. BCA, I. 13.
102. ŚS (BST), pp. 91-92.
103. ŚS, ch. II, kārikās 5-6; BCA, V. 85.
104. ŚS, ch. III, kārikā 7.
105. ŚS pp. 45-55.
106. Ibid., pp. 59-66.
107. Ibid , (BB), pp. 66-73.
108. Ibid., pp. 73-83.
109. BCA, V. 93; see I-tsing, pp. 63-64.
110. Dhammapada, verses 1-2; cf. Bhagavadgītā, VI. 36.
111. BCA, V. 1-8.
112. Ibid., V. 11; cf. Bhagavadgītā, II. 62-63, V. 7.
113. BCA, V. 12-13.
114. Ibid., V. 14-15, 18-23.
115. Ibid., V. 24; ŚS (BB), pp. 116-117.

116. Ibid., kārikās 8-10; BCA, V. 25-31.
117. Dhammapada, verses 1-2; SN, I, p. 37.
118. BCA, V. 35-51 (abridged); ŚS, ch. VI and kārikās 8-13.
119. BCA, V. 52-54.
120. Ibid., V.57-58; cf. Bhagavadgītā, II, 58—"The man of stilled mind withdraws his senses from all objects just as a tortoise draws in its limbs from every side."
121. BCA, V. 74-78; cf. ŚS (BB), pp. 147 f.
122. BCA, V. 79-83; cf. ŚS (BST), p. 6; SS (BB), pp. 125-126.
123. See Saddharmapuṇḍarīkasūtra, ch. III; Bhagavadgītā, XVIII. 67, etc.
124. BCA, V. 86-93; cf. ŚS (BB), pp. 78-83.
125. BCA, V. 97-109.
126. Cf. Dhammapada, verse 184—khantī paramaṃ tapo titikkhā.
127. BCA, VI. 1-2; ŚS, ch. 9.
128. BCA, VI. 3-6.
129. ŚS (BST), p. 100, quotation from the Dharmasaṃgītisūtra; see also Dharma-saṃgraha, 107. The second type of forbearance, dharmanidhyāna-kṣānti, is further sub-divided into three—(i) ghoṣānuga-dharmakṣānti (ii) anulomiki°, and (iii) anutpattika°.
130. Poussin in ERE, vol. II, p. 751; see N. Dutt, Aspects, pp. 40,94, 273; for an explanation of anutpattika dharmakṣānti see ŚS, ed. by Bendall, p. 212 and note 3.
131. BCA, VI. 9.
132. BCA, VI. 12-14; ŚS (BB), p. 180.
133. BCA, VI. 16-21; cf. The Imitation of Christ, p. 38—"It is good for us to encounter troubles and adversities from time to time, for trouble often compels a man to search his own heart."
134. BCA, VI. 34-45; Bhagavadgītā, II. 62-63, III. 37; The Imitation of Christ, pp. 33-34—"True peace of heart can be found only by resisting the passions, not by yielding to them."
135. BCA, VI. 41-49, ERE, vol. II, loc. cit.
136. BCA, VI. 74-76.
137. Ibid., VI. 83; cf. Bhagavadgītā, V. 7.
138. BCA, VI. 90-94. Ibid., VI. 99-100—"Indeed, those who oppose my praise do protect me from following into the hell; I, who am desirous of liberation, can have no hatred with them."
139. BCA, VI. 112-125.
140. Ibid., VI. 126-127; cf. Bhagavadgītā, X. 39.
141. BCA, VI. 128-134.
142. Ibid., VII. I; ŚS (BST), p. 105.
143. BCA, VII. 2.
144. Ibid., VII, 3-21; see ŚS, ch. XVI (BB, pp. 273f) where ten ways in which a Bodhisattva displays energy are enumerated.
145. BCA, VII. 31-60; BCAP, pp. 124-131; cf. ERE, vol. II, p. 752.
146. BCA, VII. 63-75; BCAP, pp. 131-145; ŚS, chs. X and XVI, study of the Buddhavacana and avoiding the study of the material sciences are among the means of increasing energy.
147. BCA, VIII. 2-4.
148. See DN, Satipaṭṭhānasutta; Dharma-saṃgraha, 44.
149. BCA, IX; ŚS (BST), pp. 112-130.
150. Cf. The Imitation of Christ, p. 29—"If you desire to know or learn anything to your advantage then take delight in being unknown and unregarded."
151. BCA, VIII. 4-24; cf. Wordsworth's 'Lucy Poems', but closer is T. W. Emerson's 'Good-bye'—
"Good-bye, proud world I'm going home,
Thou art not my friend and I'm not thine."
152. BCA, VIII. 26.
153. Ibid., VIII 27-29; cf. The Imitation of Christ, bk. I, ch. 20—

"Whoever is resolved to live an inward and spiritual life must, with Jesus, withdraw from the crowd."

154. BCA, VIII. 40-43; many more verses are devoted to the analysis of 'love' (kāma), and the poet comes to the conclusion that the living beings are no better than the skeletons heaped in the cemetery. The 23rd ch. of bk. I of The Imitation of Christ, entitled 'A Meditation on Death' and Buddhagoṣa's 'Meditation on Death' (Visuddhimagga), are perhaps the nearest parallels.

155. ERE, vol. II, p. 752.

156. BCA, VIII. 90-103; ŚS, kārikā I; ERE, vol. II, p. 753. For more cogent arguments and systematic analysis of 'not-self' theory see Candrakīrti, CŚV, pp. 69 f.; Madhyamakaśāstra, ch. XVIII; TS, ch. VII-VIII.

157. BCA, VIII. 104-109.

158. Ibid., BCA, VIII, 111-112, 136, 140, 170.

159. Ibid., VIII. 171-173; Bhagavadgītā, VI. 4-5.

160. BCA, IX. 1; cf. Bhagavadgītā, IV. 33-34.

161. Nyāyabindu, I. 1; cf. Bhagavadgītā, IV. 39.

162. Prajñāpāramitā-piṇḍārtha, opening line, prajñāpāramitā jñānaṃ advayam sā tathāgataḥ.

163. BCA, IX. 54-56.

164. ŚS, ch. XIX.

165. BCA, IX. 168; ŚS, kārikā 21.

166. BCA, IX. 152 f.

167. Ibid., IX. 1-5.

168. BCA, X. 11-57 (summarized).

169. MBT, II. 2, SOR vol. IX.

170. See D. T. Suzuki, Zen and Japanese Culture; Introduction to Zen Buddhism; Essays in Zen Buddhism, vols. I-III, etc., W. Pachow, 'Zen Buddhism and Bodhidharma' in IHQ, vol. XXX11, 1956, pp. 221-229.

171. G. Tucci, MBT, II, pp. 8-9.

172. The most exhaustive work on the history of this Debate is that of P. Demieville, Le concile de Lhasa. But as pointed out by G. Tucci, op. cit., p. 32, it was held in bSam-yas and not in Lhasa.

173. MBT, II, pp. 5-41.

174. Bhāvanākrama, pp. 157, 187-189.

175. MBT, II, p. 192; cf. ŚS (BST), p. 8; Gaṇḍavyūhasūtra, p. 396.

176. MBT, II, pp. 157-158; 192-193; cf. BCA, I. 15.

177. MBT, II, p. 194. Vimalakīrtinirdeśa and Gayāśīrṣa are cited as authorities for this view.

178. MBT, II, pp. 159, 195 f.

179. Ibid., pp. 160, 198; see Kamalaśīla's comment on verse 3338 of TS. The Triple Gnosis is lucidly explained in Vasubandhu's Bodhicittotpādasūtraśāstra, pp. 228 f.

180. MBT, II, pp. 164 ff; cf. Bhagavadgītā, VI. 34-35.

181. MBT, II, p. 166; cf. ŚS (BB), pp. 47, 51, 181-184.

182. MBT, II, pp. 166-167.

183. Ibid., pp. 167 f.

184. GST (GOS), p. 12; Sekoddeśaṭikā, p. 24; Two Vajrayāna Works (GOS), pp. 17, 57 f.

185. Cittaviśuddhi-prakaraṇa, verse 10.

186. GST (GOS), p. 27.

187. Ibid., pp. 14, 20, 26, 102, 120.

188. Two Vajrayāna Works, p. 23.

189. Op. cit., verse 6.

190. Ibid., verses 17-18, 26-31.

191. Buddhist Texts Through the Ages, p. 227.

192. MS cited by S. B. Dasgupta, An Introduction to Tantric Buddhism, pp. 188 ff.

193. History of Dharmaśāstra, vol. V, pt. II, pp. 1029-1030, quoting Swāmī Vivekānanda, Complete Works, vol. III, pp. 248-268.

194. An Introduction to Buddhist Esoterism, pp. 168-169.
195. Pārānandasūtra (GOS), pp. 1-3, 13; Śaktisaṃgamatantra (GOS), Tārākhaṇḍa, ch. 36, verses 18-20; Kulārṇava, ch. V, verse 48; Rājataraṅgiṇī, VII. 278; Mohaparājaya (GOS), p. 100; Mahānirvāṇatantra, XI. 105; Śāradātilaka, XXIII. 137-141; Śaktisaṃgamatantra, Kālīkhaṇḍa, VIII. 102-106; Matsya Purāṇa, chs. 93, 139-148; Agni Purāṇa, ch. 138. etc.

CHAPTER VI

1. Already in the 4th century B.C. Aristotle noticed the controversy with regard to the subjects, ideals and fields of education, Politics, VIII. 2; the controversy continues today, see John Dewey, Reconstruction in Philosophy, Introduction, p. 13; M. K. Gandhi, An Autobiography, pp. 245-253.
2. Mahābhārata, Ādiparvan, I. 1; IX. 25, etc.
3. R. K. Mookerjee, Ancient Indian Education, pp. 477 f., 490 f.
4. S.V. Venkatesvara, Indian Culture Through the Ages, vol. I, p. 161.
5. See P. V. Kane, History of Dharmaśāstra, vol. I, Introduction; S. Radhakrishnan, The Hindu View of Life; A. S. Altekar, Sources of Hindu Dharma, pp. 5 f.
6. Even Kauṭilya, an unscrupulous political thinker, places ānvīkṣikī at the head of vidyās, Arthaśāstra, II. 1.
7. Bhagavadgītā, IV. 33.
8. Mahābhārata, XII. 399.6.
9. Hitopadeśa, Mitralābha, V. 6.
10. Mahāvagga, p. 15.
11. Ibid., pp. 42ff, 56ff.
12. Mookerjee, op. cit., Plate XIX. p. 452.
13. E. J. Thomas, 'Education in Early Buddhist Schools' in Buddhistic Studies, ed. by B. C. Law, ch. VIII.
14. A. S. Altekar, Education in Ancient India, pp. 231, 234.
15. Mahāvagga, p. 6.
16. Cf. AN, I, pp. 213 ff. on a threefold training in morality (sīla), contemplation (samādhi) and insight (paññā).
17. Dhammapada, verses 109, 204; Dharma-saṃgraha, 48; I-tsing, ch. 23.
18. Studies in the Origins of Buddhism, p. 331.
19. Dharmānanda Kosambī, Pārśvanātha kā Cāturyāma Dharma, pp. 17 f.
20. I-tsing, ch. 19.
21. Ibid., pp. 105-106.
22. Dharma-saṃgraha, 72.
23. Ibid., 16.
24. Ibid., 64.
25. See MASI, no. 66; and I-tsing, Introduction.
26. Ibid., p. 169; Yuan Chwang, I,155 f.
27. Life, p. 112.
28. Ibid., 166-167.
29. Ibid., p. 111.
30. I-tsing, p. 170 f.
31. Life, p. 125.
32. I-tsing, pp. 14-15, 64, 205.
33. History of Bengal, I, p. 414.
34. Harṣacarita eka Adhyayana, pp. 122, 237.
35. Life, p. 80.
36. Yuan Chwang, I, 226.
37. Ibid., p. 296.
38. Yuan Chwang, II, 227.
39. I-tsing, pp. 177-178.

40. I-tsing, pp. 103-104.
41. I-tsing, pp. 116-117; cp. Bhagavadgītā, IV. 33.
42. I-tsing, p. 120.
43. Yuan Chwang, I, 154-155.
44. I-tsing, pp. 170-174.
45. The Adhyardhaśataka of Mātṛceta has been ed. by K. P. Jayaswal and R. Sāṃkṛtyāyana, Appendix to JBORS, vol. XXIII; Sanskrit fragments found in Turfan ed. by A.F.R. Hoernle, Manuscript Remains, vol. I, 1916; D. R. Shackleton-Bailey (ed. & tr.), Śatapañcāsatkastotra.
46. I-tsing, pp. 157-160.
47. Ibid., p. 162-164; cf. Winternitz, HIL, II, pp. 273 f.
48. I-tsing pp. 165-166.
49. Ibid., pp. 175-180.
50. Ibid., p. 64; Yuan Chwang, I, 162.
51. I-tsing, pp. 181 f.
52. Ibid., pp. 183-184.
53. Mookerjee, op cit., p. 460.
54. Altekar, op. cit.,p. 231.
55. I-tsing, p. 208.
56. I-tsing, p. 177.
57. Yuan Chwang, II, 165.
58. I-tsing, p. 154.
59. Life, p. 112.
60. Mookerjee, op. cit., p. 565; cf. D. G. Apte, Universities in Ancient India, p. 35.
61. Yuan Chwang, II, p. 165.
62. MASI, no. 66, pp. 79, 81.
63. Life, pp. 112, 177.
64. Ibid., p 112
65. See S. C. Vidyābhūṣana, History of Indian Logic, p. 516; also by him, Medieval School of Indian Logic, p. 146.
66. Si-yu-ki, Introduction, p. 9.
67. I-tsing, p. XVII.
68. Epigraphia Indica, vol. XVII, 1923-24, pp. 31 f.
69. See Life, pp. 153, 156, 160; Yuan Chwang II, 165; I-tsing, pp. 181 f.; Si-yu-ki, pp. 385-386; Bu-ston, II, pp. 134; 135-136, 161 f.; Tārānātha (Schiefner), pp. 147 ff, 163 ff.
70. Cunningham, AGI, p. 317; Altekar, op. cit., p. 125.
71. Indian Antiquary, vol. IV, p. 174; vol. VI, pp. 9 ff.; vol. V, p. 206.
72. Yuan Chwang, II, 206.
73. Ibid., II, 246; Life, p. 159.
74. I-tsing, pp. 177-178.
75. Cf. Guṇasena's Grant in Indian Antiquary, vol. VII, pp. 67 f.—saddharmasya pustakopacayārthaṃ etc.
76. Kathāsaritsāgara, XXXII. 42-43.
77. Tārānātha (Schiefner), p. 217; R. Sāṃkṛtyāyana, Purātattva Nibandhāvalī, pp. 221 f.
78. Sragdharāstotra, p. 50; Svayaṃbhū Purāṇa, VI. 320-321.
79. Pag Sam Jon Zang, pp. LXXI, LXXV.
80. History of Bengal, I, pp. 115, 417.
81. S. C. Vidyabhūṣana, History of Indian Logic, pp. 519-520; S. C. Das, Indian Pandits in Tibet, JBTS, vol. I, pt. I, p. 10-12; Phaṇīndranāth Bose, Indian Teachers of Buddhist Universities, pp. 35-84.
82. Bu-ston, pp. 156-157; History of Bengal, I, p. 417.
83. MBT, II, Introduction.
84. Life, pp. 69-71.
85. Ibid., p. 76; Yuan Chwang, I, 291 ff.
86. Life, pp. 79-81; Yuan Chwang, I, 32 ff.
87. Life, p. 84.
88. Harṣacarita, bk. VIII; V. S. Agrawala, op. cit., pp. 190 ff.

89. L'itineraire d' Ou K'ong, ed. and tr. by S.Levi and Chavannes, Journal Astiatic, 1895, pp. 341-84, a short summary in English by N. Dutt in Gilgit Manuscripts, vol. I, pp. 36-37.

90. I-tsing wrote an account of them which was translated into French from the Chinese by E. Chavannes and published from Paris in 1894. The title of this work is 'Memoire on the Chinese Pilgrims who went in search of the Law to Western Countries'. See a short summary of it by S. Beal in the Life, Introduction.

91. Vide Beal's summary of I-tsing's 'Memoire' in the Life, pp. XXVII-XXXIX; History of Bengal, I, p. 417.

92. Blue Annals, I, pp. 39-40; D. L. Snellgrove, Buddhist Himalaya, pp. 141 f.; V. Bhattacharya, Bhoṭa-Prakāśa, pp. XIX ff.; 2500 Years of Buddhism, p. 74.

CHAPTER VII

1. E. Conze, Buddhist Thought, p. 265, seems to lament this development in Buddhism.

2. Saddharmapuṇḍarīka, pp. 21 f.

3. Prasannapadā (BB), pp. 55-56.

4. Such scholars, of course, learnt these languages in Tibet and China.

5. See Life, p. 113, where political unrest in Ceylon is alluded to; see G. C. Mendis, The Early History of Ceylon, p. 50.

6. P. C. Bagchi, 'Foreign Elements in the Tantra' in IHQ, vol. VII, 1931.

7. Wrongly pronounced as 'sandhyābhāṣā' and translated as 'twilight language'. The correct form is 'sandhābhāṣā', see Saddharmapuṇḍarīka-sūtra, ch. II et. seq.; modern discussions by V. Bhattacharya in IHQ, vol. IV, pp. 287 ff.; P. C. Bagchi in IHQ, vol. VI, pp. 389ff.; F. Edgerton, JAOS, 1937, pp. 185 ff.; Agehananda Bharati, The Tantric Tradition, pp. 164 ff.

8. R. Sāṃkṛtyāyana, Purātattva Nibandhāvalī, ch. X, pp. 131 f.

9. R. Sāṃkṛtyāyana, Bauddha Saṃskriti, pp. 302f., 401f.; P.K. Mukherjee, Indian Literature in China and the Far East; P. C. Bagchi, India and China, B. Nanjio, Catalogue; Yoshimura, The Denkar-ma catalogue; P. N. Bose, op. cit.; S. C. Das, op. cit.; G. Tucci in MBT, II, Introduction.

10. Yuan Chwang, II, 215, 227, I-tsing, pp. 179-181; H. Ui, Vaiśeṣika Philosophy, p, 2; HCIP, III, p. 286; Takakusu, Essentials of Buddhist Philosophy, p. 85.

11. Yuan Chwang, II, 155.

12. On the life and works of Candrakīrti, see Bu-ston, II, pp. 134ff; Tārānātha (Schiefner), p. 147ff.; Blue Annals, I, pp. 298, 335; II, pp. 882, 909. Three of his works have been published, the Prasannapadā or Mādhyamikavṛtti in BB (a fresh edition in BST, no. 10); most of the chapters of the Prasannapadā have been translated and studied by Stcherbatsky, Schayer, J. W. de Jong and Jacques May (see Bibliography); Madhyamakāvatāra, Tibetan text ed. in BB IX, and partly translated into French by Poussin in Le Museon; ch. VI of it restored into Sanskrit by N. A. Śāstri in JOR; the Catuḥśatak-vṛtti, chs. VIII-XVI (large extracts only), published by V. Bhattacharya along with the Catuḥśataka.

13. All these works of Dharmakīrti are extant in Tibetan. The following have appeared in print—Nyāyabindu, ed. in BB, also in Kāśī Series; Eng. tr. by Stcherbatsky in BL, vol. II; Santānāntarasiddhi, Tibetan text ed. by Stcherbatsky in BB, and a Russian tr. by the same savant, an English tr. from this Russian was published in the Journal of the Greater India Society; Vādanyāya with Śāntarakṣita's Ṭīkā, ed. by R. Sāṃkṛtyāyana; Pramāṇavārttika-bhāṣyaṃ, ed. by R. Sāṃkṛtyāyana; Pramāṇavārttikam (I chapter) with Svavṛtti and super-commentaries, ed. by the same scholar; a critical edition of the First Chapter with auto-commentary of this text has been

ed. by R. Gnoli in SOR, vol. XXIII; Sambandhaparīkṣā, ed. and tr. by Frauwallner in WZKM; Pramāṇaviniścaya (I chapter), Tibetan text, Skt. fragments and German tr. by Tilmann Vetter; Hetubindu, Tibetan text, Skt. and German tr. by Ernst Steinkellner. Recently Yusho Miyasaka has edited the Skt. and Tibetan texts of the Pramāṇavārttika in Acta Indologica, vol. II. On the life and works of Dharmakīrti see Bu-ston, II, pp. 152-155; Tārānātha (Schiefner), pp. 175-185; Pag Sam Jon Zang, p. 106; S. C. Vidyābhūṣaṇa, pp. 303-306; Stcherbatsky, BL, I, pp. 34-39; R. Gnoli, SOR, vol. XXIII, Introduction; R. Sāṃkṛtyāyana, Bauddha Darśana, pp. 130-133.

14. Tārānātha (Schiefner), pp. 176-177; Vidyābhūṣaṇa, op. cit., pp. 305-306, R. C. Majumdar, History of Bengal, I, p. 186.
15. I-tsing, pp. 181-182.
16. Bu-ston, II, p. 152; Blue Annals, I, p. 346.
17. Stcherbatsky, BL, p. 37; R. Sāṃkṛtyāyana, Bauddha Darśana, pp. 132 f.
18. R. Sāṃkṛtyāyana (ed.), Pramāṇavārttika, Introduction, p. 11.
19. Bu-ston, II, p. 154.
20. Pag Sam Jon Zang, p. 106.
21. Vidyābhūṣaṇa, op. cit., p. 307.
22. See Bu-ston, II, pp. 161-166; Tārānātha (Schiefner), pp. 162-167; Pag Sam Jon Zang, pp. CXLVII, 120; for a fragmentary Sanskrit biography, see H. P. Śāstrī, 'Śāntideva' in Indian Antiquary, vol. XLII, 1913, pp. 50-51.
23. R. Sāṃkṛtyāyana, Purātattvanibandhāvalī, ch. on '84 Siddhas', Siddha no. 41.
24. See Cordier, Catalogue, II, p. 140, 230, 241; cf. History of Bengal, I, p. 331.
25. Indian Antiquary, 1913, p. 51; B. Bhattacharyya in JBORS, 1928, p. 355.
26. R. Sāṃkṛtyāyana, Purātattvanibandhāvalī, p. 146.
27. Ibid., p. 123; Tārānātha (Schiefner), p. 249.
28. Bu-ston, II, p. 163; Indian Antiquary, 1913, p. 50.
29. Does this refer to Śīlāditya, son-in-law of Harṣa ? History knows no son of Harṣa. On Śīlāditya see above Chapter II.
30. TS, Foreword, p. XXIII.
31. Bu-ston, II, p. 163; Tārānātha (Schiefner), p. 166.
32. Studies in Āryadeva and his Catuḥśataka, p. 54.
33. Winternitz, HIL, II, p. 366, note 1; Bendall's ed., p. IV; Vaidya's ed., p. VII.
34. One by C. Bendall in BB, I, reprinted in Indo-Iranian Journal, vol. I, another by P. L. Vaidya in BST, no. 11, the 27 kārikās have been separately edited with an Eng. tr. by L. M. Joshi.
35. By C. Bendall and W. H. D. Rouse in Indian Texts Series.
36. Winternitz, op. cit., II, p. 370.
37. See Vaidya's ed. of ŚS, Appendix, pp. 197-206; Bunyu Nanjio, A Catalogue of the Chinese Translation of the Buddhist Tripitaka; The Tibetan Tripitaka (Peking Edition), Catalogue and Index, ed. by D. T. Suzuki.
38. Fragments of Sanskrit version have been published in A. F. R. Hoernle's Manuscript Remains of Buddhist Literature, vol. I.
39. Ed. by D. T. Suzuki and H. Idzumi; ed. by P. L. Vaidya in BST, no. 5. Gaṇḍavyūhasūtra is quoted also in Bhāvanākrama of Kamalaśīla, BCAP of Prajñākaramati and Āloka of Haribhadra.
40. Ed. in Gilgit Manuscripts, vols. II-III, by N. Dutt; ed. in BST, no. 2, by P. L. Vaidya.
41. Ed. by J. Rahder; ed. by P. L. Vaidya in BST, no. 7.
42. Ed. by Cowell and Neil; ed. by P. L. Vaidya in BST, no. 20.
43. Ed. by A. C. Banerjee.
44. Ed. by R. L. Mitra in BI; ed. by U. Wogihara; ed. by P. L. Vaidya in BST, no. 4; tr. by E. Conze in BI.

45. A Mahāsāṃghika Prātimokṣasūtra has been ed. by W. Pachow and R. Misra.

46. It is the 56th ch. of the Gaṇḍavyūhasūtra, ed. by H. Idzumi in Eastern Buddhist, vol. V.

47. The Mahāsāṃghika Lokottaravāda version of this text has been edited by Gustav Roth.

48. Ed. by N. Dutt in Gilgit Manuscripts, vol. I, 1939; also ed. in BST, no. 17, by P. L. Vaidya.

49. A Baroda manuscript bears the name which is said to be a Dhāraṇi.

50. I-tsing, p. 64, says that Rāhulamitra used to recite this sūtra daily and it contained 700 verses.

51. Fragments published in Hoernle's Manuscript Remains of Buddhist Literature.

52. Ed. by L. Finot in BB; ed. by P. L. Vaidya in BST, no. 17; Eng. tr. by J. Ensink.

53. Ed. by B. Nanjio; ed. by P. L. Vaidya in BST, no. 3; ed. by D. T. Suzuki; a critical and detailed study of the Sutra by D. T. Suzuki, Studies in the Lankāvatāra.

54. Ed. by R. L. Mitra in BI; ed. by S. Lefmann; ed. by P. L. Vaidya in BST, no. 1.

55. Ed. by F. Max Müller; ed. and tr. by E. Conze with an Introduction, SOR, XIII; ed. also by N. P. Chakravarti in MBT, I, and by P. L. Vaidya in BST, no. 17.

56. Quoted in Kamalaśīla's Bhāvanākrama, MBT, II,p.194; Fragments of Sanskrit text discovered by Pelliot from Central Asia; tr. into Skt. by Bhikkhu Pasadika, into French by E. Lamotte and into English by Charles Luk.

57. Ed. by P. L. Vaidya in BST, no. 17, earlier edns. by Poussin and by N. A. Śāstrī.

58. Tr. into Eng. by S. Beal and into French by E. Lamotte. The text translated by Charles Luk seems to be a different one.

59. Does it refer to the Sarvāstivāda Vinaya or to the Pali Vinaya ?

60. Eng. tr. by Alex Wayman.

61. Edited 1) by H. Kern and B. Nanjio, 2) by U. Wogihara, 3) by N. Dutt, and 4) by P. L. Vaidya; Eng. tr. by H. Kern.

62. See Lin-Li-Kouang, L'Aide-Memoire de la Vraie Loi.

63. Mentioned by Hsuan-tsang and I-tsing; partly edited by N. Dutt in Gilgit Manuscript, vols. II, III and IV, and by S. Bagchi under the title Mulasarvāstivāda-vinayavastu.

64. Edns. by S. C. Das (ch. I-XV), by B. Nanjio and H. Idzumi, by J. Nobel, by S. Bagchi in BST, no. 8.

65. Edns. by I. P. Minayeff in Zapiski, IV; by Poussin, chapters I-IX with Pañjikā in BI; full text with Prajñākara's Pañjikā ed. by P. L. Vaidya in BST, no. 12; BCA of Śāntideva has been translated into French by Poussin, into Italian by Tucci, into German by R. Schmidt, into English (summary only) by L. D. Barnett, and again by Marion L. Matics, and into Hindi by Śāntibhikṣu Śāstrī.

66. Bu-ston, II, p. 166.

67. Quoted also in the Bhāvanākrama, p. 194.

68. Cf. Bhārasutta, SN, I, pp. 261-262.

69. Cf. Jātakamāla, Jātaka 8.

70. Ed. by P. C. Ghosh in BI, (only first fourteen chapters).

71. It contains quotations from 60 Sūtras.

72. BCAP, pp. 301-309; the Prajñāpāramitāstava is attributed to Nāgārjuna also called Rāhulamitra; it is published in BST, no. 4, pp. 1-2. footnote; tr. by E. Conze in Buddhist Scriptures; ed. and tr. into Hindi by me in Dharmadūta, 1966.

73. Life, pp. 106-109, 157-160; Yuan Chwang, II, 109, 165; I-tsing, p. 181.

74. Cordier, Catalogue, pt. III, p. 365; History of Bengal, I, p. 331.

75. The letters of Hsüan-tsang and his Indian friends are translated

by P. C. Bagchi and published in JUPHS, XVIII, 1945, pp. 74 ff., and also in India and China, pp. 82 ff.

76. Life, pp. 157-158.
77. Ibid., pp. 153-154; Si-yu-ki, pp. 367-368.
78. Life, pp. 159ff.
79. See Prabandhacintāmaṇī, tr. by C. H. Tawney, p. 198; the Bhartṛharinirveda in JAOS, XXV, 1904, pp. 197ff.; Winternitz, HIL, vol. III, pt. I, p. 150, and A. B. Keith, History of Sanskrit Literature, p. 178 do not attach any historical value to these legends.
80. Tārānātha (Schiefner), p. 197; Mystic Tales, pp. 25-26.
81. I-tsing, pp. 178-180.
82. See JBBRAS, vol. 26, 1951, pp. 147-149; Indo-Iranian Journal, vol. IV, nos. 2-3, 1960, p. 177.
83. Ed. by Pandit Manavalli, and also by K. A. Subramanya Iyer.
84. see S. K. Bhandarkar's Catalogue of Manuscripts in Deccan College, p. 146; Takakusu's 'Additional Notes' in I-tsing.
85. I-tsing, pp. 178-180.
86. History of Sanskrit Literature, pp. 277, 286.
87. Subhāṣita-triśatī or Śrī Bhartṛharikṛta Śatakatrayam, ed. by D. D. Kosambi and N. R. Acharya, pp. 143-144; Vairāgyaśataka, verses 49-50.
88. Ibid., verse 32; cf. I-tsing, p. 180, where Bhartṛhari is seen admitting his lack of continence.
89. Ibid., p. 183.
90. See Jātakamālā, Jātaka 9.
91. I-tsing, p. 164.
92. Rājataraṅgiṇī, I, 176.
93. Pag Sam Jon Zang, pt. I, pp. 95-96, reproduced in S. C. Vidyābhūṣaṇa, History of Indian Logic, pp. 334-335.
94. Ed. by Manavalli, II, pp. 489-490.
95. History of Bengal, I, p. 299.
96. Tārānātha (Schiefner), p. 148ff.
97. Pag Sam Jon Zang, pp. XI, 95ff.
98. Cordier, Catalogue, pt. II, p. 302.
99. Ed. by B. Liebich; the same scholar has summarized the bibliography of Cāndravyākaraṇa and its accessory literature in Indian Antiquary, 1896, pp. 103-105.
100. Winternitz, HIL, III, p. 183; Keith, Sanskrit Drama, p. 168.
101. Ed. by I. P. Minayeff in Zapiski, vol. IV, pp. 29ff.
102. S. C. Vidyābhūṣaṇa (ed.), Sragdharā-stotra in BI, Introduction, pp. XX f.
103. S. C. Vidyābhūṣaṇa, History of Indian Logic, p. 336.
104. I-tsing, p. 183; the verse belongs to Śiṣyalekha-dharma-kāvya of Candra and is quoted by Vallabhadeva in Subhāṣitāvali (P. Peterson's edn.), verse 3368; cf. H. Wenzel in JRAS, 1889, pp. 1133f.; G.K. Nariman, Literary History of Sanskrit Buddhism, p. 290.
105. Pag Sam Jon Zang, pt. I, pp. XCIX, 49; pt. II, p. 112.
106. P. C. Bagchi in IHQ, vol. VI, 1930, p.582; A. H. Franke, Antiquities of Indian Tibet, pt. II, pp. 87-88; D. L. Snellgrove, Buddhist Himalaya, p. 173.
107. See Waddell, Lamaism, pp. 20, 24, 25, 279 ff.
108. Bauddha Sanskriti, pp. 404-405; Purātattvanibandhāvalī, p. 181.
109. Blue Annals, I, p. 44.
110. Bu-ston, II, p. 189.
111. Tombs of the Tibetan Kings, SOR, I, 1950, pp. 44, 81, 95.
112. G. Tucci, MBT, II, Introduction, pp. 5 ff.; D. L. Snellgrove, Buddhist Himalaya, pp. 154-155.
113. Tattva-saṃgraha (TS), ed. by E. Krishnamacharya; tr. by Gaṅgānātha Jhā. The original Sanskrit manuscript of the TS was discovered by G. Bühler in 1873 in a 'bhāṇḍār' in Jaisalmer. The Tibetan translation by a Kashmiri scholar Guṇākara Śrībhadra exists in Tenjur.

114. Bu-ston, II, p. 136; Tāranātha (Schiefner), pp. 204-205.
115. Ed. by R. Sāṃkṛtyāyana along with the mūla of Dharmakīrti.
116. See R. S. Y. Chi, Buddhist Formal Logic, A Study of Dignāga's Hetucakra and K'uei-chi's Great Commentary on the Nyāyapraveśa.
117. They are—Aṣṭatathāgata-stotra; Vajradhara-saṃgīti-bhagavat-stotra-ṭikā; and Hevajrodbhava-kurukullyāyāha-pañcamahopadeśa.
118. Central Library, Baroda, MS no. 13124; cf. B. Bhattacharyya, Foreword to TS, pp. XX-XXII.
119. Bu-ston, II, pp. 195 f.; cf. Blue Annals, I, p. 41.
120. See G. Tucci in MBT, II, pp. 5-154.
121. Ed. by E. Krishnamacharya; Eng. tr. by G. Jha.
122. Bu-ston, II, p. 136.
123. Ed. by G. Tucci in MBT, II, 1958.
124. E. Obermiller in Journal of the Greater Indian Society, vol. II, 1935, pp. 1-11. The third Bhāvanākrama has been recently edited and published by G. Tucci.
125. The Tibetan and Chinese versions have been translated into French by E. Lamotte and P. Demieville in Le Concile de Lhasa, pp. 333-353.
126. All these three texts have been edited and translated by Blonay.
127. Edited with Jinarakṣita's commentary and two Tibetan versions by S. C. Vidyābhūṣaṇa.
128. Tāranātha (Schiefner), pp. 168ff.
129. Pag Sam Jon Zang, p. 102.
130. Tāranātha (Schiefner); Pag Sam Jon Zang, p. 102; Jinarakṣita's account in Vidyābhūṣaṇa's edn. of Sragdharā-stotra, Introduction, pp. XXVIII-XXX.
131. Tāranātha (Schiefner), pp. 195-198.
132. This text, called Pramāṇavārttika-bhāṣyam, has been ed. by R. Sāṃkṛtyāyana.
133. This book is translated by W. W. Rockhill in Life of the Buddha, pp. 181ff.
134. Tibetan text ed. in BI.
135. Tibetan text ed. in BI by Stcherbatsky and translated into Russian by the same scholar.
136. See Dharmottara-pradīpa of Durveka Miśra.
137. Bu-ston, II, 155.
138. Ibid., II, p. 155.
139. Blue Annals, I, p. 346.
140. Pramāṇa-samuccaya-vṛtti, called Viśālāmalavatī, extant in Tibetan; portions of it are translated by Stcherbatsky in B L, I, pp. 461 ff.
141. This text has been translated into Sanskrit by N. A. Śāstrī and partly published in the Bulletin of Tibetology. Kalyāṇarakṣita is possibly identical with Bhadant Śubhagupta, criticized by Kamalaśīla in the Tattva-saṅgrahapañjikā.
142. For his life and works see Tāranātha (Schiefner), pp. 146-147, Pag Sam Jon Zang, pp. 90, 101, 118 (pt. I).
143. Nyāyamañjarī, ed. by Gangādhara Śāstrī, ch. VII, p. 462.
144. Vasantasena, king of Nepal of a copper plate grant of the year 435 (?) is placed in A. D. 513 by R. C. Majumdar, HCIP, III, p. 84; but see S. C. Vidyābhūṣaṇa, History of Indian Logic, p. 322; the inscription in question is reported in Indian Antiquary, vol. IX, p. 167.
145. Mentioned by W. W. Rockhill, op. cit., p. 228.
146. Ed. by R. Sāṃkṛtyāyana.
147. Dharmottarapradīpa, pp. 5, 31, 32, 61.
148. Ibid., Introduction, p. XXV.
149. Ibid., pp. 5, 31, 32, 61.
150. Nyāyaviniścaya-vivaraṇa, pp. 526, 530-531.
151. Dharmottarapradīpa, pp. 5, 31.
152. Purātattvanibandhāvalī, p. 181.

153. Ed. by Sukhlalji Sanghavi and Muni Sri Jinavijaya in GOS, no. CXIII, 1949, see Introduction, p. XI.
154. Ibid., p. 87, 327.
155. Ibid., p. 189.
156. Bu-ston, II, p. 155.
157. Blue Annals, I, p. 346.
158. Stcherbatsky, BL, I, p. 41.
159. Rājataraṅgiṇī, IV. 498.
160. HCIP, IV, p. 114.
161. Rājataraṅgiṇī, IV. 489, 495-496.
162. Ed. by P. Peterson in BI; ed. by Chandraśekhara Śāstrī in Kāśī Sanskrit Series, no. 22; Eng. tr. by Stcherbatsky.
163. Vidyābhūṣaṇa, History of Indian Logic, p. 330, transcribes the title of this text as Pramāṇaparīkṣā; the text is referred to in the Dharmottarapradīpa, p. 24, as Prāmāṇyaparīkṣā; R. Sāṃkṛtyāyana (edn. of Vādanyāya, Appendix F, p. 11) mentions two texts of Pramāṇaparīkṣā extant in Tibetan.
164. Bu-ston, II, p. 158.
165. R. C. Majumdar, History of Bengal, I, p. 177.
166. Blue Annals, I, 367; Bu-ston, II, p. 159.
167. Tārānātha (Schiefner), pp. 229-232; HCIP, IV, pp. 270-271; Pag Sam Jon Zang, p. XCIV.
168. Ed. by G. Tucci; ed. by U. Wogihara; also ed. by P. L. Vaidya.
169. N. Dutt (ed.), Pañcaviṃśatisāhasrikā Prajñāpāramitā, Introduction, pp. VII-XIII; cf. also P. L. Vaidya in BST, no. 4, Introduction.
170. Bu-ston, II, p. 158.
171. Blue Annals, I, pp. 31, 367.
172. See the colophon of the Abhisamayālaṅkārāloka, GOS, LXIII, pp. 563-64; HCIP, IV, p. 270; History of Bengal, I, p. 417.
173. Cordier, Catalogue, pt. 2, Tenjur, I-LXX (rGyud section), a good index to it in H. P. Śāstrī, Bauddha Gān O Dohā, Appendix; see also R. Sāṃkṛtyāyana, Purātattvanibandhāvalī, chs. 9-10; the account in Winternitz, HIL, II, pp. 375 ff. is now quite superseded; see M. Shahidullah, Les Chants Mystique; B. Bhattacharyya, Sādhanamālā, Introduction; Dohākośa, ed. by P. C. Bagchi; Dohākośa (of Saraha), ed. by R. Sāṃkṛityāyana; Caryāgītikośa, ed. by P. C. Bacghi and Śantibhikṣu Śāstrī; see also S. B. Dasgupta, Obscure Religious Cults.
174. D. L. Snellgrove, Hevajratantra, I, Introduction, pp. 12-13.
175. R. Sāṃkṛtyāyana (ed.), Dohākośa, Bhūmikā, pp. 16-17.
176. See Sādhanamālā, vol. I, pp. 193f., 265f. The Ekajaṭāsādhana was brought from Tibet (Bhoṭa) by Nāgārjuna.
177. See IHQ, vol. VII, pp. 740 f; vol. VIII, pp. 790 f.
178. Tibetan text with Sanskrit restoration by P. B. Patel in IHQ, vol. VIII, 1932; see also G. Tucci in JRAS, 1932.
179. Ed. by La Vallee Poussin.
180. Ed. by B. Bhattacharyya.
181. Published in Sādhanamālā, II, pp. 353f.
182. Bu-ston, II, pp. 159-160.
183. Long extracts from its Sanskrit manuscript in H. P. Śāstrī, Descriptive Catalogue of Sanskrit Manuscripts in the Asiatic Society of Bengal, vol. I, pp. 131-141; published by American Oriental Society.
184. Tibetan text ed. in Tantric Texts, vol. XI. Eng. tr. by Kazi Dawa Samdup.
185. See H. P. Śāstrī, Notices of Sanskrit Manuscripts, 2nd series, I, pp. XXIX f
186. Ed. by I. P. Minayeff in Zapiski de la societe Archaeologique, pt. II, fasc. III, pp. 236f.
187. Ed. and tr. into French by S. K. Karpeles in Journal Asiatique, 1919, pp. 357-465.

188. Bauddha-stotra-saṃgraha, vol. I, Introduction, pp. I-XXVIII.
189. Ed. by N. Dutt in Gilgit Manuscripts, vol. I, pp. 36-40.
190. Ibid., pp. 43-46.
191. Ibid., pp. 59-89.
192. Nanjio, Catalogue, p. 435.
193. Takakusu, I-tsing's Record, Introduction, p. XXXVII.
194. JUPHS, XVIII, 1945, p. 87. The Kośa here refers to Vasubandhu's work; the other work, Nyāyānusāra, is that of Saṃghabhadra.
195. R. Sāṃkṛtyāyana, Bauddha Saṃskriti, p. 341; for a list of other Chinese and Central Asian Buddhist scholar-translators see Ibid., pp. 334-335.
196. M. Anesaki in ERE, vol. IV, p. 840; Winternitz, HIL, II, p. 399.
197. According to A. K. Nilakantha Śāstrī, Foreign Notices of South India, p. 17, Vajrabodhi was the teacher of the Pallava King Narasingh-varman II.
198. See W. Pachow in the University of Ceylon Review, vol. XII, 1954, pp. 3-4.
199. Ibid., and Journal of the Greater India Society, vol. XVII, 1958, pp. 1-22.
200. R. Sāṃkṛtyāyana, Bauddha Saṃskriti, p. 346.
201. The Denkarma, an oldest catalogue of the Tibetan Buddhist canon, ed. with notes by S. Yoshimura.
202. MBT, II, pp. 45-47.

CHAPTER VIII

1. I-tsing, pp. 7-8.
2. Ibid., pp. 14-15.
3. Yuan Chwang, I, 297, 301, 355; II, 81, 136, 199, 241, 248. 341,
4. BCA, V. 89.
5. Life, pp. 159, 165; TSP, Eng. tr. , p. 242.
6. Life, pp. 159-60.
7. Ibid., pp. 175-76.
8. BCA, IX. 42, 49.
9. Bhāvanākrama, pp. 172-73.
10. T. R. V. Murti, Central Philosophy of Buddhism, pp. 144 ff. G. C. Pande, Bauddha Dharma, p. 394.
11. On his life see Yuan Chwang, II, 215-224, who makes him a contemporary of Dharmapāla, the teacher of Śīlabhadra. Bhāvaviveka, therefore, seems to have lived in the 6th century A. D. and not in 5th as is held by N. Peri and Winternitz. He wrote (1) Mahāyāna-karatala-ratna-śāstra, (2) Mādhyamaka-hṛdaya with auto-commentary called Tarkajvālā (3) Mādhyamakārtha-saṃgraha and (4) Prajñāpradīpa, a commentary on the MŚ of Nāgārjuna.
12. Little is known about his life. He wrote a commentary on the MŚ of Nāgārjuna, which exists in Tibetan version; its first chapter restored by Indumati Datar in JBBRAS (n.s.), vol. 26, pt. 2, 1951, pp. 129-139.
13. Bu-ston, II, p. 135 and Obermiller's note; Murti, op. cit., pp. 95, 98; Takakusu, Essentials of Buddhist Philosophy, p. 101.
14. This information is given by Khai-ḍub, cited by E. Obermiller in Bu-ston, II, pp. 135-136, note.
15. Peking edition of this text is cited by Y. Kajiyama in his paper 'Bhāvaviveka and the Prāsaṅgika School' in Nava Nalanda Mahāvihāra Research Publication, vol. I, pp. 310, 313 et. seq.
16. Bhāvaviveka did not believe that the system of 'dialectics' alone can serve the purpose of asserting the Absolute Truth. The system of 'dialectics' seeks to reduce every thesis to contradictions. E. Conze observes: "Dialectics is that form of logic which, without denying the validity of the

principles of contradiction, maintains that all truth must be expressed in the form of self-contradictory statements." Buddhist Thought in India, p. 162.

17. Karatalaratna, ch. I; Y. Kajiyama, op. cit., p. 291.
18. Cf. Vigrahavyāvartani, verse 29; MŚ, XIII. 8.
19. Karatalaratna, p. 35; Y. Kajiyama, op. cit., p. 293.
20. Yuan Chwang, II, 215.
21. Visvabharati Annals, II, p. 10.
22. Bu-ston, II, p. 135.
23. Karatalaratna, pp. 34-35.
24. Prasannapadā (BB), p. 25.
25. Ibid., pp. 351-353.
26. Ibid., p. 26 (on 1.4); Y. Kajiyama, op. cit., p. 309; Murti, op, cit., pp. 95-96.
27. Prasannapadā (BB), p. 55.
28. BCA, IX. 2; BCAP, pp. 170-177.
29. See my edition and Hindi tr. of the Madhyamakārtha-saṃgraha in Dharmadūta, vol. 29, pp. 54f.
30. BCA, IX. 53-54, 56, 152, 168.
31. Ibid., IX. 41.
32. BCAP, pp. 203.
33. BCA, IX. 42.
34. Ibid., IX. 43. BCAP, p. 205 'quoting the Adhyāśayasaṃcodanasūtra, gives the following four marks of an authentic scripture—(i) it should be meaningful and not meaningless, (ii) it should embody righteousness and not unrighteousness, (iii) it should help lessening the miseries and should not increase the same, and (iv) it should praise nirvāṇa and not saṃsāra.
35. BCA, IX. 44; I-tsing, pp. 6-7; BCAP, p. 206.
36. BCA, IX. 45.
37. Ibid., IX. 46-49; BCAP, pp. 208-209.
38. BCA, IX, 50-52.
39. Ibid., IX. 53-56.
40. This had been done already by Nāgārjuna, MŚ, chs. I, III-IV, V; Dvādaśamukhaśāstra, chs. I, II, XI; and by Āryadeva, CŚ, chs. IX, XI,XIII, XV.
41. See Abhidharmakośakārikā; Abhidharmāmṛta of Ghoṣaka; Y, Sogen, Systems, ch. III; Stcherbatsky, Central Conception of Buddhism and the Meaning of the word 'Dharma'; E. Conze, Buddhist Thought, pp. 178-191; see also Takakusu, 'Sarvāstivāda', ERE, vol. XI, pp. 198-200.
42. Abhidharmakośa, III, 18, 28; the theory of dharmas means that if something appears, such and such result will follow, asmin sati, idam bhavati, i.e. dependent origination.
43. TSP, p. 155.
44. Prasannapadā, p. 78.
45. Buddhist Texts, ed. by E. Conze, p. 168; cf. SN, II, p. 207.
46. Quoted from Abhidharmakośa in Prasannapadā, p. 145; CŚV, p. 232.
47. Prasannapadā, p. 146; MŚ, VII. 2.
48. Prasannapadā, p. 545.
49. CŚV, p. 246.
50. Ibid., p. 238.
51. Ibid., pp. 197-198.
52. CŚV, pp. 35-36.
53. Ibid., p. 113.
54. Ibid., p. 114.
55. Ibid., pp. 110-120, 122.
56. BCA, IX. 142.
57. BCAP, pp. 268-270.
58. Ibid.
59. BCA, IX. 143.

60. BCAP, p. 270.
61. BCA, IX. 145-149; cf. MŚ, I, IV, and the whole of the Dvādaśamukhaśāstra; CŚ, chs. IX, XI, and XV. The Traikālyavāda is attacked also by Śāntarakṣita, TS, ch. XXI.
62. Vijñaptimātratāsiddhi, verses 1-3; Prasannapadā, pp. 61ff.; Madhyamakāvatāra, VI, 45ff.; Navaśloki, verse 7 (11) in MBT, I, pp. 217, 228.
63. See AN, I, p. 10; Buddhist Texts, ed. E. Conze, p. 33.
64. Prasannapadā, p. 276; BCAP, p. 194.
65. Prasannapadā, p. 275.
66. BCA, IX. 7; Madhyamakāvatāra, pp. 59ff.
67. BCAP, p. 188.
68. Madhyamakāvatāra, VI. 46.
69. BCA, IX. 16.
70. Ibid., IX. 18.
71. BCAP, p. 190. This argument is also pressed by Śāntarakṣita, TS, verse 2001.
72. BCA, IX. 22-23.
73. Ibid., IX, 24.
74. Ibid., IX. 25; BCAP, pp. 192-193.
75. BCA, IX. 26; BCAP, p. 193.
76. His work, Madhyāntavibhāgasūtrabhāṣyaṭikā, pt. I, is ed. by V. Bhattacharya and G. Tucci. I-tsing, p. 181, places him along with Dharmapāla and Śīlabhadra.
77. G. Tucci, Aspects of the Doctrines of Maitreyanātha and Asaṅga, pp. 29-31.
78. Ibid., pp. 33-35; Madhyāntavibhāgasūtrabhāṣyaṭīkā, pp. 12-13.
79. The work had two parts, one of twenty verses (Viṃśatikā) and another of thirty verses (Triṃśikā); ed. with Yuan Chwang's Siddhi by Vallee Poussin, Vijñaptimātratāsiddhi La Siddhi de Hiuan Tsang; also Deux Traites de Vasubandhu, ed. par S. Levi; see Ācārya Narendradeva, Bauddha Dharma Darśana, pp. 422 ff.; G. C. Pande, Bauddha Dharma, pp. 425-450.
80. Takakusu, Essentials of Buddhist Philosophy, p. 85, observes that there were, in India, three lines of transmission of Yogācāra Idealism after the death of Vasubandhu: (i) The line of Diṅnāga, Agotra, and Dharmapāla, whose centre was Nālandā. Śīlabhadra, and his Chinese pupil Hsüan-tsang, belonged to this line. (ii) The line of Guṇamati and Sthiramati whose centre was Valabhī University. Paramārtha belonged to this line. (iii) Third line was that of Nanda, whose tenet was followed by Paramārtha and Jayasena, who instructed Hsüan-tsang on certain questions. This last line did not flourish much in India.
81. Partly restored into Sanskrit by R. Sāṃkṛtyāyana in JBORS, vols. XIX-XX.
82. Takakusu, op. cit., p. 87; Winternitz, HIL, II, p. 360, note 4.
83. Vijñaptimātratāsiddhi Deux Traites de Vasubandhu, kārikā 17, p. 35; Vijñaptimātratāsiddhi La Siddhi de Hiuan Tsang, kārikā 17, pp. 416, 419.
84. Sthiramati's Triṃśikā-bhāṣya in Deux Traites, pp. 35-36.
85. Takakusu, Essentials, p. 87.
86. La Siddhi etc., p. 133.
87. Ibid., p. 131.
88. Nyāyamañjarī, ed. in Vizianagaram Sanskrit Series, vol. I, p. 72; vol. II, p. 50.
89. Life, pp. 67, 199; Yuan Chwang, I, 245; II, 286-289; Si-yu-ki, p. 181.
90. Tārānātha (Schiefner), p. 78.
91. Sanskrit fragments published by H. Lüders, Leipzig, 1926.
92. Winternitz, HIL, II, pp. 267, 269.
93. See the Cultural Heritage of India, vol. I, p. 473.
94. In his paper 'Dārṣṭāntika, Sautrāntika and Sarvāstivādin' in IHQ, vol. XVI, no. 2, pp. 246 ff.

95. Ibid.. see Poussin, 'Sautrāntika' in ERE, vol. XI, p. 213.
96. AK-vyākhyā on I. 20.
97. Karatalaratna, II, p. 72.
98. Prasannapadā (BB), pp. 61, 263, 281f.
99. BrSŚ, II, 2, 18.
100. Ṣaḍdarśana-samuccaya, p. 3.
101. Sarvadarśanasaṃgraha, Eng. tr. by Cowell and Gough, pp. 27 f.
102. Poussin in ERE, vol.XI, p. 214; Stcherbatsky, BL, I, p.29, note I.
103. Sarvadarśanasaṃgraha, Eng. tr. pp. 26-29 (abridged).
104. Prasannapadā, p. 281; ERE, vol. XI, p. 214; Stcherbatsky, Central Conception, pp. 62ff.
105. According to Stcherbatsky, BL, I, p. 529, the Sautrāntikas "were apparently the first to assume the reality of a thing-in-itself behind the outward phenomenon".
106. Vādavidhi, Vādavidhāna, and Vādahṛdaya.
107. Cf.J. Przyluski in IHQ, vol. XVI, p. 251—"the formula sarvamasti proves a liking for metaphysical subtlety"; see also the remarks of G. C. Pande, Bauddha Dharma, p. 284.
108. Yuan Chwang, I, 355-56; Tārānātha (Schiefner), p. 4, 67.
109. Sphuṭārthā-Abhidharmakośavyākhyā, ed. by U. Wogihara; ed. by N. N. Law and N. Dutt; also ed. by D. Sāstrī.
110. Winternitz, HIL, II, p. 363.
111. Ibid., note 1.
112. S. C. Vidyābhūṣaṇa, op. cit., pp. 130f.
113. E. Frauwallner, Date of Vasubandhu,p. 63.
114. Yuan Chwang, II, 209-213; Life, p. 136; I-tsing, pp. 181, 186; Tārānātha (Schiefner), pp. 130-135.
115. See Winternitz, HIL, p. 262; Stcherbatsky, BL, I, pp. 31-32; R. Sāṃkṛtyāyana, Purātattvanibandhāvalī, p. 177. The alleged reference to Diṅnāga in the Meghadūta, pūrvamegha, verse 14, of Kālidāsa, is taken as an evidence for 5th century date. It may be noted, however, that the phrase 'dignāgānāṃ' may mean 'the guardians (nāgas) of the (four) quarters', and not necessarily the logician. Moreover, the date of Kālidāsa is largely a matter of conjecture.
116. I-tsing p. 181; Vidyābhūṣaṇa, op. cit., pp. 272, 506.
117. Ibid., pp. 276-296, and by the same writer, 'Diṅnāga and his Pramāṇasamuccaya' in JASB, vol. I, no. 9, 1905; H. N. Randle, Fragments from Diṅnāga, pp. 3-4; H. R. Rangaswami Iyangar, Bhartṛhari and Diṅnāga', JBBRAS, (n.s.), vol. 26, 1950, pp. 147-149; see also M. Hattori, Dignaga on Perception, and R. S. Y. Chi, Buddhist Formal Logic.
118. I-tsing, pp. 186-187, gives a list of 8 logical works of Diṅnāga, most of them are extant in Tibetan and Chinese translations. Diṅnāga's Ālambanaparīkṣā is restored by N. A. Śāstrī; his Prajñāpāramitā-piṇḍārtha is ed. by G. Tucci, JRAS, 1947, re-edited by P. L. Vaidya in BST, no. 4; several extracts from his works quoted by Uddyotakara and others have been collected and translated by H. N. Randle in'Fragments from Diṅnāga '; Nyāyapraveśa, ed. by A. B. Dhruva, formerly ascribed to Diṅnāga, is now known to be a work of Śaṃkarasvāmin (550 A.D.).
119. Yuan Chwang, II, 209-210.
120. See Keith, Buddhist Philosophy, p. 305; summary of Ālaṃbanaparīkṣā in BL, I, pp. 518-521.
121. Pramāṇasamuccaya, I, 14, cited by Frauwallner in SOR, III, p. 63; cf. also BL, I, pp. 32-33.
122. Blue Annals, I, p. 346.
123. BL, I, p. 32, note 1.
124. On the Naiyāyika realism see Sadānanda Bhādurī, Nyāya-Vaiśeṣika Metaphysics.
125. Fragments from Diṅnāga, pp. 71 ff.
126. Diṅnāga's views are criticized by Uddyotakara in Nyāyavārttika,

pp. 60f., and by Vācaspati Miśra in Nyāyavārttika-tātparyaṭīkā, pp. 2-3 205 etc.

127. Pratyakṣam kalpanāpoḍham nāmajātyādyasaṃyuktaṃ, Fragments, pp. 8 f.; Nyāyavārttika, I. 1-4, II. 2-4; Jwālā Prasād, History of Indian Epistemology, pp. 206-207.

128. Fragments, p. 21; Nyāyavārttika, p. 56; Nyāyavārttika-tātparyaṭīkā, pp. 120, 127; H. N. Randle, Indian Logic in the Early Schools, p. 155.

129. See Fragments, pp. 48 ff.; Randle, Indian Logic, pp. 310, 317; Diṅnāga's Nyāyamukha (Nyāyadvāra) quoted in TSP, Eng., tr. pp. 618-625.

130. Vidyābhūṣaṇa, op. cit., pp. 280, 282, 295; Randle, Indian Logic, p. 181; Keith, Buddhist Philosophy, p. 307.

131. See Isshi Yamada, 'Pramāṇavārttika and Pramāṇaviniścaya' in Journal of Indian and Buddhist Studies, vol. VIII, 1960, pp. 41-45.

132. Nyāyabindu, I, 1-3; BL, I, pp. 148f.; BL, II, pp. 12-14.

133. Nyāyasūtra, I, 1.4—artha-indriyasannikarṣa-utpannam.

134. Nyāyabindu-ṭīkā, ch. I; BL, I. p. 150.

135. Ibid.

136. Pramāṇavārttika, III. 125—pratyakṣam kalpanāpoḍhaṃ pratyakṣeṇaiva siddhyati.

137. Nyāyabindu, p. 13; BL, II, p. 26.

138. Nyāyabindu, p. 14; BL, II, p. 29; cf. BCA, IX. 18.

139. Nyāyabindu, p. 14; BL, II, p. 30; cf. Mahāvagga, pp. 9-10.

140. Nyāyabindu, p. 15; BL, II, p. 33.

141. Nyāyabindu-ṭīkā, p. 15; BL, II, p. 33.

142. BL, II, p. 33, note 3.

143. See Stcherbatsky, Buddhist Conception of Nirvāṇa, pp. 149ff.

144. Nyāyabindu-ṭīkā, p. 16; BL, II, p. 36.

145. Nyāyabindu, p. 17; BL, II, p. 36.

146. Nyāyabindu, p. 17; BL, II, p. 37.

147. Nyāyabindu, II, 1-3; BL, II, pp. 47-48.

148. Nyāyabindu, II, 5-7; BL, II, pp. 51-56

149. Pramāṇavārttikaṃ, First Chapter, ed. by Gnoli, p. 2—ta ete kārya-svabhāvā'nupalabdhilakṣaṇāstrayo hetavaḥ.

150. Nyāyabindu, II, 11-18; BL, II, pp. 60-67.

151. Nyāyabindu, III, 1; BL, II, pp. 109ff.

152. BL, p. 13; BL, II, pp. 328-329, note 7.

153. Jan Yan Shadpa, quoted in BL, II p. 329.

154. Nyāyabindu, I. 19; Sarva-darśana-saṃgraha, Eng. tr. p. 24, where Dharmakīrti is quoted by name.

155. Pramāṇavārttika-bhāṣyaṃ, p. 388, verses, 335-336; p. 397, verses 354-55; p. 415 verse 398, on 'sva-saṃvitti niyama; p. 425, on 'sva-saṃvedana-cintā.'

156. Ibid., p. 429, verse 427.

157. cf. Tattva-saṃgraha, verses 2026-2028, and Satkari Mookerjee, Buddhist Philosophy of Universal Flux, pp. 325-326.

158. Ānandāśrama Skt. Series, no. 51, p. 13.

159. TS, verses 3628-29, 3635-36.

160. Blue Annals, I, p. 54.

161. Bu-ston, II, pp. 135-136; foot note by E. Obermiller.

162. Bu-ston, II, pp. 135.

163. MBT, II, Introduction, pp. 5-6, 39.

164. B. Bhattacharyya, Foreword to TS, vol. I, pp. XXI-XXII. The Tenjur does not mention this text.

165. TS verses 2000—4, 2009-12; TS, Eng. tr. pp. 949-51, 953-54.

166. MBT, II, pp. 172-73.

167. TS and TSP, Eng. tr., vol. II, pp. 964, 987-88, verses 2083-84.

168. Bu-ston, II, p. 135.

169. Ibid., and Blue Annals, I, p. 34.

170. Yuan Chwang, II, 215.

171. Bu-ston, II, p. 136.
172. See Karatalaratna, ch. I, pp. 17-19; Madhyamakārthasaṃgraha, verses 6-8.
173. TS, verse 1393; Eng. tr., p. 690.
174. TSP, Eng. tr., p. 691.
175. Karatalaratna, II, 106, p. 84—animittatvāt animittaikalakṣaṇacaryayā sarvadharmān bhāvayitvā advaye avatarati; cf.Bhāvanākrama, 16, 18 (MBT, II, pp. 168-214)—tato cittaṃ grāhyagrāhaka-viviktaṃadvayaṃ eva cittaṃ iti vicārayet advaya-lakṣaṇe tathatālambane sthitivā tadapi citta-mātraṃ atikramet.
176. TS, verse 350; Eng. tr., p. 227.
177. TSP, tr., p. 228.
178. TS, verses 288, 390.
179. TSP, pp. 140, 151.
180. Nyāyabindu, III, verses 12, 13, 15; BL, II, pp. 122-125.
181. TS, verses 378; see Stcherbatsky's excellent discussion in BL, I, p. 92.
182. TS, tr., p. 239.
183. TSP, tr., p. 242; Kamalaśīla regarded the Vaibhāṣikas as heretics who cannot be regarded as followers of the Buddha.
184. TS, verses 385, 392-394.
185. Stcherbatsky, BL, I, p. 147.
186. Ed. by H. P. Sāstrī in BI; Anantalal Thakur's ed. in Ratnakīrtinandhāvalī.
187. Nyāyavārttika-tātparyaṭīkā, pp. 483ff.
188. BL, I, pp. 477ff.; S. Mookerjee, op. cit., p. 132.
189. Pramāṇa-samuccaya, v. 1; BL, I, p. 459.
190. Ibid., p. 458.
191. Ibid., p. 461; Pramāṇa-samuccaya-vṛtti, v. 11.
192. BL, I, p. 463.
193. TS, p. 1—śūnyamāropitākāra śabdapratyaya gocaraṃ.
194. Ibid., verse 869.
195. BL, I, p. 471.
196. TS, verse 870.
197. Ibid., verse 872.
198. Ibid., verses 873-875; Eng. tr., pp. 470-472.
199. TS, verses 879-880; Eng. tr., pp. 475, 479.
200. TS, verse 1211; Eng. tr., p. 613.
201. TS, verse, 6; TSP, p. 10.
202. BL, I, p. 119, note 2.
203. TS, p. 177—sattaiva vyāpṛtiḥ, i.e. "the mere presence of the cause is its work."
204. TSP, p. 140; Eng. tr., p. 242. The older Buddhists, who were not conversant with logic, posited an eternal empty space (ākāśa), and held it everlasting like their Nirvāṇa. The older Buddhists were the Abhidharmikas, the Sarvāstivādins, who maintained that the two nirodhas (pratisaṃkhyā° and apratisaṃkhyā°) and ākāśa are asaṃskṛt a dharmas. See Abhidharmakośa-kārikā, I, 5-6. Kamalaśīla says that "they were not Buddha's followers".
205. See AK, III, 18, 28 with auto-commentary.
206. TSP, p. 399; BL, I, p. 126.
207. Nyāyabindu-ṭīkā (BI), p. 69; BL, I, p. 127.
208. Ibid.
209. TS, verses 509-510, 515-517; Eng. tr. p. 300-302.
210. TSP, p. 176; Eng. tr., p. 303.
211. TSP, pp. 176-177; Eng. tr. pp. 304-305; see BL, p. 121.
212. Viṃśatikā, verses 1-2. Vasubandhu in his auto-commentary quotes the following —citta-mātraṃ bho jinaputrāḥ yadut traidhātukam iti sūtrāt.
213. TSP, p. 550; Eng. tr., p. 936.
214. Ibid.; BL, I, p. 513.
215. TS, verses 1967-1971; TSP, pp. 550-551; Eng. tr. pp. 937-938.

216. Cf. Kumārila's reply in ŚV, Śūnyavāda, 219—"that one thing should have one and only one form is not a Divine Edict.'
217. TSP, pp. 550-52; BL, I, 514.
218. TSP, pp. 556-57; Eng. tr., pp. 944-47.
219. TS, verse 1997.
220. TS, verses 328-330; Eng. tr., pp. 213-214.
221. TSP, Eng. tr., pp. 214-215.
222. Ibid., p. 949.
223. TS, verses 2000-2.
224. TSP, Eng. tr., pp. 949-50.
225. TS, verse 2006.
226. TSP, p. 559; BL, I, p. 527.
227. TS, verse 2012; Eng. tr., p. 954.
228. TS, verse 2034; Eng. tr., p. 967.
229. TS, verse 2084; Eng. tr., p. 988.
230. Bhāvanākrama (MBT, II), pp. 211, and 173.
231. ChUp, VI. 1; BrUp, II, 4, 5.
232. Cūlamāluṅkyaputtasutta, MN, II, pp. 107 ff.; Milindapañha, IV, I. 19-27, pp. 105 ff.
233. CŚ, VIII. 16, p. 19.
234. Ācārāṅgasūtra, SBE, vol. XXII, I. 3-4.
235. ŚV, Eng. tr. by G. Jha, pp. 38-41.
236. TS, verse 6.
237. ŚV, Eng. tr., p. 38; cf. TS, verse 3186.
238. Pramāṇavārttika, II, 32-35.
239. Ibid., II, 148.
240. CŚV, XII, 7, 146; Prasannapadā, p. 55.
241. Santānāntarasiddhi quoted in BL, I, p. 339.
242. TSP, Eng. tr., pp. 1441-42.
243. TS, verses 3276-77; Eng. tr., pp. 1448-49.
244. TS, verse 3282; TSP, Eng. tr., p. 1453.
245. TS, verse 3290; Eng. tr., p. 1455 and TSP thereto.
246. TS, verses 3318-19; TSP, Eng. tr., p. 1466-67.
247. TS, verse 3322; Eng. tr., p. 1468.
248. TS, verses 3335-36; Eng. tr., pp. 1472-73.
249. TSP, Eng. tr., p. 1474.
250. TS, verses 3340-44; Eng. tr., pp. 1483-85.
251. TS, verse 3627; Eng. tr. p. 1569.
252. TS, verses 3628-29; Eng. tr., p. 1573. See E.A. Solomon, "The Problem of Omniscience (sarvajñatva)" in ALB, vol. XXVI, 1962, pp. 36 ff.; S. Mookerjee, "The Omniscient as the Founder of a Religion" in Nava Nalanda Mahavihara Research Publication, II, 1960, pp. 1-44.

CHAPTER IX

1. The following texts and translations have been utilized in this section—Mimāṃsā-ślokavārttika of Kumārila-Bhaṭṭapāda with the commentary; Nyāyaratnākara, of Pārthasārathi Miśra, ed. by Rāma Sāstrī Tailanga, Chaukhamba Sanskrit Series, no. 3, fasc. I-III, Benaras, 1898; abbreviated as ŚV-Text, Eng.tr. of the Ślokavārttika by Gangānātha Jhā, Asiatic Society of Bengal, Calcutta, 1909, abbreviated as Tr.
2. ŚV Text (Nirālambanavāda), verses 1-4; Tr., p. 119.
3. ŚV-Text, 5; Tr. p. 119.
4. Vide MŚ, XXVI.8; XXIV.10; Madhyamakāvatāra, VI. 28; Madhyamakārtha-saṃgraha; BCA, IX. 2. Pārthasārathi actually quotes MŚ, XXIV. 8 in his commentary on ŚV-Text, 5.
5. ŚV-Text, 5-10; Tr. pp. 119-120.
6. Viṃśatikā of Vasubandhu, verses 3-4.
7. ŚV-Text, 11-13; Tr., p. 120.
8. See MŚ, ch. III-V; Dvādaśamukhaśāstra, pp. 185 f.; CŚ, chs. IX, XIII and CŚV thereon; BCA, IX, 75, 86, 147 ff.

9. ŚV-Text, 14-16; Tr., p. 120.
10. ŚV-Text, 17-18; Tr. p. 121. A classical treatment of this subject in TS, ch. XXIII.
11. ŚV-Text, 19.
12. Ibid., 20-22; Tr., p. 121. 'It has been declared', and 'it has been said', these sentences refer to the earlier contents of the Bhāṣya. Kumārila gives here the pūrvapakṣa or the statement of the Buddhist view in the light of the Buddhist's objections raised against the definition of perception as given in the Sūtra (of Jaimini), and the two kinds of falsities as given by the Bhāṣyakāra (Śabara). The pūrvapakṣa passage of the Bhāṣya runs thus—'nanu sarva eva nirālambanaḥ svapnavat pratyayaḥ pratyayasyāpī nirālambanatā svabhāva upalakṣitaḥ svapne jāgrato 'pi stambha, iti vā kuḍyam iti vā pratyaya eva bhavati. tasmāt so'pi nirālambanaḥ' (quoted by G. Jhā in ŚV-Tr., p. 121, note). Now, first connection of this pūrvapakṣa (with the Mīmāṃsā theory) is that it objects to the definition of sense-perception as embodied in the Aphorism. The second connection is this that the Vṛtti has said that there are only two kinds of false notions—(1) that of which the origin is faulty, and (ii) that which is contradicted by subsequent stronger cognition. It is to the latter that the pūrvapakṣa (i.e. the Buddhist) objects on the ground that all cognitions are equally false. On some references to Buddhist philosophy in Śabarabhāṣya, see Kṣetreśacandra Chaṭṭopādhyāya's paper in Jhā Commemoration Volume, Poona, 1937, pp. 115-127.
13. ŚV-Text, 23; Tr., p. 121.
14. ŚV-Text, 25; Tr., p. 122. On the doctrine of sva-saṃvedana, see Nyāyabindu, I. 10; Pramāṇavārttika-bhāṣyam, p. 425, and p. 429; TS, verses 2001-12.
15. ŚV-Text, 31; Tr., p. 123.
16. ŚV-Text, 32; Tr., p. 123. On Buddhist view of perception, see Fragments from Diṅnāga, Fragment A; Nyāyabindu, I, 4; TS, Eng. Tr. pp. 614 ff.
17. ŚV-Text, 34—gṛhitamātrabādhe tu svapakṣo'pi na siddhyati.
18. ŚV-Text, 35-37; Tr., p. 124.
19. ŚV-Text, 38; Tr., p. 124.
20. ŚV-Text, 39.
21. Ibid., 39-40.
22. Ibid., p. 47; Tr., p. 126.
23. ŚV-Text, 48. On the Buddhist view of apoha, see above chapter VIII.
24. ŚV-Text, 49; Tr., p. 126.
25. ŚV-Text, 50; Tr., p. 126.
26. ŚV-Text, 51; Tr., p. 127.
27. ŚV-Text, 53; Tr., p. 127.
28. ŚV-Text, 54; Tr., p. 127.
29. ŚV-Text, 55-56; Tr., p. 127. On the Mīmāṃsā theory of sense-perception, see ŚV, Pratyakṣa Sūtra, and on its criticism as a reply to Kumārila's objections, see TS, verses 1286-92; Eng. Tr., pp. 645-648.
30. ŚV-Text, 57; Tr., p.127; see Sarvadarśana-saṃgraha, Eng. tr., p. 27 where this argument is pressed by the Sautrāntika against the Vijñānavādin.
31. ŚV-Text, 58-68 (abridged); SV-Tr., pp. 128-130.
32. Cf. Laṃkāvatārasūtra, III. 65; X, 58.
33. ŚV-Text, 69-72 (abridged); Tr., p. 130.
34. ŚV-Text, 74.
35. ŚV-Text, 79-81; Tr., pp. 131-32.
36. ŚV-Text, 82-83.
37. ŚV-Text, 85-87 (abridged); Tr., p. 132.

38. ŚV-Text, 88-89; Tr., p. 133.

39. ŚV-Text, 89-91.

40. Ibid., 91-94.

41. ŚV-Text, 107-109; Tr., pp. 136-137. As already noted, the verse numbers of ŚV-Text are those of the Nirālambanavāda Section of the ŚV.

42. ŚV-Text, 107-113; Tr., pp. 136-137.

43. ŚV-Text, 113-117; Tr., p. 137.

44. ŚV-Text, 178-179; Tr., p. 144.

45. ŚV-Text, 180-181; Tr., p. 145.

46. ŚV-Text, 181-185. On the Buddhist doctrine of momentariness of things, see TS, ch. VIII with Pañjikā.

47. ŚV-Text, 187-188; Tr., p. 146.

48. ŚV-Text, 189-190.

49. ŚV-Text, 193-195; Tr., p. 147.

50. ŚV-Text, 195-196.

51. ŚV-Text, 198-99; Tr., p. 147.

52. Tr., p. 148. See the counter criticism of all the above arguments in TS and TSP, Eng. tr., pp. 711 f., 949 f.

53. In this Section the verse numbers of SV-Text refer to those of the Śūnyavāda Section of the ŚV, and G. Jhā's Eng. tr. is cited according to page numbers.

54. ŚV-Text, verses 2-4; Tr., p. 148; see TS, verses 2001-12.

55. ŚV-Text, 5-8; Tr., pp. 148-149.

56. ŚV-Text, 9. On the sole reality of consciousness, see Pramāṇa-vārttika-bhāṣya, verses 335-336, 398 etc.; TS, Eng., tr., pp. 985, 988, 992 etc.

57. ŚV-Text 10-15; Tr., p. 149.

58. ŚV-Text, 15-18; Tr., pp. 149-150.

59. ŚV-Text, 19-22; Tr., p. 150; a better statement of these views in TS, verses 2012-22; Eng . tr., pp. 954-58.

60. ŚV-Text, 23-25.

61. Ibid., 26-27; Tr., p. 150; see the same verse (27) in TS, verse 2025.

62. ŚV-Text 28-32; Tr., p. 151.

63. ŚV- Text, 34-35; Tr., p. 151; cp. TS, verse 2022.

64. ŚV-Text, 36-39; contra. Sautrāntika view in Sarvadarśana-saṃgraha, Eng. tr., pp. 27-28.

65. ŚV-Text, 40; Tr., p. 152.

66. ŚV-Text, 41-45; Tr., p. 152.

67. ŚV-Text, 48-51; Tr., p. 153.

68. ŚV-Text, 53-55; Tr., p. 153.

69. ŚV-Text, 58-59, and the Nyāyaratnākara on these verses.

70. ŚV-Text, 59-61; Tr., p. 154.

71. ŚV-Text, 62-63.

72. This argument is advanced by Śāntarakṣita also in TS, verses 2001-2.

73. ŚV-Text, 64-67.

74. Ibid., 74.

75. Ibid., 77; Tr., p. 156.

76. ŚV-Text, 78; Tr., p. 156.

77. ŚV-Text, 119-121; Tr. pp. 161-162.

78. ŚV-Text, 128-129., Tr., p. 163. See counter-criticism in TS, ch. XXIII, Eng. tr., pp. 855 ff.

79. ŚV-Text, 131-133; Tr., p. 163.
80. ŚV-Text, 136. See the reply in TS, ch. XVI, Eng. tr., pp. 493 ff.
81. ŚV-Text 149-150; Tr., p. 165.
82. ŚV-Text, 151-155 (abridged).
83. ŚV-Text, 156-158.
84. ŚV-Text 159-161; Tr., p. 167.
85. ŚV-Text, 184-187; Tr., p. 170; cp. TS, verses 2012-16; also BCA, IX with Pañjikā where this argument is advanced and supported with citations from Sūtras attributed to the Buddha.
86. ŚV-Text, 197; Tr., p. 171.
87. ŚV-Text, 219; Tr., p. 175; cp. TS, verses 2033-2084.
88. ŚV-Text, 246; Tr., p. 179.
89. Tantravārttika (Eng. tr.), Introduction, p. IX.
90. The text and English translations utilized in the following account are : Brahmasūtra Śaṃkara-bhāṣyam, ed. by N.R. Āchārya, abbreviated as BrSŚ; Vedāntasūtras with the commentary of Śaṃkarācārya, tr. into English by George Thibaut, pt. I in SBE, vol. XXXIV (abbreviated as Thibaut, I); and occasional use has been made of V. H. Date's Vedānta Explained, vol. I.
91. Some sources of Sarvāstivāda: Jñāna-prasthānasūtra of Kātyāyanīputra, pt. I, restored by Śāntibhikṣu Śāstrī; Abhidharmāmṛta of Ghoṣaka, restored by the same scholar; L'abhidharmakośa de Vasubandhu, French tr. by Poussin; Abhidharmakośa, with Bhāṣya and Sphuṭārthā; CŚ, ch. IX; TS, ch. VIII; Sogen, Systems, ch. III; J. Takakusu in JRAS, 1905 and in ERE, vol. XI, pp. 193f.; A. C. Banerjee, Sarvāstivāda Literature.
92. BrSŚ, II, 2. 18; Thibaut, I, p. 402.
93. See Stcherbatsky, Central Conception, pp. 5 f.
94. BrSŚ, II, 2. 18, pp. 239-240; see however, Sogen, op. cit.
95. See DN, Poṭṭhapādasutta and Pratītyasamutpāda-vibhaṅganirdeśasūtra; Abhidharmāmṛta, ch. VIII.
96. BrSŚ, II, 2.19, p. 240.
97. This refers to Śaṃkara's criticism of the Vaiśeṣika system in BrSŚ, II, 2. 11-17, pp. 229-238.
98. Ibid., II, 2. 19; see counter-criticism from Sarvāstivāda view in Sogen, op. cit., pp. 140-142.
99. BrSŚ, II, 2. 20; Date, Vedānta Explained, p. 318; replies in Sogen, op. cit., pp. 136-137.
100. This imaginary piece of pūrvapakṣa is improbable; no Buddhist, even for argument's sake, can conceive of things originating without causes.
101. Cf. MŚ, I. 2f.
102. BrSŚ, II, 2 21, p. 242.
103. On asaṃskṛta-dharmas, see Abhidharmāmṛta of Ghoṣaka, ch. XVI, section 24.
104. BrSŚ, II, 2. 22; Thibaut, I, pp. 410-411.
105. Vide TaitUp, II. 1; R.E. Hume, Thirteen Upaniṣads, p. 283.
106. Sphuṭārthā-Abhidharmakośa-vyākhyā, on I. 5—vāyur bho Gautama kva pratiṣṭhitaḥ ? ākāśe pratiṣṭhitaḥ.
107. BrSŚ, II, 2. 24, pp. 243-244; Thibaut, I, pp. 412-413.
108. BrSŚ, II, 2. 25; Thibaut, I, pp. 413-415.
109. BrSŚ, II, 2. 26; Thibaut, I, pp. 415-417.

110. BrSŚ, II, 2-28, p. 247—nāsau Sugatābhiprāyaḥ, kasya tu vijñānaikaskandhavādā evābhipretaḥ.

111. Pramāṇavārttika-bhāṣyaṃ, pp. 388, 416.

112. BrSŚ, II, 2. 28; Thibaut, I, pp. 418-421.

113. This argument, as we have seen, is also pressed by the Sautrāntika and Kumārila against the Vijñānavādin.

114. This 'dilemma' is presented best in TS, verses 1993-97.

115. BrSŚ, II, 2. 28, p. 249.

116. BrSŚ, pp. 249-250; Thibaut, I, pp. 420-424.

117. BrSŚ, II, 2. 29; Date, op. cit., I, p. 331.

118. The anvaya and vyatireka, i.e. the positive and negative judgements, whereby the Buddhist supports his view are rather in Vedāntist favour, BrSŚ, II, 2. 30, p. 251; Thibaut, I, pp. 425-426.

119. BrSŚ, p. 251.

120. BrSŚ, II, 2. 31; Thibaut, I, pp. 426-427.

121. BrSŚ, II, 2. 32, p. 252.

122. See Brahmajālasutta in DN, I, pp. 12f., 30 f.; MŚ opening verses, and MŚ, V. 8—astitvaṃ ye tu paśyanti nāstitvaṃ cālpabuddhayaḥ,
bhāvānāṃ te na paśyanti draṣṭavyopaśamam śivaṃ.
See also BCA, IX.2; BCAP, pp. 171-177; Madhyamakāvatāra, VI. 23, and TS opening verses.

123. S. Radhakrishnan, Indian Philosophy, II, p. 473.

124. Gopīnātha Kavirāja, Preliminary Essay, p. x in Eng. tr. of Tantravārttika by G. Jhā.

125. Sogen, Systems, pp. 129.

126. See e.g. TSP, pp. 10, 140, 175-76.

127. Śaṃkara's language reminds us of several anti-Buddhist passages in Brāhmanical texts. He has made the following remark—api ca bāhyārtha vijñāna śūnyavāda trayam itaretara viruddhaṃ upadiśatā Sugatena spaṣṭīkṛtamātmano'saṃbaddhapralāpitvaṃ, pradveṣo vā prajāsu viruddhārtha pratipattyā vimuhyeyurimāḥ prajā iti. sarvathā apyanādaraṇīyo'yaṃ Sugatasamayaḥ śreyaskāmairityabhiprāyaḥ (BrSŚ, II, 2. 32, p. 252). Cf. Tantravārttika, p. 203—smaryante ca purāṇeṣu dharmaviluptihetavaḥ /
kalau Śākyādayasteṣāṃ ko vākyam śrotumarhati //
and Bhāgavata Purāṇa, I. 3. 24—
kalau saṃpravṛtte saṃmohāya suradviṣām/
Buddhanāmnā janasutaḥ kīkaṭeṣu bhaviṣyati//
and Śaktisaṃgamatantra (GOS), Kālīkhaṇḍa, I. 17—
āvirbhavati deveśi divyaughadvārataḥ śive /
Bauddhapāṣaṇḍanāśārthaṃ sampradāyārthameva ca //

128. See Āgamaśāstra, ed. by Vidhusekhara Bhattacharya, Introduction; Stcherbatsky, Buddhist Conception of Nirvāṇa, p. 38; S. N. Dasgupta, History of Indian Philosophy, I, p. 495; and below Chapter XIII.

CHAPTER X

1. BrSŚ, II, 11, speaks of Sāṃkhya as tantra—smṛtiśca tantrākhyā paramarṣipraṇītā; at BrSŚ, II, 2. 32, Buddhist thought is called 'vaināśikatantravyavahāra'. Sāṃkhyakārikā, verse 70 calls the system a tantra propagated by various sages.

2. Amarakośa, p. 1. The word 'tantra' in the sense of loom is traceable to the Vedic texts. Thus the term is used in Ṛgveda, X. 71.9; Atharvaveda, X. 7.42; and Taittirīya Brāhmaṇa, II. 5.5.3, and possibly stands for a loom

and cognate paraphernalia. As is well known, the 15th adhikaraṇa of Kauṭilya's Arthaśāstra is captioned 'tantrayukti', where 32 yuktis or propositions are enumerated. It seems that the Arthaśāstra uses the word 'tantra' in the sense of a system or 'śāstra', so that the given 32 propositions give an exposition of that system. According to the Bhāṣya of Śabara on the Mīmāṃsāsūtra of Jaimini (XI. 4.1) 'when an action or a thing, once done, becomes beneficial in several matters, that is known as tantra—yat sakṛtkṛtaṃ bahūnāṃ upakaroti tat tantraṃ uccyate, e.g. a lamp placed amidst many priests. P. V. Kane has drawn our attention to the occurrence of this word in some other Brāhmanical works, see History of Dharmaśāstra, vol. V, pt. II, p. 1033 and notes. We know that the esoteric texts, called Tantras, must have come into existence long before the time of Aparārka and the Bhāgavata Purāṇa.

Among the late grammarians we find a peculiar sense of the term, e.g. Patañjali's Vyākaraṇa-mahābhāṣya with Kaiyaṭa's Pradīpa and Nāgeśa's Uddyota on I. 1.6, p. 330—arthadvayabodhecchayā ekasya sakṛduccāraṇaṃ iti tantraṃ.

3. John Woodroffe, Shakti and Shākta, pp. 18-19; cp. Cultural Heritage of India, vol. IV, p. 211.

4. Monier-Williams, Sanskrit-Enlgish Dictionary, p. 436.

5. S. C. Das, Tibetan-English Dictionary, p. 318.

6. H. P. Śāstrī, Notices of Sanskrit Manuscripts, vol. 1, Preface, p. XXIV, says that 'the word tantra means shortening abbreviation'.

7. See Gopīnātha Kavirāja, Bharatiya Sanskriti aur Sādhanā, pt. I, ch. 17 on 'Mantravijñāna'; M. B. Jhaveri, Comparative and Critical Study of Mantraśāstra.

8. See G. Tucci, Theory and Practice of the Maṇḍala.

9. See Evans-Wentz, Tibetan Yoga and Secret Doctrines; P. H. Pott, Yoga and Tantra.

10. S. B. Dasgupta, An Introduction to Tantric Buddhism; Anagarika Govinda, Foundations of Tibetan Mysticism; B. Bhattacharyya, Buddhist Iconography; by the same author, Introduction to Buddhist Esoterism; Gopinatha Kaviraja, Tāntrika Vaṅmaya mein Śāktadṛṣṭi; Agehananda Bharati, The Tantric Tradition; John Blofeld, The Tantric Mysticism of Tibet; Herbert V. Guenther and Ghogyam Trungpa, The Dawn of Tantra.

11. Guhyasamāja-tantra, ch. I; Hevajra-tantra, ch. I; Rāmānuja says, in Srī Bhāṣya, II. 2-43, that the Lord Himself composed the Pāñcarātra-śāstra. See O. Schrader, Introduction to the Pāñcarātra.

12. Padmavajra in his Guhyasiddhi, manuscript cited by B. Bhattacharyya, Introduction to Buddhist Esoterism, p. 70, says: śrīsamājāt paraṃ nāsti ratnabhūtaṃ tridhātuke.

13. Kullūka Bhaṭṭa on Manu, II. 1—śrutiśca dvividhā vaidikī tāntrikī ca.

14. Bhāgavata Purāṇa, XI. 3. 47-48; XI. 5. 28; see R. C. Hazra, Purāṇic Records on Hindu Rites and Customs, pp. 260 ff.

15. See Chintaharana Chakravarti, Tantras: Studies on their Religion and Literature, ch. II; L. M. Joshi, 'Protohistoric Origins of Esoterism in India' in Proceedings of the Indian History Congress, XXVIth Session, Ranchi, 1964.

16. N. N. Vasu, Modern Buddhism and Its Followers in Orissa, Introduction by H. P. Sāstrī, pp. 10-11.

17. Buddhist Esoterism, p. 43; Sādhanamālā, vol. 11, p. XXXVI.

18. 'Foreign Elements in the Tantra' in IHQ, vol. VII, 1931.

19. BrSŚ, II. 2, 7-8.

20. Modern Buddhism, Introduction, pp. 10-11.

21. Bhāratīya Sanskriti aur Sādhanā, pt. I, see two chs. on Tāntrika Bauddha Sādhanā.

22. On the cult of the Mother Goddess in the ancient world, see Will Durant, Our Oriental Heritage, chs. VII, VIII, IX, XXIII.

23. John Marshall (ed.), Mohenjodaro and the Indus Civilization, vol. I, pp. 48-58.

24. Ibid., pp. 52 f, plate XII. 17.
25. Ibid., pp. 44-45, plate XCIV. 6, 8.
26. See Benjamin Rowland, Art and Architecture of India, pp. 21-23, plate 60.
27. A. Banerji Śāstrī, "The Naṭī of Pāṭaliputra' in IHQ, vol. IX, 1933, pp. 164-165 and plate.
28. B. Rowland, op. cit., pp. 21-23.
29. H. Hartland on Phallism in ERE, vol. IX, pp. 815 f.
30. Vidhusekhara Bhattacharya, 'Phallic Worship in the Veda' in IHQ, vol. IX, 1933, pp. 103f.; Ṛgveda,VII. 21.5 and X. 10.99 on śiśnadeva; cf. A.P. Karmarkar, 'The Liṅga Cult in Ancient India' in B. C. Law Volume, pt. I, pp. 456ff.
31. Marshall, op. cit., pp. 48-78.
32. Bruce-Foote, Collection of Indian Prehistoric and Protohistoric Antiquities, pp. 20, 61, 139.
33. D. D. Kosambi. 'Urvaśī and Purūravas' reprinted in Indian Studies, Past and Present, vol. I, no. 1, pp. 144, 163, 175; by the same scholar 'On the Origin of Brahmin Gotras' in JBBRAS, (n.s.), vol. 26, 1950, pp. 55, 72, etc.
34. A. B. Keith, Religion and Philosophy of the Veda and Upaniṣads, pp. 61, 71, 184, 200, 260ff.; pp. 379ff.
35. A. A. Macdonell in ERE, vol. VIII, p. 311.
36. Ṛgveda, VII. 104. 15.
37. Ibid., VII. 76. 4.
38. Ibid., X. 136. 2.
39. A. A. Macdonell, in ERE, vol. VIII, p. 314. Mention may be made in this context of the hymn of Lopāmudrā and Agastya in Ṛgveda, I. 179.
40. Keith, op. cit., pp. 181-182; G. C. Pande, Origins of Buddhism, pp. 260-261.
41. Śatapatha Brāhmaṇa, XIII. 4. 3. 7-8. Keith, op. cit., p. 180.
42. Ṛgveda, VI.47. 18; cp. Bhagavadgītā, VII. 14—daivī hyeṣā guṇamayī mama māyā duratyayā.
43. ŚvetUp, VI. 10—māyāṃ tu prakṛtiṃ vidyān māyinaṃ tu maheśvaraṃ.
44. M. Winternitz, HIL, I, p. 185.
45. Keith, op. cit., p. 312; vide Śatapatha Brāhmaṇa, I. 43.11 ff.
46. P. C. Bagchi in Cultural Heritage of India, vol. IV, p. 213.
47. TaitUp, I. 7.
48. BṛUp. I. 1.1.
49. ChUp, VIII, 1. 3.
50. Ibid., II. 13. 3
51. ŚvetUp, II. 12'; G. C. Pande, Bauddha Dharma, p. 461.
52. ChUp. V. 7.1; V. 8. 1-2; BṛUp, VI, 2. 12-13.
53. Ṛgveda X. 90-16—yajñena yajñaṃ ayajanta devāḥ.
54. Bhagavadgītā, IV. 25.
55. ChUp, III. 17, espl. verse 3; Ṛgveda, I. 164. 150; Keith, op. cit., pp. 221, 218. Agnīṣoma is a dual deity; on the secrets of yajña, see Gopinātha Kavirāja, Bhāratīya Sanskriti Aur Sādhanā, pt. I, pp. 166-190.
56. ChUp, VIII. 3. 1-10.
57. ŚvetUp, 1. 4-5; G. C. Pande, Bauddha Dharma, p. 441.
58. BṛUp, IV. 3. 21-22.
59. John Woodroffe, Principles of Tantra, p. XXVII, says that Tantra "is that development of the Vaidikakarma-kāṇḍa which under the name of the Tantra-śāstra is the scripture of the Kali Age". In the opinion of Charles Eliot , Hinduism and Buddhism, vol. II, p. 190, "Tantrism is a species of religious magic, differing from the Vedic sacrifices in method rather than principle". According to Monier-Williams , Hinduism, p. 88, Tantrika doctrine owed its origin to the popularity of the Sāṃkya theory of puruṣa and prakṛti. Gopinātha Kavirāja points out that the Tāntrika Mantraśāstra is rooted in Vedic religion.

60 Sekoddeśa-ṭīkā, pp. 2-4—'srīdhānye niyatamantranayadeśanāsthāne', etc. and the following is quoted from the Mūlatantra (?)—
gṛdhrakūṭe yathāśāstaḥ prajñāpāramitānaye /
tathā mantranaye proktā śrīdhānye dharmadeśanā //
gṛdhrakūṭe mahaśaile prajñāpāramitānayaṃ /
sandeśya bodhisattvānāṃ mahāyānaṃ niruttaraṃ //
61. Blue Annals, II, p. 754, note 1.
62. Rāhula Sāṃkṛtyāyana, Purātattvanibandhāvalī, p. 113, note 3.
63. Mañjuśrīmūlakalpa, p. 88.
64. GST, chs. V and XVII.
65. Sādhanamālā, vol. I, p. 248.
66. Ibid., p. 334—prajñādisādhanaṃ idaṃ sugatopadiṣṭaṃ.
67 Ibid., p. 335.
68. The Cultural Heritage of India, vol. IV, p. 225.
69. ERE, vol. XII, p. 196.
70. GST, p. 1.
71. Hevajra-tantra, I, p. 47.
72. Buddhist Esoterism, p. 19; also in his Introduction to Two Vajrayāna Works, p. X.
73. Sādhanamālā, II, Introduction, pp. XVI-XVII.
74. See Winternitz, 'Notes on the Guhyasamāja Tantra and the Age of the Tantras' in IHQ, vol. IX, 1933, pp. 1 f.; P. C. Bagchi, 'Reviews on Sādhanamālā' in IHQ, vol. VI, 1930; S. B. Dasgupta, Obscure Religious Cults, p. 19; G.Tucci, 'Some Glosses upon the Guhyasamāja' in Melanges, Chinois et Bauddhiques, vol. III, 1934-35.
75. Buddhist Esoterism, p. 18; Buddhist Iconography, p. 9.
76. TS, verses 3486-87; Eng. tr., p. 1527.
77. Vaiśeṣikasūtra, 2—yato abhyudayaniḥśreyasasiddhiḥ sa dharmaḥ,
78. Winternitz in IHQ, vol. IX, p. 9.
79. S. Mookerjee, Buddhist Philosophy of Universal Flux, p. XI.
80. TS, verse 3588.
tāpācchedācca nikaṣāt suvarṇaṃ iva paṇḍitaiḥ /
parīkṣya bhikṣavo grāhyaṃ madvaco na tu gauravāt //
81. MN, I, pp. 389f.
82. AN, I, pp. 174f.
83. MN, I, pp. 333-343.
84. DN, III, pp. 46, 61.
85. MN, I, pp. 209f.
86. DN, I, pp. 183f.
87. Ibid., pp. 10-12, 60-61 etc. Tīracchānavijjā includes bhūtavijjā or bhūtakamma, visavijjā, arts dealing with manes and poisons. Cullavagga, pp. 199-200, records Piṇḍola Bhāradvāja's feat of sorcery which is condemned by the Buddha.
88. Blue Annals, I, p. 102.
89. Tārānātha's Mystic Tales, pp. 9-10; IHQ, vol. XXX, 1954, p. 94.
90. Sekoddeśa-ṭīkā, pp. 2-4.
91. DN, III, pp. 150f.
92. Milindapañha, p. 153; Gopīnātha Kavirāja and G. C. Pande are of the opinion that the especial emphasis on ānāpānasati (cf. DN, Satipaṭṭhānasutta) may be viewed as a possible source of later Tāntrika Yoga.
93. Si-yu-ki, p. 381.
94. ŚS, Vaidya's edition, p. 79 (Bendall's edition, p. 142)—'vidyādharapiṭakopanibaddhaṃ sarvabhayarakṣārthaṃ prayuñjita. tadyathā—aṭṭe, baṭṭe, naṭṭe, kunaṭṭe, ṭake, ṭhake, tharake, urumati, rurumatituruhili mili sarvajñodupadagga, namo sabbasammāsaṃbuddhāṇaṃ, sijjhantu me mantapadā svāhā.'
95. Lalitavistara, p. 1.
96. Samādhirājasūtra, p. 250, verse 100.
97. HCIP, IV, pp. 260, 360 note 6.
98. Saddharmapuṇḍarīkasūtra, pp. 234-235.

99. Gilgit Manuscripts, vol. I, pp. 55-58, 67, 71.
100. Kāraṇḍavyūha, p. 301.
101. Divyāvadāna, p. 118.
102. JUPHS, vol. XV, 1942, pp. 24-27.
103. D. T. Suzuku's Eng. tr., ch. IX on spells.
104. Bodhisattvabhūmi, ed. by U. Wogihara, pp. 272-274.
105. Si-yu-ki, pp. 426-427.
106. Gilgit Manuscripts, I, p. 40; HCIP, IV, p. 20. See a valuable paper by E. Conze, 'Tantric Prajñāpāramitā Texts' in Sino-Indian Studies, vol. V, pt. 2, pp. 100-22.
107. Mañjuśrīmūlakalpa, ed. in TSS, nos. 70, 76, 84; pt. I, Introduction, and pp. 87-94.
108. Mahāyānasūtrasaṃgraha, vol. I, pp. 93-99.
109. ŚS, Bendall's edition, pp. 142, 155, 173, 188, 256, 257.
110. Buddhist Esoterism, p. 56.
111. Winternitz, HIL, II, p. 381.
112. Buddhist Esoterism, p. 56; cp. Yogasūtra, I, 27, 'om' symbolizes the Lord.
113. See Petavatthu, KN, II, pp. 135f.; Lalitavistara, p. 111; H. Kern, Manual, pp. 59-60; Poussin in ERE, XII, p. 194.
114. See John Marshall, The Monuments of Sānchī; B. M. Barua, Bharhut; G. Yazdani, Ajanṭā; Debala Mitra, Ajanṭā; A.Grünwedel, Buddhist Art of India; John Marshall, Buddhist Art of Gāndhāra; V. S. Agrawala, Catalogue of the Mathurā Museum; A. K. Coomaraswamy, Yakṣas.
115. See J. Fergusson, Tree and Serpent Worship; J. Ph. Vogel, Indian Serpent Lore.
116. Lalitavistara, pp. 1-2, 111.
117. See JUPHS, vol. VI, 1933, pp. 81f. figure 13.
118. A. K. Coomaraswamy, Yakṣas, I, p. 29.
119. Aṣṭasāhasrikā, Eng. tr., pp. 93, 140-142.
120. Mahāyānasūtrasaṃgraha, vol. I, p. 329.
121. Four lokapālas are known to the DN, III, Āṭānāṭiyasutta, pp. 150 f. and fifteen yakṣas, including yakṣiṇīs, are mentioned in Bharhut inscriptions.
122. Quoted in ŚS, ed. by Bendall, p. 286.
123. Mahāyānasūtrālaṅkāra, IX, 77.
124. ŚS (edition Bendall's), pp. 155, 142, 14, 9, 175,175, 314, 8, 133, 9, 346, 371.
125. Dharmasaṃgītisūtra, quoted in SŚ (Bendall's edition), p. 286.
126. Kathāvatthu, XXIII. 219. 1, p. 535—ekābhippāyena methuno dhammo paṭisevitabbo.
127. Upāyakauśalyasūtra, quoted in ŚS (Bendall's edition), p .167.
128. Dharmasaṃgītisūtra, quoted in ŚS (Bendall's edition), p. 322-Buddhā bhagavanto mahatpuṇyajñāna sambhāra mahāmaitri mahākaruṇā-gocarā. . . .saṃsāra-nirvāṇa-vimuktā. . . . . .
129. Āryadeva's Cittaviśuddhiprakaraṇa, verses 6,33.
130. See Vajracchedikā and Adhyardha-śatikā, opening lines.
131. Yuan Chwang, II, 107; HCIP, IV, p. 261.
132. Mahāyānasūtrasaṃgraha, pp. 175-176, espl. verses 11, 17—prajñāpāramitārūpaṃ bodhicittasya lakṣaṇam.
133. Advayavajra-saṃgraha, p. 28.
134. Mahāyānasūtālaṅkāra, IX, 45-46—

pratiṣṭhāya parāvṛttau vibhutvaṃ labhyate paraṃ /
apratiṣṭhitanirvāṇaṃ Buddhānāmacale pade //
maithunasya parāvṛttau vibhutvaṃ labhyate param /
Buddhasaukhya vihāre'tha dārā saṃkleśadarśane //

The controversy surrounds the phrase 'parāvṛtti of sexual act' (maithunasya parāvṛttau); S. Levi said that it refers to "the mystic couples of Buddhas and Bodhisattvas which have so much impo rtance in Tantrism". M. Winternitz in IHQ, vol. IX, p. 1, questioned this translation and gave the meaning of parāvṛtti as "turning aside, discard". P. C. Bagchi, Studies in the Tantras, pt. I, p. 92, suggested that parāvṛtti of maithuna refers to the enjoyment of bliss similar to that arising from that act. Gopinātha Kavirāia in Foreword to B. Upadhyaya's Bauddha Darśana Mīmāṃsā, p. 14, holds that parāvṛtti means the 'process of sublimation' or 'reversion'.

135. Winternitz in IHQ, vol. IX, pp. 1f.; S.K. De in Indian Studies-Past and Present, vol. I, pp. 570f.; N. Dutt in Foreword to N. K. Sahu's Buddhism in Orissa, pp. XIf.

136. See GST, Introduction; JASB, vol. XXVI, pp. 128f.; Bhāratīya Saṃskriti Aur Sādhanā, pp. 512 ff.; Bauddha Dharma, pp. 464-65; Purātattvanibandhāvalī, pp. 111-112.

137. See L. M. Joshi, 'Life and Times of the Mādhyamika Philosopher Nāgārjuna' in Maha Bodhi, vol. 73, nos. 1-2, 1965.

138. Rājataraṅgiṇī, I, 173.

139. W. Y. Evans-Wentz, Tibetan Yoga and Secret Doctrines, pp. 344f.; by the same scholar, Tibetan Book of The Great Liberation, pp. 156-157.

140. Yuan Chwang, II, 201; I-tsing, pp. 34-35; Harṣacarita, Eng. tr., p. 252; Mañjuśrīmūlakalpa, pp. 616f.

141. E. Lamotte, Le Traite de la grande Vertue de Sagesse de Nāgārjuna.

142. Yuan Chwang, I, 365f.; ERE, vol. II, p. 62.

143. Si-yu-ki, pp. 248-249; Winternitz, HIL, II, pp. 352ff.; Maitreyanātha is mentioned in a stone inscription of Nalanda. The inscription is found on the pedestal of a Buddha image locally called Ḍhelvā Bābā.

144. G. Tucci, Aspects of the Doctrines of Maitreya(nātha) and Asaṅga, pp. 1-18.

145. Ed. by E. H. Johnston and T. Chaudhari; Eng. tr. by E. Obermiller; see also J. Takasaki, A Study of the Ratnagotravibhāga.

146. Adhyāśayasaṃcodanasūtra, quoted in ŚS, p. 12—yatkiñcin Maitreya subhāṣitaṃ sarvaṃ tad Buddhabhāṣitam.

147. Abhidharmasamuccaya, pp. 106-107; cf. G. C. Pande, Bauddha Dharma, p. 465.

148. Si-yu-ki, pp. 248-249.

149. Tārānātha (Schiefner),p. 201; Kern, Manual, p. 133.

150. Sādhanamālā. vol. I, no. 159, p. 321, the colophon to this Sādhana reads—prajñāpāramitā-sādhanaṃ samāptaṃ kṛtiriyaṃ ācārya Asaṅgapādānām.

151. GST, Introduction, p. XXXIV; Buddhist Iconography, pp. 12-13.

152. 'Animadversiones Indicae', II in JASB, vol. XXVI, 1930, pp. 129f.

153. On the date and doctrines of Harivarman, see Y. Sogen, Systems, ch. IV, pp. 172 f.

154. JASB, vol. XXVI, pp. 129-130.

155. IHQ, vol. IX, 1933, pp. 1 f.

156. The Mahāsāṃghika group of Buddhists had buried the eggs not only of the Mahāyāna but also of the Vajrayāna. Buddhist esoterism seems to have sprung up from the Lokottaravāda docetism in Āndhradeśa in cir., 150 B.C. But it took centuries to emerge out as a system.

157. Kāraṇḍavyūhasūrtra, pp. 292 ff., 300-304.

158. Gilgit Manuscripts, vol. I, pp. 13-14; ed. also in BST, no. 17, see pp. 168-169.

159. JUPHS, vol. XV, pp. 26 f.

160. Gilgit Manuscripts, vol. I, pp. 44-45.

161. Ibid., pp. 60-62; cf. B. Bhattacharyya, Indian Buddhist Iconography, pp. 129-131.

162. Gilgit Manuscripts, vol I, pp. 48ff. The text opens with these lines—evaṃ mayā śrutaṃ ekasmin samaye Potalakaparvate Āryāvalokiteśvarāyatane divyamaṇiratne śrī-Indranīlamaye puṣpasaṃstṛte devasiṃhāsane Bhagavān sārdha mahatā bhikṣu saṃghena.

163. See JRAS, 1912, pp. 62 f.; F. A. R. Hoernle, op, cit., vol. I, pp. 52 ff.; Winternitz, HIL, II, p. 387.

164. ŚS, Appendix I, pp. 197-205.

165. Ed. by T. Gaṇapati Śāstrī in TSS.
166. GST, Introduction, pp. XXXII-XXXVIII.
167. See Winternitz, HIL, II, p. 397; in IHQ, vol. IX, pp. 5-6; K.P. Jayaswal, An Imperial History of India, Introduction, p. 3; N. Dutt in HCIP, IV, p. 262; Przyluski in BEFEO, XXIII, 1923, p. 306.
168. Mañjuśrīmūlakalpa, I, p. 38; GST, Introduction, p. XXXIII.
169. IHQ, vol. IX, p. 5.
170. Mañjuśrīmūlakalpa, pp. 384-385; B. Bhattacharyya himself knows these facts, GST, Introduction, p. XXXVI.
171. R. Sāṃkṛtyāyana, Purātattvanibandhāvalī, pp. 106-113.
172. IHQ, vol. IX, p. 8.
173. S. Levi's edition of the Mahāmāyūri in Journal Asiatique, 1915, p. 370; see also Yuan Chwang, I, on Gāndhāra and Uḍḍiyāna.
174. Yuan Chwang, I, 221; Si-yu-ki, pp. 162-163.
175. J. F. Fleet (ed. and tr.), Corpus Inscriptionum Indicarum, vol. III, p. 78.
176. Ibid., pp. 72-78.
177. Ibid., pp. 47-48.
178. Bṛhatsaṃhitā, ed. by S. Dvivedi, 59. 19; cf. J. N. Banerjea, Development of Hindu Iconography, pp. 230, 494.
179. Life, pp. 86-88. The Śakti-worshippers, who sacrificed human beings for propitiating the goddess, are known to the Bodhicaryāvatāra of Śāntideva and the Rājataraṅgiṇī of Kalhaṇa.
180. R. Sāṃkṛtyāyana, Purātattvanibandhāvalī, p. 18.
181. O. Schrader, Introduction to Pāñcarātra, p. 31.
182. Mahābhārata, Sāntiparvan, 218. 11-12.
183. P. Peterson's edn., pp. 32, 224-228.
184. Harṣacarita, bk. III (Chaukhamba edition), pp. 165 ff.
185. Ed. by S. P. Pandit and N. B. Utgikar, verses 46, 297, 1091.
186. Rājataraṅgiṇī, III. 267; IV. 94, 112, 153. 162, 246-251.
187. See R. Sāṃkṛtyāyana in Journal Asiatique for 1934, pp. 200ff. and Purātattvanibandhāvalī, pp. 106f.
188. Sādhanamālā, II, pp. 455; Hevajra-tantra, Eng. tr., p. 70 also mentions 3 of them and other kṣetras.
189. See D. C. Sircar, Sākta Pīṭhas in JASB (L), XIV, pp. 8ff.
190. Aṣṭasāhasrikā, BST, no. 4, p. 112 (R. L. Mitra's edition, p. 225; E. Conze's tr., p. 79)—ime khalu punaḥ Śāriputra ṣaṭpāramitā pratisaṃyuktāḥ sūtrāntāstathāgatasyātyayena dakṣiṇāpathe pracariṣyanti, dakṣiṇāpathātpunareva vartanyāṃ pracariśyanti, vartanyāḥ punaruttarāpathe pracariṣyanti. Haribhadra in his Āloka, says, vartanyāṃ iti pūrvadeśe.
191. Sekoddeśa-tīkā, pp. 3-4—Śrīdhānye niyata mantranayadeśanā sthāne; the following is quoted from the Mūlatantra—Gṛdhrakūṭe yathāśāstaḥ prajñāpāramitānaye / tathāmantranaye proktā Srīdhānye dharmadeśanā //
192. See Laṅkāvatārasūtra, p. 118.

dakṣiṇāpatha vedalyāṃ bhiṣuḥ śrīmān mahāyaśaḥ /
nāgāhvayaḥ sa nāmnā tu sadasatpakṣadārakaḥ //
prakāśya loke madyānaṃ mahāyānamanuttaraṃ /

Harṣacarita, bk. VIII (Chaukhamba edition, 1958), p. 440, also associates Nāgārjuna with the Nāgarāja, Nāgaloka and with king Sātavāhana who was the 'Lord of the three seas'.
193. Yuan Chwang, II, 200-206; Si yu-ki,-pp. 414-419; I-tsing, p. 159.
194. Si-yu-ki, p. 331.
195. Epigraphia Indica, vol. XX, pp. 1-37; vol. XXI, pp. 61-71; Ancient India, no. 16, 1962, pp. 65ff.
196. N. Dutt, Aspects, p. 39.
197. Mañjuśrīmūlakalpa, p. 175; cf. Purātattvanibandhāvalī, p. 108.
198. Mañjuśrīmūlakalpa, p. 88—

Śrīparvate mahāśaile dakṣiṇāpathasañjñike /
Śrīdhānyakaṭake caitye jinadhātudhare bhuvi //
Sidhyante tatra mantrā vai kṣipraṃ sarvārthakarmau /

199. Gaṇḍavyūhasūtra, BST, no. 5, pp. VII, 39—dakṣiṇāpathe Dhanyākaraṃ nāma mahānagaram............Dhanyākarasya mahānagarasya pūrveṇa vicitrasāradhvajavyūha nāma mahāvanaṣaṇḍaṃ pūrva Buddhādhyuṣita caityaṃ........; p. 394—Dhanyākarānnagarādupādāya sarvadakṣiṇāpathamaṭan daśottaraṃ kalyāṇamitraśataṃ....

200. Yuan Chwang, II, 215; Bu-ston, II, p. 164, says that Śāntideva went to Srīparvata to learn and perform the miracles.

201. Yuan Chwang, II, 229.

202. Gilgit Manuscripts, vol. I, p. 68, 70; Tārānātha (Schiefner) pp. 132, 157.

203. Yuan Chwang, II, 229, AGI, p. 549; N. L. De, Geographical Dictionary, p. 132; Gilgit Manuscripts, vol. I, p. 69.

204. Cf. Story of Buddhism with special reference to South India, pp. 39, 41.

205. Nikāya-saṃgraha, pp. 8.9; Purāttatvanibandhāvalī, p. 107, 115, 116.

206. Harṣacarita (Chaukhamba edition), bk. I, p. 9—sakalapraṇayi manoratha siddhi Srīparvato Harṣaḥ.

207. Kādaṃbarī, P. Peterson's edition, pp. 224-228; Nirnaya Sagar Press edition, p. 399.

208. Mālatīmādhava, Acts, I, VIII, X.

209. Rājataraṅgiṇī, III. 267; IV. 390.

210. L. A. Waddell, Lamaism, p. 15; G. Tucci in East and West, vol. IX, pp. 279ff.; S. Levi, in Journal Asiatique, 1915, pp. 105 f; P. C. Bagchi in IHQ, vol. VI, pp. 576 ff.

211. N. K. Sahu, op cit., pp. 142 f.

212. H. Lüders, List of Brāhmī Inscriptions, no. 62.

213. Life, p. 66.

214. Fa-hsien, p. 11.

215. Yuan Chwang, I, 225-226.

216. D N, I, pp. 12, 61 etc.

217. Mahābhārata, Śāntiparvan, 335. 8-12.

218. Yuan Chwang, I, 227; A. Foucher, Etudes sur l' iconographie bouddhique, pp. 121, 148.

219. Yuan Chwang, I, 227-237; cp. Jātakamālā, Jātaka nos. 2, 8, 28 and 30.

220. J. Ph. Vogel, Antiquities of Chamba State, vol. I, plates 4f.

221. H. Goetz. 'Antiquities of Chamba State: An Art Historical Outline' in JUPHS, vol. I, 1953, pp. 76f.

222. J. Przyluski, 'An Ancient People of Panjab: the Udumbaras' in Indian Studies—Past & Present, vol. I, 1960, pp. 729 f.

223. Tārānātha's Mystic Tales, p. 23; Evans-Wentz, Tibetan Yoga, p. 153; Blue Annals, II, p. 753; Waddell, Lamaism, p. 15.

224. Rājataraṅgiṇī, IV. 211.

225. GST, Introduction, pp. XXXIIf.

226. IHQ, vol. IX, pp. 6-7.

227. HCIP, IV, p. 262; Foreword to N. K. Sahu's Buddhism in Orissa, p. XI.

228. Bauddha Dharma, p. 469.

229. H. P. Sāstrī, Descriptive Catalogue of Sanskrit Manuscripts, Asiatic Society of Bengal, vol. I, Buddhist Manuscripts, pp. 17f; N. Dutt in HCIP, IV, p. 360, note 17.

230. Thomas Watters and C. Bendall in ŚS (ed. by Bendall), p. 274; Winternitz in IHQ, vol. IX, pp. 1-2.

231. G. Roerich, Biography of Dharmasvāmīn, pp. 107, 110.

232. Blue Annals II, p. 753.

233. Sādhanamālā, volume I, p. 267; the colophon to the Ekajaṭā Sādhana reads—Ekajaṭā sādhanaṃ samāptaṃ, Ārya-nāgārjuna-pādair Bhoṭeṣu uddhṛtaṃ; also p. 193 where the Vajratārā Sādhana is attributed to Nāgārjuna.

234. GST, p. 88—vajraikajaṭāṃ nāma mahāsarpāparājita vāgvajragrīṃ.

235. Ibid., Introduction, pp. XXXI f.
236. It is to be noted that Bhagini and Ḍākinī Tantras are mentioned by Dharmakīrti in Pramāṇavārttika-svavṛtti, ed. by R. Sāṃkṛtyāyana, p. 578; ed. by Gnoli, p. 163.
237. GST, pp. 1, 154, 172; Sekoddeśa-ṭīkā, pp. 3-5.
238. Blue Annals, II, p. 753; the Sarvatathāgata-tattva-saṃgraha is extant in Tibetan. An old Sanskrit MS. of it has been found in Nepal as reported by D. L. Snellgrove, Hevajra-tantra, I, p. 18.
239. Tārānātha (Schiefner), p. 188.
240. Hevajra-tantra, I, pp. 19f., 50f., 66f., 170, 114f.
241. Ed. with Tibetan and Chinese versions and Eng. tr. MBT, pt. I.
242. Blue Annals, II, p. 753.
243. Ibid., pp. 754-755.
244. Ibid., pp.867-869.
245. Ibid., p. 868.
246. See his paper 'A Sanskrit Biography of the Siddhas and some questions connected with Nāgārjuna' in JASB, XXVI, 1930, pp. 138-158.
247. See his learned paper 'L'Origine du Vajrayāna des 84 Siddhas', in Journal Asiatique, 1934, pp. 209-230; Hindi version in Purātattvanibandhāvalī, pp. 109-130.
248. JASB, XXVI, 1930, p. 132.
249. Cf. Satya Prakāśa, Prācīna Bhārata mein Rasāyana kā Itihāsa, ch. XII, pp. 209f.
250. Kabīra-granthāvali, Nāgarī Pracāriṇī Sabhā's edn., p. 54.
251. Gorakṣa-siddhānta-saṃgraha, (Banaras edn.) p. 40; Haṭhayoga-pradīpikā, I. 5-8, pp. 6-7; cf. Hajārī Prasād Dvivedī, Nātha Sampradāya kā Itihāsa.
252. Cultural Heritage of India, vol. IV, p. 274.
253. IHQ, March, 1929, pp. 14-30; Epigraphia Indica, vol. XXVI, pp. 247f.
254. See History of Bengal, I, chapters XI-XII, pp. 304f.
255. R. Sāṃkṛtyāyana, Purātattvanibandhāvalī, table on pp. 120-125; cf. P. C. Bagchi in the Cultural Heritage of India, vol. IV, p. 274.
256. TS, Foreword, pp. XCV-XCVI; Sādhanamālā, II, Introduction, p. XLIII; JBORS, XIV; pp. 341-357; Buddhist Esoterism, pp. 65.
257. Journal of Assam Research Society, vol. II, p. 47.
258. K. L. Barua, in the Journal of the Assam Research Society, vol. II, pp. 47-85; Maheshwar Neog in IHQ, vol. XXVII, pp. 146-147.
259. Mystic Tales, p. 8.
260. Ibid., p. 9; Blue Annals, I, p. 35, 344.
261. S. C. De, 'The Orissa Museum Image Inscription of the time of Śubhākaradeva' in Proceedings of Indian History Congress, 1949, pp. 66ff.
262. Nāgārjuna, the author of the Sādhanas, seems to be different from Nāgārjuna the author of a Ratiśāsra.
263. Purātattvanibandhāvalī, p. 121.
264. Blue Annals, II, p. 753.
265. Mystic Tales, p. 9; S. K. Pathak, 'Life of Nāgārjuna from the Pag Sam Jon Zang', IHQ, vol. XXX, p. 93.
266. Sādhanamālā, II, Introduction, p. CVI.
267. JASB, XXVI, p. 139.
268. Sādhanamālā, II, Introduction, p. XCV.
269. JASB, XXVI, p. 141.
270. Mystic Tales. p. 9.
271. Ibid., p. 46.
272. Ibid., p. 11.
273. Mystic Tales, p. 11
274. HCIP, IV, p. 267.
275. Ibid., IV, pp. 112, 117.
276. See G. Tucci in East and West, vol. 9, 1958, pp. 280, 324.
277. Hevajra-tantra, I, Introduction, p. 12.

278. Mystic Tales, pp. 18-20.
279. Bauddha Gān O Dohā, Introduction.
280. Origin and Development of Bengali Language, p. 81.
281. TSP, p. 905, commentary on TS, verse 3487.
282. Tārānātha (Schiefner), p. 275.
283. Sekoddeśa-ṭīkā, pp. 2-5.
284. Advayavajra-saṃgraha, p. 14—mahāyānaṃ ca dvividhaṃ pāramitānayo mantranayaśceti. tatra pāramitānayaḥ sautrāntika-yogācāramādhyamika-sthityā vyākhyāyate. mantranayastu yogācāra mādhyamikasthityā vyākhyāyate.
285. Ibid., pp. 21, 28.
286. Bu-ston, I, pp. 39-40.
287. Blue Annals, I, p. 102
288. See Csoma de Koros, Life and Teachings of Buddha, Appendix on Literature of Tibet, pp. 104ff.; F. W. Thomas, Indianism and Its Expansion, pp. 82ff.; R. Sāṃkṛtyāyana, Tibbat mein Bauddha Dharma, pp. 48f., G. Tucci, 'The Debate of bSam-yas' in MBT, II.
289. Blue Annals, I, p. 102, note 1.
290. Waddell, Lamaism, p. 152.
291. Tārānātha (Schiefner), pp. 201, 275.
292. See Evans-Wentz, Tibetan Yoga, pp. 155f.; Kazi Dawa Samdup, Śrīcakrasambhāra-tantra, Introduction; D. L. Snellgrove, Buddhist Himalaya.

CHAPTER XI

1. Advayavajra-saṃgraha, p. 14.
2. GST, p. 12—
sarvabhāvavigataṃ skandhadhātvāyatana-grāhyagrāhakavarjitaṃ /
dharmanairātmyasamatayā svacittamādyanutpannaṃ śūnyatābhāvaṃ //
3. Ibid.—
anutpanneṣu dharmeṣu na bhāvo na ca bhāvanā /
ākāśapadayogena iti bhāvaḥ pragīyate //
4. Prajñopāyaviniścayasiddhi, I.3.
5. Ibid., I, 9—
varaṃ hi bhāva saṃkalpo na tvabhāvakalpanā /
nirvāti jvalito dīpo nirvṛtaḥ kāṃ gatiṃ vrajet //
6. Ibid., I. 10.
7. Ibid., II, p. 7.
8. Hevajra-tantra, pt. I, p. 60.
9. MŚ, opening lines—
anirodhamanutpādamanucchedamaśāśvataṃ /
anekārthamanānārthamanāgamamanirgamam //
10. Hevajra-tantra, pt. II, p. 160.
11. Jñānasiddhi, I, 47-48—
apratiṣṭhaṃ yathākāśam vyāpi lakṣaṇavarjitam /
idaṃ tat paramaṃ tattvaṃ vajrajñānamanuttaram //
khyātāsamantabhadreti mahāmudrā ca sañjitā /
dharmakāyaṃ idaṃ jñeyamādarśajñānaṃ ityapi //
12. Prajñopāyaviniścayasiddhi, 1.14—
parāmarṣaṇayogena dharmāṇāṃ niḥsvabhāvatā /
jñānajñeyavibhāgena prajñā tattvaṃ taducyate //
13. GST, pp. 37-38.
14. MŚ, XXV, 19—
na saṃsārasya nirvāṇāt kiñcidasti viśeṣaṇam /
na nirvāṇasya saṃsārāt kiñcidasti viśeṣaṇam //
15. Ibid., XXII, 16—
Tathāgato yatsvabhāvastatsvabhāvam idaṃ jagat /
Tathāgato niḥsvabhāvo niḥsvabhāvam idaṃ jagat ./
16. Aṣṭasāhasrikā Prajñāpāramitāsūtra, p. 177—sarvakalpavikalpaprahīṇo hi Tathāgataḥ; cp. Vajracchedikā Prajñāpāramitāsūtra, ed. by E. Conze, p. 57—Dharmato Buddhā draṣṭavyā dharmakāyā hi nāyakāḥ/

dharmatā ca na vijñeyā na sā śakyā vijānituṃ // cf. Haribhadra, Āloka BST, no. 4 p. 282.

17. Hevajratantra, pt. I, p. 104.
18. Ibid., p. 107.
19. Prajñopāyaviniścayasiddhi, IV. 22.
20. Ibid., IV. 23—
 prabhāsvaraṃ kalpanayā vimuktaṃ prahīṇarāgādimalapralepam /
 grāhyaṃ na ca grāhakamagramattvaṃ tadeva nirvāṇavaraṃ jagād //
cp. AN, I, p. 10—pabhassaraṃ idaṃ, bhikkhave, cittaṃ taṃ ca kho āgantukehi upakkilesehi upakkiliṭṭhaṃ.
21. Advayavajra-saṃgraha, p. 37—
 dṛḍhaṃ sāraṃ asauśīryaṃ acchedyābhedyalakṣaṇam /
 adāhi avināśi ca śūnyatā vajraṃ ucyate //
22. Ibid., p. 24—
 vajreṇa śūnyatā proktā sattvena jñānamātratā /
 tādātmyaṃ anayoḥ siddhaṃ vajrasattva svabhāvataḥ //
23. Hevajratantra, pt. I, p. 47.
24. GST, pp. 1 f.
25. Quoted by D. L. Snellgrove in Hevajratantra, pt. I, p. 47, note.
26. Hevajratantra, pt. I, pp. 92, 117; GST, opening lines; Jñānasıddhi, opening lines.
27. Cittaviśuddhiprakaraṇa, verse 10—
 manaḥ pūrvaṅgamanā dharmāḥ manaḥ śreṣṭhā manojavāḥ /
 manasā hi prasannena bhāṣate vā karoti vā //
cp. Dhammapada, verse 1—
 manopubbaṅgamā dhammā manoseṭṭhā manomayā /
 manasā ce paduṭṭhena karoti vā bhāsati vā
 tatonaṃ dukkhamanveti cakkamiva vahato padaṃ //
28. Dohākośa, ed. by P. C. Bagchi, p. 23.
29. Buddhist Texts, ed. and tr. by E. Conze and others, p. 230.
30. Navaślokī, ed. by G. Tucci, MBT, I, pp. 217, 228—
 pratibiṃbanibhaṃ grāhyamanādicittasaṃbhavaṃ /
 tadākāraṃ ca vijñānaṃ anyonyapratibiṃbavat //
31. So Sāstrī in N. N. Vasu's Modern Buddhism, Introduction, pp. 10-11; Poussin in ERE, vol. XII, p. 193; L. A. Waddell, Lamaism, p. 14; Gopīnātha Kavirāja, Bhāratīya Sanskriti aur Sādhanā, pt. I, p. 534; B. Bhattacharyya, Introduction to Buddhist Esoterism, p. 53; S. B. Dasgupta, Introduction to Tantric Buddhism, pp. 3-4; M. Winternitz in IHQ, vol. IX, pp. 1 f. etc.
32. D. L. Snellgrove in Hevajratantra, pt. I, p. 44; Lāmā Anāgarika Govinda, Foundations of Tibetan Mysticism, pp. 94f.
33. Ibid., pp. 96-97.
34. Ibid., p. 98.
35. Hevajratantra, pt. I, p. 76.
36. First Bhāvanākrama, MBT, II, pp. 194-195—Bodhisattvasya prajñopāyarūpa pratipattir na prajñāmātraṃ na upāya mātraṃ. yathā Āryavimalakīrtinirdeśe, 'prajñārahita upāya, upāyarahitā ca prajñā bodhisattvānāṃ bandhanam' iti uktaṃ upāyasahitaprajñā prajñā-sahita upāya mokṣatvena varṇitaḥ. Āryagayāśīrṣe ca uktaṃ. 'dvāvimau—bodhisattvānāṃ saṃkṣiptau mārgau dvābhyāṃ mārgābhyāṃ samanvāgatā bodhisattvāḥ mahāsattvāḥ........katamau dvau ? upāyaśca prajñā ca' iti. Such is the opinion of Kamalaśīla (800 A.D.) who was the Professor of Tantra in the University of Nālandā and one of the putative fathers of 'Tibetan mysticism'.
37. MŚ, XXII. 16; XXV. 19.
38. Hevajratantra, pt. I, p. 104.
39. Prajñāpāramitā-piṇḍārtha, opening line BST, no. 4, p. 263—prajñāpāramitā jñānaṃ advayaṃ sā tathāgataḥ. cp. Prajñāpāramitāstava of Nāgārjuna, BST, no. 4, p. 1—ākāśamiva nirlepaṃ niṣprapañcaṃ nirakṣaram, yastvāma paśyati bhāvena sa paśyati Tathāgataḥ.

40. GST, pp. 28, 154; according to Snellgrove, Hevajratantra, I, p. 44, note 1, the word occurs also in the Sanskrit manuscript of the Sarvatathāgatatattvasaṃgraha.
41. Hevajratantra, Introduction, p. 44.
42. Bhāratīya Sanskriti aur Sādhanā, pt. I, p. 534.
43. On Bodhicitta in Mahāyāna see ŚS, ch. I; my ed. and tr. of ŚS kārikās; BCA, I, 9-12; Gaṇḍavyūhasūtra, ch. 54; Bodhicittotpāda-sūtraśāstra, p. 209.
44. GST, pp. 11-13.
45. Ibid., p. 153—
anādinidhanaṃ śāntaṃ bhāvābhāvakṣayaṃ vibhum /
śūnyatākaruṇābhinnaṃ bodhicittaṃ iti smṛtam //
46. Cittaviśuddhiprakaraṇa., verse 1 :—
anādinidhanaṃ śāntaṃ bhāvābhāvavivarjitam /
nirvikalpaṃ nirālambamanavasthitamadvayam //
47. Prajñopāyaviniścayasiddhi, IV. 17—
etaddvayamityuktaṃ bodhicittaṃ idaṃ param /
vajraṃ Śrīvajrasattvaṃ ca Saṃbuddho bodhireva ca //
48. Ibid., II. 29—
nityaṃ prabhāsvaraṃ śuddhaṃ bodhicittaṃ jinālayam /
sarvadharmamayaṃ divyaṃ nikhilāspadakāraṇam //
49. Ibid., I, 20—
na dvayaṃ nādvayaṃ śāntaṃ śivaṃ sarvatra saṃsthitam /
pratyātmavedyamacalaṃ prajñopāyamanākulam //
50. Ibid., IV. 11—
nirālaṃbapade prajñā nirālaṃbā mahākṛpā /
ekībhūtā dhiyā sārdhaṃ gagane gaganaṃ yathā //
51. Jñānasiddhi, p. 72-75.
52. Hevajratantra, pt. I, pp. 64, 76, 97.
53. Evans-Wentz, Tibetan Book of the Great Liberation, p. 129.
54. Ibid., p 148.
55. Anāgārika Govinda, Tibetan Mysticism, p. 19, quoted from H. Zimmer, Ewiges Indien, p. 81.
56. Gopīnātha Kavirāia, op. cit., pp. 323f.
57. B. Bhattacharyya, Buddhist Esoterism, p. 56.
58. Yogasūtra, I. 27—tasya vācakaḥ praṇavaḥ.
59. Muṇḍaka Up., II. 4.
60. Tārānātha's Chos ḥbyung, p. 82, cited in Hevajratantra, pt. I, p. 11.
61. Tibetan Book of the Great Liberation, p. 141, note 1; cp. Tibetan Book of the Dead. pp. 220-222.
62. See however, Kumārila, Tantravārttika, G. Jhā's Eng. tr., vol. I, p. 99—"all mantras have meanigns, some are known some unknown".
63. GST, pp. 81, 84, 91.
64. Hevajratantra, pt. I, pp. 50-51, 116-118.
65. Sādhanamālā, vol. II, pp. 558, 560, 581.
66. Ibid., p. 575—kimastyasādhyaṃ mantrāṇāṁ yojitānām yathāvidhi; cf. Tārānātha, Mystic Tales, pp. 12ff.
67. Sādhanamālā, vol. I, p. 334—viśvavismāpane śaktirasmādasyopajāyate.
68. Ibid., p. 270—ayaṃ mantrarājo buddhatvamapi dadāti kiṃ punaranyāḥ siddhayaḥ.
69. Ibid., p. 87—gardabho'pi granthaśatatraya gṛhṇāti.
70. Ibid., vol. II, p. 600.—sarvabuddhasya mantrarājasya balidānena puṇyasaṃbhāraṃ gaṇayituṃ na samartho buddho rātrindivamavichhinnadhārayā devā api tat puṇyaṃ gaṇayitum na samarthāḥ.
71. Ibid., vol. I, p. 31.
72. Ibid., vol. I, p 62.
73. GST, pp. 27 ff.
74. Hevajratantra, pt. I, pp. 50 ff.

75. Sekoddeśa-ṭīkā, p. 24 (the pupil addresses his preceptor in the following words)—
namaste kālacakrāya sarvāvaraṇa hānaye /
paramākṣarasukhāpūrṇa jñānakāya namo'stu te //
śūnyatākaruṇābhinnaṃ bodhicittaṃ yadakṣaram /
tena sekena me nātha prasādaṃ kuru sāmpratam //
putradārādibhiḥ sārdhaṃ dāso'haṃ tava sarvadā /
ābodhimaṇḍaparyantaṃ nānyo'sti śaraṇaṃ mama //

76. GST, p. 20—ācāryanindanaparā naiva siddhyanti sādhane.

77. Advayasiddhi of Lakṣamīṃkarādevi (MS. preserved in Central Library, Baroda), quoted by B. Bhattacharyya, Introduction, Buddhist Esoterism, p. 77, note 3. —ācāryātparataraṃ nāsti trailokye sacarācare, yasya prasādāt prāpyante siddhayo'nekadhā buddhaiḥ.

78. Sādhanamālā, vol. II, p. 586:—
ācārye yaḥ sadā dveṣī kupito ratnatraye'pi yaḥ /
anekasattvavidhvaṃsī mahākālena khādyate //

79. Hevajratantra, p. I, p. 65.

80. Jñānasiddhi, pp. 12, 71, 72.

81. Ibid., p. 33, verse 23 —
guruprasādo yasyāsti sa labhet tattvamuttamam /
anyathā kliśyate bālāḥ cirakāla vimohitāḥ //

82. Only 312 sādhanas have been so far printed in the Sādhanamālā, 2 vols, GOS, 26, 41.

83. Sādhanamālā, vol. I, pp. 183, 224; ERE, vol. XII, p. 196; A. Foucher, Etude sur' Iconographic Bouddhique, pt. II, pp. 8f.

84. GST, p. 165.

85. Ibid., p. 162—
sevāvidhānaṃ prathamaṃ dvitīyamupasādhanam /
sādhanantu tṛtīyaṃ vai mahāsādhanaṃ caturthakam //
See Gopīnātha Kavirāja, op. cit., chs 37-38.

86. GST, pp. 162-63—
sāmānyottamabhedena sevā tu dvividhā bhavet /
vajracatuṣkeṇa sāmānyamuttamaṃ jñānāmṛtena ca //
prathamaṃ śūnyatābodhiṃ dvitīyaṃ bījasamhṛtaṃ /
tṛtīyaṃ bimbaniṣpattiścaturthaṃ nyāsamakṣaram //

87. GST, pp. 163-64—
pratyāhārastathā dhyānaṃ prāṇāyāmo'tha dhāraṇā /
anusmṛtiḥ samādhiśca ṣaḍaṅgo yoga ucyate //

88. Yogasūtra, II. 54.

89. Ibid., III. 2.

90. Ibid., II. 49.

91. Ibid., III. 1.

92. Ibid., III. 3.

93. Hevajratantra, pt. I, pp. 63. 66.

94. See Ibid., p. 61 and contrast GST, p. 6.

95. In the Hevajratantra, pt. I, p. 96, she is called 'Prajñā of 16 years.'

96. She might be of any caste or outcaste, sister, daughter or another's wife; vide Two Vajrayāna Works, pp. 22-23, 39ff.; Sekoddeśaṭikā, pp. 23f.

97. What is condemned as a 'moral anarchy' among men and women, is the accepted order among these yogins who, being 'beyond good and evil wander like lions'. For instances of disregard to moral rules, see GST, pp. 26, 120, 161 etc.; Two Vajrayāna Works, pp. 32, 33, 38, 39; Cittaviśuddhiprakaraṇa, verses 6, 17-19.

98. Hevajratantra, pt. I. pp. 65-66.

99. See Winternitz in IHQ, vol. IX, 1933, p. 4; B. Bhattacharyya, Two Vajrayāna Works, Introduction, p. XIII; V. Bhattacharya in IHQ, 1928, pp. 287ff.; F. Edgerton in JAOS, vol. 57, pp. 185ff.;—Buddhist Hybrid Sanskrit Dictionary, p. 556; Agehananda Bharati, The Tantric Tradition, pp. 164f.

100. Hevajratantra, pt. I, p. 66, note 1.

101. F. Edgerton, Dictionary, p. 556.
102. Caryāgītikośa, ed. by P. C. Bagchi and Śāntibhikṣu Śāstrī, pp. XIX-XX.
103. Ibid., p. XXII.
104. Advayavajra-saṃgraha p. 24.
105. Caryāgītikośa, p. XXI.
106. Hevajratantra, pt. I, p. 62; see Roy Andrew Miller, 'Buddhist Hybrid Sanskrit Āli, Kāli as Grammatical Terms in Tibet', Harvard Journal of Asiatic Studies, vol. XXVI, 1966, pp. 125 ff.
107. Hevajratantra, pt. I, p. 63.
108. Ibid., pp. 66-67.
109. GST, p. 7; cf. Hevajratantra, pt. I, pp. 81f.
110. G. Tucci, Maṇḍala, p. 23.
111. Ibid.
112. Hevajratantra, pt. I, p. 97.
113. G. Tucci, Maṇḍala, pp. 45-50.
114. Two Vajrayāna Works, p. 41; Sādhanamālā, vol. I, p. 318; vol. II, p. 544.
115. Ibid., vol. I, pp.173, 224; cf. G. Tucci, Maṇḍala, pp. 30-34; Anāgārika Govinda, op. cit., p. 181.
116. B. Bhattacharyya holds, Buddhist Esoterism, p.120, that "the varied, extensive and diversified pantheon of the Northern Buddhists owes its origin to Tantric Buddhism or Vajrayāna". This remark should be modified in view of the fact that Nāgas, Kinnaras, Gandharvas, Yakṣas, Devas, etc. were recognized by the earliest Buddhists, and a large number of celestial or mythical Buddhas and Bodhisattvas were worshipped by the Buddhists before the emergence of the Vajrayāna.
117. Poussin in ERE, vol. I, 'Ādibuddha' pp. 93f; L.A. Waddell, Lamaism, p. 131; Csoma de Koros in JASB, II, 1833, pp. 57ff.; B. Bhattacharyya, Buddhist Iconography, pp. 42f.; A. K. Gordon, Iconography of Tibetan Lamaism, pp. 49f.; see the Svayambhu Purāṇa, ed. by H. P. Śāstrī. It may be pointed out that the Buddha is already called Svayamabhū (self-born) in the Buddhacarita of Aśvaghoṣa, XVI, 64, and the Saddharmapuṇḍarīka sūtra, II. 47, 56, pp. 30-31.
118. Hevajratantra, pt. I, p. 117; cf. Buddhacarita, XVI. 69; Saddharmapuṇḍarīka, has 'lokapitā', 'khalveṣāṃ sattvānāṃ pitā', pp. 53-54, 62 among the epithets of Buddha.
119. GST, pp. 5-10; cf. Niṣpannayogāvali, pp. 16-17.
120. See A. K. Gordon, op. cit., p. 52; S. B. Dasgupta, Tantric Buddhism, p. 87.
121. Hevajratantra, pt. I, pp. 118, 128.
122. Ibid., pp. 61, 119.
123. Jñānasiddhi, p. 41.
124. S. B. Dasgupta, Obscure Religious Cults, chs. II, IV; also Tantric Buddhism, p. 134.
125. Mahāyānasūtrasaṃgraha, vol. I, p. 175—
 ataḥ sarvaṃ idaṃ tyaktvā divyaṃ svargamahāsukham/
 bhāvayet satataṃ prajño bodhicittaṃ prabhāsvaram //
 niḥsvabhāvaṃ nirālaṃbaṃ sarvaśūnyaṃ nirālayam /
 prapañcasamatikrāntaṃ bodhicittasya lakṣaṇam //
126. Dhammapada, verses 203-204,—
 jighacchā paramā rogā, saṃkhārā paramā dukhā /
 etaṃ ñatvā yathābhūtaṃ, nibbāṇaṃ paramaṃ sukhaṃ //
 ārogya paramā lābhā, santuṭṭhī paramaṃ dhanaṃ /
 vissāsa paramā ñāti, nibbāṇaṃ paramaṃ sukhaṃ //
127. Udāna, VIII, 3.6, KN, I, p. 163—
 atthi, bhikkhave, ajātaṃ abhūtaṃ akataṃ asaṃkhataṃ.
128. G. C. Pande, Origins of Buddhism, pp. 443f., where numerous views on Nirvāṇa, ancient and modern, are discussed; see also E. Conze,

Buddhist Thought in India, pp. 69-79. This short account of Nirvāṇa seems to be so far the best and the most faithful modern discussion.

129. Advayavajra-saṃgraha, p. 50—
vajrasattvaṃ namaskṛtya prajñopāyasvarūpiṇam /
mahāsukhādvayaṃ vakṣye vastu tattvaṃ samāsataḥ //
130. Sādhanamālā, vol. II, p. 491; Hevajratantra, pt. I, p. 110 and plate.
131. Prajñopāya-viniścaya-siddhi, p. 6—
anantasukharūpatvāt Srī Mahāsukhasaṃjñitam /
132. Jñānasiddhi, VII. 1.
133. Ibid., VII. 3. p. 57—
sarva tāthāgataṃ jñānaṃ svasaṃvedyasvabhāvakam /
sarvasaukhyāgra bhūtatvāt mahāsukhaṃ iti smṛtam //
134. Dohā-kośa of Saraha, ed. by R. Sāṃkṛtyāyana, p. 12—
jahiṅ maṇa pavaṇa ṇa sañcarai, ravisasi ṇāhi pavesa /
tahiṅ baḍha citta visāma karu, Sarahaiṅ kahia uaesa //
ekka karu mā veṇṇi karu, mā karu viṇṇi visesa /
ekkaiṅ raṅge rañjiā, tihuaṇā sa alāsesa //
āiṇa anta ṇa majjhatahi, ṇau bhava ṇau ṇivvāṇa /
ehu so paramamahāsuha, ṇau para ṇau appāṇa //
Cf. Udāna, VIII, 1, 2, KN, I, p. 162—
atthi, bhikkhave, tadāyatanaṃ yattha neva paṭhavī
na āpo na tejo na vāyo na ākāsānañcāyatanaṃ
na viññāṇañcāyatanaṃ na akiñcaññāyatanaṃ na
nevasaññānasaññāyatanaṃ nāyaṃ loko na
paraloko na ubho candimasuriyā.....etc.
135. Hevajratantra, pt. I, pp. 54, 59, 66.
136. Ibid., pp. 94, 96; Snellgrove's Introduction, pp. 11-12.
137. Dohā-kośa of Saraha, Bhūmikā and the first seven dohās.
138. Kern, Manual, p. 133.
139. R. L. Mitra, Sanskrit Buddhist Literature of Nepal, pp. 261-264.
140. Eliot, Hinduism and Buddhism II, p. 124.
141. Winternitz, HIL, II, pp. 388-389.
142. Vallee Poussin in ERE, XII, p. 195.
143. B. Bhattacharyya in Sādhanamālā, vol. II, Introduction, p.XXII.
144. Introduction to Esoteric Buddhism, Preface.
145. Hevajratantra, pt. I, pp. 90, 96.
146. Mahācaṇḍaroṣaṇa as quoted in ERE, vol. XII, p. 196.
147. Cittaviśuddhiprakaraṇa, verses 36-38; GST pp. 26-27, 155.
148. GST, pp. 161 f.; Hevajratantra, pt. I, p. 94.
149. JASB, XXVI, 1930, p. 128.
150. Theory and Practice of the Maṇḍala, Preface. Some problems of the study of Esoteric Buddhism are raised by E. Conze in Buddhist Thought in India, pp. 270f.
151. Bhāratīya Sanskṛti aur Sādhanā, chs. II, XIV-XVII, XXXVII-XXXVIII.
152. Hevajratantra, pt. I, Introduction, pp. 6-10.
153. Foundations of Tibetan Mysticism; see also E. Conze, 'Recent Work on Tantric and Zen Buddhism' in Middle Way, XXXV, 1960, pp. 93f.; H. V. Guenther, Life and Teachings of Nāropa; Gopīnātha Kavirāja, Tāntrika Vāṅmaya mein Śāktadṛṣṭi; Agehanada Bharati, The Tantric Tradition; H. V. Guenther and Chogyam Trungpa, The Dawn of Tantra.
154. Gopīnātha Kavirāja in his Preface to G. Jhā's Eng. tr. of Tantravārttika, vol. I, p. vi.

CHAPTER XII

1. Fa-hsien, p. 29.
2. Ibid., p. 36.
3. Ibid., p. 40.

4. Ibid., p. 41.
5. Ibid., p. 30.
6. Yuan Chwang, II, 63.
7. Ibid., I, 340; Life, pp. 179-180.
8. Ibid., I, 226.
9. Ibid., 199.
10. Ibid., 240, 248, 256.
11. Si-yu-ki, p. 195.
12. N. Dutt, Gilgit Manusrcripts, vol. I, Introduction.
13. Yuan Chwang, II, 252.
14. Ibid., I, 314.
15. Fa-hsien, p. 20.
16. Yuan Chwang, I, 301.
17. Ibid., 318, 322, 320, 330, 331. 333, 359, 361, 366, 373 and 377.
18. Ibid., II, 47.
19. Ibid., 86f.; Life, pp.105.; J.N. Sammadar, The Glories of Magadha.
20. Fa-hsien, pp. 65-66; Yuan Chwang, II 190; I-tsing, pp. 44, 155.
21. Yuan Chwang, II, 184, 187, 191.
22. Ibid., 186; Life, pp. 170-172.
23. Cf. N. K. Sahu, op. cit.
24. Yuan Chwang, II, 136, 193. 196, 198.
25. A. Aiyappan and P. R. Srinivasan, op. cit.
26. Yuan Chwang, II, 214, 224, 226, 228.
27. Ibid., 245-252; see above Chapter II.
28. I-tsing, p. 52.
29. Ibid.
30. P. C. Bagchi, 'Decline of Buddhism in India and its Causes' in Asutosh Mukerjee Silver Jubilee Volumes, vol. III, p. 412.
31. R. C. Mitra, The Decline of Buddhism in India, p. 2.
32. Cullavagga, pp. 376; Brewster, Life of Gotama the Buddha, p. 119.
33. Bu-ston, II, pp. 102-103.
34. Theragāthā, verses 949-980, KN, II, pp. 362f.
35. Ibid., 400-447, KN, II, pp. 455f.
36. Rāṣṭrapālaparipṛcchāsūtra in BST, no. 17, pp. 136f.
37. Yuan Chwang, I, 204-205.
38. Ibid., II, 115.
39. Life, pp. 154-155.
40. Tabqāt-i-nāsirī, Eng. tr. by H. G. Raverty, p. 552.
41. A. Ghosh, Nālandā, p. 26.
42. Yuan Chwang, I, 371-372.
43. Ibid., I, 240.
44. Ibid., II, 252; Si-yu-ki, pp. 461-462.
45. Rājataraṅgiṇī, III. 12.
46. For example the cases of Seyyasaka, Assaji and Punabbasu of Kiṭāgiri, Cullavagga, pp. 18-19; of Channa, Ibid., p. 40; of Subhadda, Ibid., p. 406. The followers of Devadatta are said to have been engaged in manufacturing the weapons of war, Rockhill, op. cit., p. 92. In the Theragāthā (KN, II, p. 361) we are told that "they who once forsook wealth, wife and child, now do evil for the sake of a spoon-ful of rice." One of the "ten heresies" (dasavatthūni) of Vesālian bhikṣus was concerning wealth and money, jātarūpa-rajata, Cullavagga, p. 416. Bhavya reports that "the bhikṣus of Vaiśāli said—'Venerable sirs, enjoy yourselves', and they made enjoyment lawful," Rockhill, op. cit., p. 171. According to a Theravādin author, Moggaliputta Tissa, the Vetullas (Vaitulyakas, authors of the Vaipulya Sūtras ?) had laid down as a rule the following—ekādhippāyena methuno dhaṃmo paṭisevitabbo........para dāro gantabbo, Kathāvatthu, XXIII. 219. 1, p. 535. Another Theravādin author, Mahānāma, reports that Aśoka expelled 60,000 bogus monks who practised many things contrary to the Vinaya, Mahāvaṃsa, ch. V, 270-271. Such instances could be multiplied from diverse sources.

47. I-tsing, p. 179. Though a devout Buddhist and no mean scholar, Bhartṛhari became seven times a monk and returned as many times to the life of a householder.
48. Mālatīmādhava, Act I, scene 1, et seq.
49. A. A. Macdonell, History of Sanskrit Literature, p. 80.
50. Bulletin of the School of Oriental and African Studies, vol. V, pp. 697-717; HCIP, vol. III, p. 260; already Kauṭilya had prescribed the services of bhikṣukī (nun) for espionage, Arthaśāstra, I. 11, gūḍhapuruṣaniyoga.
51. Mālavikāgnimitra, Act I, et seq.
52. Caturbhāṇī or Śṛṅgārahāṭa, ed. by V. S. Agrawala and Motichandra; F. W. Thomas placed it in 7th century, A.D. JRAS, Centenary Supplement, 1924, p. 136.
53. Caturbhāṇī, pp. 14, 157-158.
54. Ibid., pp. 31-35.
55. B. Nanjio, Catalogue, no. 465; cf. BEFEO, vol. V, pp. 296-299.
56. I-tsing, p. 61.
57. Ibid., p. 194.
58. Bu-ston, II, pp. 171f.
59. Bhagavadajjukam, pp. 4, 13 as quoted in Visvabharati Annals, VI, p. 141.
60. I-tsing, pp. 194-195.
61. Rāṣṛṭapālaparipṛcchāsūtra, pp. 137-138.
62. Winternitz, HIL, II, p. 331.
63. Eliot and Dowson, History of India as told by her own Historians, vol. I, p. 147.
64. Mṛcchakaṭika, Acts, VII-VIII; cf.S. Mookerjee, 'Ujjainī in Mṛcchakaṭika', B. C. Law Volume, pt. I, pp. 416-418.
65. Yuan Chwang, I, 162.
66. Cullavagga, pp. 283f., 406f; Rockhill, Life of Buddha, pp. 187f; Life, p. 176; Yuan Chwang, I, 32, 325, 373; II 100, 252.
67. I-tsing, pp. 6-7; Yuan Chwang, II, 191.
68. Ibid., II, 258.
69. Life, pp. 159, 165.
70. BCA, IX. 15 ff.
71. CŚV, chs. IX, XI.
72. TS and TSP, Eng. tr., pp. 217ff.
73. Eliot, Hinduism and Buddhism, vol. II, p. 6.
74. I-tsing, p. 14.
75. Yuan Chwang, II, 252; Rājataraṅgiṇī, III. 12; Eliot and Dowson op. cit., p. 147.
76. GST, p. 37.
77. See Dhammapada, verse 90 and contrast Hevajratantra, pt. I, p. 104, and Prajñopāyaviniścayasiddhi, p. 23.
78. Cittaviśuddhiprakaraṇa, verses 6, 19, 33; GST, pp. 26, 120; Hevajratantra, pt. I, pp. 65, 71, 91, 96; Jñānasiddhi, pp. 32, 50 etc.
79. I-tsing, p. 52; see also S. Beal, Catena, pp. 410-411; Waddell, Lamaism, p. 14; Eliot, Hinduism and Buddhism, II, pp. 129-130.
80. Some historical instances of Brahmanical hostility to Buddha and Buddhism prior to our period are—Kasī Bhāradvāja's contempt for Buddha KN, I, p. 280; Aggika Bhāradvāja called Buddha an 'outcaste', Ibid., p. 287; Buddha did not get a grain of food in the village of the brāhmaṇas, SN, I, Piṇḍasutta; brāhmaṇa Soṇadaṇḍa hesitated to salute Buddha in public lest his community might ex-communicate him, DN, I, p. 97; 'heretics' or Brāhmanical followers are said to have killed Moggalāna, Dhammapadaṭṭhakathā, III. 65; 'heretics' or Brāhmanical dogmtists are said to have murdered the philosopher Āryadeva, Sogen, Systems pp. 187f; King Gautamiputra Sātakarṇi who considered himself 'eka bamhaṇa', 'unique brāhmaṇa', is known to have "crushed the pride of the kṣatriyas" (khatiya dapa māna, madanasa) and to have "stopped the mixing of castes", D. C. Sircar Select Inscriptions, vol. I, pp. 196-198. This was apparently an anti-Buddhist

measure adopted by the King. Hsüan-tsang has described, rather mysteriously, the murder of the philosopher Nāgārjuna by a Sātavāhana king, Yuan Chwang, II, 201. I think that this Sātavāhana prince is identifiable with the 'eka bamhaṇa'. The rich laity continued to patronize Buddhism despite the Brahmanical rule of the Sātavāhanas and hence the growth of Buddhist art in the Deccan in early centuries A. D. Baudhāyana Dharmasūtra, II. 6. 30 says that the āśrama called pravṛajyā (ascetic ordination) was introduced by an asura (demon) who was not on good terms with the gods. I believe that 'the gods' here are the priestly orthodox brāhmaṇas who were often called bhūdevas, 'gods on earth', and who were always angry with Buddha and his followers. The Rāmāyaṇa, Ayodhyākāṇḍa, 109, 34 denounces Buddha as an atheist. The Purāṇas display a similar attitude of hostility and disdain for Buddhism; see e.g., R. K. Chaudhary, 'Heretical Sects in the Purāṇas,' ABORI, XXXVII, 1957, pp. 234ff.

81. Bu-ston, II, p. 153.
82. Yājñavalkyasmṛti, I, 271-272.
83. Agni Purāṇa, XVI. 1, 3.
84. Vāyu Purāṇa, L XXVIII, 58-59.
85. Viṣṇu Purāṇa, (III) XVIII. 13-18.
86. Cf. S. Mookerjee, Philsophy of Universal Flux, p. XXXVII.
87. Nyāyavārttika, Introductory stanza.
88. ŚV, pp. 163ff.
89. Tantravārttika, Eng. tr., vol. I, Introduction; Śaṃkaravijaya of Ānandagiri, Calcutta edn., p. 235; see also Eliot, Hinduism and Buddhism, II, pp. 110-270.
90. Yuan Chwang, II, 250.
91. Mṛcchakaṭika, Act. VIII.
92. Bu-ston, II, p. 152; Tārānātha (Schiefner), p. 177 and note.
93. P. Menon, History of Kerala, vol. I, p. 453; f.n. 1; P. C. Alexander, Buddhism in Kerala, pp. 179 f.
94. Bauddha Dharma, p. 492.
95. 'Preliminary Essay : Tantravārttika and its Author' in Eng. tr. of Tantravārttika, vol. I, pp. VI-VII.
96. BrSŚ, pp. 239, 252.
97. U. Dhammaratana, "The Reason for Anti-Buddhist Propaganda in Brahmanical Literature', in Maha Bodhi, vol. 62, pp. 421f.
98. Mādhava's Śaṃkaradigvijaya, I, 93; R. Sāṃkṛtyāyana, Buddhacaryā, Introduction, pp. 11-12, tries to refute this tradition without giving any convincing reasons.
99. Journal of Mythic Society, p. 151; Eliot, Hinduism and Buddhism, II, p. 211.
100. Visvabharati Annals, VI, p. 129.
101. Ibid., p. 130.
102. BrSŚ, II, 2.32.
103. Devībhāgavata Purāṇa, I, 3.21.
104. Bhāgavata Purāṇa, I. 4. 25, 29.
105. Mārkaṇḍeya Purāṇa, chs. 95, 14-15, 19-20.
106. Matsya Purāṇa, chs. 52, 12.
107. Viṣṇu Purāṇa, III. 18, 9-12; VI. 18.
108. Matsya Purāṇa, chs. 24, 43-49.
109. S. Radhakrishnan, Indian Philosophy, I, p. 609.
110. History of Bengal, I, pp. 397f., 414f.
111. Tārānātha (Schiefner), ch. XXVIII; cf. Eliot, Hinduism and Buddhism, vol. II, p. III.
112. Visvabharati Annals, VI, p. 56.
113. MASI, no. 26, p. 5.
114. ABORI, vol. XIV, 1932-33, pp. 200-221.
115. R. C. Hazra, op. cit., pp. 41-42; P. V. Kane, History of Dharmaśāstra, vol. V, pt. II, pp. 992-998.
116. S. Radhakrishnan, 'Foreword' to 2500 Years of Buddhism, pp.

XIV-XV. But Radhakrishnan's observations (p. IX) that Buddha "was born, grew up, and died a Hindu. He was restating with a new emphasis the ancient ideals of the Indo-Āryan civilization", and that (p.XIII) "Buddhism did not start as a new and independent religion. It was an offshoot of the more ancient faith of the Hindus, perhaps a schism or a heresy," are not in keeping with historical facts. The term 'Hindu' is misleading in the context of the most ancient religious thought of India; it originated as a name of a geographical locality, the districts on the river Indus (Greek 'Indos', 'Sinthos', Persian 'Hindu' for the Vedic 'Sindhu'). Later on the Turks called India by the name of Hindustān; but prior to the 12th century A.D. there is no proof that the word 'Hindu' had any other meaning except that of a geographical entity. What is now known as 'Hinduism' is in fact a conglomeration of diverse elements born of centuries of growth of Vedic religion or Brāhmaṇism with a very large mass of Buddhist and Jainist elements. 'Hinduism' is properly speaking 'Purāṇicism', a product of early medieval India. It has incorporated in its body more than half of Buddhism, some doctrines of Jainism, and a few elements of Zoroastrianism and Christianity, while it still traces its authority and sources to the Saṃhitās, Brāhmaṇas and Upaniṣads. In no sense can the word be applied to Buddha, and his doctrine in its original form was "Śramanism" as different and distinguished from 'Brāhmaṇism'. Megasthenes knew only these two classes of Indian religious protagonists, whom he mentioned as 'Brahmanes' (Brāhmaṇas) and 'Sarmanes' (Sramaṇas), J. W. McCrindle, Ancient India as described by Megasthenes and Arrian, Calcutta, 1926, pp. 97, 104-105. Aśoka in his inscriptions regularly mentions the 'Samaṇas' and 'Bamaṇas', and Patañjali on Aṣṭādhyāyī, II. 4.9, clearly points out the antagonism between them. Buddha was a Śramaṇic Indian (Bhāratīya) and not a Brāhmanical Indo-Āryan. The term Hindu is not a name of any race or tribe; such a tribe never existed in history; it is a geographical name; and before 1200 A.D. no Indian religion was known as Hinduism. Today all those Indians who follow Brahmanism-Purāṇicism, Jainism, and Buddhism and dwell in India are generally called 'Hindus'. The term 'Hindu' has assumed today a communal sense which never existed in ancient India.

117. S. Mookerjee in the Cultural Heritage of India, vol. I, p. 587.

118. Cf. the story which Yuan Chwang (I, 288 f.) relates concerning King Bālāditya of Magadha against the Hūṇa tyrant Mihirakula. No such examples for Buddhism are known to subsequent periods.

119. The destruction of the Sākyas by the ruthless arms of king Viḍuḍabha of Kosala in the last year of Buddha's existence on earth, is too well known, Rockhill, op. cit, pp. 117f. The most violent persecution of Buddhists was at the hands of the brāhmaṇa ruler Puśyamitra Śuṅga (cir. 187-151 B.C.). An avowed enemy of Buddhism and a fanatic champion of Brahmanism, he murdered his sovereign the Maurya Bṛhadratha, usurped the throne of Pāṭaliputra, waged a cruel war against the helpless Buddhist monks, and announced a prize of 100 gold pieces (dīnāra śataṃ) for each head of a bhikṣu; he destroyed or burnt the vihāras from Pāṭaliputra to Śākala (from Magadha to Panjab). This tradition, which has all the force of a historical fact, is recorded in (i) Divyāvadāna, Cambridge edn., p.434; BST edn., p. 282; (ii) Āryamañjuśrīmūlakalpa, pp. 619-620; (iii) Chinese and (iv) Japanese Buddhist traditions place Puṣyamitra at the head of the list of persecutors (Journal of the Deptt. of Letters, vol. I, p. 19); (v) Tārānātha (Schiefner), p. 81, dwells at length on this episode. The argument that the Buddhist monuments of Sāñcī and Bharhut were raised during the reign of Śuṅgas, does not exonerate Puṣymitra from the blame; the monuments were the creation of the local officers, artisans, guild-leaders and the wealthy laity and not of any Śuṅga king.

120. Yuan Chwang, I, 211-212.

121. Ibid., I, 288 f.

122. Rājataraṅgiṇī, I. 289.

123. Ibid., I. 304.

124. Ibid, I, 305-307.
125. See Asutosh Mukerjee Silver Jubilee Volumes, vol. III, p. 407.
126. K. P. Jayaswal, An Imperial History of India in a Sanskrit Text, pp. 52-53; Text verses 778-779.
127. Yuan Chwang, I, 288-289.
128. Rājataraṅgiṇī, I, 309-310.
129. Yuan Chwang, I, 290.
130. Ibid.
131. Ancient India, no. 9, p. 146.
132. Joseph Edkins, Chinese Buddhism, p. 99.
133. K. P. Jayaswal, op. cit., pp. 49-50.
134. History of Bengal, I, p. 67; J. N. Banerjea, Development of Hindu Iconography, pp. 152, 271, plate IX, figure 12.
135. Harṣacarita, bk. VI, Chaukhamba edn., p. 321—Gauḍādhipena-mitthyopacārocitaviśvāsam.
136. For other views on Śaśāṅka and Buddhism, see R. C. Majumdar in History of Bengal. I, pp. 59-68 and in HCIP, III, pp. 80-81; R. S. Tripathi, History of Kanauj, pp. 102-105; R. K. Mookerjee, Harṣa, ch. II, note; R. G. Basak in IHQ, vol. VIII, 1932, pp. 1-20.
137. Yuan Chwang, I, 343; II, 43, 92, 115-116; Si-yu-ki, pp. 236. 290, 326, 349.
138. K. P. Jayaswal, op. cit., p. 59; Text of ch. 53, verses 715-718; see B. M. Barua, Gayā and Buddha Gayā, II, pp. 12f.
139. R. C. Majumdar, History of Bengal, I, p. 67, note 2.
140. Smith, Early History of India, p. 368.
141. Radhakrishnan, Indian Philosophy, I, p. 609.
142. B. M. Barua, Prolegomena to a History of Buddhist Philosophy, p. 19.
143. P. C. Bagchi in Asutosh Mukerjee Volumes, vol. III, pp. 420-421.
144. The Cultural Heritage of India, vol. IV, pp. 47-48.
145. Visvabharati Annals, vol. VI, pp. 150-155.
146. Le Nepal, II, p. 317.
147. See H. P. Śāstrī, Discovery of Living Buddhism in Bengal; N.N. Vasu, Modern Buddhism and its followers in Orissa; S. K. Chatterjee. 'Buddhist Survivals in Bengal' in B. C. Law Volume, I, pp. 75-87; The Cultural Heritage of India, vol. IV, chs. 16-19, pp. 273-299; S.B. Dasgupta, Obscure Religious Cults, pp. 259 f. A critical and comprehensive study of the inter-relations between Brāhmanism and Buddhism and a survey of Buddhist lagacy in Indian Culture are still wanting. It is regrettable that majority of Brahmanical scholars have not been able to correctly appreciate Buddhism.
148. Bauddha Dharma, pp. 491-492.
149. N. Dutt in Buddha Jayanti Souvenir, p. 97.
150. Eliot, Hinduism and Buddhism, vol. II, p. 120.
151. Ātmatattvaviveka, ed. by Ḍhuṇḍhirāja Śāstrī, p. 417.
152. R. C. Mitra, op. cit., pp. 149-151.
153. S. Radhakrishnan, Foreword, pp. IX, XIII in 2500 Years of Buddhism. P. V. Kane has also asserted this Brāhmanical theory of the origins of Buddhism, see History of Dharmaśāstra, vol. V, pt. II, pp. 1003-1030. I have examined and criticized these views in my Brāhmanism, Buddhism and Hinduism.
154. G. C. Pande, Studies in the Origins of Buddhism, ch. VIII; H. Zimmer, Philosophies of India, pp. 595, 600; and Vedic Index, vol. II, pp. 167-168, 185, 342-344, for an idea of the munis, yatis and vrātyas, the non-Brāhmanical fore-runners of Jainism and Buddhism; see also my chapters in the History of Punjab, vol. I.
155. Ch. Up., II, 23-1.
156. Cf. E. J. Thomas, History of Buddhist Thought, p. 90; A. B. Keith, Religion and Philosophy of the Veda and Upaniṣads, II, p. 502; E. W. Hopkins in JAOS, vol. XXII, p. 336. Brāhmanical dislike of saṃnyāsa or

asceticism in evident from Aitareya Brāhmaṇa, 33. 11; Baudhāyana Dharmasūtra, II, 6.30 and Yājñavalkyasmṛti, I, 270-272.

157. E. J. Thomas, loc. cit.; Keith, op. cit; pp. 558-559; Bhikkhu J. Kashyap, DN, vol. I, Introduction, p. XXII; O. H. de A. Wijesekera, 'A Pali Reference to Brāhmaṇacaraṇas' in ALB, vol. XX, pp. 294ff.

158. R. C. Mitra, op. cit., pp. 153-154.

159. Umesha Mishra, in the Journal of the Gaṅgānātha Jhā Research Institute, vol. IX, pt. I, 1951, pp. 111-122. See my criticism of his views in the same Journal's vol. XXI.

160. P. V. Kane, History of Dharmaśāstra, vol. V, pt. II, pp. 1004-5.

161. The Upaniṣads contain a fusion of Vedic and pre-Vedic, Brāhmanic and Śramanic cultures; they attack the Vedas and the sacrificial way, but retain a great deal of Brāhmanical theories at the same time; they incorporate many non-Brāhmanic elements such as yoga, meditation and ascetic ideals. Sculptures of ascetics in meditation have been discovered from Mohenjo-daro and Harappā which date from cir. 2500-2000 B.C. (cf. John Marshall, Mohenjo-daro and the Indus Civilization, vol. I, pp. 48-58, plates XII. 17 c; XVI. 29; CXVIII. 11). Munis, yatis and vrātyas are mentioned in Vedic texts, and we are told that their beliefs and practices were foreign to central Vedic culture, the sacrificial culture, and their ideals were opposed to those of the brāhmaṇas. These non-Vedic people were most likely the remnants of the pre-Āryan Harappan population (see Ṛgveda, X. 136, 2-4-5 on muni; Atharvaveda, VII. 74-1 on deva-muni; Aitareya Brāhmaṇa, VI. 33, 3 on muni Aitasa; Pañcaviṃśa Brāhmaṇa, XIV. 4, 7 on muni-maraṇa; Ṛgveda, VIII. 3, 9; VIII. 6, 18; X. 7 on yatis; Taittirīya Saṃhita, II, 9-2; VI. 2, 7, 5; Kāṭhaka Saṃhitā, VIII. 5; XI. 5; Pañcaviṃśa Br. VIII, 1.4; XIII. 4, 16; Aitareya Br., VII. 28. 1, on yatis; Vājasaneyī Saṃhitā, XXX. 8 and Taittrīya Br, 1II. 4, 5, 1; Pañcaviṃśa Br. XVII 1, 4 and Atharvaveda, XV, 1, 1 foll. on vrātyas; also A. A. Macdonell and A. B. Keith, Vedic Index, vol. II, pp. 167-168; 185, and 342-344).

CHAPTER XIII

1. Brahmanism, Buddhism and Hinduism, ch. II; Aspects of Buddhism in Indian History, ch. II.

2. S. N. Dasgupta, A History of Indian Philosophy, vol. I, p. 82.

3. The evidence is discussed in my God's Alternative: A Study of Swami Vivekananda's Attitude to Buddhism, ch. II.

4. Bṛhadāraṇyaka Upaniṣad, II, 4.12; Dīghanikāya, I, 190.

5. Muṇḍaka Upaniṣad, II. 1.5; III. 2.5; Dhammapada, verses 93, 420.

6. Myth and Reality, p. 16; Kashi Nath Upadhyaya, Early Buddhism and the Bhagavadgītā, still places this text between 500 and 400 B.C., an impossible date. He does not refer to the scientific studies of Kosambi and ignores archaeological evidence bearing on the early history of the Kṛṣṇa cult. The central point in the chronology of the Gītā is the date of the emergence of Kṛṣṇa-bhakti. The Garuḍa Pillar Inscription of Heliodoros found at Vidiśā (cir. 100 B.C.) suggests that the Epic Kṛṣṇa had not been identified with 'devadevasa Vāsudevasa' even in the first century B.C. The identification is first made in the Bhagavadgītā (X. 37) in which Visṇu-Kṛṣṇa says 'I am Vāsudeva among Vṛṣṇis' (Vṛṣṇīnām Vāsudevo'smi). The doctrines of the Bhagavadgītā bear remarkable resemblance to those of the Saddharmapuṇḍarīkasūtra, a text first translated into Chinese early in the second century A.D. The Gītā can hardly be earlier than this date.

7. Bhagavadgītā, VI, 15. Edgerton's translation.

8. V. V. Gokhale, 'Krishna and the Buddhist Literature' in The Cultural Forum, vol. 36, New Delhi, 1968, p. 73.

9. Bhagavadgītā, II. 16.

10. Ibid., XIV. 20.

11. V. V. Gokhale, op. cit.
12. Sacred Books of the East, vol. X, pt. I, pp. 6. 16-17 28-29, 33, 36-37, etc.
13. Dhammapada, verse 9.
14. Mahābhārata, XII. 568 (after Max Müller).
15. Dhammapada, verse 47.
16. Mahābhārata, Śāntiparvan, verse 9939.
17. Dhammapada, verses 160 and 379.
18. Bhagavadgītā, VI. 5-6; cp. also Dhammapada, verse 165.
19. Dhammapada, verse 109.
20. Manusmṛti, II. 21.
21. Dhammapada, verse 131 and Manusmṛti, V. 45; also cp. Dhammapada verse 150 with Manusmṛti, VI. 76.
22. P. V. Bapat, 2500 years of Buddhism, pp. 6, 477.
23. Arnold Toynbee, A Study of History, abridged by D.C. Somervell, vol. I, p. 431.
24. Ibid., p. 544.
25. Ahirbudhnya-saṃhitā, vol. I, ch. 33, verse 17, p. 302.
26. Central Philosophy of Buddhism, pp. 116-17.
27. Bhāratīya Saṃskṛti aur Sādhanā, pt. I, pp. 132-33.
28. S. N. Dasgupta, History of Indian Philosophy, vol. I, p. 422; S. Radhakrishnan, Indian Philosophy, vol. II, p. 452.
29. Śaṃkara's commentary on Gauḍapādakārikā, p. 214; cf. S. N. Dasgupta, op. cit., pp. 422-23.
30. Saṃyuttanikāya, I, Arhantasutta, p. 15—loke samaññaṃ kusalo viditvā, vohāramattena so vohareyyā; cf. MŚ, XXIV. 8-10, C. Ś, VIII, 8; Madhyamakāvatāra, VI. 23-28; Madhyamaka-vṛtti (BB), pp. 55-56; Madhyamakārthasaṃgraha, 1-2; BCA, IX. 2.
31. Cf. Mahāvagga, pp. 13-15; Majjhimanikāya, I, Mūlapariyāyasutta, pp. 3-10; Madhyamakaśāstra, ch. XXIII with Prasannapadā; Nettippakaraṇa, p. 85; Saṃyuttanikāya, I Upaniyasutta, p.4; Visuddhimagga, p. 587; Vajracchedikā Prajñāpāramitā, pp. 35, 42, 48; see E. Conze, Buddhist Thought in India, pp. 40-46.
32. Saṃyuttanikāya, III, pp. 50-51; Dīghanikāya I, p. 17; III, p. 30; Aṅguttaranikāya, I, p. 279.
33. Mahāvagga, pp. 34f, Ādittapariyāya.
34. Dīghanikāya, I. pp. 51-52, 151f.
35. Cf. Saṃdhinirmocanasūtra (tr. by E. Lamottee); Laṅkāvatārasūtra; D. T. Suzuki, Studies in the Lankāvatāra; G. Tucci, Aspects of the Doctrines of Maitreya (nātha); S. Levi (ed.), Deux Traites de Vasubandhu; Prajñāpāramitāpiṇḍārtha.
36. V. Bhattacharya, Āgamaśāstra, p. 33, where numerous parallels from Buddhist sources are cited.
37. Ibid., pp. 38-43.
38. S. N. Dasgupta, op. cit., p. 425 and note.
39. V. Bhattacharya, op. cit., pp. 92-98.
40. S. Radhakrishnan, op. cit., p. 465 and note 2.
41. S. N. Dasgupta, Indian Idealism, p. 154. See also his A History of Indian Philosophy, vol. II, pp. 165-170.
42. Stcherbatsky, The Conception of Buddhist Nirvana, p. 63.
43. The Complete Works of Swami Vivekananda, vol. V, p. 279.
44. The Padma-purāṇa, Uttarakhanda, 263-70-71 refers to the Buddhist doctrine (Bauddhaśāstra), identifies it with the doctrine of illusion (māyāvāda) and condemns both as 'false' (asat). The teachers of māyāvāda are called 'hidden Buddhists' (prachhanna bauddha). See Asoka Chatterjee, Padma Purāṇa—A Study, p. 90.

45. Yogarājopaniṣad, verse 14.
46. Yogavāsiṣṭha-Rāmāyaṇa, II. 5, 6-7, 16.
47. Ibid., III. 9.59. See S. N. Dasgupta, op. cit. vol. II, p. 234.
48. Haṭhayogapradīpikā, IV. 3-4, 7, 10, 56, 74.
49. Kabīragranthāvalī, p. 206; Guru Granth Sāhib, pp. 857, 1035.
50. S. Radhakrishnan in 2500 Years of Buddhism, p. XIV.
51. N. Aiyaswami in 2500 Years of Buddhism, pp. 308-312.
52. Suniti Kumar Chatterji, Nalinaksha Dutt, A.D. Pusalker and Nirmal Kumar Bose in The Cultural Heritage of India, vol. I, pp. lix, lxiii.
53. V. V. Gokhale, op. cit., p. 72.
54. Satkari Mookerjee in The Cultural Heritage of India, vol. I, p. 575.
55. The Complete Works of Swami Vivekananda, vol. V, pp. 229, 311, 316, 401.
56. Ibid., vol. VI, pp. 507-509.
57. Svayambhūpurāṇa, ed. by H. P. Śāstrī, p. 1, where the words Buddha, Dharma, Svayambhū, Dharmadhātu, Śūnyarūpa, etc. are used as synonyms.
58. See N. K. Bhattasali in the Annual Report of the Dacca Museum for 1939-40, pp. 7-8; D. C. Sircar, Studies in the Religious Life of Ancient and Medieval India, pp. 190-200.
59. N. N. Vasu, Modern Buddhism and Its Followers in Orissa, Hindi tr. under the title, Bhaktimārgi Bauddha Dharma by Narmadesvara Chaturvedi.
60. Maheshwar Neog, 'The Worhsip of Dharma in Assam' in Journal of the Asiatic Society of Bengal (Letters), vol. XVII, 1951, pp. 219-224.
61. Śūnyapurāṇa, ed. by N. N. Vasu, Calcutta, Vangiya Sahitya Parisad, 1909.
62. See his Obscure Religious Cults, pp. 259-300, 399-412.
63. Ibid., pp. 260-261.
64. See Sukumar Sen in B.C. Law Volume, pt. I; K. P. Chattopadhyay, 'Dharma Worship' in Journal of the Royal Asiatic Society of Bengal (Letters) vol. VIII, 1942, pp. 99-135.
65. Hinduism and Buddhism, vol. II, p. 175.
66. Complete Works, vol. III, p. 264.
67. M. Winternitz, History of Indian Literature, vol. III, part 1, Eng. tr. by Subhadra Jha, p. 39.
68. Ibid., p. 198.
69. E. Obermiller, Bu-ston's History of Buddhism, pt. II, p. 166.
70. M. Winternitz, op. cit., vol. III, pt. 2, 457.
71. Cf. The Subhāsitaratanakośa of Vidyākara, ed. by D. D. Kosambi and V. V. Gokhale; translated under the title, An Anthology of Sanskrit Court Poetry by Daniel H. H. Ingalls.
72. A. L. Basham, The wonder that was India, p. 256, says that 'even if judged only by his posthumous effects on the world at large he was certainly the greatest man to have been born in India.'
73. Antiquity, vol. XXII, no. 89, March 1949, p. 5.
74. Dhammapada, verse 354; Aśoka, Rock Edict XI.
75. John Marshall (ed.), The Monuments of Sāñchī, vol. I, pp. 264 ff.
76. Thomas Watters, On Yuan Chwang's Travels in India, vol. II, p. 146.
77. Memoires of the Archaeological Survey of India, no. 66, p. 79—āgama-kalā-vikhyātavidvad-janāḥ.
78. Mahāvaṃsa, XXV. 3.
79. Dīghanikāya, vol. II, pp. 58-60.
80. See L. M. Joshi in Mahā Bodhi Journal, vol. 73, pp. 115-116.
81. Cf. Gokuldas De, Democracy in Early Buddhist Saṃgha; R. C. Majumdar, Corporate Life in Ancient India, ch. IV.
82. Quoted after Sten Konow, Corpus Inscriptionum Indicarum, vol. II, p. LXVII.

83. Dīghanikāya, vol. I, Kūṭadantasutta.
84. See L. M. Joshi in Journal of Oriental Institute, vol. XIV pp. 156-157.
85. D. C. Sircar, Select Inscriptions, p. 187.
86. See 'Social Perspective of Buddhist Soteriology' in Religion and Society, vol. VIII, no. 3, pp. 59-68.
87. Buddhism and Society: A Great Tradition and Its Burmese Vicissitudes, pp. 11-12.
88. A. K. Warder, Indian Buddhism p. 157.
89. A Study of History, abridged by D. C. Somervell, vol. I, p. 350.

ABBREVIATIONS

ABORI *Annals of the Bhandarkar Oriental Research Institute*
AGI *Ancient Geography of India* by Cunningham
ALB *Adyar Library Bulletin*
ASI *Archaeological Survey of India*
ASIR *Archaeological Survey of India Annual Reports*
BB Bibliotheca Buddhica
BCA *Bodhicaryāvatāra*
BCAP *Bodhicaryāvatāra-pañjikā*
BEFEO *Bulletin de l'Ecole francaise d' Extreme-Orient*
BI Bibliotheca Indica
BL *Buddhist Logic* by Stcherbatsky
BORI Bhandarkar Oriental Research Institute
BrSŚ *Brahmasūtra-Śaṃkarabhāṣya*
BST Buddhist Sanskrit Texts
CŚ *Catuḥśataka*
CŚV *Catuḥśataka-vṛtti*
DPPN *Dictionary of Pali Proper Names*
EMB *Early Monastic Buddhism*
ERE *Encyclopaedia of Religion and Ethics*
GOS Gaekwad Oriental Series
GST *Guhyasamājatantra*
HCIP *History and Culture of the Indian People*
HIL *History of Indian Literature*
HOS Harvard Oriental Series
IHQ *Indian Historical Quarterly*
JAOS *Journal of the American Oriental Society*
JASB *Journal of the Asiatic Society of Bengal* (New Series
JBBRAS *Journal of the Bombay Branch of the Royal Asiatic Society*
JBORS *Journal of the Bihar and Orissa Research Society*
JBRS *Journal of the Bihar Research Society*
JBTS *Journal of the Buddhist Text Society*
JRAS *Journal of the Royal Asiatic Society*
JUPHS *Journal of the U.P. Historical Society*
KN *Khuddakanikāya*
MASI Memoirs of the Archaeological Survey of India

MBT	*Minor Buddhist Texts*
SBB	Sacred Books of the Buddhists
SBE	Sacred Books of the East
SOR	Serie Oriental Roma
ŚS	*Śikṣāsamuccaya*
ŚV	*Ślokavārttika*
TS	*Tattvasaṃgraha*
TSP	*Tattvasaṃgraha-pañjikā*
TSS	Trivandrum Sanskrit Series
WZKM	*Wiener Zeitschrift für die Kunde des Morgenlandes*

BIBLIOGRAPHY

ORIGINAL TEXTS AND TRANSLATIONS

Abhidharmakośa-bhāṣya, ed. by P. Pradhan, Patna, K. P. Jayaswal Research Institute, 1967; French tr. by Louis de La Vallee Poussin, *L'Abhidharmakośa de Vasubandhu*, 6 vols., Paris-Louvain, 1923-31; Hindi tr. by Narendradeva, pts. 1 & 2, Allahabad, Hindustani Academy, 1958, 1973.

Abhidharmakośa: bhāṣya-sphuṭārthā-sahitam, ed. by D. Sastri, 4 vols., Varanasi, 1970-73; ed. by U. Wogihara, *Sphuṭārthā Abhidharmakośavyākhyā*, Tokyo, 1932-36.

Abhidharmakośakārikā, ed. by V. V. Gokhale in *JBBRAS*, vol. XXII, Bombay, 1946.

Abhidharmāmṛta, restored by Shanti Bhikshu Shastri, *Visvabharati Annals*, vol. V, Santiniketan, 1953.

Abhidharmasamuccaya, ed. by P. Pradhan, Santiniketan, Visvabharati, 1950; French tr. by W. Rahula, *Le compendium de la super-doctrine d'Asanga*, Paris, 1971.

Abhisamayālaṃkāra-ālokavyākhyā, ed. by G. Tucci, GOS, vol. LXII, Baroda, 1932; ed. by P. L. Vaidya, BST, no. 4, Darbhanga, 1960.

Abhisamayālaṃkāravṛtti of Arya Vimuktisena (first *abhisamaya*), ed. by Corrado Pensa, SOR, vol. XXXVII, Rome, 1967.

Ācārangasūtra, tr. by H. Jacobi, SBE, vol. XXII, Delhi, Motilal Banarsidass, 1964 (reprint).

Adhyardhaśataka of Mātṛceta, ed. by K. P. Jayaswal and R. Sāmkṛtyāyana, Appendix to *JBORS*, vol. XXIII.

Advayasiddhi, ed. by Malati J. Shendge, Baroda, Oriental Institute, 1964.

Advayavajra-saṃgraha, ed. by H.P. Sastri, GOS, vol. XL, Baroda, 1927.

Āgamaśāstra, ed. and tr. by V. Bhattacharya, Calcutta, University of Calcutta, 1943.

Agnipurāṇa, published in Anandasrama Sanskrit Series, no. 41, Poona.

Ahirbudhnya-saṃhitā, ed. by M. D. Ramanujacharya, revised by

V. Krishnamacharya, vol. I, Adyar Library Series, Madras, 1966.

Aitareya Brāhmaṇa, published in Anandasrama Sanskrit Series, no. 32, Poona; Eng. tr. by A. B. Keith, HOS, vol. 25, Harvard University Press, Cambridge, 1920.

Akṣara-śatakam: *The Hundred Letters*, tr. by V. V. Gokhale, Heidelberg, 1930.

Ālambanaparīkṣā with *Vṛtti*, restored from Tibetan by N. Aiyaswami Sastri, Madras, Adyar Library, 1942.

Amarakośa, ed. by N. G. Sardesai and D. G. Padhye, Poona, 1940.

Aṅguttaranikāya, ed. by J. Kashyap, Devanagari Pali Series, Nalanda, 1960.

Apadāna, ed. by J. Kashyap in *KN*, vols. VI-VII, Devanagari Pali Series, Nalanda, 1959.

Apohasiddhi, ed. by H. P. Sastri in *Six Buddhist Nyāya Tracts in Sanskrit*, BI, Calcutta, 1910; ed. by A. L. Thakur in *Ratnakīrtinibandhāvali*, Patna, K. P. Jayaswal Research Institute, 1957.

Arthaśāstra, ed. by Ramateja Sastri, Varanasi, Pandit Pustakalaya, Samvat 2016; Eng. tr. by R. Shamasastri, Mysore, 1915.

Arthaviniścayasūtra, ed. by P. L. Vaidya, BST, no. 17, Darbhanga, 1961; ed. by N. H. Samtani, Patna, K. P. Jayaswal Research Institute, 1971.

Aṣṭādaśasāhasrikā Prajñāpāramitā (chs. 55 to 70), ed. and tr. by E. Conze, SOR, vol. XXVI, Rome, 1962.

Aṣṭādhyāyi, ed. by Harishankara Pandeya, Patna, 1937.

Aṣṭasāhasrikā Prajñāpāramitā, ed. by P. L. Vaidya, BST, no. 4, Darbhanga, 1960; tr. by E. Conze, BI, Calcutta, 1958.

Atharvaveda, tr. by W. D. Whitney, 2 vols., Delhi, Motilal Banarsidass, 1962 (reprint).

Ātmatattvaviveka, ed. by Ḍhuṇḍirāja Sastri, Varanasi, Chaukhamba, 1936.

Avadānaśataka, ed. by P. L. Vaidya, BST, no. 19, Darbhanga, 1958.

Bāhyārthasiddhikārikā, tr. into Sanskrit and English by N. A. Sastri, partly published in the *Bulletin of Tibetology*, vol. IV, no. 2, Gangtok, 1967.

Bauddhastotra-saṃgraha, vol. I, *Sragdharāstotra,* ed. by S. C. Vidyabhusana, BI, Calcutta, 1908.

Baudhāyana Dharmasūtra, tr. by Georg Bühler, SBE, vol. II, Delhi, Motilal Banarsidass, 1965 (reprint).

Bhagavadgītā with Śaṃkara's Commentary, published by Motilal Banarsidass, Delhi, 1964; tr. by F. Edgerton, *Bhagavadgītā: Translated and Interpreted* New York, Harper Torchbooks, 1964.

Bhāgavatapurāṇa, published by the Gita Press, Gorakhpur, Samvat 2014.

Bhagavatī-prajñāpāramitā-piṇḍārtha, ed. and tr. by G. Tucci in *MBT*, pt. I, SOR, vol. IX-1, Rome, 1956.

Bhaiṣajyagurū-vaidūryaprabharājasūtra, ed. by P. L. Vaidya in BST, no. 17, Darbhanga, 1961.

Bhāvanākrama (*prathama*), ed. by G. Tucci in *MBT*, pt. II, SOR, vol. IX-2, Rome, 1958.

Bhāvanākrama (*uttara*), ed. by G. Tucci in *MBT*, pt. III, SOR, vol. XLIII, Rome, 1971.

Bhikṣuṇī-vinaya (of the Mahāsāṃghika-Lokottaravāda), ed. by Gustav Roth, Patna, K. P. Jayaswal Research Institute, 1970.

Biography of Dharmasvāmī, tr. by George Roerich, Patna, K. P. Jayaswal Research Institute, 1959.

Blue Annals, tr. by George Roerich, 2 vols., Calcutta, Asiatic Society, 1949, 1953.

Bodhicaryāvatāra with *Pañjikā*, ed. by P. L. Vaidya, BST, no. 12, Darbhanga, 1960; Hindi tr. by Shanti Bhikshu Shastri, Lucknow, Buddha Vihara, 1955; tr. by Marion L. Matics, *Entering the Path of Enlightenment,* New York, Macmillan Co., 1970.

Bodhicittotpādasūtraśāstra, restored into Sanskrit by Shanti Bhikshu Shastri, *Visvabharati Annals,* vol. II, Santiniketan, 1949.

Bodhisattvabhūmi, ed. by Nalinaksha Dutt, Patna, K. P. Jayaswal Research Institute, 1966.

Brahmasūtra-Śaṃkarabhāṣya, ed. by N. R. Acharya, Bombay, Nirnaya Sagar Press, 1948 (third edition); tr. by George Thibaut, *The Vedāntasūtras*, 2 pts., SBE, vols. XXXIV and XXXVIII, Delhi, Motilal Banarsidass, 1962 (reprint).

Brahmasūtra-Śrībhāṣya, tr. by George Thibaut, *The Vedānta-*

sūtras with Rāmānuja's Commentary, SBE, vol. XLVIII, Delhi, Motilal Banarsidass, 1962 (reprint).

Bṛhatsaṃhitā, ed. by H. Kern, BI, Calcutta, 1865.

Buddhapālita-mūlamadhyamakavṛtti (first chapter), restored into Sanskrit by Indumati Datar in *JBBRAS*, new series, vol. 26, Bombay, 1950.

Buddhism in Translations, tr. by Henry Clarke Warren, Cambridge, Harvard University Press, 1896.

Buddhist Scriptures, tr. by Edward Conze, London-Baltimore, Penguin Classics, 1959.

Buddhist Texts Through the Ages, tr. by Edward Conze, I. B. Horner, D. L. Snellgrove and Arthur Waley, Oxford, Bruno Cassirer, 1954.

Bu-ston's History of Buddhism, tr. by E. Obermiller, 2 pts., Tokyo, Suzuki Research Foundation, 1962 (reprint).

Caṇḍamahāroṣaṇa-tantra, ed. and tr. by Christopher S. George, American Oriental Series, vol. 56, New Haven, 1974.

Cāndravyākaraṇa of Candragomin, ed. by K. C. Chatterji, 2 pts., Poona, Deccan College, 1953, 1961.

Caryāgītikośa, ed. and annotated by P. C. Bagchi and Shanti Bhikshu Shastri, Santiniketan, Visvabharati, 1956.

(*A*) *Catena of Buddhist Scriptures from the Chinese*, tr. by S. Beal, London, 1871.

Catuḥśataka (chs. VIII-XVI), restored into Sanskrit by V. Bhattacharya, Santiniketan, Visvabharati, 1931; restored into Sanskrit with French tr. (chs. VIII-XVI) by P. L. Vaidya, Paris, 1923.

Catuḥśataka-vṛitti (chs. VIII-XVI), copious extracts restored from Tibetan by V. Bhattacharya, Santiniketan, Visvabharati, 1931.

Catuḥstava, Tibetan text with Sanskrit restoration by P. B. Patel in IHQ, vol. VIII, Calcutta, 1932.

Caturbhāṇī (*Śṛṅgārahāṭa*), ed. and tr. into Hindi by Motichandra and V. S. Agrawala, Bombay, 1960.

Chāndogya Upaniṣad, Gorakhpur, Gita Press; ed. in the *Upaniṣatsaṃgraha*, Delhi, Motilal Banarsidass, 1970.

Cittaviśuddhiprakaraṇa, ed. by P. B. Patel, Santiniketan, Visvabharati, 1949.

Complete Works of Swami Vivekananda, 8 vols., Mayavati Memorial Edition, Calcutta, Advaita Ashrama, 1948-1953.

Cullavagga, ed. by J. Kashyap, Devanagari Pali Series, Nalanda, 1956; tr. by T. W. Rhys Davids and H. Oldenberg, SBE, vols. XVII and XX, Delhi, Motilal Banarsidass, 1965 (reprint).

Ḍākārṇava, ed. by N. N. Chaudhuri, Calcutta Sanskrit Series, no. 8, Calcutta, 1935.

Daśabhūmikasūtra, ed. by P. L. Vaidya, BST, no. 7, Darbhanga, 1967.

Dhammapada, ed. by J. Kashyap in *KN*, vol. I, Devanagari Pali Series, Nalanda, 1959; tr. by Max Müller, SBE, vol. X, part I, Delhi, Motilal Banarsidass, 1964 (reprint).

Dhammasaṃgaṇi, ed. by J. Kashyap, Devanagari Pali Series, Nalanda, 1960.

Dharmapūjāvidhi of Raghunandan, ed. by Nanigopal, Calcutta, 1917.

Dharmasaṃgraha, ed. by P. L. Vaidya in *Mahāyānasūtra-saṃgraha,* vol. I, BST, no. 17, Darbhanga, 1961.

Dharmottarapradīpa of Durvekamiśra, ed. by Dalsukhbhai Malvania, Patna, K. P. Jayaswal Research Institute, 1955.

Dīghanikāya, ed. by J. Kashyap, 3 vols., Devanagari Pali Series, Nalanda, 1960; Hindi tr. by R. Sāṃkṛtyāyana, Sarnath, 1936; Eng. tr. by T. W. Rhys Davids, *Dialogues of the Buddha,* 3 pts., London, Luzac & Co., 1969 (reprint).

Dīpavaṃsa, ed. and tr. by B. C. Law in *Ceylon Historical Journal,* vol. VII, Colombo, 1959.

Divyāvadāna, ed. by E. B. Cowell and R. A. Neil, Cambridge, 1886; ed. by P. L. Vaidya, BST, no. 20, Darbhanga, 1959.

Dohākośa, ed. by P. C. Bagchi, Calcutta, 1938.

Dohākośa of Sarahapāda, ed. with Tibetan version and Hindi tr. by R. Sāṃkṛtyāyana, Patna, Rastrabhasa Parisad, 1957.

Dvādaśamukhaśāstra, restored into Sanskrit by N. Aiyaswami Sastri, *Visvabharati Annals,* vol. VI, Santiniketan, 1954.

Early Indian Buddhist Schools, a translation of the Hsüan Chwang Version of Vasumitra's Treatise, tr. by J. Masuda, *Asia Major*, vol. II, 1925.

Fragments from Diṅnāga, ed. and tr. by H. N. Randle, London, 1926.

Fundamentals of the Buddhist Tantra, tr. by Ferdinand Lessing and Alex Wayman, The Hague, Mouton & Co., 1968.

Gaṇḍavyūhasūtra, ed. by P. L. Vaidya, BST, no. 5, Darbhanga, 1960.

(*The*) *Gāndhārī Dharmapada,* ed. by John Brough, London, Oxford University Press, 1962.

Gauḍapādakārikā, ed. and tr. by R. D. Karmarkar, BORI, Poona, 1953.

Gauḍavaho, ed. by S. P. Pandit and N. B. Utgikar, BORI, Poona, 1927.

Gilgit Manuscripts, ed. by N. Dutt with the assistance of Pandit Shivnath Shastri, 5 vols., Srinagar, 1949-50.

Gorakṣasiddhānta-saṃgraha, ed. by Gopinatha Kaviraja, Varanasi, n.d.

Guhyasamājatantra, ed. by B. Bhattacharyya, GOS, vol. LIII, Baroda, 1931; ed. by S. Bagchi, BST, no. 9, Darbhanga, 1965.

Guru Granth Sāhib (Sabdārtha edition), 4 vols., Amritsar, Shiromani Gurdwara Prabandhak Kameṭi, 1969 (reprint).

Harṣacarita, Varanasi, Chowkhamba, 1958; tr. by E. B. Cowell and F. W. Thomas, London, 1897 (based on Nirnaya Sagar Press edn. of 1892).

Haṭhayogapradīpikā, ed. and tr. by Brahmanand, Madras, Adyar Library, 1972 (reprint).

Hevajratantra, ed. and tr. by D. L. Snellgrove, 2 vols., London, Oxford University Press, 1959.

Hetubindu, Tibetan text, Sanskrit restoration and German tr. by Ernst Steinkellner, 2 vols. Vienna, Bohlaus, 1962.

Hetubindutīkā of Bhaṭṭa Arcaṭa with the *Āloka* of Durvekamiśra, ed. by Sukhlal Sanghavi and Muni Jinavijaya, GOS, vol. CXIII, Baroda, 1949.

Hitopadeśa, ed. by P. Peterson, Bombay, 1887.

(*The*) *Imitation of Christ,* Thomas A. Kempis, tr. by Lee Sherley-Price, Baltimore, Penguin Classics, 1959 (reprint).

Īśvara-pratyabhijñā-vivti-ṛvimarśinī, ed. in Kashmir Series of Texts and Studies, nos. LX, LXII, LXV, Bombay, 1938-43.

Jātakamālā, ed. by P. L. Vaidya, BST, no. 21, Darbhanga, 1959; tr. by J. S. Speyer, Delhi, Motilal Banarsidass, 1971 (reprint).

(*The*) *Jewel Ornament of Liberation,* tr. by H. V. Guenther, Berkeley, Shambala Publications, 1971.

Jñānaprasthāna-śāstra, pt. I, restored by Shanti Bhikshu Shastri, Santiniketan, Visvabharati, 1957.

Jñānasiddhi, ed. by B. Bhattacharyya, GOS, vol. XLIX, Baroda, 1929.

Jñānaśrīmitra-nibandhāvalī, ed. by A. L. Thakur, Patna, K. P. Jayaswal Research Institute, 1959.

Kabīragranthāvalī, ed. by Shyamsundar Das, Varanasi, Nagari Pracharini Sabha, 1965.

Kādambarī, ed. by P. Peterson, Bombay, 1889.

Kalpanāmaṇḍiṭṭikā, Sanskrit fragments, ed. by H. Lüders Leipzig, 1926.

Kāraṇḍavyūhasūtra, ed. by P. L. Vaidya, BST, no. 17, Darbhanga, 1961.

Karuṇāpuṇḍarīkasūtra, ed. by Isshi Yamada, 2 vols., London, University of London, 1968.

Kāṭhakasaṃhitā, ed. by H. von Leopold von Schroeder, Wiesbaden, Franz Steiner Verlage, 1971 (reprint).

Kathāsaritsāgara, ed. by Durga Prasad, Bombay, 1903; tr. by C. H. Tawney and ed. by N. M. Penzer, 10 vols., Delhi, Motilal Banarsidass, 1968 (reprint).

Kathāvatthu, ed. by J. Kashyap, Devanagari Pali Series, Nalanda, 1961.

Kaulajñānanirṇaya and Some Minor Texts of Matsyendranātha, ed. by P. C. Bagchi, Calcutta, Calcutta University, 1934.

Kavīndravacanasamuccaya, ed. by F. W. Thomas, BI, Calcutta, 1912.

Khuddakanikāya, ed. by J. Kashyap, 7 vols., Devanagari Pali Series, Nalanda, 1954.

Kulārṇavatantra, ed. by A. Avalon, London, Luzac & Co., 1917.

Lalitavistara, ed. by P. L. Vaidya, BST, no. 1, Darbhanga, 1958.

Laṃkāvatārasūtra, ed. by P. L. Vaidya, BST, no. 3, Darbhanga, 1963; tr. by D. T. Suzuki, London, Routledge & Kegan Paul, 1968 (reprint).

Large Sūtra on Perfect Wisdom, pt. I, tr. by Edward Conze, London, Luzac & Co., 1961.

La Siddhi de Hiuen-tsang, French tr. by Louis de la Vallée Poussin, Paris, Geuthner, 1928-1948.

Le Compendium de la Super-doctrine, French, tr. by Walpola Rahula, Paris, 1971.

Le petit traite de Vasubandhu—Nāgārjuna sur les trois natures,

French tr. by Vallée Poussin, *Melanges Chinois et Bouddhiques,* vol. II, Bruxelles, 1932-1933.

Les Chants Mystiques de Kāṇha et de Saraha, ed. and tr. by M. Shahidullah, Paris, 1928.

Le Traite de la Grand Vertu de Sagesse de Nāgārjuna, 3 vols. French tr. by Etienne Lamotte, Louvain, Institut Orientaliste, 1944, 1949, 1971.

Life of Hiuen-Tsiang by Shaman Hwui Li, tr. by Samuel Beal, London, 1914.

L'itineraire d' Ou Kong, ed. and tr. by Sylvain Levi and E. Chavannese, *Journal Asiatique,* Paris, 1895.

Lokeśvaraśataka, ed. and tr. by S. K. Karpeles in *Journal Asiatique,* 1919.

L'origine de sectes bouddhiques d'apres Paramārtha, French tr. by Paul Demieville, *Melanges Chinois et Bouddhiques,* vol. I, Bruxelles, 1931-32.

Madhyamakahṛdaya, ch. II, ed. by V. V. Gokhale in *Indo-Iranian Journal,* vol. XIV, 1972; ch. VIII, ed. by Hajime Nakamura in the *Adyar Library Bulletin,* vol. XXXIX, 1975.

Madhyamakārtha-saṃgraha, Sanskrit restoration by N. Aiyaswami Sastri in the *Journal of Oriental Research,* vol. V, Madras, 1931; Hindi tr. by L. M. Joshi in *Dharmadūta,* vol. 29, July-August, Sarnath, 1964.

Madhyamakaśāstra, ed. by P. L. Vaidya, BST, no. 10, Darbhanga, 1960; tr. by Federick J. Streng, *Emptiness—A Study in Religious Meaning,* Nashville, Abindon Press, 1967.

Madhyamakāvatāra, ch. VI, restored into Sanskrit by N. Aiyaswami Sastri in the *Journal of Oriental Research,* vol. IV, 1930; vol. V, 1931; and vol. VI, 1932.

Madhyāntavibhāga-bhāṣya, ed. by G. M. Nagao, Tokyo, Suzuki Research Foundation, 1964.

Madhyāntavibhāga-ṭīkā, ed. by S. Yamaguchi, Tokyo, Suzuki Research Foundation, 1966 (reprint).

Mahābhārata, text and Hindi tr., 6 vols., Gorakhpur, Gita Press, 1963-64.

Mahāmāyūri, ed. by S. Levi in the *Journal Asiatique,* 1915, partly reprinted in *JUPHS,* vol. XV, pt. 2, 1942.

Mahānirvāṇatantra, published by Adi Brahma Samaj, Calcutta, 1876; tr. by Arthur Avalon, London, 1913.

Mahāvagga, ed. by J. Kashyap, Devanagari Pali Series, Nalanda,

1956; tr. by I. B. Horner, *The Book of the Discipline*, vol. IV, London, Luzac & Co., 1962 (reprint).

Mahāvaṃso, ed. by N. K. Bhagvat, Bombay, University of Bombay, 1959 (second edition); tr. by W. Geiger, London, Pali Text Society, 1912.

Mahāvastu, ed. by E. Senart, 3 vols., Paris, 1882-1897; ed. by S. Bagchi, pt. I, BST, no. 14, Darbhanga; tr. by J. J. Jones, 3 vols., London, Luzac & Co., 1949, 1953, 1956.

Mahāvyutpatti, ed. by R. Sakaki, 2 vols., Tokyo, Suzuki Research Foundation, 1962.

Mahāyānakaratalaratnaśāstra, restored into Sanskrit by N. Aiyaswami, *Visvabharati Annals,* vol. II, Santiniketan, 1949.

Mahāyānasūtrālaṃkāra, ed. by S. Levi, Paris, 1907; ed. by S. Bagchi, BST, no. 13, Darbhanga, 1970.

Mahāyānasūtrasaṃgraha, vols. 1-2, ed. by P. L. Vaidya, BST, nos. 17-18, Darbhanga, 1961, 1964.

Mahāyānaviṃśikā, ed. and tr. by Giuseppe Tucci in *MBT*, pt. I SOR, vol. IX, Rome, 1956.

Mahāyānottaratantraśāstra or *Ratnagotra-vibhāgaśāstra,* ed. by E. H. Johnston, Patna, 1950; tr. by Jikido Takasaki, Rome, SOR, vol. XXXIII, 1966.

Majjhimanikāya, ed. by J. Kashyap, 3 vols., Devanagari Pali Series, Nalanda, 1958; tr. by I. B. Horner, *Middle Length Sayings,* 3 vols., London, Luzac & Co., 1967, 1970 (reprint); Hindi tr. by R. Sāṃkṛtyāyana, Sarnath, Mahabodhi Sabha, 1964 (reprint).

Mālatīmādhava, ed. and tr. by M. R. Kale, Bombay, 1928 (second edition).

Mālavikāgnimitra, ed. by K. P. Parab, Bombay Sanskrit Series, Bombay, 1915.

Mañjuśrimūlakalpa, ed. by T. Ganapati Sastri, 3 vols., TSS, nos. LXX, LXXVI, LXXXIV, 1920, 1922, 1925; ed. by P. L. Vaidya, BST, no. 18, Darbhanga, 1964.

Manuscript Remains of Buddhist Literature found in Eastern Turkistan, ed. by A. F. R. Hoernle, vol. I, Oxford, 1916.

Manusmṛti, Varanasi, Pandita Pustakālaya, 1947; tr. by Georg Bühler, SBE, vol. 25, Delhi, Motilal Banarsidass, 1964 (reprint).

Mārkaṇḍeyapurāṇa, ed. by K. M. Banerjee, Calcutta, BI, 1862; tr. by F. E. Pargiter, BI, Calcutta, 1888-1905.

Matsyapurāṇa, published in Anandasrama Sanskrit Series, no. 54, Poona.

Mattavilāsa-prahasana, ed. by T. Ganapati Sastri, TSS, no. 55, 1917.

Meghadūta, ed. by E. Hultzsch, London, 1911; tr. by G. J. Somayaji, Madras, 1934.

Memoire compose a l' epoque de la grand dynastie Tang sur les religieux eminents qui allerent chercher la loi dans les pays d' occident, par I-tsing, French tr. by Edouard Chavannese, Paris, 1894.

Milindapañho, ed. by R. D. Vadekar, Bombay, University of Bombay, 1940; tr. by T. W. Rhys Davids, SBE, vols. 35-36, Delhi, Motilal Banarsidass, 1964 (reprint).

Mīmāṃsā-ślokavārttika with the Nyāyaratnākara, ed. R. S. Sastri and other Panditas of Benares, Varanasi, Chaukhamba, 1898.

Mīmāmsāsūtra with Śabarabhāṣya, published in the *Mīmāṃsā Darśana,* BI, Calcutta, 1889.

Mṛcchakaṭika, ed. by Vidyasagar, Calcutta, 1891 (second edition).

Mūlasarvāstivādavinayavastu, ed. by N. Dutt in *Gilgit Manuscripts;* ed. by S. Bagchi, BST, no. 16, Darbhanga, 1967.

Muṇḍaka Upaniṣad, ed. by Jagdish Sastri in *Upaniṣatsaṃgraha,* Delhi, Motilal Banarsidass, 1970.

Mystic Tales of Lama Tārānātha, tr. by Bhupendranath Datta, Calcutta, 1944.

Nairātmyaparipṛcchā, ed. by P. L. Vaidya in BST, no. 17, Darbhanga, 1961.

Navaśloki, ed. by Giuseppe Tucci in *MBT,* pt. I, SOR, vol. IX, Rome, 1956.

Nettippakaraṇa, ed. by E. Hardy, London, Pali Text Society, 1961 (reprint).

Nikāyasaṃgraha, ed. by de Silva, Gunasekera and Gunawardhana, Colombo, Ceylon Government Press, 1907.

Niṣpannayogāvalī, ed. by B. Bhattacharyya, GOS, vol. CIX, Baroda, 1949.

Northern India According to Shui-Ching-Chu, tr. by L. Petech, SOR, vol. II, Rome, 1950.

Nyāyabindu with *Nyāyabinduṭīkā,* ed. by Chandrasekhara Sastri, Kasi Sanskrit Series, Varanasi, 1954 (second edition);

tr. by Stcherbatsky in *Buddhist Logic,* vol. II, The Hague, Mouton & Co., 1958 (reprint).

Nyāyamañjarī, ed. by Gangadhara Sastri, Kasi Sanskrit Series, Varanasi, 1936.

Nyāyamukha, tr. by Giuseppe Tucci, Heidelberg, 1930.

Nyāyapraveśa, ed. by A. B. Dhruva, GOS, vol. 37, Baroda, 1930.

Nyāyasūtra with *Nyāyabhāṣya,* ed. by Ganganatha Jha, Poona Oriented Series, Poona, 1939.

Nyāyavārttika, ed. by Vindhyesvari Prasad Dvivedi, Kasi Sanskrit Series, Varanasi, 1926.

Nyāyavārttika-tātparyaṭīkā, ed. by Rajesvara Sastri Dravid, Kasi Sanskrit Series, Varanasi, 1925-1926.

Nyāyaviniścayavivaraṇa, ed. by Mahendrakumar Jain, Varanasi, Jnanapitha, 1949.

On Yuan Chwang's Travels in India, tr. by Thomas Watters, 2 vols., Delhi, Munshiram Manoharlal, 1961 (reprint).

Padma-purāṇa, ed. by V. N. Mandlick, Anandasrama Sanskrit Series, no. 28, Poona, 1849.

Pag-sam-jon-zañ of Sumpa mkhan-po, ed. by S. C. Das, Calcutta, 1908.

Pañcakrama, ed. by Louis de la Vallée Poussin, Gand, 1896.

Pañcaviṃśa Brāhmaṇa, ed. in BI, Calcutta, 1870-1877.

Pañcaviṃśati-sāhasrikā-prajñāpāramitā, ch. I, ed. by N. Dutt, Calcutta Oriental Series, no. 28, Calcutta, 1934.

Pāramitāsamāsa of Āryaśūra, ed. and tr. by Alfonsa Ferrari, *Annali Lateransi,* vol. X, Rome, 1946.

Patañjalimahābhāṣya with Kaiyaṭa's *Pradīpa* and Nāgeśa's *Uddyota,* Bombay, Nirnaya Sagar Press, 1951 (fifth edition).

Path of Freedom (*Vimuttimagga*), tr. by N. R. M. Ehara, Soma Thera and Kheminda Thera, Colombo, 1961.

Petavatthu, ed. by J. Kashyap in *KN,* vol. II, Devanagari Pali Series, Nalanda, 1959.

Prajñāpāramitā-piṇḍārtha, ed. by G. Tucci in *JRAS,* London, 1947; ed. by P. L. Vaidya, BST, no. 4, Darbhanga, 1960.

(*The*) *Prajñāpāramitās,* ed. by G. Tucci, GOS, vol. 62, Baroda, 1934.

Prajñāpāramitāstava, ed. by P. L. Vaidya in BST, no. 4, Darbhanga, 1960.

Prajñopāyaviniścaya-siddhi, ed. by B. Bhattacharyya, GOS, vol. XLIX, Baroda, 1929.

Pramāṇasamuccaya, ch. I, restored by H. R. Rangaswamy Iyengar, Mysore, 1930; the first chapter, *Pratyakṣapariccheda,* of this work has been translated and studied by M. Hattori, *Dignāga on Perception,* HOS, vol. 47, Cambridge, 1968.

Pramāṇavārttika, ch. I with autocommentary of Dharmakīrti, ed. by R. Gnoli, SOR, vol. XXXII, Rome, 1960.

Pramāṇavārttika with the commentary of Manorathanandin, ed. by R. Sāṃkṛtyāyana, *JBORS,* vols. XXIV, XXVI, Patna, 1938-40; ed. by D. Sastri, Varanasi, 1968.

Pramāṇavārttika-bhāṣyam or *Vārttikālaṃkāra,* ed. by R. Sāṃkṛtyāyana, Patna, K. P. Jayaswal Research Institute, 1953.

Pramāṇavārttika-kārikā, Sanskrit and Tibetan Texts, ed. by Usho Miyasaka, *Acta Indologica,* vol. II, Naritasan Shinshoji, 1971-72

Pramāṇavārttika-svārthānumāna-pariccheda with *Svavṛtti* of Dharmakīrti and *Svavṛtti-ṭīkā* by Karṇakagomin, ed. by R. Sāṃkṛtyayāna, Allahabad, Kitab Mahal, 1943; *Svārthānumāna-pariccheda* has been edited also by Dalsukhbhai Malvania, Varanasi, Hindu University, 1959.

Pramāṇaviniścaya, ch. I (*pratyakṣam*), Tibetan text with German tr. of Sanskrit fragments by Tilmann Vetter, Vienna, Austrian Academy of Sciences, 1966.

Prasannapadā or *Madhyamaka-vṛtti,* ed. by Louis de la Vallée Poussin in *BB,* St. Petersburg, 1931; ed. by P. L. Vaidya, BST, no. 10, Darbhanga, 1960; chs. 1 & 25 tr. by Stcherbatsky, *Conception of Buddhist Nirvāṇa;* chs. 2-9, 11, 26 & 27 tr. by Jacques May, *Candrakīrti : Prasannapadā-madhyamaka-vṛtti,* Paris, 1958; chs. 5, 10, 12-16 tr. by S. Schayer, *Ausgewablte Kapitel aus der Prasannapadā,* Krakowie, 1939; ch. 17 tr. by E. Lamotte, *Melanges Chinois et Bouddhiques,* vol. IV, 1936; chs. 18-22 tr. by J. W. de Jong, *Chinq chapitres de la Prasannapadā,* Buddhica Memoires, no. IX, Paris, 1949.

Rājataraṅgiṇi, Sanskrit Text with Hindi tr. Pandit Pustakalaya, Varanasi, 1960; ed. and tr. by M. A. Stein, 2 vols., Delhi, 1961 (reprint).

Rāṣṭrapāla-paripṛcchāsūtra, ed. by P. L. Vaidya, BST, no. 17, Darbhanga, 1961; tr. by J. Ensink, Zwolle, 1952.

Ratnakīrtinibandhāvali, ed. by A. L. Thakur, Patna, K. P. Jayaswal Research Institute, 1957.

Ratnāvali, ed. and tr. by G. Tucci, *JRAS*, London, 1934; ed. by P. L. Vaidya, BST, no. 10, Darbhanga, 1960.

(*A*) *Record of the Buddhist Religion as practised in India and the Malay Archipelago by I-tsing,* tr. by J. Takakusu, Delhi, Munshiram Manoharlal, 1966 (reprint).

Ṛgveda, 6 vols., ed by Max Müller, London, 1859-72; tr. by R. T. H. Griffith, 2 vols., Varanasi, Chaukhamba, 1964 (reprint).

Ṣaḍ-darśana-samuccaya with *Ṭīkā* of Manibhadra, ed. by Goswami Damodar Sastri, Varanasi, Chaukhamba, 1957 (third edition).

Saddharmapuṇḍarīkasūtra, ed. by P. L. Vaidya, BST, no. 6, Darbhanga, 1960; tr. by H. Kern, SBE, vol. XXI, Delhi, Motilal Banarsidass, 1966 (reprint).

Sādhanamālā, 2 vols., ed. by B. Bhattacharyya, GOS, vols. XXVI and XLI, Baroda, 1925, 1926.

Śaktisaṃgamatantra, 3 vols., ed. by B. Bhattacharyya, GOS, vols. LXI, XCI, CIV, Baroda, 1932-1947.

Śālistambasūtra, restored by N. A. Sastri, Madras, Adyar Library, 1950; reproduced in BST, no. 17, Darbhanga, 1961.

Samādhirājasūtra, ed. by P. L. Vaidya, BST, no. 2, Darbhanga, 1961.

Samayabhedoparacana-cakra, tr. by W. W. Rockhill in *The Life of the Buddha,* Varanasi, Orientalia Indica, 1972 (reprint).

Sambandhaparīkṣā with Śaṃkarānanda's commentary, ed. with German tr. by E. Frauwallner, *WZKM*, vol. XLI, 1934.

Śaṃkaradigvijaya of Mādhava, published in Anandasrama Sanskrit Series, no. 22, Poona.

Sāṃkhyakārikā with Gauḍapāda's *Bhāṣya,* ed. by Ḍhuṇḍhirāja Sastri, Varanasi, Chaukhamba, 1960 (reprint); tr. by John Davies, Calcutta, 1957 (reprint).

Sammitīya-nikāya-śāstra, tr. by K. Venkataramanan, *Visvabharati Annals,* vol. V, Santiniketan, 1953.

Saṃyuttanikāya, 4 vols., ed. by J. Kashyap, Devanagari Pali Series, Nalanda, 1959.

Sandhinirmocanasūtra, Tibetan text and French tr. by E. Lamotte, Louvain, 1935.

Santānāntarasiddhi with Vinītadeva's commentary, Tibetan text ed. by Stcherbatsky, *BB,* 1916; Russian tr. by Stcherbatsky, St. Petersburg, 1922.

Sarva-darśanasaṃgraha, Anandasrama Sanskrit Series, no. 51, Poona, 1928; tr. by E. B. Cowell and A. E. Gough, Varanasi, Chaukhamba, 1961 (reprint).

Śatapañcāsatkastotra of Mātṛceta, Sanskrit, Chinese and Tibetan texts with tr. by D. R. Shackleton-Bailey, Cambridge, 1951.

Śatapatha Brāhmaṇa, tr. by Julius Eggeling, SBE, vols. XII, XXVI, XLI, XLIII, XLIV, Delhi, Motilal Banarsidass, 1965 (reprint).

Śatasāhasrikāprajñāpāramitā, chs. I-XII, ed. by P. Ghosh, BI, Calcutta, 1902-1914.

Sekoddeśaṭīkā, ed. by M. E. Carelli, GOS, vol. XC, Baroda, 1941.

Śikṣāsamuccaya, ed. by Cecil Bendall, The Hague, Mouton & Co., 1957 (reprint); ed. by P. L. Vaidya, BST, no. 11, Darbhanga, 1960; tr. by W. H. D. Rouse and Cecil Bendall, London, 1922.

Śikṣāsamuccaya-kārikā, ed. and tr. by L. M. Joshi, Sarnath, Maha Bodhi Sabha, 1965.

Si-yu-ki or *Buddhist Records of the Western World,* 4 pts., tr. by Samuel Beal, Calcutta, 1957 (reprint).

Ślokavārttika, ed. by Rama Sastri Tailang, Varanasi, Chaukhamba, 1898; tr. by Ganganatha Jha, Calcutta, Asiatic Society, 1909.

Some Sayings of the Buddha According to the Pali Canon, tr. by F. L. Woodward, London, Oxford Classics, 1955 (reprint).

Sragdharāstotra with Jinarakṣita's commentary and two Tibetan versions, ed. by S. C. Vidyabhusana, BI, Calcutta, 1908.

Śrīcakrasambhāra-tantra (ch. I), tr. by Kazi Dawa Samdup, *Tantric Texts,* vol. VII, London, 1919.

Subhāṣitaratnakośa, ed. by V. V. Gokhale and D. D. Kosambi, HOS, vol. 42, Cambridge, 1957; tr. by Daniel H. H. Ingalls, HOS, vol. 44, Cambridge, 1965.

Subhāṣitatriśati or *Nītiśataka, Vairāgyaśataka* and *Śṛṅgāraśataka,* ed. by D. D. Kosambi and N. R. Acharya, Bombay, Nirnaya Sagar Press, 1957.

Sukhāvatīvyūhasūtra, ed. by P. L. Vaidya, BST, no. 17, Darbhanga, 1961.

Śūnyapurāṇa, ed. by N. N. Basu, Calcutta, Vangiya Sahitya Parisat, 1909.

Suprabhātastotra, ed. by I. P. Minayeff in *Zapiski de la societe Archaeologique,* t. II, fasc. III.

Śūraṅgamasamādhisūtra, French tr. by E. Lamotte, Louvain, 1965 (reprint).

Śūraṅgamasūtra, tr. by S. Beal in *Catena*; tr. by Charles Luk, London, Rider & Co., 1966.

Suttanipāta, ed. by J. Kashyap in *KN*, vol. I, Devanagari Pali Series, Nalanda, 1959.

Suvarṇaprabhāsasūtra, ed. by S. Bagchi, BST, no. 8, Darbhanga, 1967; tr. by R. E. Emmerick, *The Sūtra of Golden Light,* London, Luzac & Co., 1970.

Suvikrāntavikramī-paripṛcchā, ed. by Ryusho Hikata, Fukuoka, 1958; ed. by P. L. Vaidya, BST, no. 17, Darbhanga, 1961.

Śvetāśvatara Upaniṣad, ed. by Jagadish Sastri in *Upaniṣatasaṃgraha,* Delhi, Motilal Banarsidass, 1970.

Svayambhūpurāṇa, ed. by H. P. Sastri, BI, Calcutta, 1894-1900.

Tabqāt-i-nāsiri, tr. by H. G. Raverty, Calcutta, 1881.

Taittirīya-Brāhmaṇa, published in Anandasrama Sanskrit Series, Poona, 1899.

Taittirīya Upaniṣad, published in *Upaniṣatsaṃgraha,* Delhi, Motilal Banarsidass, 1964.

Tantravārttika, tr. by Ganganatha Jha, 2 vols., Calcutta, Asiatic Society, 1924.

Tārānātha's History of Buddhism in India, tr. by Lama Chimpa and Alaka Chattopadhyaya, Simla, Indian Institute of Advanced Study, 1970; German tr. Antonius Schiefner, *Geschichte des Buddhismus in Indien,* St. Petersburg, 1869; partly tr. by U. N. Ghoshal and N. Dutt and published in *IHQ*, vols. VII, VIII, X, XXVII, XXVIII; Hindi tr. by Lama Rigzin Lundup, Patna, K. P. Jayaswal Research Institute, 1971.

Tarkabhāṣā, tr. by Y. Kajiyama, *An Introduction to Buddhist Philosophy,* Kyoto, 1966.

Tattvasaṃgraha with the *Pañjikā,* ed. by Ember Kṛṣṇāmācārya, 2 vols., GOS, nos. XXX-XXX, Baroda, 1926; ed. by D. Shastri, 2 vols., Varanasi, 1968; tr. by Ganganatha Jha, 2 vols., GOS, nos. LXXX and LXXXII, 1937, 1939.

Theragāthā and *Therīgāthā,* ed. by J. Kashyap in *KN*, vol. II, Nalanda, Devanagari Pali Series, 1959; tr. by C. A. F. Rhys Davids, *Psalms of the Early Buddhists,* London, Luzac & Co., 1964 (reprint).

Thirteen Principal Upaniṣads, tr. by R. E. Hume, Madras, Oxford University Press, 1958 (reprint of second edition).

Travels of Fa-hsien, tr. by H. A. Giles, Cambridge, 1923; tr. by James Legge, *A Record of Buddhistic Kingdoms,* New York, Dover Publications, 1965 (reprint).

Udāna, ed. by J. Kashyap in *KN*, vol. I, Devanagari Pali Series, Nalanda, 1959.

Upaniṣatsaṃgraha, ed. by Jagadish Sastri, Delhi, Motilal Banarsidass, 1964.

Vādanyāya, ed. by Rāhula Sāṃkṛtyāyana, Sarnath, Maha Bodhi Sabha, 1936; ed. by D. Shastri, Varanasi, 1972.

Vājasaneyi Saṃhitā, ed. by A. Weber, London, 1852.

Vajracchedikā Prajñāpāramitā, ed. and tr. by Edward Conze, SOR, vol. XIII, Rome, 1957.

Vākyapadīya, ed. by Pandita Manavalli, Benares, 1884-1887; ed. by K. A. Subramanya Iyer, *kānda,* III, Poona, Deccan College, 1963.

Vāyu-purāṇa, published in Anandasrama Sanskrit Series, no. 49, Poona, 1906.

Vedānta Explained (tr. of *Brahmasūtra Śaṃkara-bhāṣya*), by V. H. Date, 2 vols., Bombay, 1954.

Vedāntasūtras with Śaṃkara's commentary, tr. by George Thibaut, SBE, vols. 34, 38, Delhi, Motilal Banarsidass, 1965 (reprint).

Vigrahavyāvartanī, ed. by P. L. Vaidya in BST, no. 10, Darbhanga, 1960; tr. by Frederick J. Streng in *Emptiness, A study in Religious Meaning,* Nashville, Abingdon Press, 1967.

Vijñaptimātratāsiddhi Deux Traites de Vasubandhu, ed. and tr. by S. Levi, Paris, 1925.

Viṃśatikā-vijñaptimātratāsiddhi, Sanskrit and Tibetan texts ed. by N. Aiyaswami Sastri, Gangtok, Namgyal Institute of Tibetology, 1954.

Viṣṇu-purāṇa, published by the Gita Press, Gorakhpur, Samvat 2017; tr. by H. H. Wilson, Calcutta, Punthi Pustak, 1961 (reprint).

Visuddhimagga, ed. by Dharmananda Kosambi and H. C. Warren, HOS, vol. 41, Cambridge, 1950; tr. by Ñāṇamoli, *The Path of Purification,* Colombo, A. Semage, 1964.

(*The*) *Way of Mindfulness,* tr. by Soma Thera, Kandy, Buddhist Publication Society, 1967 (third edition).

(*The*) *Way of the Buddha,* Govt. of India Publications Division, Delhi, 1956.

(*The*) *Wisdom Gone Beyond, An Anthology of Buddhist Texts,* by various hands, Bangkok, Social Science Association Press, 1966.

Yājñavalkya-smṛti, Anandasrama Sanskrit Series, no. 46, Poona, 1903-1904.

Yogācārabhūmi, ed. by Vidhushekhara Bhattacharya, Calcutta, University of Calcutta, 1957.

Yogarājoponiṣat, ed. in the *Upaniṣatsaṃgraha,* Delhi Motilal Banarsidass, 1970.

Yogasūtra, published by the Gita Press, Gorakhpur, Samvat 2007.

Yogavāsiṣṭha Rāmāyaṇa, Nirṇaya Sagar Press, Bombay, 1911.

MODERN WORKS

A. Aiyappan and P. R. Srinivasan, *Story of Buddhism with Special Reference to South India,* Madras, Government of Madras, 1960.

A. A. Macdonell, *A History of Sanskrit Literature,* Delhi, Motilal Banarsidass, 1960 (reprint).

A. Banerji-Sastri, 'The Naṭī of Pāṭaliputra' in *IHQ,* vol. IX, 1933.

A. B. Keith, *Buddhist Philosophy in India and Ceylon,* Oxford, Clarendon Press, 1923.

—*Religion and Philosophy of the Veda and Upanishads,* 2 pts., HOS, vols. 31-32, Cambridge, 1925.

A. B. Keith and A. A. Macdonell, *Vedic Index,* 2 vols. Delhi, Motilal Banarsidass, 1958 (reprint).

A. C. Banerjee, *The Sarvāstivāda Literature,* Calcutta, 1957.

A. Foucher, *Etude sur l' Iconographie Bouddhique*. 2 vols., Paris, 1900, 1905.
—*La vie du Bouddha,* Paris, Payot, 1949.
—*The Beginnings of Buddhist Art,* London, 1918.
Agehananda Bharati, *The Tantric Tradition,* London, Rider & Co., 1969 (reprint).
A. Getty, *The Gods of Northern Buddhism,* Oxford, 1928.
A. Ghosh, *Nalanda,* New Delhi, 1959 (fourth edition).
A. Grünwedel, *Buddhist Art in India,* London, 1901.
A. K. Gordon, *The Iconography of Tibetan Lamaism,* New York, 1939.
Akira Hirakawa, 'The Rise of Mahāyāna Buddhism' in *Memoirs of the Toyo Bunko,* no. 22, Tokyo, 1963.
A. K. Warder, *Indian Buddhism,* Delhi, Motilal Banarsidass, 1970.
A. L. Basham, *The Wonder that was India,* New York, Macmillan Co., 1954.
Alexander Cunningham, *Ancient Geography of India,* Varanasi, Indological Book House, 1963 (reprint).
—*Maha Bodhi or the Great Buddhist Temple at Bodh Gaya,* London, 1892.
—*The Stupa of Bharhut,* London, 1879.
Alex Wayman, 'The significance of Mantras from the Veda down to Buddhist Tantric Practice' in *ALB*, vol. XXXIX, Madras, 1975.
—'The Twenty Praises of Tārā, a syncretism of Śaivism and Buddhism' in *JBRS*, vol. XLV, Patna, 1959.
Alicia Matsunaga, *The Buddhist Philosophy of Assimilation,* Tokyo, Sophia University, 1969.
Andre Bareau, *Les Sectes Bouddhiques du petit vehicule,* Saigon, 1955.
Andrew Vostrikov, 'Nyāyavārttika of Uddyotakara and Vādanyāya of Dharmakīrti' in *IHQ*, vol. XI, 1935.
Aparna Banerji, *Traces of Buddhism in South India,* Calcutta, Scientific Book Agency, 1970.
A. P. Karmarkar, 'The Linga Cult in Ancient India' in *B. C. Law Volume,* pt. I, Calcutta, 1945.
Arnold J. Toynbee, *A Study of History,* 2 vols., abridged by D. C. Somervell, New York, Dell Publishing Co., 1969.

Arthur Waley, 'New Light on Buddhism in Medieval India' in *Melanges Chinois et Bouddhiques,* vol. I, Bruxelles, 1931-32.
—*The Real Tripitaka,* London, George Allen & Unwin, 1952.
A. S. Altekar, *Education in Ancient India,* Varanasi, Nandkishore Brothers, 1957.
—*Sources of Hindu Dharma,* Sholapur, D. A. V. College, 1953.
A. S. Geden, 'Kanakamuni' in *ERE*, vol. VII.
—'Monasticism' in *ERE*, vol. VIII
Ashok Kumar Chatterjee, *The Yogācāra Idealism,* Varanasi, Banaras Hindu University, 1962.
Asoke Chatterjee, *Padma Purāṇa—A Study*, Calcutta, Sanskrit College, 1969.
Baldeva Upadhyaya, *Bauddha Darśana Mīmāṃsā,* Varanasi, Chaukhamba, 1954.
B. C. Law (ed.), *Buddhistic Studies,* Calcutta, 1932.
—*Life and Works of Buddhaghosa,* Calcutta Oriental Series, no. 9, Calcutta, 1923.
—*Kauśāmbī in Ancient Literature,* MASI, no. 60, 1939.
—*Śrāvastī in Ancient Literature,* MASI, no. 50, 1935.
—*Rājagriha in Ancient Literature,* MASI, no. 58, 1938.
—'Contemporary Indian and Ceylonese Kings' in *JBBRAS*, vol. 26, Bombay, 1950.
Benimadhab Barua, *Gayā and Buddha-Gayā,* 2 vols, Calcutta, 1931-34.
Benjamin Rowland, *The Art and Architecture of India,* London Baltimore, The Penguin Books, 1959 (reprint).
Benoytosh Bhattacharyya, *The Indian Buddhist Iconography,* Calcutta, K. L. Mukhopadhyaya, 1958 (second edition).
—*An Introduction to Buddhist Esoterism,* Mysore, Oxford University Press, 1932.
Bhikshu Sangharakshita, *A Survey of Buddhism,* Bangalore, Indian Institute of World Culture, 1966 (third edition).
—*The Three Jewels,* London, Rider & Co., 1967.
Binayak Misra, *Dynasties of Medieval Orissa,* Calcutta, 1933.
B. L. Suzuki, *Mahāyāna Buddhism,* London, 1959.
B. Majumdar, *A Guide to Sarnath,* Delhi, 1937.
B. N. Misra, 'The Three Bodhisattva Images from Nalanda' in *JUPHS*, (n.s.), vol. I, Lucknow, 1953.
Bunyu Nanjio, *A Catalogue of the Chinese Translation of the Buddhist Tripitaka,* Oxford, 1883.

C. A. F. Rhys Davids, 'Asceticism in *ERE*, vol. II.

C. C. Dasgupta, *Paharpur and its Monuments,* Calcutta, K. L. Mukhopadhyaya, 1961.

Charles Eliot, *Hinduism and Buddhism,* 3 vols., London, Routledge and Kegan Paul, 1921.

Chintaharan Chakravarti, *Tantras: Studies on their Religion and Literature*, Calcutta, Punthi, 1963.

Daisetz Teitaro Suzuki, *Essays in Zen Buddhism,* Series I-III, London, Rider & Co., 1949, 1953.

—*Outlines of Mahāyāna Buddhism,* New York, Schocken Books, 1963 (reprint).

—Studies in the Lankāvatāra Sūtra, London, Routledge & Kegan Paul, 1968 (reprint).

—*Tibetan Tripitaka, Catalogue and Index,* Tokyo, Suzuki Research Foundation, 1962.

D. B. Disalkar, *Selections from Sanskrit Inscriptions,* Rajkot, 1925.

—'Wala Museum Plates' in *JBBRAS* (n.s.), vol. I, Bombay, 1924.

D. C. Sircar, *Select Inscriptions*, vol. I, Calcutta, University of Calcutta Press, 1942.

—*Studies in the Religious Life of Ancient and Medieval India,* Delhi, Motilal Banarsidass, 1971.

—*The Śākta Pīṭhas in JASB,* vol. XIV, Calcutta, 1948.

D. D. Kosambi, *Myth and Reality,* Bombay, Popular Prakashan, 1962.

—'On the Origin of Brahmin Gotras' in *JBBRAS*. vol. 26 (n.s.), Bombay, 1950.

Debala Mitra, *Ajanta,* Delhi, Department of Archaeology, 1959.

Dharmananda Kosambi, *Pārśvanātha kā Cāturyāma Dharma,* Bombay, 1957.

Dharmarakshita, *Kuśīnagara kā Itihāsa,* Kuśinagara, 1951.

—*Sāranātha kā Itihāsa,* Varanasi, Nandkishore Brothers, 1961.

Dietrich Seckel, *The Art of Buddhism,* New York, Crown Publishers, 1964.

D. L. Snellgnove, *Buddhist Himalaya,* Oxford, 1957.

D. R. Bhandarkar, *A List of the Inscriptions of Northern India in Brāhmī and its derivative scripts from about* 200 *A.C. in Epigraphic Indica,* vols. XIX-XXIII, Appendix.

—*Aśoka,* Calcutta, University of Calcutta, 1955 (third edition).

—(ed.) *B.C. Law Volume,* pt. I, Calcutta, 1945; pt. II, Poona, 1946.

E. A. Solomon, 'The Problem of Omniscience' in the *Adyar Library Bulletin,* vol. XVI, Madras, 1962.

Edward Conze, *A Short History of Buddhism,* Bombay, Chetna Ltd., 1961.

—*Buddhism, its Essence and Development,* Oxford, Bruno Cassirer, 1951.

—*Buddhist Meditation,* London, Allen & Unwin, 1956.

—*Buddhist Thought in India,* London, Allen & Unwin, 1962.

—*Materials for a Dictionary of the Prajñāpāramitā Literature,* Tokyo, Suzuki Research Foundation, 1967.

—*The Prajñāpāramitā Literature,* The Hague, Mouton & Co., 1960.

—'The Tantric Prajñāpāramitā Texts' in *Sino-Indian Studies,* vol. V, pt. 2, 1957.

—*Thirty Years of Buddhist Studies,* Oxford, Bruno Cassirer, 1967.

E. Frauwallner, *Die Philosophie des Buddhismus,* Berlin, 1958.

—*History of Indian Philosophy,* 2 vols., tr. by V. M. Bedekar, Delhi, Motilal Banarsidass, 1973.

—*On the Date of the Buddhist Master of the Law Vasubandhu,* SOR, vol. III, Rome, 1951.

—*The Earliest Vinaya and Beginnings of Buddhist Literature,* SOR, vol. VIII, Rome, 1956.

E. J. Thomas, 'Education in Early Buddhist Schools' in *Buddhistic Studies,* ed. by B. C. Law, Calcutta, 1931.

—*The History of Buddhist Thought,* London, Routledge & Kegan Paul, 1967 (reprint).

—*The Life of the Buddha as Legend and History,* London, Routledge and Kegan Paul, 1969 (reprint).

E. Obermiller, 'A Study of Twenty Aspects of Śūnyatā' in *IHQ,* vol. IX, Calcutta, 1933.

Erich Zürcher, *The Buddhist Conquest of China,* 2 vols., Leiden, E. J. Brill, 1959.

Ernst Waldschmidt, *Von Cylon Bis Turfan, Schriften zur Geschichte, Literature, Religion und Kunst des indischen Kulturaumes,* Göttingen, 1967.

F. Edgerton, *Buddhist Hybrid Sanskrit Dictionary,* Delhi, Motilal Banarsidass, 1970 (reprint).

—'Sandhābhāṣā' in *JAOS,* vol. 57, Baltimore, 1937.

—'Dominant Ideas in the Formation of Indian Culture' in *JAOS,* vol. 62, Baltimore, 1942.

F. Kielhorn, *A List of the Inscriptions of Northern India from about* 400 A.D. *Epigraphia Indica,* vol. V, Appendix I with Supplement, 1896-1899, 1905-1906.

F. W. Thomas, *Indianism and its Expansion,* Calcutta, University of Calcutta, 1944.

G. C. Mendis, *The Early History of Ceylon,* Calcutta, 1947 (eighth edition).

Geoffrey Parrinder, *Avatar and Incarnation,* London, Faber & Faber, 1970.

Giuseppe Tucci, *On Some Aspects of the Doctrines of Maitreya (nātha) and Asaṅga,* Calcutta, University of Calcutta, 1930.

—*Theory and Practice of the Maṇḍala,* London, Rider & Co., 1969.

G. K. Nariman, *Literary History of Sanskrit Buddhism,* Bombay, 1923.

Gokuldas De, *Democracy in Early Buddhist Saṃgha,* Calcutta, University of Calcutta, 1954.

Gopinatha Kaviraja, *Bhāratīya Saṃskṛti aur Sādhanā,* pt. I, Patna, Bihar Rastrabhasa Parisad, 1963.

—'Mystic Significance of Evaṃ' in *The Journal of the Ganganatha Jha Research Institute,* vol. II, pt. I, 1944.

Govind Chandra Pande, *Studies in the Origins of Buddhism,* Allahabad. University of Allahabad, 1957.

G. P. Malalasekera, *Dictionary of Pali Proper Names,* 2 vols., London, Luzac & Co., 1960 (reprint).

G. R. Sharma, *Excavations at Kauśāmbī,* Allahabad, 1960.

Guy Richard Welbon, *The Buddhist Nirvana and its Western Interpreters,* Chicago, University of Chicago Press, 1968.

G. Yazdani, *Ajantā* (Text and Plates), vols.. I-IV, Oxford, 1930-1955.

Hajari Prasad Dvivedi, *Nātha Sampradāya kā Itihāsa,* Varanasi, Naivedya Niketan, 1966 (second edition).

H. A. Jāschke, *A Tibetan-English Dictionary,* New York, Frederick Ungar Publishing Co., 1965 (reprint).

Hajime Nakamura 'Historical Studies of the Coming into Existence of Mahāyānasūtras' in *Bulletin of the Okurayama Oriental Research Institute,* no. 2, 1957.

—*Buddhism in Comparative Light,* New Delhi, Islam and the Modern Age Society, 1975.

Haraprasad Sastri, '*The Northern Buddhism*' in *IHQ*, vol. I, 1925.

—*Discovery of Living Buddhist in Bengal,* Calcutta, 1897.

—*A Descriptive Catalogue of Sanskrit Manuscripts,* vol. I, Buddhist Manuscripts, Calcutta, 1917.

—*Notices of Sanskrit Manuscripts,* Second Series, pt. I, Calcutta, 1907.

—'Literary History of the Pāla Period' in *JBORS*, vol. V, Patna, 1919.

—'*Śāntideva*' in *Indian Antiquary,* vol. XLII, 1913.

Hardayal, *The Bodhisattva Doctrine in Buddhist Sanskrit Literature,* Delhi, Motilal Banarsidass, 1970 (reprint).

H. C. Raychaudhuri, *Political History of Ancient India,* Calcutta, University of Calcutta, 1953 (sixth edition).

H. D. Sankalia, *The University of Nalanda,* Madras, 1934.

Heimo Rau, 'Multiple Arms in Indian God-Images' in *Adyar Library Bulletin,* vol. XXXIV, 1975.

Helmut Hoffmann, *The Religions of Tibet,* London, Allen & Unwin, 1961.

Hermann Goetz, 'Antiquity of Chamba State: An Art Historical Outline, in *JUPHS* (n.s.), vol. I, Lucknow, 1953.

—*Kashmir and the Indian Himalayas,* Wiesbaden, Otto Harrassowitz, 1969.

H. Hartland, 'Phallism' in *ERE,* vol. IX.

H. Heras, 'The Royal Patrons of the University of Nalanda' in *JBORS,* vol. XIV, Patna 1928.

Hiralal (Rai Bhadur), *Descriptive List of Inscriptions in the Central Provinces and Berar,* Nagpur, 1916.

Hirananda Sastri, *Nalanda and Its Epigraphic Material,* MASI, no. 66, Calcutta, 1942.

H. Kern, *Manual of Indian Buddhism,* Varanasi, Indological Book House, 1968 (reprint).

H. Lüders, *A List of Brahmi Inscriptions* in *Epigraphia Indica,* vol. X, Appendix.

H. M. Eliot and John Dowson, *History of India as told by its own Historians,* vol. I, Allahabad, Kitab Mahal, n.d.

H. N. Randle, *Indian Logic in the Early Schools,* Allahabad, Oxford University Press, 1930.

H. R. R. Iyengar, 'Bhartṛhari and Diṅnāga' in *JBBRAS,* (n.s.), vol. 26, Bombay, 1950.

H. Ui, *Vaiśeṣika Philosophy*, Varanasi, Chaukhamba, 1961 (reprint).

H. Ui, M. Suzuki, Y. Kanakura and T. Tada, *A Complete Catalogue of the Tibetan Buddhist Canons,* Sendai, Tohoku Imperial University, 1934.

H. V. Guenther, *Yuganaddha: The Tantric View Life,* Varanasi, Chaukhamba, 1952.

—*The Life and Teachings of Nāropa,* New York, Oxford University Press, 1968.

—*Treasures on the Tibetan Middle Way,* Leiden, E. J. Brill, 1969.

—*The Royal Song of Saraha,* Seattle, University of Washington, 1969.

—*Buddhist Philosophy in Theory and Practice,* Baltimore, Penguin Books, 1972.

H. Zimmer, *Myths and Symbols in Indian Art and Civilization,* New York, Bollingen Series, no. VI, 1953.

—*Philosophies of India,* ed. by J. Campbell, NewYork, Meridian Books, 1960 (reprint).

—*Ewiges Indien,* Zürich, 1930.

—*The Art of Indian Asia, Its Mythology and Transformation,* 2 vols., New York, Bollingen Series, nos. 39-40, 1956.

Isshi Yamada, 'Pramāṇavārttika and Pramāṇaviniścaya' in *Journal of Indian and Buddhist Studies,* vol. VIII, no. 2, Tokyo, 1960.

Jacques May, '*La philosophie bouddhiques idealiste*' in *Etudes asiatiques*, vol. 25, 1971.

James Fergusson, *The Tree and Serpent Worship,* London, 1873.

James Fergusson and James Burgess, *The Cave Temples of India,* London, 1880

James Hastings (ed.), *The Encyclopaedia of Religion and Ethics,* vols. I-XII, Edinbourgh, T. & T Clark, 1908-1926.

Jan Yun Hua, 'Kashmir's Contribution to the Expansion of Buddhism in the Far East' in *IHQ*, vol. XXXVII, Calcutta, 1961.

Jean Przyluski, 'Uposatha, A Babylonian Element in Indian Culture' in *IHQ*, Calcutta, 1936.

—'Dārṣṭāntika, Sautrāntika and Sarvāstivādin' in *IHQ*, vol. XVI, Calcutta, 1940.

—'An Ancient People of Panjab: The Udumbaras' in *Indian Studies*: *Past and Present,* vol. I, 1960.

J. Griffiths, *Paintings in the Buddhist Cave Temples of Ajantā*, 2 vols., London, 1896-1897.

J. N. Banerjea, *The Development of Hindu Iconography*, Calcutta, University of Calcutta, 1956 (second edition).

J. N. Ganhar and P.N. Ganhar, *Buddhism in Kashmir and Ladakh*, Delhi, 1956.

John Blofeld, *The Tantric Mysticism of Tibet*, New York, E. P. Dutton & Co., 1970.

John Dewey, *Reconstruction in Philosophy*, Boston, Beacon Press, 1948.

John F. Fleet, *Corpus Inscriptionum Indicarum*, vol. III, Calcutta 1888.

John Marshall, *The Buddhist Art of Gāndhāra*, Cambridge, 1960.

John Marshall *et al*, *The Monuments of Sānchi*, vols. I-III, Delhi, 1940.

John Woodroffe, *Principles of Tantra*, Madras, 1950.

—*Shakti and Shakta*, Madras, 1951.

J. Ph. Vogel, *Antiquities of Chamba State*, pt. I, ASI, New Imperial Series, vol. XXXVI, Calcutta, 1911.

—*Indian Serpent Lore*, London, Arthur Probsthain, 1926.

—*Buddhist Art in India, Ceylon and Java*, Eng. tr. by A. J. Barnouw, Oxford, 1936.

J. Takakusu, *The Essentials of Buddhist Philosophy*, Bombay, Asia Publishing House, 1956.

—'Sarvāstivāda' in *ERE*, vol. XI.

J. Takakusu and M. Anesaki; 'Dhyāna' in *ERE*, vol. IV.

Jwala Prasad, *History of Indian Epistemology*, Delhi, Munshiram Manoharlal. 1958 (reprint).

J. W. de Jong, 'The Problem of the Absolute in the Madhyamaka School' in *Journal of Indian Philosophy*, vol. II, 1972.

—'A Brief History of Buddhist Studies in Europe and America' in *The Eastern Buddhist*, (n.s.),vol VII Kyoto, 1974.

J. W. Hauer, *Die Dhārani in nordischen Buddhismus*, Sttutgart, 1927.

J. W. McCrindle, *Ancient India as Described by Megasthenes and Arrian*, Calcutta, 1926.

K. A. Nilakanta Sastri, 'An Episode in the History of Buddhism in South India' in *B. C. Law Volume*, pt. I, Calcutta, 1945.

—*Foreign Notices of South India*, Madras, 1939.

K. C. Chattopadhyaya, 'Religious Suicide at Prayaga' in *JUPHS*, vol. X, pt. I, Lucknow, 1937.

—'References to Buddhist Philosophy in the Śābarabhāṣya' in *Ganganatha Jha Commemoration Volume*, Poona, 1937.

Kenneth K. S. Chen, *Buddhism in China*, Princeton, University of Princeton Press, 1964.

Kenneth W. Morgan (ed.), *The Path of the Buddha*, New York, Ronald Press, 1956.

K. M. Munshi, *Glory That was Gūrjaradeśa*, 2 vols., Bombay, Bharatiya Vidya Bhavan, 1955.

K. N. Jayatilleke, *Early Buddhist Theory of Knowledge*, London, Allen & Unwin, 1963.

K. N. Upadhyaya, *Early Buddhism and the Bhagavadgītā*, Delhi, Motilal Banarsidass, 1971.

K. P. Chattopadhyaya, 'Dharma Worship' in *JRASB* (Letters), vol. VIII, 1942.

K. P. Jayaswal, *An Imperial History of India in a Sanskrit Text*, Lahore, 1934.

K. V. Ramanan, *Nāgārjuna's Philosophy As Presented in the Mahāprajñāpāramitāśāstra*, Routland, E. Tuttle, 1966.

Lal Mani Joshi (ed.), *History of the Punjab*, vol. I, Patiala, Punjabi University, 1976.

—*God's Alternative—A Study of Vivekananda's Attitude to Buddhism*, Cape Cod, Claude Stark & Co., 1977.

—*Brahmanism, Buddhism and Hinduism*, Kandy, Buddhist Publication Society, 1973.

—'Social Perspective of Buddhist Soteriology' in *Religion and Society*, vol. VIII, no. 3, Bangalore, 1971.

—'Truth: A Buddhist Perspective' in *The Journal of Religious Studies*, vol. IV, Patiala, 1972.

—'A Survey of the Conception of Bodhicitta' in *The Journal of Religious Studies*, vol. III, Patiala 1971.

—'Our Republican Heritage' in *The Mahabodhi*, vol. 73, 1965.

—'Original Homes of Tāntrika Buddhism' in *Journal of the Oriental Institute*, vol. XVII, Baroda, 1967.

—'Buddhist Gleanings from the Rājataraṅgiṇī' in *Journal of the Oriental Institute*, vol. XIV, Baroda, 1964.

—'Reviews on some Alleged Causes of the Decline of Buddhism in India' in *The Journal of the Ganganatha Jha Research Institute*, vol. XXII, Allahabad, 1966-1967.

Lama Anagarika Govinda, *The Psychological Attitude of Early Buddhism,* London, Rider & Co., 1969 (reprint).
—*Foundations of Tibetan Mysticism,* London, Rider & Co., 1960.
Lama Chimpa and Alaka Chattopadhyaya, *Atiśa and Tibet,* Calcutta, 1967.
L. A. Waddell, *The Buddhism of Tibet and Lamaism* New Delhi, Heritage Publishers, 1974 (reprint).
—'Jewel' in *ERE,* vol. VIII.
Lokesh Chandra, *Bhota-Sanskrit Abhidhāna,* 2 vols., Kyoto, Rinsen Book Co., 1971 (reprint).
Louis De La Vallée Poussin, *La Morale Bouddhique,* Paris Novelle Librarie Nationale, 1972.
—*The Way to Nirvāṇa,* Cambridge, Cambridge University Press, 1917.
—'Bodhisattva' in *ERE,* vol. II.
—'Tantrism' in *ERE,* vol. XII.
—'Ādibuddha' in *ERE,* vol. I.
—'Mahāyāna' in *ERE,* vol. VIII.
—*Le dogme et la philosophie du bouddhisme,* Paris, 1930.
Masaaki Hattori, *Dignāga on Perception,* Cambridge, Harvard University Press, 1968.
Maurice Winternitz, *A History of Indian Literature*, vol. II. tr. by S. Ketkar and H. Kohn, New Delhi, Oriental Reprint Corporation, 1972; vol. III, pts. 1-2, tr. by Subhadra Jha, Delhi, Motilal Banarsidass, 1963, 1967.
—'Notes on the Guhyasamāja-Tantra and the Age of the Tantras' in the *IHQ*, vol. IX, Calcutta, 1933.
M. B. Jhaveri, *Comparative and Critical Study of Mantraśāstra*, Ahmedabad, 1944.
Melford E. Spiro, *Buddhism and Society, A Great Tradition and its Burmese Vicissitudes,* London, Allen & Unwin, 1971.
Mervyin Sprung (d.), *Problem of Two Truths in Buddhism and Vedānta,* Dordrecht-Boston, D. Reidel Publishing Co., 1973.
M. H. Kuraishi and A. Ghosh, *A Guide to Rajgir,* Delhi, Department of Archaeology, 1951 (third edition).
Mircea Eliade, *Yoga, Immortality and Freedom,* tr. by W. R. Trask, Princeton, Bollingen Series, no. 56, 1969 (second edition).
Mitsuyoshi Saigusa, *Studien zum Mahāprajñāpāramitā* (*Upadeśa*) *Śāstra,* Tokyo, 1969.

M. K. Gandhi, *An Autobiography or the Story of My Experiments with Truth,* tr. by Mahadev Desai, Ahmedabad, Navajivan Publishing House, 1949.

Monier Williams, *A Sanskrit-English Dictionary,* Delhi, Motilal Banarsidass, 1968 (reprint).

Mortimer Wheeler, *The Indus Civilization,* Cambridge, Cambridge University Press, 1968 (third edition).

Nagin J. Shah, *Akalaṅka's Criticism of Dharmakīrti's Philosophy: A Study,* Ahmedabad, L. D. Institute of Indology, 1967.

Nalinaksha Dutt, *Early Monastic Buddhism,* 2 vols., Calcutta, 1941, 1945.

Aspects of Mahāyāna Buddhism and its Relation to Hīnayāna, London, Luzac & Co., 1930.

Narendradeva, *Bauddha Dharma Darśana,* Patna, Bihar Rāṣtrabhāṣā Parisad, 1956.

N. K. Bhattasali, *Iconography of Buddhist and Brahmanical Sculptures in the Dacca Museum,* Dacca, 1929.

N. K. Sahu, *Buddhism in Orissa,* Bhubaneswar, Utkal University, 1958.

N. N. Dasgupta, *'Uḍḍiyāna and Sāhore'* in *IHQ,* vol. XI, Calcutta, 1935.

N. N. Ghosh, *Early History of Kauśāṃbī,* Allahabad, 1935.

N. N. Law, 'Some Images and Traces of Mahāyāna in Chittagong' in *IHQ*, vol. VIII, Calcutta, 1932.

N. N. Vasu, *Modern Buddhism and its Followers in Orissa,* Calcutta, 1911.

Noel Peri, 'Hārīti: La Mere de Demons' in *BEFEO*, vol. XVIII, 1917.

Nolan Pliny Jacobson, *Buddhism, The Religion of Analysis,* London, Allen & Unwin, 1966.

Nundolal De, *Geographical Dictionary of Ancient and Medieval India,* London, Luzac & Co., 1927.

Nyanaponika Thera, *The Heart of Buddhist Meditation,* London, Rider & Co., 1962.

O. H. de A. Wijesekera, 'A Pāli Reference to Brāhmaṇa-caraṇas' in *ALB*, vol. XX, Madras, 1956.

—'The Concept of Viññāṇa in Theravāda Buddhism' in *JAOS*, vol. 84, 1964.

Otto Schrader, *An Introduction to Pāñcarātra,* Adyar, 1916.

P. B. Desai, 'Buddhist Antiquities of Karṇāṭaka' in *The Journal of Indian History,* vol. 32, 1954.
P. C. Alexander, *Buddhism in Kerala,* Annamalainagar, 1949.
P. C. Bagchi, *Studies in the Tantras,* pt. I, Calcutta, 1939.
—'Sandhābhāṣā' in *IHQ*, vol. IV, Calcutta, 1928.
—'Reviews on Sādhanamālā' in *IHQ*, vol. IV, Calcutta, 1930.
—'Foreign Elements in the Tantra' in *IHQ*, vol. VII, Calcutta, 1931.
—'Decline of Buddhsim in India and its Causes' in *Asutosh Mukerjee Silver Jubilee Volumes,* vol. III, Calcutta, University of Calcutta, 1928.
—'Letters of Hsüan-tsang' in *JUPHS*, vol. XVII, Lucknow, 1945.
—*India and China,* Bombay, 1950 (second edition).
P. Cordier, *Catalogue du Fonds Tibetain de la Bibliotheque Nationale,* 2e partie, Index du Bstan-Hgyur, Paris, 1909.
Phanindra Nath Bose, *Indian Teachers of Buddhist Universities,* Madras, 1925.
P. H. Pott, *Yoga and Tantra,* tr. by Rodney Needham, The Hague, Martinus Nijhoff, 1966.
P. K. Mukherje, *Indian Literature in China and the Far East,* Bombay, 1949.
P. V. Kane, *History of Dharmaśāstra,* vol. V, pt. 2, Poona, Bhandarkar Institute, 1962.
Rāhula Sāṃkṛtyāyana, *Purātattva Nibandhāvalī*, Allahabad, 1958 (second edition).
—*Buddhacaryā,* Saranatha, Maha Bodhi Sabha, 1952.
—*Tibbata Mein Bauddha Dharma,* Allahabad, 1948.
R. B. Foote, *Collection of Indian Prehistoric and Protohistoric Antiquities,* Madras, 1916.
R. C. Hazra, *Studies in the Purānic Records on Hindu Rites and Customs,* University of Dacca, Bulletin no. XX, Dacca, 1940.
R. C. Majumdar, *Corporate Life in Ancient India,* Calcutta, 1922.
R. C. Majumdar and A. D. Pusalker (ed.), *The History and Culture of the Indian People,* vols. I-IV, Bombay, Bharatiya Vidya Bhavan, 1951-1957.
R. C. Zaehner (ed.), *The Concise Encyclopaedia of Living Faiths,* Boston, Beacon, Press, 1968.

R. D. Banerji, *The Eastern Indian School of Medieval Sculpture*, Delhi, 1933.

R. G. Basak, *Aśokan Inscriptions,* Calcutta, Progressive Publishers, 1959.

—'Śaśāṅka, King of Bengal' in *IHQ*, vol. VIII, Calcutta, 1932.

R. H. L. Slater, *Paradox and Nirvāṇa,* Chicago, University of Chicago Press, 1951.

Ria Kloppenborg, *The Paccekabuddha, A Buddhist Ascetic*, Leiden, E. J. Brill, 1974.

Richard H. Robinson, *Early Mādhyamika in India and China*, Madison, University of Wisconsin Press, 1967.

—*The Buddhist Religion,* Belmont, Dickenson Publishing Co., 1970.

R. K. Chaudhary, 'Heretical Sects in the Purāṇas' in *ABORI*. vol. XXXVII, Poona, 1957.

R. Kimura, 'A Historical Study of the Terms Hīnayāna and Mahāyāna etc.' in *The Journal of the Department of Letters*, vol. XII, Calcutta, 1925.

R. K. Mookerji, *Ancient Indian Education,* Delhi, Motilal Banarsidass, 1951 (reprint).

—*Men and Thought in Ancient India*, Bombay, 1957 (second edition).

—*Harṣa,* Delhi, Motilal Banarsidass, 1965 (reprint).

—'A Note on the History of Tea' in *JUPHS*, vol. XII, Lucknow, 1935.

R. L. Mitra, *Sanskrit Buddhist Literature of Nepal*, Calcutta, 1882.

R. N. Saletore, 'Divākaramitra, His Date and Monastery' in the *Proceedings of the Indian History Congress,* Eighth Session, Annamalainagar, 1945.

S. K. Bhandarkar, *Catalogue of Manuscripts in Deccan College*, Bombay, 1886.

S. K. Chatterji, *Origin and Development of Bengali Language*, 2 vols., Calcutta, 1926.

—'Buddhist Survivals in Bengal' in *B. C. Law Volume,* pt. I, Calcutta, 1945.

S. K. De, 'Bengal's Contribution to Sanskrit Literature' in *Indian Studies: Past & Present,* vol. I, no. 4, 1960.

S. K. Pathak, 'Life of Nāgārjuna (from Pag Sam Jon Zang)' in *IHQ*, vol. XXX, Calcutta, 1954.

S. K. Saraswati, *A Survey of Indian Sculpture,* Calcutta, 1958.

S. N. Dasgupta, *A History of Indian Philosophy,* vols. I-V, Delhi, Motilal Banarsidass, 1975 (reprint).

—*Indian Idealism,* Cambridge, Cambridge University Press, 1962 (reprint).

S. Radhakrishnan, *Indian Philosophy,* 2 vols., London, Allen & Unwin, 1923, 1927.

S. Radhakrishnan *et al* (ed.), *The Cultural Heritage of India,* vols. I-IV, Calcutta, Ramakrishna Mission Institute of Culture, 1958 (second edition).

S. Schayer, 'Precanonical Buddhism' in *Archiv Orientalni,* vol. VII, Prague, 1938.

—*Pāla and Sena Sculpture,* Calcutta, 1929.

—*The Art of India Through the Ages,* London, 1955 (second edition).

Sten Konow, *Corpus Inscriptionum Indicarum,* vol. II, Varanasi, Indological Book House, 1969 (reprint).

—*A Survey of Painting in the Deccan,* London, 1937.

Sukumar Dutt, *Early Buddhist Monachism,* Bombay, Asia Publishing House, 1960 (revised edition).

—*Buddhist Monks and Monasteries of India,* London, Allen and Unwin, 1962.

—*Buddhism in East Asia,* New Delhi, Indian Council for Cultural Relations, 1966.

Sukumar Sen, 'Is the Cult of Dharma a Living Relic of Buddhism in Bengal ?' in *B. C. Law Volume,* pt. I, Calcutta, 1945.

Roy Andrew Miller, 'Buddhist Hybrid Sanskrit *Āli, Kāli,* as Grammatical Terms in Tibet', *Harvard Journal of Asiatic Studies,* vol. 26, 1965-66.

R. P. Chanda, *Medieval Indian Sculpture in the British Museum,* London, 1936.

R. S. Tripathi, *History of Kanauj,* Delhi, Motilal Banarsidass, 1964 (reprint).

Satkari Mookerjee, *Buddhist Philosophy of Universal Flux,* Calcutta, University of Calcutta, 1936.

—'The Absolutists' Standpoint in Logic' in *Nava Nālandā Mahāvihāra Research Publication,* vol. I, Nalānda, 1957.

—'The Omniscient as the Founder of Religion' in *Nava Nālandā Mahāvihāra Research Publication,* vol. II, Nalanda, 1960.

—'Ujjainī in the Mṛcchakaṭika' in *B. C. Law Volume,* pt. I, Calcutta, 1945.

—'Buddhism in Indian Life and Thought' in *The Cultural Heritage of India,* vol. I, Calcutta, The Ramakrishna Mission Institute of Culture, 1958.

Satya Prakash, *Prācīna Bhārata mein Rasāyana kā Itihāsa,* Lucknow, Hindi Samiti.

S. B. Dasgupta, *An Introduction to Tantric Buddhism,* Calcutta, University of Calcutta, 1958 (second edition).

—*Obscure Religious Cults,* Calcutta, K. L. Mukhopadhyaya, 1962 (second edition).

S. C. Das, *Indian Pandits in the Land of Snow,* Calcutta, 1893.

—*Tibetan-English Dictionary,* Alipore, West Bengal Government Press, 1960 (reprint).

S. C. De, 'The Orissa Museum Image Inscription of the time of Śubhakaradeva' in *Proceedings of the Indian History Congress,* Twelfth Session, 1949'.

S. C. Goswami, 'Hidden Traces of Buddhism in Assam' in *IHQ,* vol. II,Calcutta, 1927.

S. C. Vidyabhusana, *A History of Indian Logic,* Delhi, Motilal Banarsidass, 1971 (reprint).

—'Sarvajñamitra—a Tantric Buddhist Author of Kashmir in the 8th Century A. D.' in *JASB* (n.s.), vol. I, 1905.

Shyam Sundar Das, *Prācīna Lekha Maṇi Mālā,* Banaras, Nāgari Pracāriṇī Sabhā, 1903.

S. V. Venkateswara, *Indian Culture Through the Ages,* vol. I, Mysore, 1928.

Sylvain Levi, *Le Nepal,* 3 vols., Paris, 1905-1906.

Th. Stcherbatsky, *Buddhist Logic,* 2 vols., Bibliotheca Buddhica, vol. XXV, pts. 1-2, Leningrad, USSR Academy of Sciences, 1930-1932.

—*The Central Conception of Buddhism and the Meaning of the Word "Dharma",* London, Royal Asiatic Society, 1923.

—*The Conception of Buddhist Nirvāṇa,* Leningrad, USSR Academy of Sciences, 1927.

—*The Soul Theory of the Buddhists,* Varanasi, Bharatiya Vidya Prakasan, 1970 (reprint).

T. R. V. Murti, *The Central Philosophy of Buddhism,* London, Allen & Unwin, 1955.

T. W. Rhys Davids, 'Buddhaghosa' in *ERE*, vol. II.

T. W. Rhys Davids & W. Stede, *The Pali Text Society's Pali-English Dictionary,* London, Luzac & Co. 1966 (reprint).

U. Dhammaratana, 'The Reason For Anti-Buddhist Propaganda in Brahmanical Literature' in *The Maha Bodhi,* vol. 62, 1954.

Umesha Mishra, 'Influence of the Teachings of the Buddha and the Causes of the Decline of Buddhism in India' in *The Journal of the Ganganatha Jha Research Institute,* vol. IX, pt. I, 1951.

Unarai Wogihara, 'Vasubandhu' in *ERE*, vol. XII.

Vidhushekhara Bhattacharya, 'Sandhābhāṣā' in *IHQ*, vol. IV, Calcutta, 1928.

Vincent A. Smith, *A History of Fine Art in India and Ceylon,* Oxford, 1911.

Vishvanath Prasad Varma, *Early Buddhism and its Origins,* Delhi, Munshiram Manoharlal, 1973.

V. R. R. Dikshitar, 'Buddhism in Āndhradeśa' in *B. C. Law Volume,* pt. I, Calcutta, 1945.

V. S. Agrawala, *Harṣacarita eka Sāṃskritika Adhyayana,* Patna, Bihar Rāṣṭrabhāṣā Pariṣad, 1953.

—*Sārnātha,* Delhi, Department of Archaeology, 1957 (reprint).

—'Geographical Contents of the *Mahāmāyūrī'* in *JUPHS,* vol. XV, pt. 2, Lucknow, 1942.

—*Catalogue of the Mathura Museum,* published in *JUPHS,* vol. XXIII, Lucknow, 1950.

V. V. Gokhale, 'Krishna and the Buddhist Literature' in *The Cultural Forum,* vol. 36, New Delhi, April 1968.

Walpola Rahula, *What the Buddha Taught,* New York, Grove Press, 1959.

W. M. McGovern, *An Introduction to Mahāyāna Buddhism,* London, 1922.

W. Pachow, *A Comparative Study of the Prātimokṣa,* Santiniketan, Sino-Indian Cultural Society, 1955.

—'Voyage of Buddhist Missions to South-East Asia and the Far-East' in *Journal of the Greater India Society,* vol. XVII, Calcutta, 1958.

W. W. Rockhill, *The Life of the Buddha and the Early History of His Order,* Varanasi, Orientalia Indica, 1972 (reprint).

Yamakami Sogen, *Systems of Buddhistic Thought,* Calcutta, University of Calcutta, 1912.

Y. Kajiyama, 'Bhāvaviveka and the Prāsaṅgika School' in *Nava Nālandā Mahāvihāra Research Publication,* vol. I, Nalanda, 1957.

INDEX